AGENT ORANGE AND VIETNAM:

An Annotated Bibliography

by
CAROLINE D. HARNLY

The Scarecrow Press, Inc.
Metuchen, N.J., & London
1988

British Library Cataloguing-in-Publication data available

Library of Congress Cataloging-in-Publication Data

Harnly, Caroline D.
    Agent Orange and Vietnam : an annotated bibliography /
by Caroline D. Harnly.
        p.   cm.
    Includes index.
    ISBN 0-8108-2174-5
    1. Agent Orange--Bibliography. 2. Veterans--United
States--Bibliography. 3. Vietnamese Conflict, 1961-1975--
United States--Bibliography. I. Title.
Z6724.C5H38 1988
[UG447]
016.3551 ' 156 ' 097--dc19   88-22657

ACKNOWLEDGMENTS

The author is deeply grateful for all of the help extended to her in obtaining the material listed in this bibliography -- especially the Interlibrary Services Department of San Francisco State University's J. Paul Leonard Library. A big thank you is also extended to Henok Yared, Assistant Systems Software Specialist at the J. Paul Leonard Library, for his assistance in the production of this book and to Brian Aveney, former Systems Librarian at San Francisco State University, for assuring the author she could learn how to do word processing. The author would also like to thank Cynthia Hall, a reference librarian at the J. Paul Leonard Library, for her editorial assistance. In addition the author would like to acknowledge the release time the administration of San Francisco State University granted her to work on the bibliography during the Spring 1986 semester.

TABLE OF CONTENTS

INTRODUCTION

The Agent Orange issue continues to be one of the many unresolved issues of the Vietnam War. Although Agent Orange is only one of six defoliants used by the U.S. military during the Vietnam War, when the words "Agent Orange" are used most people are referring to the use of all of these defoliants in Vietnam, as Agent Orange was the most heavily used. The U.S. military used these defoliants in Vietnam from 1961-1971 in order to destroy jungle growth and crops. Agent Orange's name is derived from the orange stripe that was painted around the 55 gallon barrels in which it was stored. It was a combination of 2,4-D (2,4-dichlorophenoxyacetic acid) and 2,4,5-T (n-butyl esters of 2,4,5-trichlorophenoxyacetic acid) and was contaminated with 2,3,7,8-tetrachloro-p-dioxin. In addition to Agent Orange, Agents White, Blue, Purple, Pink and Green were used. Agents Purple, Pink and Green were basically not used after 1964. The Air Force conducted this program under the name Operation Ranch Hand. Their motto was "Only You Can Prevent Forests." In addition to the Operation Ranch Hand crew members, many ground troops were also exposed to Agent Orange. Australian as well as American troops were exposed. In all about 17.7 million gallons were sprayed on over five million acres. Over 32 percent of South Vietnam's upland forests were sprayed more than once. It has been estimated that one-fifth of Vietnam's mangrove forest was destroyed. 500,000 acres of crops were also sprayed.

Scientists began to express concern about the ecological effects this spraying was having. The American Association for the Advancement of Science and the National Academy of Sciences both sponsored trips to Vietnam to study the situation. Reports also began to be received about ill health in Vietnamese exposed to Agent Orange and birth defects in their offspring. Many scientists and politicians also came to believe that the military use of herbicides was an act of chemical warfare and therefore a violation of the Geneva Protocol of 1925. The U.S. military has maintained that the use of defoliants was effective militarily, not harmful to humans and not a violation of the Geneva Protocol.

Vietnam veterans first began to be concerned about the possible effects of exposure to Agent Orange when Maude deVictor, a former Veterans Administration claims officer in Chicago, found similarities in the health complaints among the veterans with whom she was working. On March 23, 1978, WBBM-TV in Chicago aired a documentary of the subject. On November 10, 1986, a made-for-television movie, starring Alfre Woodard and John Ritter, based on Maude deVictor's story entitled "Unnatural Causes" was shown. At the end of 1978, Paul Reutershan, who has since died of cancer, filed the first lawsuit against the manufacturers of Agent Orange. Several veterans' groups such as the Veterans of Foreign Wars of the USA, the Disabled American Veterans, Citizen Soldier, the National Veterans Law Center, and Agent Orange Victims International, have been active over the years in attempting to get the federal government to accept responsibility for the veterans' problems which they believe to be the result of exposure to Agent Orange and in the litigation against the manufacturers of Agent Orange which was settled out of court on May 7, 1984. Michael Ryan, whose daughter Kerry was born with multiple birth defects, summed up the feelings of many veterans involved in this issue when he stated, "I was there when my country needed me, where is my country now that I need help?"[1]

The most frequent health complaints veterans exposed to Agent Orange have include: skin conditions, cancers, fatigue and/or nervousness, numbness in extremities, vision and/or hearing impairments, birth defects in their offspring and reduced libido. In general the Veterans Administration has not granted disability claims except for chloracne. The Air Force has been conducting an epidemiological investigation of the former Ranch Hand crew members. Congress, in 1981, mandated that veterans be provided with free medical care at Veterans Administration facilities for "Agent Orange-type illnesses" based on the presumption that exposure to Agent Orange caused the illness. Scientific evidence of causality is not needed. This legislation also called for the Veterans Administration to establish an Agent Orange Registry. Congress also passed legislation requiring the Veterans Administration to conduct an epidemiological study. The control of this study has been passed to the Centers for Disease Control. It is now doubtful that this study will ever be conducted as the Centers for Disease Control feel that they will not be able to find substantial numbers of veterans who received high levels of exposure to Agent Orange. In 1984 the Centers for Disease Control released the results of a study on the risks of Vietnam veterans' fathering babies with birth defects. This study found that Vietnam veterans including those exposed to Agent Orange are not at greater risk for fathering babies with birth defects when all types of birth defects are combined. Congress passed the Agent Orange and Atomic Veterans Relief Act in 1984. This legislation requires the Veterans Administration to grant disability payments to Vietnam veterans suffering from soft tissue sarcomas, porphyria cutanea tarda and chloracne. Other responses to veterans' concerns included the establishment by the White House of an Intragency Agent Orange Working Group and by Veterans Administration of an

---

1"Where Is My Country?" Time 115 (February 25, 1980):20.

Advisory Committee on Health-Related Effects of Herbicides and by the formation in many states of their own Agent Orange commissions.

The litigation battle against the manufacturers of Agent Orange started in 1978 and still has not been resolved. In May 1984 the veterans settled out of court for $180 million. Fairness hearings were held and the court ruled that the settlement was reasonable and in the public interest. Those veterans who opted out of the settlement have had their cases dismissed. Most of the settlement has been upheld by the Court of Appeals. However, none of the money in the settlement has of yet been distributed. Both the veterans and their families and the chemical manufacturers have filed suits against the United States government. These suits have all been dismissed.

This bibliography is an expansion of a bibliography I wrote entitled <u>Agent Orange and the Vietnam Veteran: An Annotated Bibliography</u> which was published by Vance Bibliographies in 1985. All of the citations listed in that bibliography are included in this volume. This bibliography includes citations to material from books, journals, technical reports, transcripts of television news programs and newspapers written for specialized audiences such as the <u>New York Law Journal</u>, the <u>Air Force Times</u>, or the <u>Chemical Marketing Reporter</u>. General newspaper articles have been excluded because of their quantity. The reader is referred to the major newspaper indexes, such as the <u>New York Times, Los Angeles Times, Washington Post</u>, or the <u>National Newspaper Index</u> for citations to newspaper articles. Only material written in English or material written in a foreign language which has an English-language abstract has been included. A few citations to audio and video cassettes have been included. Citations to material that is still classified as secret by the U.S. government have not been included. Aside from citations to articles from legal journals, no other legal material has been cited. Material on the health effects of exposure to 2,3,5-T and 2,4-D in general has not been included. For a bibliography on this topic the reader is referred to <u>Review of Literature on Herbicides Including Phenoxy Herbicides and Associated Dioxins</u> (see entry 1243) which has been prepared under a contract from the Veterans Administration first by JRB Associates and now by Clement Associates. Every attempt has been made to include all published material written before 1987. A few citations to material written in 1987 have been included. The reader should be able to locate all the material listed in America's major research libraries, through the interlibrary loan system, or by writing the appropriate governmental agency.

The readers of this bibliography may also be interested in a collection that is housed in the Special Collections Department of the National Agricultural Library. This collection was donated by Dr. Alvin Young. The collection consists of newspaper articles, journal reprints, technical reports, Congressional hearing testimony, government documents, and other research materials on the effects of phenoxy herbicides and their associated dioxins. Approximately two-thirds of the materials in the collection are on the effects of Agent Orange on plants and animals. Dr. Young has developed a card-file subject index to his collection. He amassed this literature in the process of spending over twenty years in the U.S. Air Force and at the Veterans Administration researching this topic. Dr. Young is currently with the Office of Science and Technology Policy, Executive Office of the President.

Caroline D. Harnly
Reference Librarian
San Francisco State
University

November 1987

DESCRIPTION OF CHAPTER CONTENTS

This bibliography is divided into six chapters -- two of which have been divided into subchapters. Within each chapter or subchapter the entries are listed in alphabetical order by author or title if no author is known. Each reference will be found in the chapter or subchapter that most closely represents its primary focus. If a reference could have been entered into one of two chapters or subchapters, the citation and annotation will be listed in one chapter or subchapter and a see reference will be found in the other. If a reference could have been entered into one of three or more chapters or subchapters, it will be listed in one of the two general discussion sections. A description of the contents of each chapter follows.

I. General Discussions
    This chapter includes references to material that discusses all aspects of the Agent Orange issue without going into depth about any one aspect or that could have been listed in three or more of the other chapters.

II.   Ethical and Political Issues
       A. Military Justifications for the Spraying
    This subchapter includes references to material that mentions how Operation Ranch Hand was carried out, whether or not the sprayings were effective militarily, the amount and composition of the herbicides used, the use of military records to determine the areas that were sprayed, and the phaseout of the spraying program.
       B. The Efforts to Stop the Use of Agent Orange in Vietnam and the Debate on the Legality of Its Use
    This subchapter includes references to material that refers to the objections of many scientists to the defoliation and their efforts to stop the sprayings, the link between the military spraying of herbicides and the Geneva Protocol of 1925, the issue of whether or not the sprayings were an act of chemical warfare and the debates in Congress.

III. The Effects on Vietnam's Ecology
    This chapter includes references to material which details the effects of the sprayings on Vietnam's soil, plants and animals, the effects of the crop destruction program, and the findings of the reports prepared by such organizations as the American Association for the Advancement of Science and the National Academy of Sciences.

IV. The Health Effects and the Societal Costs of Exposure on the Vietnamese

This chapter includes references to material which notes the effects of the sprayings on the health of the Vietnamese, the possibility of a link between Agent Orange and birth defects in the offspring of exposed Vietnamese, and how the Vietnamese felt about the sprayings.

V. The Disposal of the Leftover Agent Orange

This chapter includes references to material which mentions the debate over what to do with the Agent Orange that was left after the defoliation missions were stopped and how the leftover Agent Orange was incinerated. The references to the studies that were conducted on how the storing of Agent Orange at various sites in the United States affected the environment of these sites and how the incineration of Agent Orange affected the environment of Johnson Island have not been included in this bibliography.

VI. The Effects on the Vietnam Veteran
    A. General Discussions

This subchapter includes references to material that provides an overview on the effects of exposure to Agent Orange on both the American and Australian Vietnam veteran and the civilians who served in Vietnam.

    B. Health Effects of Exposure

This subchapter includes references to material that discusses the concerns those who served in Vietnam and their families have as to what possible effects exposure to Agent Orange will have on the health of those who served in Vietnam and their offspring. References to the findings of studies such as the Air Force's study of the Operation Ranch Hand personnel are also included.

    C. Efforts to Involve State and Federal Governments

This subchapter includes references to material that refers to the efforts made to get state and federal governments involved in the issue, legislation that has been passed, efforts made by the Veterans Administration to respond to veterans' concerns, reports issued by the General Accounting Office, and studies that have been undertaken by various governmental agencies such as the epidemiological study which was originally undertaken by the Veterans Administration and is now being conducted by the Centers for Disease Control. References to the findings of any of these studies are listed in the Health Effects of Exposure subchapter.

    D. The Agent Orange Litigation

This subchapter includes references to material that details all of the events and issues involved in the litigation through the Spring 1987 approval of the May 1984 out of court settlement and most of the plans for the disposition of the settlement fund by the Second U.S. Circuit Court of Appeals.

GENERAL DISCUSSIONS

0001 Adler, J. et al. "Search for an Orange Thread." Newsweek,
v. 95, no. 24, June 16, 1980, p. 56. An account of the
spraying of Agent Orange between 1965 and 1970, the symptoms
veterans are experiencing, the problem of getting the
Veterans Administration to grant disability payments, the Air
Force's study of Operation Ranch Hand veterans, and a class-
action lawsuit brought by the veterans against the chemical
companies who manufactured Agent Orange.

0002 "Agent O - History & Consequences of Agent Orange." CBS
News Daily News Broadcasts, new ser., v. 10, no. 129, p. 33
(morning news). A history of the Agent Orange issue is
given.

0003 "Agent Orange: a Family Album." Mother Jones, v. 8, no. 9,
November 1983, p. 40-44. This article consists of
photographs of American and Vietnamese families haunted by
the tragedies of Agent Orange exposure.

0004 "Agent Orange: a Search for Answers." [transcript] B.
Kurtis, reporter. Chicago: WBBM-TV, 1978. 30p. Reprinted
in "Percy Calls for Full Investigation of Agent Orange."
Congressional Record, v. 125, pt. 11, June 5, 1979, p. 13465-
13474. This documentary was aired on WBBM on March 23,
1978. It was one of the first examinations by the media of
the connection between Vietnam service and Agent Orange.
The program details how M. deVictor began to uncover the
connection, the spraying of the defoliant in Vietnam and the
ecological damage done to the country, some to the studies
that have been done on the adverse effects of exposure to
dioxin, and the personal stories of several veterans who are
suffering from a variety of illnesses or have children born
with birth defects which the veterans believe are a result of
their exposure to Agent Orange.

0005 Aufderheide, P. "New Film Gets to the Root Problem." In
These Times, v. 8, no. 19, April 11, 1984, p. 9. The
documentary, The Secret Agent, made by J. Ochs on the dioxin
controversy is reviewed. The film goes beyond the events and
examines how our attitudes about progress, corporate
research, and military actions make us willing to gamble with
our society's future.

1

0006   Australia. Senate Standing Committee on Science and the
       Environment. Pesticides and the Health of Australian Vietnam
       Veterans: First Report. Canberra: Australian Government
       Publishing Service, November 1982. 240p. The Senate asked
       the Standing Committee on Science and the Environment on
       October 15, 1981 to study the effects of pesticides on the
       ecology, humans and animal health. The first issue the
       Committee was charged to examine was the possible effects of
       exposure to Agent Orange by the Australian Vietnam veteran.
       This document contains the Committee's report and
       recommendations on this issue. The Committee examined the
       degree to which Australian veterans were exposed to
       pesticides, research into the health effects of exposure to
       pesticides, epidemiological studies being conducted by the
       Commonwealth Institute of Health, legislation covering
       compensation for disabilities related to war service and
       possible health effects on the Vietnamese.

0007   Bac, H.A. See Ho Mai Bac.

0008   Barber, B. "Orange in Nam." Omni, v. 6, no. 10, July 1984,
       p. 18+. The author summarizes the conference held in 1983 in
       North Vietnam to discuss the effects of the use of Agent
       Orange in Vietnam on the land, people, plants and animals.
       Also mentioned are the studies being conducted by the
       Australians, the U.S. Air Force and the Centers for Disease
       Control, and the out of court settlement.

0009   Bengelsdorf, I.S. "The American Way of Defoliation." U.S.
       Catholic and Jubilee, v. 34, no. 6, October 1968, p. 15-16.
       The growing criticism of scientists to the use of defoliants
       in Vietnam is noted as well as the Department of Defense's
       reasons for using the defoliants. In response to the growing
       criticism the Department of Defense has given a contract to
       the Midwest Research Institute. The author notes one tragic
       result of the use of defoliants was that Vietnam used to grow
       not only enough rice to feed their people but enough to
       export as well - now that is no longer true. They must now
       have rice imported to them.

0010   "Blight that Failed." Newsweek, v. 77, no. 2, January 11,
       1971, p. 79. The results of the American Association for the
       Advancement of Science's study of the use of herbicides in
       Vietnam were reported in Chicago recently. Conclusive
       evidence that the use of the herbicides affected the health
       of the civilian population was found. The report also found
       that about half of Vietnam's mangrove trees have been
       destroyed and that the Army has destroyed enough crops to
       feed 600,000 people for a year. The White House has
       announced that it will begin an orderly yet rapid phaseout of
       the herbicide program.

0011 **Boulle, P. Ears of the Jungle. Translated by M. Dorby and L. Cole. New York: Vanguard Pr., 1972. 224p.** The ears of the jungle are sensors that are meant to help American forces pick up the sounds of truck convoys on the Ho Chi Minh Trail. The heroine, Aunt Ngha, rearranges the sensors so that the American bombing raids and defoliation missions actually end up clearing the jungle for future peacetime uses. Aunt Ngha is the intelligence chief for Uncle Ho, President of the Democratic Republic of North Vietnam. At one point in the story, the general responsible for defoliating the jungle flies into a rage when he catches his personal gardener using weed killer on the gravel outside his bungalow.

0012 **Buckingham, W.A., Jr. "Operation Ranch Hand: Herbicides in Southeast Asia." Air University Review, v. 34, no. 5, July/ August 1983, p. 42-53.** This article is a retrospective evaluation of Operation Ranch Hand derived from the author's book, Operation Ranch Hand: the Air Force and Herbicides in Southeast Asia. Also mentioned is the 1967 study by the Midwest Research Institute, the 1974 National Academy of Science's study, the 1967 Rand Corporation report, the Air Force's study of Ranch Hand veterans, the epidemiological study that is now under the supervision of the Centers for Disease Control and the media interest in the issue.

0013 **Buckingham, W.A., Jr. Operation Ranch Hand: the Air Force and Herbicides in Southeast Asia 1961-1971. Washington: GPO, 1982. 253p.** The author details the controversy over the military, political and ecological effects of the spraying of herbicides in Southeast Asia both within the government and among the public. The policy developed for this operation and the technical difficulties in spraying the herbicides are also discussed. Also mentioned is the continuing debate over the ecological and health effects of the operation.

0014 **Cahalane, R. "Agent Orange: Vets Die from Vietnam War Chemicals." Militant, v. 44, no. 26, July 22, 1980, p. 11.** The story of the spraying of defoliants and Operation ranch Hand is told. Speakers at the recent forum "The Legacy of Chemical Warfare in Vietnam: Agent Orange" in Boston told of the health difficulties veterans exposed to Agent Orange are having and the problems they are having getting the government to acknowledge the problem.

0015 **California. Department of Veterans Affairs. Agent Orange. Sacramento: The Department, [n.d.] 3p.** The Agent Orange issue is analyzed including the details on the spraying of Agent Orange in Vietnam, health questions veterans have, studies being conducted to determine the possible health

effects of exposure, the class action suit and the actions
that have been taken by the Veterans Administration.

0016   Committee of Concerned Asian Scholars. "Defoliation: the
       War Against the Land and the Unborn." In The Indochina
       Story: a Fully Documented Account. New York: Pantheon
       Books, 1970, p. 111-115. The Committee of Concerned Asian
       Scholars prepared this book as an effort to bring together
       the arguments for a total and immediate American withdrawal
       from Indochina. This chapter discusses the use of herbicides
       as a military weapon in Indochina. The military's
       justification, the type of herbicides, the reports of birth
       abnormalities in South Vietnam and the ecological effects of
       the spraying.

0017   Commoner, B. "Toxicologic Time Bomb." Hospital Practice, v.
       13, no. 6, June 1978, p. 56+. Reprinted as "Dioxin: the
       Vietnam Connection; Agent Orange." In Science Digest, v. 84,
       no. 4, October 1978, p. 58-61. The information presented in
       an hour-long documentary produced by WBBM-TV in Chicago on
       the Agent Orange issue is recounted.

0018   Cookson, J. and J. Nottingham. Survey of Chemical and
       Biological Warfare. London: Sheed and Ward, 1969. vii,
       376p. This book documents the past and present use of
       chemical and biological weapons in warfare and assesses the
       effects of these weapons. The use of defoliants and
       herbicides in Vietnam is described on pages 26-52. The
       development of the defoliation program, the types of
       herbicides used, the consequences of drift and
       miscalculation, the amount of herbicides used and the
       protests against their use in Vietnam are all noted on these
       pages. What is known about the effects of defoliants on
       plants, animals, the soil and man is detailed on pages 223-
       252. The authors then apply this knowledge to what has
       happened in Vietnam. In addition the Midwest Research
       Institute's report and other American data are critiqued.

0019   Cornell University. Air War Study Group. The Air War in
       Indochina. Ed. by R. Littauer and N. Uphoff. Rev. ed.
       Boston: Beacon Pr., 1972. xxi, 289p. Chapter 8 reprinted
       in "The Geneva Protocol-II." Congressional Record, v. 117,
       pt. 33, November 29, 1971, p. 43211-43214. This study group
       examined the manner in which American air power was used in
       Indochina. The composition and mode of action of the
       chemicals used and the ecological impact the spraying of
       these chemicals had on Vietnam are summarized on pages 91-93
       and discussed in detail on pages 241-263. The legal issues
       surrounding the military use of herbicides in Vietnam are
       discussed on pages 134-136.

0020 Crone, H.D. "The Public's Perception of the Herbicide
      Problem." In Chemicals & Society: a Guide to the New
      Chemical Age. New York: Cambridge University Pr., 1986, p.
      180-193. This chapter is part of a book which attempts to
      provide a balanced evaluation of the problems resulting from
      the vastly increased use of chemicals over the last forty
      years. In this chapter the author discusses the difficulty
      in presenting the 2,4,5-T, dioxin and Agent Orange issue to
      the public accurately.

0021 Crossland, J. "Dioxin: the Lingering Controversy."
      Ecologist, v. 10, no. 3, March 1980, p. 87-93. This article
      includes a brief mention of the Agent Orange issue.

0022 Davidson, J.H. "What We Can Learn from the 2,4,5-T
      Controversy." In Weed Control in Forest Management. Ed. by
      H.A. Holt and B.C. Fischer. West Lafayette, Ind.: Purdue
      Research Foundation, 1981, p. 272-279. The author is a
      proponent of the use of 2,4,5-T and reviews the debate over
      its use including its use during the Vietnam War and the
      studies that have been conducted thus far.

0023 Davis, D.E. "Herbicides in Peace and War." Bioscience, v.
      29, no. 2, February 1979, p. 84+. The history of the
      development of phenoxy herbicides and how they came to be
      used in the Vietnam War is given. The author also discusses
      the concern that developed about the ecological and human
      effects the spraying of Agent Orange had on Vietnam and its
      people. Also noted are the efforts scientists made to get
      the sprayings halted.

0024 Davis, D.E. "The 2,4,5-T Story - Is This the End?" Weeds
      Today, v. 5, no. 2, Spring 1974, p. 12-13+. The story of the
      trials and tribulations of 2,4,5-T is told. 2,4,5-T first
      came under criticism as a result of its use in Vietnam. The
      Bionetics Laboratory study is mentioned. The decision by the
      federal government to ban 2,4,5-T and the efforts being made
      by the Dow Chemical and Hercules Chemical companies to get
      its use restored are noted. The problem of what to do with
      the leftover Agent Orange is also mentioned.

0025 "Defoliants in Vietnam: the Background." VFW Magazine, v.
      70, no. 5, February 1983, p. 47. W.A. Buckingham's recently
      published account of Operation Ranch Hand is summarized.

0026 Diaz-Colon, J.D. and R.W. Bovey. Selected Bibliography of
      the Phenoxy Herbicides. VII. Military Uses. (Miscellaneous
      Publication, no. 1387) College Station, Tex.: Texas
      Agricultural Experiment Station, July 1978. 26p. This
      bibliography lists a selected number of materials on the

military uses of defoliants with particular reference to the
phenoxy herbicides.

0027 "Dioxin Levels of Herbicide Are Called Relatively Low."
American Medical News, v. 26, no. 34, September 16, 1983, p.
22. At the recent American Chemical Society meeting, A.L.
Young stated that Agent Orange contains much lower levels of
dioxin than herbicides used earlier in the Vietnam War
although the quantity used is much higher.

0028 "Do 'Agent Orange' Herbicides Destroy People as Well as
Plants?: the Evidence Mounts." People, v. 11, no. 23, June
11, 1979, p. 28-31. The story of exposure to Agent Orange in
Vietnam, Italy, Wisconsin and Missouri.

0029 Dux, J. and P.J. Young. Agent Orange: the Bitter Harvest.
Sydney: Hodder and Stoughton, 1980. 285p. An account of
the use of defoliants in southeast Asia and the realization
that those exposed to Agent Orange may suffer long-term
health effects as a result is given. Also recounted are the
efforts to get the Australian and American governments to
acknowledge the problem.

0030 Ehrlich, P.R. and Holdren, J.P. "Starvation as a Policy."
Saturday Review, v. 54, no. 49, December 4, 1971, p. 91. The
findings of the American Association for the Advancement of
Science's Herbicide Assessment Commission's study are
mentioned in terms of the health effects on the Vietnamese
and the ecological damage done to Vietnam. Also mentioned
are the ecological effects of the use of Rome plows and
bombs. Ecocide has not been limited to Vietnam. Defoliants
have also been used in Cambodia. The moral aspects of the
use of herbicides are also discussed.

0031 "Environmental Warfare." Congressional Record, v. 116, pt.
22, August 25, 1970, p. 30000-30012. Senator G. Nelson (D-
Wisc.) and Senator T.J. McIntyre (D-N.H.) discuss the use of
herbicides in Vietnam and the debate over its military value,
the ecological effects on Vietnam and the effects on the
health of the Vietnamese. The Senators had an article by
F.H. Tschirley which appeared in the February 21, 1969 issue
of Science (See 0626) inserted in the Record.

0032 Ewalt, G., Jr. "Agent Orange and the Effects of the
Herbicide Program." In Vietnam Reconsidered: Lessons from a
War. Ed. by H.E. Salisbury. New York: Harper and Row,
1984, p. 192-195. The material in this book is drawn from a
four day conference which took place from February 6-9, 1983
at the University of Southern California. The conference
debated the human, political, moral, social and philosophical

lessons learned from the Vietnam War. The author of this paper tells about the problems veterans are experiencing in trying to find out if they were in areas sprayed by herbicides, the health problems veterans have which they believe to be related to their exposure to Agent Orange. The military reasons for using the herbicides are also noted. The amount of herbicides used in Vietnam are detailed in Appendix 2 (pages 326-329).

0033 "Fall-out from Vietnam War Continues." New Scientist, v. 97, no. 1346, February 24, 1983, p. 506. The U.S. State Department has been accused of trying to sabotage the recent conference in Ho Chi Minh City. They evidently rather strongly urged officials from two U.N. agencies not to attend.

0034 Feeny, P. with J. Allaway. "The Ecological Impact of the Air War." In Vietnam and America: a Documented History. By M.E. Gettleman et al. New York: Grove Pr., 1985, p. 461-469. This book includes documents on every aspect of the Vietnam experience and notes, an introduction and an abstract precede each document. The authors of this chapter based their article on and reprinted portions of "The Ecological Impact of the Air War" by the Air War Study Group of Cornell University (See 0019) which discusses the composition of the herbicides used and the ecological effects the sprayings had on Vietnam. The authors also note the out of court settlement, the health effects of exposure to the herbicides and congressional efforts regarding this issue.

0035 Fuchs, G. "Opening Address." Peace and the Sciences, no. 3, 1982, p. 1-4. The author presented this paper as the opening address of the Round Table on Chemical Weapons and Disarmament held in Vienna on May 14, 1982. This address gives a history of the development of chemical weapons and a lengthy overview of the use of defoliants by the U.S. military during the Vietnam War. The health problems of both Vietnamese and soldiers exposed to the defoliants and the ecological effects of the sprayings are briefly mentioned.

0036 Galston, A.W. "Warfare with Herbicides in Vietnam." In Patient Earth. Ed. by J. Harte and R.H. Socolow. New York: Holt Rinehart & Winston, 1971, p. 136-150. This book describes ten case studies on environmental problems in contemporary America of which the use of herbicides in Vietnam is one. The amount of herbicides sprayed in Vietnam is detailed along with the debate over their use including whether their use is a violation of the Geneva Protocol, and the effects of the sprayings on plant life and man.

0037   Gimlin, H. "Chemical-biological Weaponry: Use of Tear Gas
       and Defoliants in Viet Nam War." Editorial Research Reports,
       v. 1, no. 23, June 18, 1969, p. 468-469. The use of tear gas
       and defoliants in Vietnam by the U.S. military is discussed
       in this section of an article on the history of the use of
       chemical-biological weapons and the debate on whether or not
       they should be used. The military justifications for using
       these weapons is explained. The findings of the report
       prepared by the Midwest Research Institute are noted. The
       author also mentions the concerns the American scientific
       community have about the use of these weapons.

0038   Gough, M. Dioxin, Agent Orange: the Facts. New York:
       Plenum Pr., 1986. 289p. The author examines the studies
       that have been conducted on the health effects of exposure to
       dioxin and the controversies the results of these studies
       have generated. The health effects of exposure by Vietnam
       veterans to Agent Orange are discussed on pages 43-120. A
       summary of Operation Ranch Hand, the ecological effects of
       the use of the herbicides on Vietnam and the controversy
       Operation Ranch Hand created is also included.

0039   Grossman, K. "Out of War They Came." In The Poison
       Controversy. Sag Harbor, N.Y.: Permanent Pr., 1983, p. 55-
       62. This chapter gives a little bit of background on the
       military use of herbicides, details the health problems many
       veterans are having, the Agent Orange litigation and how some
       veterans have come to feel emotionally about the military's
       spraying program.

0040   Grummer, G. "Genocide with Herbicides." In Truth about U.S.
       Aggression in Vietnam: GDR Authors Unmask Imperialist
       Crimes. Berlin: Vietnam Commission of the Afro-Asian
       Solidarity Committee of the German Democratic Republic, 1972,
       p. 96-125. The collection of essays that make up this book
       expose the illegal aggression of United States imperialism in
       Indochina. The essay by this author details the types of
       chemical used and the ecological damage done to Vietnam. The
       author believes that the destruction of the forests has led
       to an increase in the number of cases of malaria and has
       endangered Vietnam's medicinal plants. He also mentions the
       health effects of exposure to herbicides on the Vietnamese.

0041   Grummer, G. Herbicides in Vietnam. Berlin: Afro-Asian
       Solidarity Committee of the German Democratic Republic,
       1969. 191p. This book examines the way the military use of
       herbicides in Vietnam affected plants, animals and human
       beings. Also discussed are the ethical issues involved, the
       legal issues involved, and the reports prepared by the
       American Association for the Advancement of Science and the
       Midwest Research Institute.

0042 **Gunby, P. "Dispute Over Some Herbicides Rages in Wake of Agent Orange."** JAMA, **v. 241, no. 14, April 6, 1979, p. 1443-1444.** The Agent Orange controversy continues. The Veterans Administration has begun a project to determine if dioxin is retained in human tissues. The 1974 National Academy of Sciences report on the effects of herbicides in Vietnam is discussed. The suits against the manufacturers of Agent Orange are noted. Researchers at the University of Illinois at the Medical Center in Chicago plan to develop a computerized case study of Vietnam veterans who may have been exposed as well as their spouses and children.

0043 **Hansen, J.C. "The Vietnam Veteran vs. Agent Orange: the War that Lingers."** GAO Review, **v. 16, no. 2, Spring 1981, p. 29-36.** A general article on the Agent Orange situation. It focuses on the use of Agent Orange in Vietnam, some of the early congressional hearings and General Accounting Office reports, efforts to determine who was exposed to Agent Orange, scientific studies on the health effects of exposure, the lawsuit against the manufacturers of Agent Orange and what the Veterans Administration is doing for veterans.

0044 **Hay, A. "2,4,5-T in Cambodia and Laos."** In The Chemical Scythe: Lessons of 2,4,5-T and Dioxin. **New York: Plenum Pr., 1982, p. 187-197.** In this chapter the defoliation missions were carried out in Cambodia and Laos as well as Vietnam. How these missions were carried out, who authorized them, the ecological effects and the effects of the health of the Cambodians and Laotians are all noted.

0045 **Hay, A. "Vietnam and 2,4,5-T."** In The Chemical Scythe: Lessons of 2,4,5-T and Dioxin. **New York: Plenum Pr., 1982, p. 147-185.** In this chapter the spraying operation, ecological damage, the health effects attributed to Agent Orange and litigation brought by some Vietnam veterans against the manufacturers of the defoliant are all thoroughly discussed.

0046 **Hay, A. et al. "The Poison Cloud Hanging Over Europe."** New Scientist, **v. 93, no. 1296, March 11, 1982, p. 630-635.** How the various types of chemical weapons have been developed and when they should be used is noted. This article was written in response to a renewed concern over chemical weapons. As part of this article the author discusses the use of herbicides during the Vietnam War. The rationale of the program, and the health effects on the Vietnamese and the Vietnam veteran are all mentioned.

0047 **Hayes, M.K. "Agent Orange."** In Health Effects of Herbicide 2,4,5-T. **Updated ed. New York: American Council on Science**

and Health, July 1981, p. 88-91. This paper was prepared as
a result of the controversy surrounding the suspension of
2,4,5-T by the Environmental Protection Agency and attempts
to present a balanced and unbiased assessment of this public
health issue. This chapter detail the composition and
amounts of the various herbicides used, the concerns of
veterans exposed to Agent Orange, the research studies that
are underway, and the litigation against the manufacturers of
Agent Orange.

0048   "Herbicide Report Leaked to Avert DOD Mishandling." Science
        & Government Report, v. 4, no. 5, March 1, 1974, p. 5-6.
        Portions of the National Academy of Sciences' report on the
        military use of herbicides in Vietnam have been deliberately
        leaked to the press because of fears that the Defense
        Department would attempt to obscure or discredit the report.
        The Academy found extensive damage and evidence of lethal
        effects on Montagnard children and noted this in the report.
        The Academy's review panel had the study group rewrite
        portions of the report to clear up technical inaccuracies,
        etc. If not for this review panel the DOD might actually
        have gotten a report they could have lived with.

0049   "Herbicides Controversy May Flare Anew." Chemical and
        Engineering News, v. 46, no. 41, September 23, 1968, p. 28-
        30. The Department of Defense's position on their use of
        herbicides in Vietnam is reviewed and the efforts the
        American Association for the Advancement of Science is making
        to get the Department of Defense to halt the spraying are
        noted. The findings of the Midwest Research Institute's
        study are mentioned.

0050   "Herbicides; Viet Weapon." Oil, Paint and Drug Reporter, v.
        187, no. 14, April 5, 1965, p. 3+. Herbicides are being used
        as a military weapon in the Vietnam War to destroy many types
        of plant life. Military officials emphasize that the
        herbicides will not harm animals, people, soil or water.

0051   Herman, E.S. "U.S. vs NFL-DRV Atrocities." In Atrocities in
        Vietnam: Myths and Realities. Philadelphia: Pilgrim Pr.,
        1970, p. 41-88. In this book the author first discusses the
        meaning of atrocities and analyzes atrocities committed by
        all sides in the Vietnam Conflict. Then in chapter three on
        pages 75-83 the author discusses the use of defoliants. The
        effects of the ecology and the health of the Vietnamese is
        mentioned as well as the relationship between the use of
        defoliants and the Geneva Protocol. Also mentioned is the
        fact that local farmers sometimes accidently have their crops
        destroyed as a result of the defoliating missions.

0052   Hersh, S.M. "CBW in Combat: Vietnam." In Chemical and
       Biological Warfare: America's Hidden Arsenal. Indianapolis:
       Bobbs-Merrill Co., 1968, p. 144-187. Summarized as "Chemical
       Warfare in Vietnam." In Crimes of War: a Legal, Political-
       documentary, and Psychological Inquiry into the
       Responsibility of Leaders, Citizens, and Soldiers for
       Criminal Acts in War. Ed. by R.A. Falk, G. Kolko and R.J.
       Lifton. New York: Random House, 1971, p. 285-290. This
       book discusses the development of chemical and biological
       weapons in the United States. This chapter details the
       military use of herbicides and gases in Vietnam. The section
       detailing the use of herbicides discusses the thinking that
       led up to the decision to use herbicides militarily, how
       Operation Ranch Hand was carried out, efforts of South
       Vietnamese farmers to get compensated for their destroyed
       crops and the ecological effects of the sprayings.

0053   Hersh, S.M. "Our Chemical War." New York Review of Books,
       v. 10, no. 8, April 25, 1968, p. 31-36. A history of the use
       of defoliants is given and the debate over their use and
       their military effectiveness, the accidental destruction of
       crops, the problems farmers are having in getting reimbursed,
       the ecological concerns, and the health problems Vietnamese
       exposed to the defoliants are having are all discussed.

0054   Ho Mai Bac. "What Are the Defoliating Agents?" South
       Vietnam in Struggle, no. 53, February 1, 1970, p. 4. Some
       background information on the defoliation program is given.
       The ecological damage done and the health problems some
       Vietnamese are having as a result of being exposed are noted.

0055   Hodgkin, D.C. "Chemical Warfare." Bulletin of Peace
       Proposals, v. 2, no. 1, 1971, p. 68. The author discusses
       the findings of the reports prepared by the American
       Association for the Advancement of Science and the National
       Cancer Institute and details the current plans for
       defoliation. The herbicide program has been an ecological
       disaster and one of the agents used has been shown to cause
       birth defects.

0056   Holden, C. "Agent Orange Furor Continues to Build."
       [editorial] Science, v. 205, no. 4408, August 24, 1979, p.
       770-772. The story of how the Agent Orange issue developed
       is told. Also mentioned are some of the studies that have
       been started on the effects of exposure to herbicides and the
       position the Veterans Administration has taken on this issue.

0057   Horne, J. "Tracking Agent Orange: Vietnam Vets Battle an
       Insidious Foe." Life, v. 4, no. 12, December 1981, p. 65-70.
       Several Vietnam veterans describe the health problems and

birth defects their children have which the veterans believe
to be the result of their exposure to Agent Orange. Also
described is the foot-dragging by the Veterans
Administration, background information on the spraying of
Agent Orange in Vietnam, a class action lawsuit brought by V.
Yannacone, and an epidemiological study that Dr. G. Spivey of
the University of California at Los Angeles Medical School
has been commissioned to do. However, Dr. Spivey has
irritated veterans by stating, "The fear which is generated
by the current publicity is very likely to be the most
serious consequence of the use of Agent Orange."

0058   Lacey, P. and V.A. Lacey. "Agent Orange: Government
       Responsibility for the Military Use of Phenoxy Herbicides."
       Journal of Legal Medicine, v. 3, no. 1, March 1982, p. 137-
       178. Thoroughly discussed in this article is the use of
       Agent Orange in Vietnam, the health effects of TCDD, the lack
       of assistance from the Veterans Administration or the
       Congress, how the courts have approached claims involving
       military personnel, and how the Feres doctrine and the
       concept of government contract defense have been applied in
       the Agent Orange litigation. The authors believe that no
       government contract defense exists in this case.

0059   Lederer, E. "Report of the Sub-committee on Chemical Warfare
       in Vietnam." In Against the Crime of Silence: Proceedings
       of the International War Crimes Tribunal. Ed. by J. Duffet.
       New York: Simon and Schuster, 1968, p. 338-366. This book
       contains the proceedings of a tribunal which was held to bear
       witness to the crimes committed against the Vietnamese during
       the Vietnamese War. This paper discusses the controversy
       over the use of defoliants, the nutritional and social
       aspects of the crop destruction program and the toxicity of
       herbicides on man and animals.

0060   Lederer, E. "Report on Chemical Warfare in Vietnam." In
       Prevent the Crime of Silence: Reports from the Sessions of
       the International War Crimes Tribunal Founded by Bertrand
       Russell. Ed. by P. Limqueco, P. Weiss and K. Coates.
       London: Allen Lane, 1971, p. 203-225. This book contains
       selected and edited reports from a tribunal which was held to
       decide whether the accusations of war crimes levelled against
       the governments of the United States, South Korea, New
       Zealand and Australia during the Vietnam War were justified.
       The tribunal decided they were. This paper discusses the
       controversy over the use of defoliants, the reasons why the
       military decided to use defoliants, the ecological effects of
       the use of defoliants, the nutritional and social aspects of
       the crop destruction program and the toxicity of herbicides
       on man and animals.

0061 Lentz, L.H. and A. Sorenson. "Patches: the Hole Story." <u>Air Reservist</u>, v. 32, no. 10, September-October 1980, p. 14-15. The story of "Patches," a C-123 who when she left combat became part of the 12th Air Commando Squadron (RANCH HAND) and is now on display at the Air Force Museum at Wright Patterson Air Force Base, Ohio.

0062 Lewy, G. "Defoliation and Crop Destruction." In <u>America in Vietnam</u>. New York: Oxford University Pr., 1978, p. 257-266. The author wrote this book in order to examine the factual uncertainties and moral ambiguities of the American involvement in Vietnam. This section discusses the debate on whether or not the spraying of defoliants by the U.S. military violated the Geneva Protocol, the ecological effects of the sprayings, the health effects of the spraying on the Vietnamese, the findings of the studies by the National Academy of Sciences and the American Association for the Advancement of Science, and the adverse political effects of the crop destruction program.

0063 McCulloch, J. <u>The Politics of Agent Orange: an Annotated Chronology</u>. (Parliament of the Commonwealth of Australia. Department of the Parliamentary Library. Basic Paper no. 9) Canberra: Department of the Parliamentary Library, 1983. iv, 65p. The author provides a chronology of the history of the use of chemical agents in war and attempts to limit the use of these weapons; the history of the Vietnam War and Australian involvement; the history of the use of herbicides as part of the Vietnam War by the United States and her allies; the history of the "Agent Orange" issue in terms of the effects of exposure to this chemical on the health of veterans; a history of the response by the Australian government; the history of the herbicides used in Vietnam and their involvement in industrial accidents; and a history of similar instances of chemical contamination. The author also summarizes the findings of the major documents that have been published on the ecological and human effects of the herbicides that were used in Vietnam.

0064 McCulloch, J. <u>The Politics of Agent Orange: the Australian Experience</u>. Richmond, Vic.: Heinemann, 1984. xvii, 252p. This book thoroughly examines the Agent Orange issue from the Australian point of view. When, where, why and how the defoliants were used, the effects on the land and people of Vietnam, the effects on the Australian soldiers who served in Vietnam, and the efforts these soldiers are making to get the courts and governments to respond to their plight are all detailed.

0065 McDaniel, C.G. "Herbicides in Vietnam: Violating the Laws,

Starving Our Allies." Christian Century, v. 88, no. 6,
February 10, 1971, p. 195-197. The findings of the American
Association for the Advancement of Science's Herbicides
Assessment Commission are summarized. Defoliants will no
longer be used in Vietnam. The report considers the
ecological damage, the reactions of the Vietnamese farmer and
the legal implications in regards to the Geneva Protocol.

0066   McGrady, M. "Defoliation." In Dove in Vietnam. New York:
Funk & Wagnalls, 1968, p. 71-88. The author is a staff
writer for Newsday. He traveled to Vietnam and wrote of his
impressions of the war as he felt that the coverage of the
war was critical enough. This chapter tells of the
controversy surrounding Operation Ranch Hand.

0067   MacPherson, M. "Agent Orange." In Long Time Passing:
Vietnam and the Haunted Generation. New York: Doubleday,
1984, p. 586-601. The health effects, especially birth
defects in the offspring of American and Australian Vietnam
veterans and Vietnamese exposed to Agent Orange, are
detailed. Also noted is the litigation, the efforts to get
the Veterans Administration and Congress to do something, the
history of the epidemiological study which is now in the
hands of the Centers for Disease Control, and the Air Force's
study of the Operation Ranch Hand crew members.

0068   Maitland, T. and S. Weiss. "The Coming of Agent Orange." In
Raising the Stakes. (The Vietnam Experience) Boston:
Boston Publishing Company, 1982, p. 134. The research behind
the development of the herbicides used in Vietnam, how the
missions that constituted Operation Ranch Hand were carried
out and the beginning of the debate of the concern about the
ecological and health effects of the spraying. The findings
of the Bionetics Research Laboratories' study are also noted.

0069   Massachusetts. General Court. Science Resource Office. What
Information Does the SRO Have Concerning Agent Orange?
Boston: The Office, 1980? 5p. A bibliography of reports
and newspaper and journal articles.

0070   Mays, R.H. "Dioxin: Deadly or Deceptive?" Environmental
Forum, v. 2, no. 10, February 1984, p. 13-21. The author
reviews what is known about dioxin. The use of Agent Orange
in Vietnam is integrated into this article.

0071   Melman, S., ed. "Defoliants and Crop Destruction." In In
the Name of America. New York: Clergy and Laymen
Concerned About Vietnam, 1968, p. 283-304. This book
examines what the authors believe to be the breakdown of
moral constraint by the United States and Allied military
personnel in Vietnam and then to compare the conduct of

American operations in Vietnam with the laws of war. In this
chapter excerpts from newspapers, news services, periodicals,
and treaties are used to illustrate how the use of defoliants
in Vietnam are part of this breakdown of moral constraint.
These excerpts detail the amount of land sprayed, the
military justifications, and the ecological and moral
concerns of scientists.

0072   Merrill, S. and M. Simpson. Agent Orange: Veterans'
        Complaints and Studies of Health Effects. Rev. ed. (Report
        no. 1B83043) Washington: U.S. Library of Congress.
        Congressional Research Service, May 10, 1984. 19p. This
        paper provides background information on the spraying
        operation in Vietnam, the health effects of phenoxy
        herbicides, the efforts made by the Veterans Administration
        to respond to veterans' complaints, current or proposed
        studies on the health effects of Agent Orange, the state
        commissions that have been established and congressional
        action that has been taken. A short bibliography and a
        listing of federal organizations involved with Agent Orange
        are included.

0073   Meselson, M.S. et al. "Background Materials on Defoliation in
        Vietnam." In The Effects of Modern Weapons on the Human
        Environment in Indochina: Documents Presented at a Hearing
        Organized by the International Commission in Cooperation with
        the Stockholm Conference on Vietnam and the Swedish
        Committee for Vietnam. Stockholm: International Commission
        of Enquiry into U.S. Crimes in Indochina, 1972, p. 8:1-8:19.
        This report consists of an excerpt from the preliminary
        report of the Herbicide Assessment Commission of the
        American Association for the Advancement of Science,
        extracts from the background material presented by the
        Commission at the 1970 annual meeting of the American
        Association for the Advancement of Science and extracts from
        a letter from the Commission to Ambassador E. Bunker. This
        material discusses the ecological effects of the military use
        of herbicides, the health effects on the Vietnamese, the
        effectiveness of the crop destruction program, the types of
        herbicides used and the area treated.

0074   Meyers, B.F. "Soldier of Orange: the Administrative,
        Diplomatic, Legislative, and Litigatory Impact of Herbicide
        Agent Orange in South Vietnam." Boston College
        Environmental Affairs Law Review, v. 8, no. 2, 1979, p. 159-
        199. This is an exhaustive review of the Agent Orange issue.
        Included in this review are the following aspects of the
        issue: the history of the development and use of the
        defoliant, the termination of its use in Vietnam, the
        disposal of the leftover defoliant, the accusation by some

that the use of the defoliants violated the Geneva Protocol
of 1925, congressional action regarding dioxin, the
complaints of veterans as to their responses to exposure, and
the litigation brought by the veterans against the
manufacturers of Agent Orange. Some of the issues involved
in the litigation are examined: federal common law, the
trust fund, private cause of action, and the United State
government as a third party defendant.

0075   Mody, N. "Chemical Warfare in Vietnam." Economic and
       Political Weekly, v. 5, no. 24, June 13, 1970, p. 948-949.
       The U.S. military's use of chemicals including defoliants as
       part of the Vietnam War is summarized. The possible effects
       on farmlands, people and ecology are noted.

0076   Mokhiber, R. "Agent Orange: Bringing the Battle Home."
       Multinational Monitor, v. 8, no. 4, April 1987, p. 11-13.
       The author discusses many aspects of the Agent Orange issue.
       Specifically the litigation against the manufacturers of
       Agent Orange, the health effects of the sprayings on both the
       veterans and the Vietnamese, the ecological effects the
       sprayings have had on Vietnam and how the missions were
       carried out are mentioned.

0077   Murphy, S., A. Hay and S. Rose. No Fire, No Thunder: the
       Threat of Chemical and Biological Weapons. New York:
       Monthly Review Press, 1984. ix, 145p. This book describes
       what the authors believe to be the beginnings of a new
       chemical weapons race, the status of chemical and biological
       weapons in international law, how these weapons came to be
       produced and how restrictions have come to be imposed on
       their use. The military use of herbicides during the Vietnam
       War is mentioned on pages 22-23, 52, 64-65, 78 and 103. The
       health effects on the Vietnamese and the legal implications
       of the use of herbicides are briefly mentioned.

0078   Neilands, J.B. "Vietnam: Progress of the Chemical War."
       Asian Survey, v. 10, no. 3, March 1970, p. 209-229. The
       military use of herbicides in Vietnam is explained as part of
       a survey on the use of chemical weapons in Vietnam. The
       ecological effects of the spraying and the birth defects
       which may be a result of the sprayings as well as criticism
       that has developed as a result of this effort.

0079   "New York Times Readers Deceived on Defoliation Report."
       AIM Report, v. 3, no. 3, March 1974, p. 1-3. This article
       reviews they way the news media reported the findings of the
       National Academy of Sciences' study. The New York Times
       printed two articles on the findings of the study. The AIM
       Report believes these two articles are very inaccurate and
       misleading and explains why they believe this.

0080 "Nixon Selling Agent Orange for Paramilitary Operations in
      Brazil." Nola Express, no. 131, May 11, 1973-May 24, 1973,
      p. 7. One of the options for what to do with the leftover
      Agent Orange is to sell it to one of the two interested
      American corporations who want to market it to Latin America,
      in particular Brazil. Also mentioned is what the Agent
      Orange did to the Vietnamese people and to Vietnam.

0081 "Overall Summary Report, International Symposium on
      Herbicides and Defoliants in War: the Long-term Effects on
      Man and Nature: Ho Chi Minh City 13-20 January 1983." U.S.
      Committee for Scientific Cooperation with Vietnam. Bulletin,
      v. 2, no. 1, Spring 1983, p. 1-5. The four general topics
      discussed at the International Symposium on Herbicides and
      Defoliants in War and the ten subject areas the majority of
      the participants were able to reach agreement on are
      summarized. These areas of agreement include: Operation
      Ranch Hand was chemical warfare, nature and natural resources
      in Vietnam were substantially damaged, no definitive answers
      are known about the health effects of exposure and that
      studies should be continued.

0082 Pfeiffer, E.W. "Operation Ranch Hand: the U.S. Herbicide
      Program." Bulletin of the Atomic Scientists, v. 38, no. 5,
      May 1982, p. 20-24. Reprinted in New World Review, v. 51,
      no. 3, May-June 1983, p. 20-23. All but twenty pages of the
      500-page history on Operation Ranch Hand by M.A.
      Buckingham were recently declassified and are summarized in
      this article.

0083 Pian, C. "Defoliation in Vietnam." Indochina Chronicle, no.
      5, September 15, 1971, p. 8-12. An exhaustive review of the
      use of defoliants in Vietnam by the U.S. military including
      the debate over the ecological damage done, the medical
      problems caused by the spraying and the difficulties farmers
      faced in getting compensation if their farms were accidently
      sprayed.

0084 Regenstein, L. "Agent Orange and Vietnam: a Preview of
      What's Happening Here?" In American the Poisoned: How
      Deadly Chemicals Are Destroying Our Environment, Our
      Wildlife, Ourselves and How We Can Survive! Washington:
      Acropolis Books, 1982, p. 57-61. This book discusses the
      pervasive presence in our society of chemicals that may be
      killing and disabling Americans. This chapter details the
      health problems veterans believe to be caused as a result of
      their exposure to Agent Orange and efforts veterans are
      making to get the government to respond to their concerns
      about having been exposed to Agent Orange. The National
      Academy of Sciences' report is also mentioned which details

the ecological damage done to Vietnam and the health effects
on the Montagnard people.

0085 Reissner, W. "Legacy of U.S. Chemical War on Vietnam:
Lasting Damage to People and Environment in Both Countries."
Intercontinental Press, v. 21, no. 12, June 27, 1983, p. 357-
359. Background information on Operation Ranch Hand, the
insistence by the Pentagon that the defoliants were safe for
humans and the cover-ups by Dow are noted. Also included is
a discussion of a conference held in Ho Chi Minh City in
January entitled, "International Symposium on the Lasting
Consequence on Man and Nature of the Herbicides and
Defoliants Used in Vietnam During the American War."

0086 Reissner, W. "'Only You Can Prevent Forests': U.S. Tries to
Hide Dioxin's Effects." Militant, v. 47, no. 24, July 1,
1983, p. 12. Background information on Operation Ranch Hand
is given. The class action suit against the manufacturers of
Agent Orange is also mentioned. Between February 1982 and
1983, 369,000 visits to Veterans Administration clinics were
made by veterans for treatment for health problems veterans
believed were caused by Agent Orange exposure.

0087 Ridgeway, J. "Agent Orange: Settlement or Sellout?"
Village Voice, v. 29, no. 21, May 22, 1984, p. 22-23. The
author feels that the settlement is pretty pathetic. The
concerns of the veterans about the settlement are given.
Also noted is the history of the manufacture of Agent Orange
and the evidence that the manufacturers and the federal
government knew about its potentials hazards. Also noted are
the effects Agent Orange is having on the health of the
Vietnamese. However, the settlement may push the federal
government into passing legislation granting treatment to all
veterans exposed to Agent Orange.

0088 Rose, S. "The Real Significance of CBW." New Perspectives,
v. 1, no. 3, December 1971, p. 53-57. The author discusses
the development of chemical and biological weapons and the
political ramifications of the use of these weapons. The
ecological effects on Vietnam and the health problems
Vietnamese have experienced as a result of the U.S. military
use of herbicides in Vietnam are noted.

0089 Rose, S. "Real Significance of CBW." Instant Research on
Peace & Violence, no. 1, 1972, p. 9-16. As part of this
article on the use, development and consequences of chemical
and biological weapons in Vietnam, the use of defoliants by
the U.S. military is mentioned. The ecological effects on
Vietnam and the health effects on the Vietnamese of these
sprayings are also noted.

0090 "6 Pounds of US Toxic Chemicals Per Population Head." <u>South
Vietnam in Struggle</u>, no. 73, September 10, 1970, p. 5.
Senator G. Nelson (D-Wisc.) has denounced the increased use
of herbicides in Vietnam. The United States has now sprayed
over 100 million pounds of herbicide, or six pounds per head
of population. He also has wondered why the United States is
trying to destroy Vietnam's environment while it is claiming
to "defend Vietnam."

0091 Smith, M.J., Jr. <u>Air War, Southeast Asia, 1961-1973: an
Annotated Bibliography and 16mm Film Guide</u>. Metuchen, N.J.:
Scarecrow Press, 1979. xviii, 298p. This book is an
annotated bibliography of 3113 items on the American air
effort in Southeast Asia. Items are listed by author and
there is a subject index. The author attempted to exclude
the political side of the topic. Chapters on 16mm films and
photographs are included. Operation Ranch Hand is one of the
topics included in this bibliography.

0092 Stockholm International Peace Research Institute. "Chemical
Warfare: 1961-1970: Indo-china: the Use of Anti-plant
Chemicals." In <u>The Problem of Chemical and Biological
Warfare, Volume I</u>. New York: Humanities Pr., 1971, p. 162-
185. This volume describes the technology underlying
chemical and biological warfare and the constraints which
affect the use of chemical and biological weapons. This
section discusses how the U.S. military carried out Operation
Ranch Hand, the amount and types of herbicides used, the
areas sprayed, whether the program was militarily effective
and the concern over the possible ecological effects on
Vietnam and health effects on the Vietnamese.

0093 <u>Straight Talk on Agent Orange</u>. [S.l.]: S & K Data, 1985.
8p. This pamphlet is written in a question and answer
format. The military's use of herbicides in Vietnam,the
types of herbicides used, the amounts used, and how they were
distributed, etc. are explained. Also described is what is
known about the health effects of exposure. The conclusion
of this pamphlet is that a long-term study of the health
risks of Agent Orange exposure is needed.

0094 Summers, H.G., Jr. "Agent Orange." In <u>Vietnam War Almanac</u>.
New York: Facts on File, 1985, p. 66-68. The use of Agent
Orange in Vietnam, the lawsuit brought by Vietnam veterans
and the studies being conducted by the Veterans
Administration and the Centers of Disease Control are all
noted. A chart of the amounts and types herbicides sprayed
and when they were sprayed is included.

0095 "Talk of the Town: Notes and Comment." <u>New Yorker</u>, v. 50,

no. 5, March 25, 1974, p. 29-31. The report prepared by the
National Academy of Sciences on the effects of the use of
herbicides in Vietnam is summarized. The report discusses
the effects the use of these herbicides has had on Vietnam's
environment and its people. The criticism this report has
received is noted. Also discussed is the debate over the
ratification of the Geneva Protocol of 1925 and whether or
not the Protocol bans the use of herbicides in war.

0096   "The 2,4,5-T Rumble: What Is It All About." Down to Earth,
       v. 32, no. 2, 1976, p. 21-24. The Dow Chemical Company's
       position is that the charges leveled against 2,4,5-T are
       false.

0097   Uhl, M. and T. Ensign. GI Guinea Pigs: How the Pentagon
       Exposed Our Troops to Dangers More Deadly than War: Agent
       Orange and Atomic Radiation. New York: Playboy Pr., 1980.
       256p. The second half of this book discusses the Operation
       Ranch Hand mission, the effects the spraying of Agent Orange
       had on the soldiers, and the efforts the Vietnam veterans
       have made to get the government to accept responsibility for
       the effects Agent Orange has had on their health and their
       children's health.

0098   "U.S. Chemical Warfare in South Viet Nam (as Seen by
       American Scientists)." Vietnam Courier, v. 7, no. 251,
       January 12, 1970, p. 2+. An account of the statements made
       by American scientists at the American Association for the
       Advancement of Science meeting held recently in Boston and a
       summary of an article that appeared in the French newspaper
       Le Monde are given. These accounts detail the amount of
       chemicals used, the concerns over the ecological and health
       damages and the recent halt to the use of Agent Orange.

0099   U.S. Congress. House. Committee on Armed Services. "Use of
       Herbicides and Tear Gas in Vietnam. I. Herbicides." In
       Hearings on Military Posture and Legislation to Authorize
       Appropriations During Fiscal Year 1971. Hearing, 91st Cong.,
       2nd sess., February-April 1970. Washington: GPO, 1970, p.
       vii-vii following p. 8667. Responses were given to questions
       on the types of herbicides used in Vietnam, the quantities
       used, the amount of land sprayed, and the possible ecological
       damage and possible health effects as part of this set of
       hearings on Department of Defense appropriations for FY1971.

0100   U.S. Congress. House. Committee on Foreign Affairs.
       Subcommittee on National Security Policy and Scientific
       Developments. Chemical Biological Warfare: U.S. Policies
       and International Effects. Hearing, 91st Cong., 1st sess.,
       November 18 and 20 and December 2, 9, 18 and 19, 1969.

Washington: GPO, 1970. v, 513p. This series of hearings was held to discuss U.S. chemical-biological warfare policy as the Senate will soon begin debating the possible ratification of the Geneva Protocol. Many of the witnesses testify on the ecological and health effects, military justifications and how claims are processed regarding the use of herbicides in Vietnam. G. Bunn's 1969 article from the Wisconsin Law Review (See 0288) is included on pages 304-345.

0101 U.S. Congress. House. Committee on Foreign Affairs. Subcommittee on National Security Policy and Scientific Developments. Chemical-biological Warfare: U.S. Policies and International Effects. Report, 91st Cong., 2nd sess., May 16, 1970. Washington: GPO, 1970. vii, 41p. This report was prepared by the Subcommittee as a result of hearings (See 0360) the Subcommittee held on November 18 and 20 and December 2, 9, 18 and 19, 1969. Pages 5 and 6 of this report discuss the use of herbicides in Vietnam and the possible health and ecological effects of their spraying.

0102 U.S. Congress. House. Committee on Veterans' Affairs. Agent Orange in Vietnam: Report on Mission to Vietnam. Report, 98th Cong., 2nd sess., January 31, 1984. Washington: GPO, 1984. iii, 10p. Representative D. Edwards (D-CA) reports on his trip to Vietnam to investigate the effects of Agent Orange on the environment and the health of the Vietnamese people and includes findings and recommendations. His recommendations are that there should be an international study conducted in the living laboratory of Vietnam itself, that the United States should smooth the way for such a study, and that compensation and health care must be provided for affected veterans.

0103 U.S. Congress. House. Committee on Veterans' Affairs. Report on Congressional Delegation to Southeast Asia to the Committee on Veterans' Affairs. Report, 98th Cong., 2nd sess. Washington: GPO, 1985. v, 22p. Representative G.V. Montgomery (D-Miss.) headed a delegation of six members on a trip to Indochina from December 6-17, 1984. Issues discussed with high officials of all countries visited, representatives of the U.S. State Department and the Veterans Administration, and military officials in Hawaii and the Philippines included: Agent Orange, Amerasian children, MIAs and the status of Vietnamese still being held in reeducation camps.

0104 U.S. Library of Congress. Foreign Affairs Division. "Military Use of Herbicides." In Impact of the Vietnam War. Prepared for the Use of Committee on Foreign Relations, United States Senate. Report, 92nd Cong., 1st sess. Washington: GPO, 1971, p. 10-13. This article is part of a

survey prepared by the Library of Congress as an attempt to
detail the human and material costs incurred as a result of
the war in Indochina. In this article the findings of the
studies conducted by the American Association for the
Advancement of Science and the Bionetics Research
Laboratories are mentioned. A history of the use of
defoliants in Vietnam is also given.

0105 **U.S. Office of the President. Science Advisory Committee.
Panel on Herbicides. Report on 2,4,5-T. Washington: GPO,
1971. vii, 68p.** The Panel conducted a review of the
herbicide 2,4,5-T, examined what is known scientifically
about the chemical so that policy judgements can be made and
made a series of recommendations. Pages 34-36 detail how
much 2,4,5-T was used in Vietnam and why the military felt it
was important to carry out this operation. Page 47 mentions
the reports of birth defects in Vietnam. Pages 60-64 detail
what is known about the residues of 2,4-D and 2,4,5-T that
were left in the environment as a result of the sprayings in
Vietnam.

0106 **U.S. Veterans Administration. Veterans Administration
Continuing Education Conference on Herbicide Orange (2nd).
Proceedings. 1980. 79p. Available from NTIS: PB 82-
119017.** The topics of the papers presented include: use of
herbicides in South Vietnam from 1861-1971; the recognition
and significance of chloracne; the epidemiological study
mandated by Public Law 96-151; the legal aspects of Agent
Orange; and the future and public information aspects of
Agent Orange.

0107 **U.S. Veterans Administration Medical Center, St. Louis.
Agent Orange: a Search for Answers. Content specialist:
B.M. Shepard. Washington: Veterans Administration, 1981. 1
videocassette.** This videocassette was developed for Vietnam
veterans and their families who are concerned about the Agent
Orange issue. The tactical reasons why Agent Orange was
sprayed, the locations of the sprayings, what is known about
and agreed upon about the health effects of exposure, how
veterans may have been exposed, what the Veterans
Administration is doing, and the results of studies conducted
thus far are all explained. The program concludes by stating
the only proven symptom of dioxin exposure is chloracne and
that no good scientific evidence of birth defects or cancer
as the result of exposure to Agent Orange exists.

0108 **"An Unsettling Settlement." Environmental Action, v. 16, no.
1, June 1984, p. 8.** This article discusses the issues that
remain now that the class action suit has been settled out of
court. These include the issue of the federal government's
liability and the Vietnamese.

0109 "Use of Defoliants in Vietnam: a Stain on Our National
      Conscience." Congressional Record, v. 116, pt. 6, March 18,
      1970, p. 7803-7804. Senator S.M. Young (D-Ohio) urges a halt
      to the use of defoliants in Vietnam. He mentions the effects
      of the sprayings on crops and people. He also states that
      the crop destruction program is starving the civilian
      population. There are deformed babies being born. Water
      buffalo and other livestock are being destroyed. The Senator
      spoke regarding the effects of the sprayings he personally
      witnessed when he visited Vietnam in early 1968.

0110 Vandermeer, J. "Ecological Warfare: Long-term Consequences
      of Aerial Herbicide Application in Vietnam." Science for the
      People, v. 15, no. 5, September/October 1983, p. 11-16. The
      recently released official Air Force history of Operation
      Ranch Hand, the ecological damage done to Vietnam as a result
      of the spraying of Agent Orange, and the effects on human
      health of exposure to the defoliant are discussed. The
      author calls for a ban on ecological warfare.

0111 van Strum, C. "Herbicides: a Faustian Bargain."
      CoEvolution Quarterly, no. 21, Spring 1979, p. 22-25. What
      is known about the toxicity of phenoxy herbicides is
      explained. The reports of birth defects among the Vietnamese
      and the reports of health problems among veterans are
      mentioned. The author also presents some alternatives to the
      use of herbicides in forests.

0112 Verwey, W.D. "The Nature of Anti-plant Agents as
      Distinguished from Chemical and Biological Warfare Agents:
      the Criterion of Toxicity." In Riot Control Agents and
      Herbicides in War: Their Humanitarian, Toxicological,
      Ecological, Military, Polemological and Legal Aspects.
      Leyden, Netherlands: A.W. Sijthoff International Publ. Co.,
      1977, p. 83-154. The debate concerning the use of herbicides
      during the Vietnam War is intermingled in this text on all
      aspects of the use of riot control agents and anti-plant
      agents in war. On pages 99-154 of this chapter entitled,
      "Anti-plant Agents in Military Practice, or Lessons from the
      Vietnam War," the effects of the sprayings on Vietnam's
      ecology and the health of the Vietnamese people are
      mentioned. The reasons why the U.S. government felt
      justified in undertaking Operation Ranch Hand are also noted.

0113 "Vietnam: a Chemical Hiroshima." [editorial] Inside Asia,
      no. 9, July 1986, p. 4. This editorial reflects on the
      ecological effects on Vietnam and the health effects on the
      Vietnamese the spraying of Agent Orange during the Vietnam
      War had then and continues to have today. The reasons why
      the U.S. military felt it was necessary to use defoliants are
      also noted.

0114   Vietnam (Democratic Republic). Commission for Investigation
        on the American Imperialists' War Crimes in Vietnam.
        "Chemical Warfare." In <u>American Crimes in Vietnam</u>. Hanoi?:
        The Commission, 1966, p. 21-24. This article mentions the
        effects the spraying of the herbicides has had as well as the
        types and amounts of herbicides sprayed. The article also
        states that the United States is daily using methods that
        Hitler himself did not dare to use.

0115   "Vietnam Hosts Dioxin Symposium." <u>Citizen Soldier</u>, no. 5,
        May 1983, p. 1-2. An International Symposium on Herbicides
        and Defoliants in War was held in Ho Chi Minh City recently.
        Papers presented at this conference discussed the effects of
        the sprayings on Vietnam's ecology, the effects of the
        sprayings on the health of the Vietnamese and the Vietnam
        veteran. Field trips were also taken to some of the areas
        that were sprayed.

0116   Weisburd, A. "U.S. Agent Orange Sowed Bitter Fruit, Bitter
        Harvest." <u>Guardian</u>, v. 35, no. 40, July 27, 1983, p. 20.
        The author reports on the International Trade Union
        Conference Against Chemical and Biological Weapons which
        was held in Ho Chi Minh City recently.

0117   Westing, A.H. "Bibliography: Herbicides as Weapons in South
        Vietnam." <u>Bioscience</u>, v. 21, no. 24, December 15, 1971, p.
        1225-1227. A listing of the materials on this topic that
        have come to the author's attention through October 1971.

0118   Westing, A.H. <u>Herbicides as Weapons: a Bibliography</u>.
        (Political Issues Series v. 3, no. 1) Los Angeles: Center
        for the Study of Armament and Disarmament, California State
        University, 1973. vi, 36p. This bibliography lists the
        materials the author has used in his research on the effects
        of the use of herbicides by U.S. military in Vietnam.

0119   Westing, A.H. "Poisoning Plants for Peace." <u>Friends
        Journal</u>, v. 16, no. 7, April 1, 1970, p. 193-194. Reprinted
        in <u>Vermont Freeman</u>, v. 2, no. 4, January 30-February 1, 1970,
        p. 7-9; in <u>Ecocide in Indochina: the Ecology of War</u>. Ed. by
        B. Weisberg. San Francisco: Canfield Pr., 1970, p. 72-74;
        and in <u>Not Since the Romans Salted the Land: Chemical
        Warfare in S.E. Asia</u> by J.B. Neilands <u>et al</u>. Ithaca, N.Y.:
        Glad Day Pr., 1970, p. 16-17. The Operation Ranch Hand
        program and the ecological havoc that is being created in
        Vietnam as a result of the spraying are discussed. The
        National Cancer Institute's study on the health effects of
        exposure to 2,4,5-T and 2,4-D is noted. Severe restrictions
        have been placed on the use of 2,4,5-T in the United States
        but it is still being sprayed by the Defense Department in

Vietnam. The author believes the United States must put a
stop to the spraying in Vietnam.

0120   Westing, A.H. "The New Killers; War Against Vegetation in
       Vietnam." Vermont Freeman, v. 3, no. 20, Latter October
       1971, p. 18-19. Reprinted as "War Against Vegetation in Viet
       Nam." Science Today, v. 6, no. 8, February 1972, p. 43-46.
       The author discusses whether the military use of herbicides
       as part of Operation Ranch Hand during the Vietnam War was a
       tactical success. The health effects of exposure to the
       herbicides on the Vietnamese and the amount of crops
       destroyed as a result of Operation Ranch Hand are also
       discussed. The concentration of the herbicides used is also
       noted.

0121   Whiteside, T. with foreword by G. Wild. Defoliation: What
       Are Our Herbicides Doing to Us? New York: a Ballantine/
       Friends of the Earth Book, 1970. 168p. This book describes
       the use of defoliants by the U.S. military in Southeast Asia
       in the 1960's and the growing realization that these
       defoliants could have damaged the health of veterans and
       Southeast Asians. In addition the author notes the efforts
       that are being made to get the government to act on the use
       of 2,4,5-T. Included are the texts of relevant reports.

0122   Whiteside, T. "Department of Amplification." New Yorker, v.
       46, no. 4, March 14, 1970, p. 124-129. Reprinted in Effects
       of 2,4,5-T on Man and the Environment. Hearing, 91st Cong.,
       2nd sess., April 7 and 15, 1970. U.S. Congress. Senate.
       Committee on Commerce. Subcommittee on Energy, Natural
       Resources, and the Environment. Washington: GPO, 1970, p.
       123-126 and in Effects of 2,4,5-T on Man and the Environment.
       Hearing, 91st Cong., 2nd sess., June 17 and 18, 1970. U.S.
       Congress. Senate. Committee on Commerce. Subcommittee on
       Energy, Natural Resources, and the Environment. Washington:
       GPO, 1970, p. 105-108. The continued use of Agent Orange in
       the United States as well as Vietnam is discussed. The
       concern over the human health effects of exposure to both
       veterans and Vietnamese are expressed. Also mentioned are
       the findings of the study conducted by the Bionetics Research
       Laboratories.

0123   Whiteside, T. "Department of Amplification." New Yorker, v.
       46, no. 20, July 4, 1970, p. 64-66+. Reprinted in Effects of
       2,4,5-T on Man and the Environment. Hearing, 91st Cong., 2nd
       sess., June 17 and 18, 1970. U.S. Congress. Senate.
       Committee on Commerce. Subcommittee on Energy, Natural
       Resources, and the Environment. Washington: GPO, 1970, p.
       108-112. The history of the herbicide spraying in Vietnam is
       noted and the effectiveness of the program is questioned.

Also mentioned is the ecological damage done to Vietnam as a
result of the spraying. The debate over whether the military
use of herbicides is banned by the Geneva Protocol is also
mentioned.

0124   Whiteside, T. "Department of Amplification." New Yorker, v.
       47, no. 26, August 14, 1971, p. 54+. The findings of a study
       conducted by a National Academy of Sciences committee on the
       effects of the use of herbicides in Vietnam are summarized.
       The use of herbicides in Vietnam will be phased out. The
       debate over whether the military use of herbicides is banned
       by the Geneva Protocol is also mentioned.

0125   Whiteside, T. "Reporter at Large: Defoliation." New
       Yorker, v. 45, no. 51, February 7, 1970, p. 32-38+.
       Reprinted in "CBW, Health and the Environment."
       Congressional Record, v. 116, pt. 3, February 9, 1970, p.
       2976-2983. Reprinted in "Herbicides and Defoliants in
       Vietnam: a Critical Review." Congressional Record, v. 116,
       pt. 3, February 10, 1970, p. 3064-3071; in "Congressional
       Responsibilities and the Hidden Policies of Southeast Asia."
       Congressional Record, v. 116, pt. 5, March 3, 1970, p. 5609-
       5624; in Effects of 2,4,5-T on Man and the Environment.
       Hearing, 91st Cong., 2nd sess., April 7 and 15, 1970. U.S.
       Congress. Senate. Committee on Commerce. Subcommittee on
       Energy, Natural Resources, and the Environment. Washington:
       GPO, 1970, p. 107-123; and in Effects of 2,4,5-T on Man and
       the Environment. Hearing, 91st Cong., 2nd sess., June 17 and
       18, 1970. U.S. Congress. Senate. Committee on Commerce.
       Subcommittee on Energy, Natural Resources, and the
       Environment. Washington: GPO, 1970, p. 89-105. The history
       of the defoliation project is given and the possible health
       effects of the spraying on the Vietnamese and the ecological
       effects on Vietnam are mentioned. The results of the
       findings of a study conducted by the Bionetics Research
       Laboratories are mentioned.

0126   Whiteside, T. The Withering Rain: America's Herbicidal
       Folly. New York: Dutton, 1971. 224p. This book discusses
       the use of 2,4,5-T as part of the Vietnam War and here in the
       United States and the the concerns that have arisen over the
       ecological and health effects of the use of this chemical and
       is a revision of the author's book, Defoliation (See 0121).
       The author also mentions the effects of the crop destruction
       program, the findings of the report prepared by the Bionetics
       Research Laboratory, and the issue of whether or not the
       Geneva Protocol applies to the sprayings of herbicides in
       Vietnam. The appendices include the text of testimonies
       given by A.H. Westing, A.W. Galston and Admiral Lemos before
       congressional committees, a table detailing the composition

of the chemicals used in Vietnam, a list of the areas sprayed, and the text of a resolution passed by the American Association for the Advancement of Science.

0127 Wilber, C.G. "Agent Orange and Dioxin: Do 2.4 Million Plaintiffs Have a Cause of Action." Trauma, v. 22, no. 1, June 1980, p. 11-77. An extremely detailed examination of the composition of 2,4-D, 2,4,5-T, TCDD, and Agent Orange; the cases involving exposure to these herbicides; and the studies that have been done or are in progress on the possible adverse effects of exposure. The author believes that there are serious deficiencies in any litigation case involving Agent Orange from a scientific point of view.

0128 Wisconsin. Department of Health and Social Services. Questions and Answers about Agent Orange. Madison: The Department, 1980. pamphlet. This pamphlet discusses the following points: one, how Agent Orange was used in Vietnam; two, how Agent Orange may have been absorbed; three, reported health effects and symptoms resulting from exposure; four, how one might determine whether exposure occurred; five, possible actions to be taken if exposed; and six, known technical facts regarding Agent Orange and its contaminant, dioxin.

0129 Wright, T.C., comp. Agent Orange, TCDD. (LC Science Tracer Bullet TB 79-10) Washington: U.S. Library of Congress. Science and Technology Division. Reference Section, 1979. 9p. The author has compiled a list of references and has explained how to find information on the TCDD, Agent Orange, dioxin and 2,4,5-T controversies.

0130 Yannacone, V.J., Jr. "Dioxin: Molecule of Death." Trial, v. 17, no. 12, December 1981, p. 30-37. The author gives an in depth account of the use of chemical defoliants by the United States including the use of Agent Orange in Vietnam and the growing realization that exposure to dioxin could be hazardous to the health of humans and to the environment.

0131 Young, A.L. "Dioxin: a Case Study of Conflict Between Science and Social Concerns." American Chemical Society. Abstracts of Papers, v. 188, 1984, #CHAL 0016. The author discusses whether or not the issues surrounding the use of 2,3,7,8 tetrachlorodibenzo-p-dioxin can be resolved by science alone.

0132 Young, A.L. "Use of Herbicides in South Vietnam, 1961-1971." Western Society of Weed Science, Proceedings, v. 34, 1981, p. 27-35. The author describes the herbicides used in South Vietnam by the U.S. military. He details the amounts used, the areas sprayed, the methods employed to do the spraying, the possibility of exposure by military personnel and the environmental effects of the sprayings. The author believes that the procedures employed for the spraying of the herbicides precluded any physical contact with the herbicides by most military personnel and that it is highly unlikely that there will be any environmental generation of TCDD from residues through thermal or photolytic processes.

0133   Young, A.L. et al. The Toxicology, Environmental Fate, and Human Risk of Herbicide Orange and Its Associated Dioxins. October 1978. 262p. Available from NTIS: AD-A062 143/3 GA. Included in this report is a review of the use of herbicides in South Vietnam from 1962 to 1972 with an emphasis on Agent Orange. To determine the potential for exposure to Agent Orange, the at risk U.S. military population is defined. Also included is a discussion of the environmental and occupational risks in disposing of Agent Orange, a review of studies of suspected TCDD poisoning, and an evaluation of the potential human risk for those who might have been in areas sprayed with Agent Orange.

ETHICAL AND POLITICAL ISSUES

MILITARY JUSTIFICATIONS FOR THE SPRAYING

0134 "The Agent Orange Affair." Time, v. 96, no. 18, November 2, 1970, p. 39-40. It appears that despite the Department of Defense's suspension of the use of Agent Orange some Army units have still been spraying it.

0135 "Agent Orange Was Tested in Canada." New Scientist, v. 89, no. 1239, February 5, 1981, p. 324. It has been revealed that Canada's armed forces helped the U.S. Army develop the chemical defoliants that were used in the Vietnam War during 1966 and 1967.

0136 "Aid for Congressional Case Workers and Vietnam Veterans - Agent Orange and the Vietnam Map Book." Congressional Record, v. 127, no. 189, January 6, 1982, p. E6015. Representative F.H. Stark (D-CA) discusses the map book prepared by the Winter Soldier Archive which will help veterans determine if they were exposed to Agent Orange while serving in Vietnam. Representative Stark's office was actively involved in the project.

0137 "Alpha-picoline for Herbicides: Most Natural Slated for Dow, with Government's Blessing." Oil, Paint and Drug Reporter, v. 191, no. 24, June 12, 1967, p. 5+. Almost all of the natural alpha-picoline being made in the United States is going to the Dow Chemical Company so that Dow can fill its government priority orders for its "Tordon" herbicide which is being used as a defoliant in Vietnam.

0138 "American Troops Use Agent Orange, Banned Defoliant in Vietnam." (See 0271)

0139 Armstrong, R. "Vietnam: 'Believe Me, He Can Kill You.'" Saturday Evening Post, v. 240, no. 6, March 25, 1967, p. 29-35+. The author discusses the strategy employed to fight the North Vietnamese and a soldier's life in Vietnam. On pages 30-31 the author mentions Operation Ranch Hand and how the missions are conducted.

0140 "Army Herbicide Study." Congressional Record, v. 118, pt.

22, August 18, 1972, p. 29253-29255. Representative L. Aspin
(D-Wisc.) had an article by J. Fuller and T. O'Brien from the
August 13, 1972 issue of the Washington Post inserted in the
Record. The Army evidently, despite what happened in
Vietnam, wants to continue to use herbicides as a weapon in
future wars.

0141   "Army Scientist Defends Defoliant Use in Vietnam." Chemical
and Engineering News, v. 46, no. 3, January 15, 1968, p. 17.
At a recent Northeastern Weed Control Conference in New
York City, Dr. C.E. Minarik, director of the plant science
laboratory at Fort Detrick, Md., defended the use of
herbicides as defoliants in Vietnam. He stated that the
defoliation operation had saved combat lives and offered some
beneficial by-products to the South Vietnamese civilians such
as release of land for agricultural purposes and improved
commerce in isolated village areas. Operation Ranch Hand
will have no long term ecological effects.

0142   Atkinson, J.D. "Counterguerrilla Warfare." Ordnance, v. 48,
no. 262, January-February 1964, p. 434-436. This discussion
of the efforts to apply technology to guerrilla warfare
includes the effort to use defoliants in Vietnam. It would
appear that the results in this particular area have been
surprisingly good especially if measured against the
Communist propaganda reaction.

0143   Australia. Minister for Defence. Report on the Use of
Herbicides, Insecticides & Other Chemicals by the Australian
Army in South Vietnam. Presented to the Parliament by the
Rt. Hon. I. Sinclair. Canberra: Australian Government
Publishing Service, 1982. 1 v. (various paginations). This
report was prepared in order to provide as complete a review
as the Australian Army records examined would allow of all of
the aspects of the policy regarding the use of pesticides
(including herbicides, defoliants and insecticides) and other
chemical substances in South Vietnam.

0144   Beecher, W. "Chemicals vs. the Viet Cong — 'Right,' or
'Wrong'?" National Guardsman, v. 20, no. 2, February 1966,
p. 2-6. The military use of tear gas and herbicides in
Vietnam by the United States is described and whether or not
they have made effective weapons is discussed.

0145   Berger, C., ed. The United States Air Force in Southeast
Asia, 1961-1973: an Illustrated Account. rev. ed.
Washington: Office of Air Force History, 1984. xiv, 383p.
This book is a history of air activity in the Vietnam War.
The defoliation missions are mentioned on p. 6, 11-13, 15,
205 and 245. Includes photographs.

0146 Betts, R. and F. Denton. <u>An Evaluation of Chemical Crop Destruction in Vietnam</u>. October 1967. 41p. Available from NTIS: AD 779 790/5. This report is based on the analysis of data from 206 interviews with ex-Viet Cong and non-Viet Cong civilians. It examines the effectiveness of chemical crop destruction as a means of denying food to the Viet Cong. The report concludes that chemical destruction of crops does not affect the food supply of the Viet Cong but the peasants are very bitter about the crop destruction program and suggests ways to lessen the peasants' feelings of hostility.

0147 Bevan, W. "AAAS Council Meeting, 1970." (See 0282)

0148 Brightman, C. "The 'Weed Killers.'" <u>Viet-Report</u>, v. 2, no. 4-5, June/July 1966, p. 9-14+. The author describes the development of an American chemical warfare policy in general and the use of chemicals as part of the Vietnam War including the use of herbicides to destroy jungle and crops. The article includes tables listing the chemical compounds used in Vietnam, the military codes, disseminated form, military purpose, incapacitating effects, disabling effects, military advantages, military disadvantages and use in Vietnam.

0149 Brown, D. "Nixon's War: a New Escalation." <u>Amex--Canada</u>, v. 3, no. 3, March/April 1972, p. 24-27. As part of this discussion on how President Nixon is escalating the Vietnam War, the damage done by the use of Agent Orange is noted. The defoliant has been sprayed in Laos and Cambodia and the United States is supplying the defoliant to the Saigon Air Force.

0150 Brown, D.E. "The Use of Herbicides in War: a Political/ Military Analysis." In <u>The Control of Chemical and Biological Weapons</u>. New York: Carnegie Endowment for International Peace, 1971, p. 39-63. This book is the result of a study undertaken by the Endowment to examine the issues surrounding the new policies enunciated by President Nixon in the field of chemical and biological warfare. D. Brown's paper examines the military value, political implications and ecological effects of the use of herbicides in Vietnam.

0151 Browne, M.W. "American Gadgets." In <u>The New Face of War</u>. Indianapolis: Bobbs-Merrill Co., 1965, p. 30-39. This book was written in order to help give Americans an understanding of how a war like Vietnam War is fought. Pages 35-38 of this chapter detail how the defoliation missions were carried out and how the Viet Cong used these missions as a propaganda tool.

0152 "C-123s Defoliate Jungle Stronghold of Viet Cong." <u>Aviation</u>

Week and Space Technology, v. 86, no. 19, May 8, 1967, p. 82-85. This article consists of a series of photographs of the C123 aircraft inflight as the Air Force carried out the defoliating missions.

0153 "CBW: What's Being Done in Vietnam?" Scientific Research, v. 3, no. 23, November 11, 1968, p. 26. The composition of the five herbicides used in Vietnam is noted. There is growing concern about the long-term effects of Agent Blue (cacodylic acid.)

0154 Castleman, M. "Options for Vietnam Veterans." Medical Selfcare, no. 31, November-December 1985, p. 14-16. C. Smith, a part-time English professor at the University of San Francisco and co-author of The Vietnam Map Book, has transformed the HERBS data into the Agent Orange Database with the help of two friends who worked for Apple Computer. The database can be used by Vietnam veterans so they can make a relative-risk evaluation of exposure to Agent Orange.

0155 Cecil, P.F. Herbicidal Warfare: the Ranch Hand Project in Vietnam. New York: Praeger Pub., 1986. xiii, 289p. The author describes the Ranch Hand mission and the controversies surrounding it and the processes by which the political and military decisions were reached concerning herbicidal warfare. The author served with Ranch Hand.

0156 "Chemical and Biological Warfare: Questions to be Answered." Congressional Record, v. 115, pt. 6, April 1, 1969, p. 8159-8170. Representative R.D. McCarthy (D-N.Y.) discusses the questions he has regarding chemical and biological warfare. As part of his remarks he includes a letter listing his questions to the Secretaries of Defense and State. He also had the text of a report prepared by Brig. Gen. J.A. Hebbeler on policy issues involving these weapons inserted. Both the letter and the report mention in part the issue of the use of herbicides in Vietnam. Representative McCarthy also had an article from the February 21, 1969 issue of Science by F.H. Tschirley (See 0626) inserted in the Record.

0157 "Chemical Herbicides for Defoliation." Congressional Record, v. 114, pt. 18, July 30, 1968, p. 24153-24155. Senator J.S. Clark (D-PA) expresses concern over the Air Force's request of $70.8 million for the defoliation program in light of the obligations facing Congress to reduce federal expenditures. The Senator also had an article from the July 19, 1968 issue of Science by D.K. Price et al. (See 0600) inserted in the Record.

0158 "Chemicals and Vietnam: No Word on Petition but Defoliant Gets Scare." (See 0300)

0159   Christian, R.S. and J.K. White. "Battlefield Records
       Management and Its Relationship with the Agent Orange Study."
       Chemosphere, v. 12, no. 4-5, 1983, p. 761-768. The
       difficulty in obtaining accurate records of who was exposed
       to Agent Orange is explained.

0160   Collins, C.V. Herbicide Operations in Southeast Asia, July
       1961-June 1967. October 11, 1967. v, 94p. Available from
       NTIS: AD 779 796. The author explains the reasons why
       herbicide operations were begun in Vietnam, the present scope
       of operations, how the herbicide operations have been
       expanded and could be even further expanded, and the results
       of the operations.

0161   "DOD Lags in Vietnam Herbicide Phase-out." Biomedical News,
       v. 2, no. 3, March 1971, p. 1+. The Department of Defense
       has slowly begun to comply with the White House's order to
       phaseout the use of herbicides in Vietnam. This came about
       as a result of the American Association for the Advancement
       of Science's study. A progress report on the National
       Research Council's study is given.

0162   Davis, L.N. "Stoking the Engines of War." In The Corporate
       Alchemists: Profit Takers and Problem Makers in the Chemical
       Industry. New York: Morrow, 1984, p. 88-104. This book
       examines how chemical companies function; how the chemical
       industry originated, developed, and grew; the plastics,
       pharmaceutical and pesticide sectors of the chemical industry
       today; the consequences of the growth of the chemical
       industry, in particular the escalation of dangerous products,
       accidents and wastes; and the reasons why we have been
       assaulted with enough chemicals to drown us all. On page 103
       of this chapter, the chemical industry's involvement in
       supplying herbicides for use in the Vietnam War is discussed.

0163   Davis, P.M. "The Agent Orange Litigation: a Learning
       Experience - Part I." (See 2051)

0164   Deedy, J. "The Deflowering Process." (See 0304)

0165   "Defoliant Raids Suspended." Facts on File, v. 30, no. 1547,
       June 18-24, 1970, p. 437-438. Defoliant raids were suspended
       in April.

0166   "Defoliants, a Closed Case?" (See 0305)

0167   "Defoliants and Herbicides: AF Wants More in Vietnam." Oil,
       Paint and Drug Reporter, v. 193, no. 21, May 20, 1968, p. 5.
       The Air Force is asking for an appropriation for FY1969 of
       $70.8 million for herbicides to use in Vietnam. This is an

increase from $45.9 million this year and $38.8 million for
FY 1967.

0168   "Defoliation, Dow and Vietnam." (See 0474)

0169   **"Defoliation: Secret Army Study Urges Use in Future Wars."**
       Science and Government Report, v. 2, no. 11, August 18, 1972,
       p. 1+. Reprinted in "Defoliant Study Reported."
       Congressional Record, v. 118, pt. 22, August 18, 1972, p.
       29243-29244. The U.S. Army Corps of Engineers has secretly
       prepared scenarios which would use herbicides to destroy
       foliage in combat situations. The reports review the use of
       herbicides in Vietnam and based on interviews of officers
       strongly argues in behalf of herbicides on the grounds of
       military utility. The results of the questionnaires given to
       the officers are given. The conclusion of a computer
       analysis of the defoliation operations is that that these
       interviews provide an inconsistent picture of the advantages
       and disadvantages of spraying herbicides from fixed-wing
       aircraft.

0170   **Delmore, F.J. "Importance of Defoliation in**
       Counterinsurgency Operations." In Proceedings of the First
       Defoliation Conference: 29-30 July 1963. Comp. by V.Z.
       Mattie. January 1964, p. 11-13. Available from NTIS: AD-
       427874. This conference provided government and industry an
       opportunity to exchange ideas which could result in new
       herbicides for military programs and new commercial products
       and an opportunity to exchange research results. In this
       paper the author explains why a defoliation program is
       essential for the American military.

0171   **Donnelley, D. "Letter." Bioscience, v. 17, no. 1, January**
       1967, p. 10. The author is the Assistant Secretary of State
       and this letter is a response to the plant physiologists'
       September 6, 1966 letter to President Johnson on behalf of
       the President. The letter explains why the herbicides are
       being used and that they are not harmful to people, animals,
       soil or water.

0172   **Dougherty, J.M. The Use of Herbicides in Southeast Asia and**
       Its Criticism. Maxwell A.F.B.: Air War College, 1972. iv,
       58p. This report traces the development of the Operation
       Ranch Hand program. It also examines the criticism the
       program received and concluded that the criticism is invalid
       and that it was militarily effective.

0173   **"Drafting a Weed Killer." Business Week, no. 1964, April 22,**
       1967, p. 37. The Defense Department has increased the use of
       defoliants in Vietnam to the point that there could be a

serious commercial shortage of 2,4,5-T in the United States. This shortage will be felt keenly by ranchers and utility companies.

0174 "An End to Hanoi's Jungle Sanctuary?" U.S. News & World Report, v. 61, no. 14, October 3, 1966, p. 21. Defoliants are being used in Vietnam to clear the jungle cover that conceals Communist operations. There is talk that the defoliant spraying is being expanded into the demilitarized zone. It takes about 30 days for the defoliants to do their work and they are harmless to humans.

0175 "Extensive Chemical Warfare Against Civilians." Vietnam Courier, v. 6, no. 203, February 10, 1969, p. 4. The use of chemical to destroy crops in 1968 is summarized.

0176 Fair, S.D. "No Place to Hide: How Defoliants Expose the Viet Cong." Army, v. 14, no. 2, September 1963, p. 54-55. Reprinted in Armed Forces Chemical Journal, v. 18, no. 1, March 1964, p. 5-6. The use of defoliants is an effective weapon in the war against the Viet Cong. The Communists as to be expected have exploited this use for their own propaganda purposes by saying that the defoliants are harmful to the health of humans and cause the death of animals.

0177 Futrell, R.F. "Tactical Air Command, Mule Train, and Ranch Hand." In The Advisory Years to 1965. Washington: U.S. Air Force. Office of Air Force History, 1981, p. 103-117. This book details the Air Force's involvement in Southeast Asia from the end of World War II to 1965. In this chapter the author details the circumstances that led to the start up of these programs.

0178 Galston, A.W. "Changing the Environment: Herbicides in Vietnam II." (See 0501)

0179 Galston, A.W. "Defoliants." (See 0502)

0180 Galston, A.W. "Herbicides in Vietnam." (See 0503)

0181 Galston, A.W. et al. "Letter to President Lyndon B. Johnson." Bioscience, v. 17, no. 1, January 1967, p. 10. The text of a letter dated September 6, 1966 to President Johnson expressing concerns about the military use of herbicides in Vietnam signed by 12 plant physiologists is given.

0182 Gonzales, A.F., Jr. "Defoliation: a Controversial U.S. Mission in Vietnam." Data on Defense and Civil Systems, v. 13, no. 10, October 1968, p. 12-15. An account of how the

spraying missions of Operation Ranch Hand are accomplished.
Also discussed is the debate as to whether or not the
defoliation program is a form of chemical warfare.

0183 "Government Begins Buildup of Defoliants to Meet Increasing
      Use in Vietnam." Chemical and Engineering News, v. 46, no.
      23, May 27, 1968, p. 26-27. The military's planned
      escalation of the defoliation program is discussed.

0184 Gruchow, N. "Curbs on 2,4,5-T Use Imposed." Science, v.
      168, no. 3930, April 24, 1970, p. 453. The federal
      government has announced that the domestic use of 2,4,5-T
      will be halted and that its use as a defoliant in Vietnam
      will be suspended.

0185 "Hanoi Charges U.S. Raids." Facts on File, v. 31, no. 1578,
      January 21-27, 1971, p. 42. Hanoi has charged the United
      States conducted almost daily bombing and defoliating
      missions in North Vietnam between January 4 and 17.

0186 Harris, R. and J. Paxman. "The Rise and Rise of Chemical
      Weapons." In A Higher Form of Killing: the Secret Story of
      Chemical and Biological Warfare. New York: Hill and Wang,
      1982, p. 173-196. This book examines the development of
      chemical and biological weapons. Pages 190-193 of this
      chapter discuss how Operation Ranch Hand was carried out and
      the suspected effects on veterans' health.

0187 Harvey, F. "Tan Son Nhut." In Air War: Vietnam. New York:
      Bantam Books, 1967, p. 39-43. This book is an expansion of
      an article the author wrote for Flying magazine. The author
      examines all of the aspects of the air war in Vietnam and in
      this chapter details how Operation Ranch Hand was carried
      out. Also mentioned is the fact that the defoliant
      permanently sterilizes the soil, and the problems local
      farmers encounter in getting compensated when their crops are
      destroyed as a result of the defoliating missions are noted.

0188 Harvey, F. "Operation 'Ranch Hand.'" Flying, v. 79, no. 5,
      November 1966, p. 56. The purpose of Operation Ranch Hand
      and how the missions are carried out are detailed. Comments
      from Maj. R. Dresser, USAF, Commander of Operation Ranch
      Hand are included.

0189 Hay, A. "U.S. Defense Department Destroys Evidence of
      Vietnam Devastation." Nature, v. 279, no. 5715, June 21,
      1979, p. 662. The Department of Defense has destroyed the
      photographs used by the National Academy of Sciences as part
      of its assessment of the effects of the use of herbicides in
      Vietnam.

0190 Hay, J. "Ghosts of Poison Past." Macleans, v. 94, no. 5,
      February 2, 1981, p. 29-30. Because a U.S. Army document had
      to be released under the U.S. Freedom of Information Act, it
      has been learned that Canadian Forces Base Gagetown served as
      a test site in 1966 and 1967 for preliminary sprayings of
      Agent Orange as it had vegetation densities similar to those
      in Southeast Asia.

0191 Hay, J.H., Jr. "Dak To (November-December 1967)." In
      Vietnam Studies: Tactical and Materiel Innovations.
      Washington: GPO, 1974, p. 78-96. This book details some of
      the tactical and materiel innovations developed in Vietnam
      from the point of view of the infantry division commander.
      Pages 89-95 of this chapter discuss the considerations
      involved in the carrying out of Operation Ranch Hand.

0192 "Herbicide Hassle: the Army Fires Back." Chemical Week, v.
      102, no. 2, January 13, 1968, p. 67-68. At a recent
      Northeastern Weed Control Conference, C. Minarik of the
      Army's Fort Dietrick (MD) Chemical Warfare Center defended
      the use of defoliants in Vietnam and presented the Defense
      Department's first public response to recent criticism about
      Operation Ranch Hand.

0193 "Herbicide Program in Vietnam." Congressional Record, v.
      116, pt. 22, August 25, 1970, p. 29932-29933. Senator T.J.
      McIntyre (D-N.H.) had inserted in the Record the December
      1969 testimony of Rear Adm. W.E. Lemos before the House's
      Committee on Foreign Affairs' Subcommittee on National
      Security Policy and Scientific Developments concerning the
      contribution the use of herbicides is making to the saving of
      American lives in Vietnam.

0194 "Herbicide Use Restricted." Facts on File, v. 30, no. 1538,
      April 16-22, 1970, p. 264. Three federal agencies have
      announced a halt to the use of 2,4,5-T including the Defense
      Department's use of Agent Orange in Vietnam. Agent White
      and picloram will now be the only herbicides used in Vietnam.

0195 Hill, H. "'Only You Can Prevent Forests.'" Guardian, v. 21,
      no. 31, May 3, 1969, p. 17. Figures are given for the amount
      of herbicides used and the number of acres destroyed as part
      of Operation Ranch Hand from 1962-1968.

0196 Hilsman, R. "And How Do You Know If You're Winning?" In
      To Move a Nation: the Politics of Foreign Policy in the
      Administration of John F. Kennedy. Garden City, N.Y.:
      Doubleday, 1967. p. 440-467. This book examines the
      politics of how policy was made in the Kennedy Administration
      with regards to foreign affairs. Pages 442-443 of this

chapter detail some of the debate behind the decision to use defoliants in Vietnam.

0197   Hoard, B. "Vets Mobilize Micro to Attack Agent Orange: but Face Cash Crisis." Computerworld, v. 15, no. 24, June 15, 1981, p. 6. Vietnam veterans in Vermont are attempting to computerize military data on the sprayings of Agent Orange in order to pinpoint pertinent facts. Right now they are using an Apple II but would like to raise the money to buy a TRS-80 Model III. The veterans hope to distribute their program nationwide on diskette.

0198   Howard, J.D. "Herbicides in Support of Counterinsurgency Operations: a Cost-effectiveness Study." Masters Thesis, Naval Postgraduate School, 1972. 127p. Available from NTIS: AD 745 180. The author develops costs, effectiveness criteria and cost-effectiveness ratios for military herbicide systems and three alternatives which would accomplish the goals of foliage removal and crop destruction in Vietnam-type situations. The author concludes that the most cost-effective solution is a mix of spraying herbicides from aircraft and land clearing tractors.

0199   House, W.B. et al. Assessment of Ecological Effects of Extensive or Repeated Use of Herbicides. (See 0529)

0200   "The Immediate Danger of Defoliation Program." Congressional Record, v. 116, pt. 9, April 15, 1970, p. 11861-11862. Representative R.D. McCarthy (D-N.Y.) expresses his joy given the findings of the Bionetics Laboratories study that the use of 2,4,5-T will be banned in the United States and that the Department of Defense will soon announce a ban on its use in Vietnam.

0201   Jordan, C. "Uncovering Charlie: Spray Destroys Hiding Places of Viet Cong." Air Force Times, v. 26, no. 39, May 11, 1966, p. 14. How the missions of Operation Ranch Hand are carried out is discussed.

0202   Kolko, G. "Escalation of Chemical Warfare and War Against Civilians." Solidarity with Vietnam, no. 49, June 1969, p. 4-5. The escalation of the use of herbicides in Vietnam is detailed.

0203   Krepinevich, A.F., Jr. "Defoliation." In The Army and Vietnam. Baltimore: Johns Hopkins University Press, 1986, p. 210-213. The military effectiveness of the defoliation operations is debated in this section of this book which examines how little, as an institution, the U.S. Army anticipated and prepared for the kind of war the Vietnam War turned out to be.

0204   Langer, E. "Chemical and Biological Warfare (II): the
       Weapons and the Policies." (See 0351)

0205   McCarthy, R.D. "War Against Food and Foliage." (See 0550)

0206   **McConnell, A.F., Jr. "Mission: Ranch Hand." Air University
       Review, v. 21, no. 2, January-February 1970, p. 89-94.** A
       discussion of how Operation Ranch Hand came into existence
       and why a defoliation program was needed.

0207   McElheny, V. "Herbicides in Vietnam: Juggernaut Out of
       Control." (See 0551)

0208   **Mayer, J. "Starvation as a Weapon - Herbicides in Vietnam,
       I." Scientist and Citizen, v. 9, no. 7, August-September
       1967, p. 115-121. Reprinted in Ecocide in Indochina: the
       Ecology of War. Ed. by B. Weisberg. San Francisco:
       Canfield Pr., 1970, p. 78-88.** The author discusses whether
       or not the crop destruction aspect of the military spraying
       of herbicides has accomplished its military purpose. The
       author contends that all it is doing is starving the civilian
       population, not the Viet Cong soldiers.

0209   **Meek, S.L. "An Estimate of the Relative Exposure of U.S. Air
       Force Crewmembers to Agent Orange." Masters Thesis,
       University of Washington, 1981. iii, 33p.** This masters
       thesis examines the extent to which the Ranch Hand crew
       members were exposed to Agent Orange during the actual
       spraying missions and whether exposure to Agent Orange
       differed significantly as a function of crew position. The
       author concluded that the flight mechanic's exposure was at
       least six times as great as the other crew members.

0210   **Military Assistance Command, Vietnam. Evaluation of
       Herbicide Operations in the Republic of Vietnam as of 30
       April 1966. July 12, 1966. 1 volume (various paginations).
       Available from NTIS: AD 779 792.** This report reviews
       existing evidence concerning the military use of herbicides
       in Vietnam and concludes that at this time, militarily, the
       advantages outweigh the disadvantages. However, the
       unintentional destruction of civilian crops as a result of
       the sprayings has caused resentment towards the United States
       and the GVN.

0211   **Military Assistance Command, Vietnam. Evaluation of
       Herbicide Operations in the Republic of Vietnam (September
       1962-September 1963). Prepared by P.G. Olenchuk, R.T. Burke
       and O.K. Henderson. October 10, 1963. 55p. Available from
       NTIS: AD 779 795.** This evaluation concludes that the use of
       herbicides has been almost 100 percent effective in the

physical destruction of crops and have a direct and
continuing favorable impact on military and civilian
activities in Vietnam. The authors believe that the use of
herbicides should be continued if certain guidelines are
employed.

0212 Military Assistance Command, Vietnam. The Herbicide Policy
Review: Report for March-May 1968. August 20, 1968. vii,
129p. Available from NTIS: AD 779 794. The American
Ambassador to Vietnam appointed a special committee to
review the efficacy of herbicide operations in Vietnam. This
is their report. The Committee found that the benefits of
the program outweighed any problems that have resulted and
that the crop destruction program should be continued but
that the defoliation operations should be held to a minimum.
The Committee also found that the ecological impact of the
herbicide operations was not serious.

0213 Military Assistance Command, Vietnam. Military Operations:
Herbicide Operations. August 12, 1969. 19p. Available from
NTIS: AD 779 793. This directive was written to ensure that
the herbicide program in Vietnam was being conducted in
accordance with the conditions of the Report on the Herbicide
Policy Review (See 0212) of 1968. It spells out the
policies, responsibilities and procedures governing the
operational deployment of herbicides with this Command.

0214 "Military Use of Herbicides." Congressional Record, v. 116,
pt. 22, August 17, 1970, p. 29219-29220. Senator G. Nelson
(D-Wisc.) expressed his concern over the use of defoliants in
Cambodia and had a August 16, 1970 article from the
Washington Star by S. Hersh and a August 16, 1970 article
from the Philadelphia Bulletin by J.R. Kerney inserted in the
Record.

0215 Minarik, C.E. "The Use of Herbicides in Vietnam."
Northeastern Weed Control Conference. Proceedings, v. 22,
1968, p. 1-5. The author uses excerpts from newspaper
articles to describe how Operation Ranch Hand is carried out
and its effectiveness. The author believes the military
value of herbicides and defoliants has been proven.

0216 "NAS, AAAS to Report on Vietnam Defoliation." (See 0560)

0217 Neilands, J.B. "Chemical Warfare." (See 0367)

0218 Neilands, J.B. "Ecocide in Vietnam." In Why Are We Still in
Vietnam? Ed. by S. Brown and L. Acklund. New York:
Vintage, 1970, p. 87-97. This book focuses on the premises
and consequences of the current American policy toward

Vietnam and detail what the authors believe to be alternative policies. This article describes the types and amounts of herbicides which were used in Vietnam, the American government's contention that the use of herbicides does not violate the Geneva Protocol and how much the government knew about the toxicity of 2,4,5-T before they banned the use of Agent Orange in Vietnam.

0219 Nelson, B. "Herbicides: Order on 2,4,5-T Issued at Unusually High Level." Science, v. 166, no. 3908, November 21, 1969, p. 977-979. The White House Science Adviser, L. DuBridge, announced a partial curtailment of the use of 2,4,5-T. This action appears to be in response to recent studies indicating that herbicides such as 2,4,5-T and 2,4-D may cause birth defects in animals and the controversy surrounding the use of the herbicides in Vietnam. The Defense Department will hereafter restrict its use of 2,4,5-T to unpopulated areas. The Defense Department however said that there will be no change in the policy governing the use of 2,4,5-T as it already complies with this recent White House directive.

0220 "New Weapon for Jungle War." Congressional Record, v. 111, pt. 5, April 1, 1965, p. 6776-6777. Representative R.C. Pucinski (D-Ill.) spoke in support of the use of defoliants in Vietnam and had an article by C. Nidodemus from the Chicago Daily News inserted in the Record.

0221 Newman, S. "Herbicide or Genocide - Which Cide Are They On." (See 0374)

0222 "Nixon's Chemical Warfare in South Vietnam." Vietnam Courier, v. 6, no. 246, December 8, 1969, p. 3-4. This article consists of excerpts from a communique issued on November 18, 1969 by the South Viet Nam Committee to Denounce US-Puppets' War Crimes. This communique is an accounting of the instances where the United States has sprayed chemicals to destroy crops in the delta provinces such as My Tho, Ben Tre, Tay Ninh, Tra Vinh, Thu Dau Mot, Can Tho, etc.

0223 "Operation Ranch Hand." Weeds Trees and Turf, v. 8, no. 3, March 1969, p. 20-22. The purpose of Operation Ranch Hand and how the defoliation missions are carried out are described.

0224 "Operation Wasteland." (See 0574)

0225 Orians, G.H. and E.W. Pfeiffer. "Defoliants: Orange, White, and Blue." (See 0576)

0226 **"Pentagon Drops Defoliant Contract."** Science, v. 163, no.
3868, February 14, 1969, p. 656. The Department of Defense
has cancelled plans to renovate an old chemical plant near
St. Louis which was to be used to produce herbicides. The
plant was to have produced eight million gallons of
defoliants for Vietnam. But the Department of Defense has
cancelled these plans because the civilian industry is
producing enough herbicides to meet the Department of
Defense's need. The defoliation program will continue
despite criticism from some scientists.

0227 **"Pentagon Purchases."** Chemical Week, v. 100, no. 13, April
1, 1967, p. 36. The Pentagon is asking for $39.5 million to
purchase defoliants to use in Vietnam - a nearly fourfold
increase from the $10 million spent in fiscal 1966.
Production of these defoliants is already at capacity.
Farmers will have problems obtaining these chemicals. The
Pentagon is asking for $49.5 million in fiscal 1968.

0228 **"Pesticides on the Batttlefront."** Farm Chemicals, v. 129,
no. 6, June 1966, p. 53. Farm Chemicals questioned the
Department of Defense about the defoliation project underway
in Vietnam. Their responses are listed in this article. The
questions concern the chemicals being used, the frequency of
application, the type of aircraft used, the amount of acreage
sprayed and other ways pesticides are being used in Vietnam.

0229 **Pruden, W., Jr. "The Special Spray Flight - Defoliating the
Jungles in Vietnam."** National Observer (Silver Spring, MD),
v. 5, no. 9, February 28, 1966, p. 1+. The author details
how the defoliating missions are carried out by explaining
the types of planes used, how the spraying is done and the
method in which approval for a target was obtained. He
accompanied a crew on one of the flights. The crop
destruction aspect of the program and how the Viet Cong tried
to use this as a propaganda weapon are also mentioned.

0230 **Shade, R.A. "Management of the Department of Defense
Vietnam Herbicide Management Program."** Masters Thesis,
George Washington University, 1969. iv, 75p. This thesis
examines the decision making process the Department of
Defense used in managing the program to acquire herbicides
for the military to use in Vietnam, the alternatives
available to meet the military demand for herbicides, the
impact the decision to pre-empt the herbicide supply for
military use had on the civilian sector and the factors that
caused the military demand for the herbicides to exceed
supply.

0231 **Shapley, D. "Herbicides: DOD Study of Viet Use Damns with
Faint Praise."** Science, v. 177, no. 4051, September 1, 1972,

p. 776-779. Reprinted in "Senate Resolution 48: Submission of a Resolution Relating to a Comprehensive Interpretation for the Geneva Protocol." Congressional Record, v. 119, pt. 2, January 29, 1973, p. 2430-2432. The Army Corps of Engineers Strategic Studies Group has concluded that herbicides were of only limited usefulness in the Vietnam War.

0232 Shook, H.W. Defoliation Operations in Southeast Asia. Maxwell A.F.B.: Air Command & Staff College, 1969. vi, 108p. This study examines the development of defoliation operations in Southeast Asia and their overall impact. The author concludes that while the concepts behind the operations are sound and their overall effectiveness have been militarily beneficial, certain discrepancies still exist.

0233 "Silent Weapons: Role of Chemicals in Lower Case Warfare." Army Digest, v. 23, no. 11, November 1968, p. 6-11. Most of this article discusses the use of riot control gases in Vietnam. The use of herbicides in Vietnam is also mentioned and how they help the Army fight the war against the Viet Cong.

0234 Skierkowski, P. "One More Job for Army Aviation." USA Army Aviation Digest, v. 13, no. 6, July 1967, p. 6-7. How Army Aviation adapted their planes and helicopters in order to spray defoliants and dispense riot control agents and ensure the safety of their pilots is described.

0235 Smith, C. and D. Watkins. The Vietnam Map Book: a Selp-help Guide to Herbicide Exposure. Berkeley, CA: Winter Soldier Archive, 1981. 107p. This book contains the necessary maps and information for a Vietnam veteran to determine if he was exposed to Agent Orange or not. The book also discusses the approach taken by the Veterans Administration in dealing with the problem, obstacles put in the authors' way in obtaining the information on where the spraying took place and the possible health risks of being exposed to Agent Orange.

0236 Smith, C. and D. Watkins. "What's New on the Vietnam Map Book." Citizen Soldier, no. 4, 1982, p. 5. The Vietnam Map Book documents where Agents Orange, White and Blue were sprayed in Vietnam. The reactions of veterans and government officials to the book are related.

0237 "Spraying Step-up." Chemical Week, v. 99, no. 7, August 13, 1966, p. 98. The spraying of defoliants in Vietnam is on the increase. The reasons why defoliation is carried out is explained. The amount of land that has been sprayed, the

rate the chemicals are been applied, which chemicals are
being used and who supplied the chemicals are all mentioned.

0238   "Statement on US Intensification of Chemical Warfare in South
       Viet Nam." South Vietnam in Struggle, no. 91, March 10,
       1971, p. 2. The Committee for Denunciation of the US
       Imperialists' and Their Henchman's War Crimes in South Viet
       Nam denounces President Nixon's statement that defoliation
       operations will be discontinued except for inaccessible areas
       and around military installations as deceptive due to the
       fact that nearly all of South Vietnam fits into the
       exception.

0239   "Stepped-up US Chemical Warfare." South Vietnam in Struggle,
       no. 133, January 31, 1972, p. 2. Although the use of
       herbicides has been ordered stopped, this article lists
       several incidences in 1971 where sprayings took place. Also
       massive amounts of the herbicides continued to be stored in
       South Vietnam.

0240   "Suspension." Scientific American, v. 223, no. 2, August
       1970, p. 46. The use of defoliants in South Vietnam has been
       suspended and may not be resumed on a large scale. The
       planes will be used to fly captured material out of Cambodia
       for right now.

0241   "The Talk of the Town: Notes and Comment." New Yorker, v.
       47, no. 53, February 19, 1972, p. 31-32. Reprinted in "The
       Talk of the Town." Congressional Record, v. 118, pt. 4,
       February 17, 1972, p. 4351. The decision to stop using 2,4-
       D and 2,4,5-T in Vietnam and what to with the remaining
       chemicals are discussed.

0242   Thant, U. et al. Chemical and Bacteriological (Biological)
       Weapons and the Effects of Their Possible Use: Report of the
       Secretary General. (See 0619)

0243   "They Are Even More Ruthless Than Hitler!" For Vietnam:
       Tricontinental Committee of Support to the People of Viet Nam
       Bulletin, v. 2, no. 4, 1967, p. 26-35. This article is taken
       from the Black Book on Viet Nam which was prepared by the
       Committee for the Denunciation of the War Crimes of the U.S.
       The poison gases, napalm, white phosphorus and herbicides
       used by the "U.S. Imperialists" in hope of subduing "the
       patriotic South Vietnamese people" are described.

0244   "2,4,5-T Is Going the Way of DDT: Nixed in Home and Aquatic
       Areas; Is Taken Out of Action in Vietnam." Oil, Paint and
       Drug Reporter, v. 197, no. 16, April 20, 1970, p. 3+. The
       use of Agent Orange in Vietnam has been suspended.

0245 "The USAF 'Deniability' Factor: Spraying Was Obliterated."
      Citizen Soldier, no. 5, May 1983, p. 7. An Operation Ranch
      Hand veteran details his experiences in Vietnam and the fact
      that the sprayings did not stop in February 1970. He
      questions if this means that veterans who were exposed in the
      time period from February 1970 to the end of 1971 will be
      told by the Veterans Administration and the Air Force that
      they were not exposed as the HERBS tapes show that the last
      spraying took place on February 28, 1970.

0246 "U.S. Chemical Warfare Intensified in South Vietnam."
      Vietnam Courier, v. 6, no. 219, June 2, 1969, p. 5. The
      spraying of chemicals to destroy crops has intensified since
      President Nixon took office.

0247 U.S. Congress. Joint Committee on Defense Production.
      "Herbicides for Southeast Asia." In Seventeenth Annual
      Report of the Activities of the Joint Committee on Defense
      Production. Report, 90th Cong., 2nd sess., January 15, 1968.
      Washington: GPO, 1968, p. 12-13, 420. The efforts being
      made to meet the ever increasing need for herbicides for
      military use in Southeast Asia are described.

0248 "U.S. Defoliant Ban Defied." Facts on File, v. 30, no. 1567,
      November 5-11, 1970, p. 817. The herbicide 2,4,5-T has
      evidently been used several times recently in Vietnam despite
      the fact that the Defense Department has ordered a ban on its
      use in Vietnam. The leftover Agent Orange will be stored in
      Vietnam for right now. Agents White and Blue have not been
      banned.

0249 U.S. Department of the Army. Employment of Riot Control
      Agents, Flame, Smoke, Anti-plant Agents and Personnel
      Detectors in Counter-guerrilla Operations. (U.S. Department
      of the Army Training Circular no. TC 3-16) Washington:
      Headquarters, Department of the Army, 1969. 85p. In this
      book the Army provides guidance on the employment of riot
      control agents, flame, smoke, antiplant agents and personnel
      detectors in counterguerrilla operations. Chapter 5,
      "Antiplant Agent Operations," on pages 62-68 and Appendices C
      and D on pages 80 and 81 describe Agents Orange, Blue, White
      and several soil sterilants. The rate of application, safety
      precautions and the effects on foliage for each agent are
      also noted.

0250 "U.S. to Curb Herbicide Use." Facts on File, v. 30, no.
      1574, December 24-30, 1970, p. 961. The United States has
      announced that herbicide operations in Vietnam will be phased
      out.

0251   "U.S. to Step Up Vietnam Defoliation." <u>Agricultural</u>
        <u>Chemicals</u>, v. 21, no. 10, October 1966, p. 65. Despite the
        efforts of 22 leading American scientists to stop the
        chemical defoliation missions in Vietnam, the Pentagon is
        taking steps to triple the number of aircraft spraying the
        defoliant.

0252   "Use of Herbicides in Viet-Nam to be Phased Out." <u>Department</u>
        <u>of State Bulletin</u>, v. 64, no. 1647, January 18, 1971, p. 77.
        A copy of a White House press release dated December 26, 1970
        which the Department of Defense had compiled with the
        President's direction to reduce the use of herbicides in
        Vietnam and the ban on the use of Agent Orange continues to
        be in effect.

0253   "Vegetation Destruction in Vietnam Will Hamper Vegetation
        Control in the U.S." <u>Chemical Engineering</u>, v. 74, no. 9,
        April 24, 1967, p. 88. As a result of the Department of
        Defense's buying such large amounts of herbicides for use in
        Vietnam, there is a shortage of herbicides for domestic use.
        The government is studying ways to solve this problem.

0254   "Vietnam: Buildup." <u>Newsweek</u>, v. 58, no. 22, November 27,
        1961, p. 40. The line between American assistance and
        participation is beginning to blur. The Americans are
        showing Vietnamese fliers how to spray chemicals that turn
        rice fields in Communist-held areas yellow.

0255   "Vietnam Defoliation." <u>Science News</u>, v. 99, no. 2, January
        9, 1971, p. 29. The release of the first report of the
        findings of the American Association for the Advancement of
        Science's Herbicides Assessment Commission coincides with the
        announcement by the White House that the use of herbicides in
        Vietnam will be phased out. The American Association for the
        Advancement of Science's study found that one-fifth of South
        Vietnam's mangrove forests have been destroyed.

0256   "'Vietnam Order of Battle' May Figure in Agent Orange Suits."
        <u>Publishers Weekly</u>, v. 220, no. 25, December 18, 1981, p. 44.
        <u>Vietnam Order of Battle</u> by S.L. Stanton, a book published by
        the U.S. News & World Report Book Division, is being used by
        veterans to determine if they served in troops that had come
        in contact with Agent Orange.

0257   "Vietnam: Today, Tomorrow." <u>Chemical Week</u>, v. 98, no. 13,
        March 26, 1966, p. 43-46+. This article was written to
        inform businessmen on what they need to know about the
        domestic impact of the Vietnam War, the role of chemicals in
        the war and the future of Vietnam's CPI. Page 46 of this
        article details how the herbicide spraying missions are

conducted and why the military thinks the sprayings are a good idea.

0258 "War Herbicides Ban Issued." Facts on File, v. 35, no. 1797, April 19, 1975, p. 253. An executive order has been signed by President Ford stating that it will be national policy that first use of herbicides in war will be limited to clearing away vegetation within U.S. base defense perimeters.

0259 Warren, W.F. A Review of the Herbicide Program in South Vietnam. August 1968. 69p. Available from NTIS: AD 779 797. This report gives a history of the military use of herbicides, details the development of their use in Vietnam, provides an assessment of the psychological effects of the crop destruction program and gives the results of the herbicides operations.

0260 Warren, W.F., L.L. Henry and R.D. Johnston. Crop Destruction Operation in RVN During CY 1967. December 23, 1967. ii, 38p. Available from NTIS: AD 779 798. The authors detail the operations and objectives of the crop destruction program, comment on the effectiveness of the program and detail the results of the program. They conclude that the crop destruction operations are an integral, essential and effective part of the effort in Vietnam.

0261 Westing, A.H. "Chemical and Biological Weapons: Past and Present." Peace and the Sciences, no. 3, 1982, p. 25-37. The author gives an overview of the use of chemical weapons and mentions the Agent Orange issue and why the military chose to use it.

0262 Westing, A.H. "Introduction to the Aerial Application of Herbicides for Military Purposes." Aerial Applicator, v. 11, no. 1, January-February 1973, p. 10. The author gives a very brief history of the use of herbicides in war including Vietnam and provides a very short bibliography.

0263 Westing, A.H. "Laotian Postscript." [letter] Nature, v. 294, no. 5842, December 17, 1981, p. 606. The author details the amount of spraying of herbicides that has been done in Laos. Approximately 1,600 cubic meters of herbicides have been dispensed and about 83 percent was Agent Orange.

0264 Winchester, J.H. "Cargo Planes in the Vietnam War." NATO's Fifteen Nations, v. 11, no. 4, August-September 1966, p. 50-53. A portion of this article discusses how the C-123 airplanes carry out the Ranch Hand missions. Although the Viet Cong tell their troops and the Vietnamese villagers that these chemicals are poisonous to humans, it is known that this is of course not true.

0265   Wolfe, W.H. "Epidemiology and Toxicology of Agent Orange."
       (See 1272)

0266   **World Health Organization. "Anti-plant Agents." In** Health
       Aspects of Chemical and Biological Weapons: Report of a
       WHO Group of Consultants. Geneva: The Organization, 1970.
       132p. This report attempts to analyze the health effects of
       the possible use of chemical and biological weapons on
       civilians at different levels of social and economic
       development and what this means for the World Health
       Organization and its member states. In this chapter the
       types of anti-plant agents and their formulations used in
       Vietnam and what is known about their toxicological
       properties are discussed.

THE EFFORTS TO STOP THE USE OF AGENT ORANGE IN VIETNAM AND THE DEBATE ON THE LEGALITY OF ITS USE

0267   **"AAAS Sets Up Group to Study Environmental Changes by
       Man."** Chemical and Engineering News v. 46, no. 2, January
       8, 1968, p. 16. The American Association for the Advancement
       of Science has set up a committee to study environmental
       alteration. The first item of business for this committee is
       to review the report prepared by the Midwest Research
       Institute.

0268   **"AAAS Team Will Go to Vietnam."** Scientific Research, v. 4,
       no. 23, November 10, 1969, p. 11. The go ahead has been
       given by the American Association for the Advancement of
       Science's Board for J.E. Cantlon, provost of Michigan State
       University, to begin putting a team together to study the
       effects of the military use of herbicides in Vietnam. Some
       of the debate the American Association for the Advancement of
       Sciences has gone through to get to this point is noted.

0269   **"AP Discloses Large-scale Use of Poison Chemicals in South
       Viet Nam."** Solidarity with Vietnam, no. 59, June 1970, p.
       19. The Associated Press says that the American ruling
       circles have admitted that 2,4,5-T and its contaminant may
       produce abnormal developments in unborn animals and that the
       consequences of the use of chemical poisons are
       unforeseeable. The Vietnamese people sternly condemn and
       denounce to public opinion this monstrous crime.

0270   **"American Scientists Denounce US Chemical Warfare in South
       Vietnam."** South Vietnam in Struggle, no. 52, January 15,

1970, p. 9. At a recent American Association for the
Advancement of Science meeting several scientists opposed the
use of toxic chemicals including herbicides in Vietnam,
citing the ecological damage they have done.

0271   "American Troops Use Agent Orange, Banned Defoliant, in
        Vietnam." Congressional Record, v. 116, pt. 29, November 25,
        1970, p. 38846. Senator S.M. Young (D-Ohio) comments on the
        fact that Agent Orange is continuing to be spraying in
        Vietnam despite the fact that its use was ordered suspended
        in April. Senator Young calls for the ratification of the
        Geneva Protocol and for the dismantling of our biological and
        chemical warfare establishment.

0272   Anderson, F.E., Jr. Is the Use of Herbicides in Limited War
        Justified. November 2, 1970. 14p. Available from NTIS: AD
        774 204. The author examines the opposition that has
        developed to the military use of herbicides in Vietnam from
        military, scientific, political and legal standpoints. The
        author states that while opposition to the use of the
        herbicides seems to be based on scientific speculation and
        strained legalities, the use of this rather humane weapon has
        been discontinued.

0273   "Are Tear Gas and Herbicides Permitted Weapons?"
        Congressional Record, v. 116, pt. 15, June 18, 1970, p.
        20567-20569. Representative D.M. Fraser (D-Minn.) discussed
        his concern over the fact that the Geneva Protocol had not
        been submitted to the Senate for ratification and had J.
        Goldblatt's article from the April 1970 issue of Bulletin of
        the Atomic Scientists (See 0328) inserted in the Record.

0274   "The Atrocities Nixon Condones and Continues." I.F. Stone's
        Weekly, v. 17, no. 23, December 15, 1969, p. 1+. The health
        effects and ethical considerations of the anti-crop program
        in South Vietnam are discussed.

0275   "Authorization of Appropriations for Military Procurement and
        Other Purposes." Congressional Record, v. 116, pt. 22,
        August 26, 1970, p. 30036-30055. The discussion on the floor
        of the Senate on the Nelson-Goodell Amendment which would
        call a halt to the use of herbicides in Vietnam is given. It
        was defeated.

0276   "Authorization of Appropriations for Military Procurement and
        Other Purposes." Congressional Record, v. 116, pt. 22,
        August 27, 1970, p. 30222-30227. Amendment no. 863 to the
        military authorization bill for FY 1971 was co-sponsored by
        Senator C.E. Goodell (R-N.Y.) and Senator G. Nelson (D-
        Wisc.). This amendment would limit the use of chemical

herbicides in war especially in Vietnam. The Senate debate
on this amendment is given on these pages. The amendment was
defeated.

0277   "Authorization of Appropriations for Military Procurement
       During Fiscal Year 1971 - Amendment." (See 0427)

0278   Bach, P.V. "Law and the Use of Chemical Warfare in Vietnam."
       Scientific World, v. 15, no. 6, 1971, p. 12-14. The author
       presented this paper at the International Scientists
       Conference on U.S. Chemical Warfare in Viet Nam. The author
       discusses what he believes to be the United States' disregard
       for international law by using chemical weapons such as
       herbicides in Vietnam.

0279   Bach, P.V. "The Legal Viewpoint." Vietnamese Studies, no.
       29, 1971, p. 27-35. The entire issue of this journal
       consists of documents of the International Conference of
       Scientists on U.S. Chemical Warfare in Viet Nam. The author
       discusses whether or not the United States has a legal right
       to conduct chemical warfare (including the use of herbicides
       and tear gas) in Vietnam.

0280   "Ban Leaves Loophole." Chemical Week, v. 116, no. 1, January
       1, 1975, p. 12. The Senate has approved the 1925 Geneva
       Protocol which bans the use of chemical weapons. However,
       the Senate left in the loophole that tear gas and herbicides
       were not to be considered chemical weapons and could be used
       in the future, in order to get the White House to ratify the
       protocol. The Senate, however, did get the White House to
       agree that tear gas and herbicides as "national policy" would
       only be used as defensive weapons.

0281   Baxter, R.R. and T. Buergenthal. "Legal Aspects of the
       Geneva Protocol of 1925." American Journal of International
       Law, v. 64, no. 4, October 1970, p. 853-879. Slightly
       revised in The Control of Chemical and Biological Weapons.
       New York: Carnegie Endowment for International Peace, 1971,
       p. 1-38, which was reprinted in The Geneva Protocol of 1925.
       U.S. Congress. Senate. Committee on Foreign Relations.
       Hearing, 92nd Cong., 1st sess., March 5, 16, 18, 19, 22, and
       26, 1971. Washington: GPO, p. 118-155. This article
       describes the obligations that a nation which ratifies the
       Geneva Protocol agrees to, what the United States will need
       to do if it decides it does not want to accept all of the
       obligations and what legal problems it will encounter if it
       decides to do this. The article also discusses if tear gas
       and anti-plant chemicals were meant to be excluded.

0282   Bevan, W. "AAAS Council Meeting, 1970." Science, v. 171, no. 3972, February 19, 1971, p. 709-711. The American Association for the Advancement of Science's Council meeting of December 30, 1970 is summarized. The Herbicide Assessment Commission updated the Council on the work they accomplished thus far. The Council passed a resolution on the use of chemical defoliants in Vietnam, commending the United States government on its announcement that the use of herbicides in Vietnam will be phased out.

0283 Bixler, G. "Chemical Control of Weeds in Vietnam." [editorial] Chemical and Engineering News, v. 46, no. 8, February 19, 1968, p. 5. The author contends that those who are against the military use of herbicides in Vietnam would do well to base their protests on fact rather than emotion.

0284 Boffey, P.M. "Defoliation: the Academy as Shield for the Pentagon." In The Brain Bank of America: an Inquiry into the Politics of Science. New York: McGraw-Hill, 1975, p. 143-164. This book is the result of an investigation into the workings of the National Academy of Sciences by R. Nader's Center for Study of Responsive Law. This chapter details the story behind the report prepared by the Academy's Committee on the Effects of Herbicides in Vietnam. The author believes that the Academy failed to act as an impartial overseer of the herbicide program.

0285 Boffey, P.M. "Herbicides in Vietnam: AAAS Study Runs into Military Roadblock." Science, v. 170, no. 3953, October 2, 1970, p. 42-45. The difficulties the American Association for the Advancement of Science has had in obtaining information for their study on the military use of herbicides in Vietnam is discussed.

0286 Brown, D.E. "The Use of Herbicides in War: a Political/ Military Analysis." (See 0150)

0287 Brown, T.L. "Herbicides in Vietnam." [letter] Chemical and Engineering News, v. 46, no. 14, March 25, 1968, p. 7. This letter was written response to G. Bixler's editorial (See 0283) from the February 19, 1968 issue of this journal. T.L. Brown feels the editorial was entirely inadequate. The defoliation operation is causing starvation and malnutrition among the Vietnamese people.

0288 Bunn, G. "Banning Poison Gas and Germ Warfare: Should the U.S. Agree?" Wisconsin Law Review, v. 1969, no. 2, 1969, p. 375-420. Reprinted in The Geneva Protocol of 1925. U.S. Congress. Senate. Committee on Foreign Relations. Hearing, 92nd Cong., 1st sess., March 5, 16, 18, 19, 22, and 26, 1971. Washington: GPO, 1972, p. 72-117, and in Chemical and

Biological Warfare: U.S. Policies and International Effects. U.S. Congress. House. Committee on Foreign Affairs. Subcommittee on National Security Policy and Scientific Developments. Hearing, 91st Cong., 1st sess., November 18 and 20 and December 2, 9, 18 and 19, 1969. Washington: GPO, 1970, p. 304-345. This article discusses the Geneva Protocol in terms of whether or not its principles have become so widely accepted that they apply to the United States even though the United States has not signed the protocol. Pages 406-409 discuss whether or not the use of herbicides in Vietnam violates the Protocol. The author feels there is doubt about whether herbicides were meant to be prohibited. The United States feels that the use of herbicides is not a violation of the treaty.

0289   Burchan, L.T. "Defoliation Effects on Forest Ecology." (See 0445)

0290   "CBW and National Security." Congressional Record, v. 115, pt. 24, November 3, 1969, p. 32737-32746. Representative J.R. Dellenback (R-Ore.) had inserted into the Record a report prepared by an informal study group on the strategic and tactical implications of chemical weapons which includes a mention of the issues surrounding the use of defoliants as a weapon on page 32741. Representative H.W. Robison (R-N.Y.) then had a speech on what American policy on chemical and biological weapons should be, delivered by M.S. Meselson, inserted in the Record. Representative C.A. Mosher (R-Ohio) spoke and announced that the President has decided to limit the use of 2,4,5-T. Representative F.D. Schwengel (R-Iowa) also spoke on the issue of chemical and biological weapon proliferation.

0291   "CBW in Vietnam." Congressional Record, v. 117, pt. 23, August 6, 1971, p. 30694-30695. Representative J.R. Dellenback (R-Ore.) summarized the position that he has taken over the years on the use of herbicides as a weapon in Vietnam. He is disappointed that the Administration has chosen to interpret the Geneva Protocol as not banning the use of herbicides. Representative Dellenback wishes that the protocol would have been interpreted as banning these weapons.

0292   "CW in Vietnam? Defoliants and Tear Gas." Senior Scholastic, v. 94, no. 3, February 7, 1969, p. 7. The debate over the use of herbicides and tear gas in Vietnam and how this relates to the Geneva Protocol is explained.

0293   Calder, N. "War by Weedkiller." New Statesman, v. 75, no. 1924, January 26, 1968, p. 106. The protests lodged by scientists over the use of defoliants in South Vietnam and the environmental studies underway by the National Academy of Sciences and the American Association for the Advancement of Science are noted.

0294 Cecil, P.F. <u>Herbicidal Warfare: the Ranch Hand Project in Vietnam</u>. (See 0155)

0295 Chamlin, G.R. "Vietnam Defoliation Saves Lives." (See 0453)

0296 **"Chemical & Biological Warfare."** <u>Facts on File</u>, v. 29, no. 1518, November 27-December 3, 1969, p. 772-773. Although President Nixon has renounced the use of biological weapons, he has pledged to continue to use tear gas and defoliants in Vietnam. A House subcommittee has begun consideration of the Geneva Protocol of 1925.

0297 **"Chemical and Biological Warfare Policies and Practices."** <u>Congressional Record</u>, v. 115, pt. 7, April 21, 1969, p. 9732-9739. Representative R.D. McCarthy (D-N.Y.) spoke at length on American policy towards chemical and biological weapons. On pages 9736 and 9738 the Department of Defense and State answer questions in letter form put to them by the Congressman on American use of defoliants in Vietnam.

0298 **"Chemical-biological Warfare."** <u>Congressional Record</u>, v. 115, pt. 12, June 16, 1969, p. 16029-16033. Representative E.I. Koch (D-N.Y.) spoke in support of House Joint Resolution 691 which calls for a study of the environmental impacts of the use of defoliants in Vietnam. He also had three articles from the <u>New York Times</u> inserted in the <u>Record</u>.

0299 **"Chemical, Biological Weapons."** <u>Science</u>, v. 153, no. 3743, September 23, 1966, p. 1508. Twenty-two scientists have petitioned President Johnson to stop the use of tear gas and defoliants in Vietnam.

0300 **"Chemicals and Vietnam: No Word on Petition but Defoliant Gets Scarce."** <u>Scientific Research</u>, v. 2, no. 6, June 1967, p. 39. There has been no substantive reply to the petition 5,000 scientists sent to President Johnson protesting the use of chemical and biological weapons in Vietnam. However, they can be heartened by the fact that the Administration is in short supply of 2,4,5-T. In order to rectify this the Pentagon is moving ahead with plans to intensify the defoliation program and President Johnson has told his Office of Emergency Planning to make sure that the military gets all the 2,4,5-T it needs.

0301 **Clarke, R. <u>The Silent Weapons</u>. New York: David McKay Co.,**

1968. xiv, 270p. This book examines the objectives of
chemical warfare, the types of weapons that may be feasible
and the potential dangers they represent. On pages 145-146
the use of herbicides in Vietnam are discussed. On pages
212-223 the protests against the herbicides program by
scientific organizations such as the Federation of American
Scientists and the Society for Social Responsibility in
Science are detailed.

0302 "Condemnation of US Chemical War." South Vietnam in
Struggle, no. 84, January 1, 1971, p. 2. The statement
prepared by the attendees of the recent International
Conference on Scientists on the Chemical War in Vietnam is
given. The statement discusses the damage done by toxic
gases and herbicides and the belief that the use of these
weapons are a violation of the Geneva Protocol.

0303 "DOD Lags in Vietnam Herbicide Phase-out." (See 0161)

0304 Deedy, J. "The Deflowering Process." Commonweal, v. 90, no.
11, May 30, 1969, p. 306. Figures on the amount of
defoliants used in Vietnam are given and the moral
implications of the military use of defoliants in Vietnam are
discussed.

0305 "Defoliants, a Closed Case?" [editorial] Commonweal, v. 93,
no. 15, January 15, 1971, p. 363-364. The American
Association for the Advancement of Science's herbicide study
is finished. One positive effect is the announcement of the
phasing out of the use of defoliants in Vietnam. The study
confirms the influence the intellectual community can exert
on war policy given the opportunity. The study also adds
evidence to the fact that the United States violated the
spirit of the Geneva Protocol if not the law when the
military used herbicides in Vietnam.

0306 Dixon, B. "Refoliation." Spectator, v. 232, no. 7593,
January 5, 1974, p. 11. How A. Galston came to feel partly
responsible for the consequences of the use of herbicides as
a weapon in the Vietnam War and what he did about it is
described. Now that the war is over he is the moving force
behind the founding of Scientists' Institute for Public
Information. This organization is composed of scientists who
would like to help Vietnam get back on its feet.

0307 Do Xuan Sang. "U.S. Crime of Chemical Warfare in South Viet
Nam." In U.S. War Crimes in Vietnam. Hanoi: Juridical
Sciences Institute Under the Viet Nam State Commission of
Social Sciences, 1968, p. 217-249. In this book the
Juridical Sciences Institute under the Viet Nam State

Commission of Social Sciences deals with American war crimes as a whole and then with specific crimes. The author of this paper describes the use of chemical warfare including defoliants by the United States, the attempts at justification of the use of these weapons by the United States and how international law applies to these weapons. The use of these weapons have hurt the Vietnamese people but not their morale.

0308   "Doubts on Defoliants." Chemical Week, v. 101, no. 22, November 25, 1967, p. 32. Criticism has started to emerge over the use of defoliants in Vietnam and the effects it may have on the Vietnamese people and their land.

0309   Dougherty, J.M. The Use of Herbicides in Southeast Asia and Its Criticism. (See 0172)

0310   Edsall, J. et al. "Statement on the Use of Chemical Agents in the Viet Nam War." SSRS Newsletter, no. 162, February 1966, p. 3. The text of a statement denouncing the use of chemical agents for the destruction of crops by American forces in Vietnam is given. The statement urges the President to proclaim that the use of these agents by armed forces is forbidden. The statement is signed by J. Edsall and 28 other people.

0311   "The Effect of Herbicides in Vietnam." Congressional Record, v. 118, pt. 6, March 3, 1972, p. 6826-6834. Senator L.M. Bentsen, Jr. (D-Tex.) inserted in the Record a statement by Senator T.J. McIntyre (D-N.H.) and other materials Senator McIntyre wished printed on the National Academy of Sciences' study of the effects of the use of herbicides in Vietnam.

0312   "FAS Statement on Biological and Chemical Warfare." Bulletin of the Atomic Scientists, v. 20, no. 8, October 1964, p. 46-47. The text of a statement approved at the spring council meeting of the Federation of American Scientists. It calls for a ban on the research and development of chemical and biological weapons and no first use of such weapons. The statement also expresses concern about reports that defoliants are being used in Vietnam.

0313   Fair, S.D. "No Place to Hide: How Defoliants Expose the Viet Cong." (See 0176)

0314   Falk, R.A. "Environmental Warfare and Ecocide: Facts, Appraisal and Proposals." Revue Belge de Droit International, v. 9, no. 1, 1973, p. 1-27. Reprinted in Bulletin of Peace Proposals, v. 4, no. 1, 1973, p. 80-96. The author examines the use of herbicides, Rome plows,

bombardment, artillery fire and weather modification
techniques in Indochina to assess whether they violate
existing criteria of legal judgement. The author feels that
the Geneva Protocol bans the use of herbicides. However, in
order to clarify international law and to take steps to stop
the ecological devastation the author has drafted "A Proposed
International Convention on the Crime," "Protocol on
Environmental Warfare," "Peoples' Petition of Redress on
Ecocide and Environmental Warfare" and a petition addressed
to the Secretary General.

0315   "5,000 Scientists Petition Against Use of CBR." [editorial]
       Fellowship, v. 33, no. 4, April 1967, p. 3. Five thousand
       scientists have petitioned the White House asking for an
       immediate over-all review of American policy on chemical and
       biological warfare. Specifically, the petition included a
       plea for a halt to the use of anti-personnel and anti-crop
       chemical weapons in Vietnam.

0316   Friend, J.H.E. "War by Ecocide: Some Legal Observations."
       In The Effects of Modern Weapons on the Human Environment
       in Indochina: Documents Presented at a Hearing Organized by
       the International Commission in Cooperation with the
       Stockholm Conference on Vietnam and the Swedish Committee
       for Vietnam. Stockholm: International Commission of Enquiry
       into U.S. Crimes in Indochina, 1972, p. 2:1-2:26. In this
       report the term ecocide is defined and how the use of
       herbicides in Vietnam fits into that definition. Also the
       legality of the use of herbicides is discussed and how the
       Geneva Protocol applies to the use of herbicides in Vietnam.

0317   Galston, A.W. "Herbicide Study." [letter] Science, v. 177,
       no. 4051, September 1, 1972, p. 745. The author replies to
       H.J. Lewis' letter (See 0354) which appeared in this issue of
       Science. A.W. Galston remains concerned about the fact that
       the National Academy of Sciences' study is being funded by
       the Department of Defense, the group that was responsible for
       the spraying in the first place!

0318   Galston, A.W. "Lesser of Two Evils." (See 0504)

0319   Galston, A.W. "Military Uses of Herbicides in Vietnam." New
       Scientist, v. 38, no. 601, June 13, 1968, p. 583-584. The
       objections scientists have to the defoliation program center
       on the ecological effects, the health effects on the
       Vietnamese, the moral implications of the crop destruction
       program and on the military's failure to warn the civilian
       population to take adequate precautions against exposure.

0320   Galston, A.W. "Plants, People, and Politics." Bioscience,

v. 20, no. 7, April 1, 1970, p. 405-410. Reprinted in <u>Plant Science Bulletin</u>, v. 16, no. 1, March 1970, p. 1-7. The author presented this address at the 1969 Botanical Society of American's annual banquet as its retiring president. A.W. Galston discusses the public responsibility of the botanist which includes speaking out against the use of botanical knowledge for destructive rather than constructive ends such as the military use of herbicides in Vietnam. The ecological damage done to Vietnam is mentioned as well as statements made by the federal government that the use of defoliants does not violate the Geneva Protocol and legislation pending in Congress.

0321   Galston, A.W. "Science and Social Responsibility: a Case History." <u>New York Academy of Science. Annals</u>, v. 196, no. 4, June 7, 1972, p. 223-235. The author presented this paper at a conference on the social responsibility of scientists sponsored by the Academy's Section of Science and Public Policy. The ecological effects of the military use of herbicides in Vietnam is detailed. The legal implications of the use of herbicides in Vietnam is also mentioned. In addition the author tells of his efforts to protest the use of herbicides as a weapon in Vietnam.

0322   Galston, A.W. "Science in Review: On the Use and Misuse of Science." <u>Yale Review</u>, v. 60, no. 3, Spring 1971, p. 458-463. Reprinted as "Education of a Scientific Innocent." <u>Natural History</u>, v. 80, no. 6, June-July 1971, p. 16-18+. The author discusses the need for scientists to be socially responsible and how his search for a substance which would function as an antigrowth hormone led to the formulation of defoliants which would later be used in massive quantities in Vietnam.

0323   "Geneva Protocol Endorsed." <u>Facts on File</u>, v. 30, no. 1555, August 20-August 26, 1970, p. 608. President Nixon has asked the Senate to ratify the Geneva Protocol but has stated that he does not believe that the use of tear gas and defoliants fall within the agreement's jurisdiction.

0324   "The Geneva Protocol of 1925." <u>Congressional Record</u>, v. 117, pt. 14, June 8, 1971, p. 18694-18695. Senator J.W. Fulbright (D-Ark.) summarizes the position of the Foreign Relations Committee on the Geneva Protocol. The Committee asked the Senator to write to the President and ask the President to give his interpretation of the Protocol further consideration. The text of this letter is inserted in the <u>Record</u>.

0325   "Geneva Protocol of 1925 Submitted to the Senate."

Congressional Record, v. 116, pt. 22, August 21, 1970, p. 29708. Senator J.W. Fulbright (D-Ark.) is pleased that the Geneva Protocol of 1925 has been submitted to the Senate. He would have preferred it if the Administration had interpreted the Protocol to exclude the use of herbicides and harassing gases. However, the Senate can still act on the amendment proposed by Senators G. Nelson (D-Wisc.) and C.E. Goodell (R-N.Y.).

0326   "The Geneva Protocol-II." Congressional Record, v. 117, pt. 33, November 29, 1971, p. 43211-43214. Senator H.H. Humphrey (D-Minn.) calls on the Administration to change its mind on the ratification of the Geneva Protocol and support a broad interpretation of the Protocol. The Senator had an article from the October 10, 1971 issue of the New York Times by H. Mitgang, Chapter 8 from Air War in Indochina (See 0019) and a statement from the Canadian Ambassador to the Conference of the Committee on Disarmament at Geneva inserted in the Record.

0327   Genocide Crime in South Vietnam. Hanoi: "Liberation" Editions, March 1963. 32p. This pamphlet consists of a statement denouncing the use of defoliants in Vietnam and a discussion of the beginnings of protests by scientists. A statement by the South Vietnam Liberation National Front demanding that these operations cease is also included.

0328   Goldblat, J. "Are Tear Gas and Herbicides Permitted Weapons?" Bulletin of the Atomic Scientists, v. 26, no. 4, April 1970, p. 13-16. Reprinted in Congressional Record, v. 116, pt. 15, June 18, 1970, p. 20567-20569. This article examines whether or not the American position that the Geneva Protocol does not apply to the use of tear gas and herbicides in Vietnam is correct. The author believes that the Protocol does ban the use of these weapons.

0329   Gonzales, A.F. "Defoliation: a Controversial U.S. Mission in Vietnam." (See 0182)

0330   Graham, E. "Letter." SSRS Newsletter, no. 200, June 1969, p. 2. The author addresses two questions in this letter concerning the use of chemical weapons in Vietnam. The questions are: "Isn't chemical defoliation justified if it saves American soldiers' lives?" and "Is a napalm victim any deader than one killed with a rifle?"

0331   Graham, F., Jr. "The Toxic Field of Mars." (See 0510)

0332   Greenberg, D.S. "Defoliation: AAAS Study Delayed by Resignations from Committee." Science, v. 159, no. 3817,

February 23, 1968, p. 857-859. The study group known as the
Committee on Environmental Alteration appointed by the
American Association for the Advancement of Science to begin
a study of chemical and biological agents that affect the
environment has been delayed in starting its work as two of
its four members have resigned. The inspiration for forming
the committee came from concern about the military
defoliation program in Vietnam. A group of scientists with
the National Academy of Sciences-National Research Council
have evaluated the report prepared by the Midwest Research
Institute on the adverse long-term effects of herbicides.
They found that the Institute had done a credible job but not
much is known about the ecological effects of herbicides.

0333 **Griswold, D. "Agent Orange: the Humanitarian Poison."**
Workers World, v. 21, no. 24, June 15, 1979, p. 3+.
Scientists first warned the world about the toxic properties
of Agent Orange over a decade ago.

0334 Grummer, G. "Chemical Weapons Can Also Not Improve the
Aggressor's Position." (See 0513)

0335 **Hamilton, A. "CBW: Nixon Initiative on Treaty Anticipates**
Congressional Critics." Science, v. 166, no. 3910, December
5, 1969, p. 1249-1250. President Nixon has asked the Senate
to ratify the Geneva Protocol of 1925. However, he does not
believe that the use of herbicides and tear gas are outside
the scope of the treaty.

0336 **Handorf, H.H. "Chemical and Biological Warfare: Is**
Propriety the Issue?" [letter] Science, v. 155, no. 3767,
March 10, 1967, p. 1198-1199. The author wrote this letter
in order to respond to E. Langer's article from the January
20, 1967 issue (See 0351) of this journal. H.H. Handorf
feels that while the military use of defoliants destroys the
environment this is preferable to the increased sacrifice of
American lives.

0337 **Harmer, R.M. "Only We Can Prevent Forests." In Unfit for**
Human Consumption. Englewood Cliffs, N.J.: Prentice-Hall,
1971, p. 68-71. The efforts being made by some scientists to
stop the military use of herbicides in Vietnam are described.
Also Vietnamese scientists were not given any information
about what was sprayed. Three million dollars in damage
claims has been paid to Vietnamese by the United State
government. The government is also considering a $12 million
claim made by the Cambodian government for damage done to
that country's rubber trees by a defoliation mission.

0338 **"Herbicide Assessment Commission." American Association for**

the Advancement of Science. Bulletin, v. 15, no. 3, September
1970, p. 7. The work completed thus far by this commission
is noted.

0339 "Herbicides and the Geneva Protocol." Congressional Record,
v. 117, pt. 6, March 24, 1971, p. 7757-7759. Senator W.
Mondale (D-Minn.) states that the Geneva Protocol would be
interpreted in such a way as to ban the use of herbicides as
a weapon. He had Senator G. Nelson's (D-Wisc.) testimony
before the Foreign Relations Committee on this issue inserted
in the Record.

0340 "Herbicides, Defoliants; Vietnam Study Urged." Oil, Paint
and Drug Reporter, v. 197, no. 1, January 5, 1970, p. 47.
The American Association for the Advancement of Science has
asked Dr. M. Meselson of Harvard University to conduct a
study to determine what effects the use of herbicides and
defoliants in Vietnam has had besides stripping the land of
plant growth and exposing the enemy.

0341 "Herbicides in Vietnam." Bioscience, v. 20, no. 19, October
1, 1970, p. 1070. An attempt to ban the use of herbicides in
Vietnam was defeated in the Senate by a vote of 22-62 in late
August.

0342 "Herbicides in Vietnam: Senate Vetoes Ban Idea." Oil, Paint
and Drug Reporter, v. 198, no. 9, August 31, 1970, p. 5+.
The Senate has defeated an amendment to a military bill that
would have banned the military use of herbicides in South
Vietnam.

0343 Hippel, F.V. and J. Primack. "Public Interest Science."
Science, v. 177, no. 4055, September 29, 1972, p. 1166-1171.
This two section article discusses the impact scientists have
had on the federal policy-making process regarding
technology. One section details how the executive branch
exploits scientists by not providing them all the information
they need and the other section is on how scientists can
counterbalance politicians by giving the public and Congress
the information they need to make decisions. In this second
section mention is made of the fact the government may have
indeed known about the hazards of 2,4,5-T and chose to ignore
them when they sprayed defoliants in Vietnam. However,
scientists helped inform the public through its American
Association for the Advancement of Science study.

0344 Ito, Y. "Japanese View on Defoliation." [letter] Science,
v. 162, no. 3853, November 1, 1968, p. 513-514. At the 15th
general meeting of the Ecological Society of Japan which was
held recently in Ueda City a resolution was passed demanding

the United States stop the military use of herbicides and forest burning in Vietnam.

0345 Johnstone, L.C. "Ecocide and the Geneva Protocol." Foreign Affairs, v. 49, no. 4, July 1971, p. 711-720. Reprinted in "Senate Resolution 154: Submission of a Resolution Relating to a Comprehensive Interpretation for the Geneva Protocol." Congressional Record, v. 117, pt. 20, July 23, 1971, p. 26931-26934. The debate over whether the United States should ratify the Geneva Protocol with the understanding that the Protocol does not ban the use of herbicides or tear gas is given. Also mentioned are the reasons why the United States does not want to see these weapons prohibited. The author feels that the United States should ratify the protocol with the understanding that all the war use of all gases, bacteriological weapons and herbicides would be banned.

0346 Jones, F.D. "The Defoliant Story: a Cautionary Tale." Your Environment, v. 1, no. 4, Autumn 1970, p. 118-123. The misuse of defoliants is detailed. The use of Agent Orange in Vietnam is cited as one of several instances of this misuse.

0347 Kanegis, A. "U.S. CBW Policy." Liberation, v. 15, no. 9, November 1970, p. 11-19. President Nixon's chemical and biological warfare policy is examined. Statements President Nixon has made declaring that the use of herbicides and defoliants will not be banned are given.

0348 Kelley, J.B. "Ravaged Soil of Vietnam." (See 0535)

0349 Lamade, W. "Fact, Not Sensationalism, Needed in Pesticide Evaluation." Agricultural Chemicals, v. 25, no. 12, December 1970, p. 23. The Weed Science Society of American has spoken out in opposition to the results of a study conducted by Bionetics Laboratories. They do not feel that the doses of 2,4,5-T studied were representative of commercial grades. They feel that emotionalism needs to be reduced or eliminated concerning the use of herbicides.

0350 Langer, E. "CBW, Vietnam Evoke Scientist's Concern." Science, v. 155, no. 3760, January 20, 1967, p. 302. Thousands of scientists have signed a petition urging President Johnson to stop using anti-personnel and anti-crop chemical weapons in Vietnam. Several scientific societies have also passed resolutions and many scientists have sent private communications to the President and the Pentagon on this issue.

0351 Langer, E. "Chemical and Biological Warfare (II): the

Weapons and the Policies." Science, v. 155, no. 3760,
January 20, 1967, p. 299-303. As part of a general article
on the biological and chemical weapons that the United States
has developed and the American policies on using such
weapons, the debate as to whether the United States is using
such weapons in Vietnam is mentioned. Government officials
deny that such weapons are being used but they do admit that
more than 150,000 acres have been treated with herbicides and
that riot control agents have been used.

0352   Leopold, A.C. "Defoliation." [editorial] Bioscience, v. 18,
       no. 9, September 1968, p. 853. The author finds it an
       intellectual embarrassment that some members of the
       scientific community place the biological consequences of
       using herbicides over the saving of the lives of American
       soldiers.

0353   Leuba, C. "Defoliants: Orange, White, and Blue." (See
       0544)

0354   Lewis, H.J. "Herbicide Study." [letter] Science, v. 177,
       no. 4051, September 1, 1972, p. 745. This letter was written
       in order to correct some of the statements A.W. Galston made
       in his book review of Harvest of Death. A.W. Galston implies
       that the grant given to the National Academy of Sciences to
       study the effects of the use of herbicides was made at the
       initiative of the Department of Defense. It was not; it was
       made at the initiative of Congress. The Academy did not turn
       to the Department of Defense.

0355   McCarthy, R.D. "War Against Food and Foliage." (See 0550)

0356   McElheny, V. "Herbicides in Vietnam: Juggernaut Out of
       Control." (See 0551)

0357   Marini, J. "Herbicides in Vietnam." [letter] Chemical and
       Engineering News, v. 46, no. 14, March 25, 1968, p. 7. This
       letter was written in response to G. Bixler's editorial (See
       0283) which appeared in the February 19, 1968 issue of this
       journal. J. Marini feels that it is irresponsible to compare
       the military use of chemical defoliants to controlling weeds
       with a hoe.

0358   Mayer, J. "Crop Destruction in Vietnam." [letter] Science,
       v. 152, no. 3720, April 15, 1966, p. 291. The author
       addresses the practical and ethical implications of using
       chemicals to destroy crops in Vietnam in this letter. He is
       opposed to the use of these chemicals.

0359   Mayer, J. "Starvation as a Weapon - Herbicides in Vietnam,
       I." (See 0208)

0360 Meselson, M. "Chemical and Biological Warfare." <u>Scientific American</u>, v. 222, no. 5, May 1970, p. 15-25. The author discusses the issue of whether or not the use of irritant gases and antiplant agents are banned by the Geneva Protocol and the development of chemical and biological weapons.

0361 Meselson, M. and P. Doty. "Chemical and Biological Warfare." <u>American Academy of Arts and Sciences. Bulletin</u>, v. 23, no. 4, January 1970, p. 2-14. The authors discuss the issues surrounding the American policy of chemical and biological warfare. The reasons why the United States should ratify the Geneva Protocol are given. Also discussed is if the United States does ratify the Geneva Protocol will it be ratified with the understanding that the use of herbicides and tear gas will not be banned. The use of herbicides and tear gas by the U.S. military in Vietnam is noted.

0362 "Meselson to Head Herbicides Study." <u>Science</u>, v. 167, no. 3914, January 2, 1970, p. 37. M. Meselson, a professor at Harvard University, has been appointed by the Council of the American Association for the Advancement of Science to head a committee to design a plan for a study of the effects of the use of defoliants and herbicides by the U.S. military on the land and people of Vietnam.

0363 "The Military Language." [editorial] <u>Manas</u>, v. 24, no. 13, March 31, 1971, p. 4. This editorial reports on the findings of the study conducted by the American Association for the Advancement of Science on the effects of the use of defoliants by the U.S. military in Vietnam. A <u>New York Times</u> article on this study is quoted. This article states that "...the United States military in Vietnam have made it a general practice to treat mass methods of death and destruction as abstractions."

0364 "Military Procurement Authorizations, 1972." <u>Congressional Record</u>, v. 117, pt. 27, October 6, 1971, p. 35249-35283. On pages 35274-35280 there is a discussion of the progress that has been made by the National Academy of Sciences in its study of the effects of the use of herbicides by the United States in Vietnam. Also discussed is the funding the Academy will need in order to complete its study.

0365 Moore, J.N. "Ratification of the Geneva Protocol on Gas and Bacteriological Warfare: a Legal and Political Analysis." <u>Virginia Law Review</u>, v. 58, no. 3, March 1972, p. 419-509. The implications of the proposed ratification by President Nixon of the Geneva Protocol of 1925 is discussed. However, the United States does not consider that the ratification of this protocol as banning the use of chemical herbicides or riot-control gases in Vietnam.

0366 Nechayuk, L. "Weapons of 'Civilised' Barbarians." Soviet
      Military Review, no. 8, August 1971, p. 52-54. The author
      denounces the use of chemical weapons such as herbicides by
      the United States in Vietnam and the fact that the use of
      these weapons violates international law.

0367 Neilands, J.B. "Chemical Warfare." In The Social
      Responsibility of the Scientist. Ed. by M. Brown. New York:
      Free Press, 1971, p. 81-94. The essays in this volume are
      based on lectures given for a course at the University of
      California, Berkeley on the role of scientists in society.
      This essay describes the types and amounts of chemical
      weapons including herbicides used in Vietnam and the
      relationship of the use of these weapons to international
      law. The author concludes by stating that the use of
      herbicides violates several international laws and by using
      these herbicides the United States is guilty of crimes
      against humanity and that the Geneva Protocol should be
      ratified by all nations.

0368 Neilands, J.B. "Chemical Warfare in Vietnam." Peace and the
      Sciences, no. 3, July-September 1969, p. 24-35. The author
      discusses the use of several chemical agents by the United
      States as part of the Vietnam War and the relationship
      between their use and international law. This is the text of
      a speech given as part of the Stockholm Conference on Vietnam
      Emergency Action which was held May 16-18, 1969.

0369 Neilands, J.B. "Ecocide in Vietnam." (See 0218)

0370 Neilands, J.B. "More on Forest Defoliation." [letter]
      Science, v. 161, no. 3845, September 6, 1968, p. 965. The
      author believes that the use of herbicides in Vietnam
      violates the Geneva Protocol of 1925.

0371 Neilands, J.B. "Survey of Chemical and Related Weapons."
      Naturwissenchaften, v. 60, no. 4, April 1973, p. 177-183.
      The history of the use of chemical weapons in war is given
      including the use of herbicides in Vietnam. The United
      States is almost the only nation that has not ratified the
      Geneva Protocol of 1925 primarily due to the debate over
      whether the use of herbicides and tear gas is banned by the
      Protocol.

0372 Neilands, J.B. "Vietnam: Progress of the Chemical War."
      Asian Survey, v. 10, no. 3, March 1970, p. 209-229.
      Reprinted in Not Since the Romans Salted the Land: Chemical
      Warfare in S.E. Asia. By J.B. Neilands et al. Ithaca, N.Y.:
      Glad Day Pr., 1970, p. 3-15. The controversy surrounding the
      gas and herbicide warfare being conducted by the Americans in

Vietnam is noted. Also mentioned is the concern over the ecological damage the spraying of herbicides is doing to Vietnam.

0373   Nelson, B. "Herbicides in Vietnam: AAAS Board Seeks Field Study." Science, v. 163, no. 3862, January 3, 1969, p. 58-59. The American Association for the Advancement of Science's Board of Directors has authorized the Association's staff to convene a group of interested national and international scientific organizations to develop a plan for a field study of the long-term and short-term ecological effects of the use of herbicides in Vietnam. The reports given at the Association's recent meeting in Dallas on the use of herbicides in Vietnam are summarized.

0374   Newman, S. "Herbicide or Genocide - Which Cide Are They On." Science for the People, v. 3, no. 1, February 1971, p. 13. A summary of a panel discussion entitled "Implications of Continued Military Use of Herbicides in South East Asia" which was held at a recent American Association for the Advancement of Science's annual meeting is given. Both sides of the issue of whether or not the use of herbicides was militarily effective and whether or not this use was legal were presented.

0375   "On Chemical Warfare in Vietnam." Congressional Record, v. 115, pt. 8, April 30, 1969, p. 10833. Representative E.I. Koch (D-N.Y.) and R.D. McCarthy (D-N.Y.) are introducing a resolution calling for a joint commission with the participation of the United States, Republic of South Vietnam and International Commission for Supervision and Control in Vietnam to be established to study use and effects of anticrop sprays and chemical defoliants in Vietnam.

0376   "One Man's Meat." New Republic, v. 148, no. 12 (issue no. 2522), March 23, 1963, p. 5-6. Concern is expressed over the existence of the Ranch Hand program. Is it a violation of the Geneva Protocol? Isn't the spraying affecting peasants as well as guerillas?

0377   "Passing the Biological Buck." Nation, v. 206, no. 11, March 11, 1968, p. 325. The review of the Midwest Research Institute's study which will take place by the American Association for the Advancement of Science and the National Research Council is discussed. The debate over this review which is occurring within the Association for the Advancement of Science is also mentioned.

0378   Phan van Bach. See Bach, P.V.

0379 "Plant Physiologists Regret Chemical Herbicides." SSRS
      Newsletter, no. 172, December 1966, p. 1. The text of a
      petition to President Johnson by a dozen plant physiologists
      expressing their misgivings concerning the alleged use of
      herbicides for the destruction of food crops and for
      defoliation operations in Vietnam. Also included is the text
      of the State Department's reply.

0380 Primack, J. and F. von Hippel. "Matthew Meselson and the
      United States Policy on Chemical and Biological Warfare." In
      Advice and Dissent: Scientists in the Political Arena. New
      York: Basic Books, 1974, p. 143-164. This book examines how
      scientists have been following through on their political
      responsibilities. This chapter describes M. Meselson's
      battle against chemical and biological warfare including his
      work with the American Association for the Advancement of
      Science's Herbicide Assessment Commission.

0381 "Prohibition of the Use of Herbicides in Vietnam."
      Congressional Record, v. 116, pt. 22, August 24, 1970, p.
      29835-29837. Senator T.J. McIntyre (D-N.H.) spoke on the
      deliberations the Armed Services Committee has had on the use
      of herbicides. The Committee decided putting an end to the
      use of herbicides in Vietnam would be ill-advised. The
      Senator had inserted in the Record some of responses made by
      the Department of Defense to the questions put to them by the
      Committee on the use of herbicides in Vietnam.

0382 "Protest Declaration of GDR Scientists Against the Use of
      Chemical Substances in Vietnam." In Truth About U.S.
      Aggression in Vietnam; GDR Authors Unmask Imperialist
      Crimes. East Berlin: Vietnam Commission of the Afro-Asian
      Solidarity Committee of the German Democratic Republic,
      1972, p. 84-86. This article consists of a statement signed
      by a dozen East German scientists protesting the use of
      chemical weapons (including herbicides) by the United States
      in Vietnam.

0383 Robinson, C. "U.S. Undermines Gas War Ban." Recon., v. 3,
      no. 2, February 1975, p. 6-7+. The author discusses the
      Senate's recent ratification of the Geneva Protocol and the
      unfortunate fact that the United States has refused to ban
      the use of a variety of chemical and biological weapons in
      war including the use of herbicides as was done in Vietnam.

0384 Rosenhead, J. "CRW and Disarmament." Labour Monthly, v.
      52, no. 1, January 1970, p. 15-18. Upon closer examination,
      President Nixon's recent request to the Congress that the
      Geneva Protocol be ratified is not a reversal of American
      policy on chemical and biological warfare. President Nixon

does not regard the Geneva Protocol as banning the use of herbicides or riot control gases in war.

0385   Sachs, R.M. "Vietnam: AAAS Herbicide Study." [letter] Science, v. 170, no. 3962, December 4, 1970, p. 1034+. This letter was written in response to P. Boffey's article (See 0285) from the October 2, 1970 issue of this journal. R.M. Sachs does not feel that any of the American Association for the Advancement of Science's scientists presented an objective view of the use of herbicides in Vietnam. These scientists examined only the damage and did not look for any benefits which might have resulted from this project.

0386   Sang, D.X. See Do Xuan Sang.

0387   "Scientists Decry 'Chemical Warfare'." Chemical and Engineering News, v. 44, no. 4, January 24, 1966, p. 26. Twenty-nine scientists, all from New England, last week issued a statement directed to President Johnson protesting the use of crop-killing chemicals by American forces in Vietnam.

0388   "Scientists Protest Viet Crop Destruction." Science, v. 151, no. 3708, January 21, 1966, p. 309. A recent statement issued by 29 scientists and physicians from Harvard, the Massachusetts Institute of Technology and several nearby institutions protests the use of crop-destroying chemicals by American forces in Vietnam.

0389   "Senate OKs 1925 Germ Warfare Ban." Facts on File, v. 34, no. 1780, December 21, 1974, p. 1042-1043. The Senate has voted 90-0 to ratify the 1925 Geneva Protocol banning biological and chemical warfare. There was considerable delay in ratifying the Protocol due to the debate over the question of whether or not tear gas and herbicides were banned by the Protocol. The White House interpretation on this is that the "first use" of these two materials would not take place except in limited circumstances.

0390   "Senate Resolution 48: Submission of a Resolution Relating to a Comprehensive Interpretation for the Geneva Protocol." Congressional Record, v. 119, pt. 2, January 29, 1973, p. 2430-2432. Senator H.H. Humphrey (D-Minn.) reintroduced his resolution calling for the ratification of the Geneva Protocol without qualification. The text of his resolution is included. It was referred to the Committee on Foreign Relations. Senator Humphrey had a copy of D. Shapley's article from the September 1, 1972 issue of Science (See 0231) inserted in the Record.

0391   "Senate Resolution 158: Submission of a Resolution Relating
       to the Geneva Protocol." Congressional Record, v. 117, pt.
       21, July 27, 1971, p. 27435-27438. Senator E.W. Brooke (R-
       Mass.) discusses the debate on whether or not the Geneva
       Protocol bans the use of chemical herbicides and riot control
       agents. He offers Resolution 158 which would have this issue
       submitted to the International Court of Justice and force the
       United States to comply with the Court's decision. The
       Senator also had a letter dated April 15, 1971 addressed to
       the President from Senator Fulbright inserted in the Record.

0392   "Senate Resolution 154: Submission of a Resolution Relating
       to a Comprehensive Interpretation for the Geneva Protocol."
       Congressional Record, v. 117, pt. 20, July 23, 1971, p.
       26931-26934. Senator H.H. Humphrey (D-Minn.) submitted S.
       Res. 154 which calls for the ratification of the Geneva
       Protocol. This resolution calls for a broad interpretation
       of the Protocol and a banning of the military use of
       herbicides and tear gas. The Senator had an article by L.C.
       Johnstone from the July 1971 issue of Foreign Affairs (See
       0345) inserted in the Record.

0393   Shapley, D. "Herbicide Panel Short on Fieldwork." Science,
       v. 180, no. 4093, June 29, 1973, p. 1350. The Chair and the
       Executive Director of the National Academy of Science's
       Committee on the Effects of Herbicides in Vietnam have both
       admitted that they were not able to make field studies in
       Vietnam on the scale and depth they would have liked and that
       because of this their results will be less definitive than
       expected. The Committee will give its final report to the
       Secretary of Defense on August 31.

0394   "Statements on Introduced Bills and Resolutions."
       Congressional Record, v. 118, pt. 2, January 28, 1972, p.
       1634-1640. On pages 1634-1636 Senator G. Nelson (D-Wisc.)
       explains why he introduced S. 3084, the Vietnam War
       Ecological Damage Assessment Act of 1972. The text of the
       bill is included. This bill would ask that the President
       contract with the National Academy of Sciences to study the
       ecological damage done to Indochina as a result of the
       weapons used by the American Armed Forces. This bill was
       referred to the Committee on Foreign Relations.

0395   Stockholm International Peace Research Institute. The
       Problem of Chemical and Biological Warfare, Volume 3. New
       York: Humanities Pr., 1973. 194p. Pages 67-80 and 134-135
       discuss how the Geneva Protocol and customary prohibition
       apply to the military use of herbicides by the United States
       during the Vietnam War.

0396 Synge, A. "Chemical and Biological Warfare." New
      Blackfriars, v. 50, no. 585, February 1969, p. 256-263. The
      author summarizes the material presented at a recent
      international conference on biological and chemical warfare
      held in London, discusses the legal issues and the United
      States' position on the Geneva Protocol, and presents
      arguments against the use of chemical and biological weapons.
      Interwoven into this examination is the debate on the use of
      herbicides in Vietnam.

0397 Szabo, S.S. "Defoliation of Vietnamese Forests." (See 0618)

0398 Tauss, K.H. "Herbicides in Vietnam." [letter] Chemical and
      Engineering News, v. 46, no. 14, March 25, 1968, p. 7. This
      letter was written in response to G. Bixler's letter (See
      0283) which appeared in the February 19, 1968 issue of this
      journal. K.H. Tauss feels that the use of defoliants is not
      comparable to controlling weeds with a hoe.

0399 "2,4,5-T: Where Next." [letter] Lancet, v. 2, no. 8152,
      November 24, 1979, p. 1114-1115. This editorial states that
      instead of crying wolf over 2,4,5-T as there is no wolf, we
      instead should be working at improving working conditions,
      monitoring worker safety and maintaining product purity.

0400 "US Chemical Warfare Universally Condemned." South
      Vietnam in Struggle, no. 88, February 10, 1971, p. 8. At
      the conference held on December 10 to consider the use of
      chemical weapons in Vietnam by the United States, several
      Vietnamese scientists told of the health effects of exposure
      to the herbicides. The attendees also denounced the United
      States for using Indochina as a chemical laboratory.

0401 U.S. Congress. House. Committee on Foreign Affairs.
      Subcommittee on National Security, Policy and Scientific
      Developments. U.S. Chemical Warfare Policy. Hearing, 93rd
      Cong., 2nd sess., May 1, 2, 7, 9, and 14, 1974. Washington:
      GPO, 1974. vi, 379p. These hearings were held to discuss
      American chemical warfare policy, especially the future
      status of herbicides and tear gas which needs to be resolved
      so that the Senate can move toward ratification of the Geneva
      Protocol. Almost all of the witnesses as part of their
      testimony mentioned the use of herbicides in Vietnam and how
      this affects possible ratification of the Geneva Protocol.
      On pages 251-293 there is a summary of the National Academy
      of Sciences' study.

0402 U.S. Congress. Senate. Committee on Appropriations.
      Subcommittee on Department of Defense Appropriations.
      Department of Defense Appropriations for FY 71. Part I.

Hearing, 91st Cong., 2nd sess., February 20, 24, April 13, 14, 15, May 11, 12, 13, 15, 20, 1970. Washington: GPO, 1970. ii, 1174, xiip. These hearings were held to debate the Department of Defense's budget request for FY 71. On pages 1143-1158 M. Meselson testifies against the funding of chemical weapons and invokes the Geneva Protocol. He also urges the President to ratify the Geneva Protocol without restrictions.

0403   U.S. Congress. Senate. Committee on Foreign Relations. Geneva Protocol of 1925. Hearing, 92nd Cong., 1st sess., March 5, 16, 18, 19, 22, and 26, 1971. Washington: GPO, 1972. vii, 439p. This hearing was held to reconsider the Geneva Protocol, especially the issue of how the use of herbicides and tear gas apply to the Protocol. Nearly all of the witnesses mention the use of herbicides in Vietnam and its impact on Vietnam. They also mention the applicability of the military use of herbicides to the Geneva Protocol. A.H. Westing (pages 234-260) and M. Meselson (p. 353-377) mention in their testimonies the ecological effects of the U.S. military's use of herbicides in Vietnam. G. Bunn's 1969 article from the Wisconsin Law Review (See 0288), the Preliminary Report from the American Association for the Advancement of Science's Herbicides Assessment Commission (See 0556) and T. Aaronson's article from the March 1971 issue of Environment (See 0419) are included as part of these hearings.

0404   U.S. Congress. Senate. Committee on Foreign Relations. Prohibition of Chemical and Biological Weapons. Hearing, 93rd Cong., 2nd sess., December 10, 1974. Washington: GPO, 1974. iii, 71p. This hearing was held to further consider the issue of the ratification of the Geneva Protocol. Interspersed in the testimony is the issue of the military use of herbicides and whether or not they should be banned.

0405   "U.S. to Step Up Vietnam Defoliation." (See 0251)

0406   "Use of Chemical-biological Weapons in Vietnam Justified, According to Survey." Industrial Research, v. 9, no. 2, February 1967, p. 115. The majority of scientists and engineers responding to this magazine's opinion poll on the use of chemical and biological agents in Vietnam feel that use of these agents is justified in certain specific instances. Four out of five feel that the use of herbicides in Vietnam is justified.

0407   "The Use of Defoliants in Vietnam Is a Stain on Our National Conscience." Congressional Record, v. 116, pt. 33, December 30, 1970, p. 44024-44026. Senator S.M. Young (D-Ohio) spoke

on the Geneva Protocol, the fact that the use of herbicides
in Vietnam has continued and the findings of commission of
the American Association for the Advancement of Science.
Senator Young calls for an immediate halt to the use of
defoliants. The Senator had an article by V. Cohn from the
December 30, 1970 issue of the Washington Post inserted in
the Record.

0408 Vinnedge, H.H. "Lets Hear It for Pollution, (If It's in
      Asia)." New Republic, v. 163, no. 16, October 17, 1970, p.
      14-15. The author discusses the debate taking place in the
      Senate about a motion to stop the use of herbicides as a
      weapon in Vietnam. The author expresses his consternation at
      the lack of concern by some Senators about the long-term
      effects of the spraying.

0409 Wald, G. "Can Corporations Be Tried for War Crimes?"
      Current, no. 120, August 1970, p. 56-63. The author is a
      plaintiff in a test case in the U.S. District Court system to
      determine if the Nuremberg Principles of World War II can be
      expanded to the concept of corporate responsibility so that
      the manufacturers of the chemical weapons, including
      defoliants, being used in Vietnam can be tried for war
      crimes.

0410 Wald, G. "The Leaves Fall, the Blood Flows." Saturday
      Review, v. 53, no. 23, June 6, 1970, p. 28-29. Reprinted in
      "The Costs of Defoliation." Congressional Record, v. 116,
      pt. 14, June 12, 1970, p. 19599-19600. The author feels that
      some of the methods the U.S. military is using in Vietnam are
      not justified. He believes that the use of herbicides in
      Vietnam violates the Geneva Protocol and that herbicides as
      they are being used in Vietnam are lethal weapons.

0411 "We Americans Should Lead in Outlawing Poison Gas and
      Biological Methods of Warfare." Congressional Record, v.
      116, pt. 15, June 17, 1970, p. 20079-20080. Senator S.M.
      Young (D-Ohio) spoke in favor of ratifying the Geneva
      Protocol. The Senator spoke of the effects of defoliants on
      the Vietnamese people and what he had seen when he went to
      Vietnam in early 1968.

0412 Westing, A.H. "AAAS Herbicide Assessment Commission."
      [letter] Science, v. 179, no. 4080, March 30, 1973, p. 1278-
      1279. In this letter the author summarizes the activities of
      the American Association for the Advancement of Science's
      Herbicide Assessment Commission. A final report of the
      Commission will be published in 1973 or 1974.

0413 Westing, A.H. "Ecological Considerations Regarding Massive

Environmental Contamination with 2,3,7,8-tetrachlorodibenzo-para-dioxin." (See 0660)

0414   Westing, A.H. "Herbicides as Agents of Chemical Warfare:
       Their Impact in Relation to the Geneva Protocol of 1925."
       Environmental Affairs, v. 1, no. 3, November 1971, p. 578-
       586. Reprinted in The Geneva Protocol of 1925. U.S.
       Congress. Senate. Committee on Foreign Relations. Hearing,
       92nd Cong., 1st sess., March 5, 16, 18, 19, 22, and 26, 1971.
       Washington: GPO, p. 239-246. The author argues that the
       military uses of herbicides should be included in the weapons
       that are banned under the Geneva Protocol and that the United
       States should ratify the Protocol with this inclusion. The
       environmental damage done to Vietnam as a result of the U.S.
       military's use of herbicides is also discussed.

0415   Westing, A.H. "Vietnam: AAAS Herbicide Study." [letter]
       Science, v. 170, no. 3962, December 4, 1970, p. 1036-1037.
       This letter was written in response to R.M. Sachs' letter
       (See 0385) which appeared in this issue of Science. A.H.
       Westing responds to R.M. Sachs by stating that he believes
       the American Association for the Advancement of Sciences has
       conducted an objective study and that Sachs' personal
       political and moral views are irrelevant to the American
       Association for the Advancement of Science's study.

0416   Westing, A.H. "Widespread, Long-lasting and Severe..." (See
       0678)

0417   "World Environment Meeting Held in Stockholm." Editorials on
       File, v. 3, no. 11, June 1-June 15, 1972, p. 762-767. A
       United Nations-sponsored World Conference on the Human
       Environment was held this month in Stockholm. The issue of
       the military use of defoliants by the United States in
       Vietnam was raised at the conference. Editorials from the
       Boston Globe, San Francisco Chronicle, and the Dayton Daily
       News comment on this issue.

0418   Yannacone, V.J., Jr. "Chemical Defoliation or Chemical
       Warfare?" University of Toledo Law Journal, v. 13, no. 4,
       Summer 1982, p. 1260-1270. The lead attorney for the
       plaintiffs in the Agent Orange litigation debates whether or
       not the use of chemical defoliants should be considered an
       act of "chemical-biological warfare."

0419 Aaronson, T. "Tour of Vietnam." Environment, v. 13, no. 2, March 1971, p. 34-43. Reprinted in "Ecological Destruction in Vietnam." Congressional Record, v. 117, pt. 6, March 25, 1971, p. 8184-8187 and in The Geneva Protocol of 1925. Hearing, 92nd Cong., 1st sess., March 5, 16, 18, 19, 22, and, 26, 1971. U.S. Congress. Senate. Committee on Foreign Relations. Washington: GPO, 1972, p. 396-403. Summarized in "Ravaged Land." Manas, v. 24, no. 24, June 16, 1971. p. 6-7. The preliminary findings of the American Association for the Advancement of Science's Herbicide Assessment Commission are detailed. The report mentions the ecological damage done to Vietnam and the health effects of exposure on the Vietnamese people.

0420 "Academy Reports on Vietnam Herbicide Damage." Nature, v. 248, no. 5445, March 15, 1974, p. 186-188. The conclusions of the National Academy of Sciences report detailing the ecological damage to Vietnam and the health effects on the Vietnamese as a result the herbicidal sprayings by the U.S. military are given.

0421 Adamson, L. "Spray Now Pay Later." Environmental Action, v. 6, no. 4, July 6, 1974, p. 8-13. What has come to be known about the hazards of spraying 2,4,5-T is summarized. The findings of the report prepared by the National Academy of Sciences are mentioned.

0422 Agarwal, A. "Vietnam After the Storm." New Scientist, v. 102, no. 1409, May 10, 1984, p. 10-14. This article describes Vietnam's efforts to recover from the war. The efforts to recover from the effects of the use of defoliants by the U.S. military are described on page 13. In addition to the efforts to reforest the areas and to plant crops, the medical effects of exposure are mentioned.

0423 Allman, T.D. "How to Kill the Earth." Far Eastern Economic Review, v. 77, no. 34, August 19, 1972, p. 12-13. Summarized by C. Conner as "Reading from Left to Right." International Socialist Review, v. 33, no. 9, October 1972, p. 6. The effects the defoliating and bombing the U.S. military did in Southeast Asia on this area's soils are noted.

0424 American Association for the Advancement of Science. Effects

of the Large-scale Use of Herbicides and Defoliants in
Vietnam: Implications of Continued Military Use of
Herbicides in South East Asia. Washington: The Association,
1970. 4 cassette tapes. The Herbicide Assessment Commission
provided a preliminary description of their findings at a
panel discussion with a question and answer period during the
137th Meeting of the American Association for the Advancement
of Science. The findings focused on the health effects on
animals and humans, effects on tropical hardwood and mangrove
forests, on crops and on the food chain.

0425 "American Scientists Denounce US Chemical Warfare in South
      Vietnam." (See 0270)

0426 "Army Scientist Defends Defoliant Use in Vietnam." (See
      0141)

0427 "Authorization of Appropriations for Military Procurement
      During Fiscal Year 1971 - Amendment." Congressional Record,
      v. 116, pt. 18, July 16, 1970, p. 24661-24670. Senator G.
      Nelson (D-Wisc.) discusses an amendment he is co-authoring
      with Senator C.E. Goodell (R-N.Y.) which would prohibit the
      military use of antiplant chemical weapons. He also
      discusses the debate over the military value of the use of
      defoliants, the ecological effects of these weapons and the
      report prepared by F.H. Tschirley. Senator Nelson also
      submitted the text of an article G.H. Orians and E.W.
      Pfieffer (See 0577) which appeared in a recent issue of
      Science and an article by R. Blumenthal which appeared in a
      recent issue of the New York Times.

0428 Baghat, H. "Vietnam: Where No Birds Sing." New
      Internationalist, no. 29, July 1975, p. 18-20. The author
      discusses the effects the U.S. military's use of herbicides
      during the Vietnam War had on the Vietnamese people, fauna
      and flora.

0429 Barnaby, F. "Environmental Warfare." Bulletin of the Atomic
      Scientists, v. 32, no. 5, May 1976, p. 36-43. Included in
      this article on the beginnings of concern on the
      environmental effects of wars are statements on how the
      various ways (including using herbicides) the U.S. military
      altered Vietnam's environment during the Vietnam War.

0430 Barnaby, F. "Towards Environmental Warfare." New Scientist,
      v. 69, no. 981, p. 6-8. As a result of the Vietnam War there
      continues to be a concern about the environmental impact of
      war. A. Westing's research on the environmental effects of
      herbicides is mentioned.

0431   Barnaby, F. "Weather Modification or Warfare?" Current, no.
       182, April 1976, p. 55-59. A general discussion of Soviet
       proposals to ban military techniques that modify the
       environment and on ways the use of these techniques including
       the use of herbicides modified the environment of Vietnam
       during the Vietnam War.

0432   Bass, A.B. "One Scientist's Crusade: a Portrait of Matthew
       Meselson." Technology Review, v. 89, no. 3, April 1986, p.
       42-54. Matthew Meselson was one of the first scientists to
       be concerned about the ecological effects of Agent Orange in
       Vietnam. Today he is researching the controversy over the
       "yellow rain" incidences in Southeast Asia.

0433   Baughman, R. and M. Meselson. "Analytical Method for
       Detecting TCDD (Dioxin): Levels of TCDD in Samples from
       Vietnam." Environmental Health Perspectives, experimental
       issue no. 5, September 1973, p. 27-35. The authors developed
       a method for detecting TCDD in animal tissues. They
       collected fish and crustacean samples in South Vietnam near
       areas heavily sprayed with 2,4,5-T. The authors feel that
       TCDD may have accumulated to biologically significant levels
       in the South Vietnamese food chains in areas sprayed with
       herbicides.

0434   Bendix, S. "Eyewitness Report from Vietnam." Freedom News,
       v. 6, no. 3, March 1972, p. 8. The efforts E.W. Pfeiffer is
       making to determine the ecological damage done to Vietnam
       because of the use of defoliants by the U.S. military are
       detailed.

0435   Bethel, J.S. et al. "Military Defoliation of Vietnam
       Forests." American Forests, v. 81, no. 1, January 1975, p.
       26-30+. This article details the work and findings of the
       Forestry Study Team of the National Academy of Sciences'
       Committee on the Effects of Herbicides in Vietnam. There was
       some dissent between committee members on the study teams'
       findings. The authors conclude by stating that the greatest
       effect of the military's use on herbicides on Vietnam's
       forests is not reflected in estimates of merchantable timber
       loss but rather in the open forests which were just beginning
       to recover from abandonment from shifting agriculture.

0436   Bethel, J.S. et al. "Timber Losses from Military Use of
       Herbicides on the Inland Forests of South Vietnam." Journal
       of Forestry, v. 73, no. 4, April 1975, p. 228-233. This
       report is based on the findings of the National Academy of
       Sciences' Committee on the Effects of Herbicides in Vietnam's
       Forestry Study Team. The team estimated that between one-
       half and two million cubic meters of currently merchantable

timber and between 5.6 and 11.9 million cubic meters of noncommercial species trees, immature commercial trees and crownwood were destroyed.

0437 Boffey, P.M. "Defense Issues Summary of Defoliation Issue." Science, v. 159, no. 3815, February 9, 1968, p. 613. The Department of Defense contracted with the Midwest Research Institute to prepare a state of knowledge on the ecological impact of the herbicides used for defoliation and crop destruction in Vietnam. The Department of Defense has recently released a summary digest of this report. This summary states that the ecological changes resulting from the use of defoliants in Vietnam have not yet reached the proportion of ecological disturbance caused by man's use of fire, the ax and the plow to clear land and improve agricultural production.

0438 Boffey, P.M. "Herbicides in Vietnam: AAAS Study Finds Widespread Devastation." Science, v. 171, no. 3966, January 8, 1971, p. 43-47. The preliminary report of the American Association for the Advancement of Science's Herbicide Assessment Commission was presented to the American Association for the Advancement of Science's annual convention last week. The findings of this Commission are summarized in this report. The Commission believes the use of defoliants has caused extremely serious harm to Vietnam and that there is evidence of shocking deficiencies in the precautions taken by U.S. military authorities. The Commission has found that about one-fifth to one-half of the mangrove forests have been destroyed, about one-half of the mature hardwood forests north and west of Saigon are dead, the crop destruction program has been a total failure and there is no evidence of adverse health effects.

0439 Braun, S. "Professor Westing Counts the Craters." Saturday Review, v. 55, no. 34, August 19, 1972, p. 18-20. The author interviewed Professor A. Westing who has done extensive research on the ecological effects of the use of bombs, herbicides and bulldozers by the U.S. military in Vietnam.

0440 Briantais, J.M. "Action of Defoliants and Herbicides on Plants: Their Utilization in Viet Nam." Vietnamese Studies, no. 29, 1971, p. 141-149. The entire issue of this journal consists of documents from the International Conference of Scientists on U.S. Chemical Warfare in Viet Nam. The author of this paper discusses how the defoliants used by the U.S. military chemically act on plants in Vietnam.

0441 Brindley, T. "A Legacy of Poison." Far Eastern Economic Review, v. 79, no. 9, March 5, 1973, p. 22-24. The destruction caused by the U.S. military defoliating, bulldozing and bombing Vietnam is detailed and the effects these military activities are having on the soil, water cycle, plant and animal life are described.

0442   Brown, D. "Nixon's War: a New Escalation." (See 0149)

0443   Brown, D.E. "The Use of Herbicides in War: a Political/ Military Analysis." (See 0150)

0444   Bulletin of the Union of Vietnamese Intellectuals in France. "Chemical Warfare by U.S. Troops in South Viet Nam." Vietnamese Studies, no. 29, 1971, p. 113-128. The entire issue of this journal consists of documents from the International Conference of Scientists on U.S. Chemical Warfare in Viet Nam. The authors of this paper discuss the ecological effects of the use of various chemicals - including Agent Orange - and toxic gases by the U.S. military are having on Vietnam.

0445   Burchan, L.T. "Defoliation Effects on Forest Ecology." [letter] Science, v. 161, no. 3837, July 12, 1968, p. 109. This letter was written in response to T.O. Perry's letter (See 0588) in the May 10, 1968 issue of this journal. L.T. Burchan does not agree that the use of defoliants in Vietnam will severely damage the ecology. The author asks why it is any more objectionable or morally reprehensible to use these chemicals, which have been licensed as safe for use by the general public, in Vietnam where the ideals of the free world are at stake than it is to use them for industrial and agricultural purposes at home.

0446   Burchett, W. "Defoliation Destroying Rural Vietnam." Guardian, v. 22, no. 21, February 21, 1970, p. 8. The author reports on a press conference given in Paris on December 19, 1969 and on papers given at the Paris peace talks on the concern of many regarding the amount of defoliants that have been sprayed in Vietnam and the possible ecological consequences and health effects on the Vietnamese people of the sprayings.

0447   Burchett, W. "South Viet-nam: War Against Trees." New Times (Moscow), no. 25, June 20, 1962, p. 24-26. The author in his interviews of South Vietnamese inquired about the spraying of chemicals on trees and crops and the effects the spraying had.

0448   Burchett, W.G. "War on Food Crops." In Vietnam: Inside Story of the Guerilla War. New York: International Publishers, 1965, p. 207-209. In this book the author tells

of his travels in the areas controlled by the National Front
of Liberation of South Vietnam in 1963 and 1964. In this
chapter the author tells in part the effects the use of
herbicides by the U.S. military has had on crops and people.

0449 Byast, T.H. and R.J. Hance. "Degradation 2,4,5-T by South
Vietnamese Soils Incubated in the Laboratory." Bulletin of
Environmental Contamination and Toxicology, v. 14, no. 1,
July 1975, p. 71-76. Some soils samples taken from areas in
South Vietnam that were thought to have received applications
of Agent Orange and were examined to obtain an indication of
the ability these soils had to degrade 2,4,5-T. The authors
determined that it was possible, in the four soils studied,
for 2,4,5-T to be degraded at levels at least as high as 15
ppm or about twice the rate of military applications in
Vietnam.

0450 Calder, N. "War by Weed Killer." (See 0293)

0451 Cameron, J. "Consequences of Artificial Defoliation in
Southeast Asia." Commonwealth Forestry Review, v. 51, no.
148 (no. 2), June 1972, p. 132-136. This paper examines the
use of chemical defoliants in Southeast Asia and the possible
environmental consequences arising from their use.

0452 Carlson, E.A. "International Symposium on Herbicides in the
Vietnam War: an Appraisal." Bioscience, v. 33, no. 8,
September 1983, p. 507-512. A delegate to the recent
International Symposium on Herbicides and Defoliants in War
held in Ho Chi Minh City summarizes the papers presented.
The conference dealt almost entirely with the effects of the
sprayings on Vietnam's ecology and the health of the
Vietnamese. The author was relieved to find that politics
was kept to a minimum.

0453 Chamlin, G.R. "Vietnam Defoliation Saves Lives." [letter]
Science, v. 170, no. 3963, December 11, 1970, p. 1156. The
author writes to state that G.H. Orians and E.W. Pfeiffer's
article (See 0577) of May 1, 1970 and letter (See 0579) of
September 11, 1970 do not constitute good science and that
the life of a tree is nothing compared to the life of an
American soldier.

0454 "Chemical and Biological Warfare Policies and Practices."
(See 0297)

0455 "Chemical-biological Warfare." (See 0298)

0456 "Chemical Destruction in Indochina." SSRS Newsletter, no. 2
(old ser. no. 209), 1971, p. 3. The findings of two studies

on the ecological effects of the military use of herbicides
in Vietnam are summarized. At a conference on chemical
warfare in Paris a team of physicians stated that they
believe that the chromosomes of some Vietnamese have been
altered as a result of having been exposed to these
herbicides.

0457   "Chemical Warfare's Toll." Indochina Chronicle, no. 49, May-
       June 1976, p. 6. This article notes the effects of the
       spraying of herbicides on Vietnam's forests, crops and on the
       health of the Vietnamese.

0458   "The Chemically Poisonous Products' Effects on Particular
       Agricultural Products." In Ecocide in Indochina: the
       Ecology of War. Ed. by B. Weisberg. San Francisco: Canfield
       Press, 1970, p. 75-77. The effects of the spraying of
       herbicides by the U.S. military on the following Vietnamese
       plants and crops are noted: manioc, rice, sweet potato,
       maize, coconut palms, jacquiers, banana trees, anganiers and
       letchiers, heveas, ricin, cotton and tobacco.

0459   Clarke, R. "Ecological War." (See 0706)

0460   Concerned Architects and Planners, UCLA. "Ecological Effects
       of the Vietnam War." American Institute of Planners.
       Journal, v. 38, no. 5, September 1972, p. 297-307. The
       authors discuss the social and physical destruction in
       Vietnam as the result of bombing, defoliation and forced
       urbanization and present a cost benefit analysis of the war.

0461   Constable, J.D. "Visit to Vietnam." Oryx, v. 16, no. 3,
       February 1982, p. 249-254. The author details what he was
       able to learn about wildlife in Vietnam during a visit to
       that country. The effects of the U.S. military's spraying of
       herbicides are briefly mentioned.

0462   Constable, J. and M. Meselson. "Ecological Impact of Large-
       scale Defoliation in Vietnam." Sierra Club Bulletin, v. 56,
       no. 4, April 1971, p. 4-9. Reprinted in "Ecocide in
       Indochina." Congressional Record, v. 117, pt. 13, June 2,
       1971, p. 17692-17694. The authors describe how the American
       Association for the Advancement of Science's Herbicides
       Assessment Committee went about conducting their study on the
       ecological effects of the use of herbicides in Vietnam and
       the findings of this committee as to the effects of the
       spraying on the mangrove forests, the upland forests and the
       health of the Vietnamese people. The authors also mention
       the effects of the crop destruction program.

0463   Constable, J.D. et al. "AAAS and NAS Herbicide Reports."

[letter] Science, v. 186, no. 4164, November 15, 1974, p.
584+. The authors who constituted the American Association
for the Advancement of Science's Herbicide Assessment
Commission respond to K.V. Thimann's letter (See 0631) from
the July 19, 1974 issue of this journal in which he stated
that the National Academy of Sciences' committee completely
failed to find evidence to support the claims of the American
Association for the Advancement of Science's Herbicide
Commission. The authors of this letter cite specific
examples of where the reports agree. These examples involve
the issues of birth defects and stillbirths, herbicide
residues in soil, reported deaths of Montagnards, effects on
inland forests and mangrove forests, bamboo invasion, and
effects of the crop destruction program.

0464   Cook, R.E. "Completely Destroyed." Yale Alumni Magazine, v.
       34, no. 8, 1970, p. 26-29. The author was part of the team
       of scientists that was sent to Vietnam by the American
       Association for the Advancement of Science to study the
       ecological and civil consequences of the defoliation and crop
       destruction. The author was particularly interested in the
       effects of the spraying on the mangrove forests.

0465   Cook, R.E., W. Haseltine and A.W. Galston. "What Have We
       Done to Vietnam?" New Republic, v. 162, no. 2, January 10,
       1970, p. 18-21. Reprinted in Ecocide in Indochina: the
       Ecology of War. Ed. by B. Weisberg. San Francisco:
       Canfield Press, 1970, p. 89-94; and in "Environmental Warfare
       in Vietnam." Congressional Record, v. 116, pt. 3, February
       19, 1970, p. 4111-4112. The authors summarize the concerns
       scientists have had about the environmental effects of the
       use of herbicides as a weapon in Vietnam and note the studies
       that have been done this far on the health effects of
       exposure to these compounds.

0466   Council for Agricultural Science and Technology. Effect of
       Herbicides in Vietnam and Their Relation to Herbicide Use in
       the United States. (Report no. 46) Ames, Iowa: The
       Council, 1975. 14p. This pamphlet is mostly a summary of
       the National Academy of Sciences' report. There is also a
       brief section on herbicide use in the United States.

0467   "Counterbriefing on U.S. Policy in Indochina." Congressional
       Record, v. 118, pt. 3, February 14, 1972, p. 3824-3833.
       Representative D.M. Fraser (D-Minn.) details a
       counterbriefing held by a group of House members primarily
       for editors and broadcasters brought to Washington to attend
       meetings on U.S. foreign policy. Accounts of the meeting and
       a transcript of a tape recording made of the counterbriefing
       are included. The counterbriefing was entirely on the

Vietnam War. The transcript of E. Pfeiffer's description of
the ecological damage done to Vietnam by bombs, herbicides
and bulldozing is on pages 3832-3833.

0468 **"DOD Report on Defoliants Unlikely to Still Critics."**
<u>Chemical and Engineering News</u>, v. 46, no. 7, February 12,
1968, p. 12-13. The findings of the study prepared by the
Midwest Research Institute on the ecological effects of
herbicides are given. They will do little to still the
debate on the use of defoliants in Vietnam.

0469 Dat, D.H. See Duong Hong Dat.

0470 **Davis, G.M. "Defoliation in Vietnam: Assessing the Damage."**
<u>Frontiers</u>, v. 38, no. 2, Winter 1973, p. 18-24. The author
was a member of the team of scientists that went to Vietnam
to assess the ecological damage done to that country as a
result of the spraying of herbicides by the U.S. military for
the National Research Council. The author surveyed the Rung
Sat Special Zone and focused his studies on the effects of
the spraying on mollusks. None of the molluscan species are
considered to be extinct or endangered and no abnormalities
were found. He also states that the mangroves will recover
and that the damage done by the sprayings is not
irreversible.

0471 **"Defoliant Fallout Lingers in South Vietnam."** <u>Science
Digest</u>, v. 76, no. 2, August 1974, p. 20-21. The findings of
the National Academy of Sciences' report on the effects of
the use of herbicides during the Vietnam War on Vietnam's
ecology and the health of the Vietnamese are mentioned.

0472 **"Defoliants: Use Still Controversial."** <u>Chemical and
Engineering News</u>, v. 46, no. 50, November 25, 1968, p. 13.
The September issue of <u>Scientist and Citizen</u> contains a
report on the use of picloram which takes issue with the
Department of Defense's contentions that picloram and the
other herbicides being used in Vietnam will not cause any
long-term threat to Vietnam's ecology.

0473 **"Defoliating Viet Nam."** <u>Time</u>, v. 91, no. 8, February 23,
1968, p. 70. The results of the study by the Midwest
Research Institute have been released. The report concludes
that there is no evidence that there will be long-term damage
to South Vietnam's plants and animal life as a result of the
spraying of herbicides.

0474 **"Defoliation, Dow and Vietnam."** <u>Peace News</u>, no. 1729, August
15, 1969, p. front cover, 5. The ecological effects of the
defoliation by the U.S. military in Vietnam and Cambodia are

given. The military justifications of this program are also
noted.

0475   "Defoliation Effect May Last 100 Yr." Intercontinental
       Press, v. 12, no. 9, March 11, 1974, p. 258. The report
       prepared by the National Academy of Sciences is summarized.
       The report stated that it may take 100 years for the mangrove
       area to be reforested.

0476   "Defoliation in Chicago." Scientific American, v. 224, no.
       2, February 1971, p. 44-45. The American Association for the
       Advancement of Science's committee's investigation into the
       physiological, genetic and ecological hazards of the Agent
       Orange spraying on the inhabitants of Vietnam is discussed.

0477   "Defoliation in South Vietnam." National Academy of
       Sciences. New Report, v. 24, no. 3-4, March/April 1974, p.
       1+. The complete text of the summary and recommendations
       sections of the National Research Council's Committee on the
       Effects of Herbicides in Vietnam's summary report constitute
       this article.

0478   "Defoliation in Vietnam." Editorials on File, v. 2, no. 1,
       January 1-15, 1971, p. 11-16. This article consists of
       editorials commenting on the results of the study conducted
       by the American Association for the Advancement of Sciences'
       Herbicides Assessment Commission.

0479   "Defoliation: the Nondefinitive Report." Science News, v.
       93, no. 8, February 24, 1968, p. 185. The findings of the
       Midwest Research Institute's study on the use of herbicides
       in Vietnam are given. The report fails to draw any
       definitive conclusions. Many scientists are concerned about
       the effects of the use of herbicides on endangered species.

0480   "Defoliation: What Happens to Nature?" Senior Scholastic,
       v. 93, no. 5, October 11, 1968, p. 10. The concern
       scientists have on the effects the spraying of herbicides
       will have on the environment is discussed. The reports
       prepared by F. Tschirley and the Midwest Research Institute
       conclude that these effects will not be serious. The
       American Association for the Advancement of Science has
       disputed their findings and has requested that a field study
       be conducted under the auspices of the United Nations.

0481   "Dioxin: a Potential Chemical-warfare Agent." SIPRI
       Yearbook, World Armaments and Disarmament, 1977, p. 86-102.
       Excerpted as "The Dioxin Curse." Atlas - World Press Review,
       v. 24, no. 11, November 1977, p. 13-15. As part of a review
       article of the ecological effects of dioxin as a military

weapon, the effects of the use of Agent Orange during the
Vietnam War are mentioned on pages 92-93 and 95-96. The
health effects of Agent Orange on the Vietnamese are
mentioned on page 98.

0482   "Dioxin From Defoliation Found in Vietnam Fish." Science
       News, v. 103, no. 18, May 5, 1973, p. 287. Samples taken by
       the American Association for the Advancement of Sciences'
       Herbicide Assessment Commission of river fish, shellfish and
       mother's milk were frozen and brought back to the United
       States. The fish samples have now been analyzed and TCDD
       has been found in all of the samples taken from the coastal
       and inland areas of Vietnam.

0483   "Dioxin in Vietnam's Rivers." Marine Pollution Bulletin, v.
       4, no. 6, June 1973, p. 83. M. Meselson has found dioxin in
       fish and shellfish from the rivers and coastline of Vietnam.
       The highest dioxin content was found in catfish.

0484   Duke, J.A. and J.T. McGinnis. "Vietnam Refoliation."
       [letter] Science, v. 170, no. 3960, November 20, 1970, p.
       807. As a result of all the articles that have been written
       on the effects of defoliation on Vietnam, the authors have
       developed a 10 point research program which would contribute
       to a successful ecological rehabilitation of Vietnam.

0485   Duong Hong Dat. "Effects of Herbicides and Defoliants on the
       Fauna and Flora of South Vietnam." [preliminary survey]
       Vietnamese Studies, no. 29, 1971, p. 45-52. The entire issue
       of this journal consists of documents from the International
       Conference of Scientists on U.S. Chemical Warfare in Viet
       Nam. The author of this paper discusses the on the spot
       observations made on the effects of the chemical warfare
       (including Agent Orange) conducted by the U.S. military on
       the fauna and flora of South Vietnam. The author offers
       these preliminary findings in hopes that they will lead to a
       more thorough study.

0486   "Ecocide: a Strategy of War." Friends Journal, v. 28, no.
       19, December 15, 1982, p. 28-29. A motion picture filmed and
       narrated by E.W. Pfeiffer and distributed by Green Mountain
       Post films is reviewed. The film is a compilation of the
       footage Pfeiffer took during his five trips to Vietnam to
       study the effects on the ecology of the area of the various
       chemicals and other weapons used by the U.S. military.

0487   "Ecocide in Indochina." Congressional Record, v. 117, pt.
       13, June 2, 1971, p. 17692-17694. Representative R.W.
       Kastenmeier (D-Wisc.) had J. Constable and M. Meselson's
       article from the April 1971 issue of the Sierra Club Bulletin

(See 0462) inserted in the Record. Representative
Kastenmeier believes that all Americans should be ashamed and
saddened by this willful destruction of another people's home
environment.

0488   "Ecological Destruction in Vietnam." Congressional Record,
        v. 117, pt. 6, March 25, 1971, p. 8133-8187. Representative
        R.W. Kastenmeier (D-Wisc.) had A.H. Westing's article from
        the March 1971 issue of Natural History (See 0658) and T.
        Aaronson's article from the March 1971 issue of Environment
        (See 0419) inserted in the Record. Representative
        Kastenmeier feels that the American conscience will be
        bothered by this brutal action for years to come.

0489   "Ecological Effects of the War in Vietnam." Congressional
        Record, v. 116, pt. 11, May 12, 1970, p. 15260-12566.
        Representative J. Dellenback (R-Ore.) had an article by G.H.
        Orians and E.W. Pfeiffer from the May 1, 1970 issue of
        Science (See 0577) inserted in the Record. Representative
        Dellenback stated that he has written to the President asking
        that a Vietnam Ecology Commission be established consisting
        of American and Vietnamese scientists.

0490   "Ecological Warfare." Scientific American, v. 218, no. 1,
        January 1968, p. 44-46. The articles by J. Mayer and A.W.
        Galston from a recent issue of Scientist and Citizen are
        summarized.

0491   "The Ecology of War." Scientific American, v. 223, no. 1,
        July 1970, p. 48-49. The article by G.H. Orians and E.W.
        Pfeiffer from the May 1, 1970 issue of Science is summarized.

0492   "Effects of Chemical Warfare in South Vietnam." In Wasted
        Nations: Report of the International Commission of Enquiry
        into United States Crimes in Indochina, June 20-25, 1971.
        Ed. by F. Browning and D. Forman. New York: Harper & Row,
        1972, p. 115-137. This article is part of the task force's
        report and discusses the effects of the U.S. military's use
        of herbicides on Vietnam's forests, animal and crops and on
        the health of the Vietnamese.

0493   Egler, F.A. "Herbicides and Vegetation Management: Vietnam
        and Defoliation." Ecology, v. 49, no. 6, Autumn 1968, p.
        1212-1215. The author reviews the report prepared by the
        Midwest Research Institute.

0494   Ehrlich, P., A.H. Ehrlich and J.P. Holdren. "Herbicides and
        Ecosystems." In Human Ecology: Problems and Solutions. San
        Francisco: W.H. Freeman, 1973, p. 181-183. These pages from
        this general text on human ecology examine the possible

effects of the military use of defoliants in Vietnam on plant
and animal life.

0495   Ehrlich, P., A.H. Ehrlich and J.P. Holdren. "Ecocide in
       Indochina." In Ecoscience: Population, Resources,
       Environment. 3rd ed. San Francisco: W.H. Freeman, 1977, p.
       653-656. This book attempts to provide an understanding of
       the population-resource-environment predicament and to
       present possible strategies for dealing with it. These pages
       of this book discuss the ecological effects of the military
       use of herbicides, bombs and Rome plows in Indochina.

0496   "The Everyday Devastation of Rural Vietnam." Peace News, v.
       7, no. 1852, January 7, 1972, p. 7. Recent reports by the
       Stockholm International Peace Research Institute and the
       American Association for the Advancement of Science
       document the damage done to rural Vietnam through the use of
       herbicides to fight the war.

0497   Fall, B.B. "'This Isn't Munich, It's Spain': a Vietnam
       Album." Ramparts, v. 4, no. 8, December 1965, p. 23-29. In
       this article describing the brutality of the Vietnam War, the
       author, based on his observations, describes on page 24 the
       effects of the defoliation project on Vietnam's trees.

0498   Fineberg, R. "U.S. Herbicide Created More Damage in
       Vietnam Than Revealed by the Pentagon's Tests, Claims New
       Defense Dept.-funded Report." Win, v. 8, no. 8, May 1, 1972,
       p. 31. It may take as long as five years for a herbicide-
       treated tree to die, the National Academy of Sciences'
       Committee on the Effects of Herbicides in Vietnam has found.
       Earlier reports which stated that about one-fifth of South
       Vietnam's forests were defoliated did not take this fact into
       consideration.

0499   Flamm, B.R. and J.H. Cravens. "Effects of War Damage on the
       Forest Resources of South Vietnam." Journal of Forestry, v.
       69, no. 11, November 1971, p. 784-789. Reprinted in "Vietnam
       War Ecological Assessment Act of 1972." Congressional
       Record, v. 118, pt. 10, April 11, 1972, p. 12241-12244. The
       authors describe the ecological damage done to the forests of
       Vietnam as the result of the spraying of herbicides by the
       U.S. military. The efforts of the U.S. Mission's Herbicide
       Review Committee and F. Tschirley to study the effects of the
       use of defoliants are mentioned.

0500   Futrell, R.F. "Diffusion of Air Assets." In The Advisory
       Years to 1965. Washington: U.S. Air Force. Office of Air
       Force History, 1981, p. 236-252. This chapter in this book
       detailing the Air Force's involvement in Southeast Asia from

the end of World War II to 1965 discusses the crop
destruction aspects of the herbicide spraying program.

0501   Galston, A.W. "Changing the Environment: Herbicides in
       Vietnam II." Scientist and Citizen, v. 9, no. 7, August-
       September 1967, p. 122-129. Reprinted in Yale Scientific
       Magazine, v. 42, no. 7, April 1968, p. 4-7+. How the
       spraying of herbicides by the U.S. military in Vietnam is
       done and the effect on the plants sprayed are described.
       Concerns about the defoliants getting into food chain and how
       the soil might be changed are discussed. Also the economic
       effects on farmers who have had their crops destroyed
       accidently are noted.

0502   Galston, A.W. "Defoliants." In CBW: Chemical and
       Biological Warfare. Ed. by S. Rose. Boston: Beacon Press,
       1969, p. 62-75. This paper was presented at a conference
       held in London at which an international group of scientists
       discussed the current state of chemical and biological
       warfare and ways to control its spread and is based on data
       which first appeared in the August-September 1967 issue of
       Scientist and Citizen (See 0501). The author discussed how
       the spraying of herbicides was done by the U.S. military and
       the effects of the spraying on plant life and expressed
       concern about the defoliant possibly getting into the food
       chain and how the soil might be changed.

0503   Galston, A.W. "Herbicides in Vietnam." New Republic, v.
       157, no. 22, November 25, 1967, p. 19-21. The author
       explains the concerns he has about the effects the military
       use of herbicides in Vietnam will have on Vietnam's
       environment. He also gives the military's reasons for
       launching this program, how Operation Ranch Hand is carried
       out and the amount of herbicides that have been used thus
       far.

0504   Galston, A.W. "Lesser of Two Evils." [letter] Science, v.
       164, no. 3878, April 25, 1969, p. 373. A.W. Galston wrote
       this letter in order to respond to an announcement about the
       Department of Defense's cancellation of plans to reactivate a
       herbicide manufacturing plant in St. Louis and F. Tschirley's
       article (See 0626) of February 21. A.W. Galston calls for
       the herbicide spraying program to be rigorously limited or
       halted.

0505   Galston, A.W. "Plants, People, and Politics." (See 0320)

0506   Galston, A.W. "Science and Social Responsibility: a Case
       History." (See 0321)

0507   Galston, A.W. "Ungreening of South Vietnam." Natural
       History, v. 83, no. 6, June-July 1974, p. 10+. A summary of
       the report, "The Effects of Herbicides in South Vietnam,"
       prepared by a committee of the National Academy of Sciences
       is given. The report shed no light on the issue of human
       exposure to defoliants.

0508   Gilbert, L.E., P.H. Raven and P.R. Ehrlich. "More on Forest
       Defoliation." [letter] Science, v. 161, no. 3845, September
       6, 1968, p. 964-965. This letter was written in response to
       T.D. Newton's letter (See 0566) of July 12, 1968. The
       authors of this letter do not believe that there will be no
       serious ecological damage done to Vietnam as a result of the
       military use of herbicides. In fact, they believe that
       certain animal populations will become extinct.

0509   Grabelsky, J. "Dioxin: War Horror Coming Home to Roost."
       (See 1077)

0510   Graham, F., Jr. "The Toxic Field of Mars." In Since Silent
       Spring. Boston: Houghton Mifflin, 1970, p. 204-210. The
       seeming lack of concern for the ecological consequences of
       the spraying of herbicides in Vietnam by the Department of
       Defense is described. The findings of the Midwest Research
       Institute's report are mentioned as well as the call by
       scientific societies for the military to stop spraying the
       herbicides. The author concludes this chapter by stating
       that the myth that herbicides can be used indiscriminately
       with no ill effects on the environment has been destroyed.

0511   Greenberg, D.S. "Defoliation: AAAS Study Delayed by
       Resignations from Committee." (See 0332)

0512   Gregersen, H.M. "Westing's Loss Figure of $470 Million Too
       High." [letter] Journal of Forestry, v. 70, no. 3, March
       1972, p. 129. The author feels that A. Westing in his
       article of November 1971 (See 0667) placed too high a figure
       on the economic loss to Vietnam as a result of their forests
       being damaged by the U.S. military's use of herbicides.

0513   Grummer, G. "Chemical Weapons Can Also Not Improve the
       Aggressor's Position." In Protocol of the International
       Conference on the U.S. Aggression in Vietnam. International
       Conference on the U.S. Aggression in Vietnam (1969: Berlin)
       East Berlin: Vietnam Commission of the Afro-Asian Solidarity
       Committee of the GDR, 1969, p. 171-174. This book presents
       the papers from a conference held in Berlin on February 17,
       1969 within the framework of a scientific deliberation on
       problems facing East, South East and South Asia. The author
       of this paper discusses the ecological effects the use of

herbicides by the U.S. military had on Vietnam and whether the United States has the moral right to conduct such a program.

0514   Grummer, G. "Crime Against the Forest." In <u>Accusation from the Jungle</u>. Berlin: Vietnam Commission of the Afro-Asian Solidarity Committee of the German Democratic Republic, 1972, p. 19-23. In this chapter of this book in which the author tells of his impressions of his travels in Vietnam, the author tells of the ecological effects the use of defoliants had on plant life and the soil.

0515   Grummer, G. <u>Genocide with Herbicides: Report, Analysis, Evidence</u>. Berlin: Vietnam Commission of the Afro-Asian Solidarity Committee of the German Democratic Republik, 1971. 38, 13p. The author made a tour of the Democratic Republic of Vietnam and parts of the Republic of South Vietnam in 1970. In this report the author describes the effects the military use of herbicides has had on the plant life and the health of the Vietnamese.

0516   Handorf, H.H. "Chemical and Biological Warfare: Is Propriety the Issue?" (See 0336)

0517   Harvey, F. <u>Air War: Vietnam</u>. (See 0187)

0518   Harvey, G.R. and J.D. Mann. "Picloram in Vietnam." <u>Scientist and Citizen</u>, v. 10, no. 7, September 1968, p. 165-171. The ecological effects of the spraying of Agent White in South Vietnam are discussed.

0519   Haseltine, W., W.R. Carter and N.V. Long. "Human Suffering in Vietnam." [letter] <u>Science</u>, v. 169, no. 3940, July 3, 1970, p. 6. This letter is written in response to G.H. Orians and E.W. Pfeiffer's article (See 0577) of May 1, 1970. The authors feel that no one is addressing the human health and societal costs of the crop destruction program. Vietnamese are being forced to move into refugee camps and into Saigon. The authors want the American Association for the Advancement of Science to expand the December 1969 resolution to include the cessation of the use of all herbicides in war.

0520   Hay, A. "Ho Chi Minh Conference. Defoliants in Vietnam: the Long-term Effects." <u>Nature</u>, v. 302, no. 5905, March 17, 1983, p. 208-209. A conference recently took place in Vietnam to evaluate the long-term effects of the military use of herbicides on environment and on man. Difficulties encountered in replanting mangroves, the failure of tropical inland forests to regenerate, and the increase in the rate of liver cancer, spontaneous abortions, birth defects and chromosome aberations in the Vietnamese were just a few of the topics discussed.

0521 **"Herbicidal Warfare."** Scientific American, **v. 230, no. 4, April 1974, p. 49-50.** A committee of the National Academy of Sciences has released the results of their study on the effects of the use of herbicides in Vietnam. They concluded that it may take 100 years for the mangrove area to be reforested and that the damage to inland forests has been widespread and serious. The committee found no conclusive proof that exposure to the herbicides caused human illnesses or congenital malformations.

0522 **"Herbicide Commission Reports Extensive Damage."** Nature, **v. 229, no. 5282, January 22, 1971, p. 223-224.** The preliminary findings of the American Association for the Advancement of Science's Herbicide Assessment Commission are discussed. The Commission studied the effects on human health, on mangrove swamps, tropical hardwood forests, the effects of the crop destruction program and the distribution of the herbicides and their residues and contaminants in food chains. The Commission did not assess the military effectiveness of the use of defoliants.

0523 "Herbicides, Defoliants: Vietnam Study Urged." (See 0340)

0524 **"Herbicides Sizzle in Vietnam."** Portland Scribe, **v. 6, no. 18, June 23, 1977, p. 4.** The defoliants used in Vietnam by the U.S. military are continuing to wreak havoc in Vietnam both ecologically and health effects in man.

0525 **Hickey, G.C.** Free in the Forest: Ethnohistory of the Vietnamese Central Highlands 1954-1976. **New Haven, CT: Yale University Pr. xxi, 350p.** Appendix C (p. 308-319) of this study of the Vietnamese Central Highland people is entitled "Perceived Effects of Herbicides Used in the Highlands" and details what the Vietnamese perceived the effects of the spraying to be on the health of humans, animal life, plant life and their soil. On pages 254-256 the author tells of his work with the National Academy of Sciences' Committee on the Effects of Herbicides in Vietnam.

0526 Hoang, T.G. "Effects of the Employment of Chemical Substances in the Vietnam War." (See 0748)

0527 **Hodgkin, D.C. "The Effects of Chemical Defoliants."** Vietnamese Studies, **no. 29, 1971, p. 101-106.** The entire issue of this journal consists of documents from the International Conference of Scientists on U.S. Chemical

Warfare in Viet Nam. The author of this paper summarizes the
findings of the American Association for the Advancement of
Science's study and the findings of studies which were
presented at a recent meeting in Paris. These findings
concern the health effects and ecological effects of the use
of defoliants by the U.S. military in Vietnam.

0528   Holmberg, B. "Biological Aspects of Chemical and Biological
        Weapons." Ambio, v. 4, no. 5-6, 1975, p. 211-215. As part
        of a general article on the effects of the use of chemical
        and biological weapons, the use of herbicides by the U.S.
        military during the Vietnam War is mentioned. The author
        reviews what is known about the toxicity of these compounds
        and the biological effects of the sprayings on Vietnam.

0529   House, W.B. et al. "Military Applications of Herbicides."
        In Assessment of Ecological Effects of Extensive or Repeated
        Use of Herbicides. Kansas City, MO: Midwest Research
        Institute. December 1, 1967, p. 108-150. Available from
        NTIS: AD-824314. This chapter of this report on herbicide
        production, usage, and applications; military usage of
        herbicides in Vietnam; and the ecological effects of the use
        of herbicides describes the tests which led to the decision
        by the military to use herbicides in Vietnam, the objectives
        of the mission and the ecological effects of the sprayings.

0530   Huddle, F.P. Technology Assessment of the Vietnam Defoliant
        Matter: a Case History. Report to the U.S. Congress. House
        of Representatives. Committee on Science and Astronautics,
        Subcommittee on Science, Research, and Development, 91st
        Cong., 1st sess. Washington: GPO, August 8, 1969. 73p.
        This report examines the process the American Association for
        the Advancement of Science used to assess the ecological
        effects of the military use of defoliants in Vietnam. The
        Midwest Research Institute's study of the ecological effects
        of herbicides is also mentioned.

0531   "Impact of Use of Herbicides in War." Asian Recorder, v. 30,
        no. 13, March 26-April 1, 1974, p. 11923-11924. The National
        Academy of Sciences has finished its study of the impact of
        the military use of herbicides by the United States during
        the Vietnam War. The Academy found that the wounds to
        Vietnam's ecology will take a century to heal. Thirty-six
        percent of the mangrove forests along the coasts of South
        Vietnam have been destroyed. The report also found the
        spraying program had adverse psychological effects in that it
        turned public opinion against the United States.

0532   "Indochina Is Becoming Extinct." Augur, v. 3, no. 6,
        December 3-January 14, 1971, p. 4. The various ways in which

the United State is destroying the ecology of Vietnam due to the various types of weapons including herbicides that are being used to fight the North Vietnamese are noted.

0533 "Introduction of Bills and Joint Resolutions." Congressional Record, v. 117, pt. 2, January 28, 1972, p. 1634. Senator G.A. Nelson (D-Wisc.) introduced S. 3084 which would commission a study of the ecological damage done to Indochina as a result of the operations by the Armed Forces of the United States. This bill was referred to the Committee on Foreign Relations.

0534 Karnow, S. "Vietnam: Legacy of Desolation." New Republic, v. 170, no. 11, March 16, 1974, p. 18-19. In part, a discussion of the National Academy of Sciences' report on the effects of the U.S. military's use of herbicides on Vietnam's mangrove marshes, crops and timber industry and the health effects of exposure on the Vietnamese.

0535 Kelley, J.B. "Ravaged Soil of Vietnam." Catholic World, v. 211, no. 1262, May 1970, p. 71-73. The ecological effects on Vietnam of the defoliation done by the U.S. military and the moral questions raised by using defoliants in a war are discussed. The findings of G.H. Orians and E.W. Pfeiffer as a result of their visit to Vietnam are noted.

0536 Kemf, E. "Vietnam's Conservation Programme: Seeds of Recovery." Inside Asia, no. 9, July-August 1986, p. 33-35. The author discusses the current state of Vietnam's ecology, especially the current state of their forests. The efforts the Vietnamese government has had to make in order to attempt to restore the forests destroyed the U.S. military's use of herbicides are noted.

0537 Klaseen, T.A. "Questions Defoliation in Vietnam." [letter] Journal of Soil and Water Conservation, v. 24, no. 2, March-April 1969, p. 80. This letter was written in response to G.R. Harvey and J.D. Mann's September 1968 article (See 0518) in Scientist and Citizen. The author of this letter wonders what role soil scientists should play in doing something about this situation. No wonder the Vietnamese are disillusioned about American friendship.

0538 Klopfer, P.H. "If the Soldiers Leave, Will Dying Stop?: the Long-term Effects of Ecological Disturbances in Vietnam." Churchman, v. 184, no. 4, April 1970, p. 7-8. The effects of the military use of defoliants, in particular picloram, in Vietnam are detailed. The author discusses potential long-term effects on human development, other animals and the viability of the soil.

0539 Kotelchuck, R. "America in Vietnam: Democracy for Dead
      People." Health Pac Bulletin, no. 31, May 1971, p. 1-9.
      This article discusses how the South Vietnamese people are
      being killed by starvation, disease and dislocation and how
      the spraying of herbicides has destroyed their crops and
      forests.

0540 Kunstadter, P. "Herbicide Use in Vietnam." [letter]
      Science, v. 186, no. 4169, December 20, 1974, p. 1075. This
      letter was written in response to D. Shapley's article of
      March 22, 1974 (See 0610) and K.V. Thimann's letter of July
      19, 1974 (See 0621) concerning of the National Academy of
      Sciences' Committee on the Effects of Herbicides in Vietnam.
      The author of this letter feels that the issue is the data,
      reasoning and conclusions of the committee, not the personal
      characteristics of the committee members and panel reviewers
      and the areas of disagreement among the committee members.
      He disagrees with K.V. Thimann that the National Academy of
      Sciences failed to find evidence to collaborate the findings
      of the American Association for the Advancement of Science's
      commission. We should not only take into account the effects
      on American lives but the effects on the lives of the
      Vietnamese and Montagnard villagers as well.

0541 Lavorel, J. "Report by an Inquiry Mission on the Spraying of
      Herbicides in Cambodia." Vietnamese Studies, no. 29, p. 165-
      173. The entire issue of this journal consists of documents
      from the International Conference of Scientists on U.S.
      Chemical Warfare in Viet Nam. The author of this paper
      discusses the findings of a team of scientists who visited
      Cambodia to research the ecological effects of the spraying
      of herbicides by the U.S. military on Cambodia.

0542 Lenard, P. "The War in Indochina and the Destruction of the
      Environment." New Perspectives, v. 3, no. 1, January-April
      1973, p. 9-14. The ecological effects of the spraying of
      herbicides on Vietnam are described.

0543 Leopold, A.C. "Defoliation." (See 0352)

0544 Leuba, C. "Defoliants: Orange, White, and Blue." [letter]
      Science, v. 165, no. 3892, August 1, 1969, p. 442-443. This
      letter responds to the recent letters on the use of
      defoliants in Vietnam that express concern on the effects of
      defoliation on plants and animals. These scientists are too
      concerned about their highly specialized interests and are
      forgetting that defoliation saves American and South
      Vietnamese lives.

0545 Lewallen, J. Ecology of Devastation: Indochina. Baltimore:

Penquin Books, 1971. 179p. The author examines the effects of the Vietnam War on the natural environment, the effects of the war on the patterns of human life in Indochina, and the organizations that carry out the American portion of the war. The pages that discuss the ecological effects of the use of herbicides by the U.S. military as part of the Vietnam War are: p. 58-88, 96-101, 107-109 and 113-118.

0546 Long, N.V. "Crop Destruction in South Vietnam: Salvation Through Starvation." Thoi-Bao Ga, no.14-15, 1971, p. 5-7. The effects of the military use of herbicides on South Vietnam's crops and water buffalo are discussed.

0547 Long, N.V. "Leaf Abscission?" Bulletin of Concerned Asian Scholars (See 0761)

0548 Luce, D. and J. Sommer. Viet Nam: the Unheard Voices. Ithaca: Cornell University Press, 1969, p. 160-162. The authors served in Vietnam as part of the organization, International Voluntary Services, and compiled the feelings of their Vietnamese friends and colleagues about the dilemmas of Vietnam. On these pages the Vietnamese people discuss how they feel about the use of defoliants and the ecological effects the defoliation program had on Vietnam.

0549 Lugo, A.E. and S.C. Snedaker. "The Ecology of Mangroves." Annual Review of Ecology and Systematics, no. 5, 1974, p. 39-64. In this review article on the ecology of mangrove forests, the effects of the spraying of herbicides on the mangrove forests in Vietnam during the Vietnam war are noted.

0550 McCarthy, R.D. "War Against Food and Foliage." In Ultimate Folly: War by Pestilence, Asphyxiation and Defoliation. New York: Knopf, 1969, p. 74-98. This chapter in this text on the development of chemical and biological weapons by the United States discusses the use of herbicides in Vietnam by the U.S. military. The amounts and types used, how missions were carried out, the ecological concerns, the reports by the American Association for the Advancement of Science and the Midwest Research Institute, the anti-food campaign and the moral implications of using such weapons are all discussed. The notes at the end of the chapter include the text of a letter of protest from Cambodia, the text of H.R. Res. 691 and a letter from E.W. Pfeiffer which further explains the ecological effects of the sprayings.

0551 McElheny, V. "Herbicides in Vietnam: Juggernaut Out of Control." [editorial] Technology Review, v. 73, no. 5, March 1971, p. 12-13. Reprinted in War-related Civilian Problems in Indochina. Part I - Vietnam. Hearing, 92nd

Cong., 1st sess., April 21, 1971. U.S. Congress. Senate.
Committee on the Judiciary. Subcommittee to Investigate
Problems Connected with Refugees and Escapees. Washington:
GPO, 1971, p. 134-137. The effects of the crop destruction
program are noted. Some areas have been sprayed by mistake.
The author does not feel that it has had a significant impact
on the enemy's food supplies. The spraying also violates the
Army's own rules. The Geneva Protocol and the Herbicide
Assessment Commission of the American Association for the
Advancement of Science are also mentioned.

0552 "Massive Herbicide and Defoliant Use Requires Field Study of
      Ecology." SSRS Newsletter, no. 193, October 1968, p. 1. The
      efforts E.W. Pfeiffer is making to implement the resolution
      passed by the American Association for the Advancement of
      Science to undertake a study of the ecological effects of the
      use of herbicides in Vietnam are noted.

0553 Mayer, J. and V.M. Sidel. "Crop Destruction in Viet Nam."
      Christian Century, v. 83, no. 26, June 29, 1966, p. 829-832.
      The practical and ethical implications of the destruction of
      rice crops and grain stores by the U.S. military are
      considered. The U.S. military destroyed crops by spraying
      defoliants, preventing harvesting of crops or burning
      harvested rice. The authors conclude that crop destruction
      will hurt only the innocent - it will not disable the
      Vietcong.

0554 Members of Congress for Peace Through Law. Military Spending
      Committee. "Environmental Warfare: Anti-plant Chemical
      Weapons." In Economics of Defense: a Bipartisan Review of
      Military Spending. New York: Praeger, 1971, p. 133-145.
      This book is a bipartisan review of selected U.S. military
      programs. Members of Congress for Peace Through Law is a
      bipartisan group composed of congressmen and senators who
      study in committees ways to obtain enforceable world law.
      This chapter describes the use of defoliants in Vietnam and
      Cambodia and reviews investigations into the ecological
      effects of the spraying. The use of herbicides in the food
      denial program is also mentioned.

0555 Meselson, M.S., A.H. Westing and J.D. Constable. Background
      Material Relevant to Presentations at the 1970 Annual Meeting
      of the AAAS. Washington: American Association for the
      Advancement of Science. Herbicide Assessment Commission,
      January 14, 1971. 47p. Reprinted in "Herbicide Assessment
      Studies." Congressional Record, v. 118, pt. 6, March 3,
      1971, p. 6807-6813; and in War-related Civilian Problems in
      Indochina. Part I - Vietnam. Hearing, 92nd Cong., 1st
      sess., April 21, 1971. U.S. Congress. Senate. Committee on

the Judiciary Committee. Subcommittee to Investigate
Problems Connected with Refugees and Escapees. Washington:
GPO, 1971, p. 115-133. This document is a revision of the
report the Commission made to the 1970 American Association
for the Advancement of Science annual conference. The
Commission went to South Vietnam to research the effects of
the spraying of Agent Orange on the environment of Vietnam
and the health effects of exposure on the Vietnamese. The
found that about one-fifth of the mangrove forests have been
destroyed, about one-half of the hardwood forests north and
west of Saigon are dead, that the crop destruction program
was a failure and that there was no definite evidence of
adverse health effects.

0556   Meselson, M.S. et al. Preliminary Report of Herbicide
       Assessment Commission of the American Association for the
       Advancement of Science. Reprinted in "Herbicide Assessment
       Studies." Congressional Record, v. 118, pt. 6, March 3,
       1972, p. 6806-6807, in War-related Civilian Problems in
       Indochina. Part I - Vietnam. Hearing, 92nd Cong., 1st
       sess., April 21, 1971. U.S. Senate. Committee on the
       Judiciary. Subcommittee to Investigate Problems Connected
       with Refugees and Escapees. Washington: GPO, 1971, p. 113-
       115; and in The Geneva Protocol of 1925. Hearing, 92nd
       Cong., 1st sess., March 5, 16, 18, 19, 22, and 26, 1971.
       U.S. Senate. Committee on Foreign Relations. Washington:
       GPO, 1972, p. 354-357. This document presents the
       preliminary findings of the trip the authors made to Vietnam
       in order to identify the chief problems and makes
       recommendations on how future studies should be conducted.

0557   Military Assistance Command Vietnam. The Herbicide Policy
       Review Report for March-May 1968 (See 0212)

0558   "Mission to Vietnam." Scientific Research, v. 4, no. 12,
       June 9, 1969, p. 22-30; v. 4, no. 13, June 23, 1969, p. 26-
       30; v. 4, no. 15, July 21, 1969, p. 5. Reprinted in
       Environmental Effects of Weapons Technology. By M.
       McClintock et al. New York: Scientists' Institute for
       Public Information, 1970, p. 17-22. G.H. Orians and E.W.
       Pfeiffer are interviewed. They visited Vietnam in 1969 and
       were sponsored by the Society for Social Responsibility in
       Science. The interview centers on how the war has destroyed
       the ecology of Vietnam.

0559   Mousseau, M. "Action of Defoliants on Natural Equilibriums."
       Vietnamese Studies, no. 29, 1971, p. 129-139. The entire
       issue of this journal consists of documents from the
       International Conference of Scientists on U.S. Chemical
       Warfare in Viet Nam. The author of this paper discusses the

ecological effects of the use of chemicals -- specifically
herbicides -- by the U.S. military on Vietnam.

0560   "NAS, AAAS to Report on Vietnam Defoliation." Nature, v.
       228, no. 5267, October 10, 1970, p. 108-109. The findings of
       the study conducted by the American Association for the
       Advancement of Science are discussed in terms of the damage
       done to Vietnam's ecology. Also mentioned is the fact that
       the Department of Defense is required to commission a study
       with the National Academy of Sciences under a military
       procurement authorization bill passed by Congress.

0561   National Research Council. Committee on the Effects of
       Herbicides in Vietnam. The Effects of Herbicides in South
       Vietnam. Part A: Summary and Conclusions. Part B: Working
       Papers. Washington: National Academy of Sciences, 1974.
       The Council studied the ecological and physiological effects
       of the spraying of herbicides in South Vietnam. The
       following aspects were studied: an inventory of the sprayed
       areas by herbicide type, date, and frequency; effects on
       vegetation; persistence of herbicides in the soil, and their
       effects on soil fertility; effects on animals; effects on
       people. The Committee concluded that there was no definitive
       indication of direct damage by herbicides to human health.

0562   National Research Council. Committee on the Effects of
       Herbicides in Vietnam. Interim Report: December 1970
       Through December 1971. 1972. ii, 34p. Available from NTIS:
       AD 737 600. This report summarizes the activities of the
       Committee beginning with the signing of the contract through
       December 1971 and details the decisions made during the
       planning phase and most of the reconnaissance phase. The
       reconnaissance phase being the phase in which decisions were
       made concerning where the most suitable localities and
       materials were and what the possible range of problems and
       variables to be encountered were.

0563   Neilands, J.B. "Vietnam: Progress of the Chemical War."
       (See 0372)

0564   Neilands, J.B. et al. Harvest of Death: Chemical Warfare in
       Vietnam and Cambodia. New York: Free Press, 1972. 304p.
       Two of the four chapters deal with the use of herbicides in
       Vietnam and Cambodia. The ecological effects of the spraying
       of herbicides by the U.S. military on the crops and
       vegetation of Southeast Asia are discussed. Also included
       are excerpts from the American Association for the
       Advancement of Science's study, the Department of the Army's
       Training Circular 3-16, and statements made by President
       Nixon on chemical and biological warfare.

0565   "New Details on Chemical Warfare." Guardian, v. 22, no. 9,
       November 22, 1969, p. 16. New statistics on the damage done
       to crops and animals by the use of chemicals by the U.S.
       military have been released by the War Crimes Commission of
       the PRG. Some 500 people have died and 2.3 million acres of
       crops have been destroyed.

0566   Newton, M. "Defoliation Effects on Forest Ecology." [letter]
       Science, v. 161, no. 3837, July 12, 1968, p. 109. M. Newton
       has written this letter in response to T.O. Perry's letter
       (See 0588) of May 10, 1968 which was written in response to
       P.M. Boffey's article (See 0437) of February 9, 1968. M.
       Newton does not agree that the Department of Defense's use of
       herbicides in Vietnam constitutes biocide. One application
       of the herbicides is not enough to permanently damage the
       ecology.

0567   Ngo Vinh Long. See Long, N.V.

0568   Nguyen Khac Vien. "The Lasting Consequences of Chemical
       Warfare." Vietnam Courier, no. 2, 1983, p. 21-30. This
       report was compiled from data supplied by Vietnamese
       biologists and doctors on the occasion of the international
       symposium held on this issue in Ho Chi Minh City from January
       14-19, 1983. It details the effects of the use of defoliants
       on crops and forests and the medical problems the Vietnamese
       people have encountered.

0569   Norman, C. "Vietnam's Herbicide Legacy." (See 0775)

0570   Novick, S. "Chemical War." Environment, v. 13, no. 2, March
       1971, p. 44-47. The content of a film made in North Vietnam
       on chemical warfare in Vietnam is described. The first half
       of the film is on the military spraying of herbicides which
       shows the damage the spraying caused to forests, crop plants,
       higher animals and humans. A good deal of the film may be
       inaccurate or misleading but there is no disputing the war
       has dealt enormous destruction to the land and its people.

0571   Novick, S. "The Vietnam Herbicide Experiment." Scientist
       and Citizen, v. 10, no. 1, January-February 1968, p. 20-21.
       The author critically reviews the report prepared by the
       Midwest Research Institute at the request of the Department
       of Defense. He feels the report is very disappointing and
       does little to answer concerns about the long-term ecological
       effects of the spraying.

0572   Odum, H.T. "Status of Knowledge on Herbicide and Ecology."
       Ecology, v. 49, no. 6, Autumn 1968, p. 1215. The author
       critiques the report prepared by the Midwest Research
       Institute.

0573 "On the Trail of Dioxin." Scientific American, v. 229, no.
5, November 1973, p. 47-48. M.S. Meselson and R. Baughan
have developed methods to determine the levels of dioxin in
the Vietnamese fish samples they brought back from Vietnam
when they went to study the effects of the herbicide spraying
program as part of the American Association for the
Advancement of Science's Herbicide Assessment Commission.
These fish samples have been found to contain 200-800 parts
per trillion of dioxin.

0574 "Operation Wasteland." Time, v. 95, no. 21, May 25, 1970, p.
70-73. The debate over the possible ecological damage done
to Vietnam by the spraying of defoliants is explained. Also
mentioned is the debate on the propaganda value it has to the
Viet Cong and whether militarily it has done what it was
supposed to do.

0575 "Orange to Green." The Times Higher Education Supplement,
no. 724, September 19, 1986, p. 13. The efforts Vietnamese
scientists are making to reverse the ecological damage done
by the Vietnam War are noted. The successful replanting of
more than half of the mangrove forests destroyed by the
spraying of Agent Orange is mentioned.

0576 Orians, G.H. and E.W. Pfeiffer. "Defoliants: Orange, White,
and Blue." [letter] Science, v. 165, no. 3892, August 1,
1969, p. 442. This letter was written in response to A.W.
Galston's letter (See 0504) which appeared in the April 25,
1969 issue of this journal. The authors state that the
reason why the use of picloram is on the increase in Vietnam
is that it is much less volatile and does not drift like
Agent Orange does. Agent Orange constitutes about 50
percent, Agent White 35 percent and Agent Blue 15 percent of
the herbicides used in Vietnam.

0577 Orians, G.H. and E.W. Pfeiffer. "Ecological Effects of the
War in Vietnam." Science, v. 168, no. 3931, May 1, 1970, p.
544-554. Reprinted in "Ecological Effects of the War in
Vietnam." Congressional Record, v. 116, pt. 11, May 12,
1970, p. 15250-15256, in "Authorization of Appropriations for
Military Procurement During Fiscal Year 1971 - Amendment."
Congressional Record, v. 116, pt. 18, July 16, 1970, p.
24661-24670; and in Not Since the Romans Salted the Land:
Chemical Warfare in S.E. Asia by J.B. Neilands et al.
Ithaca, N.Y.: Glad Day Pr., 1970, p. 18-28. The effects of
the U.S. military's activities, including the use of
defoliants in Vietnam, on Vietnam's ecology are described.
These observations were made based on interviews with
military personnel and a tour of the Rung Sat Special Zone.

0578   Orians, G.H. and E.W. Pfeiffer. "Ecological Effects of the
       War in Vietnam." Indian Agricultural News Digest, v. 2, no.
       8-12, February-June 1971, p. 251-264. The findings of a
       study on the ecological effects of the use of chemicals for
       defoliation by the U.S. military during the Vietnam War are
       summarized. This study was done as a supplement to a study
       done by F.H. Tschirley in an attempt to gather data on
       aspects of the problem, including animal life where Tschirley
       had been unable to gather data first-hand.

0579   Orians, G.H. and E.W. Pfeiffer. "United States Goals in
       Vietnam." [letter] Science, v. 169, no. 3950, September 11,
       1970, p. 1030. The authors respond to W. Haseltine, W.R.
       Carter and N.V. Long's letter (See 0519) of July 3, 1970.
       G.H. Orians and E.W. Pfeiffer state that in their May 1, 1970
       article (See 0577) they dealt lightly with the possible
       health hazards of exposure because they did not learn
       anything about this issue during their trip that the
       scientific community did not already know. G.H. Orians and
       E.W. Pfeiffer agree with W. Haseltine, W.R. Carter and N.V.
       Long about the societal costs of the spraying of herbicides.

0580   "The Other War in Vietnam." Newsweek, v. 71, no. 9, February
       26, 1968, p. 56. The use of 2,4-D and 2,4,5-T by the U.S.
       military in Vietnam has caused a shortage of the herbicide
       here in the U.S. The Midwest Research Institute has released
       its study on the ecological effects of herbicides. The
       report warns that some wildlife species could be starved to
       the point of extinction. The Pentagon released a summary of
       the report before the entire report was released in which the
       possible adverse effects of defoliation were minimized and at
       one point in the summary the Pentagon even states that
       herbicides could be ecologically beneficial.

0581   "Our Poisoning of Vietnam." Congressional Record, v. 117,
       pt. 9, April 20, 1971, p. 11085-11086. Representative M.J.
       Harrington (D-Mass.) comments on the ecological damage done
       to Vietnam by the spraying of herbicides and had printed in
       the Record an article by A. Wyman entitled "Our Poisoning of
       Vietnam" which discusses the ecological damage done to
       Vietnam by the spraying. He has brought this issue up as the
       Senate will soon begin reflection on the ratification of the
       Geneva Protocol.

0582   Page, H. "Ecocidal War: the Ideal Answer to Mass
       Destruction." Not Man Apart, v. 2, no. 7, July 1972, p. 7.
       As part of the first worldwide meeting on the human
       environment in Stockholm, a panel on ecocidal war was held.
       Drs. E. Pfeiffer and A. Westing provided information to this
       panel on the ecological damage done to Vietnam by the
       spraying of herbicides and the use of Rome plows and bombs.

0583   Peck, J. "U.S. Defoliation Will Take Century to Heal." Win,
       v. 10, no. 9, March 14, 1974, p. 16. The findings of a
       report prepared by the National Academy of Sciences are
       mentioned. Also mentioned is an article published in the New
       York Times which indicated how surprised the Department of
       Defense was at the critical nature of the report.

0584   Peck, J. "US Sprays Destroy Viet Forests." Win, v. 7, no.
       4, March 1, 1971, p. 5. The American Association for the
       Advancement of Science has released a report which states
       that at least one-fifth of the 1.2 million acres of mangrove
       forests in South Vietnam have been utterly destroyed as a
       result of the herbicide sprayings. The report also states
       that the Pentagon did not observe its policy of only spraying
       food crops in sparsely populated areas. The spraying of rice
       and other crops has cut off approximately 600,000 people from
       their normal food supply.

0585   Peck, J. "Vietnam Ecocide." Edcentric: a Journal of
       Educational Change, no. 29, April 1974, p. 23. The National
       Academy of Sciences has reported to Congress on their
       findings concerning the use of herbicides during the Vietnam
       War. The report states that it will take a century for
       Vietnam to heal. Department of Defense officials were
       surprised by the critical tone of the report.

0586   "Pentagon Disputes Defoliation Study." Facts on File, v. 31,
       no. 1577, January 14-20, 1971, p.33. A Department of Defense
       spokesman stated that M.S. Meselson did not offer conclusive
       evidence in his study of the effects of the use of defoliants
       in Vietnam. Meselson stated that the mangrove forests would
       not be able to sustain new life as a result of having been
       sprayed. The spokesman also stated that the use of
       defoliants may have benefited some parts of South Vietnam's
       economy, specifically small farmers and the lumber industry.

0587   Perkins, P. "Scars of Imperialist War in Vietnam." Workers
       World, v. 17, no. 33, August 22, 1975, p. 7. A. Galston at a
       United Nations press conference reported on his findings
       concerning the ecological damage he had found in Vietnam due
       to the use of herbicides, bombs, etc. He was sponsored by
       the Scientists Institute for Public Information. The health
       of the Vietnamese people is also suffering. The liver cancer
       rate is now six times what it was prior to the war. Although
       no direct cause and effect relationship between the use of
       herbicides and cancer has been established, the author feels
       none is needed.

0588   Perry, T.O. "Vietnam: Truths of Defoliation." [letter]
       Science, v. 160, no. 3828, May 10, 1968, p. 601. This letter

was written in response to P.M. Boffey's article (See 0437) of February 9, 1968. T.O. Perry states that there can be little doubt about the short-term effects of the use of defoliants in Vietnam - they kill the green vegetation. The Department of Defense has gone beyond genocide to biocide.

0589   Pfeiffer, E.W. "Chemical Warfare in Viet Nam and the American Scientific Community." SSRS Newsletter, no. 195, January 1969, p. 1-3. Reprinted in Scientific World, v. 12, no. 6, 1968, p. 16-19. The author reviews the efforts he has made to get a study of the ecological effects of the use of herbicides in Vietnam started. The author also summarizes the findings of the study conducted by the Midwest Research Institute.

0590   Pfeiffer, E.W. "Defoliation and Bombing Effects in Vietnam." Biological Conservation, v. 2, no. 2, January 1970, p. 149-151. The ecological effects of defoliation and bombing in Vietnam as witnessed by the author and G.H. Orians in a visit to Vietnam which was sponsored by the Society for Social Responsibility in Science and the McGraw-Hill Publishing Company are summarized.

0591   Pfeiffer, E.W. "Ecological Effects of the Vietnam War." Peace and the Sciences, October-December 1969, p. 1-12. This article consists of the text of a speech given at the World Assembly for Peace in Berlin in June 1969. The author discusses the ecological effects of the use of herbicides and high explosives by the U.S. military as part of the Vietnam War.

0592   Pfeiffer, E.W. "Ecological Effects of the Vietnam War." Science Journal, v. 5, no. 2, February 1969, p. 33-38. Excerpted as "From Ecological Effects of the Vietnam War." In Ecocide in Indochina: the Ecology of War. Ed. by B. Weisberg. San Francisco: Canfield Pr., 1970, p. 33-38. The author summarizes the opinions of both government and independent American scientists on the ecological effects of the use of explosive and defoliants by the U.S. military on Vietnam's plant and animal communities and their soil.

0593   Pfeiffer, E.W. "Post-war Vietnam." Environment, v. 15, no. 9, November 1973, p. 29-33. The author and A.H. Westing visited Hanoi in late July 1973 on behalf of the Scientists' Institute for Public Information's New Scientific Aid to Indochina Task Force to learn what assistance independent American scientists might be able to give in the restoration of war damage in Indochina. The authors toured many of the devastated areas of Vietnam including areas that had been sprayed with defoliants and took soil samples for later study.

0594   Pfeiffer, E.W. "Recent Developments in Indochina and the USA
       Related to the Military Use of Herbicides." Scientific
       World, v. 15, no. 6, 1971, p. 20-23. The author describes
       what scientists have found out about the effect of the U.S.
       military's spraying of herbicides in Vietnam on Vietnam's
       ecology and the efforts scientists made to get the sprayings
       halted.

0595   Pfeiffer, E.W. "Recent Developments in Indochina and the USA
       Relating to the Military Uses of Herbicides." Vietnamese
       Studies, no. 29, 1971, p. 85-99. The entire issue of this
       journal consists of documents from the International
       Conference of Scientists on U.S. Chemical Warfare in Viet
       Nam. The author summarizes the results of recent studies on
       the effects of the herbicides used by the U.S. military in
       Vietnam on plants, animals and humans.

0596   Pfeiffer, E.W. "Some Effects on Environmental Warfare on
       Agriculture in Indochina." Agriculture & Environment, v. 2,
       no. 3, October 1975, p. 271-281. This article documents the
       extent the war had on Vietnam's forests and other
       agricultural resources. Included in this report is a
       discussion of the environmental damage done by the
       defoliation project.

0597   Pfeiffer, E.W. and A.H. Westing. "Some Ecological Effects of
       the War in Indochina." Solidarity with Vietnam, no. 33,
       October 1971, p. 16-22. Reprinted in Relevant Scientist, no.
       2, November 1972, p. 9-11. The ecological effects of the use
       of chemical weapons (including herbicides), high explosives
       and land-clearing equipment by the U.S. military as part of
       the Indochina War on Vietnam is described.

0598   Popovich, L. "Of Mice and Men: the Troubles of 2,4,5-T."
       Journal of Forestry, v. 76, no. 12, December 1978, p. 787-
       789. This is a general article which reviews the concerns of
       the spraying of herbicides in forest management. The
       findings of the National Academy of Sciences' study of the
       use of herbicides in Vietnam are briefly mentioned. Also
       mentioned is upcoming debate on the possible ban by the
       Environmental Protection Agency of 2,4,5-T in the United
       States.

0599   "A Preliminary Assessment of Herbicides and Defoliation."
       Environmental Science and Technology, v. 2, no. 3, March
       1968, p. 176-181. The Midwest Research Institute's report on
       the ecological repercussions of the U.S. military's use of
       herbicides in Vietnam is summarized and the report by the
       National Academy of Sciences is reviewed.

0600 Price, D.K. et al. "On the Use of Herbicides in Vietnam."
      Science, v. 161, no. 3838, July 19, 1968, p. 253-256.
      Reprinted in Scientist and Citizen, v. 10, no. 5, June/July
      1968, p. 118-122; and in "Chemical Herbicides for
      Defoliation." Congressional Record, v. 114, pt. 18, July 30,
      1968, p. 24153-24155. This article consists of a statement
      made by the Board of Directors of the American Association
      for the Advancement of Science which urges that a field study
      be undertaken to determine the ecological effects of the
      spraying of herbicides in Vietnam by the U.S. military. The
      article also includes supplementary statements by some of the
      Board of Directors. The Board feels that the study should be
      conducted under the auspices and direction of the United
      Nations.

0601 "Ravaging Vietnam." Nation, v. 208, no. 16, April 21, 1969,
      p. 484-485. The trip made by E.W. Pfeiffer and G.H. Orians
      to Vietnam which was sponsored by the Society for Social
      Responsibility in Science to study the ecological damage done
      by the war is commented upon. Pfeiffer and Orians found that
      while the defoliants were effective militarily the ecology of
      Vietnam paid the price. The lumber and rubber industries
      have suffered and bird life has been greatly reduced.

0602 Richards, P.W. "The Forests of South Vietnam in 1971-72: a
      Personal Account." Environmental Conservation, v. 11, no. 2,
      Summer 1984, p. 147-153. The author describes his
      participation on the U.S. Academy of Sciences' Committee on
      the Effects of Herbicides in South Vietnam during 1971-1974.
      The appearance in 1971 and 1972 of the inland and mangrove
      forests as seen from the air after having been sprayed with
      herbicides is detailed. The author also mentions what he
      perceives the future changes in southern Vietnam's forests to
      be.

0603 Russell, B. "Chemical Warfare in Vietnam." (See 0787)

0604 Russo, A.J. A Statistical Analysis of the U.S. Crop Spraying
      Program in South Vietnam. October 1967. 45p. Available
      from NTIS: AD-779 791/3. This report examines the effects
      of the chemical spraying on Viet Cong rice consumption. The
      report concludes that the crop destruction program has had an
      insignificant effect on Viet Cong rice consumption and may in
      fact be counterproductive due to the disproportionately high
      costs to the villager.

0605 "SSRS to Study Vietnam Ecology." SSRS Newsletter, no. 194,
      November-December 1968, p. 1. E.W. Pfeiffer will be going to
      Vietnam to undertake a fact-finding mission for the Society
      for Social Responsibility in Science that will hopefully be

the beginning of a study of the ecological effects of the use
of chemical agents in Vietnam. The purposes of the study
mission and the methods to be used in carrying out the study
are outlined.

0606   Schell, O., Jr. "Silent Vietnam: How We Invented Ecocide
and Killed a Country." Look, v. 35, no. 7, April 6, 1971, p.
55+. Reprinted in "Silent Vietnam." Congressional Record,
v. 117, pt. 7, March 30, 1971, p. 8505-8508. How the
environment of Vietnam has been destroyed as the result of
the weapons the U.S. military has used in the war, including
the use of herbicides, is described.

0607   Schell, O., Jr. and B. Weisberg. "Ecocide in Indochina." In
Ecocide in Indochina: the Ecology of War. Ed. by B.
Weisberg. San Francisco: Canfield Pr., 1970, p. 16-32. The
authors discuss the effects of the war, including the U.S.
military's use of herbicides, on Vietnam's ecology and on the
Vietnamese people as a result of being uprooted.

0608   "Serious Defoliant Damage in Vietnam." Science News, v. 105,
no. 11, March 16, 1974, p. 174-175. The findings of the
National Academy of Science's Committee on the Effects of
Herbicides in Vietnam's report are given. The ecological
damage is detailed. The Committee found no evidence of
direct damage to human health.

0609   Shapley, D. "Herbicides: AAAS Study Finds Dioxin in Vietnam
Fish." Science, v. 180, no. 4083, April 20, 1973, p. 285-
286. Two Harvard scientists have determined that fish and
shellfish from areas sprayed during the United States'
defoliation program in South Vietnam contain significant
quantities of dioxin.

0610   Shapley, D. "Herbicides: Academy Finds Damage in Vietnam
After a Fight of Its Own." Science, v. 183, no. 4138, March
22, 1974, p. 1177-1180. The findings of the National Academy
of Sciences' Committee on the Effects of Herbicides' report
are summarized and commented upon.

0611   "A Small War's Toll." Newsweek, v. 79, no. 24, June 12,
1972, p. 43. Reprinted in "Ecocide in Vietnam."
Congressional Record, v. 118, pt. 16, June 7, 1972, p. 19978.
The problems facing the United States diplomatically in the
world as a result of the ecological damage done by the
military's spraying of herbicides in Vietnam are noted.

0612   Somerville, M. "They Shall Inherit the Earth." In Ecocide
in Indochina: the Ecology of War. Ed. by B. Weisberg. San
Francisco: Canfield Pr., 1970, p. 64-71. The effect of the

U.S. military's use of herbicides and Rome plows on Vietnam's soils is detailed.

0613   Stanford Biology Study Group. The Destruction of Indochina: a Legacy of Our Presence. San Francisco: California Tomorrow, 1970. 8p. Reprinted in Bulletin of the Atomic Scientists, v. 27, no. 5, May 1979, p. 36-40; in Instant Research on Peace and Violence, no. 1, 1972, p. 2-8; and in Global Ecology: Readings Toward a Rational Strategy for Man. Ed. by J.P. Holdren and P.R. Erlich. New York: Harcourt Brace Javonovich, 1971, p. 146-154. Summarized in Humanist, v. 31, no. 1, January/February 1971, p. 14-17. This pamphlet describes the ecological effects of the Indochina War. In addition to mentioning the ecological effects of the use of defoliants, the pamphlet also mentions the "resource denial" program and the possibility that exposure to the defoliants is causing birth defects among the Vietnamese.

0614   "Statements on Introduced Bills and Resolutions." (See 0394)

0615   Stockholm International Peace Research Institute. "Tropical Regions: Woody Vegetation." In Warfare in a Fragile World: Military Impact on the Human Environment. Written by A.H. Westing. London: Taylor & Francis, 1980, p. 79-103. This book examines how weapons and techniques of war disrupt the environment. This section describes the impact of warfare on tropical vegetation with special emphasis placed on the effects the use of herbicides by the U.S. military in South Vietnam during the Second Indochina War had on forests and agricultural crops.

0616   "Study on Use of Herbicides in South Vietnam." Congressional Record, v. 120, pt. 4, February 28, 1974, p. 4615-4632. Senator T.J. McIntyre (D-N.H.) had the summary and conclusion of the National Academy of Sciences' report and letters discussing the follow-up studies recommended by the Academy printed in the Record.

0617   Swanson, C.W. "Reforestation in the Republic of Vietnam." Journal of Forestry, v. 73, no. 6, June 1975, p. 367-371. The author believes that the war was not the major reason why Vietnam's forests came to be deforested. Except for the mangroves the use of herbicides did a minimum of actual deforestation. The deforestation was caused by itinerant cultivation, uncontrolled forest fires, indiscriminate clearing and lumbering by the Japanese. The author then describes the efforts that are currently underway to reforest Vietnam.

0618   Szabo, S.S. "Defoliation of Vietnames Forests." [letter]

Bioscience, v. 22, no. 5, May 1972, p. 273. This letter was
written in response to A.H. Westing's article (See 0661)
from the September 1, 1971 issue of this journal. S.S. Szabo
disagrees with the entire premise of A.H. Westing's article
as his article is based largely on supposition. S.S. Szabo
states that unless you spend a lot of time trying to fight
your way through the jungle you cannot be an authority on the
merits or demerits of military defoliation. The defoliation
was done with the consent of the South Vietnam government.
Also the saving of American soldiers is of more value than
all of the timber resources in Indochina.

0619   Thant, U. et al. Chemical and Bacteriological (Biological)
       Weapons and the Effects of Their Possible Use: Report of the
       Secretary General. New York: United Nations, 1969. xiv,
       100p. Also published by New York: Ballantine, 1970. 178p.
       Pages 71-72 of this general report on chemical and biological
       weapons and the effects of their possible use discuss the use
       of defoliants in Vietnam. The amount of herbicides used and
       their ecological effects are mentioned.

0620   "There Are No More Birds in South Vietnam." St. Louis
       Outlaw, v. 2, no. 3, May 28, 1971-June 17, 1971, p. 24. This
       article was adapted from the report prepared by the Stanford
       Biology Study Group. It details how the United States is
       destroying the ecology of Vietnam by the use of herbicides,
       scrapnel, and fire and how the United States justifies these
       actions and the long-term effects of these actions.

0621   Thimann, K.V. "Herbicides in Vietnam." [letter] Science, v.
       185, no. 4147, July 19, 1974, p. 207. This letter was
       written to correct some of the information D. Shapley gave in
       his March 22, 1974 article (See 0610) on the National Academy
       of Sciences' Committee on the Effects of Herbicides' report.
       K.V. Thimann discusses some of the disagreement within the
       National Academy of Sciences regarding this report. Also the
       claim D. Shapley makes that the mangrove forests will not
       regenerate is simply not true. K.V. Thimann reminds us that
       the purpose of the defoliation project was to save American
       lives.

0622   Thomas, W.L. "The Use of Herbicides in South Vietnam:
       Resultant Economic Stress and Settlement Changes." Pacific
       Viewpoint, v. 16, no. 1, 1975, p. 1-25. This paper
       describes how the National Academy of Sciences carried out
       its study of the effects of the use of herbicides in Vietnam,
       specifically the geographical aspects of the study. The
       author wrote the "Economic Stress" and "Settlement Changes"
       working papers.

0623 Thomsen, V. "Ecological Effects of the War in Vietnam."
College Press Service, no. 14, November 17, 1971, p. 2. A
speech given by E.W. Pfeiffer in St. Louis recently is
summarized. In this speech he details the ecological damage
done to Vietnam by the use of herbicidal chemicals, land
clearance and bombing. His observations are based on
personal visits to Vietnam. He specifically mentions the
destruction of the mangrove forests and the increase in birth
defects.

0624 Tinker, J. "Indochina: Ecology Which Stockholm Forgot."
New Scientist, v. 54, no. 801, June 22, 1972, p. 694-695.
Participants at the United Nations' Conference on the Human
Environment and its fringe forums expressed concerns about
the environmental effects of the war in Indochina.

0625 Tran Huu Tuog. "Intervention." [excerpt] In U.S. Military
Adventure in South Vietnam. Vietnam (Democratic Republic,
1946-). National Assembly. Hanoi: Foreign Languages
Publishing House, p. 46-49. The author tells of the effects
of the use of chemicals weapons, including defoliants, in
various provinces of South Vietnam on the people, forests and
the land.

0626 Tschirley, F.H. "Defoliation in Vietnam." Science, v. 163,
no. 3869, February 21, 1969, p. 779-786. Reprinted in Man's
Impact on Environment. Ed. by T.R. Detwyler. New York:
McGraw-Hill, 1971, p. 532-554; in "Chemical and Biological
Warfare: Questions to Be Answered." Congressional Record,
v. 115, pt. 6, April 1, 1969, p. 8166-8170; and in
"Environmental Warfare." Congressional Record, v. 116, pt.
22, August 25, 1970, p. 30000-30012. The ecological
consequences of the defoliation program in Vietnam are
assessed based on the author's observation of some of the
defoliated areas and discussions with people knowledgeable
about the areas observed. The author concludes that the
defoliation program has caused changes but they are not
irreversible. The author could not make any conclusions
about the effects of the defoliation program on animals.

0627 Tschirley, F.H. "Ecological Effects of Extensive or Repeated
Use of Herbicides." Ecology, v. 49, no. 6, Autumn 1968, p.
1211-1212. The author reviews the report prepared by the
Midwest Research Institute.

0628 Tschirley, F.H. "Herbicides in Vietnam and the United
States." Council of Agricultural Science and Technology.
News from CAST, v. 2, no. 4, September 1975, p. 51-53. The
Council's recently released report entitled "Effects of
Herbicides in Vietnam and Their Relation to Herbicide Use in

the United States" is summarized. The report discusses the
ecological effects of the use of herbicides as part of the
Vietnam War. It concludes the atypical military usage in
South Vietnam has no relation to and no bearing on the
peaceful uses of herbicides on agricultural, forest and
industrial lands.

0629   Tuan, V.H. See Vo Hoai Tuan.

0630   Tuog, T.H. See Tran Huu Tuog.

0631   "The U.S. Command Wages a Large-scale Chemical War Against
       Populated Regions: 500,000 Persons Poisoned in Ben-Tre."
       Vietnam Courier, special issue, January 31, 1966, p. 4+. An
       account is given of the effect the spraying of chemicals to
       destroy crops is having on the people, domestic animals and
       crops in the Ben Tre province.

0632   U.S. Congress. House. Committee on Foreign Affairs.
       Subcommittee on National Security Policy and Scientific
       Developments. U.S. Chemical Warfare Policy. (See 0401)

0633   U.S. Congress. Senate. Committee on Foreign Relations.
       Geneva Protocol of 1925. (See 0403)

0634   U.S. Department of the Army. Employment of Riot Control
       Agents, Flame, Smoke, Anti-plant Agents and Personnel
       Detectors in Counter-guerrilla Operations. (See 0249)

0635   "United States Experts Report on Defoliation in Cambodia."
       U.S. Department of State Bulletin, v. 61, no. 1592, December
       29, 1969, p. 635. A group of scientists who visited Cambodia
       earlier in 1969 to study the effects of herbicide sprayings
       in the Kompong Cham Province in Cambodia found that damage
       was extensive. However few, if any, rubber or fruit trees
       were killed and recovery should be well advanced by mid-1970.

0636   Vien, N.K. See Nguyen Khac Vien.

0637   Viet Nam: Destruction - War Damage. Hanoi: Foreign
       Languages Publishing House, 1977. 66p. The effects on
       Vietnam's ecology and on the health of the Vietnamese of the
       herbicidal sprayings by the U.S. military are noted.

0638   "Vietnam Defoliation." (See 0255)

0639   "Vietnam Defoliation Judged Long Lasting." Facts on File, v.
       34, no. 1740, March 16, 1984, p. 192. The study prepared by
       the National Academy of Sciences on the military use of
       herbicides in Vietnam found that damage done to the ecology

could last as long as a century. It is estimated that 36 percent of the mangrove forests along the southeast coast have been destroyed. The scientists also investigated the effects of the spraying on the health of the Montagnard tribes.

0640 "Vietnam Developments." Congressional Quarterly Weekly Report, v. 26, no. 40, October 4, 1968, p. 2671. One portion of this article is entitled "Damaged Ecology." In this section the report prepared by F.H. Tschirley's committee on the effects of the use of defoliants by the U.S. military on Vietnam's ecology is noted. The committee found substantial, but not irreparable, damage to plant and animal life.

0641 "Vietnam Foliage Hit Hard by Herbicides." Chemical and Engineering News, v. 52, no. 9, March 4, 1974, p. 6-7. The findings of the National Academy of Sciences' report on the use of herbicides in Vietnam are noted.

0642 "Vietnam Herbicide Controversy." Chemistry, v. 47, no. 6, June 1974, p. 23-25. The report recently released by the National Academy of Sciences on the use of herbicides in Vietnam is commented upon.

0643 "Vietnam: Impact of War on Its Environment." Congressional Quarterly Weekly Report, v. 30, no. 31, July 29, 1972, p. 1878-1881. The effects of the use of herbicides, bulldozing, bombs and weather modification by the U.S. military on Vietnam's environment is discussed.

0644 "Vietnam Investigates Chemical Poisoning." Militant, v. 47, no. 24, July 1, 1983, p. 12-13. The recent "International Symposium on the Lasting Consequences on Man and Nature of the Herbicides and Defoliants Used in Vietnam During the American War" conference in Ho Chi Minh City is discussed.

0645 "Vietnam Laid Waste." Ally, no. 30, October 1970, p. 2. The effects of the defoliation program on Vietnam's ecology and the crop destruction program on Vietnam's agriculture are discussed.

0646 "Vietnam War Damage." Congressional Record, v. 118, pt. 10, April 13, 1972, p. 12647-12649. Senator G.A. Nelson (D-Wisc.) recently hosted a briefing sponsored by the Council for a Liveable World. Drs. A. Westing and E. Pfeiffer spoke at this briefing on the environmental damage done to Vietnam. Dr. Westing's comments have been inserted in the Record.

0647 "Vietnam War Ecological Assessment Act of 1972."

Congressional Record, v. 118, pt. 10, April 11, 1972, p. 12241-12244. Representative D.M. Fraser (D-Minn.) had printed into the Record a letter from M.L. Kopp of Minneapolis which gives an eyewitness account of the ecological damage done to Vietnam and supports Representative Fraser's bill to have a study conducted on the ecological damage to Vietnam. B.R. Flamm and J.H. Craven's article (See 0499) in the November 1971 issue of Journal of Forestry was also inserted in the Record.

0648 "Vietnamese Ecology Battered." Chinook, v. ?, no. 26, July 16, 1970, p. 3. A report prepared by the Stanford Biological Sciences department which documents the ecological damage done to South Vietnam by the defoliants used by the U.S. military is commented upon.

0649 Vo Hoai Tuan. "Some Data on Chemical Warfare in South Viet Nam in 1969-1970." Vietnamese Studies, no. 29, 1971, p. 337-344. The entire issue of this journal consists of documents from the International Conference of Scientists on U.S. Chemical Warfare in Viet Nam. The author of this paper discusses the ecological effects and the health effects on the Vietnamese of the use of herbicides and toxic gases by the U.S. military.

0650 Wagner, R.H. "Biocides." In Environment and Man. 3rd ed. New York: Norton, 1978, p. 88-115. Pages 90-94 of Chapter Five in this general text on environmental problems detail the ecological effects of the spraying of herbicides in Vietnam.

0651 "War Herbicide Report Stirs Controversy." Chemical and Engineering News, v. 52, no. 10, March 11, 1974, p. 18-19. The controversy that has been created by the release of the report by the National Academy of Sciences is commented on.

0652 Ward, R.E. "Study Hits Vietnam Defoliants." Guardian, v. 26, no. 23, March 20, 1974, p. 17. A report drawn up at the request of Congress tells of the effects the spraying of herbicides during the Vietnam War had on Vietnam. Massive ecological damage was found as well as birth defects and deaths. The Pentagon was surprised by the critical tone of the report as there were no known "doves" on the research team. However, the report has been criticized by some scientists because they think the report understates the amount of damage.

0653 "Watching an Environmental Watchdog Watch." Environmental Science & Technology, v. 1, no. 12, December 1967, p. 971. The efforts to get a study done on the environmental effects

of the use of defoliants in Vietnam are noted. Several
American Association for the Advancement of Science
committees have been formed to study broader issues. The
National Academy of Sciences said they did not have the funds
to study the issue. The American Association for the
Advancement of Sciences then asked the Department of Defense
which contracted with the Midwest Research Institute to
conduct a study. Their study is finished and will be
reviewed by the National Academy of Sciences and then by the
American Association for the Advancement of Science.

0654   Way, J.M. and R.J. Chancellor. "Herbicides and Higher Plant
       Ecology: Part E. Military Uses." In Herbicides:
       Physiology, Biochemistry, Ecology. 2nd ed. Ed. by L.J.
       Audus. New York: Academic Pr., 1976, p. 368-369. A summary
       of the National Academy of Sciences' report is given.

0655   Weisberg, B., ed. Ecocide in Indochina: the Ecology of War.
       San Francisco: Canfield Pr., 1970. x, 241p. A collection
       of articles on the environmental effects and moral
       implications of the Vietnam War. The relevant articles (See
       0119, 0208, 0458, 0465, 0592, 0607, 0612 and 0761) are
       annotated.

0656   Westing, A.H. "Anti-plant Chemicals." In Ecological
       Consequences of the Second Indo-China War. Stockholm:
       Almqvist & Wiksell, 1976, p. 24-45. The aim of this book is
       to examine the Second Indochina War as a case study of modern
       environmental abuse. This chapter describes the use of anti-
       plant agents in Vietnam and the ecological effects of their
       use.

0657   Westing, A.H. "Crop Destruction as a Means of War."
       Bulletin of the Atomic Scientists, v. 37, no. 2, February
       1981, p. 38-42. The destruction of crops for military
       purposes in past wars is summarized. The crop destruction
       program in Vietnam is reviewed. In Vietnam several methods
       were used to destroy crops--the spraying of herbicides and
       Rome plows are specifically mentioned. The author reviews
       their effectiveness and discusses the ethical issues involved
       in such a program.

0658   Westing, A.H. "Ecocide in Indochina." Natural History, v.
       80, no. 3, March 1971, p. 56-61. Reprinted in Vermont
       Freeman, v. 3, no. 7, March 1, 1971, p. 4; in Essays Today,
       v. 7. Ed. by W.T. Moynihan. New York: Harcourt Brace
       Jovanovich, 1972, p. 54-58; in Ants, Indians, and Little
       Dinosaurs. Ed. by A. Ternes. New York: Charles Scribner's
       Sons, 1975, p. 292-297; and in "Ecological Destruction in
       Vietnam." Congressional Record, v. 117, pt. 6, March 25,

1971, p. 8183-8184. The ecological impact of the military use of herbicides, bombing and Rome plows as observed by the author during his two visits to Vietnam is discussed.

0659   Westing, A.H. "Ecocide, Our Last Gift to Vietnam." Environmental Quality Magazine, v. 4, no. 5, May 1973, p. 36-42+. Reprinted in "Ecocide in Indochina." Congressional Record, v. 119, pt. 13, May 22, 1973, p. 16468-16470. The author reviews the ecological damage done to Vietnam by the use of Rome plows, weather modification techniques, bombs and herbicides by the U.S. military.

0660   Westing, A.H. "Ecological Considerations Regarding Massive Environmental Contamination with 2,3,7,8-tetrachlorodibenzo-para-dioxin." In Chlorinated Phenoxy Acids and Their Dioxins: Mode of Action, Health Risks and Environmental Effects: Report from a Conference Arranged by the Royal Swedish Academy of Sciences, Stockholm, Sweden, 7-9 February 1977. (Ecological Bulletins, no. 27) Ed. by C. Ramel. Stockholm: NFR, 1978, p. 285-294. The details of the release of dioxin into the environment in South Vietnam. eastern Missouri, Northwest Florida and northern Italy are given as well as the ecological and social consequences of these events.

0661   Westing, A.H. "Ecological Effects of Military Defoliation on the Forests of South Vietnam." Bioscience, v. 21, no. 17, September 1, 1971, p. 893-898. The extent to which forests in Vietnam were sprayed with herbicides by the U.S. military is detailed and how the plant and animal communities have been altered as a result is explained. This paper was presented at a symposium on Possible Health Implications of the Widespread Use of Herbicides held at the American Institute of Biological Sciences in Bloomington, Indiana in August 1970.

0662   Westing, A.H. "Ecological Effects of the Military Use of Herbicides." In Ecological Effects of Pesticides. (Linnean Society Symposium Series, no. 5) Ed. by F.H. Perring and K. Mellanby. New York: Academic Pr., 1977, p. 89-94. The ecological effects of the spraying of herbicides by the U.S. military of Vietnam's upland and lowland tropical forest ecosystems are detailed.

0663   Westing, A.H. "The Environmental Aftermath of Warfare in Viet Nam." In World Armaments and Disarmament: SIPRI Yearbook, 1982. New York: Humanities Press, 1982, p. 363-389. Reprinted in Natural Resources Journal, v. 23, no. 2, April 1983, p. 365-389. The author describes the nature and pace of recovery of Vietnam's natural resources as a result

of the destruction done by the Vietnam War including the
military use of herbicides.

0664 Westing, A.H. "Environmental Consequences of the Second
Indochina War: a Case Study." Ambio, v. 4, no. 5-6, 1975,
p. 216-222. Reprinted in Strategic Digest, v. 7, no. 1-2,
January-February 1977, p. 72-81. The author discusses the
environmental effects and implications of the use of high-
explosive munitions, herbicides and landclearing tractors in
Vietnam by the U.S. military.

0665 Westing, A.H. "The Environmental Disruption of Indochina."
In The Effects of Modern Weapons on the Human Environment
in Indochina: Documents Presented at a Hearing Organized
by the International Commission in Cooperation with the
Stockholm Conference on Vietnam and the Swedish Committee
for Vietnam. Stockholm: International Commission of Enquiry
into U.S. Crimes in Indochina, 1972, p. 1:1-1:7. Summarized
in Bulletin of Peace Proposals, v. 3, no. 3, 1972, p. 230-
231. A survey article of the various issues involved in the
environmental disruption of Indochina including the military
use of herbicides.

0666 Westing, A.H. The Environmental Disruption of Indochina.
Washington: Council for a Liveable World, April 12, 1972.
4p. The author summarizes the environmental damage done by
the U.S. military's use of herbicides, Rome-plow tractors and
bombs as part of the Vietnam War.

0667 Westing, A.H. "Forestry and the War in South Vietnam."
Journal of Forestry, v. 69, no. 11, November 1971, p. 777-
783. As part of an article describing the impact of the war
on the forests resources on Vietnam, the ecological and
economic effects of the spraying of defoliants are mentioned.

0668 Westing, A.H. "Freedom from Hunger?" [letter] ADA World, v.
26, no. 7-8-9, September 1971, p. 2+. Reprinted as "Agent
Blue in Vietnam." Solidarity with Vietnam, no. 33, January
1968, p. 12-15. Herbicides are being used by the U.S.
military in Vietnam to destroy crops as well as jungles.

0669 Westing, A.H. "Herbicides as Agents of Chemical Warfare:
Their Impact in Relation to the Geneva Protocol of 1925."
(See 0414)

0670 Westing, A.H. "Herbicides in War: Current Status and Future
Doubt." Biological Conservation, v. 4, no. 5, October 1972,
p. 322-327. This article is an extensive review of the use
of herbicides as a weapon by the U.S. military in Vietnam.
The effects on forests, crops and livestock are mentioned.

0671   Westing, A., ed. Herbicides in War: the Long-term
       Ecological and Human Consequences. Philadelphia: Taylor &
       Francis, 1984. xiv, 210p. This book is an outgrowth of the
       International Symposium on Herbicides and Defoliants in War:
       the Long-term Effects on Man and Nature which was held in Ho
       Chi Minh City in January 1983. The papers discuss the
       effects of the use of herbicides during the Vietnam War by
       the U.S. military on Vietnam's environment and the health of
       the Vietnamese people.

0672   Westing, A.H. "Indochina: Prototype of Ecocide." In Air,
       Water, Earth, Fire: the Impact of the Military on the
       Environment (Sierra Club. Office of International
       Environmental Affairs. Series No. 2) by M. McClintock et al.
       San Francisco: Sierra Club, May 1974, p. 15-25. The purpose
       of this book is to examine the seemingly senseless escalation
       of the arms race and escalation of military destructiveness.
       A.H. Westing's article is on the ecological effects of the
       use of anti-crop agents by the U.S. military in Vietnam.

0673   Westing, A.H. "Not Peace on Earth." Minnesota Earth
       Journal, v. 2, no. 8, November 1972, p. 22-25. Reprinted as
       "Environmental Disruption of Indochina." Solidarity with
       Vietnam, no. 49, September 1972, p. 26-30. The author
       summarizes the ecological impact of the U.S. military use of
       herbicides, Rome plows, bombs and rainmaking as part of the
       Vietnam War.

0674   Westing, A.H. "On the Bethel Vietnam Story." [letter]
       American Forests, v. 81, no. 9, September 1975, p. 46-47.
       Reprinted as "War Damage to Vietnam Forests." [letter]
       Journal of Forestry, v. 73, no. 12, December 1975, p. 755.
       The author lists which findings of Bethel et al. in their
       January 1975 article in this journal (See 0445) he agrees
       with and which he disagrees with in terms of the timber loss
       as a result of the U.S. military's use of herbicides in
       Vietnam.

0675   Westing, A.H. "U.S. Food Destruction Program in South
       Vietnam." In The Effects of Modern Weapons on the Human
       Environment in Indochina. Stockholm: International
       Commission of Enquiry into U.S. Crimes in Indochina, 1972, p.
       9:1-9:4. Reprinted in Wasted Nations: Report of the
       International Commission of Enquiry into United States Crimes
       in Indochina, June 20-25, 1971. Ed. by F. Browning and D.
       Forman. New York: Harper & Row, 1972, p. 21-25. This
       report describes how herbicides are being used to destroy
       crops in South Vietnam and lists the amount of crops that
       have been destroyed. The purported reason for doing this was
       to deny food to the enemy soldier but civilians are being

starved also. The author calls for an immediate re-
evaluation of this program.

0676   **Westing, A.H.** "Vietnam Amplification." [letter]
       <u>Environment</u>, v. 13, no. 4, May 1971, p. 52. The author
       corrects and clarifies some of the figures given in the
       account of the American Association for the Advancement of
       Sciences' Herbicides Assessment Commission preliminary
       report.

0677   **Westing, A.H.** "Westing Reply." [letter] <u>Journal of
       Forestry</u>, v. 70, no. 3, March 1972, p. 129. A.H. Westing
       replies to H.M. Gregersen's letter in this issue (See 0512)
       which was written in response to A.H. Westing's article of
       November 1971 in this journal (See 0667). A.H. Westing
       justifies his figures for economic loss and also discusses
       the forest damage caused by bombing and shelling.

0678   **Westing, A.H.** "Widespread, Long-lasting, and Severe..."
       <u>SSRS Review</u>, v. 3, no. 1, Spring 1976, p. 2-3. The author
       discusses the ecological damage done to Vietnam as a result
       of the use of bombs and shells, Rome plows, and herbicides by
       the U.S. military. Also mentioned are proposals put forward
       by the Soviet Union and the United States that would prohibit
       the military use of environmental modification techniques.

0679   **Westing, A.H.** "Widespread, Longlasting and Severe: Forest
       Destruction During the Second Indochina War."** <u>Yale Forest
       School News</u>, v. 67, no. 1, Spring 1979, p. 6-7. The impact
       the use of high-explosive munitions, heavy landclearing
       tractors and herbicides by the U.S. military during the
       Second Indochina War had on forest lands in Vietnam is
       summarized.

0680   **Westing, A.H. and C.E. Westing.** "Endangered Species and
       Habitats of Viet Nam." <u>Environmental Conservation</u>, v. 8, no.
       1, Spring 1981, p. 59-62. The authors report on the status
       of the habitat and endangered species in Vietnam based on a
       visit made to Vietnam in August 1980.

0681   **"When the Landscape is the Enemy."** <u>Newsweek</u>, v. 80, no. 6,
       August 7, 1972, p. 24-26. The various ways including the use
       of herbicides that the United States has destroyed the
       ecology of Vietnam in fighting the war are detailed.

0682   **Whiteside, T.** "A Reporter at Large: the Pendulum and the
       Toxic Cloud." <u>New Yorker</u>, v. 53, no. 23, July 25, 1977, p.
       30-41+. A detailed discussion of the debate over the use of
       2,4,5-T throughout the world. What is mostly discussed
       regarding the use of Agent Orange in Vietnam is the concern

over what the use of Agent Orange has done to the ecology and
what to do with the leftover Agent Orange.

0683   **Willis, E.O.   "Lesser of Two Evils." [letter]   Science, v.
       164, no. 3878, April 25, 1969, p. 373-374.**   E.O. Willis wrote
       this letter in order to respond to F.H. Tschirley's article
       (See 0626) which appeared in the February 21, 1969 issue of
       this journal.   E.O. Willis responds to comments F.H.
       Tschirley made about how defoliation would not affect the
       water cycle and about the type of animals that would die off
       as a result of defoliation.   E.O. Willis calls for future
       studies to pay attention to the effects of defoliation on
       forest-adapted species not to open country ones.

0684   Winchester, J.H.   "Cargo Planes in Vietnam War."   (See 0264)

THE HEALTH EFFECTS AND THE SOCIETAL COSTS
OF EXPOSURE ON THE VIETNAMESE

0685   Aaronson, T. "Tour of Vietnam." (See 0419)

0686   "Academy Report on Vietnam Herbicide Damage." (See 0420)

0687   Agarwal, A. "Vietnam After the Storm." (See 0422)

0688   **"Agent Orange."** Congressional Record, **v. 126, pt. 6, March 27, 1980, p. 6951-6952.** Senator J. Heinz (R-PA) submitted an article from the New York Times by B. Kurtis detailing the effects of exposure to Agent Orange reported by the Vietnamese.

0689   **Alland, A., Jr. "War and Disease: an Anthropological Perspective."** Natural History, **v. 76, no. 10, December 1967, p. 58-61.** Reprinted in Bulletin of the Atomic Scientists, **v. 24, no. 6, June 1968, p. 28-31.** As part of this article on the relationship of war to disease, the author suggests there may be a link between instances of the plague and other acute infectious disease in Vietnam and the spraying of defoliants by the U.S. military.

0690   American Association for the Advancement of Science. Effects of the Large-scale Use of Herbicides and Defoliants in Vietnam: Implications of Continued Military Use of Herbicides in South East Asia. (See 0424)

0691   American Chemical Society. Dioxins, Vietnam and 15 Years. (See 0984)

0692   "The Atrocities Nixon Condones and Continues." (See 0274)

0693   Baghat, H. "Vietnam: Where No Birds Sing." (See 0428)

0694   Boffey, P.M. "Herbicides in Vietnam: AAAS Study Finds Widespread Devastation." (See 0428)

0695   Brown, T.L. "Herbicides in Vietnam." (See 0287)

0696   **Browne, M.W. "Aiding Vietnam." [letter]** Science, **v. 205, no. 4410, September 7, 1979, p. 954.** This letter was written in response to E. Cooperman and J.H. LeVan's letter (See

0712) which appeared in the August 10, 1979 issue of this
journal. M.W. Browne believes that while a joint study with
the Vietnamese on the effects of dioxin would be useful, the
assertions of Vietnamese scientists should be as rigorously
evaluated as those of any other scientist. Science is often
clouded by the official manipulation of propaganda in certain
parts of the world and dioxin is a propaganda word as well as
a chemical one.

0697   Burchett, W. "Defoliation Destroying Rural Vietnam." (See
       0446)

0698   Burchett, W.G. "The War Against Trees: Chemical Spray
       Campaign." In The Furtive War; the United States in Vietnam
       and Laos. New York: International Publishers, 1963, p. 60-
       65. This section of this book on American involvement in
       Vietnam and Laos details the use of herbicides in Vietnam
       mostly by giving accounts of the Vietnamese who witnessed the
       sprayings.

0699   Burchett, W.G. "War on Food Crops." (See 0448)

0700   Carlson, E.A. "International Symposium on Herbicides in the
       Vietnam War: an Appraisal." (See 0452)

0701   "Chemical Destruction in Indochina." (See 0456)

0702   "Chemical Warfare: a US Crime of Genocide." South Vietnam
       in Struggle, no. 83, special issue 1970, p. 10. The health
       effects of exposure to herbicides sprayed by the U.S.
       military in the Vietnamese is discussed.

0703   "Chemical Warfare's Toll." (See 0457)

0704   Chipman, M. "Herbicides in Vietnam." [letter] Science, v.
       179, no. 4078, March 16, 1973, p. 1075. This letter was
       written in response to the article by H.A. Rose and S.P.R.
       Rose (See 0783) which appeared in the August 25, 1972 issue
       of this journal. M. Chipman does not believe that the data
       gathered by H.A. Rose and S.P.R. Rose from 98 South
       Vietnamese evacuees through the use of questionnaires is
       reliable.

0705   Chu Thao. "Resuscitation of the Dead Earth." In Between Two
       Fires; the Unheard Voices of Vietnam. Comp. by Ly-qui-Chung.
       New York: Praeger, 1970, p. 53-61. The stories collected in
       this book tell about the Vietnamese who are living between
       the two fires of the Americans and the Communists. This
       story by a Saigon teacher tells how the Vietnamese feel about
       the use of defoliants by the Americans.

0706   Clarke, R. "Ecological War." In The Science of War and
       Peace. New York: McGraw-Hill, 1971, p. 145-150. This book
       discusses the reasons behind the explosion in wars. This
       section discusses the concern over the health effects of the
       Vietnamese and ecological effects on Vietnam's forests,
       animals, and soil as a result of the spraying of herbicides
       by the U.S. military.

0707   Co, N.T. See Nguyen Trinh Co.

0708   "Conflicting Philosophies of 2,4,5-T." Nature, v. 231, no.
       5304, June 25, 1971, p. 483-485. The findings of the reports
       published by the American Association for the Advancement of
       Science and the Bionetics Research Laboratory are mentioned
       and commented upon - specifically the findings regarding the
       effects of the defoliation and crop destruction programs on
       the health of the Vietnamese.

0709   Constable, J. and M. Meselson. "Ecological Impact of Large-
       scale Defoliation in Vietnam." (See 0462)

0710   Constable, J.D. and M.C. Hatch. "Reproductive Effects of
       Herbicide Exposure in Vietnam: Recent Studies by the
       Vietnamese and Others." Teratogenesis Carcinogenesis and
       Mutagenesis, v. 5, no. 4, 1985, p. 231-250. The authors
       summarize unpublished research carried out by Vietnamese
       scientists on the reproductive effects on Vietnamese exposed
       to herbicides.

0711   Constable, J.D. et al. "AAAS and NAS Herbicide Reports."
       (See 0463)

0712   Cooperman, E. and J.H. LeVan. "Scientific Cooperation with
       Vietnam." [letter] Science, v. 205, no. 4406, August 10,
       1979, p. 540+. The coordinators of the U.S. Committee for
       Scientific Cooperation with Vietnam recently visited and
       witnessed the burden the Vietnamese scientists carry in their
       efforts in trying to rebuild their war torn society. Dr.
       T.T. Tung recently toured the United States to tell of this
       work with the Vietnamese who are suffering as the result of
       being exposed to herbicides. He believes that dioxin is
       linked to lung cancer and birth defects. He would like the
       United States scientific community to help in carrying out
       epidemiological studies.

0713   Cook, R.E., Haseltine, W. and A.W. Galston. "What Have We
       Done to Vietnam?" (See 0465)

0714   Cutting, R.T. et al. Congenital Malformations, Hydatidiform
       Moles and Stillbirths in the Republic of Vietnam 1960-1969.

Washington: GPO, December 1970. ii, 29p. The U.S. Military
Assistance Command studied obstetrical records from 22
Vietnamese hospitals over a 10-year period to determine if
being exposed to Agent Orange might cause birth defects of
stillbirths. No correlation between birth defects or
stillbirths and exposure to herbicides was found.

0715 **"Dangers of Defoliation Campaign in Vietnam."** <u>Congressional</u>
<u>Record</u>, v. 116, pt. 6, March 16, 1970, p. 7415-7416.
Representative R.D. McCarthy (D-N.Y.) expressed his concerns
over reports that defoliants are having health effects on the
Vietnamese. He had an article from the March 15, 1970 issue
of the <u>New York Times</u> by R. Blumenthal printed into the
<u>Record</u>.

0716 "Defoliant Fallout Lingers in South Vietnam." (See 0471)

0717 **"Defoliants in Vietnam."** <u>Congressional Record</u>, v. 117, pt.
2, February 8, 1971, p. 2031-2032. Senator F. Church (D-ID)
had two articles printed into the <u>Record</u> on the effects of
the use of defoliants in Vietnam on the health of the
Vietnamese. Both are by B. Nelson: one was in the December
31, 1970 issue of <u>Los Angeles Times</u> and one from the January
28, 1971 issue of <u>Village Voice</u> (See 0769).

0718 "Defoliation in Chicago." (See 0476)

0719 "Dioxin: a Potential Chemical-warfare Agent." (See 0481)

0720 "Dioxin Dilemma." (See 1039)

0721 **"Dioxin: Who Cares? Ho Cares!"** <u>Berkeley Barb</u>, v. 29, no.
17, May 24-June 6, 1979, p. 3+. Dr. T.T. Tung discussed the
health problems that the Vietnamese people are having as a
result of being exposed to Agent Orange in a recent talk at
the University of California at Berkeley. Also discussed is
the federal government's failure to assume responsibility for
this problem. The health problems of James Janko, a student
at University of California at Berkeley and a Vietnam veteran
exposed to Agent Orange are described.

0722 **"Dioxins in the Environment: No Consensus on Human Health."**
<u>Chemical and Engineering News</u>, v. 63, no. 21, May 27, 1985,
p. 41-44. The American Chemical Society's Environmental
Chemistry Division sponsored a symposium on what is known
about dioxins in the environment. As part of this symposium
A. Schecter and J.J. Ryan discussed their findings on fat
samples they had obtained from Vietnamese physicians for
people from both North and South Vietnam.

0723   "Effects of Chemical Warfare in South Vietnam." (See 0492)

0724   **"Fed Poisoned Viets." Portland Scribe, v. 6, no. 25, August 11, 1977, p. 4.** Significant abnormalities were found in the chromosomes of Indochinese people exposed to Agent Orange reported medical teams at a symposium in Ho Chi Minh City recently.

0725   "Fifteen Years of Evidence: the Epidemiology of 2,4,5-T." (See 1063)

0726   **Fuchs, G. "Medical Effects of Chemical Weapons." Peace and the Sciences, no. 3, 1982, p. 52-54.** What is known about the medical effects of several types of chemical weapons, including Agent Orange, which were used in Vietnam by the U.S. military is discussed. The possible relationship between exposure to Agent Orange and liver cancer is noted.

0727   **"Further Information about Agent Orange." Congressional Record, v. 126, pt. 17, August 22, 1980, p. 22598-22609.** Senator A. Cranston (D-CA) had the following material printed in the Record: an English translation of a study by Dr. T.T. Tung on the effects of exposure to Agent Orange in the Vietnamese, the text of Senator A. Cranston's letter to the Office of Technology Assessment, the text of the Office of Technology Assessment's reply, a draft report of the Veterans Administration's fat study and the review of this study by the scientific panel of the President's Interagency Work Group.

0728   **Galston, A.W. "Herbicide Usage." [letter] Science, v. 168, no. 3939, June 26, 1970, p. 1607.** The author responds to M. Newton's and L.A. Norris' (See 0771) letter of June 26, 1970. The author states that until the question of whether or not 2,4,5-T is teratogenic is resolved that its use should be discontinued and lists the questions that need to answered regarding phenoxyacetic acid herbicides.

0729   **Galston, A.W. "Herbicides: No Margin of Safety." Science, v. 167, no. 3916, January 16, 1970, p. 237.** This letter was written in response to B. Nelson's (See 0219) article of November 21, 1969. A.W. Galston wanted to correct a statement attributed to him in this article. This correction does not change the fact that that based on body weight, pregnant women in Vietnam are receiving through the drinking water close to the minimum teratogenic dose in mice and rats.

0730   Galston, A.W. "Ungreening of South Vietnam." (See 0507)

0731   **Goldwater, M. and A. Barnett. "Wouldn't Hurt a Mouse." New**

Statesman, v. 100, no. 2579, August 22, 1980, p. 8-9. The
health problems Vietnamese exposed to Agent Orange are
having as well the birth defects and health problems their
offspring are having are noted.

0732   Griswold, D. "The Agent Orange Story: the Toll in Vietnam
        Today." Workers World, v. 21, no. 27, July 6, 1979, p. 8.
        The effects of exposure to Agent Orange on the people in
        Vietnam are noted. Dr. T.T. Tung visited the United States
        recently and told of the dramatic increases in liver cancer
        and birth defects. He feels along with other Vietnamese
        scientists that there is a direct correlation between these
        diseases and the spraying of Agent Orange.

0733   Grummer, G. "Accusation from the Jungle." In Accusation
        from the Jungle. Berlin: Vietnam Commission of the Afro-
        Asian Solidarity Committee of the German Democratic
        Republic, 1972, p. 101-108. In this chapter of this book
        in which the author tells of his impressions of his travels
        in Vietnam, the author discusses the health effects of
        exposure to herbicides.

0734   Grummer, G. "The Colour of Crime." In Accusation from the
        Jungle. Berlin: Vietnam Commission of the Afro-Asian
        Solidarity Committee of the German Democratic Republic,
        1972, p. 98-101. In this chapter of this book in which the
        author tells of his impressions of his travels in Vietnam,
        the author discusses the health effects of exposure to
        herbicides.

0735   Grummer, G. Genocide with Herbicides: Report, Analysis,
        Evidence. (See 0515)

0736   Halperin, W.E., P.A. Honchar and M.A. Fingerhut. "Dioxin:
        an Overview." American Statistician, v. 36, no. 3 pt. 2,
        August 1982, p. 285-289. This article is a literature review
        on what is known about the effects of 2,4,5-T and TCDD on
        mortality, morbidity and reproduction. Part of the public
        interest in this topic is the result of the use of Agent
        Orange in Vietnam by the U.S. military. The health effects
        studies that are being conducted on the Vietnamese are noted.

0737   Harris, R. and J. Paxman. "The Rise and Rise of Chemical
        Weapons." (See 0186)

0738   Haseltine, W., W.R. Carter and N.V. Long. "Human Suffering
        in Vietnam." (See 0519)

0739   Hay, A. "Ho Chi Minh City Conference. Defoliants in
        Vietnam: the Long-term Effects." (See 0520)

0740 Hay, A. "Informing on 2,4,5-T." Nature, v. 269, no. 5631, October 27, 1977, p. 749-750. The author reports on two recently released reports on 2,4,5-T. One of these reports was prepared by the United Kingdom's Forestry Commission and claims that there is no evidence that the defoliation spraying in Vietnam had any direct effect on humans.

0741 Hay, A. "It Kills Weeds, but What about People?" New Scientist, v. 95, no. 1314, July 15, 1982, p. 158-161. This article discusses the health effects of exposure to 2,4,5-T on various groups including the Vietnamese.

0742 Hay, A. "Vietnam's Dioxin Problem." Nature, v. 271, no. 5646, February 16, 1978, p. 597-598. The damage done to Vietnam and its people as a result of the U.S. military's use of herbicides is described. The efforts Vietnamese scientists are making to assess the damage caused by the use of these herbicides are noted.

0743 "Hearts and Minds." Technology Review, v. 73, no. 5, March 1971, p. 61. How the Montagnard people feel about the spraying is noted.

0744 "Herbicidal Warfare." (See 0521)

0745 "Herbicide Commission Reports Extensive Damage." (See 0522)

0746 "Herbicides Sizzle in Vietnam." (See 0524)

0747 Hickey, G.C. Free in the Forest: Ethnohistory of the Vietnamese Central Highlands 1954-1976. (See 0525)

0748 Hoang, T.G. "Effects of the Employment of Chemical Substances in the Vietnam War." Peace and the Sciences, no. 3, 1982, p. 38-39. The author mentions the effects of the use of defoliants in Indochina on both its land and its people. However, the United States claims that Soviet-backed forces in Afghanistan are using chemical weapons even though there is no concrete proof of this. The United States is pursuing this to cover-up the continuing arms race. The author supports the peace initiatives of the Soviet Union.

0749 Hodgkin, D.C. "The Effects of Chemical Defoliants." (See 0527)

0750 Huyen, N.X. See Nguyen Xuan Huyen.

0751 Joyce, C. "How Toxic is Dioxin? The Mystery Deepens." New Scientist, v. 110, no. 1506, May 1, 1986, p. 24. A. Schecter has examined Vietnamese from both the north and south portions of the country. He has found higher levels of TCDD and other dioxins in the fat tissue and breast milk of Vietnamese living in the southern portion of the country and known to have been exposed to Agent Orange than those living in the northern portion of the country and not exposed to Agent Orange.

0752   Karnow, S. "Vietnam: Legacy of Desolation." (See 0534)

0753   Kearns, K. and A. Dockery. "Gene Warfare Around the World: Agent Orange." Space City, v. 3, no. 6, July 13, 1971, p. 12. Personal narratives of several Vietnamese who were exposed to Agent Orange are given.

0754   Kotelchuck, R. "America in Vietnam: Democracy for Dead People." (See 0539)

0755   Kriebel, D. "Dioxins: Toxic and Still Troublesome." (See 1121)

0756   Kunstadter, P. A Study of Herbicides and Birth Defects in the Republic of Vietnam: an Analysis of Hospital Records. (Cover title: Herbicides and Birth Defects in the Republic of Vietnam) Washington: National Academy Pr., 1982. v, 73p. This study was conducted to supplement other studies that had been conducted in the past which did not have access to every needed type of material. The author tried to match the HERBS data with date of birth and place of maternal residence in an attempt to determine if there was a connection between exposure to herbicides in Vietnam and birth defects in children born to mothers exposed during pregnancy. The author concluded that a connection could neither be definitively confirmed nor could it be disproved.

0757   "A Lack of Data." Technology Review, v. 73, no. 5, March 1971, p. 61-62. The Herbicide Assessment Commission of the American Association for the Advancement of Science found that no conclusions could be made about the health effects of the spraying of herbicides by the U.S. military on the Vietnamese due to the patchiness of health records and inaccessibility of precise spraying records. What the records for the children's hospital in Saigon do show is noted.

0758   Laporte, J.R. "Effects of Dioxin Exposure." [letter] Lancet, v. 1, no. 8020, May 14, 1977, p. 1049-1050. A portion of this letter summarized Dr. T.T. Tung's findings as to the types of lesions which can be attributed to dioxin exposure. These findings are based on Dr. Tung's work with Vietnamese exposed to herbicides during the Vietnam War.

0759 "Liver Cancer Linked to Dioxin." New Scientist, v. 78, no.
      1103, May 18, 1978, p. 431. Dr. T.T. Tung believes that the
      exposure to defoliants during the Vietnam War is the reason
      why there has been an increase in liver cancer, spontaneous
      abortions and birth defects in Vietnam.

0760 Long, N.V. "Leaf Abscission?" Thoi Bao Ga, no. 5, November
      1969, p. 1-8. The health effects of exposure to herbicides
      sprayed by the U.S. military on the Vietnamese is discussed.

0761 Long, N.V. "Leaf Abscission?" Bulletin of Concerned Asian
      Scholars, v. 2, no. 2, January 1970, p. 63-72. Reprinted in
      Cambodia: the Widening War in Indochina. Ed. by J.S.
      Grant, L. Moss and J. Unger. New York: Washington Square
      Pr., 1971, p. 201-213; and in Ecocide in Indochina: the
      Ecology of War. Ed. by B. Weisberg. San Francisco:
      Canfield Pr., 1970, p. 54-63. B. Weisberg incorrectly states
      that the reprint which appears in his book is from the
      October 1969 issue of Bulletin of Concerned Asian Scholars.
      This article is a revised version of an article which
      appeared in the November 1969 issue of Thoi Bao Ga. The
      effect the defoliation by the U.S. military had on the
      Vietnamese in terms of dislocating them, their crops, their
      livestock and their health is explained.

0762 Luce, D. "Social Disruption." In The Effects of Modern
      Weapons on the Human Environment in Indochina: Documents
      Presented at a Hearing Organized by the International
      Commission in Cooperation with the Stockholm Conference on
      Vietnam and the Swedish Committee for Vietnam. Stockholm:
      International Commission of Enquiry into U.S. Crimes in
      Indochina, 1972, p. 10:1-10:5. This report was part of the
      testimony given at the Oslo session of the International
      Commission of Enquiry Into U.S. Crimes in Indochina. It in
      part describes the effects the use of herbicides has had on
      the lives of the Vietnamese and the relocation that has
      resulted. Excerpts from the question and answer period
      following the presentation are given.

0763 Mayers, P. "U.S. CVW Deforms Viet Babies." Los Angeles Free
      Press, v. 6, no. 83, December 19, 1969, p. 9. The reports of
      deformities in Vietnamese babies as a result of pregnant
      women having been in areas that had been sprayed with
      herbicides are mentioned. Congressman R.D. McCarthy (D-
      N.Y.) has denounced the use of these chemicals in Vietnam.
      A National Cancer Institute report has declared 2,4,5-T and
      2,4-D to be "probably dangerous" and "potentially dangerous."

0764 Meselson, M.S., A.H. Westing and J.D. Constable. Background
      Material Relevant to Presentations at the 1970 Annual Meeting
      of the AAAS. (See 0555)

0765   Meselson, M.S. et al. Preliminary Report of Herbicide
       Assessment Commission of the American Association for the
       Advancement of Science. (See 0556)

0766   **Murphy, J.M. "War Stress and Civilian Vietnamese: a Study
       of Psychological Effects." Acta Psychiatrica Scandinavica,
       v. 56, no. 2, August 1977, p. 92-108.** The people of the Binh
       Hoa village in Binh Duong Province north of Saigon were
       studied to determine the level of psychological disturbance
       they experienced by being forced to evacuate their homes.
       These villagers were forced to evacuate as their homes were
       in an area of massive military action including the spraying
       of large doses of herbicides. The authors concluded that the
       spraying measurably contributed to their stress.

0767   National Research Council. Committee on the Effects of
       Herbicides in Vietnam. The Effects of Herbicides in South
       Vietnam. (See 0561)

0768   Nelson, B. "Herbicides: Order on 2,4,5-T Issued at
       Unusually High Level." (See 0219)

0769   **Nelson, B. "Tu My's Children: Death by Defoliation?"
       Village Voice, v. 16, no. 4, January 28, 1971, p. 15+.
       Reprinted in "Defoliants in Vietnam." Congressional Record,
       v. 117, pt. 2, February 8, 1971, p. 2023; and "Defoliant Use
       in Vietnam." Congressional Record, v. 117, pt. 6, March 25,
       1971, p. 8101.** It has been reported that 90 infants and
       children of the Tu My village may have died as a result of
       the spraying of Agent Blue. The American Association for the
       Advancement of Science's Herbicide Assessment Commission
       did not include this incident in their report as the
       Commission has not yet scientifically proved that the
       children died as a result of the spraying. The article goes
       on to discuss other instances where the spraying of the
       herbicides has affected the health of the Vietnamese.

0770   "New Details on Chemical Warfare." (See 0565)

0771   **Newton, M. and L.A. Norris. "Herbicide Usage." [letter]
       Science, v. 168, no. 3939, June 26, 1970, p. 1606-1607.** The
       authors are responding to statements attributed to A.W.
       Galston in B. Nelson's article of November 21, 1969 (See
       0219) and A.W. Galston's letter of January 16, 1970 (See
       0729). The authors of this letter do not believe that
       pregnant women in Vietnam are receiving continuous exposures
       to the defoliants through the drinking water. The authors
       believe that the use of the herbicides should be continued.

0772   Ngo Vinh Long. See Long, N.V.

0773 Nguyen Khac Vien. "The Lasting Consequences of Chemical
      Warfare." (See 0568)

0774 **Nguyen Trinh Co and Nguyen Xuan Huyen. "Genetic Defects
      Resulting from the Large-scale and Repeated Use of Defoliants
      in South Vietnam." In ABC Weapons, Disarmament and the
      Responsibility of Scientists: Report on an International
      Conference of the World Federation of Scientific Workers
      Berlin (GDR), 21st-23rd November 1971. Ed. by K. Baudisch.
      Berlin: Executive Council of Gewerkschaft Wissenschaft for
      the World Federation of Scientific Workers, 1971?, p. 27-31.**
      The authors present their findings of a study showing what
      they believe to be the link between chromosome damage in
      deformed South Vietnamese children and exposure to defoliants
      sprayed by the U.S. military.

0775 **Norman, C. "Vietnam's Herbicide Legacy." Science, v. 219,
      no. 4589, March 11, 1983, p. 1196-1197.** The author reports
      on the recent international conference held in Ho Chi Minh
      City on herbicides and defoliants in war. Specifically
      mentioned is how Vietnam is recovering ecologically and the
      studies that have been conducted on the effects of the
      sprayings on the health of the Vietnamese.

0776 Orians, G.H. and E.W. Pfeiffer. "United States Goals in
      Vietnam." (See 0579)

0777 Perkins, P. "Scars of Imperialist War in Vietnam." (See
      0587)

0778 Pfeiffer, E.W. "Recent Developments in Indochina and the USA
      Relating to the Military Uses of Herbicides." (See 0595)

0779 **Pomeroy, W. "British Issue Call: 'Compensate Vietnamese
      Victims of Agent Orange.'" Vietnam Today, v. 7, no. 1,
      January/March 1985, p. 5.** The British organization, Medical
      and Scientific Aid for Vietnam, Laos and Kampuchea
      (MSAVLK), has launched a drive to try to win compensation
      for Vietnamese victims of the spraying of Agent Orange by
      the U.S. military from the United States government.

0780 **Raloff, J. "Dioxin: Is Everyone Contaminated?" Science
      News, v. 128, no. 2, July 13, 1985, p. 26-29.** The ongoing
      research on the health effects of exposure to dioxin,
      including studies that A. Schecter and J.J. Ryan have
      conducted measuring dioxin and furans in the adipose tissues
      of Vietnamese who were exposed to Agent Orange, is detailed.

0781 **Rand Corporation. Rand Vietnam Interview Series H:
      Villagers' Impressions of Herbicide Operations. March 1972.**

653p. **Available from NTIS: AD 741 309.** Forty-three South
Vietnamese villagers were interviewed regarding their
impressions of the spraying of herbicides by the U.S.
military and what they felt the effects and psychological
implications of these sprayings were on village food
supplies.

0782   Rogers, J. **"Agent Orange in Vietnam: America's Shared
Legacy."** Indochina Issues, no. 60, September 1985, p. 1-7.
What is known about the effects of Agent Orange exposure on
the health of the Vietnamese is commented upon.

0783   Rose, H.A. and S.P.R. Rose. **"Chemical Spraying as Reported
by Refugees from South Vietnam."** Science, v. 177, no. 4050,
August 25, 1972, p. 710-712. The health effects of chemical
exposure to herbicides in South Vietnam as reported by 98
refugees interviewed in Hanoi are noted.

0784   Rose, H. and S. Rose. **"Herbicides in Vietnam."** [letter]
Science, v. 179, no. 4078, March 16, 1973, p. 1075. The
authors respond to the letters of March 16, 1973 (See 0704
and 0786) which were written in response to their August 25,
1972 (See 0783) report. They feel that the use of
questionnaires is a routine method of data collection in the
social sciences and that they just reported symptoms and did
not try to define them neurologically. They also feel that
they did mention abortions and monstrous births in their
report.

0785   Rose, S. **"Defoliants, Herbicides and Racism."** New
Scientist, v. 82, no. 1151, April 19, 1979, p. 206. The
author discusses his research into the health effects of
exposure on the Vietnamese. He published his findings in
Science. The author mentions the fact that veterans are
filing claims for health problems as a result of exposure.

0786   Runeckles, V.C. **"Herbicides in Vietnam."** [letter] Science,
v. 179, no. 4078, March 16, 1973, p. 1075. This letter was
written in response to H. Rose and S. Rose's letter (See
0784) of August 25, 1972. V.C. Runeckles takes issue with
the abstract to the report inferring that monstrous births
have occurred in South Vietnam as a result of herbicidal
sprayings in Vietnam when the text does not make any mention
of these births.

0787   Russell, B. **"Chemical Warfare in Vietnam."** [letter] New
Republic, v. 149, no. 1 (issue no. 2537), July 6, 1963, p.
30-31. The author wants to call attention to a report
prepared by the South Vietnam Liberation Red Cross detailing
the effects of the spraying of chemicals including herbicides
on humans, animals and crops.

0788   Schecter, A.J., J.J. Ryan and J.D. Constable. "Chlorinated
       Dibenzo-p-dioxin and Dibenzofuran Levels in Human Adipose
       Tissue and Milk Samples from the North and South of Vietnam."
       Chemosphere, v. 15, no. 9-12, 1986, p. 1613-1620. The
       authors analyzed adipose tissue samples from Vietnamese
       living in the northern and southern portions of Vietnam.
       They found that 2,3,7,8-TCDD has persisted in Vietnamese even
       15 years after the last application of Agent Orange.

0789   Schecter, A. et al. "Chlorinated Dibenzodioxins and
       Dibenzofurans in Human Tissues from Vietnam." [abstract]
       American Chemical Society. Abstracts of Papers, v. 189, 1985,
       #ENVR 0059. The authors collected and analyzed human
       tissues from a variety of geographical locations in Vietnam
       in 1984.

0790   Schecter, A.J. et al. "Chlorinated Dioxins and Dibenzofurans
       in Human Tissues from Vietnam, 1983-84." In Chlorinated
       Dioxins and Dibenzofurans in Perspective. Ed. by C. Rappe,
       G. Choudhary and L.H. Keith. Chelsea, MI: Lewis Publ.,
       Inc., 1986, p. 35-50. This volume was developed from the
       proceedings of a symposium held during the 189th National
       Meeting of the American Chemical Society. The authors
       reported their findings of the examination of some breast
       milk samples from presumed Agent Orange-exposed
       Vietnamese patients and 20 adipose tissue samples from
       hospitalized Vietnamese patients undergoing surgery. There
       was no 2,3,7,8-TCDD detected in the breast milk samples.
       Higher mean levels of 2,3,7,8-TCDD were found in some of the
       adipose tissue samples from Vietnam than were previously
       found in most of the studies that have been conducted in the
       United States. The adipose tissue samples from North Vietnam
       had lower tissue levels of 2,3,7,8-TCDD than any known
       population studied thus far.

0791   "Serious Defoliant Damage in Vietnam." (See 0608)

0792   Silbergeld, E.K. and D.R. Mattison. "Experimental and
       Clinical Studies on the Reproductive Toxicology of 2,3,7,8-
       tetrachlorodibenzo-p-dioxin." (See 1200)

0793   Stanford Biology Study Group. The Destruction of Indochina:
       a Legacy of Our Presence. (See 0613)

0794   Sterling, T.D. and A.V. Arundel. "Health Effects of Phenoxy
       Herbicides: a Review." Scandinavian Journal of Work,
       Environment & Health, v. 12, no. 3, June 1986, p. 161-173.
       The authors review what has been learned from the
       epidemiologic studies that have been conducted concerning the
       health effects of exposure to phenoxy herbicides. The

studies that been conducted on the Vietnamese and Vietnam
veterans are reviewed in depth.

0795 Sterling, T.D. and A. Arundel. "Review of Recent Vietnamese
Studies on the Carcinogenic and Tetratogenic Effects of
Phenoxy Herbicide Exposure." International Journal of Health
Services, v. 16, no. 2, 1986, p. 265-278. The authors review
the methodology and results of several Vietnamese studies on
the health effects on the Vietnamese of exposure to the
herbicides sprayed by the U.S. military during the Vietnam
War. Most of the studies deal with the link between exposure
to herbicides and unfavorable outcomes of pregnancy and
incidences of liver cancer.

0796 "Studies Conflict on Herbicide's Role in Birth Defects."
American Medical News, v. 26, no. 13, April 1, 1983, p. 23.
A study by Vietnamese scientists showed an increase in birth
abnormalities among children born to North Vietnamese
soldiers who served in South Vietnam and thereby potentially
were exposed to Agent Orange. A study of Australian Vietnam
veterans showed no connection between service in Vietnam and
birth defects.

0797 "Thalidomide Effect from Defoliants?" Scientific Research,
v. 4, no. 23, November 10, 1969, p. 11-12. The Bionetics
Research Laboratories in an as of yet unpublished report
prepared for the National Cancer Institute has found that
2,4,5-T and 2,4-D are probably capable of producing gross
birth defects. This raises concerns about the health effects
of the military spraying of herbicides containing these
chemicals on the Vietnamese.

0798 Thao, C. See Chu Thao.

0799 Thomsen, V. "Ecological Effects of the War in Vietnam."
(See 0623)

0800 Ton That Tung. See Tung, T.T.

0801 Tran Huu Tuog. "Intervention." (See 0625)

0802 Tuan, V.H. See Vo Hoai Tuan.

0803 Tung, T.T. Reminiscences of a Vietnamese Surgeon. Hanoi:
Foreign Languages Publishing House. 1980. 86p. On pages
71-77 of this memoir, T.T. Tung discusses his research into
the health effects of exposure to defoliants sprayed by the
U.S. military on the Vietnamese.

0804 Tung, T.T. et al. "Le Cancer Primaire du Foie au Vietnam."

[Primary Liver Cancer in Vietnam] Chirurgie, v. 99, no. 7, May 16, 23, and 30, 1973, p. 427-436. In French with English summary. There has been an abnormal increase in Vietnam of primary carcinoma of the liver. The authors attribute this to the massive use of 2,3,7-8 tetrachlorodibenzo-p-dioxin mixed with 2,4,5-T and used as a defoliant in Vietnam.

0805   Tung, T.T. et al. "Clinical Effects of Massive and Continuous Utilization." [preliminary study] Vietnamese Studies, no. 29, 1971, p. 53-81. The entire issue of this journal consists of documents from the International Conference of Scientists on U.S. Chemical Warfare in Viet Nam. The authors present their findings of the examinations they have made of South Vietnamese who have taken refuge in North Vietnam and were exposed to herbicides and defoliants.

0806   Tuog, T.H. See Tran Huu Tuog.

0807   "2,4,5-T." American Forests, v. 76, no. 7, July 1970, p. 11. The possible effects of the use of herbicides as a military weapon in Vietnam is mentioned. Scientists have received reports of birth defects in Vietnam which could be linked to 2,4,5-T, one of the defoliants.

0808   "U.S. Chemical Warfare: a Menace to All Mankind." South Vietnam in Struggle, no. 82, December 10, 1970, p. 2. The health effects of exposure to chemical weapons including herbicides are detailed.

0809   U.S. Chemical Warfare and Its Consequences: Dossier. Hanoi: Vietnam Courier. 1980. 178p. This book presents information on the effects of exposure to herbicides used by the U.S. military during the Vietnam War on the health of the Vietnamese.

0810   "U.S. Chemical Warfare in South Viet Nam: Its Genetic Effects." Vietnam Courier, v. 7, no. 258, March 2, 1970, p. 2. Several instances of birth defects and miscarriages have been reported as a result of the U.S. military's spraying of chemicals in South Vietnam.

0811   U.S. Chemical Warfare Universally Condemned." (See 0400)

0812   "U.S. Defoliants Hit Vietnamese Infants." Militant, v. 43, no. 21, June 1, 1979, p. 24. T.T. Tung, Vietnam's Director of Science and Health, stated during a visit to the United States that the use of defoliants by the U.S. military in Vietnam has caused an increased number of birth defects and miscarriages in the Vietnamese.

0813   U.S. Veterans Administration. Advisory Committee on Health-
       Related Effects of Herbicides. <u>Transcript of Proceedings
       (Fifth Meeting, August 6, 1980)</u>. (See 1791)

0814   **"Update: Health-Orange Alert."** <u>New Internationalist,</u> **no.
       100, June 1981, p. 3.** Some of the concerns in regards to the
       use of the herbicides 2,4-D and 2,4,5-T around the world are
       expressed. In Vietnam's Hue District, after Agent Orange had
       been sprayed the rate of still births rose 50 percent. Among
       Australian Vietnam veterans one in four has fathered a
       deformed child.

0815   Vien, N.K. See Nguyen Khac Vien.

0816   **"Viet Deformities: Will We Ever Know?"** <u>Medical World News,
       v. 12, no. 4, January 29, 1971, p. 4-5.</u> The debate over the
       number of birth defects in Vietnamese children and whether or
       not exposure to Agent Orange is the cause of these birth
       defects is discussed.

0817   <u>Viet Nam: Destruction - War Damage</u>. (See 0637)

0818   "Vietnam Defoliation Judged Long Lasting." (See 0639)

0819   "Vietnam Investigates Chemical Poisoning." (See 0644)

0820   Vo Hoai Tuan. "Some Data on Chemical Warfare in South Viet
       Nam in 1969-1970." (See 0649)

0821   Wade, N. "Viets and Vets Fear Herbicide Health Effects."
       (See 1259)

0822   **Waelsch, S.G. "Responsibility of Individual Scientists."**
       <u>New York Academy of Science. Annals,</u> **v. 196, no. 4, June 7,
       1972, p. 241-242.** The author discussed the social
       responsibility of the individual scientist at a conference on
       the social responsibility of scientists sponsored by the
       Academy's Section of Science and Public Policy. As part of
       this discussion, the author tells of the study he made of
       reports and photographs from Vietnam describing congenital
       abnormalities possibly linked to 2,4,5-T.

0823   Ward, R.E. "Study Hits Vietnam Defoliants." (See 0652)

0824   Westing, A., ed. <u>Herbicides in War: the Long-term
       Ecological and Human Consequences</u>. (See 0671)

0825   **Wilson, J.G. "Teratological Potential of 2,4,5-T."** <u>Down to
       Earth, v. 28, no. 4, Spring 1973, p. 14-17.</u> This article is
       the text of an address which was given at the 25th Annual

Meeting of the Southern Weed Science Society in Dallas. The author discusses the findings of the Environmental Protection Agency's 2,4,5-T Advisory Committee's report and the criticisms which have resulted from its publication. It does not appear that the levels or 2,4,5-T to which people were exposed in Vietnam, Swedish Lapland or Globe, Arizona will create a hazard to human reproduction.

0826 World Health Organization. "Anti-plant Agents." (See 0266)

THE DISPOSAL OF THE LEFTOVER AGENT ORANGE

0827 "Agent Orange." Goodbye to All that, no. 27, March 17, 1972, p. 2. As a result of the protests over the use of Agent Orange in Vietnam, the government has halted the use of the defoliant in Vietnam. However, they have turned over the leftover defoliant to the Saigon government to use as they want.

0828 "Agent Orange." Ann Arbor Sun, no. 27, March 17-31, 1972, p. 13. The Air Force still has more than 800,000 gallons of Agent Orange in Mississippi and another 1.5 million gallons in storage in South Vietnam. They are having difficulties finding a site to dispose of it. Once a site is found 5,000 gallons will be burned a day for 468 days.

0829 "'Agent Orange' Sale Proposed by Air Force." Chemical Marketing Reporter, v. 206, no. 14, September 30, 1974, p. 5+. The Air Force has informed the Environmental Protection Agency that it intends to sell the leftover Agent Orange from the Vietnam War. They will register the herbicide with the Environmental Protection Agency before offering it for sale.

0830 "The Case for Chemical Export Controls." Congressional Record, v. 119, pt. 15, June 1, 1973, p. 19063-19065. Representative C.B. Rangel (D-N.Y.) discusses the continued use of herbicides by North and South Vietnamese forces since the cease-fire, the export of herbicides to Portugal and South Africa, the possibility of selling the leftover Agent Orange to South American countries and the ban of 2,4,5-T in the United States. Representative Rangel raised these issues as he is introducing "The Herbicide Export Control Act of 1973" and "The Chemical Warfare Prevention Act of 1973."

0831 "Cool on Incineration." Chemical Week, v. 116, no. 19, May 7, 1975, p. 19. The Environmental Protection Agency would like to look into the possibility of reprocessing the Agent Orange that the Air Force still has on hand. The Air Force wants to incinerate it on the Dutch vessel Vulcanus near Johnston Island.

0832 "Dioxin Tainted Ship." Chemical Week, v. 122, no. 23, July 7, 1978, p. 18. The Vulcanus became contaminated with small amounts of dioxin when the leftover Agent Orange from the Vietnam War was burned aboard the ship last year.

0833 "Disposal of Air Force Herbicide." Northwest Passage, v. 12,
      no. 9, April 14, 1975, p. 25. The Environmental Protection
      Agency will be holding hearings in Honolulu and San Francisco
      in the near future to discuss whether or not the Air Force
      should be allowed to incinerate the leftover Agent Orange
      from the Vietnam War in the mid-Pacific Ocean aboard the
      Dutch incinerator ship, Vulcanus. The Environmental
      Protection Agency's final decision will be based upon whether
      or not the Air Force can prove that there is no feasible
      alternative to incineration.

0834 "Fiery End for Orange." Chemical Week, v. 120, no. 23, June
      8, 1977, p. 28-29. Negotiations by Agent Chemical (Houston)
      to reprocess the leftover Agent Orange have fallen through.
      The defoliant will instead be burned on board the Vulcanus in
      the Pacific Ocean. It will cost the Air Force more than four
      million dollars to burn the herbicide.

0835 Fife, D. "Correspondence on Agent Orange in Louisiana."
      Nola Express, no. 136, July 27-August 9, 1973, p. 16. The
      correspondence between D. Fife and various government
      officials on the possibility that the leftover Agent Orange
      might be disposed of in Louisiana is reprinted.

0836 Harrington, J.F. "Herbicide Orange Surplus." [letter]
      Science, v. 180, no. 4093, June 29, 1973, p. 1320. This
      letter was written in response to D. Shapley's report (See
      0850) of April 6, 1973 regarding the possibility of the
      leftover Agent Orange being sold to the South Americans.
      J.F. Harrington thinks that it would be a good idea to sell
      the Agent Orange to the South Americans. The doses they
      would use it in would be considerably less than were used in
      Vietnam and it would be used in very rural areas.

0837 "Herbicide Destroyed." Air Force Times, v. 38, no. 9,
      September 26, 1977, p. 8. The leftover Agent Orange was
      destroyed about 120 miles from Johnston Island in the Pacific
      Ocean recently.

0838 "'Herbicide Orange' Held Salvageable by New Process that
      Absorbs TCDD." Chemical Marketing Reporter, v. 211, no. 7,
      February 14, 1977, p. 5+. Researchers at the Fish and
      Wildlife Service Fish Pesticide Laboratory in Colombia,
      Missouri have discovered a way to salvage Agent Orange and
      recover a safe herbicide. The leftover Agent Orange then
      will not need to be burned near Johnston Island in the
      Pacific Ocean.

0839 Laursen, B. "Agent Orange Turns Green." Mother Jones, v. 1,
      no. 6, August 1976, p. 9. The issue of what to do with the

leftover Agent Orange is discussed. It is possible that it
will be used as a weed killer.

0840   Lavergne, E.A. Study of Feasibility of Herbicide Orange
        Chlorinolysis. Washington: GPO, July 1974. 1 volume
        (various paginations). This report examines the feasibility
        of chlorinolysis as a method to convert the leftover Agent
        Orange into useful commercial products namely carbon
        tetrachloride, carbonyl chloride and hydrogen chloride. The
        author concludes that the process is feasible.

0841   "Method Rids Agent Orange of TCDD Contamination."
        Chemical and Engineering News, v. 55, no. 11, March 14, 1977,
        p. 25. A charcoal filtration technique developed by Fish and
        Wildlife Service chemists which may be used to remove the
        toxic TCDD from the stockpiles of Agent Orange is described.
        The Air Force would like to sell the stockpiles to a company
        that could reprocess it for sale as a commercial herbicide.

0842   Muneta, B. "Ecocide in the American Global Frontiers:
        Tribal Armies and Herbicides." Akwesasne Notes, v. 6, no. 3,
        July 1974, p. 26-27. One possibility being discussed of what
        to do with the leftover Agent Orange is to sell it to South
        American countries, specifically Brazil, for use in
        defoliating the Amazon. The author does not approve and
        feels that it is just another way the American government is
        practicing genocide.

0843   "'Nam 'Herbicide (Orange)' Can Be Made Safe." Air Force
        Times, v. 37, no. 32, March 7, 1977, p. 21. It has been
        discovered that the leftover Agent Orange can be broken down
        and converted into a safe and valuable herbicide by a process
        developed by two Fish and Wildlife Service chemists who were
        studying impurities in fish tissue. They discovered Agent
        Orange could be broken down by absorbing it onto coconut
        charcoal filters.

0844   "New Hope for Herbicide." Chemical Week, v. 117, no. 21,
        November 19, 1975, p. 15. What to do with the leftover Agent
        Orange is discussed. It is possible that it could be
        reprocessed. Other countries will not be permitted to
        purchase it.

0845   "'Orange' Burning Requested." Air Force Times, v. 32, no.
        28, February 16, 1972, p. 19. The Air Force hopes to burn
        the leftover 2.3 million gallons of Agent Orange in either
        Texas or Illinois.

0846   Princeton, I. "Incineration: Three New Ships to Burn Toxic
        Wastes." Solid Wastes Management, v. 25, no. 7, July 1982,

p. 20+. The design and equipment of three ships that dispose of hazardous wastes, including Vulcanus II which destroyed the Agent Orange leftover from the Vietnam War, are explained.

0847 **Rowen, J. "Dumping Agent Orange."** New Republic, v. 166, no. 26, June 24, 1972, p. 10-11. The plans that are being developed to dispose of the leftover herbicide are noted. One proposal involves a New Mexico oil drilling business who wants the Air Force to dump the Agent Orange down an empty well in Lea County, New Mexico. The company would dump the herbicide in a one percent solution of salt water.

0848 **"Seagoing Furnace Destroys Toxics."** EPA Journal, v. 4, no. 8, September 1978, p. 16-17. The possibility of incinerating the leftover Agent Orange at sea is discussed.

0849 **Shapley, D. "Air Force Tries Again on Agent Orange."** Science, v. 186, no. 4160, October 18, 1974, p. 244. The Air Force is still trying to get rid of its stockpile of Agent Orange. Before they can market it, the Agent Orange must be registered with the Environmental Protection Agency which so far this agency has been unwilling to do but may now be willing to do.

0850 **Shapley, D. "Herbicides: Agent Orange Stockpile May Go to the South Americans."** Science, v. 180, no. 4081, April 6, 1973, p. 43-45. The United States government is considering selling the leftover Agent Orange to Brazil, Venezuela, Paraguay and perhaps to other South American countries. The implications of this sale are discussed. The defoliant would be out of the control of the United States government once sold and could be used as a military weapon and there is the question to be resolved of whether exposure to Agent Orange has caused birth defects.

0851 "The Talk of the Town: Notes and Comment." (See 0241)

0852 **Tremblay, J.W. "The Design, Implementation, and Evaluation of the Industrial Hygiene Program Used During the Disposal of Herbicide Orange."** in Human and Environmental Risks of Chlorinated Dioxins and Related Compounds. (Environmental Science Research, v. 26) Ed. by R.E. Tucker, A.L. Young and A.P. Gray. New York: Plenum Pr., 1983, p. 749-769. This paper reviews how the incineration of the leftover Agent Orange was accomplished on board M/T Vulcanus and the industrial hygiene monitoring that took place following the incineration.

0853 "U.S. Defoliant Ban Defied." (See 0248)

0854 Walsh, J. "Odyssey of Agent Orange Ends in the Pacific."
      Science, v. 197, no. 4307, September 2, 1977, p. 966-967.
      Agent Orange will at last be disposed of by burning it aboard
      the Dutch owned incinerator ship, the Vulcanus, 120 miles
      west of Johnston Island in the Pacific Ocean.

0855 Westing, A.H. and E.W. Pfeiffer. "Use of 2,4,5-T." [letter]
      Science, v. 174, no. 4009, November 5, 1971, p. 546. The
      authors have returned recently from Vietnam and expressed
      their concern about the continued use of Agents White and
      Blue by the South Vietnamese government. They fear the South
      Vietnamese will also use the Agent Orange. There is some
      conflict as to who owns the remaining Agent Orange - the
      United States or the South Vietnam government. Now that the
      United States has stopped using Agent Orange the authors call
      for the United States to get the red tape cleared up and get
      the Agent Orange destroyed.

0856 Whiteside, T. "A Reporter at Large: the Pendulum and the
      Toxic Cloud." (See 0682)

0857 Zwerdling, D. "The Immolation of Agent Orange." New Times
      (New York), v. 9, no. 3, August 5, 1977, p. 13+. The
      incineration of the leftover Agent Orange from the Vietnam
      War is noted and the proposed ban of 2,4,5-T by the
      Environmental Protection Agency here in the United States is
      discussed.

THE EFFECTS ON THE VIETNAM VETERAN

GENERAL DISCUSSIONS

0858 "Agent Orange: the Never-ending Cost of the Vietnam War."
<u>Congressional Record</u>, v. 131, no. 94, July 16, 1985, p.
E3311-E3312. Representative F.H. Stark (D-CA) feels the out
of court settlement is inadequate. The congressman had
inserted in the <u>Record</u> an article by M. Collier which tells
the story of Tim Baumgardner who committed suicide out of
frustration in dealing with the Veterans Administration over
his disabilities which he believed were the result of
exposure to Agent Orange. He had cysts in his armpits,
dizziness, vertigo, rashes and chronic arthritis.

0859 "Agent Orange Update." <u>National Vietnam Veterans Review</u>, v.
4, no. 5, May 1984, p. 9. The Agent Orange litigation has
been settled out of court. The Veterans Administration has
updated its review and analysis of the scientific literature
on the health effects of exposure to Agent Orange and phenoxy
herbicides. The Dow Chemical Company is examining its
options regarding the responsibility of the federal
government in helping to pay for the settlement. Australian
scientists have found no convincing evidence that structural
birth defects could be caused by paternal exposure to Agent
Orange in Vietnam.

0860 "Agent Orange: Vietnam's Last Battle." <u>American Legion
Magazine</u>, v. 122, no. 2, February 1987, p. 41+. The author
discusses the link between a study of Kansas farmers exposed
to herbicides and Vietnam veterans exposed to Agent Orange.
The American Legion will release the results of its study
soon. The status of the Centers for Disease Control's study
is mentioned. Also mentioned is the Veterans
Administration's position on Agent Orange and its Agent
Orange Registry. The status of the Agent Orange settlement
is noted.

0861 "Agent Orange: View of an Exposed Veteran." <u>Congressional
Record</u>, v. 130, no. 71, May 30, 1984, p. E2494-E2495.
Representative J.P. Hammerschmidt (R-Ark.) told of the
research T. Carhart, director of the Vietnam veterans
leadership program in Connecticut, has done on the Agent

Orange issue. The congressman had inserted into the <u>Record</u>
an article by T. Carhart from the May 30, 1984 issue of the
<u>Washington Times</u>.

0862   "Aid for Congressional Case Workers and Vietnam Veterans -
       Agent Orange and the Vietnam Map Book." (See 0136)

0863   Bryan, C.D.B. "Orange Ruse." [reply] <u>New Republic</u>, v. 189,
       no. 7 & 8, August 15-22, 1983, p. 40. This letter was
       written in reply to the letter by R. Irvine (See 0891) which
       criticized his article (See 0864) reviewing the Agent Orange
       issue. C.D.B. Bryan writes to say he did explain why the
       Veterans Administration will not help veterans and to say the
       Operation Ranch Hand study is flawed.

0864   Bryan, C.D.B. "The Veterans' Ordeal." <u>New Republic</u>, v. 188,
       no. 25, June 27, 1983, p. 26-33. <u>Waiting for an Army to Die:
       the Tragedy of Agent Orange</u> by F.A. Wilcox is reviewed. The
       class action suit, the Veterans Administration's position on
       Agent Orange and the personal stories of several Vietnam
       veterans who are suffering from the ill effects of exposure
       to Agent Orange are all discussed as well.

0865   "By His Father's Hand, the Zumwalts." [transcript] J.
       Laurence, correspondent. New York: Journal Graphics, 1986.
       9p. This program was aired on ABC-TV's television program,
       20/20, on October 2, 1986. J. Laurence interviews Admiral
       Zumwalt and Elmo Zumwalt, III. The Zumwalts have recently
       published their dual autobiography entitled <u>My Father, My
       Son</u>. Admiral Zumwalt discusses the reasons why he ordered
       Agent Orange to be sprayed in the areas in which Elmo III
       served. Elmo III now has cancer and his son, Elmo IV, has
       learning disabilities. The Zumwalt family believes these
       health problems are due to Elmo III being exposed to Agent
       Orange. Elmo III's fight with cancer is discussed in
       detail.

0866   Castleman, M. "Options for Vietnam Veterans." (See 0154)

0867   Christian, R.S. and J.K. White. "Battlefield Records
       Management and Its Relationship with the Agent Orange Study."
       (See 0159)

0868   Corson, W.R. "The Vietnam Veterans Adviser." <u>Penthouse</u>, v.
       13, no. 9, May 1982, p. 100. R. Muller's visit to Hanoi with
       three other members of the Vietnam Veterans of American to
       discuss the MIA and Agent Orange issues has created quite a
       bit of controversy.

0869   Costello, G.M. "A Father's Legacy." <u>U.S. Catholic</u>, v. 52, no. 2, February 1987, p. 48-50. The author discusses how Admiral Zumwalt and Elmo Zumwalt III feel about the Agent Orange issue. Admiral Zumwalt ordered sprayings of Agent Orange in areas in which Elmo III was serving during the Vietnam War. Elmo III now has two forms of cancer and his son Elmo IV has severe learning disabilities.

0870 Council on Environmental Quality. "Veterans' Exposure to Dioxin." In Environmental Quality 1979: the Tenth Annual Report of the Council on Environmental Quality. Washington: GPO, 1979, p. 213-214. The controversy surrounding the concerns of veterans who were exposed to Agent Orange is summarized.

0871 David, P. "Dioxin Lawsuits: Agent Orange in the Courts." Nature, v. 301, no. 5921, July 7, 1983, p. 6. The American Medical Association's resolution which accuses the media of conducting an irrational "witch hunt" against dioxin, the postponement of the beginning of the trial against the manufacturers of the defoliant for another year, the results of the Ranch Hand study, the transfer of the epidemiological study to the Centers for Disease Control, and the discovery that the Dow Chemical Company was worried about the consequences of exposure to dioxin as early as 1965 are mentioned.

0872 "Dioxin: a Witches' Brew that Has Just Begun to Boil." Business Week, no. 2794, June 13, 1983, p. 128B+. The debate on whether or not exposure to Agent Orange has caused some of the health problems experienced by some Vietnam veterans is discussed. The lawsuits have hurt the stock performances of the chemical companies involved. Dow continues to insist that chloracne is the only known side effect of exposure to Agent Orange.

0873 "Double Agent." American Film, v. 9, no. 2, November 1983, p. 10. An hour-long documentary called "The Secret Agent" premiered at the New York Film Festival recently. It tells the stories of veterans exposed to Agent Orange in Vietnam and how it affected their health and families.

0874 "A Double Standard on Dioxin." National Vietnam Veterans Review, v. 3, no. 1 & 2, January/February 1983, p. 3. The same concern, commitment, and standards that were applied to the Times Beach, Missouri situation should also be applied to the Agent Orange issue.

0875 Doyle, E. and T. Maitland. "The Forgotten Veterans." In The Aftermath: 1975-1985. (The Vietnam Experience) Boston: Boston Publishing Company, 1985, p. 136-145. This article discusses the problems Vietnam veterans and their families have faced since the end of the war: Post Traumatic Stress Syndrome, Agent Orange, MIAs, etc. Regarding the Agent Orange issue, the authors mention the concern over the health effects of exposure, the Veterans Administration's position on Agent Orange, and the litigation.

0876 Dugger, C. "Endless War." Southern Exposure, v. 10, no. 2, March/April 1982, p. 48-55. The personal stories of L. Gwaltney, whose husband died of cancer due to exposure to Agent Orange in Vietnam, and Reverend Tom Champion, who is also dying of cancer due to exposure to Agent Orange in Vietnam, are told. Ms. Gwaltney founded Agent Orange Victims of Atlanta and Tom serves as its chairperson.

0877 Dutton, J.A. "Agent Orange: Has It Caused Health Problems for Veterans?" Illinois Issues, v. 7, no. 5, May 1981, p. 38. The litigation, efforts by Congress to respond to veterans' concerns, efforts by veterans to get the Veterans Administration to respond to their concerns and what is known about the health effects of exposure are all noted.

0878 Eisenberg, L. "Mine Field Ahead: a TV-movie about Agent Orange." TV Guide, v. 34, no. 45 issue 1754, November 8, 1986, p. 18-20+. The story of the making of the TV movie, "Unnatural Causes," is told. This movie is based on M. deVictor's feelings that the health problems of the Vietnam veterans she was helping were associated with exposure to Agent Orange and the efforts she made to bring this situation to the government's and the public's attention.

0879 Ensign, T. "Court Broadens Agent Orange Suits." Guardian, v. 33, no. 16, January 21, 1981, p. 4. A federal court in New York has ruled that for the purposes of the damage claims against the manufacturers of Agent Orange, all of the 2.4 million Vietnam veterans constitute a single class. The court also dismissed the counter-suit by the manufacturers to have the federal government named as a third party in the suit. The Veterans Administration continues to claim that there is no scientific evidence against Agent Orange. The proposed epidemiological study will probably not be started in 1981. Citizen Soldier hopes to publish the results of their study in a few months. Their data is being analyzed by J. Dwyer and R. Smith of the State University of New York at Stony Brook.

0880 Ensign, T. and M. Uhl. "Dioxin Poisoning Spurs Tests." In These Times, v. 3, no. 37, August 15, 1979, p. 19. The growing evidence of health problems related to Agent Orange exposure, the lack of proper examinations by the Veterans

Administration, the federal studies now underway, and the
lawsuits that have been filed are described.

0881 Epstein, S.S. "Problems of Causality, Burdens of Proof and
      and Restitution: Agent Orange Diseases." Trial, v. 19, no.
      11, November 1983, p. 91-99+. The author notes the problems
      in demonstrating causality in the Agent Orange issue. Also
      discussed are the studies that have been done to determine
      the adverse health effects of exposure in experimental
      animals and humans, the positions taken on the toxic effects
      of dioxin by veterans' organizations and Congress, and the
      lawsuits that have been filed.

0882 Felde, G. "Get the Facts on Agent Orange." Imprint, v. 29,
      no. 3, September 1982, p. 17+. A general discussion on the
      Agent Orange issue. The legal battles, research studies
      underway, and the health problems of veterans who believe
      these problems are due to exposure to Agent Orange are noted.

0883 "Four U.S. Veterans Return to Vietnam." Facts on File, v.
      41, no. 2146, December 31, 1981, p. 966. Four Vietnam
      veterans recently spent six days discussing the MIA issue and
      the long-term effects of the spraying of Agent Orange with
      the Vietnamese government.

0884 Galian, E.G. "Agent Orange: a New Approach." DAV
      Magazine, v. 25, no. 6, June 1983, p. 1+. The DAV has
      proposed a new method for dealing with the Agent Orange
      problem.

0885 Garlock, C. "Agent Orange: Local Vet Contaminated?"
      Rochester Patriot, v. 7, no. 9, May 18, 1979, p. 1+. The
      miscarriage Jerry Dennis' wife had is noted. Jerry is a
      veteran who was exposed to Agent Orange in Vietnam. Some of
      the health effects people seem to suffer from due to exposure
      are also noted. The number of Agent Orange-related lawsuits
      is growing. The Veterans Administration does not have a
      policy of checking veterans for effects of chemicals that
      were sprayed in Vietnam.

0886 Garlock, C. "Over 200 Vets Here Fear Agent Orange Contact."
      Rochester Patriot, v. 8, no. 2, January 30, 1980, p. 1+. The
      Veterans Outreach Project is trying to help local veterans
      who fear they may have been exposed to Agent Orange while
      serving in Vietnam. The Veterans Administration is
      continuing to claim the only side effect of exposure to Agent
      Orange is chloracne. On the judicial front, the chemical
      companies have filed a suit against the government placing
      the blame on the government for the misapplication of Agent
      Orange.

0887   Gorda, M.L. "Orange Ruse." [letter] New Republic, v. 189,
        no. 7 & 8, August 15-22, 1983, p. 4. This letter was written
        in order to criticize C.D.B. Bryan's review of the Agent
        Orange issue (See 0864) which appeared in the June 27, 1983
        issue of this journal. M.L. Gorda discusses the problem of
        using animal studies to verify effects on humans and the fact
        that industry is now using animal studies to prove that
        dioxin is not harmful to humans.

0888   Greenleaf, S. Fatal Obsession. New York: Dial Press, 1983.
        250p. In this novel John Marshall Tanner, a private
        investigator, attempts to determine who murdered his nephew
        Billy. Billy was a Vietnam veteran who had been exposed to
        Agent Orange while in Vietnam.

0889   Gunby, P. "Light at End of Tunnel in Orange Controversy."
        JAMA, v. 247, no. 10, March 12, 1982, p. 1382. The Air
        Force's Operation Ranch Hand study is nearing completion.
        The Veterans Administration still has not allowed any
        compensation claims based solely on exposure to Agent Orange.
        The Supreme Court has declined to hear an appeal that would
        allow Vietnam veterans to sue the manufacturers of the
        defoliant under federal law. A team of researchers at the
        University of California at Los Angeles will design an
        epidemiological study for the Veterans Administration. The
        American Medical Association's Council on Scientific Affairs
        has issued a report reviewing the possible health effects of
        Agent Orange exposure.

0890   Hoard, B. "Vets Mobilize Micro to Attack Agent Orange: but
        Face Cash Crisis." (See 0197)

0891   Irvine, R. "Orange Ruse." [letter] New Republic, v. 189,
        no. 7 & 8, August 15-22, 1983, p. 4+. This letter was
        written to criticize C.D.B. Bryan's review article on the
        Agent Orange issue (See 0864) which appeared in the June 27,
        1983 issue of this journal. R. Irvine writes to say that the
        Veterans Administration cannot help until scientific evidence
        proves that Agent Orange is the cause of veterans' health
        problems.

0892   Isenberg, D. "Agent Orange: an Ever-Intensifying
        Controversy." Guardian, v. 32, no. 30, April 30, 1980, p.
        7+. The prospects of an epidemiological study of Agent
        Orange being authorized and several congressional measures
        relating to Agent Orange being passed look dim. New Jersey
        and Illinois have established commissions to study the
        effects of Agent Orange on veterans and their children. A
        summary of several recent studies is included. The five
        chemical companies named in a class action Agent Orange suit

have filed a counter-suit naming the federal government as a
third party. The federal government still maintains that
exposure to dioxin only causes chloracne.

0893   Joeckel, C.E., Jr. "An Agent Orange Plan that Makes Sense."
       DAV Magazine, v. 26, no. 6, June 1984, p. 2-3. The out of
       court settlement will not close the book on the debate on the
       health effects of exposure to Agent Orange for veterans and
       their offspring. The Disabled American Veterans support a
       bill called the "Veterans' Dioxin and Radiation Exposure
       Compensation Standards Act" sponsored by Senators A. Simpson
       (R-WY) and A. Cranston (D-CA) which would establish
       guidelines to be used in evaluating the data and assigning
       accountability.

0894   Kubey, C. et al. "Agent Orange." In The Viet Vet Survival
       Guide: How to Cut Through the Bureaucracy and Get What
       You Need--and Are Entitled to. New York: Facts on File,
       1986, p. 81-98. This book was written to help Vietnam
       veterans figure out what they are entitled to and how to go
       about getting it. This chapter discusses the Agent Orange
       litigation and how to file a claim, what is known about the
       health effects of exposure to Agent Orange, the Veterans
       Administration's Agent Orange exam, how to file for
       compensation from the Veterans Administration, state
       programs, and the medical studies that are currently underway
       at the Department of Defense and the Centers for Disease
       Control.

0895   Leepson, M. "Continuing Agent Orange Controversy."
       Editorial Research Reports, v. 1, June 23, 1983, daily and
       reminder services section. The Agent Orange controversy is
       briefly discussed -- specifically what has happened with the
       class action suit and the bills that are before Congress.

0896   Long, J.R. and D.J. Hanson. "Dioxin Issue Focuses on Three
       Major Controversies in U.S." Chemical and Engineering News,
       v. 61, no. 23, June 6, 1983, p. 23-30+. In part details the
       debate surrounding the Agent Orange and Vietnam veteran
       issue.

0897   "MIA, 'Orange' Mission: 4 Vets Go to Vietnam." Air Force
       Times, v. 42, no. 23, December 28, 1981, p. 10. Four senior
       officials of the Vietnam Veterans of American have gone to
       Vietnam to learn more about the effects of Agent Orange
       exposure and the Missing in Action.

0898   McDonnell, T. "The War Goes on the First Combat Veterans to
       Return to Vietnam Confront Painful Legacies in Meeting
       Rooms of Hanoi and in the Streets of Saigon." Rolling Stone,

no. 365, March 18, 1982, p. 11-12+. Four members of the
Vietnam Veterans of American discuss their visit to Vietnam.
They were part of a group of people that went to Vietnam to
discuss the MIA and Agent Orange issues with the Vietnamese
government.

0899 Maiman, J.M. "Agent Orange Campaign Launched by Post."
      VFW Magazine, v. 72, no. 1, September 1984, p. 12+. The
      story of how Veterans of Foreign Wars Post 10013 in Stamford,
      Connecticut and Paul Reutershan launched the battle to get
      some answers on how exposure to Agent Orange affects veterans
      and their families.

0900 Main, J. "The Hazards of Helping Toxic Waste Victims."
      Fortune, v. 108, no. 9, October 31, 1983, p. 158-160+. In
      part a discussion of the legislation passed, the litigation,
      and the medical evidence in the Agent Orange controversy.

0901 Mason, B.A. In Country. New York: Harper and Row, 1985.
      247p. A novel about a teenager living in rural Kentucky
      whose father died in Vietnam before she was born and whose
      uncle probably was exposed to Agent Orange while he was
      serving in Vietnam. The novel deals with her feelings about
      father and her uncle.

0902 Meek, S.L. "An Estimate of the Relative Exposure of U.S.
      Air Force Crewmembers to Agent Orange." (See 0209)

0903 "National Veterans' Task Force on Agent Orange." Discharge
      Upgrading Newsletter, v. 4, no. 6, June 1979, p. 3. A
      coalition of veterans' organizations, lawyers, scientists and
      church organizations called the National Veterans' Task Force
      on Agent Orange has been formed.

0904 New York (State). Temporary Commission on Dioxin Exposure.
      What You Should Know about Dioxin. (On Cover: Dioxin,
      Agent Orange...There Are No Simple Solutions.) Albany: The
      Commission, January 1983. vii, 50p. This booklet contains a
      portion of the Interim Report of September 1982 (See 1629)
      prepared by this Commission; a section entitled "Dioxin in
      Vietnam" which tells veterans how to get a Veterans
      Administration physical exam, how to find out if they were
      exposed, how to request a tissue exam and how to file a
      claim; sections detailing the studies currently underway by
      agencies of the federal and New York state government; and
      chemical fact sheets on 2,3,7,8-TCDD and 2,4,5-T.

0905 New York (State). Temporary Commission on Dioxin Exposure.
      Final Report. Albany: The Commission, September 1983. 22p.
      and appendices. The history and development of the dioxin

exposure issue is reviewed and the Commission's fact-finding and public education efforts are summarized. The Commission's recommendations for state and federal action are included. The research that is underway is summarized. The appendices include a reprint of the <u>Interim Report</u> (See 1629), a summary of the litigation and a reprint of the <u>What You Should Know about Dioxin</u> (See 0904) pamphlet.

0906 "The Poison Harvest: Agent Orange--a Vietnam Legacy." <u>Rolling Stone</u>, no. 272, August 24, 1978, p. 31-32. The story of several veterans who were exposed to Agent Orange while in Vietnam is told. Also detailed is how M. deVictor, a claims officer for the Veterans Administration in Chicago, found a link between Agent Orange and service in Vietnam. The Veterans Administration continues to do very little for these veterans. The story of the spraying of the Freelund family farm in Wisconsin is also told.

0907 Posner, M. "Agent Orange Comes Home to Do Battle." <u>Macleans</u>, v. 93, no. 37, September 15, 1980, p. 48+. The health problems experienced by those exposed to Agent Orange, the proposed epidemiological study, the class action suit filed in a New York federal court, and efforts to get the Congress to pass legislation are all discussed.

0908 "The Price for Agent Orange." <u>Environmental Action</u>, v. 15, no. 3, September 1983, p. 8. The House will consider a bill this month which would grant Vietnam veterans who suffer from sarcoma, chloracne, or porphyria cutanea tarda benefits because it is assumed that they have these diseases because they were exposed to Agent Orange. The documentary "The Secret Agent" by Green Mountain Post Films will be premiering at the New York Film Festival on October 8. It is about Vietnam veterans suffering from Agent Orange-related diseases. Pre-trial motions are continuing in a New York federal district court.

0909 Roberson, R.L. "Agent Orange: A Critical Review and Proposal for Action." Masters Thesis, Ball State University, 1982. iii, 70p. This thesis examines several areas of interest in regards to the Agent Orange issue. These areas are: environmental public policy, who bears the burden of proof in the litigation against the manufacturers of Agent Orange and the federal government, and Agent Orange toxicological data. The author concludes that the federal government and the manufacturers of Agent Orange ought to bear the burden of proof in the litigation brought by Vietnam veterans exposed to Agent Orange.

0910 Rosen, D. "Agent Orange Returns." <u>Seven Days</u>, v. 2, no. 11,

July 1978, p. 8-9. Vietnam veterans are having problems in getting the government to accept responsibility for the health problems they are having as a result of being exposed to Agent Orange. Also noted is the documentary aired by WBBM-TV in Chicago based on the discoveries made by M. deVictor, a Chicago claims worker.

0911   Rosen, D. "Campaign to Identify GI Herbicide Poisoning Initiated." Win, v. 14, no. 19, May 25, 1978, p. 16-17. Citizen Soldier has begun a national campaign to identify Vietnam veterans suffering from herbicide exposure. The problem was first identified by M. deVictor, a Chicago Veterans Administration benefits counselor. A television special was recently aired in Chicago.

0912   Slavin, P. "The Agent Orange Settlement: What Have the Victims Really Won?" Air Force Times, v. 47, no. 17, December 8, 1986, p. 73+. The author discusses the health problems veterans feel they have as a result of being exposed to Agent Orange, the concerns they have about the May 1984 out of court settlement and the reason why Congress has been reluctant to act on this issue.

0913   Smith, C. "The Soldier-Cynics: Veterans Still Caught in a War." Southeast Asia Chronicle, no. 85, August 1982, p. 9-13. Agent Orange is just one of the issues Vietnam veterans have become cynical about.

0914   Smith, C. and D. Watkins. The Vietnam Map Book: a Self-help Guide to Herbicide Exposure (See 0235)

0915   Smith, C. and D. Watkins. "What's New on the Vietnam Map Book." (See 0236)

0916   Smith, D. "A Trail of Poison." Multinational Monitor, v. 5, no. 2, February 1984, p. 22-23. The documentary "The Secret Agent," which was produced by J. Ochs and D. Kellerand and is a Green Mountain Post Films/Human Arts Association Production, is reviewed. The film documents the struggle Vietnam veterans have waged to gain compensation for their problems which resulted from exposure to Agent Orange. It also explores the logic of the corporate system. The film is distributed by First Run Features in Cooper Station, New York. In addition it explores the Times Beach and Seveso incidents.

0917   Sypko, T.P. and G.T. Estry. "Agent Orange Update." VFW Magazine, v. 70, no. 5, February 1983, p. 46-47. Resolutions passed at the 83rd National Convention in Los Angeles are listed and the efforts the Veterans of Foreign Wars have made on the Agent Orange issue are mentioned.

0918   Thacher, S. "Vietnam War Legacy: Birth Defects and
       Illness." Science for the People, v. 12, no. 5, September/
       October 1980, p. 29-32. A general discussion of the Agent
       Orange and Vietnam veteran issue.

0919   "2,4,5-T: the Heat Goes on." Science News, v. 119, no. 16,
       April 18, 1981, p. 247. The 2,4,5-T issue is still hazy
       after 15 years of controversy. The National Veterans Task
       Force on Agent Orange will convene a conference at the
       American University campus in the near future.

0920   "The USAF 'Deniability' Factor: Spraying Was Obliterated."
       (See 0245)

0921   Uhl, M. "In the Grip of Agent Orange." Progressive, v. 50,
       no. 1, January 1984, p. 35. The author reviews Waiting for
       an Army to Die by F.A. Wilcox and is disappointed that Mr.
       Wilcox did not dig deep enough into the issue and merely
       restated what has already been reported by the mainstream
       press.

0922   Van Strum, C. A Bitter Fog: Herbicides and Human Rights.
       San Francisco: Sierra Club Books, 1983. 288p. The author
       details her discovery of the hazards of 2,4,5-T, the research
       that has been done the effects of 2,4,5-T exposure, and her
       petitions and the resulting court cases because the area she
       lives in had been sprayed with 2,4,5-T by the Forest Service
       and a county road crew. The author includes a description of
       the experiences veterans who were exposed to Agent Orange in
       Vietnam have had.

0923   "Veterans' Concern." CBS News Daily News Broadcasts, new
       ser., v. 10, no. 114, April 23, 1984, p. 7 (morning news).
       R. Muller, president of the Vietnam Veterans of America, is
       interviewed on his recent trip to Vietnam and Cambodia.
       While in these countries he discussed the issues of Agent
       Orange, Amerasian children and the MIA with the Hanoi
       government.

0924   "'Vietnam Order of Battle' May Figure in Agent Orange Suits."
       (See 0256)

0925   "Vietnam Poison Comes Home." Science for the People, v. 10,
       no. 4, July/August 1978, p. 8. The organization, Citizen
       Soldier, has established Project Search and Save to assist
       veterans and their families who might be suffering from the
       veterans' exposure to Agent Orange in Vietnam.

0926   Vietnam Veterans of America. Agent Orange. Washington:
       Vietnam Veterans of America, December 1986. 12p. This

publication discusses how persons concerned about the Agent Orange issue can help the Vietnam Veterans of American move the Veterans Administration and the federal government to give the Vietnam veteran a fair hearing. What Agent Orange is, how to file for benefits from the Veterans Administration, the settlement fund, the status of the government studies that are being conducted, where veterans and their families can get help, the Agent Orange litigation, the suit the Vietnam Veterans of America filed against the federal government, and what concerned people can do are all explained.

0927   "Vietnam Veterans Visit Hanoi." Editorials on File, v. 12, no. 24, December 16-31, 1981, p. 1440-1445. This article consists of editorials from newspapers across the country which discuss the trip four Vietnam veterans took to Hanoi to talk to Vietnamese officials about the MIA issue and the effects of exposure to Agent Orange. Some of the editorials also mention the Supreme Court's refusal to review an appeals court decision that veterans who are seeking damages for illnesses thought to be caused by exposure to Agent Orange must go through the state courts, not the federal courts.

0928   "Where Is My Country?" Time, v. 115, no. 8, February 25, 1980, p. 20. Three hundred veterans, wives, and children met recently in Long Island, New York to exchange their tales of how the exposure of Vietnam veterans to Agent Orange has changed their lives. Also recounted are efforts by V. Yannacone, Jr. to bring suit against the manufacturers of Agent Orange and the frustration veterans feel at the unwillingness of the Veterans Administration to grant disability payments. As Mike Ryan, a Vietnam veteran stated, "I was there when my country needed me, where is my country now that I need help?"

0929   "Who's to Pay?" Economist, v. 288, no. 7300, July 30-August 5, 1983, p. 24. The following aspects of the Agent Orange issue are noted: Congress has passed legislation to give the epidemiological study to the Centers for Disease Control, the Veterans Administration's reluctance to compensate the veterans, the preliminary results of the Air Force's Ranch Hand study, and the class action suit in which recently the chemical companies being sued have claimed that the government knew as much as they did about possible adverse health effects as a 1967 Rand Corporation report warned the Defense Department that Agent Orange was poisoning peasants.

0930   Wilcox, F.A. Waiting for an Army to Die: the Tragedy of Agent Orange. New York: Random House, 1983. 222p. The obstacles Vietnam veterans exposed to Agent Orange are facing in getting the government to accept responsibility for their difficulties and the medical problems they and their children have had as a result of the exposure are detailed.

0931   Zumwalt, E., Jr. and E. Zumwalt III. "Agent Orange and the Anguish of an American Family." New York Times Magazine, August 24, 1986, p. 32-34+. The Zumwalts talk about their service in Vietnam, the Admiral's decision to spray the defoliant, and Elmo III and Elmo IV's health problems which the Zumwalts believe are the result of Elmo III having been exposed to Agent Orange in Vietnam. This article was adapted from their book, My Father, My Son (See 0932).

0932   Zumwalt, E.R., Jr. and E.R. Zumwalt III with J. Pekkanen. My Father, My Son. New York: Macmillan, 1986. xii, 224p. This book tells the story of Admiral Zumwalt and Elmo III's lives which includes serving in Vietnam during the Vietnam War. Admiral Zumwalt explains why he ordered Agent Orange to be sprayed in areas in which Elmo III was in charge of river patrols. Elmo III now suffers from nodular poorly differentiated lymphoma and Hodgkin's disease. His son Elmo IV suffers from sensory integration dysfunction. The Zumwalts all feel that Elmo III's and Elmo IV's health problems are the result of Elmo III being exposed to Agent Orange. Elmo III also discusses how he feels about the Agent Orange litigation.

HEALTH EFFECTS OF EXPOSURE

0933   "ACS National Meeting: Meteorite, Agent Orange, Polymers." Chemical and Engineering News, v. 61, no. 36, September 5, 1983, p. 4. At the recent American Chemical Society meeting in Washington, D.C., A. Young of the Veterans Administration's Agent Orange Project Office detailed the results of the health effects of Vietnam service on approximately 85,000 Vietnam veterans examined as part of the Veterans Administration's Agent Orange Registry. It was found that the incidence of soft tissue sarcoma was slightly lower than in the general population.

0934   "An AMA Study Requests More Data on TCDD." Chemical Week, v. 130, no. 3, January 20, 1982, p. 18. The American Medical Association recently released its own assessment of the available literature on TCDD. The report concludes that there is still very little substantive evidence for many of the allegations.

0935   Adena, M.A. et al. "Mortality Among Vietnam Veterans
       Compared with Non-Veterans and the Australian Population."
       Medical Journal of Australia, v. 143, no. 12/13, December
       9/23, 1985, p. 541-544. The author conducted a study of
       Australians to determine if service in Vietnam influenced
       their overall death rates or those from specific causes.
       There was no evidence of higher death rates among Vietnam
       veterans.

0936   "Agent Orange." [editorial] American Family Physician, v.
       25, no. 4, April 1982, p. 91-92. The American Medical
       Association's Council on Scientific Affairs has prepared a
       technical report on Agent Orange which must be viewed as a
       significant contribution to the literature.

0937   "Agent Orange." Veterans Rights Newsletter, May-June 1982.
       (See 1302)

0938   "Agent Orange." Veterans Rights Newsletter, v. 2, no. 7-8,
       November-December 1982, p. 58-59. A list of state
       commissions on Agent Orange is given. The following items
       were also mentioned: the University Hospital at Stony Brook,
       New York is offering genetic counseling to veterans exposed
       to Agent Orange and their families; the National Academy of
       Sciences has issued its review of the protocol prepared by
       the University of California at Los Angeles for the Veterans
       Administration's study of Agent Orange exposure, in which
       several changes were recommended; the American Medical
       Association's Council of Scientific Affairs has issued a
       report on the health effects of Agent Orange and dioxin
       contaminants which asks American Medical Association
       publications to alert physicians to the signs of chloracne
       and the the possible signs and adverse effects of TCDD
       exposure.

0939   "Agent Orange." Veterans Rights Newsletter, v. 2, no. 11-12,
       March-April 1983, p. 91-92. The Australian government has
       released the results of a study they commissioned on Vietnam
       service and birth defects. Also mentioned is the legislation
       that has been introduced in the House which would compensate
       veterans suffering from three diseases believed to be caused
       by exposure to Agent Orange; the Veterans Administration has
       renewed its Agent Orange Advisory Committee for two years;
       and none of the 469 veterans who appealed their Agent Orange
       claims received compensation in 1982. One was dismissed, 403
       were denied and 63 were remanded for further development.
       Two were marked as approved. However the digest of the cases
       does not support this.

0940   "Agent Orange." CBS News Daily News Broadcasts, new ser., v.

9, no. 182, July 1, 1983, p. 7 (evening news). The Air Force
has released the results of its study on the effects of Agent
Orange on the mortality rate of veterans. There is no
evidence of an abnormal death rate among the former members
of Operation Ranch Hand.

0941 "Agent Orange." Veterans Rights Newsletter, v. 3, no. 3-4,
July-August 1983, p. 22. The following items are mentioned:
the Air Force has released the results of its study of Ranch
Hand personnel, the National Institute for Occupational
Safety and Health is studying exposure of chemical plant
workers to 2,4,5-T, the Illinois Agent Orange Commission is
holding a symposium on the health effects of defoliants and
dioxin, the state of New York has agreed to extend the
statute of limitations for Vietnam veterans filing Agent
Orange claims.

0942 "Agent Orange." CBS News Daily News Broadcasts, new ser., v.
10, no. 55, February 24, 1984, p. 5 (evening news). The Air
Force has released a report on the health of the Operation
Ranch Hand crew members. Among their findings were higher
skin cancer rates, abnormal leg pulses and a higher incidence
of early infant death in the offspring of the former crew
members than normal. The Air Force does not feel that these
findings can be linked to Agent Orange. Reaction to the
results was given by Maj. Gen. Murphy Chesney, M.D., Dep.
Surgeon General, USAF and John Tarzano of the Vietnam
Veterans of America.

0943 "Agent Orange - a Hero's Response." (See 1323)

0944 "Agent Orange: a Problem of Exposure." Science News, v.
117, no. 4, January 26, 1980, p. 55+. A high incidence of a
particular type of autoimmune antibodies was detected in
tests of blood of Vietnam veterans who believe they were
exposed to Agent Orange in Vietnam conducted at the
University of Illinois Medical Center in Chicago last fall.
The recently released General Accounting Office report on the
exposure of ground troops to Agent Orange is mentioned. The
Air Force has proposed to study the health problems of the
Operation Ranch Hand personnel.

0945 "Agent Orange Alert Issued to Physicians." American Medical
News, v. 25, no. 41, October 22-29, 1982, p. 28. The
American Medical Association has alerted physicians to watch
for adverse reactions in patients thought to have been
exposed to Agent Orange. This is in response to a report
prepared by the American Medical Association's Council on
Scientific Affairs on the health effects of exposure to Agent
Orange. The findings of this report are noted.

0946 "Agent Orange: an Ongoing Problem." Congressional Record,
      v. 126, pt. 7, April 23, 1980, p. 8917-8918. Representative
      J. LaFalce (D-N.Y.) read a letter from the wife of a Vietnam
      veteran from his district detailing her husband's medical
      problems. Representative LaFalce feels that this letter
      "...speaks for every veteran who fears Agent Orange
      exposure."

0947 "Agent Orange: Are Safe Levels Toxic?" Science Digest, v.
      91, no. 9, September 1983, p. 30. The recently released
      results of several studies indicate that the Vietnam veterans
      are correct in asserting that exposure to Agent Orange causes
      health problems.

0948 "Agent Orange 'Breakthrough' Claimed in N.J." Chemical
      Marketing Reporter, v. 230, no. 14, October 6, 1986, p. 27.
      The New Jersey Agent Orange Commission has recently
      released the results of a study that indicates that it is now
      possible to measure the amount of dioxin Vietnam veterans
      were exposed to even though it is now 10-15 years after they
      were exposed.

0949 "Agent Orange Breakthrough Reported." Air Force Times, v.
      47, no. 7, September 29, 1986, p. 2. Scientists working for
      the state of New Jersey have developed a test that determines
      the level of dioxin in veterans' bloodstreams. As a result
      it may be possible to determine who was exposed to Agent
      Orange in Vietnam and who was not.

0950 "Agent Orange Controversy." CBS News Daily News
      Broadcasts, new ser., v. 6, no. 247, September 3, 1980, p.
      17-19 (evening news). Dr. J. Moore, Deputy Director of the
      National Toxicology Program, is interviewed concerning the
      possible health effects of exposure to Agent Orange.

0951 "Agent Orange Data Seen as Limited." American Medical
      News, v. 26, no. 34, September 16, 1983, p. 22. Several
      experts stated at the recent annual meeting of the American
      Chemical Society that the medical examinations conducted on
      veterans as part of the Agent Orange Registry Program have
      resulted in data that is of limited use.

0952 "Agent Orange Effects." CBS News Daily News Broadcasts, new
      ser., v. 6, no. 246, September 2, 1980, p. 20-23 (evening
      news). Vietnam veteran Rick White tells about his health
      problems which he believes are due to having been exposed to
      Agent Orange in Vietnam and his difficulties in getting
      treated by the Veterans Administration. Also interviewed is
      Dr. G. Bogen, president of Vietline Hotline, on the health
      effects of Agent Orange exposure.

0953 "Agent Orange Effects: Air Force Study Fails to Resolve Issue." <u>Chemical and Engineering News</u>, v. 62, no. 10, March 5, 1984, p. 4. The results of an Air Force study of the Operation Ranch Hand veterans were released recently. The study did not find any ill effects that could be directly attributed to Agent Orange exposure. There were, however, two disturbing findings. Among the Ranch Hand veterans there were more cases of nonmelanotic skin cancers and the veterans reported statistically significant more birth defects in their children.

0954 "Agent Orange Effects Doubted." <u>Facts on File</u>, v. 43, no. 2233, September 2, 1983, p. 670. At a recent American Chemical Society meeting, Dr. A. Young stated that "...nothing stands out as related to dioxin or Agent Orange exposure."

0955 "Agent Orange Health Issues Raised Again." <u>Chemical and Engineering News</u>, v. 58, no. 32, August 11, 1980, p. 4. A federal intragency work group has suggested that the Air Force carry out a study of the Ranch Hand veterans to determine if they suffered adverse effects from Agent Orange exposure. This group cited studies done in Europe which show that exposure to 2,4,5-T and 2,4-D do increase the chance of developing certain types of cancer. The National Toxicology Program in a study on 200 mice has determined that "simulated" Agent Orange has no significant effect on fertility, reproduction, germ cell toxicology, or on the survival and development of the offspring of exposed animals.

0956 "Agent Orange Legislation May Pass Congress, but Questions Surround Compensation Issue." (See 1356)

0957 "Agent Orange: More Data Help Define Dioxin Danger." (See 1947)

0958 "Agent Orange: No Link to Birth Defects?" <u>Newsweek</u>, v. 104, no. 9, August 27, 1984, p. 24. The Centers for Disease Control has announced the findings of their study of birth defects in the offspring of Vietnam veterans. They found no significant link between birth defects and Agent Orange.

0959 "Agent Orange Not Cause of Psychologic Problems." <u>American Family Physician</u>, v. 28, no. 6, December 1983, p. 18. A study of 100 Vietnam veterans conducted by G.P. Korgeski and G.R. Leon at the University of Minnesota found no relationship between Agent Orange exposure and psychologic problems.

0960 "Agent Orange Pleas Fail in Appeals Court." (See 1958)

0961 "Agent Orange Rejected in Health Claims." Facts on File, v.
      45, no. 2339, September 20, 1985, p. 699. An Australian
      Royal Commission study on the claims of veterans that
      defoliants sprayed in Vietnam are the source of their health
      problems has been completed. The findings of the study
      reject the veterans' claims and describe them as "quite
      unfounded."

0962 "Agent Orange Shows Up in Fat-biopsy Studies." Chemical
      Week, v. 125, no. 25, December 18, 1979, p. 21. In fat-
      biopsy studies yet to be validated, trace levels of Agent
      Orange have been found in veterans, announced the Veterans
      Administration's Advisory Committee on Health-Related Effects
      of Herbicides recently. An interagency work group has been
      formed to study the Agent Orange issue.

0963 "Agent Orange: Still the Fog." Progressive, v. 48, no. 4,
      April 1984, p. 11. The Air Force has released the results of
      their study of the pilots and crew members who sprayed Agent
      Orange in Vietnam. The study found that these veterans are
      suffering from "minor or undetermined" ailments. The Air
      Force also acknowledged that some of the veterans have skin
      disorders, liver complications and possibly hardening of the
      arteries. The infant death rate of children of the veterans
      is three and a half times higher than among those fathered by
      other men in the same age group. The Air Force believes that
      the study gives servicemen exposed to the defoliant a clean
      bill of health.

0964 "Agent Orange Studies." Congressional Record, v. 129, no.
      128, September 29, 1983, p. S13218-S13225. Senator A.
      Cranston (D-CA) spoke on the Office of Technology
      Assessment's review of the Centers for Disease Control's
      proposed protocol of the epidemiological study, the Office of
      Technology Assessment's review of an Australian birth defects
      study, and the Agent Orange Registry. The text of Senator
      Cranston's correspondence with the Office of Technology
      Assessment, with the Veterans Administration's Chief Medical
      Director and the Centers for Disease Control's principal
      Agent Orange investigator is included. Also included are
      copies of articles from the August 30, 1983 issues of the New
      York Times and the Washington Post and from the July 11, 1983
      issue of Chemical and Engineering News. (See 1947 for the
      annotation of the last article)

0965 "Agent Orange Studies Urged." American Medical News, v. 24,
      no. 47, December 18, 1981, p. 19. The American Medical
      Association's House of Delegates stated recently that the
      studies of the toxicity and long-term effects of Agent Orange
      exposure should continue to be supported.

0966 "Agent Orange Study Finds Adverse Effects." Science News, v.
      125, no. 9, March 3, 1984, p. 132. The Air Force has
      recently released the results of their study comparing all
      1,269 Ranch Hand participants with 19,000 military-cargo
      flight-crew members who served in Vietnam during the same
      period. The study found subtle and unanticipated problems
      among the Ranch Hand veterans and their offspring.

0967 "Agent Orange Study Finds No Firm Evidence for Birth Defect
      Link." Chemical Marketing Reporter, v. 226, no. 8, August
      20, 1984, p. 3+. The Centers for Disease Control has
      recently released the report of the their findings in a study
      of the link between service in Vietnam and birth defects in
      their offspring. The study concludes that Vietnam veterans
      in general have not fathered, at higher rates than other men,
      babies with birth defects when all types of birth defects are
      combined. Elevated rates of some birth defects, however,
      were found in the offspring of veterans who may have been
      exposed to Agent Orange.

0968 "Agent Orange Study Good News for Industry." Chemical
      Marketing Reporter, v. 225, no. 9, February 27, 1984, p. 3+.
      The results of an Air Force epidemiological study of the
      Operation Ranch Hand veterans have been released. While
      several areas of questionable health were found, there were
      no symptoms of ill health which could be attributed directly
      to Agent Orange exposure.

0969 "Agent Orange Survey Conducted by the VA Fails to Back
      Claims." Chemical Marketing Reporter, v. 224, no. 10,
      September 5, 1983, p. 5+. At the American Chemical Society's
      annual meeting last week, A.L. Young of the Veterans
      Administration's Agent Orange Project Office reported that
      medical tests on approximately 85,000 Vietnam veterans have
      revealed few significant health problems. Some 25 percent
      had no health complaints about symptoms which have been
      associated with Agent Orange exposure and only 11 have soft
      tissue sarcomas.

0970 "Agent Orange: 10-year Controversy Over Health Effects on
      Humans." Congressional Quarterly Weekly Report, v. 38, no.
      8, February 23, 1980, p. 550-551. For the past 10 years
      dioxins have been a subject of controversy. The 1979
      developments concerning the Agent Orange issue are reviewed.

0971 "Agent Orange: the Persistent Uncertainty and Continuing
      Anguish Are Not Likely to End Soon." DAV Magazine, v. 22,
      no. 10, October 1980, p. 8-9. The symptoms alleged to be
      linked to Agent Orange exposure, pressure being put on the
      Veterans Administration by the DAV to get some answers and

the status of current research projects are noted. Basic
questions remain unanswered.

0972 **"Agent Orange Treatment."** Congressional Record, v. 129, no.
34, March 17, 1983, p. E1099-E1100. Representative T.A.
Daschle (D-S.D.) told of the efforts the McDonagh Medical
Center in Kansas City is making to treat Vietnam veterans
suffering from the effects of exposure to Agent Orange free
of charge. Inserted in the Record are copies of a letter
from the Medical Center to Representative Daschle and a press
release describing this program.

0973 "Agent Orange Update." American Legion Magazine, June 1982
(See 1389)

0974 **"Agent Orange Update."** Congressional Record, v. 131, no. 48,
April 23, 1985, p. S4522-S4524. Senator A. Cranston (D-CA)
had the Office of Technology Assessment's reviews of the
"Project Ranch Hand II, Mortality Update, 1984" and
"Mortality Among Vietnam Veterans in Massachusetts, 1972-83"
inserted in the Record.

0975 "Agent Orange Update." Congressional Record, February 4,
1987 (See 1392)

0976 "Agent Orange Victims." (See 1394)

0977 **"Agent Orange Was Safe."** New Scientist, v. 97, no. 1348,
March 10, 1983, p. 633. The Australian Commonwealth
Institute of Health recently completed a study of 8,517
deformed children born between 1966 and 1979 who were
matched with a healthy infant born at roughly the same time.
One hundred twenty-seven of the deformed infants were
fathered by Vietnam veterans while 123 healthy children were
fathered by veterans. The study therefore concludes that
army service in Vietnam does not increase the risk of birth
defects in the offspring of Vietnam veterans.

0978 **"Air Force Ranch Hand Morbidity Study."** Medical Service
Digest, v. 35, no. 1, Spring 1984, p. 13-14. The findings of
the morbidity report of the study of the Operation Ranch Hand
crew members are mentioned. So far the data is insufficient
to support a cause and effect relationship between Agent
Orange exposure and adverse health in the Ranch Hand crew
members. There was no significant difference between the
Ranch Handers and the comparison group. There were mixed
results in the measurement of fertility and reproductive
systems. There were no neurological problems that could be
associated with Agent Orange. Liver function tests and
clinical history data indicated mixed results. Birth defects
might be associated with herbicide exposure in some cases.

0979 "Air Force Releases Preliminary Findings on 'Ranch Hand'
      Agent Orange Investigation." DAV Magazine, v. 26, no. 4,
      April 1984, p. 9. The preliminary findings of the Air
      Force's study of the Air Force crewmen who handled Agent
      Orange have been released. No cases of soft tissue sarcoma,
      chloracne or porphyria cutanea tarda were found. No
      significant or moderate birth defects were found among the
      offspring of these crewmen.

0980 "Air Force Releases Ranch Hand Morbidity Study." National
      Vietnam Veterans Review, v. 4, no.4, April 1984, p. 9. The
      Air Force has released the first results of its study on
      mortality among the Ranch Hand crew members. The report's
      conclusion is that there is insufficient evidence to support
      a cause and effect relationship between herbicide exposure
      and adverse health among Ranch Hand crew members.

0981 "Air Force Says Herbicide No Cause for Early Deaths."
      Chemical Marketing Reporter, v. 222, no. 23, December 6,
      1982, p. 20. The Operation Ranch Hand study preliminary
      findings indicate that the mortality rate of these veterans
      is lower than that of the general population. However these
      findings should not be interpreted to mean that Agent Orange
      exposure does not cause ill effects.

0982 Aitken, L. and M. Wilhelm. "A Grim Irony Links Adm. Elmo
      Zumwalt to His Son's Cancer, but They've Closed Ranks to
      Battle Adversity." People, v. 26, no. 13, September 29,
      1986, p. 77-78+. Admiral Zumwalt and his son, Elmo III, have
      written a book entitled My Father, My Son. In this book they
      discuss their experiences during the Vietnam War and Elmo
      III's fight with cancer. Both Adm. Zumwalt and his son
      believe Elmo's cancer is due to having been exposed to Agent
      Orange which Admiral Zumwalt had ordered sprayed. Elmo
      III's son suffers from a severe learning disability. Both
      Admiral Zumwalt and his son believe that this is also the
      result of Elmo III having been exposed to Agent Orange.

0983 American Academy of Clinical Toxicology. Scientific Review
      Committee. "Commentary on 2,3,7,8-tetrachlorodibenzo-para-
      dioxin (TCDD)." Journal of Toxicology. Clinical Toxicology,
      v. 23, no. 2-3, 1985, p. 191-204. This article reviews what
      has been learned from epidemiologic studies and animal
      studies on the effects of exposure to TCDD. The studies that
      have been initiated as a result of veteran's exposure to
      Agent Orange in Vietnam are mentioned.

0984 American Chemical Society. Dioxins, Vietnam and 15 Years.
      Washington: The Society, 1985?, on side 2 of 1 sound
      cassette tape. The moderator of this discussion on the

debate regarding the health effects Vietnam veterans and
Vietnamese feel are associated with exposure to Agent Orange
is A. Smith. The moderator discusses the issue with A.
Schecter who also mentions his research on detecting traces
of dioxin in fat tissue.

0985   American Medical Association. Council on Scientific Affairs.
       "Health Effects of Agent Orange and Dioxin Contaminants."
       JAMA, v. 248, no. 15, October 15, 1982, p. 1895-1897. The
       executive summary of the report prepared by the Council on
       Scientific Affairs' Advisory Panel on Toxic Substances on
       Agent Orange is given.

0986   American Medical Association. Council on Scientific Affairs.
       Advisory Panel on Toxic Substances. The Health Effects of
       "Agent Orange" and Polychlorinated Dioxin Contaminants: an
       Update, 1984: Technical Report. Chicago: American Medical
       Association, October 1, 1984. 41, 10, 1p. Reprinted by
       Washington: GPO, 1984. This report examines the health
       effects of a variety of exposures of Agent Orange including
       the exposure of Vietnam veterans. The report concludes that
       the studies to date on the health effects of Vietnam
       veterans' exposure to Agent Orange are inconclusive.

0987   American Medical Association. Council on Scientific Affairs.
       Advisory Panel on Toxic Substances. The Health Effects of
       "Agent Orange" and Polychlorinated Dioxin Contaminants:
       Technical Report. Chicago: American Medical Association,
       October 1, 1981. 43p. This report reviews the medical
       evidence regarding the toxicity and long-term effects of
       TCDD. Studies that have been completed are critiqued and
       studies that have been started including those by the
       Veterans Administration and the Air Force are mentioned. The
       report concludes that there is nonconclusive evidence that
       neither TCDD or 2,4,5-T are mutagenic, carcinogenic or
       teratogenic in man, nor that they have caused reproductive
       difficulties in man. TCDD exposure does, however, cause
       chloracne.

0988   Andonian, J. "Possible Agent Orange Exposure in a Population
       of Incarcerated Vietnam Veterans." Masters Thesis,
       University of Wisconsin-Madison, 1982. 53p. and appendices.
       The author studied 44 Vietnam veterans and 39 Vietnam-era
       veterans without a history of exposure to Agent Orange from
       the same group of incarcerated veterans. The hypothesis that
       exposure to Agent Orange is the cause of the Vietnam
       veterans' health problems could not be established. However,
       the author found that service in Vietnam was a predictor of
       health problems.

0989 "Another Look at Dioxin." Consumers' Research Magazine, v.
67, no. 5, May 1984, p. 28. The recently released report on
the health of the more than 1,000 Operation Ranch Hand
personnel is excerpted. There is insufficient evidence to
support a cause and effect relationship between the herbicide
and adverse health in the Ranch Hand personnel.

0990 Armstrong, B. "Australians Report No Link Between Service in
Vietnam and Birth Defects Among Offspring." Epidemiology
Monitor, v. 4, no. 3, March 1983, p. 1. The Australian
Government has released the results of a study that found no
link between service in Vietnam and birth defects in their
offspring.

0991 Armstrong, B.K. "Storm in a Cup of 2,4,5-T." Medical
Journal of Australia, v. 144, no. 6, March 17, 1986, p. 284-
285. The author discusses the controversy over the manner in
which the Evatt Royal Commission treated the findings of the
studies which were conducted by O. Axelson and L. Hardell.

0992 Armstrong, B.K. and F.J. Stanley. "Birth Defects and Vietnam
Service." [editorial] Medical Journal of Australia, v. 140,
no. 7, March 31, 1984, p. 388-389. This editorial discusses
the concerns Vietnam veterans have concerning the fact that
their service in Vietnam (including being exposed to Agent
Orange) may cause them to father children with birth defects.
The authors agree with the conclusions of J.W. Donovan, R.
MacLennan and M. Adena (See 1046) that Vietnam veterans
will not father children with birth defects in any higher
numbers than other men of their generation.

0993 "'At Issue': Agent Orange." CBS News Daily News Broadcasts,
new ser., v. 8, no. 243, p. 22-24 (morning news). Whether or
not Agent Orange exposure is the cause of some Vietnam
veterans' health problems is discussed. Some of the studies
that are underway are noted.

0994 Australian Information Service. Birth Defects: Australian
Government Statement. Washington: Embassy of Australia,
February 20, 1983. 4p. This report summarizes the findings
of the report entitled "Case-control Study of Congenital
Anomalies and Vietnam Service (Birth Defects Study)" (See
1044).

0995 Australian Veterans Health Studies: The Mortality Report.
Canberra: Australian Government Publishing Service, 1984. 3
v. Part I: A Retrospective Cohort Study of Mortality Among
Australian National Servicemen of the Vietnam Conflict Era,
and a Executive Summary of the Mortality Report by M.J. Fett
et al. Part II: Factors Influencing Mortality Rates of

Australian National Servicemen of the Vietnam Conflict Era by
B.I. O'Toole, M.A. Adena and M.J. Fett. Part III: The
Relationship between Aspects of Vietnam Service and
Subsequent Mortality Among Australian National Servicemen
of the Vietnam Conflict Era by L. Forcier, H.M. Hudson and
M.J. Fett. The independent unit known as the Australian
Veterans Herbicide Studies expanded their investigation of
the effects of exposure to herbicides in veterans to an
investigation of all aspects of Vietnam service and
mortality. Their study found, in part, that the number of
deaths due to the several cancers that have been attributed
to exposure to herbicides were not significantly greater
than expected.

0996   Axelson, O. and L. Hardell. "Storm in a Cup of 2,4,5-T."
       [letter] Medical Journal of Australia, v. 144, no. 11, May
       26, 1986, p. 612-613. This letter was written in response to
       B.K. Armstrong's article of March 17, 1986 (See 0992) on the
       findings of the Evatt Royal Commission. The authors of this
       letter feel that the "scientific judgements" made by the
       Royal Commission are totally unreliable and useless.

0997   Axelson, O. and L. Hardell. "Storm in a Cup of 2,4,5-T."
       [letter] Medical Journal of Australia, v. 145, no. 6,
       September 15, 1986, p. 299. The authors of this letter
       respond to A.J. Christopher's response of September 15, 1986
       (See 1022) to their letter of May 26, 1986 (See 0997). They
       reaffirm their position and state that it is unclear to them
       why they have not been able to satisfactorily respond to
       their critics. Their arguments reflect scientific concern
       rather than a political position.

0998   Bailey, C. et al. West Virginia Vietnam Era Veterans
       Mortality Study: West Virginia Residents 1968-1983,
       Preliminary Report. Charleston, W. VA.: West Virginia
       Health Department, 1986. 30p. At the request of the West
       Virginia Agent Orange Assistance Program, a study of the
       causes of death among the state's Vietnam veterans who died
       between 1968 and 1983 was undertaken. The authors found
       strong statistical evidence which indicates that Hodgkin's
       disease, cancer of the testis and soft tissue tumors were
       more common among veterans who served in Vietnam than
       among veterans who did not.

0999   Baran, E. et al. "Somatosensory Evoked-Potential
       Abnormalities with Agent Orange." [abstract] Muscle & Nerve,
       v. 7, no. 7, September 1984, p. 571. Also
       Electroencephalography and Clinical Neurophysiology, v. 60,
       no. 5, May 1985, p. 112P. The authors obtained the
       differential surface-recorded sural, peroneal, tibial and
       median nerve somatosensory evoked potentials from 13 men who

were exposed to Agent Orange. Also performed were EEGs, visual/auditory brain-stem evoked potentials, peripheral nerve conduction studies, refractory periods of sensory nerves and EMGs. The authors conclude that Agent Orange does exert a neurotoxic effect on the central somatosensory pathway.

1000 Barr, M.M. "Apparent Progressive Axonal Dying Back Neuropathy in Vietnam Veterans." Neuroscience Letters, supplement 11, 1983, p. S29. Of the 120 Vietnam veterans and 10 farmers examined, 90 demonstrated neurological defects including distal peripheral neuropathy.

1001 Barr, M. "Post Concussion Syndrome Hypoglycemia and Agent Orange." [letter] Australian Family Physician, v. 17, no. 4, April 1983, p. 224. An examination of several veterans possibly exposed to Agent Orange showed that they had the same symptoms as patients who have post concussion syndrome and hypoglycemia.

1002 "The Battle of Agent Orange." (See 2006)

1003 Becker, M.S. "Level of Sensory Integrative Functioning in Children of Vietnam Veterans Exposed to Agent Orange." Occupational Therapy Journal of Research, v. 2, no. 4, October 1982, p. 234-244. Using the Southern California Sensory Integration Test battery and the Southern California Postrotary Nystagmus Test, the author investigated the sensory integrative functioning of six children whose fathers were exposed to Agent Orange in Vietnam. These children were matched against six control children. The results indicate that the children of the veterans are at a greater risk for sensory integrative dysfunction than children in the general population.

1004 "Bitter Legacy." CBS News Daily News Broadcasts, new ser., v.12, no. 260, September 17, 1986, p. 10-11 (morning news). The findings of a recently released study by the New Jersey Agent Orange Commission which shows that large quantities of dioxin still remains in soldiers exposed to Agent Orange in Vietnam are discussed.

1005 Black, A.L. "Dioxins as Contaminants of Herbicides: Australian Perspective." In Human and Environmental Risks of Chlorinated Dioxins and Related Compounds. (Environmental Science Research, v. 26) Ed. by R.E. Tucker, A.L. Young and A.P. Gray. New York: Plenum Pr., 1983, p. 13-16. The author presented this paper at the International Symposium on Chlorinated Dioxins and Related Compounds which was held in 1981. The debate on the health effects of the use of 2,4,5-T

in Australia including the complaints of Australian Vietnam
veterans exposed to Agent Orange in Vietnam is noted.

1006 Blackburn, A.B. "Review of the Effects of Agent Orange: a
      Psychiatric Perspective on the Controversy." Military
      Medicine, v. 148, no. 4, April 1983, p. 333-340. The author
      reviews the development of the media's interest in Agent
      Orange and the clinical studies that have been conducted.
      The controversy has affected the mental health of veterans.

1007 Bloemen, A. "Herbicides Linked to Vets' Brain Damage."
      World Environment Report, v. 8, no. 13, July 15, 1982, p. 3.
      A group of Australian neurologists have conducted a study of
      Vietnam veterans and have found a pattern of brain damage
      which links the psychological problems of these veterans to
      exposure to herbicides.

1008 Bogen, G. "Symptoms in Vietnam Veterans Exposed to Agent
      Orange." [letter] JAMA, v. 242, no. 22, November 30, 1979,
      p. 2391. The author details the results of a 10-month study
      of 78 Vietnam veterans. These veterans have in general been
      chronically ill.

1009 Booth, W. "Agent Orange Study Hits Brick Wall." Science, v.
      237, no. 4820, September 11, 1987, p. 1285-1286. The author
      details the Centers for Disease Control's involvement with
      the Agent Orange epidemiological study. It now appears based
      on new blood sera tests that neither military records or
      self-assessments of Vietnam veterans are reliable indicators
      of Agent Orange exposure. The Centers for Disease Control
      believes that they will not be able to find substantial
      numbers of veterans who received high levels of exposure to
      Agent Orange. It is doubtful that the study will ever be
      conducted.

1010 Brandt, E.N. "The CDC Study of Vietnam Veterans' Risks of
      Fathering Infants with Birth Defects." [editorial] Public
      Health Reports, v. 99, no. 6, November/December 1984, p. 529-
      530. The findings of the Centers for Disease Control's study
      on the risk of Vietnam veterans fathering children with birth
      defects are given. The most important conclusion to draw
      from the report is that, in general, Vietnam veterans are not
      at greater risk of fathering a child with birth defects. The
      author quotes a JAMA editorial which stated that these
      findings are of little consolation to those families with
      children with birth defects but perhaps these findings will
      encourage us to work harder to prevent birth defects in any
      child.

1011 "A Breakthrough on Agent Orange." Congressional Record, v.

132, no. 131, September 29, 1986, p. E3320-E3321.
Representative J.J. Florio (D-N.J.) spoke on the recently
announced findings of the New Jersey Agent Orange
Commission. These findings indicate that high levels of
dioxin can still be found in veterans who were exposed to
Agent Orange. Representative Florio had an article from the
September 18, 1986 issue of the New York Times and an article
by M. Purdy from the September 18, 1986 issue of the
Philadelphia Inquirer inserted in the Record.

1012   Breslin, P. et al. Proportionate Mortality Study of Army and
        Marine Corps Veterans of the Vietnam War. Washington:
        Veterans Administration. Office of Environmental
        Epidemiology, [1987]. 27p. The authors studied the patterns
        of mortality among 24,235 Army and Marine Corps Vietnam
        veterans with those of 25,685 non-Vietnam veterans. Among
        Army Vietnam veterans there were statistically significant
        excess deaths for motor vehicle accidents, non-motor vehicle
        accidents and accidental poisonings. Among Marine Corps
        Vietnam veterans there seemed to be an increased mortality
        from lung cancer and non-Hodgkin's lymphoma. This could be
        the result of exposure to Agent Orange but this study did not
        examine possible etiologic factors for these elevated
        malignancies. This study did not find an excess of soft
        tissue sarcomas.

1013   Brodkin, R.H. and R.A. Schwartz. "Cutaneous Signs of Dioxin
        Exposure." American Family Physician, v. 30, no. 3,
        September 1984, p. 189-194. The authors detail what has been
        learned about the skin problems resulting from exposure to
        dioxin. Veterans' exposure to Agent Orange in Vietnam has
        helped physicians learn about exposure to dioxin. The skin
        lesions commonly produced by exposure to dioxin are:
        chloracne, hyperpigmentation, hirsutism and porphyria cutanea
        tarda.

1014   Budiansky, S. "Agent Orange: Survey Spells Out Hazards."
        Nature, v. 305, no. 5929, September 1, 1983, p. 4. In a
        presentation at the recent American Chemical Society meeting,
        A. Young reported that a study of 85,000 Vietnam veterans
        found that exposure to Agent Orange does not seem to have
        caused any unusual health problems. The morbidity results of
        the Operation Ranch Hand study and the transfer of the
        epidemiological study to the Centers for Disease Control are
        also mentioned.

1015   Calesnick, B. "Dioxin and Agent Orange." American Family
        Physician, v. 29, no. 3, March 1984, p. 303-305. The
        chemistry and toxicology of Agent Orange is mentioned. Also
        noted are the studies being conducted by the Veterans

Administration, the Centers for Disease Control and several
other agencies.

1016 California. Department of Health Services. Approaches to the
      Study of Cancer Risk and Agent Orange Exposure in California
      Veterans. Sacramento: Department of Health Services,
      Preventive Health Services, June 30, 1985. 2, 29p. This
      report examines possible ways in which the California Tumor
      Registry might be used to study possible carcinogenic effects
      of Agent Orange exposure. The Department of Health Services
      feels the state of California should not undertake additional
      studies of the cancer risk from Agent Orange exposure with
      support from the General Fund but rather should continue to
      cooperate with federal studies.

1017 California. Legislature. Assembly Veterans Affairs Committee.
      Hearings July 30 and 31 and August 5 and 6, 1981 (See 1423-
      1426)

1018 Carnow, B.W. "Environmental Health" Medical and Health
      Annual, 1984, p. 226-232. In the section of this article
      entitled "Dioxin and Vietnam" (p. 229-230), the author gives
      a summary of the use of herbicides in Vietnam and the health
      concerns veterans have as a result of having been exposed to
      Agent Orange.

1019 Cashmore, A.B. "Agent Orange." [letter] Search, v. 11, no.
      6, June 1980, p. 178. This letter was written in reply to an
      editorial which appeared in the March 1980 issue of this
      journal. The author states that he has used 2,4,5-T for 30
      years and his health record is quite good.

1020 Cassimatis, N. "Agent Orange." [letter] Australian and New
      Zealand Journal of Psychiatry, v. 17, no. 1, March 1983, p.
      95. The author responds to a letter written by T. Stanley in
      the September 1982 issue of this journal (See 1207) by
      stating that the symptoms detailed in Stanley's article
      remind him of the symptoms of a group of Greek migrants he
      treated in 1977-1979 who also acted together out of a strong
      belief that they were victims and demanded justice.

1021 Chapman, L.J. Literature Review of Neurotoxic Disease
      Associated with Herbicide Orange and Related Compounds.
      Madison, WI: University of Wisconsin. Department of
      Preventative Medicine. Behavioral Toxicology and Human
      Performance Laboratory. June 1, 1981. 19p. The author
      believes when there is a strong indication of exposure to
      Agent Orange that there are increased risks of particular
      health effects which include identifiable neurobehavioral
      disorders which often persist and may grow more severe as
      time goes by.

1022   Christophers, A.J. "Storm in a Cup of 2,4,5-T." [letter]
        Medical Journal of Australia, v. 145, no. 6, September 15,
        1986, p. 298-299. This letter was written in response to O.
        Axelson and L. Hardell's letter of May 26, 1986 (See 0997)
        on what O. Axelson and L. Hardell felt to be the totally
        unreliable and useless scientific judgements of the Evatt
        Royal Commission. A.J. Christophers feels that O. Axelson
        and L. Hardell do not have a legitimate argument and agrees
        with the Commission's criticisms of L. Hardell's studies.

1023   Codario, R.A. "Agent Orange... the Curse that Lingers."
        Stars and Stripes - the National Tribune, v. 105, no. 50,
        December 16, 1982, p. 7+. The author briefly reviews why
        Agent Orange was used in Vietnam and what has been learned
        about the health effects of exposure to TCDD. The author
        then details what he has learned about the health effects of
        exposure to Agent Orange based on his examination of 350
        Vietnam veterans. His findings include the fact that 70
        percent of these veterans have peripheral nerve damage, 29
        percent have elevated liver function tests, 60 percent have
        elevated porphyrins, 71 percent have rashes, 73 percent have
        joint pain and 60 percent have gastrointestinal disturbances.

1024   Cohen, F.L. "Paternal Contributions to Birth Defects." The
        Nursing Clinics of North America, v. 21, no. 1, March 1986,
        p. 51-66. This article focuses on the male contributions to
        birth defects. The Agent Orange issue is discussed on pages
        59-60.

1025   Colton, T. "Herbicide Exposure and Cancer." [editorial]
        JAMA, v. 256, no. 9, September 5, 1986, p. 1176-1178. The
        author of this editorial compares the findings of a study by
        S.K. Hoar et al on the link between soft tissue sarcoma,
        Hodgkin's disease and non-Hodgkin's lymphoma and Kansas
        farmer's exposure to phenoxyacetic acid herbicides to similar
        studies conducted on Vietnam veterans exposed to Agent
        Orange. The results of Hoar et al's study are reported on
        pages 1141-1147 of this issue of JAMA.

1026   "Compensation for Agent Orange Victims." (See 1437)

1027   Connecticut. Department of Health Services. Vietnam
        Herbicides Information Center. A Report from the Vietnam
        Herbicides Information Center. (See 1443)

1028   Constable, J.D. and M.C. Hatch. "Agent Orange and Birth
        Defects (Continued)." [letter] New England Journal of
        Medicine, v. 310, no. 10, March 8, 1984, p. 653-654. The
        authors feel that the results of a study reported by A.
        Lipson (See 1135) have only minimal relevance to the possible
        toxic effects of exposure to Agent Orange.

1029   Cooper, C.L. et al. "Anencephaly: Agent Orange
       Implications?" National Medical Association. Journal, v. 75,
       no. 1, January 1983, p. 93-94. The authors discuss an
       incident of anencephaly and wonder if the birth defect might
       be connected to dioxin exposure.

1030   Crone, H.D. "The Factual Basis for Concern about
       Herbicides." In Chemicals & Society: a Guide to the New
       Chemical Age. New York: Cambridge University Press, 1986,
       p. 167-179. This chapter is part of a book which attempts to
       provide a balanced evaluation of the problems resulting from
       the vastly increased use of chemicals over the last 40 years.
       In this chapter the author discusses what is known about the
       toxicity of 2,4,5-T (including Agent Orange) and asbestos.

1031   Dan, B.B. "Vietnam and Birth-defects." [editorial] JAMA, v.
       252, no. 7, August 17, 1984, p. 936-937. The author
       discusses the issue of service in Vietnam including exposure
       to Agent Orange and birth defects in the offspring of
       veterans. The Centers for Disease Control's recently
       completed study on this issue is mentioned. The author
       believes that it can now be rather strongly stated that birth
       defects in the offspring of Vietnam veterans are not the
       result of their fathers' service in Vietnam.

1032   Dan, B.B. "Vietnam Veterans Risk for Fathering Children with
       Birth Defects." [letter] JAMA, v. 254, no. 5, August 2,
       1985, p. 610. The author in this letter replies to a letter
       by T.D. Sterling and A. Arundel (See 1213). While the
       results of Erickson et al's study (See 1058) show that there
       is an increase of occurrences of cleft palate and spina
       bifida in the offspring of Vietnam veterans possibly exposed
       to Agent Orange, four abnormalities had a lower incidence
       than expected. Also statistically significant results may
       not be biologically significant.

1033   Davies, N.E. "Agent Orange." [letter] Lancet, v. 2, no.
       8414, December 1, 1984, p. 1285. The author reports that he
       saw an ad in a Kansas City newspaper for a chiropractor
       stating he specialized in treating victims of Agent Orange
       exposure. The author states that only in America could you
       find a non-treatment for a non-disease.

1034   Davis, D.E. et al. "Agent Orange." Council of Agricultural
       Science and Technology. Comments from CAST, no. 10, 1978, p.
       1-5. This report is a response to 20/20's July 25, 1978
       program on Agent Orange. The authors feel the program made
       unwarranted allegations and that it has been scientifically
       proven that exposure to Agent Orange in Vietnam is not the
       cause of Vietnam veterans' health problems.

1035   Davis, J.W. "Exposure to Agent Orange." [letter] Chemical
       and Engineering News, v. 61, no. 45, November 7, 1983, p. 2.
       The author responds to some of the debate about using data
       drawn from the Agent Orange Registry to interpret the effects
       of Agent Orange exposure.

1036   Dawson, A. "No More Dioxin: Dow Chemical Stops American
       Use of Dioxin." National Vietnam Veterans Review, v. 4, no.
       3, March 1984, p. 50. The author mentions the fact that the
       manufacture of 2,4,5-T has been discontinued. The issue of
       who is responsible for the health problems Vietnam veterans
       are having as a result of being exposed to Agent Orange is
       also discussed.

1037   "Deaths No Greater for Agent Orange Handlers." Chemical and
       Engineering News, v. 63, no. 7, February 18, 1985, p. 27.
       The Air Force's mortality study of servicemen who handled
       Agent Orange continues to indicate that these men are not
       dying at a faster rate than other military personnel or
       civilians.

1038   "Defense." (See 1460)

1039   "Dioxin Dilemma." New Scientist, v. 111, no. 1527, September
       25, 1986, p. 19. Scientists at a recent symposium held in
       Fukuko, Japan debated whether or not the findings of the most
       recent studies reveal a link between exposure to dioxin
       (including Agent Orange) and a variety of diseases such as
       soft tissue sarcoma.

1040   "Dioxin Hysteria." [editorial] Wall Street Journal, May 31,
       1983, p. 28(E). Most of the scare stories about dioxin are
       exaggerated. For example, in the Air Force's study of the
       Ranch Hand veterans only three deaths are attributable to
       cancer, a lower proportion of cancer-caused deaths than in
       the control population. The idea that dioxin is a doomsday
       menace is based on some sort of psychological phenomenon
       rather than medical evidence.

1041   "Dioxin Poisons Vietnam Veterans." New Scientist, v. 78, no.
       1098, April 13, 1978, p. 69. Many Vietnam veterans feel that
       some of their injuries were caused by exposure to Agent
       Orange. The Veterans Administration feels that the claims
       they are receiving are due to a recent documentary on WBBM-
       TV in Chicago.

1042   "A Dioxin Report for Everyone." Chemical Week, v. 134, no.
       11, March 14, 1984, p. 20-21. The results of the Air Force's
       study of the Operation Ranch Hand veterans does not give
       conclusive evidence about the health effects of Agent Orange

exposure. Each side in the Agent Orange litigation are hand-picking sections of the report to use to their advantage in the upcoming trial.

1043 "Dioxin: Who Cares? Ho Cares!" (See 0721)

1044 Distelheim, R. **"There's a Time Bomb Ticking Inside Me."** Family Circle, v. 98, no. 14, October 15, 1985, p. 46+. Micki Voisard, a flight attendant with a private air transport company under contract to the U.S. government during the Vietnam War, feels her present health problems are the result of exposure to Agent Orange. She suffers from chloracne and digestive problems. Her hair has fallen out around her forehead. She has had a benign cyst removed from her right ovary, has suffered miscarriages and has an alarmingly low white blood count. The health problems of two other women who served in Vietnam are also described.

1045 **"Distributing Agent Orange Questionnaire."** Discharge Upgrading Newsletter, v. 5, no. 7-8, July-August 1980, p. 5. Several veterans' organizations are working with Dr. J. Stellman and her colleagues at Columbia University's School of Public Health to study the health effects of exposure to Agent Orange. Details on how veterans' organizations can help with the study are given.

1046 Donovan, J.W., R. MacLennan and M. Adena. **"Vietnam Service and the Risk of Congenital Anomalies."** Medical Journal of Australia, v. 140, no. 7, March 31, 1984, p. 394-397. The authors conducted a study to determine if Vietnam veterans are at a higher risk of fathering a child with a birth defect diagnosable at birth. Vietnam veterans have claimed that a high rate of birth defects in their offspring can be attributed to their exposure to Agent Orange. The authors concluded that Vietnam veterans are not any more likely to father a child with anomalies diagnosable at birth than other men.

1047 Donovan, J.W. et al. Case-control Study of Congenital Anomalies and Vietnam Service (Birth Defects Study): Report to the Minister for Veterans' Affairs. (Australian Veterans Health Studies) Canberra: Australian Government Publishing Service, January 1983. 127p. This document is the result of a study conducted by the Commonwealth Institute of Health to determine whether or not service in Vietnam was related to the risk of fathering a child with an anomaly. The study found no such connection. However, the risk of malformation was found to be higher in male children and in multiple births.

1048 "Dow Chemical Co. and Dioxin." Congressional Record, v. 129,
     no. 50, April 19, 1983, p. E1680-E1682. Representative T.A.
     Daschle (D-S.D.) submitted an article from the April 19 issue
     of the New York Times by D. Burnhan which detailed the fact
     that Dow was aware of the fact that exposure to dioxin might
     cause health problems.

1049 Dow Chemical Company. Dioxin, Agent Orange and Human
     Health. Midland, MI: The Company, 1984. v, 71 p. This
     pamphlet summarizes what is known about the health effects of
     exposure to TCDD and the studies underway to determine the
     health effects of Agent Orange exposure on the Vietnam
     veteran.

1050 Downing, D.R. "Epidemiology Division School of Aerospace
     Medicine." Medical Service Digest, v. 34, no. 5, Fall 1983,
     p. 14-17. The work and the organization of this Division are
     described. Their largest project is the study of the
     potential health effects of exposure to Agent Orange by
     Operation Ranch Hand crew members.

1051 Dyro, F.M. "Conduction Velocities and Agent Orange
     Exposure." [abstract] Muscle & Nerve, v. 7, no. 7,
     September 1984, p. 571-572. Also Electroencephalography and
     Clinical Neurophysiology, v. 60, no. 5, May 1985, p. 112P.
     Fifteen Vietnam veterans who claimed to have been exposed to
     Agent Orange were tested to determine if their paresthesia
     could be explained by peripheral neuropathy. The authors
     concluded that it could not.

1052 Ensign, T. "Agent Orange Study Released." Guardian, v. 36,
     no. 23, March 14, 1984, p. 4. The Air Force has recently
     released the findings of their two year study of Ranch Hand
     crew members. The study results indicate that the crew
     members do not have a higher mortality rate than the control
     group. They do have, however, higher rates of skin cancer
     and liver disorders and 28 of these men's children have died.
     The Air Force is assuming that if these crew members do not
     manifest health problems then the ground troops who were
     exposed have no reason to worry.

1053 Ensign, T. "The Deadly Truth about Dioxin." (See 2089)

1054 Ensign, T. and M. Uhl. "Dioxin: Uncovered by Accident, the
     Number of Cases Rising Dramatically." In These Times, v. 2,
     no. 35, July 19, 1978, p. 16. Case studies of several
     veterans exposed to Agent Orange are given and how M.
     deVictor, a Veterans Administration claims worker in Chicago,
     pieced together the symptoms of veterans to link them with
     Agent Orange is noted.

1055 Erickson, J.D. and J. Mulinare. "Agent Orange and Risks to
      Reproduction: the Limits of Epidemiology." [letter]
      Teratogenesis, Carcinogenesis, and Mutagenesis, v. 7, no. 2,
      1987, p. 197-200. The authors respond in this letter to M.C.
      Hatch and Z.A. Stein's 1986 article (See 1089) in this
      journal. The authors wish to correct misimpressions after
      reading M.C. Hatch and Z.A. Stein's article the reader may
      have been left with regarding their study.

1056 Erickson, J.D. and J. Mulinare. "Vietnam Veterans' Risk for
      Fathering Children with Birth Defects." [reply] JAMA, v.
      254, no. 5, August 2, 1985, p. 609-610. The authors, in this
      letter, reply to the August 2, 1985 letter of T.D. Sterling
      and A. Arundel (See 1213). They explain why the results of
      their study on the link between birth defects and service in
      Vietnam can not be used to show a link between possible Agent
      Orange exposure in Vietnam and birth defects and specifically
      cleft palate and spina bifida.

1057 Erickson, J.D. et al. "Design and Execution of a Very Large
      Birth-defects Case-control Study." In Prevention of Physical
      and Mental Congenital Defects: Proceedings of an
      International Conference Held in Strassbourg, France, October
      10-17, 1982. Part B: Epidemiology, Early Detection and
      Therapy, and Environmental Factors, ed. by M. Marois.
      (Progress in Clinical and Biological Research, v. 163B). New
      York: Alan R. Liss, Inc., 1985, p. 273-278. The authors
      describe the design and conduct of their birth defects and
      military service in Vietnam study which is supported by the
      Centers for Disease Control, the Veterans Administration and
      the Department of Defense.

1058 Erickson, J.D. et al. "Vietnam Veterans' Risk for Fathering
      Babies with Birth Defects." JAMA, v. 252, no. 7, August 17,
      1984, p. 903-912. Reprinted as "Agent Orange Continuum."
      Trauma: Medicine, Anatomy, Surgery for Lawyers, v. 27, no.
      1, June 1985, p. 1-10. The authors have studied Vietnam
      veterans' risks for fathering babies with major structural
      birth defects. The results of this study indicate that
      Vietnam veterans, in general, did not have increased risks of
      fathering babies with defects. With all types of birth
      defects combined, Vietnam veterans who may have been
      exposed to Agent Orange did not seem to be at greater risk of
      fathering babies with birth defects. However, the risks for
      fathering babies with a few specific types of defects seemed
      to be higher among these veterans.

1059 Erickson, J.D. et al. Vietnam Veterans' Risk for Fathering
      Babies with Birth Defects. Washington: GPO, August 1984.
      x, 370p. This study was set up to determine if Vietnam

veterans were at risk for fathering babies with major
structural birth defects. The most important conclusion that
the authors of this study reached was that no evidence could
be found that Vietnam veterans have a greater risk than other
men for fathering babies with serious structural birth
defects when all of these types of defects are combined. The
authors also concluded that there is little support for the
belief that veterans exposed to Agent Orange have an
increased risk of fathering babies when all types of birth
defects are combined.

1060 Fackelman, K. "Testing for Dioxin Exposure." Bioscience, v.
      33, no. 11, December 1983, p. 680-681. The debate on whether
      or not a method known as adipose tissue analysis should be
      used to help measure the amount of dioxin stored in the
      bodies of Vietnam veterans who may have been exposed to
      Agent Orange is discussed.

1061 Famiglietti, L. "AF: Stats Don't Show Agent Orange
      Effects." Air Force Times, v. 45, no. 32, February 25, 1985,
      p. 6. The Air Force stated in a report released recently
      that there is no statistical evidence of increased mortality
      for those who participated in Operation Ranch Hand as a
      result of being exposed to Agent Orange versus a comparison
      group.

1062 Feldman, W.S. "Agent Orange Disease: Media Hype of Life-
      threatening Reality." Legal Aspects of Medical Practice, v.
      11, no. 7, July 1983, p. 5-6. The author feels that no
      scientific proof exists to connect Agent Orange with the
      health problems experienced by Vietnam veterans and the
      situation has become an emotional reaction created by the
      media. The editor of this journal also added his comments
      and states that an in-depth epidemiological study must be
      done and that the Vietnam veteran should not blame all of his
      problems on Agent Orange.

1063 "Fifteen Years of Evidence: the Epidemiology of 2,4,5-T."
      Citizen Soldier, no. 7, June 1984, p. 3+. The findings of
      the early studies done on the health effects of the herbicide
      spraying done as part of the Vietnam War are summarized. The
      results of the Ranch Hand Study and Vietnamese and Australian
      studies are also noted.

1064 Fink, D.J. "Exposure to Agent Orange." [letter] JAMA, v.
      244, no. 10, September 5, 1980, p. 1094-1095. This letter
      criticizes G. Bogen's report, "Symptoms in Vietnam Veterans
      Exposed to Agent Orange." (See 1009)

1065 Fleck, H. "An Agent Orange: Case History." Military

Medicine, v. 150, no. 2, February 1985, p. 103-104. The
author gives the case history of a 38 year-old Vietnam
veteran whose medical problems are probably due to being
exposed to Agent Orange and suggests a neurologic basis for
his problems.

1066   Flicker, M.R. and A.L. Young. "Evaluation of Veterans for
       Agent Orange Exposure." [abstract] American Chemical
       Society. Abstracts with Papers, v. 186, 1983, #ENVR 0053.
       Data on over 110,000 Vietnam veterans including histories,
       physical examinations and laboratory analysis has been
       collected. No statistically significant health or
       reproductive effects have been discovered as of yet.

1067   Fox, J.L. "Agent Orange: Guarded Reassurance." Science, v.
       225, no. 4665, August 31, 1984, p. 909. The findings of the
       Centers for Disease Control's study on the risk of Vietnam
       veterans fathering children with birth defects are unlikely
       to still the debate about the health effects of exposure to
       Agent Orange.

1068   Fox, J.L. "Agent Orange Study Is Like a Chameleon."
       Science, v. 223, no. 4641, March 16, 1984, p. 1156-1157. The
       results of the Air Force's study of Ranch Hand veterans are
       discussed. These results have been interpreted differently
       by various groups to support opposite conclusions about the
       effects of exposure to dioxin.

1069   Fox, J.L. "Dioxin's Health Effects Remain Puzzling."
       Science, v. 221, no. 4616, September 16, 1983, p. 1161-1162.
       In part this article discusses a report given by A.L. Young
       at the recent American Chemical Society meeting in
       Washington. In his study he found no connection between
       Agent Orange and service in Vietnam.

1070   Friedman, J.M. "Does Agent Orange Cause Birth Defects?"
       Teratology, v. 29, no. 2, April 1984, p. 193-221. The
       scientific evidence regarding the genetic and teratogenic
       effects of Agent Orange and its major components is reviewed.
       Currently there is no scientific evidence which indicates
       that men previously exposed to Agent Orange are at increased
       risk of having children with birth defects, but the data
       available to assess this possibility critically are
       inadequate.

1071   "Further Information about Agent Orange." (See 0727)

1072   Gaffey, W.R. "Agent Orange and Birth Defects." [letter] New
       England Journal of Medicine, v. 309, no. 8, August 25, 1983,
       p. 492. The author mentions studies that have already been

done on the reproductive effects of exposure to dioxins and suggests that F. LaVecchio's study (See 1130) is not scientifically credible.

1073 Gale, L. "Veterans Target Dioxin." Guardian, v. 31, no. 37, June 20, 1979, p. 9. The 12th annual convention of the National Association of Concerned Veterans focused on the health problems facing Vietnam veterans who were exposed to Agent Orange.

1074 Gardner, J. "New Agent Orange Research: Answers at Last?" Nation, v. 244, no. 14, April 11, 1987, p. 460-462. The author reviews the findings of the Agent Orange studies conducted thus far and the debate over how the Centers for Disease Control's epidemiological study should be conducted.

1075 Garmon, L. "Dioxin Digest." (See 1510)

1076 Geisel, J. "Agent Orange." Business Insurance, v. 15, no. 17, April 27, 1981, p. 10. An American Council on Science and Health study states that there is no scientific evidence to justify the traditional uses of 2,4,5-T. The study did not examine the claims of Vietnam veterans that exposure to Agent Orange is the source of their health problems.

1077 Grabelsky, J. "Dioxin: War Horror Coming Home to Recover." Peace Newsletter, no. 765, April 1980, p. 15. The ecological damage done to Vietnam as a result of the spraying of Agent Orange during the Vietnam War and the possibility that spina bifida in the offspring of veterans exposed to Agent Orange could be linked to that exposure are discussed.

1078 Grady, A. "The American Way of Life." Militant, v. 45, no. 9, March 13, 1981, p. 26. The story of Edward, whose leg was shot up in Vietnam and who was in an area sprayed with Agent Orange, is told. His leg was diagnosed as cancerous in 1976 and removed in 1979. His injuries are service-connected because of the bullet wounds not because of the Agent Orange. Neither Dow nor the Veterans Administration recognizes Agent Orange as a source of cancer.

1079 Grant, W.F. "The Genotoxic Effects of 2,4,5-T." Mutation Research, v. 65, no. 2, June 1979, p. 83-119. This article considers the cytogenic, carcinogenic and teratogenic properties of 2,4,5-T. Mention of what is known about these properties of 2,4,5-T in regards to the use of Agent Orange is interwoven into this discussion.

1080 Greenwald, P. et al. "Sarcomas of Soft Tissues After Vietnam Service." National Cancer Institute. Journal, v. 73, no. 5,

November 1984, p. 1107-1110. The authors compared Vietnam
service and military service experiences of 281 men with soft
tissue sarcomas. The authors found no statistically
significant positive association between soft tissue sarcomas
and service in Vietnam, military service in general, or
exposure to Agent Orange.

1081   Gross, M.L. et al. "2,3,7,8-Tetrachlorodibenzo-p-dioxin
        Levels in Adipose Tissue of Vietnam Veterans." Environmental
        Research, v. 33, no. 1, 1984, p. 261-268. Thirty adipose
        tissue samples from veterans exposed to Agent Orange and
        control subjects were examined. TCDD was detected in levels
        ranging from 20 to 173 parts per trillion in three veterans
        who were "heavily exposed" to Agent Orange in Vietnam.

1082   Gunby, P. "More Questions Not Answers Emerge from Agent
        Orange Studies." JAMA, v. 249, no. 20, May 27, 1983, p.
        2743-2746. The recent developments in several Agent Orange
        studies are noted. Also mentioned is the report prepared by
        the American Medical Association's Council on Scientific
        Affairs. The status of the lawsuits against the
        manufacturers of Agent Orange is also noted.

1083   Gunby, P. "Plenty of Fuel for Agent Orange Dispute." (See
        1523)

1084   Hall, W. "The Agent Orange Controversy." [letter] Medical
        Journal of Australia, v. 146, no. 8, April 20, 1987, p. 453-
        454. W. Hall responds to the letters by J.K. Pollack (See
        1173) and G.F. Humphrey (See 1099) which appeared in the
        January 19, 1987 issue of this journal and were criticisms of
        W. Hall's article (See 1085) which appeared in the September
        1, 1986 issue of this journal. W. Hall believes that neither
        J.K. Pollack or G.F. Humphrey presented arguments that were
        good enough to invalidate the conclusions of the Evatt
        Commission. The author of this letter also states that all
        concerned should distinguish between the process and product
        of the Evatt Commission. Only then can Vietnam veterans and
        their families be reassured that they are not at a higher
        risk of birth defects or cancer by virtue of having served in
        Vietnam.

1085   Hall, W. "The Agent Orange Controversy After the Evatt Royal
        Commission." Medical Journal of Australia, v. 145, no. 5,
        September 1, 1986, p. 219-225. The author summarizes the
        findings of the Evatt Royal Commission's Report on the Use
        and Effects of Chemical Agents on Australian Personnel in
        Vietnam. The Commission rejects the claims of Vietnam
        veterans that exposure to Agent Orange is the cause of their
        health problems. The author also summarizes the response of

the media, the Vietnam Veterans' Association of Australia and the government to the report. The author concludes by stating that the public should be persuaded to reject the Vietnam Veterans' Association of Australia's claims about the chemicals and that this rejection will not deny Vietnam veterans fair treatment for disabilities they may have sustained as a result of serving in Vietnam.

1086 Hall, W. and D. MacPhee. "The Agent Orange Controversy in Australia: a Contribution to the Debate." Community Health Studies, v. 9, no. 2, 1985, p. 109-119. The authors examine the issue of whether or not the claims Australian Vietnam veterans are making concerning their exposure Agent Orange are correct. The authors conclude that the veterans' claims that exposure to the chemical caused birth defects in their offspring and psychiatric disorders and premature deaths among themselves do not have much evidence in their support. Also discussed is why this issue will not go away despite the fact scientists have found no evidence to support veterans' claims. The authors conclude that veterans must be treated fairly.

1087 Hall, W. and D. MacPhee. "Do Vietnam Veterans Suffer from Toxic Neurastenia?" Australian and New Zealand Journal of Psychiatry, v. 19, no. 1, March 1985, p. 19-29. The authors examine the issue of whether or not the psychiatric disorders and specifically toxic neurastenia that some Vietnam veterans are suffering from are the result of having been exposed to pesticides in Vietnam. The authors believe that the veterans' health problems are due to service in Vietnam but are not due to pesticide exposure.

1088 Hartnett, N.B. "Agent Orange." DAV Magazine, v. 21, no. 5, May 1979, p. 3. Vietnam veterans who feel they are suffering symptoms of exposure to Agent Orange are urged to contact the National Service and Legislative Headquarters of the DAV. The symptoms of dioxin poisoning are given. The Veterans Administration and other federal agencies are being very slow in accepting liability in these cases.

1089 Hatch, M.C. and Z.A. Stein. "Agent Orange and Risks to Reproduction: the Limits of Epidemiology." Teratogenesis, Carcinogenesis, and Mutagenesis, v. 6, no. 3, 1986, p. 185-202. The authors review the findings of three studies that have examined the link between exposure to Agent Orange and birth defects in their offspring. The authors feel that these studies have taken the issue as far as epidemiology can take it. It is time for scientists from other disciplines to determine the agenda.

1090   Herbert, W. "Vets Mindful of Herbicide's Effects." Science
       News, v. 124, no. 20, November 12, 1983, p. 309. G.P.
       Korgeski and G.R. Leon, two University of Minnesota
       psychologists, have studied the psychological effects of
       Agent Orange exposure on Vietnam veterans. Their conclusion
       is that while there appears to be no evidence linking actual
       exposure to dysfunction, veterans who feel that they were
       exposed to Agent Orange are experiencing a number of mental
       and emotional problems.

1091   "Herbicides, Birth Defects Unrelated, Study Claims." Chicago
       Daily Law Bulletin, v. 130, no. 161, August 16, 1984, p. 1+.
       The results of a study conducted by the Centers for Disease
       Control provide strong evidence that Vietnam veterans in
       general are not at increased risk of having babies with birth
       defects.

1092   Heyde, C.C. "The Effect on Humans of Exposure to Herbicides:
       a Contentious Contemporary Problem in Statistical Inference."
       Mathematical Scientist, v. 8, no. 2, July 1983, p. 63-73.
       The author examines the issues of model formulation and
       hypothesis testing in connection with testing for increased
       risk of disability associated with exposure to herbicides
       especially Vietnam veterans exposed to herbicides in Vietnam.

1093   Hitchens, C. "Minority Report." Nation, v. 238, no. 21,
       June 2, 1984, p. 662. Our actions often affect others.
       Admiral Zumwalt ordered the spraying of Agent Orange on the
       Camau Peninsula during the Vietnam War. His son, Elmo, was
       in charge of a river patrol in that area when it was sprayed.
       He now suffers from advanced cancer of the lymph glands. And
       his son, Russell, has "sensory integration dysfunction." The
       Admiral has stated that his feelings about the extent to
       which he was the causal agent of his son's and grandson's ill
       health are nonexistent.

1094   Hobson, L.B. "Human Effects of TCDD Exposure." Bulletin of
       Environmental Contamination and Toxicology, v. 33, no. 6,
       December 1984, p. 696-701. The author reviews the studies
       that are underway to determine the effects of exposure to
       Agent Orange and the difficulties encountered in conducting
       these studies. Also mentioned are the symptoms the veterans
       themselves have reported.

1095   Hobson, L.B. et al. "Dioxin in Body Fat and Health Status:
       a Feasibility Study." [abstract] American Chemical Society.
       Abstracts with Papers, v. 186, 1983, #ENVR 0032. TCDD was
       assayed in biopsy specimens of fat from several different
       groups of veterans, some of whom had reported exposure to
       Agent Orange, some of whom had not served in Vietnam and

some of whom had recently been exposed to Agent Orange. The authors have concluded from the preliminary study that the technique was sensitive enough to detect TCDD but questionable for proving exposure to Agent Orange in Vietnam.

1096 Hogan, M. Human Health Effects of the Phenoxy Herbicides 2,4-D and 2,4,5-T and Their Contaminant, TCDD (Dioxin): a Bibliography for the Clinician with Selected Background Materials. Milwaukee, WI: Vietnam Veterans Against the War, 1983. approximately 40p. This bibliography lists 226 articles and is divided into three parts. Part I lists medical articles on the human health effects of 2,4-D, 2,4,5-T and TCDD. Part II lists articles relevant to a broader study of 2,4-D, 2,4,5-T and TCDD. The last section lists additional articles which might be of interest to the Vietnam veteran exposed to Agent Orange.

1097 Horvath, E.P., Jr. "The Agent Orange Controversy: Physician's Dilemma." Wisconsin Medical Journal, v. 80, no. 3, March 1981, p. 16-18. The physician faces a diagnostic dilemma when treating veterans who believe they were exposed to Agent Orange due to the lack of a clearly definable syndrome of Agent Orange toxicity. All veterans who believe they were exposed to Agent Orange should have examination at Veterans Administration hospitals and participate in the Veterans Administration's Agent Orange Registry.

1098 Houts, M. "Update on Agent Orange." Trauma: Medicine, Anatomy, Surgery for Lawyers, v. 24, no. 2, August 1982, p. 101-111. The findings that have been determined thus far from the information submitted to the Agent Orange Registry are detailed.

1099 Humphrey, G.F. "The Agent Orange Controversy." [letter] Medical Journal of Australia, v. 146, no. 2, January 19, 1987, p. 115-116. The author is responding to W. Hall's article of September 1, 1986 (See 1085) on the findings of the Evatt Royal Commission. The author of this letter discusses the causes of the controversy surrounding the findings of the Evatt Royal Commission.

1100 Humphrey, G.F. "Storm in a Cup of 2,4,5-T." [letter] Medical Journal of Australia, v. 144, no. 11, May 26, 1986, p. 611-612. This letter was written in order to expand on the issues raised by B.K. Armstrong in his March 17, 1986 article (See 0991) on the controversy surrounding the findings of the Evatt Royal Commission.

1101 Illinois. Agent Orange Study Commission. Interim Report. (See 1552)

1102   Illinois. Agent Orange Study Commission. <u>Testimonies from
        Professional Hearings</u>. Springfield, Ill.: The Commission,
        February 1983. 20p. In a hearing before the Commission, R.
        Ginsberg, a toxicologist, P. Orris and A. Idris, physicians
        at Cook County Hospital in Chicago, A. Young, a toxicologist
        with the Veterans Administration, and M. O'Grady, a Veterans
        Administration environmental physician, discussed their
        concerns regarding the Agent Orange controversy.

1103   Illinois. Agent Orange Study Commission. <u>Transcript from the
        National Agent Orange Medical Symposium</u>. Springfield, Ill.:
        The Commission, May 1984. 63p. A panel of physicians and
        researchers spoke on what they have learned about Agent
        Orange exposure at the O'Hare Hilton Hotel in Chicago on
        September 24 and 25, 1983.

1104   Irey, N.S. <u>Report on Agent Orange Registry</u>. Washington:
        Armed Forces Institute of Pathology, May 1982. 19p. The
        Agent Orange Registry was established in part to conduct a
        study of the illnesses of some 800 Vietnam veterans as
        reflected in tissues removed during surgical procedures and
        in findings revealed at autopsy examinations. Analysis of
        these cases failed to reveal anything significantly unusual.
        However, two clusters of benign lymphomas and epidermal
        inclusion cysts were discovered and there were six cases with
        unusual features.

1105   Irvine, R. "The Zumwalts and Agent Orange." <u>Human Events</u>,
        v. 46, no. 50, December 13, 1986, p. 7. The author notes
        that the Zumwalts in their book <u>My Father, My Son</u> state that
        they believe that Elmo III's cancer was caused by exposure to
        Agent Orange and have been appearing on many television
        interview programs promoting their book. The media is also
        going along with the Zumwalts' assertion when the Zumwalts
        are interviewed. The author takes the media and the Zumwalts
        to task for not doing justice to scientific evidence as the
        link between Agent Orange and health problems has never been
        proven. The author discusses the out of court settlement in
        conjunction with the discussion of the lack of scientific
        evidence between exposure to Agent Orange and health
        problems and why the chemical companies settled.

1106   Jackson, S. "Agent Orange." <u>National Library of Medicine
        (U.S.) Literature Search</u>. (no. 80-30) Bethesda, MD: NLM.
        1980. 9p. This bibliography lists 99 citations from the
        MEDLINE database covering the time period of January 1972
        through December 1980.

1107   Jackson, S. "Dioxin Toxicology (Including Agent Orange)"
        <u>National Library of Medicine (U.S.) Literature Search</u>. no.

83-19) **Bethesda, MD: NLM. 1983. 11p.** This bibliography updates literature search 80-30 and lists 128 citations from the MEDLINE database for the time period of January 1981 through September 1983.

1108 Johnston, S.J. and G. Evans. "Veterans Rap Agent Orange Settlement." (See 2139)

1109 "Judge Dismisses Agent Orange Claims of Vietnam Veterans Against the U.S." (See 2141)

1110 **Kang, H. et al. "Soft-tissue Sarcoma and Military Service in Vietnam - a Case Comparison Group-analysis of Hospital Patients." [abstract] American Journal of Epidemiology, v. 122, no. 3, September 1985, p. 523-524.** This paper was presented at the 18th annual meeting of the Society for Epidemiologic Research. The authors conducted a survey to see if they could find a link between service in Vietnam and soft tissue sarcoma. They examined the cases of 214 Vietnam-era and 13,496 comparison group patients. They could not find a significant association between soft tissue sarcoma and military service in Vietnam.

1111 **Kang, H.K. et al. "Soft Tissue Sarcomas and Military Service in Vietnam: a Case Comparison Group Analysis of Hospital Patients." Journal of Occupational Medicine, v. 28, no. 12, December 1986, p. 1215-1218.** The authors examined the medical records and military personnel records of Vietnam veterans to determine if there is an association between Agent Orange exposure and soft tissue sarcoma. No statistically significant association could be found by the authors.

1112 Kansas. Department of Health and Environment. Veterans' Exposure to Chemical Agents, Including Agent Orange (Update): Report to the Governor and Legislature (See 1569)

1113 **Kaye, C.I. et al. "Evaluation of Chromosomal Damage in Males Exposed to Agent Orange and Their Families." Journal of Craniofacial Genetics and Developmental Biology, Supplement 1, 1985, p. 259-265.** The authors present the cases of 10 families where the father was exposed to Agent Orange while serving in Vietnam. Ten children born to these fathers after their exposure to Agent Orange had birth defects. However, no consistent pattern of anomalies was detected. When compared with their unexposed relatives, six of the ten fathers had increased chromosome breakage.

1114 **Kayser, K. et al. "Chronic Progredient Diffuse Alveolar Damage Probably Related to Exposure to Herbicides."**

Klinische Wochenschrift, v. 64, no. 1, January 1986, p. 44-
48. The authors present the case of a Vietnam veteran who
had been exposed to herbicides and now has severe lung tissue
damage which the authors believe may partly be the result of
the exposure to herbicides.

1115 Klein, R. "The Poison Orange." In Wounded Men and Broken
Promises. New York: Macmillan, 1981, p. 154-182. The
personal stories of several veterans suffering from ill
effects due to exposure to Agent Orange are given. The
unwillingness of the Veterans Administration to compensate
these veterans is commented upon.

1116 Kogan, M. and R. Clapp. "Mortality Among Vietnam Veterans
in Massachusetts, 1972-1983." [abstract] American Journal of
Epidemiology, v. 122, no. 3, September 1985, p. 523. This
paper was presented at the 18th annual meeting of the Society
for Epidemiologic Research. The authors did a study
comparing mortality among Massachusetts Vietnam veterans to
mortality among other veterans who did not serve in Vietnam
and all other white males who died between 1972 and 1983.
Mortality due to soft tissue sarcoma and stroke was
significantly higher in Vietnam-era veterans when compared to
the other two groups. Mortality due to motor vehicle
accidents, suicides, etc. and kidney cancer in these veterans
was also higher when compared to the other two groups.

1117 Kogan, M.D. and R.W. Clapp. Mortality Among Vietnam
Veterans in Massachusetts, 1972-1983. Boston: Massachusetts
Commission of Veterans Services. Agent Orange Program,
January 18, 1985. 28p. This study was conducted at the
request of the Massachusetts Agent Orange Program in order to
compare the causes of death among Vietnam veterans to those
of non-Vietnam veterans and non-veteran Massachusetts
residents. Among Vietnam veterans there were higher rates of
deaths due to motor vehicle accidents, suicides, kidney
cancer, stroke, and connective tissue cancer.

1118 Korgeski, G.P. Psychological, Neuropsychological and Medical
Correlates of Self-reported and Objective Ratings of
Herbicide Exposure Among Vietnam Veterans. Ph.D. Diss.,
University of Minnesota, 1981. Ann Arbor: UMI, 1981. 82-
11495. 157p. The author chose at random 100 subjects
requesting "Agent Orange screening exams" at a Veterans
Administration hospital. Based on his study of these
subjects, the author concludes that Agent Orange exposure may
be a way for veterans to explain their psychological and
medical symptoms and that the pervasive and vague nature of
their complaints may be more a function of personality
traits, especially hypochondrial traits, rather than of
actual exposure to Agent Orange.

1119   Korgeski, G.P. and G.R. Leon. "Correlates of Self-reported
       and Objectively Determined Exposure to Agent Orange."
       American Journal of Psychiatry, v. 140, no. 11, November
       1983, p. 1443-1449. One hundred veterans were given
       objective psychological tests to determine if their exposure
       to Agent Orange was the cause of their self-reported
       psychological problems. Attempts were made to determine if
       the veterans were actually exposed to Agent Orange or if the
       veterans just thought they were exposed. No correlation
       could be found between exposure and neuropsychological or
       psychological problems. The authors feel the self-reported
       medical problems could be psychosomatic.

1120   Kreul, K. "No Time to Rest." (See 1573)

1121   Kriebel, D. "Dioxins: Toxic and Still Troublesome."
       Environment, v. 23, no. 1, January/February 1981, p. 6-13.
       This paper addresses the following issues concerning dioxins:
       are they being created in significant quantities through
       combustion, what will happen to the dioxin already in the
       environment and are dioxins causing genetic damage to humans?
       The health effects of the use of Agent Orange on veterans and
       on the Vietnamese are briefly mentioned as part of this
       discussion.

1122   Kuntz, A.J. and W.F. Page. "Morbidity Among Vietnam Era
       Veterans." American Statistical Association. Social
       Statistics Section. Proceedings, 1981, p. 428-430. The
       authors examined the information collected from exams given
       in Veterans Administration medical centers. Skin problems
       turned out to be the most prevalent problem. Mental problems
       were the second.

1123   Lakshman, M.R. et al. "Absorption, Distribution and
       Metabolism of 2,3,7,8-tetrchlorodibenzo-para-dioxin (TCDD),
       the Toxic Contaminant of Agent Orange." [abstract]
       Federation Proceedings, v. 44, no. 4, March 5, 1985, p. 1117.
       The authors studied the absorption and distribution of TCDD
       in the liver and adipose tissue. They found that the liver
       was the major site of metabolism of TCDD and they found a
       negligible rate of TCDD disappearance in adipose tissue.

1124   Lathrop, G.D. et al. Air Force Health Study (Project RANCH
       HAND II). An Epidemiologic Investigation of Health Effects
       in Air Force Personnel Following Exposure to Herbicides.
       Baseline Morbidity Study Results. Interim Report. 1979-
       1982. February 24, 1984. 362p. Available from NTIS: AD-A
       138 340/5. In a study of Operation Ranch Hand personnel and
       comparison individuals, it was concluded that there is
       insufficient evidence to support a cause and effect

relationship between herbicide exposure and adverse health in
the Ranch Hand group.

1125   Lathrop, G.D. et al. "An Epidemiologic Investigation of
        Health Effects in Air Force Personnel Following Exposure to
        Herbicides." In Biological Mechanisms of Dioxin Action.
        (Banbury Report, no. 18) Ed. by A. Poland and R.D.
        Kimbrough. Cold Spring Harbor, N.Y.: Cold Spring Harbor
        Laboratory, 1984, p. 471-474. The authors explain how the
        Ranch Hand II epidemiologic study is being conducted. The
        baseline report concludes that a cause and effect
        relationship between herbicide exposure and adverse health in
        the Ranch Hand group can not be supported at this time due to
        insufficient evidence. Ranch Handers should be reassured by
        these results.

1126   Lathrop, G.D. et al. Epidemiologic Investigation of Health
        Effects in Air Force Personnel Following Exposure to
        Herbicides: Baseline Questionnaires. November 1982. 287p.
        Available from NTIS: A121 285/1. The questionnaires
        presented in this paper were used as part of the morbidity
        portion of the Air Force's study of the Operation Ranch Hand
        veterans.

1127   Lathrop, G.D. et al. Epidemiologic Investigation of Health
        Effects in Air Force Personnel Following Exposure to
        Herbicides: Study Protocol. December 1982. 198p.
        Available from NTIS: AD-A122 250/4. This report outlines
        the protocol that will be used for the Air Force's
        epidemiological study of the Operation Ranch Hand veterans.

1128   Lathrop, G.D. et al. Project RANCH HAND II. An
        Epidemiological Investigation of Health Effects in Air Force
        Personnel Following Exposure to Herbicides: Baseline
        Mortality Study Results. June 30, 1983. 70p. Available
        from NTIS: AD-A130 793/3. Reprinted in Dioxin: the Impact
        on Human Health. U.S. Congress. House. Committee on
        Science and Technology. Subcommittee on Natural Resources,
        Agriculture Research and Environment. Hearing, 98th Cong.,
        1st sess., June 30, July 13, 28, 1983. Washington: GPO,
        1984, p. 183-252. This report presents the baseline
        mortality results for the Ranch Hand Veterans Study. As of
        December 31, 1982, 50 Ranch Hand and 250 comparison
        subjects had died. The authors stress that this report
        should not be considered conclusively negative since the
        study population may not have yet reached the latency period.

1129   LaVecchio, F.A., H.M. Pashayan and W. Singer. "Agent Orange
        and Birth Defects." [letter] New England Journal of
        Medicine, v. 308, no. 12, March 24, 1983, p. 719-720. This

letter reports the analysis of 327 telephone calls for information placed to the Massachusetts Chapter of the Agent Orange Victims International's Advocacy Center. Of the 268 children of the 158 veterans reporting having children, 37 percent were reported to be "not normal." The authors also call for controlled epidemiological studies concerning birth defects in the children of Vietnam veterans.

1130 LaVecchio, F.A., H. Pashayan and W. Singer. "Agent Orange and Birth Defects." [letter] New England Journal of Medicine, v. 309, no. 8, August 25, 1983, p. 492. The authors of this letter reply to a letter by W.R. Gaffey (See 1072). They reply that they realize that their sample was biased and that there are conflicting results in the studies that have already been done. They hope their comments promote a collaborative effort among clinicians and a clinical-research methodology.

1131 Lawrence, C.E. et al. "Mortality Patterns of New York State Vietnam Veterans." American Journal of Public Health, v. 75, no. 3, March 1985, p. 277-279. The authors compared the deaths of veterans with Vietnam service who died in New York state to veterans of the Vietnam-era with no Vietnam service. The authors found no significant disease differences between Vietnam veterans and other veterans of that era and no indication of association with cause of death and exposure to herbicides in Vietnam.

1132 Lee, L.E. and L.B. Hobson. "2,3,7,8-Tetrachlorodibenzo-p-dioxin (TCDD) in Body Fat of Vietnam Veterans and Other Men." In Chlorinated Dioxins and Dibenzofurans in the Total Environment II, ed. by L.H. Keith, C. Rappe and G. Choudhary. Stoneham, MA: Butterworth Publ., 1985, p. 197-204. The authors conducted a feasibility trial study to determine if TCDD could still be found in Vietnam veterans who were exposed to Agent Orange a decade or so after the exposure. The authors found that their assay did not offer a satisfactory routine test for exposure to Agent Orange. Their results from gas chromatography-mass spectrometry could not prove Agent Orange exposure.

1133 Lewis, R. "Dioxin Danger (?)." Biology Digest, v. 11, no. 1, September 1984, p. 11-24. What is known about the health effects of exposure to TCDD is reviewed. Times Beach, Seveso, Midland, Michigan and Vietnam veterans' exposure to Agent Orange are all mentioned.

1134 Linedecker, C. with M. Ryan and M. Ryan. Kerry: Agent Orange and an American Family. New York: St. Martin's Pr., 1982. 240p. This book tells the story of Kerry Ryan who was

born with multiple birth defects. Her father was exposed to
Agent Orange while serving in Vietnam. After learning about
what symptoms others exposed to Agent Orange had, the Ryans
came to believe that the reason why their daughter was born
with such serious birth defects was that the father had been
exposed to Agent Orange in Vietnam. Also told is the story
of how the Ryans joined with other veterans and lawyers to
attempt to win recognition from the federal government that
Agent Orange is the source of their disabilities.

1135   Lipson, A. "Agent Orange and Birth Defects." [letter] New
       England Journal of Medicine, v. 309, no. 8, August 25, 1983,
       p. 491. The author reports that an independent investigation
       of Australian Vietnam veterans found no evidence that Army
       service in Vietnam was related to the risk of fathering a
       child with birth defects.

1136   Lipson, A. "Agent Orange and Birth Defects (Continued)."
       [letter] New England Journal of Medicine, v. 310, no. 10,
       March 8, 1984, p. 653-654. The author replies to a letter by
       J.D. Constable and M.C. Hatch (See 1028) and states that a
       recent study of handlers of 2,4,5,trichloropenoxyacetic acid
       concluded that an association between herbicide exposure and
       birth defects was unlikely.

1137   "Long-term Toxicity of Dioxin Still Unclear." Chemical and
       Engineering News, v. 60, no. 5, February 1, 1982, p. 19. The
       American Medical Association has recently published a report
       on the health effects of Agent Orange and other herbicides
       contaminated by polychlorinated dioxins. The report
       concludes that there is still no conclusive evidence that
       these herbicides are mutagenic, carcinogenic, or teratogenic
       in man, nor that they have caused reproductive difficulties
       in humans.

1138   McCarthy, F. "Agent Orange." [letter] American Journal of
       Forensic Medicine and Pathology, v. 4, no. 2, June 1983, p.
       191-192. This letter was written to rebut a letter written
       by F.H. Tschirley (See 1231) which was written in response to
       an article by L.G. Tedeschi (See 1225) in the June 1980 issue
       of this journal. F. McCarthy wrote to support L.G. Tedeschi
       and mentions the American Medical Association's report on
       Agent Orange.

1139   McDaniel, H.G. "The Agent Orange Controversy." [letter]
       Alabama Journal of Medical Sciences, v. 17, no. 3-4, July-
       October 1980, p. 256-257. In this letter the author notes
       the study of the Ranch Hand veterans that is being conducted
       and examinations that are being performed at Veterans
       Administration health clinics. It is the author's belief

that Agent Orange was not a significant health hazard to
soldiers who served in Vietnam. The medical profession
should reassure those who seek advice and encourage them to
participate in the Veterans Administration's examinations.

1140 **McKinley, T.W. Georgia Agent Orange Survey of Vietnam
Veterans: Summary.** Atlanta: Georgia Department of Human
Resources, July 1983. i, 8p. This report details the
findings of a questionnaire survey conducted by the Georgia
Department of Human Resources of Vietnam veterans now
residing in the state of Georgia who were exposed to Agent
Orange during the Vietnam War.

1141 **MacPhee, D.M. and W. Hall.** "Long-term Hazards of Exposure
to Environmental Chemicals: the Case of Vietnam Veterans and
Agent Orange." Search, v. 16, no. 5/6, June/July 1985, p.
146-148. The authors review what has been found out about
the relationship between exposure to Agent Orange and service
in Vietnam. It is known that the claims of veterans that
their offspring's birth defects were caused by exposure to
Agent Orange can be rejected, that the carcinogenic potential
of exposure to Agent Orange may be misplaced and that there
has not been an unexpected increase in mortality among
Vietnam veterans.

1142 **Magee, D.** "Long War of Wayne Felde." Nation, v. 234, no. 1,
January 2-9, 1982, p. 11-14. The story of Wayne Felde who
has been sentenced to death for the 1978 killing of a
Shreveport policeman, is given. It is felt that his behavior
problems may, in part, be due to exposure to Agent Orange in
Vietnam. The Veterans Administration has now been ordered
by the Congress to give priority treatment to Vietnam
veterans who may have been exposed to Agent Orange.

1143 Mahler, K. "Agent Orange Studies Continue at CDC." (See
1589)

1144 **Maiman, J.M.** "Veterans Need Compassion of Physicians in
Addressing Agent Orange Concerns." American Medical News,
v. 27, no. 12, March 23/30, 1984, p. 33. The debate on
whether Agent Orange has caused the health problems of some
Vietnam veterans is summarized. But regardless of the
outcome of the debate, the needs of these veterans are real
and immediate. The author calls on physicians to assume a
leadership role in seeing that these veterans and their
families are treated with compassion and given quality care
while they wait for answers on Agent Orange.

1145 **"Medical Society Offering Instruction on Agent Orange."**
American Medical News, v. 26, no. 33, September 9, 1983, p.

6. The Pennsylvania State Medical Society has established a physician education program to teach MDs how to detect, diagnose and treat Vietnam veterans who complain of illnesses the veterans believe to be caused by exposure to Agent Orange.

1146   Meier, B. "Agent Orange Study Fails to Quiet Debate on Birth-defect Issue." Wall Street Journal, August 17, 1984, p. 24(E), p. 25(W). Although the birth defects study does not show an overall increase in birth defects among offspring of Vietnam veterans, it does show an increase in certain defects such as spinal malformations and congenital tumors in offspring of veterans believed to have received the highest amount of exposure to Agent Orange. This finding has caused a lot of debate among scientists, lawyers and veterans. It will not affect the outcome of the out of court settlement.

1147   Meier, B. "Link Between Agent Orange, Birth Defects Isn't Found by Federal Study, Sources Say." Wall Street Journal, August 16, 1984, p. 2(E), p. 2(W). The results of the long awaited study on the children of Vietnam veterans will be released soon and will not show a conclusive link between birth defects and exposure of the fathers to Agent Orange in Vietnam.

1148   Mitter, N.S., L.I. Gardner and J. Welsh-Sloan. "A Previously Unreported De Novo Fragile Site [Fra(2)(Q37)] in a Boy with Developmental Delay, Hypotonia and Dysmorphism." Pediatric Research, v. 19, no. 4 pt. 2, April 1985, p. 251A. The father of the boy whose case history is noted in this abstract was exposed to Agent Orange in Vietnam. The boy at 21 months had hypertelorism, epidanthal folds, pectus excavatum, hammer-toe deformities of the great toes and a head that appeared small. His GTS-banded, peripheral cultured lympocytes revealed a karyotype of 46,XY,fra(2)(q37) while his parents had normal karotypes. In all of the cells examined, the fragility on chromosome 2 was present.

1149   Mulcahy, M.T. "Chromosome Aberrations and 'Agent Orange.'" [letter] Medical Journal of Australia, v. 2, no. 10, November 15, 1980, p. 573-574. The author examined several Vietnam veterans who claimed to have been exposed to Agent Orange in Vietnam to determine if this exposure resulted in chromosome damage. The author found that there was no higher level of chromosome damage in these men than in a control group.

1150   Musselman, K.G. "Patient Men Have Waited Too Long." (See 1616)

1151   Myers, P.W. "The Ranch Hand Health Effects Study." Air
       Force Policy Letter for Commanders. Supplement, November
       1980, p. 37-39. The text of the presentation made by the Air
       Force Surgeon General to the Subcommittee on Medical
       Facilities and Benefits of the House Veterans Affairs
       Committee on September 16, 1980 is given. Dr. Myers
       commented on the Air Force activities to date on the
       epidemiological study of the Ranch Hand personnel.

1152   "New Agent Orange Study: No Evidence of Birth Defects."
       Chemical and Engineering News, v. 62, no. 34, p. 6. The
       results of the Centers for Disease Control's study of the
       risks of Vietnam veterans, particularly those who may have
       been exposed to Agent Orange, in fathering children with
       birth defects have been released recently. It was found that
       when all types of birth defects are combined these veterans
       were no more likely than other men of fathering children with
       serious birth defects. However, certain types of birth
       defects were found more frequently than would be expected.

1153   "New Agent Orange Warning Urged by Veterans." (See 1622)

1154   "New Blood Test Can Measure Level of Dioxin." Air Force
       Times, v. 47, no. 45, June 22, 1987, p. 24. The Centers for
       Disease Control has developed a test which can determine the
       amount of dioxin that is remaining in the body fat of the
       Vietnam veterans who were exposed to Agent Orange. The Air
       Force's School of Aerospace Medicine is now using this test
       as part of its Ranch Hand II study.

1155   "New Jersey Agent Orange Commission Work Yields New Test
       for Dioxin Exposure." Congressional Record, v. 132, no. 141,
       October 14, 1986, p. E3613-E3614. Representative J.J. Florio
       (D-N.J.) again raised the issue of the findings of the New
       Jersey Agent Orange Commission which showed that high levels
       of dioxin can still be detected in veterans exposed to Agent
       Orange. Representative Florio had an article by E. Eckholm
       from the October 14, 1986 issue of the New York Times
       inserted in the Record.

1156   New Jersey. State Commission on Agent Orange. The Point Man
       Project on Agent Orange: Report to the New Jersey
       Legislature. Trenton, N.J.: The Commission, 1984. 16p.
       This booklet gives the protocol, in layman's language, of the
       Point Man project which is a study to measure the blood
       dioxin levels in Vietnam veterans who were heavily exposed to
       Agent Orange during the Vietnam War.

1157   New York (State). Department of Health. Dioxin Exposure:
       Report to the Governor & Legislature: Article 24-B, Public

Health Law. Albany, N.Y.: The Department, April 1982. 93p.
This report consists of an abstract and a report of progress
of three ongoing studies conducted by this department. They
are: a Vietnam veteran proportionate mortality study, an
epidemiological study of soft tissue sarcoma in men who are
aged in the range that would have made them eligible to serve
in Vietnam, and a study of exposure to herbicides by state
highway maintenance workers. The Department feels it is too
early to assess the impact of these studies. Complete
protocols for the studies are included in the appendices.

1158 New York (State). Temporary Commission on Dioxin Exposure.
      Interim Report. (See 1629)

1159 Newell, J. "New Research Links Agent Orange with Cancers."
      [editorial] New Scientist, v. 105, no. 1442, February 7,
      1985, p. 6. A study conducted by the Massachusetts
      Department of Health has found that Agent Orange could be the
      cause of cancer among Vietnam-era veterans.

1160 "No Health Danger Seen in Defoliant." Air Force Times, v.
      39, no. 14, October 30, 1978, p. 28. Major General D.
      Dettinger, the Air Force Deputy Surgeon General, in testimony
      before the House Veterans Affairs Subcommittee on Medical
      Affairs and Benefits stated that there are no serious long-
      term health effects from exposure to Agent Orange. He said
      that veterans complaining of chloracne, cancer, hypertension,
      loss of sex drive, etc. should look elsewhere to find the
      cause of their health problems.

1161 "No Increased Defect Rate for Vets' Offspring: CDC."
      American Medical News, v. 27, no. 32, August 24/31, 1984, p.
      10. The findings of a Centers for Disease Control report
      seem to indicate that Vietnam veterans do not have an
      increased risk for fathering children with major birth
      defects nor do veterans with greater estimated exposure to
      Agent Orange although this is based on weaker evidence than
      the conclusion about Vietnam veterans in general.

1162 "No Link Between Agent Orange and Birth Defects." Jet, v.
      66, no. 26, September 3, 1984, p. 33. The Centers for
      Disease Control has released the results of a study which
      shows that there is no link between fathers exposed to Agent
      Orange in Vietnam and birth defects in their children.
      However, the study did indicate there was a correlation
      between exposure and several specific types of cancer. The
      Centers for Disease Control stated this could be the result
      of chance. Veterans feel the study was biased as it was
      funded by the government and that not enough veterans'
      children were included in the study.

1163 Novack, B. and J. Fisher. "Agent Orange Exposure." [letter] Plastic and Reconstructive Surgery, v. 74, no. 4, October 1984, p. 577. The authors are requesting that anyone who has cared for patients exposed to Agent Orange displaying diffuse and aggressive patterns of basal cell carcinoma write to them as they know of two such patients.

1164 "Of Mice and Men." Environmental Action, v. 12, no. 3, September 1980, p. 14. A National Institute of Environmental Health Sciences study on mice exposed to Agent Orange in varying doses found no effect on fertility of male mice and no birth defects in offspring. Families of veterans exposed to Agent Orange contend that exposure to Agent Orange does cause birth defects.

1165 O'Toole, B.I. "The Feasibility of Ascertaining Exposure to Pesticides by Self Report in Australian Vietnam Veterans." Community Health Studies, v. 9, no. 2, 1985, p. 120-130. The author examined the possibility of developing a subjective measurement of exposure to herbicides and insecticides among Australian soldiers serving in Vietnam.

1166 O'Toole, B.I. et al. "A Comparison of Costs and Data Quality of Three Health Survey Methods: Mail, Telephone and Personal Home Interview." American Journal of Epidemiology, v. 124, no. 2, August 1986, p. 317-328. In order to study the effects of exposure of Australian Vietnam veterans to Agent Orange the authors examined what type of survey would ensure them of getting the best results. Of the 600 veterans studied, 200 received a self-administered questionnaire, 200 were interviewed by telephone and 200 were interviewed in their home. The costs were the lowest for the mail mode but items were omitted, produced less reliable results for questions about environmental exposure and underreporting of medical conditions. No mode differences were observed in the reliability of answers (which was high) to medical questions.

1167 Page, W.F., S.C. Gee and A.J. Kuntz. Protocol for the Vietnam Veteran Mortality Study. Washington: Veterans Administration, 1983. 111p. This document presents the original protocol of the proposed Vietnam Mortality Study and includes the background and experience of the authors up to the pilot study phase.

1168 Parson, E.R. "Narcissistic Injury in Vietnam Vets: the Role of Post-traumatic Stress Disorder, 'Agent Orange' Anxiety, and the Repatriation Experience." Stars and Stripes - the National Tribune, v. 105, no. 46, November 18, 1982, p. 1+. The author describes the symptoms of narcissistic injury and the three sources of narcissistic injury found in Vietnam

veterans: Post Traumatic Stress Disorder, Agent Orange
Anxiety and the Homecoming.

1169   **Pennsylvania. Vietnam Herbicides Information Commission.**
       <u>Toxic Herbicide Exposure (Agent Orange): the Physician's</u>
       <u>Resource</u>. Harrisburg, PA: The Commission, 1984. 8p. This
       document was prepared to assist physicians who are treating
       Vietnam veterans who may have been exposed to Agent Orange.
       Physicians are told about chloracne, the Veterans
       Administration's Agent Orange examination, and state and
       Veterans Administration services available to the
       Pennsylvania Vietnam veteran who was exposed to Agent
       Orange.

1170   **"Pentagon Disputes Link Between Herbicide Ailments."**
       <u>American Medical News,</u> v. 27, no. 12, March 23/30, 1984, p.
       33. The Air Force has released the results of their
       Operation Ranch Hand veterans study. The Air Force maintains
       that while Vietnam veterans who were exposed to Agent Orange
       have more health problems than normal, the defoliant cannot
       be clearly linked to the observed ailments. Not all
       scientists agree with the Air Force's conclusions.

1171   **Petryka, Z.J., C.A. Pierach and R.A. Codario. "HPLC Urinary**
       Porphyrins' Profiles After Exposure to 2,4-D and 2,4,5-T."
       [abstract] <u>Federation Proceedings</u>, v. 41, no. 4, March 5,
       1982, p. 1210. Reverse phase HPLC was used to analyze the
       urinary porphyrins in 73 urines of Vietnam veterans exposed
       to Agent Orange. Porphyrinuria was frequently found which
       probably reflects liver damage.

1172   "The Poisoned Trail of Agent Orange." (See 1659)

1173   **Pollak, J.K. "The Agent Orange Controversy."** [letter]
       <u>Medical Journal of Australia</u>, v. 146, no. 2, January 19,
       1987, p. 115. The author is responding to W. Hall's article
       of September 1, 1986 (See 1085) on the findings of the Evatt
       Royal Commission. The author of this letter points out some
       of the errors, misinformation and mistakes he believes the
       Evatt Royal Commission report contains.

1174   **Pollei, S. et al. "Follow-up Chest Radiographs in Vietnam**
       Veterans: Are They Useful?" <u>Radiology</u>, v. 161, no. 1,
       October 1986, p. 101-102. The question of whether those
       Americans who served in Vietnam show cardiovascular or
       pulmonary effects of that service that can be determined on
       long-term follow-up chest radiographs was examined. The
       authors found that the veterans did not suffer from an
       increased number of abnormalities that could be determined on
       follow-up chest radiographs. The subset of these veterans

who were probably exposed to Agent Orange also did not appear to be at a greater risk than the control population.

1175 **"Prejudice and Agent Orange."** [editorial] American Medical News, v. 24, no. 41, October 30, 1981, p. 4. Dr. G.H. Spivey, the leader of the University of California at Los Angeles research team which will design a study to examine whether or not exposure to Agent Orange is the cause of some Vietnam veterans' health problems, has testified before a California Assembly Legislative Committee that there is little evidence linking Agent Orange to human health problems. Veterans' groups would now like to oust Dr. Spivey. The editorial states as the study will be reviewed by independent scientific panels, Dr. Spivey should be allowed to design the study.

1176 **Preslan, M.W., G.R. Beauchamp and Z.N. Zakov. "Congenital Glaucoma and Retinal Dysplasia."** Journal of Pediatric Opthalmology and Strabismus, v. 22, no. 5, September/October 1985, p. 166-170. The case history of a one month old white male is given. The child has an enlarged eye, elevated intraocular pressure, prominent iris vasculature and leukocoria. The child is completely normal except for his left eye. He is the second child born to a Vietnam veteran who was exposed to Agent Orange.

1177 **Raloff, J. "Agent Orange and Birth Defects Risk."** Science News, v. 126, no. 8, August 25, 1984, p. 117. The findings of the Centers for Disease Control's study of the risk of birth defects posed by exposure to Agent Orange in Vietnam are mentioned. The study concludes that the total incidence of birth defects among children born to Vietnam veterans was not greater than other groups. However, a few specific diseases occurred with greater frequency than would have been expected. The author states that only "weak" conclusions concerning Agent Orange exposure are possible from this study.

1178 Raloff, J. "Agent Orange: What Isn't Settled." (See 2252)

1179 **Raloff, J. "Dioxin's 'Fingerprint' Lingers for Decades."** Science News, v. 130, no. 14, October 4, 1986, p. 212. Scientists have been able to prove that dioxin contamination remains in body fat for more than 20-30 years after exposure. This may help Vietnam veterans who were exposed to Agent Orange prove that their health problems are the result of that exposure.

1180 **"Ranch Hand Deaths Parallel Control Group's."** Air Force Times, v. 46, no. 24, December 30, 1985, p. 6. The Air

Force's study of Ranch Hand crew members continues to show that these crew members are not dying at a rate greater than men who were not exposed to Agent Orange.

1181   Reiches, N.A. and J.V. Gaeuman. Ohio Vietnam Veterans Medical Examination Reporting Program: Final Report. Columbus, Ohio: Ohio Board of Regents, January 1985. 19p. This report was submitted to the Ohio Agent Orange Advisory Council and examines the results from a survey of 155 Vietnam veterans about their exposure to Agent Orange. The Council decided against doing an exhaustive state study due to programmatic and methodological concerns and because of the epidemiological study being conducted by the Centers for Disease Control. This report also summarizes the findings of studies that have been conducted in other states, the Centers for Disease Control, and the Australian Department of Health and what is known about the toxicology of Agent Orange.

1182   Rellahan, W. The Agent Orange Program. (R & S Report no. 45) Honolulu, Hawaii: Hawaii State Department of Health. Research and Statistics Office, September 1983. 22p. The research being done by the State of Hawaii's Agent Orange Program is discussed. A survey conducted by this program has found that persons that believe they were exposed to Agent Orange in Vietnam suffer more health problems than those who are not sure if they were exposed or are sure they were not exposed.

1183   Rellahan, W. Aspects of the Health of Hawaii's Vietnam-era Veterans Reflecting the Impact of the Vietnam Experience. (R & S Report, no. 53) Honolulu, Hawaii: Hawaii State Department of Health. Research and Statistics Office, July 1985. 24p. The author surveyed 418 Vietnam-era veterans presently living in Hawaii and found that their health was significantly different from the health of those who have not served in the Vietnam theatre. The author also attempted to determine the extent to which the veterans had been exposed to Agent Orange.

1184   "Representative Kemp Cosponsors Bill to Assist Vietnam Veterans." (See 1682)

1185   Roby, E. "Dow Study Challenges Claims by Vets of Agent Orange Harm." Los Angeles Daily Journal, v. 93, no. 262, December 29, 1980, p. 2. The Dow Chemical Company has reported the result of a new statistical study which challenges the claims of veterans exposed to Agent Orange who have sired children who have birth defects due to that exposure. The study found no link between Dow employees exposed to dioxins and the outcome of pregnancies among the workers' wives.

1186 "Rochester Wife: 'We Thought My Husband Was a Survivor'..."
      Rochester Patriot, v. 8, no. 9, May 16, 1980, p. 2. A
      Rochester veteran took his life last Christmas morning. He
      had been suffering from symptoms similar to those other
      veterans had experienced due to Agent Orange exposure in
      Vietnam.

1187 Roehm, D.C. "Effects of a Program of Sauna Baths and
      Megavitamins of Adipose DDE and PCB's and on Clearing of
      Symptoms of Agent Orange (Dioxin) Toxicity." [abstract]
      Clinical Research, v. 31, no. 2, April 1983, p. 243A. A 33
      year old Vietnam veteran with a history of exposure to Agent
      Orange and suggestive resulting symptoms was placed on a 37
      day regimen of dry sauna, brisk muscular exercise, and
      vitamin and mineral dietary supplements. The treatment was
      rated as successful by the subject.

1188 Rose, S. "Defoliants, Herbicides and Racism." (See 0785)

1189 Royal Commission on the Use and Effects of Chemical Agents
      on Australian Personnel in Vietnam. Final Report. Canberra:
      Australian Government Publications Service, July 1985, 9v.
      In 1983 this Commission was established to inquire into the
      use and effects of chemical agents on Australian personnel in
      Vietnam and was headed by P.G. Evatt. The nine volumes of
      this report are: v. 1: Introduction and Exposure; v. 2:
      Toxicology and General Health; v. 3: Birth Anomalies; v. 4:
      Cancer; v. 5: Mental Well-being; v. 6: Mortality, Class
      Action VVAA and Section 47; v. 7: Benefits and Treatment; v.
      8: Conclusions, Recommendations and Epilogue; and v. 9:
      Exhibits and Bibliography. The main conclusion of the report
      is that Australian Vietnam veterans were not exposed to Agent
      Orange at dosage levels which would be likely to cause any
      long-term health effects. No valid scientific study has ever
      found a link between birth defects and the fathers' exposure
      to Agent Orange. The report also states that Agent Orange is
      not guilty and that this news should be shouted from the
      roof-tops.

1190 Rubin, L. and A. Davison. "Agent Orange: Effects Remain
      Long." In These Times, v. 2, no. 35, July 19, 1978, p. 15.
      Despite the claims of the Veterans Administration and the
      manufacturers of Agent Orange, medical researchers believe
      that the following are symptoms of exposure to dioxin:
      chloracne rash, liver abcesses, numbness in limbs,
      personality change, soreness in joints, miscarriage, still-
      births and birth defects in offspring. The only symptom the
      Veterans Administration acknowledges is chloracne.

1191 "A Rush to Judgement on Agent Orange Issue." (See 1692)

1192   Saracci, R. "Storm in a Cup of 2,4,5-T." [letter] Medical
        Journal of Australia, v. 144, no. 11, May 26, 1986, p. 611.
        This letter was written in order to clarify some of the
        points made by B.K. Armstrong in his March 17, 1986 article
        (See 0991) on the controversy surrounding the Evatt Royal
        Commission's report.

1193   Sarma, P.R. and J. Jacobs. "Thoracic Soft-tissue Sarcoma in
        Vietnam Veterans Exposed to Agent Orange." [letter] New
        England Journal of Medicine, v. 306, no. 18, May 6, 1982, p.
        1109. Reprinted in Citizen Soldier, no. 4, 1982, p. 5; in
        "Important New Data on Agent Orange." Congressional Record,
        v. 128, pt. 7, May 12, 1982, p. 9773; and in "Soft Tissue
        Cancers and Vietnam Veterans" Congressional Record, v. 128,
        no. 122, September 15, 1982, p. E4195-E4197. The authors
        tell in this letter about three Vietnam veterans exposed to
        Agent Orange who each have thoracic soft tissue sarcoma.

1194   Schacter, L. et al. "Adenocarcinoma of the Lung in Vietnam
        Veterans Younger Than 35 Years." [letter] JAMA, v. 251, no.
        5, February 3, 1983, p. 604. Two cases of adenocarcinoma of
        the lung in Vietnam veterans younger that 35 years are
        reported. These two cases may or may not be linked to
        herbicide exposure in Vietnam. Both were two-pack-a-day
        cigarette smokers.

1195   Schulz, C.O., P.K. LaGoy and M.B. Paxton. "Reviewing the
        Literature on the Health Effects of Phenoxy Herbicides and
        Associated Dioxins." Chemosphere, v. 15, no. 9-12, 1986, p.
        2099-2102. The authors review the nature and results of the
        literature search that was conducted for the Veterans
        Administration by Clement Associates, Inc. in order to
        compile volumes three and four of the "Review of Literature
        on Herbicides, Including Phenoxy Herbicides and Associated
        Dioxins."

1196   Sellar, J. "Agent Orange: Australian Study Continues."
        [editorial] Nature, v. 310, no. 5978, August 16, 1984, p.
        534. The studies underway by the Australian government to
        determine the effects of exposure to Agent Orange by the
        Australian Vietnam veteran are noted.

1197   Shepard, B.M. "Health-related Problems to TCDD." In
        Accidental Exposure to Dioxins: Human Health Aspects. Ed.
        by F. Coulston and F. Pocchiari. New York: Academic Pr.,
        1983, p. 229-230. This paper was presented at an
        International Forum on Human Health Aspects of Accidental
        Chemical Exposure to Dioxins -- Strategy for Environmental
        and Community Protection held in Bethesda, Maryland in
        October 1981. The authors mention some of the studies that

are being done on the health effects of exposure to Agent
Orange by Vietnam veterans. Discussion of the authors' paper
follows on pages 231-232.

1198   Shepard, B.M. and A.L. Young. "Dioxins as Contaminants of
        Herbicides: the U.S. Perspective." In Human and
        Environmental Risks of Chlorinated Dioxins and Related
        Compounds. Ed. by R.E. Tucker, A.L. Young and A.P. Gray.
        (Environmental Science Research, v. 26). New York: Plenum
        Pr., 1983, p. 3-11. This paper was presented at an
        International Symposium on Chlorinated Dioxins and Related
        Compounds which was held in 1981. The authors summarize the
        various health studies on the effects of the use of Agent
        Orange in Vietnam that are being conducted in the United
        States.

1199   Sherry, C.J. "Agent Orange. Why is Dioxin Dangerous?
        National Guard, v. 39, no. 2, February 1985, p. 16-18. This
        article examines what is known about the potential health
        effects of having been exposed to Agent Orange.

1200   Silbergeld, E.K. and D.R. Mattison. "Experimental and
        Clinical Studies on the Reproductive Technology of 2,3,7,8-
        tetrachlorodibenzo-p-dioxin." American Journal of Industrial
        Medicine, v. 11, no. 2, 1987, p. 131-144. As part of a
        review of the recent experimental and clinical studies of the
        effects of 2,3,7,8-tetrachlorodibenzodioxin on reproduction,
        what is known about the reproductive effects of exposure to
        Agent Orange on Vietnam veterans and the Vietnamese is noted.

1201   Silberner, J. "Common Herbicide Linked to Cancer." Science
        News v. 130, no. 11, September 13, 1986, p. 167+. A study
        has been conducted which has revealed a connection between
        exposure to 2,4-D and non-Hodgkin's lymphoma in Kansas
        farmers. Vietnam veterans will be interested in this study
        as 2,4-D is a component in Agent Orange. The Veterans
        Administration will be reviewing their Operation Ranch Hand
        crew members study to determine if anyone who has developed
        non-Hodgkin's lymphoma is due disability benefits.

1202   Smith, C. and D. Watkins. "Herbicide Alert." Short-timers
        Journal, no. 3, 1983, p. 8+. The story of Mike Rego, a
        Vietnam veteran who was exposed to Agent Orange, is told. He
        is suffering from pityriasis ruba pilaris, a relatively rare
        psoriasis-like disease.

1203   Smith, R.A. Politics and Science in Public Health Disputes:
        Two Case Studies of Public Advocacy Research. Ph.d. Diss.,
        State University of New York-Stony Brook, 1984. Ann Arbor:
        UMI, 1985. 85-15322. ix, 234, 71p. The impact of issue-

oriented public advocacy groups on public health policy and
the importance of including social factors in current
epidemiological investigations is discussed with specific
reference to two cases: the infant formula and Agent Orange
controversies. The role of institutional science and
scientists in public health disputes is also noted. The
results of a study commissioned by Citizen Soldier on the
possible adverse health effects of exposure to Agent Orange
are given.

1204 "Soft Tissue Cancers and Vietnam Veterans." (See 1710)

1205 Sommer, A. Birth Defects and Genetic Counseling.
Washington: GPO, 1985. 1 volume (various paginations).
This booklet was prepared by the Agent Orange Projects Office
of the Veterans Administration's Department of Medicine and
Surgery in order to give those (especially veterans who were
exposed to Agent Orange) concerned about the connection
between birth defects and human exposure to phenoxy
herbicides and dioxin a better understanding of this issue
and the etiology of birth defects. The findings of the
Centers for Disease Control's study of the risk of Vietnam
veterans fathering offspring with birth defects are
summarized.

1206 Stanley, J.S. et al. "Analytical Methods for Measurement of
Polychlorinated Dibenzo-p-dioxins (PCDDs) in Human Adipose
Tissue." American Chemical Society. Abstracts of Papers, v.
186, 1983, #ENVR 0054. In order to further the scientific
knowledge of the long-term health effects of exposure to
Agent Orange by Vietnam veterans the Environmental
Protection Agency's Office of Toxic Substances and the
Veterans Administration are working cooperatively to identify
analytical methods for detecting PCDDs in human adipose
tissue.

1207 Stanley, T. "Vietnam Veterans." [letter] Australian and New
Zealand Journal of Psychiatry, v. 16, no. 3, September 1982,
p. 196-197. The author believes that the psychiatric
problems several of the Vietnam veterans he has treated have
are connected to Agent Orange exposure.

1208 Stellman, S.D. "VA Registrants Exposed to Agent Orange."
[letter] Chemical and Engineering News, v. 61, no. 49,
December 5, 1983, p. 4+. The author feels the data gathered
from the Agent Orange Registry should not be used to make
definitive conclusions about the effects of exposure to Agent
Orange.

1209 Stellman, S.D. and J.M. Stellman. "Estimation of Exposure to
Agent Orange and Other Defoliants Among American Troops

in Vietnam: a Methodological Approach." <u>American Journal of Industrial Medicine</u>, v. 9, no. 4, 1986, p. 305-321. Reprinted in U.S. Congress. House. Committee on Veterans Affairs, Subcommittee on Hospitals and Health Care. <u>Agent Orange Studies</u>. Hearing, 99th Cong., 2nd sess., July 31, 1986. Washington: GPO, 1986, p. 115-131. Based on the Department of Defense's HERBs tapes the authors have developed a probability exposure index in order to classify the likelihood of exposure to herbicides in South Vietnam. This index would be well suited in determining exposure to herbicides in South Vietnam as part of future epidemiological studies on Vietnam veterans who were exposed to Agent Orange.

1210   Stellman, S. and J. Stellman. "Health Problems Among 535 Vietnam Veterans Potentially Exposed to Toxic Herbicides." [abstract] <u>American Journal of Epidemiology</u>, v. 112, no. 3, September 1980, p. 444. The results of a nationwide mail survey which was conducted among 535 Vietnam veterans are noted. One-third of the men reported skin conditions such as recurrent acne. Congenital anomalies in men fathering at least one child after service in Vietnam were nearly twice as great among the men with these skin conditions as among those without these conditions.

1211   Sterling, T.D. and A. Arundel. "The C.D.C. Birth Defects Study: a Critique." <u>Citizen Soldier</u>, no. 8, April 1985, p. 5. The authors agree that the Centers for Disease Control's study shows that there is not a link between service in Vietnam and birth defects in the servicemen's offspring but do not agree with the conclusion that there is no evidence of a link between Vietnam veterans' exposure to Agent Orange and birth defects in their offspring.

1212   Sterling, T.D. and A.L. Arundel. "Health Effects of Phenoxy Herbicides: a Review." (See 0794)

1213   Sterling, T.D. and A. Arundel. "Vietnam Veterans Risk for Fathering Children with Birth Defects." [letter] <u>JAMA</u>, v. 254, no. 5, August 2, 1985, p. 609. The authors of this letter express concern that Erickson <u>et al</u>. (<u>JAMA</u>, August 17, 1984. See 1058) have used the results of their study on the possible link between service in Vietnam and birth defects in servicemen's offspring to prove that there is no link between Agent Orange and birth defects in the offspring of Vietnam veterans. Erickson's study shows an increase in cleft palate and spina bifida in the offspring of Vietnam veterans possibly exposed to Agent Orange.

1214   Stevens, K.M. "Agent Orange Toxicity: a Quantitative

Perspective." Human Toxicology, v. 1, no. 1, 1981, p. 31-39.
The author quantitatively examined the data concerning the
exposure of Vietnam veterans to Agent Orange and has
concluded that the dioxin in Agent Orange could not have
caused systematic illnesses in the veterans or birth defects
in their children.

1215   Strahan, R. "Agent Orange." [editorial] Search, v. 11, no.
3, March 1980, p. 49. This editorial suggests that males
subject to the draft for Vietnam but not called up would make
a near-perfect control group for a study to measure the
effects of Agent Orange exposure.

1216   Strange, J.R. and W.E. Kerr. "Teratogenic and Toxicological
Examination on 2,4,5-T in Developing Chick Embryos."
Toxicology, v. 6, no. 1, June 1976, p. 35-40. Chick embryos
and fertilized chick eggs were exposed to 2,4,5-T. No
teratological or developmental anomalies were found when
serial sections of sacrificed embryos were examined. This
study was conducted due to the concern over the use of Agent
Orange in Vietnam.

1217   "Studies Conflict on Herbicide's Role in Birth Defects."
(See 0796)

1218   "Studies of the Texas Agent Orange Commission Issued."
National Vietnam Veterans Review, v. 4, no. 4, April 1984, p.
3. The preliminary findings of three studies conducted by
the University of Texas in conjunction with the Texas
Department of Health on Vietnam veterans exposed to Agent
Orange are given. There was no difference found between the
percent of cells with chromosome breaks or the number of
breaks per cell between Vietnam veterans and matched
controls. No difference between the number of sperm,
appearance of sperm or fluorescent bodies of sperm between
Vietnam veterans and matched controls was found. The percent
of active T-RFC was higher among veterans than among
controls.

1219   "Study Should 'Reassure' Agent Orange Participants." Air
Force Times, v. 44, no. 34, March 12, 1984, p. 10. A study
conducted at the Air Force's School of Aerospace Medicine at
Brooks Air Force Base, Texas has concluded that there are
only minor differences between the health of aircrew and
ground crew members exposed to Agent Orange and that of a
control group not exposed. The Ranch Hand veterans had
slightly more skin cancers, liver diseases and a lower self-
perception of health. There were also more neonatal deaths
among veterans' children.

1220 "Symposium Updates Health Effects of Dioxins, Benzofurans."
Chemical and Engineering News, v. 61, no. 37, September 12,
1983, p. 26-30. Reprinted in "Agent Orange Studies."
Congressional Record, v. 129, no. 128, September 29, 1983, p.
S13218-S13225. In part, a detailed discussion of the report
presented by A.L. Young of the Veterans Administration's
Agent Orange Project Office at the recent American Chemical
Society's meeting in Washington, D.C. The report details the
results of a study comparing the health of approximately
85,000 veterans who served in Vietnam. The results of the
study indicate that the veterans on the Veterans
Administration's Agent Orange Registry seem to be as healthy
as other United States men of the same age.

1221 Tamburro, C.H. and B. Miller. "Etiological Factors in
Chronic Liver Injury in Phenoxy Herbicide Exposed Vietnam
Veterans." [abstract] Hepatology, v. 6, no. 4, July-August
1986, p. 785. The authors examined the cases of 100 veterans
who had hepatotoxic injury and who had applied to the Agent
Orange Registry. They concluded that in these cases the
veterans' chronic liver abnormalities were due to viral or
alcoholic causality and not to exposure to herbicides and
their TCDD contaminant.

1222 Tamburro, C.H. and B. Miller. "Etiological Factors in
Chronic Liver Injury in Vietnam Veterans Exposed to Agent
Orange." [abstract] Hepatology, v. 5, no. 5, September-
October 1985, p. 990. The authors studied hepatotoxic injury
in Vietnam veterans who reported they were exposed to Agent
Orange and concluded that the chronic liver abnormalities
among the veterans applying to the Agent Orange Registry are
mainly due to viral or alcoholic causality and not to
exposure to Agent Orange.

1223 Tedeschi, L.G. "Agent Orange." [letter] American Journal of
Forensic Medicine and Pathology, v. 4, no. 2, June 1983, p.
192. The author replies to the letters by F.H. Tschirley
(See 1231) and F. McCarthy (See 1138) which were written in
response to his June 1980 article (See 1225) by commenting on
the widely divergent opinion on the Agent Orange issue.

1224 Tedeschi, L.G. "Agent Orange: Update." American Journal of
Forensic Medicine and Pathology, v. 4, no. 4, December 1983,
p. 319-321. In the time since the author wrote his review on
dioxin in the June 1980 issue of this journal, the difficulty
in extracting true scientific data from emotionalism and
sensationalism remains. The author reviews the results of
studies that have been published in the last few years and
believes that more definitive and conclusive studies need
still to be done before this issue can be put to rest.

1225 Tedeschi, L.G. "Dioxin: a Case in Point." <u>American Journal</u>
       <u>of Forensic Medicine and Pathology</u>, v. 1, no. 2, June 1980,
       p. 145-148. The toxic results of the spraying of Agent
       Orange in Vietnam are detailed. Complete acceptance by
       medical and governmental communities has been spotty, slow
       and inconsistent which has led to a feeling of frustration
       and futility for the Agent Orange victims. The government
       needs to create an Agent Orange registry.

1226 Texas. Department of Health. Texas Veterans Agent Orange
       Assistance Program. <u>Annual Report - 1983</u>. (See 1740)

1227 Texas. Department of Health. Texas Veterans Agent Orange
       Assistance Program. <u>Annual Report - 1985</u>. (See 1741)

1228 Theiler, P. "A Vietnam Aftermath: the Untold Story of Women
       and Agent Orange." <u>Common Cause</u>, v. 10, no. 6, November-
       December 1984, p. 28-34. Women who went to Vietnam as
       nurses, Red Cross workers and served in other capacities may
       have been exposed to Agent Orange. These women are being
       ignored in the debate over whether or not the health problems
       of those who went to Vietnam are caused by exposure to Agent
       Orange. The Centers for Disease Control's study will not
       included any of these women. The efforts women veterans and
       women who served in Vietnam as civilians are making to get
       the government to listen to them and their health problems
       are described.

1229 Thomasson, W.A. "Deadly Legacy: Dioxin and the Vietnam
       Veteran." <u>Bulletin of the Atomic Scientists</u>, v. 35, no. 5,
       May 1979, p. 15-19. What little is known about the health
       effects Vietnam veterans exposed to Agent Orange might be is
       noted.

1230 Trojan, J. "Front Row Center." <u>Wilson Library Bulletin</u>, v.
       57, no. 1, September 1982, p. 64-65. One of the reviewed
       films is Jim Gamborne's <u>Agent Orange: a Story of Dignity and</u>
       <u>Doubt</u> which tells the story of several veterans who were
       exposed to Agent Orange while serving in Vietnam. Particular
       attention is paid to the Ted Tallas family. Ted has severe
       skin lesions and has fathered several deformed babies, now
       dead, and a disabled son. The daughter conceived before he
       went to Vietnam is healthy.

1231 Tschirley, F.H. "Agent Orange." [letter] <u>American Journal</u>
       <u>of Forensic Medicine and Pathology</u>, v. 4, no. 2, June 1983,
       p. 190-191. This letter was written in response to L.G.
       Tedeschi's article (See 1225) which appeared in the June 1980
       issue of this journal. Tschirley wished to correct what he
       felt were several inaccuracies in Tedeschi's article.

1232   Uhl, M. "What Do You Have to Do to Prove You're Sick?
        Die?" Win, v. 16, no. 8, May 15, 1980, p. 8-11. This
        article consists of letters sent to the author from veterans
        and veterans' wives detailing the veterans' physical and
        mental problems and the birth defects of their children which
        they believe to be caused as a result of the veterans being
        exposed to Agent Orange.

1233   Uhl, M. and T. Ensign. "Blowing the Whistle on Agent
        Orange." (See 1748)

1234   U.S. Centers for Disease Control. Protocol for Epidemiologic
        Studies of the Health of Vietnam Veterans. Atlanta: Centers
        for Disease Control, November 1983. 101p. The protocols for
        three studies that the Centers for Disease Control proposed
        to conduct are presented. The three studies are: Cohort
        Study of the Long-term Effects of Exposure to Agent Orange in
        Vietnam, Cohort Study of the Long-term Health Effects of
        Military Service in Vietnam, and Case-control Study to
        Determine the Risks for Selected Cancers Among Vietnam
        Veterans.

1235   U.S. Congress. House. Committee on Science and Technology,
        Subcommittee on Natural Resources, Agriculture Research and
        Environment. Dioxin: the Impact on Human Health. Hearing,
        98th Cong., 1st sess., June 30, July 13, 28, 1983.
        Washington: GPO, 1984. iii, 252p. This hearing was held to
        evaluate the available evidence on the effects of dioxin on
        human health. Pages 27-69 contain the testimony of Dr. B.
        Shepard, Veterans Administration; L. Hobson and Maj. A.
        Young, Air Force; J. Moore, National Institute of
        Environmental Health Studies; Dr. V. Houk and Dr. R.
        Kimbrough, Centers for Disease Control, about the studies
        underway on the effects of exposure to Agent Orange on the
        Vietnam veteran. The witnesses responded to questions from
        the members of the subcommittee. Pages 148-181 contain the
        testimony of J. Sommer and P. Egin, American Legion; L.
        Milford, National Veterans Law Center, Maj. General M.
        Chesterton, Air Force; and Maj. J. Spey, Ranch Hand Vietnam
        Association, about the studies underway on the effects of
        exposure to Agent Orange on the Vietnam veteran.

1236   U.S. Congress. House. Committee on Veterans' Affairs,
        Subcommittee on Hospitals and Health Care. Centers for
        Disease Control Birth Defects Study. Hearing, 98th Cong.,
        2nd sess., October 3, 1984. Washington: GPO, 1984. iii,
        90p. The Subcommittee met to hear testimony from the Centers
        for Disease Control, the Office of Technology Assessment and
        the Science Panel of the Agent Orange Working Group
        concerning the report entitled "Vietnam Veterans' Risk for

Fathering Babies with Birth Defects." Also included is a
review of the article which appeared in the August 17, 1984
issue of JAMA (See 1058) and full report by the Office of
Technology Assessment. The Office basically supports the
report and finds no justification for initiating more studies
at this time.

1237 U.S. Congress. House. Committee on Veterans' Affairs,
      Subcommittee on Medical Facilities and Benefits.
      Herbicide "Agent Orange". Hearing, 95th Cong., 2nd sess.,
      October 11, 1978. Washington: GPO, 1979. iii, 62p. This
      hearing was held by the Subcommittee because of their concern
      about the possible adverse health effects exposure to Agent
      Orange may have had on Vietnam veterans. Testimony was
      heard from various officials of the Executive Branch.

1238 U.S. Congress. House. Committee on Veterans' Affairs,
      Subcommittee on Medical Facilities and Benefits. Oversight
      Hearing to Receive Testimony on Agent Orange. Hearing, 96th
      Cong., 2nd sess., February 25, 1980. Washington: GPO, 1980.
      iii, 121p. This hearing was held to receive testimony of
      officials from various offices of the Executive Branch to
      determine what has been learned and done since the meeting
      held by the Subcommittee on October 11, 1978.

1239 U.S. Congress. House. Committee on Veterans' Affairs,
      Subcommittee on Medical Facilities and Benefits. Oversight
      Hearing to Receive Testimony on Agent Orange. Hearing, 96th
      Cong., 2nd sess., July 22, 1980. Washington: GPO, 1981. v,
      459p. This is the third oversight hearing the Subcommittee
      has held on the Agent Orange issue. Testimony was heard from
      two congressmen, scientists and representatives of veterans'
      organizations. Those testifying focused on whether exposure
      to dioxin causes health problems in humans.

1240 U.S. Congress. House. Committee on Veterans' Affairs,
      Subcommittee on Medical Facilities and Benefits. Scientific
      Community Report on Agent Orange. Hearing, 96th Cong., 2nd
      sess., September 16, 1980. Washington: GPO, 1981. iii,
      145p. This hearing was the fourth of a series of hearings
      the Subcommittee held on the Agent Orange. Testimony at this
      hearing focused on the most current scientific information
      concerning the possible long-term health effects of exposure
      to dioxin.

1241 U.S. Environmental Protection Agency. Advisory Committee on
      2,4,5-T. Report of the Advisory Committee on 2,4,5-T to the
      Administrator of the Environmental Protection Agency.
      Washington: GPO, May 7, 1971. 2, 76p. This Committee was
      given the charge of examining whether or not the use of

2,4,5-T does in fact constitute an imminent health hazard
especially to pregnant women. Pages 51-58 and 71-72 examine
the issue of the reports of increased occurrence of
congenital malformations and/or stillbirths in human beings
as a result of the military use of 2,4,5-T in Vietnam. The
Committee concludes that 2,4,5-T as presently produced and as
applied according to regulations in force prior to April
1970, represents no hazard to human reproduction.

1242 **U.S. General Accounting Office.** Health Effects of Exposure
to Herbicide Orange in South Vietnam Should Be Resolved.
(Its Report to Congress - H). Washington: General
Accounting Office, 1979. 38p. This report recommends that
the Department of Defense with the assistance of an
interagency group conduct a survey of any long-term effects
on military personnel who were likely to have been exposed to
herbicides in South Vietnam. The report details what is
known about the health effects of TCDD and the federal
response to the herbicide concerns of Vietnam veterans.

1243 **U.S. Veterans Administration.** Review of Literature on
Herbicides, Including Phenoxy Herbicides and Associated
Dioxins. Washington: GPO, 1981- . This set of reports
which was prepared by JRB Associates and then by Clement
Associates under contract from the Veterans Administration
critically reviews the worldwide literature on all of the
herbicides used in Vietnam and to present a balanced and
critical review. An annotated bibliography is provided with
each review. There are presently eight volumes in the set.

1244 **U.S. Veterans Administration.** Synopsis of Scientific
Literature on Phenoxy Herbicides and Associated Dioxins.
Washington: GPO, 1985- . These volumes summarize in
laymen's terms the information found in Review of Literature
on Herbicides, Including Phenoxy Herbicides and Associated
Dioxins and were prepared for the Veterans Administration by
Clement Associates. The emphasis in these volumes is on the
health problems that have associated with exposure to Agent
Orange. There are presently three volumes in the set.

1245 U.S. Veterans Administration. Worried About Agent Orange?
(See 1782)

1246 U.S. Veterans Administration. Advisory Committee on Health-
Related Effects of Herbicides. Transcript of Proceedings,
1st - 25th Meetings (See 1787-1811)

1247 U.S. Veterans Administration. Veterans' Advisory Committee
on Environmental Hazards. [Transcript and Minutes of the
Meetings of the Committee and Scientific Council] (See 1814-
1820)

1248 "Update: Health-Orange Alert." (See 0814)

1249 **"Veterans Criticize Study on Agent Orange."** <u>American Medical
       News</u>, v. 26, no. 25, July 1-8, 1983, p. 19. The preliminary
       findings of the Air Force's study of Ranch Hand veterans
       indicate that they are not dying at a significantly higher
       rate than a control group. Veterans' organizations disagree
       with the findings. V. Yannacone, Jr. called the study "...a
       patent fraud."

1250 "Veterans Form Agent Orange Task Force." (See 1854)

1251 **"Viet Vets Study."** <u>CBS News Daily News Broadcasts</u>, new ser.,
       v. 11, no. 28, p. 17 (morning news). State Representative
       Vallely of Massachusetts discusses the results of a study on
       the death rates of white Vietnam veterans in Massachusetts.

1252 **"Vietnam Veteran Study Begins in February."** <u>American Legion
       Magazine</u>, v. 116, no. 1, January 1984, p. 27. The final part
       of the Columbia University-American Legion Study of Vietnam
       Era Veterans will begin this month. The primary researchers
       are Drs. S. and J. Stellman. Exposure to Agent Orange is one
       of the issues that will be examined in the survey.

1253 "Vietnam Veterans and Agent Orange." <u>Congressional Record</u>,
       March 25, 1980 (See 1873)

1254 **"Vietnam Veterans' Risks for Fathering Babies with Birth
       Defects."** <u>Morbidity and Mortality Weekly Report</u>, v. 33, no.
       32, August 17, 1984, p. 457-459. The methods used in
       conducting and the results of the Centers for Disease
       Control's study on the Vietnam veterans' risks for fathering
       babies with serious structural birth defects are reported.
       The study found that there is no evidence to indicate that
       Vietnam veterans have a greater risk than other men of
       fathering babies when all types of serious structural birth
       defects are combined. In an editorial note, it is stated
       that it is difficult to assess whether the few statistically
       significant associations found in this study between birth
       defects and possible Agent Orange exposure reflect true
       effects of exposure or whether they are merely chance
       occurrences.

1255 **"Vietnam Veterans: Study Doubts Birth Defect Risk."** <u>Facts
       on File</u>, v. 44, no. 2285, August 31, 1984, p. 640-641. The
       Centers for Disease Control has issued the results of a study
       which found that Vietnam veterans are at no greater risk of
       fathering children with birth defects but that veterans who
       believed they were exposed to Agent Orange had a slightly
       statistically higher chance of fathering children with spina
       bifida, cleft palate and certain rare deformities.

1256   "Vietnam Veterans Tell Their Herbicide Horror Stories."
       [editorial] New Scientist, v. 101, no. 1397, February 16,
       1984, p. 7. At hearings held by an Australian Royal
       Commission, Australian Vietnam veterans told about the health
       problems they have which they believe to be due to Agent
       Orange exposure.

1257   "Vietnam Vets Health Endangered by Exposure to Agent
       Orange." Congressional Record, v. 124, pt. 8, April 18,
       1978, p. 10590. Representative F.H. Stark (D-CA) submitted
       an article from the Stars and Stripes for insertion in the
       Record and discussed the need for congressmen to warn
       veterans in their districts about the possible health effects
       of exposure and to urge them to file claims with the Veterans
       Administration if they have health problems.

1258   Wade, N. "Agent Orange Again." [editorial] Science, v. 207,
       no. 4426, January 4, 1980, p. 41. L.E. Lee of the Veterans
       Administration has done a study in which he found traces of
       dioxin in the fat tissues of Vietnam veterans.

1259   Wade, N. "Viets and Vets Fear Herbicide Health Effects."
       Science, v. 204, no. 4395, May 25, 1979, p. 817. At a
       seminar sponsored by the Federation of American Scientists,
       T.T. Tung told of the effects of exposure to Agent Orange on
       the Vietnamese people. Vietnam veterans have begun
       complaining of ill health due to exposure to Agent Orange.
       CAVEAT, a Chicago-based organization, claims to represent
       2,000 veterans suffering from symptoms attributed to
       herbicide exposure.

1260   Watson, I.P.B. "Vietnam Veterans." [letter] Australian and
       New Zealand Journal of Psychiatry, v. 17, no. 1, March 1983,
       p. 93-94. The author responds to a letter written by T.
       Stanley (See 1207) and an article written by B. Boman which
       appeared in the September 1982 issue of this journal. Watson
       agrees that those who were exposed to Agent Orange may be
       using this exposure as a way of denying their problems or may
       be the victims of an unresolved national sense of guilt.

1261   Weerasinghe, N.C.A. et al. "Levels of 2,3,7,8-
       tetrachlorodibenzo-p-dioxin (2,3,7,8-TCDD) in Adipose Tissue
       of U.S. Vietnam Veterans Seeking Medical Assistance."
       Chemosphere, v. 15, no. 9-12, 1986, p. 1787-1794. The
       authors screened 13 Vietnam veterans for 2,3,7,8-TCDD in
       adipose tissue. These veterans had sought medical assistance
       and all had some of the medical problems that have been
       ascribed to 2,3,7,8-TCDD exposure. The authors found no
       significant difference between the tissue levels of these
       veterans and the person from the control group.

1262   Weigand, D.A. "Agent Orange and Skin Rash - a Different
       Experience." [letter] JAMA, v. 243, no. 14, April 11, 1980,
       p. 1422-1423. The author responds to G. Bogen's letter (See
       1009) which appeared in the November 30, 1979 issue of this
       journal which tells of his experiences treating 78 Vietnam
       veterans. Weigand has had entirely different experiences
       with the 16 veterans he has treated.

1263   Weintraub, P. "Agent Orange Mystery." Omni, v. 4, no. 11,
       August 1982, p. 14+. The efforts Dr. R. Codario is making to
       determine the biochemical link between the illnesses various
       Vietnam veterans he has examined have and Agent Orange are
       noted.

1264   Weissberg, A. "Agent Orange: Continuing Horror of Vietnam."
       Militant, v. 43, no. 48, December 14, 1979, p. 27. The
       effects the spraying of Agent Orange in Vietnam has had on
       the health of several veterans and their families are noted.
       The Pentagon has tried to dismiss this problem but a recent
       report by the General Accounting Office has exposed the
       cover-up by the military.

1265   Wendt, A.S. Agent Orange: 1985 Final Report. Des Moines,
       Iowa: Iowa State Department of Health, 1985. 53, [29]p. In
       1983 the Iowa Agent Orange Program was established.
       The purpose of this program was to develop a reporting system
       for Vietnam veterans who may have been exposed to Agent
       Orange and to compile statistical information based on these
       reports. This document details the program's findings.
       There appear to be an abnormal number of birth defects,
       premature births, miscarriages and fetal deaths. 120 cases
       of cancer were reported. The physical problems most often
       reported concerned skin, gastrointestinal and sleep
       impairments. However emotional and adjustment difficulties
       were the most frequently reported health problems.

1266   West, A.M. and C.A. Leon. "Health Needs of the Vietnam
       Veteran Exposed to Agent Orange." Nurse Practitioner, v. 11,
       no. 11, November 1986, p. 33+. The authors review what is
       known about the health effects of exposure to dioxin. They
       then list the psychological and physical problems that have
       come to be associated with Vietnam veterans' exposure to
       Agent Orange. Suggestions for how the nurse practitioner can
       help veterans who could have been exposed to Agent Orange are
       also given.

1267   Whelan, E.M. "Deadly Dioxin?" In Toxic Terror. Ottawa,
       Ill.: Jameson Books, 1985, p. 171-192. In this chapter from
       a book which focuses on and assesses the risks associated
       with various hazards, the author examines the Agent Orange

litigation and the claims of veterans that exposure to Agent
Orange is the cause of their health problems. The author
believes that Agent Orange is not the cause of their health
problems.

1268   Whelan, E. "'Orange' Case Best Feasible Solution." (See
       2368)

1269   **Willis, G. "Ranch Hand Deaths for 1986 Parallel Earlier
       Years."** Air Force Times, **v. 47, no. 28, February 23, 1987,
       p. 15.** The latest mortality report from the Air Force's
       Operation Ranch Hand study shows that the Ranch Handers are
       still not dying at a faster rate than the control group. The
       controversy on whether this means anything about ground troop
       exposure is discussed. Also noted is the fact that
       differences have been found between the health of Ranch Hand
       officers and enlisted men.

1270   **Wolfe, L.S. "Chemical and Biological Warfare: Medical
       Effects and Consequences."** McGill Law Journal, **v. 28, no. 3,
       July 1983, p. 732-749.** A portion of this article briefly
       reviews the chemical and medical facts and issues of the
       Agent Orange problem.

1271   **Wolfe, W.H. "Agent Orange in Perspective." Inland Empire
       Agricultural Chemical Association Conference. Spokane,
       Washington. December 10, 1980. 6p.** In this presentation
       the author gives a summary of the spraying of the various
       herbicides in Vietnam and the known medical effects of
       phenoxy herbicides and TCDD. He states that while there is
       no evidence of serious long-term health effects other than
       chloracne associated with TCDD exposure neither is there
       strong evidence for lack of effect. He concludes by stating
       that scientists must present their evidence to the public in
       an unbiased manner without jargon or highly technical
       explanations in order for their opinions to be accepted.

1272   **Wolfe, W.H. "Epidemiology and Toxicology of Agent Orange."
       In** Conference on Environmental Toxicology. Proceedings. **Ed.
       by J.D. MacEwen and E.H. Vernot. August 1984. p. 300-306.
       Available from NTIS: AD-P 004 038/6.** This presentation
       details the history of the military use of herbicides during
       the Vietnam War and reviews what is known about the medical
       effects of exposure to phenoxy herbicides and TCDD. It then
       summarizes the findings made thus far in the Air Force's
       morbidity study of the Operation Ranch Hand crew members.
       Thus far the Operation Ranch Hand crew members do not have
       a higher mortality rate than the matched comparison group.
       While statistically nonsignificant, there is a higher death
       rate due to liver disorders among the Ranch Handers.

1273   Wolfe, W.H. and J.E. Michalek. Ranch Hand II. An
       Epidemiologic Investigation of Health Effects in Air Force
       Personnel Following Exposure to Herbicides. Mortality Update
       - 1985. November 29, 1985. iii, 43p. Available from NTIS:
       AD-A163 237/1. This study reports the findings of the third
       mortality analysis performed as part of the Ranch Hand II
       Project. There is no evidence of increased mortality as a
       result of having participated in Operation Ranch Hand. As of
       December 31, 1984, 55 Ranch Handers and 285 comparison
       subjects have died.

1274   Wolfe, W.H. et al. "An Epidemiologic Investigation of Health
       Effects in Air Force Personnel Following Exposure to
       Herbicides and Associated Dioxins." Chemosphere, v. 14, no.
       6-7, 1985, p. 707-716. This paper presents the results of
       the epidemiological study the Air Force is conducting of the
       personnel who took part in Operation Ranch Hand. The authors
       conclude that they do not feel there is sufficient evidence
       to confirm that there is a cause and effect relationship
       between adverse health in the Ranch Hand group and Agent
       Orange exposure.

1275   Wolfe, W.H. et al. Epidemiologic Investigation of Health
       Effects in Air Force Personnel Following Exposure to
       Herbicides: Mortality Update - 1986. December 26, 1986.
       12p. Available from NTIS: AD-A 175 453/0. This report
       provides summary statistics only for the deaths which
       occurred among the Operation Ranch Hand crew members
       through 1985. As of December 31, 1985, 59 Ranch Handers and
       312 comparison subjects had died. This suggests that the
       findings of earlier reports are still valid: there is no
       statistically significant difference between the Ranch
       Handers and their matched comparison in terms of mortality.

1276   Wolfe, W.H. et al. "An Epidemiological Investigation of the
       Health Effects of Herbicide Orange." [abstract] American
       Chemical Society. Abstracts of Papers, v. 189, 1985, #ENVR
       0067. The authors are conducting a study of Ranch Hand crew
       members and the effects of their exposure to Agent Orange.
       They have concluded that, at this time, there is insufficient
       evidence to support a cause and effect relationship between
       herbicide exposure and adverse health in the Ranch Hand
       group.

1277   Wolfe, W.H. et al. Project Ranch Hand II. An Epidemiologic
       Investigation of Health Effects in Air Force Personnel
       Following Exposure to Herbicides. Mortality Update - 1984.
       December 10, 1984. 55p. Available from NTIS: AD-A162
       687/8. This study reports the findings of the second
       mortality analysis performed as part of the Ranch Hand II

Project. This second study still shows that there is no evidence of increased mortality as a result of having participated in Operation Ranch Hand. As of December 31, 1983, 54 Ranch Handers and 265 comparison subjects had died.

1278 Young, A.L. Agent Orange at the Crossroads of Science and Social Concern. May 1981. 69p. Available from NTIS: AD-A102 611/1. This report discusses the issue of whether or not Agent Orange is responsible for the health problems reported among Vietnam veterans. Examination of the scientific data suggests three possible conclusions. One, long-term adverse effects associated with exposure to the defoliant are low. Two, disease stemming from exposure to the herbicide is low. Three, the medical problems reported by some Vietnam veterans do not stem from exposure to Agent Orange. The author, therefore, concludes that the factors that drive the Agent Orange controversy are not based on scientific truth but rather by social, political and legal concerns.

1279 Young, A.L. "Analysis of Dioxins and Furans in Human Adipose Tissue." In Public Health Risks of the Dioxins: Proceedings of a Symposium Held in New York City on Oct. 19-20, 1983 by the Life Sciences and Public Policy Program of the Rockefeller University. Ed. by W.W. Lowrance. New York: The Rockefeller University dist. by Los Altos, CA: William Kaufmann, 1984, p. 63-75. This symposium was convened to examine the scientific issues surrounding the effects of low level exposure to dioxins on humans. In this paper the author examines efforts to determine the levels of TCDD in the adipose tissue of those exposed in Seveso, Italy; Ohio; the Great Lakes in Canada; and Vietnam veterans exposed to Agent Orange.

1280 Young, A.L. "Health Assessments of Herbicides: a Case Study of the Phenoxy Herbicides." [abstract] Weed Science Society of America. Abstracts, 1984, p. 120-121. The author describes the difficulties in developing epidemiological studies on the effects of exposure of veterans to Agent Orange in Vietnam. The author also describes many of the studies currently underway.

1281 Young, A.L., H.K. Kang and B.M. Shepard. "Chlorinated Dioxins as Herbicide Contaminants." ES&T: Environmental Science & Technology, v. 17, no. 11, November 1983, p. 530A-540A. This article reviews the studies and health issues surrounding the Agent Orange controversy and discusses in detail a study that was conducted to analyze human fat for traces of TCDD.

1282 Young, A.L., H.K. Kang and B.M. Shepard. "Rationale and Description of the Federally Sponsored Epidemiological Research in the United States on the Phenoxy Herbicides and Chlorinated Dioxin Contaminants." In Chlorinated Dioxins and Dibenzofurans in the Total Environment II. Ed. by L.H. Keith, C. Rappe and G. Choudhary. Stoneham, MA: Butterworth Publ., 1985, p. 155-166. The authors summarize the findings of current federally sponsored scientific research studies concerning exposure to phenoxy herbicides and their associated dioxin contaminants, especially 2,3,7,8-TCDD. The studies underway on the health problems Vietnam veterans feel are associated with exposure to Agent Orange are summarized on pages 159-164.

1283 Young, A.L. and B.M. Shepard. "A Review of Ongoing Epidemiologic Research in the USA on the Phenoxy Herbicides and Chlorinated Dioxin Contaminants." Chemosphere, v. 12, no. 4-5, 1983, p. 749-760. Some of the current federally sponsored investigations into the health effects of exposure to Agent Orange by Vietnam veterans are described. Specifically mentioned are the TCDD Assay of Human Adipose Tissue Study, the Vietnam Veteran Mortality Study, the Vietnam Experience Twin Study, the Birth Defects and Military Service in Vietnam Study, the Air Force Health Study, and the Epidemiologic Study of Ground Troops Exposed to Agent Orange. The Veterans Administration is firmly committed to working with other federal agencies and the private sector in attempting to find answers to as many questions as possible on the issue.

1284 Young, A.L., B.M. Shepard and H.K. Kang. "Rationale and Description of the Federally-sponsored Epidemiologic Research in the United States on the Phenoxy Herbicides and Chlorinated Dioxin Contaminants." [abstract] American Chemical Society. Abstracts of Papers, v. 186, 1983, #ENVR 0052. The Veterans Administration and the Centers for Disease Control have initiated extensive studies on the health effects of exposure of Agent Orange on Vietnam veterans. These studies have been undertaken as it is necessary to determine the long-term effects of such exposure. Mortality, morbidity, reproduction and body burden levels of TCDD must be studied. Also underway are efforts to clarify the relationship of soft tissue sarcoma and chlorophenol exposure.

1285 Young, A.L. et al. "Health Surveillance of Vietnam Veterans Claiming Agent Orange Exposure." In Chlorinated Dioxins and Dibenzofurans in the Total Environment II. Ed. by L.H. Keith, C. Rappe and G. Choudhary. Stoneham, MA: Butterworth Publ., 1985, p. 167-180. The authors review the health studies of Vietnam veterans exposed to Agent Orange being conducted by the Veterans Administration in cooperation with other federal agencies, state health agencies and private researchers.

1286 Zumwalt, E., III. as told to J. Grossman. "A War with Hope." Health, v. 19, no. 6, June 1987, p. 86+. Elmo III tells of his battle with non-Hodgkin's and Hodgkin's disease. He believes he has these diseases because he served in areas that were sprayed with Agent Orange in Vietnam. His son has sensory integration dysfunction which Elmo III also believes is due to his exposure to Agent Orange. Elmo III also mentions how he feels about the out of court settlement.

EFFORTS TO INVOLVE STATE AND FEDERAL GOVERNMENTS

1287 "AF, HEW Studying 'Orange.'" Air Force Times, v. 39, no. 47, June 18, 1979, p. 27. The Air Force and the Department of Health, Education and Welfare have both begun studies on Agent Orange exposure. The Air Force will be studying Ranch Hand personnel and the Department of Health, Education and Welfare will be studying an accident which took place 30 years ago at a Monsanto plant in West Virginia.

1288 "Additional Evidence on Agent Orange." Congressional Record, v. 126, pt. 12, June 20, 1980, p. 16018. Senator J. Heinz (R-PA) inserted in the Record the texts of two articles from the June 20, 1980 issue of the Washington Post which raise further questions about the consequences of Agent Orange exposure. Senator Heinz will soon be introducing legislation which will be designed to help veterans exposed to Agent Orange.

1289 Addlestone, D.F. "Developments in Veterans Programs in 1981." Clearinghouse Review, v. 15, no. 9, January 1982, p. 781-787. A portion of this article discusses the little progress that has been made in the courts, with the Congress, with the Veterans Administration and with the Defense Department on the Agent Orange issue 1981. In the courts most of the litigation concerned the chemical companies' argument that they are immune from liability because of the government contract defense. Also a temporary restraining order was not granted to prevent the Veterans Administration from proceeding with a health study. Each house in Congress passed different measures designed to improve Veterans Administration medical treatment to those veterans exposed to

Agent Orange. But the Veterans Administration will only give hospital care if they decide "credible medical evidence" exists linking health problems to Agent Orange. Both the Veterans Administration and the Defense Department are still firm in their belief that there are not health problems associated with exposure to Agent Orange.

1290   "Agent Orange." CBS News Daily News Broadcasts, new ser., v. 4, no. 284, October 11, 1978, p. 11 (evening news). The Veterans Administration says they have received claims from 500 veterans who believe their health problems are a result of having been exposed to Agent Orange in Vietnam. Eight claims have been allowed, 72 have been rejected and the rest are pending.

1291   "Agent Orange." Discharge Upgrading Newsletter, v. 4, no. 10, October 1979, p. 6. The General Accounting Office has released a report stating that Congress should direct the Department of Defense, the Veterans Administration, the Department of Health, Education and Welfare or the Environmental Protection Agency to determine whether a study of the health effects of exposure to Agent Orange is needed. A judge in New York has ruled that the suit brought against the manufacturers of Agent Orange by Vietnam veterans exposed to Agent Orange cannot be dismissed.

1292   "Agent Orange." Congressional Record, v. 126, pt. 1, January 30, 1980, p. 1329-1330. Representative T. Daschle (D-S.D.) introduced H.R. 6377 which would amend title 38 to provide a presumption of service-connection for the occurrence of certain diseases in veterans exposed to phenoxy herbicides contaminated by dioxins. The text of the resolution is included.

1293   "Agent Orange." Congressional Record, v. 126, pt. 6, April 1, 1980, p. 7343. Senator M. Baucus (D-Mont.) stated that veterans have a right to expect that the Agent Orange issue will be dealt with immediately, effectively and compassionately. He also read into the Record an editorial from the Washington Post lamenting the fact that the Veterans Administration has not done this.

1294   "Agent Orange." Congressional Record, v. 126, pt. 6, April 1, 1980, p. 7464-7465. Representative T. Harkin (D-Iowa) spoke about his concern regarding the Agent Orange issue and expressed his hope that the Veterans Administration will soon have a study underway on the effects of Agent Orange exposure.

1295   "Agent Orange." Congressional Record, v. 126, pt. 8, May 1,

1980, p. 9660. Representative A.E. Ertel (D-PA) stated that as he is convinced there is a cause and effect relationship between exposure to Agent Orange in Vietnam and the development of neurological disorders, he has decided to co-sponsor H.R. 6377.

1296 "Agent Orange." CBS News Daily News Broadcasts, new ser., v. 6, no. 128, May 7, 1980, p. 9-11 (evening news). A group of veterans have filed a suit asking that a Veterans Administration study on the effects of exposure to Agent Orange be halted as the veterans feel that the proposed study is inadequate. This report goes on to detail the frustration many veterans feel with the Veterans Administration over the issue of exposure to Agent Orange. The stories of Charlie Poole and Charlie Hartz are told.

1297 "Agent Orange." Congressional Record, v. 126, pt. 16, July 31, 1980, p. 20938. Representative T. Daschle (D-S.D.) summarized the testimony heard on July 22 at a hearing held by the House Veterans' Affairs Committee's Subcommittee on Medical Facilities and Benefits and submitted the text of an article on the hearing from the July 27, 1980 issue of the Washington Post.

1298 "Agent Orange." CBS News Daily News Broadcasts, new ser., v. 6, no. 270, September 26, 1980, p. 12-13 (morning news). This report details the debate in a Congressional subcommittee hearing on how to get the Veterans Administration to accept ailments resulting from exposure to Agent Orange as service-connected and therefore make veterans eligible for disability compensation payments.

1299 "Agent Orange." Veterans Rights Newsletter, v. 1, no. 4, August 1981, p. 28. Illinois has established an Agent Orange Commission in their state. The Coalition for New York Vietnam Veterans Organizations was formed following a meeting of the National Veterans Task Force on Agent Orange. Veterans who have been diagnosed as having cancer and believe they were exposed to Agent Orange should have their doctor send a tissue specimen to the Armed Forces Institute of Pathology.

1300 "Agent Orange." Veterans Rights Newsletter, v. 1, no. 7-8, November-December 1981, p. 59. The Texas Attorney General has offered his assistance to veterans who were exposed to Agent Orange. The Veterans Administration has just released a scientific review of the literature on Agent Orange. The Supreme Court refused to hear an appeal sought by veterans regarding state statute of limitations laws. The protocol submitted by Dr. Spivey has been rejected by the Centers for Disease Control.

1301 **"Agent Orange."** <u>Veterans Rights Newsletter</u>**, v. 1, no. 9-10,
January-February 1982, p. 74.** The National Cancer Institute
has released the results from oral and dermal studies which
found that TCDD exposure causes cancer, the Veterans
Administration is withholding the second draft protocol of
the Agent Orange epidemiological study, a history of
Operation Ranch Hand has been published and in both
California and Oklahoma Agent Orange legislation has been
introduced.

1302 **"Agent Orange."** <u>Veterans Rights Newsletter</u>**, v. 2, no. 1-2,
May-June 1982, p. 7.** The Australian Repatriation Review
Tribunal has ruled that the government must pay a pension to
the widow of a Vietnam veteran who died of malignant
lymphoma. A recent issue of the <u>New England Journal of
Medicine</u> contains a letter to the editor detailing three
cases of thoracic soft tissue sarcoma in Vietnam veterans who
had been in areas sprayed with defoliants. The Veterans
Administration's Office of Public and Consumer Affairs has
now published three pamphlets on Agent Orange. The topic of
the Veterans Administration's epidemiological study was
brought up at a recent meeting of the Veterans
Administration's Agent Orange Advisory Committee.

1303 **"Agent Orange."** <u>CBS News Daily News Broadcasts</u>**, new ser., v.
8, no. 281, October 8, 1982, p. 4 (morning news).** Seventeen
states have formed Agent Orange commissions. The New York
Commission has developed an outreach program which includes
a television commercial, posters and brochures. Dow Chemical
Company went to court to try to block the program but failed.

1304 **"Agent Orange."** <u>CBS News Daily News Broadcasts</u>**, new ser., v.
8, no. 313, November 9, 1982, p. 12 (evening news).** The
National Academy of Sciences has found serious flaws in the
Veterans Administration's proposed epidemiological study on
Agent Orange which will add yet another delay to the start of
this study.

1305 **"Agent Orange."** <u>CBS News Daily News Broadcasts</u>**, new ser., v.
8, no. 316, November 12, 1982, p. 14 (evening news).** A five
day tribute to Vietnam veterans included a seminar on Agent
Orange. G. Sinclair, a veteran with five children with birth
defects, stated that veterans want an admission that Agent
Orange has caused their health problems - not money.

1306 "Agent Orange." <u>Veterans Rights Newsletter</u>, November-
December 1982 (See 0938)

1307 **"Agent Orange."** <u>U.S. Air Force. Office of the Judge Advocate
General of the Air Force. Reporter</u>**, v. 11, no. 6, December**

1982, p. 186. HQ USAF/JACC will continue to be responsible
for all Agent Orange litigation. If the Air Force becomes a
defendant, a move for dismissal will have to be sought. The
Department of Defense is opposed to using government
resources to notify the class involved in the Agent Orange
litigation.

1308 "Agent Orange." CBS News Daily News Broadcasts, new ser., v.
      9, no. 6, January 6, 1983, p. 13 (evening news). Sixteen
      thousand veterans have filed claims for compensation for
      health problems due to exposure to Agent Orange. However,
      the Veterans Administration will not acknowledge that Agent
      Orange is a cause of long term health problems.

1309 "Agent Orange." CBS News Daily News Broadcasts, new ser., v.
      9, no. 67, March 8, 1983, p. 8 (evening news). The Veterans
      Administration will not compensate nearly 17,000 veterans who
      believe that their health problems are a result of exposure
      to Agent Orange. The Veterans Administration says that there
      is not proof that Agent Orange is the cause of their health
      problems. One hundred and thirteen members of the House
      have introduced a bill which will grant compensation for
      certain diseases even if the veteran cannot prove the disease
      is Agent Orange-related.

1310 "Agent Orange." Veterans Rights Newsletter, March-April 1983
      (See 0939)

1311 "Agent Orange." Veterans Rights Newsletter, v. 3, no. 1-2,
      May-June 1983, p. 12. The activities of the Agent Orange
      commissions in Connecticut, Illinois and Indiana are noted.
      The Senate is considering several bills on Agent Orange.

1312 "Agent Orange." [editorial] Los Angeles Daily Journal, v.
      96, no. 147, July 25, 1983, p. 4. Veterans Administration
      Chief Walters opposes granting compensation to veterans who
      believe exposure to Agent Orange is the cause of their health
      problems until science speaks as one voice on the issue.
      Opposition in Congress to bills that would compensate
      veterans also seem to be based on the belief that the
      herbicides will not pan out to be the cause of the diseases.
      Congress should be willing to give the benefit of the doubt
      and spend nominal sums in compensation.

1313 "Agent Orange." Veterans Rights Newsletter, July-August 1983
      (See 0941)

1314 "Agent Orange." Veterans Rights Newsletter, v. 3, no. 5-6,
      September-October 1983, p. 43-44. The court has released to
      the public hundreds of pages from previously sealed documents

in the Agent Orange litigation. These documents show that
both the manufacturers and the government were aware of the
hazards of dioxin. The American Legion has attacked a report
given by A.L. Young at a recent American Chemical Society
meeting on his findings of the results of examinations
entered on the Agent Orange Registry as "...totally
irresponsible and misleading." Governor Deukmejian of
California has vetoed a bill which would established a state
Agent Orange commission in California.

1315   "Agent Orange." Veterans Rights Newsletter, v. 3, no. 7-8,
November-December 1983, p. 60. The Veterans Administration's
Advisory Committee on Health-Related Effects of Herbicides
has recommended that the Veterans Administration stop showing
a videotape to Veterans Administration workers on Agent
Orange. The Committee said it was too condescending, painted
too rosy a picture and reinforced stereotypes of Vietnam
veterans. Publicity will be out soon to tell veterans how to
"opt-out" of the litigation if they so desire and Washington
State has an Agent Orange toll-free hotline.

1316   "Agent Orange." Congressional Record, v. 130, no. 7, January
31, 1984, p. E219. Representative M.R. Oaker (D-Ohio) spoke
on why she supported the passage of H.R. 1961, the Agent
Orange and Atomic Veterans Relief Act.

1317   "Agent Orange." Congressional Record, v. 130, no. 9,
February 2, 1984, p. E311. Representative G.B.H. Solomon (R-
N.Y.) spoke on why he is pleased the H.R. 1961, the Agent
Orange and Atomic Veterans Relief Act, has passed the House.

1318   "Agent Orange." Congressional Record, v. 130, no. 64, May
16, 1984, p. E2192. Representative T.A. Daschle (D-S.D.)
submitted the text of an editorial from the Washington Post
by P. Geyelin which states that the federal government has
not dealt in good faith on the Agent Orange issue.
Representative Daschle agrees with the author of this
editorial and urges the Senate to take positive action on the
issue of service-connection to certain diseases as the House
did with the passage of HR 1961.

1319   "Agent Orange." Congress Watcher, July 1984, p. 7. The
Senate has passed a bill that would require the Veterans
Administration to establish guidelines for compensating
Vietnam veterans to Agent Orange. The House has passed a
similar bill and the measure will now be sent to conference.

1320   "Agent Orange." Veterans Rights Newsletter, v. 4, no. 11-12,
March-April 1985, p. 96-97. The first meeting of the
advisory committee mandated by the Veterans Dioxin and

Radiation Exposure Compensation Standards Act was held
recently. The Massachusetts Agent Orange Program has
recently released the results of their study.

1321 "Agent Orange." Veterans Rights Newsletter, January-February
      1986 (See 1915)

1322 **"Agent Orange." Veterans Rights Newsletter, v. 6, no. 1-2,
      May-June 1986, p. 10-11.** The findings of a recent General
      Accounting Office report which re-examined how well the
      Veterans Administration's Agent Orange examination and
      registry program is working are detailed. Problems still
      remain.

1323 **"Agent Orange - a Hero's Response." Congressional Record, v.
      129, no. 97, July 13, 1983, p. E3454-3455.** Representative B.
      Edgar (D-PA) discussed the hearings that have been held by
      the Veterans' Affairs Subcommittee on Compensation, Pension
      and Insurance on the Agent Orange issue. Included in this
      article is the testimony Sammy Lee Davis, a Vietnam veteran,
      presented this subcommittee concerning the health effects of
      Agent Orange exposure.

1324 "Agent Orange: a Problem of Exposure." (See 0944)

1325 "Agent Orange Accord Nears Approval...as Vets' Compensation
      Bill Passes." (See 1917)

1326 **"Agent Orange and Atomic Veterans Relief Act." Congressional
      Record, v. 130, no. 6, January 30, 1984, p. H217-H227.** The
      debate on the House floor on H.R. 1961, the Agent Orange and
      Atomic Veterans Relief Act, is given. The text of the bill
      is also included. The bill as amended was passed by voice
      vote.

1327 **"Agent Orange and Atomic Veterans Relief Act." Congressional
      Record, v. 130, no. 7, January 31, 1984, p. E191-E192.**
      Representative R.J. McGrath (R-N.Y.) spoke on why he supports
      the passage of H.R. 1961, the Agent Orange and Atomic
      Veterans Relief Act.

1328 **"Agent Orange and Atomic Veterans Relief Act." Congressional
      Record, v. 130, no. 7, January 31, 1984, p. E193-E194.**
      Representative J.M. Jeffords (R-Vt.) spoke on why he supports
      the passage of H.R. 1961, the Agent Orange and Atomic
      Veterans Relief Act.

1329 **"The Agent Orange and Atomic Veterans Relief Act."
      Congressional Record, v.130, no. 7, January 31, 1984, p.
      E195-E196.** Representative L. Stokes (D-Ohio) spoke on why he

supports the passage of H.R. 1961, the Agent Orange and Atomic Veterans Relief Act.

1330 "Agent Orange and Atomic Veterans Relief Act." Congressional Record, v.130, no. 7, January 31, 1984, p. E215. Representative M. Leland (D-Tex.) spoke on why he supported the passage of H.R. 1961, the Agent Orange and Atomic Veterans Relief Act.

1331 "Agent Orange and Atomic Veterans Relief, H.R. 1961." Congressional Record, v. 130, no. 7, January 31, 1984, p. H300-H306. Further House floor comment on H.R. 1961, the Agent Orange and Atomic Veterans Relief Act, is given.

1332 "Agent Orange and Atomic Vets' Bill Passes House." Veterans Rights Newsletter, v. 3, no. 9-10, January-February 1984, p. 77. H.R. 1961 has passed the House. This legislation allows Vietnam veterans who are suffering from soft tissue sarcoma, chloracne or porphyria cutanea tarda to receive a disability allowance or survivors to receive a death allowance.

1333 "Agent Orange & Vet Benefits." Editorials on File, v. 12, no. 11, June 1-15, 1981, p. 662-666. This article consists of editorials from newspapers across the country which discuss the legislation passed by Congress requiring the Veterans Administration to provide medical care to Vietnam veterans who were exposed to Agent Orange and the recent sit-in veterans held at a Veterans Administration hospital in Los Angeles to protest inadequate medical care.

1334 "Agent Orange Answers Still Four Years Away." DAV Magazine, v. 24, no. 1, January 1982, p. 8-9. The progress that has been made so far in the design of the epidemiological study that will be done at the University of California at Los Angeles and what has been so far by the Veterans Administration is discussed. Complete answers are still at least four years away.

1335 "Agent Orange Bill Helps Our Veterans." Congressional Record, v. 130, no. 70, May 24, 1984, p. S6481-S6482. Senator Sasser (D-Tenn.) spoke in favor of the passage of S.1651, the Veterans' Dioxin and Radiation Exposure Compensation Standards Act and urges expeditious conference action on this bill.

1336 "Agent Orange Bill Passes in Senate: Study to Expand." Chemical Marketing Reporter, v. 219, no. 25, June 22, 1981, p. 5+. In legislation comparable to that passed by the House, the Senate has unanimously passed a bill which grants health-care eligibility and outpatient care priority to veterans exposed to Agent Orange in Vietnam. The bill also provides for an expansion of the on-going study of exposure to Agent Orange. The House and Senate will now need to reach a compromise on their two bills.

1337 "Agent Orange and Budget Reconciliation." Congressional Record, v. 126, pt. 9, May 13, 1980, p. 11060-11062. Representative R. Roberts (D-Tex.) feels that scientists have not been able to show a cause and effect relationship between Agent Orange and certain diseases and that the Veterans Administration and the House Committee on Veterans' Affairs have acted responsibly. He does not see how his colleagues can support H.R. 6377 which would presume a connection between certain disabilities and Agent Orange exposure now that the House Committee on Veterans' Affairs must slash $400 million from ongoing veterans' entitlements.

1338 "Agent Orange Caravan." Congressional Record, v. 129, no. 117, September 13, 1983, p. E4248. Representative M. Kaptur (D-Ohio) spoke about the Agent Orange Caravan and its stop in Toledo which was organized by Mike Flowers, President of the Vietnam Veterans of Toledo.

1339 "Agent Orange Care Promised." American Medical News, v. 23, no. 41, October 24, 1980, p. 13. The Veterans Administration has promised that medical care to those concerned about exposure to Agent Orange will not be delayed while the defoliant is being investigated.

1340 "Agent Orange Clarification." Congressional Record, v. 127, pt. 17, September 24, 1981, p. 21987-21988. Representative J. Dunn (R-Mich.) clarifies some statements that have been made about which soldiers may have been exposed to Agent Orange.

1341 "Agent Orange Compensation." Congressional Record, v. 129, no. 27, March 8, 1983, p. H929-H931. Representative T.A. Daschle (D-S.D.) introduced H.R. 1961 on behalf of 111 of his colleagues. This bill would provide presumption of service connection for certain diseases related to exposure to herbicides or other environmental hazards and conditions in veterans who served in Southeast Asia during the Vietnam era. The text of the bill is included.

1342 "Agent Orange Compensation Limits Urged." American Medical News, v. 26, no. 27, July 22-29, 1983, p. 17. Dr. J.R. Beljan, the chairman of the American Medical Association's Advisory Panel on Toxic Substances, feels that Vietnam veterans should not receive compensation for exposure to Agent Orange until a causal relationship between exposure and injury can be established scientifically.

1343 "Agent Orange Controversy Continues." Congressional Record,
      v. 126, pt. 5, March 25, 1980, p. 6580. Representative R.
      Edgar (D-PA) addressed the House stating his concern that not
      enough was being done for the veterans exposed to Agent
      Orange. He had an editorial from the Philadelphia Bulletin
      inserted in the Record.

1344 "Agent Orange: Decision Day." (See 1929)

1345 "Agent Orange Delay Granted." Chemical Marketing Reporter,
      v. 219, no. 19, May 11, 1981, p. 7+. The Veterans
      Administration has announced that a research team at the
      University of California at Los Angeles has been awarded a
      contract to design an epidemiological study to determine
      what, if any, adverse medical effects Vietnam veterans have
      suffered as a result of being exposed to Agent Orange.

1346 "Agent Orange Design Submitted to VA." DAV Magazine, v. 24,
      no. 6, June 1982, p. 9. The final design of the University
      of California at Los Angeles' epidemiological study has been
      submitted to the Veterans Administration's Central Office.
      The DAV's demand for a scientifically sound study is
      repeated.

1347 "Agent Orange Dispute." CBS News Daily News Broadcasts,
      new ser., v. 10, no. 230, August 17, 1984, p. 3 (morning
      news). Reaction to the recently released Centers for Disease
      Control report on the link between birth defects and service
      in Vietnam is given.

1348 "Agent Orange Find Moves Senator." National Underwriter:
      Property & Casualty Insurance Edition, v. 88, no. 34, August
      24, 1984, p. 3+. Senator A. Cranston (D-CA) will offer an
      amendment to a veterans bill as a response to the results of
      a Centers for Disease Control study which found that there
      was a statistically significant risk for Vietnam veterans to
      father children with spina bifida, cleft lip and certain
      benign and malignant tumors. The legislation will direct the
      Veterans Administration to develop and evaluate various
      methods for providing medical care, rehabilitation and
      compensation to affected children. The Administrator of
      Veterans Affairs would be required to report back to Congress
      by early next year.

1349 "Agent Orange Funds Voted." American Medical News, v. 24,
      no. 25, July 3, 1981, p. 8. The Senate recently approved
      legislation providing federal financing for treatment of
      veterans exposed to Agent Orange.

1350 "Agent Orange Herbicide Is Studied as a Cause of Vietnam

Veterans' Ills." Chemical Marketing Reporter, v. 215, no.
23, June 4, 1979, p. 4+. The Defense Department has
announced that it will carry out a year long study of the
1,200 Vietnam veterans who were part of Operation Ranch
Hand. The studies being conducted by the Veterans
Administration are also noted.

1351 "Agent Orange: Identifying the Problem." American Legion
Magazine, v. 112, no. 1, January 1982, p. 34-37. This
article discusses what Agent Orange is, how a Veterans
Administration Medical Administration Service employee in
Chicago began noticing recurring problems in many of the
Vietnam veterans she was working with, the claims that have
been filed with the Veterans Administration and the Veterans
Administration's official position on Agent Orange.

1352 "Agent Orange: in Search of Answers." American Legion
Magazine, v. 112, no. 2, February 1982, p. 46-49. The
purpose of the Agent Orange Working Group and the status of
the Veterans Administration's epidemiological study, the
Operation Ranch Hand study and other scientific studies are
noted.

1353 "Agent Orange Law 'a Step in the Right Direction.'" American
Legion, v. 118, no. 1, January 1985, p. 29. The Legion's
reaction to recently passed legislation stating that there is
a presumed connection between exposure to Agent Orange and
certain diseases is given.

1354 "Agent Orange Legacy." CBS News Daily News Broadcasts, new
ser., v. 10, no. 347, December 12, 1984, p. 8-9 (evening
news). A study being conducted by an independent New Jersey
agency on the effects of exposure to Agent Orange is
discussed.

1355 "Agent Orange Legislation." Congressional Record, v. 129,
no. 27, March 8, 1983, p. H892. Representative B. Richardson
(D-N.M.) is cosponsoring the legislation sponsored by
Representative Daschle (D-S.D.). We must stop ignoring
Vietnam veterans and the Veterans Administration should stop
treating them in such a humiliating way. This legislation
will not cost too much.

1356 "Agent Orange Legislation May Pass Congress, but Questions
Surround Compensation Issue." DAV Magazine, v. 25, no. 9,
September 1983, p. 6-8. Current activity in Congress to deal
with legislation introduced concerning the Agent Orange issue
is remarked upon. The Air Force's study of Ranch Hand crews
who sprayed Agent Orange in Vietnam has been finished. A
study of death rates has determined that these veterans have
experienced higher death rates than other veterans.

1357   "Agent Orange Legislation: Necessary but Not Enough."
<u>Congressional Record</u>, v. 130, no. 7, January 31, 1984, p.
E188-E189. Representative B.L. Dorgan (D-S.D.) spoke on why
he supported H.R. 1961, the Agent Orange and Atomic Veterans
Relief Act, and on the legislation he feels still needs to be
passed.

1358   "Agent Orange Legislation Signed by the President." <u>Chemical
Marketing Reporter</u>, v. 226, no. 18, October 29, 1984, p. 5.
The President has signed legislation which will grant
compensation to Vietnam veterans who developed chloracne or
porphyria cutanea tarda within one year of leaving Vietnam.
This is the first time the government has acknowledged that
exposure to Agent Orange may have harmed troops.

1359   "Agent Orange Linked to Cancer." <u>Black Panther</u>, v. 20, no.
5, April 21, 1980, p. 7. According to five studies released
on Capitol Hill recently, Agent Orange exposure probably
causes cancer in humans.

1360   "The Agent Orange March." [editorial] <u>Wall Street Journal</u>,
August 12, 1983, p. 20(E), p. 16(W). Reprinted in <u>Los
Angeles Daily Journal</u>, v. 96, no. 163, August 16, 1983, p. 4.
When Congress returns in September they will still have a
bill on Agent Orange compensation to deal with. The
editorial states that compensation should not be made until
it is established that Agent Orange has caused the
disabilities, illnesses and birth defects attributed to it by
using the responsible method this society has for dealing
with such difficult and disputed issues.

1361   "Agent Orange Measure Signed." <u>American Medical News</u>, v.
24, no. 26, July 19, 1981, p. 22. A state law has been
passed in New York that authorizes Vietnam veterans to sue
for damages resulting from exposure to Agent Orange despite
expiration of the statute of limitations.

1362   "Agent Orange Moves to CDC." <u>American Family Physician</u>, v.
26, no. 6, December 1982, p. 18. As a result of the
criticism the Veterans Administration has received, the
epidemiological study on the effects of exposure to Agent
Orange has been turned over to the Centers for Disease
Control.

1363   "Agent Orange, Patient Visits Linked by VA." <u>American
Medical News</u>, v. 26, no. 18, May 13, 1983, p. 34. More than
369,000 visits have been made to Veterans Administration
hospitals by Vietnam veterans for illnesses that could have
been caused by exposure to Agent Orange.

1364 "Agent Orange Pilot Test Nearly Ready." DAV Magazine, v. 24, no. 8, August 1982, p. 10. A pilot test of the Veterans Administration's epidemiological study may be ready for implementation in fiscal year 1982.

1365 "Agent Orange: Progress but Not Much." Congressional Record, v. 127, pt. 18, October 14, 1981, p. 24051-24052. Representative T.A. Daschle (D-S.D.) had inserted an article Representative R.W. Edgar (D-PA) wrote for the October 6, 1981 issue of the Philadelphia Inquirer. Representative Edgar discusses the implications of the recently released information regarding the fact that American troops were exposed to Agent Orange because U.S. aircraft were required on occasion to dump the herbicide in emergency situations on them. Representative Daschle is upset that the Air Force withheld this information because the design of the Veterans Administration's epidemiological study will have to be altered and this means further delay of a study that has already been delayed many times.

1366 "Agent Orange 'Protocol' Criticized." Veterans Rights Newsletter, v. 1, no. 5-6, September-October 1981, p. 40-41. This article consists of an excerpt of a letter written by the National Veterans Task Force on Agent Orange to Dr. B. Shepard of the Veterans Administration criticizing the draft protocol submitted by Dr. G. Spivey.

1367 "Agent Orange, PTSD Measures Awaiting President's Signature." [editorial] National Vietnam Veterans Review, v. 4, no. 8, [n.d.], p. 2. In the final days of the 98th Congress H.R. 1961, the Veterans' Dioxin and Radiation Exposure Compensation Standards Act, was approved. The Act will provide a disability allowance to Vietnam veterans who within one year of departure from Vietnam developed chloracne or porphyria cutanea tarda. Congress also approved the Veterans' Health Care Act of 1984. Both bills are now awaiting the President's endorsement.

1368 "Agent Orange Relief Act." Congressional Record, v. 129, no. 8, February 2, 1983, p. S853-S864. Senator A. Spector (R-PA) is reintroducing the Vietnam Veterans' Agent Orange Relief Act. This bill would grant compensation for an ailment caused by Agent Orange exposure as established by credible medical opinion. The text of S. 374 is included.

1369 "Agent Orange Research Urged by Two Groups." American Medical News, v. 24, no. 18, May 8, 1981, p. 14X. The Veterans Administration and the inter-agency task force on Agent Orange have both endorsed legislation to expand research on the health problems of Vietnam veterans beyond those caused by exposure to Agent Orange. The Air Force has begun a study of the Operation Ranch Hand veterans. Legal action by various veterans' groups have developed the start of a government study which would research the effects of Agent Orange on veterans.

1370 **"Agent Orange Science Study and Lawsuit Settled."** Veterans Rights Newsletter, v. 6, no. 3-4, July-August 1986, p. 17+. The Agent Orange Working Group has been examining the issue of whether or not the Centers for Disease Control's study should proceed. The problem is determining whether veterans were exposed to Agent Orange or not. No further planning of the Distribution Plan will be done until the Second Circuit Court decides the pending appeals to the settlement.

1371 "Agent Orange Settlement." Congressional Record (See 1966)

1372 **"Agent Orange Settlement - a Hollow Victory."** Congressional Record, v. 130, no. 69 part I, May 23, 1984, p. E2389-E2390. Representative M. Biaggi (D-N.Y.) spoke on the problem of getting the federal government to own up to its responsibilities for veterans exposed to Agent Orange. The settlement is very nice but it still does not address this issue. Eighteen thousand veterans seeking complete medical care have sued the Veterans Administration. Representative Biaggi submitted a May 18, 1984 article from the Gannett Westchester newspapers to the Record.

1373 "Agent Orange Shows Up in Fat-biopsy Studies." (See 0962)

1374 "Agent Orange Studies." (See 0964)

1375 **"Agent Orange: Studies Find Cancer Link."** Rochester Patriot, v. 8, no. 9, May 16, 1980, p. 2. Congressmen D. Bonior (D-Mich.) and T. Daschle (D-S.D.) have made known the results of five studies done in Sweden and West Germany. The two publicized these studies as the Veterans Administration continues to state that there is no link between Agent Orange exposure and cancer.

1376 **"Agent Orange Study."** Congressional Record, v. 125, pt. 12, June 20, 1979, p. 15693. Senator C.H. Percy (R-Ill.) spoke in support of S. 1039 which would authorize the Department of Health, Education and Welfare to conduct a study of the health effects of exposure to Agent Orange.

1377 **"Agent Orange Study."** Congressional Record, v. 127, pt. 5, April 8, 1981, p. 7051-7052. Representative T. Railsback (R-Ill.) has introduced legislation asking that the Secretary of Health and Human Services arrange for an independent study of exposure to Agent Orange and that it should be conducted by the National Academy of Sciences. Representative Railsback feels that the Veterans Administration does not have sufficient credibility to conduct the study. The text of his bill is included.

1378   "Agent Orange Study May Be Given to CDC." DAV Magazine, v. 24, no. 11, November 1982, p. 14. There is a possibility that the epidemiological study on Agent Orange will be transferred to the Centers for Disease Control.

1379   "Agent Orange Study Rejected." Science News, v. 120, no. 24, December 12, 1981, p. 377. Office of Technology Assessment reviewers want more detail from the University of California at Los Angeles research team who designed an epidemiological study of Vietnam veterans who may have been exposed to Agent Orange and the reviewers question whether or not the study's objectives can be accomplished in a double-blinded fashion.

1380   "Agent Orange Study Reset." Facts on File, v. 42, no. 2188, October 22, 1982, p. 780. The responsibility for the study of the health effects of exposure of Vietnam veterans to Agent Orange has been turned over to the Centers for Disease Control.

1381   "Agent Orange Study Reset." Editorials on File, v. 13, no. 21, November 1-15, 1982, p. 1293-1295. This article consists of editorials from newspapers from around the country which discuss the fact that the epidemiological study on exposure to Agent Orange has been transferred from the Veterans Administration to the Centers for Disease Control and the findings of a General Accounting Office report on the medical examinations given by the Veterans Administration to veterans who believe they were exposed to Agent Orange.

1382   "Agent Orange Study Under CDC Control Now Backed by VA." Chemical Marketing Reporter, v. 222, no. 16, October 18, 1982, p. 4+. Veterans Administration Administrator Nimmo is trying to work out arrangements for the Centers for Disease Control to take over control of the epidemiological study to determine if exposure to Agent Orange is the cause of some Vietnam veterans' health problems. The Veterans Administration has been accused of deliberately stalling the study.

1383   "Agent Orange Study Will Be Pressed Despite Veterans Administration." Chemical Marketing Reporter, v. 227, no. 1, January 7, 1985, p. 5+. The Veterans Administration has agreed not to cancel a major Agent Orange research project at least until the study is reviewed by the Office of Technology Assessment.

1384 "Agent Orange: the Continuing Vietnam War." <u>Congressional Record</u>, v. 126, pt. 8, April 30, 1980, p. 9528.
Representative L. Panetta (D-CA) spoke in favor of H.R. 6377 which would include Agent Orange in the list of Veterans Administration recognized diseases which are presumed to be service-connected.

1385 "Agent Orange: the Persistent Uncertainty and Continuing Anguish Are Not likely to End Soon." (See 0971)

1386 "Agent Orange: Time Bomb...or Dud?" <u>American Legion Magazine</u>, v. 112, no. 3, March 1982, p. 34-37. The efforts veterans are making on Capitol Hill to get legislators to respond to the Agent Orange problem and the American Legion's position on Agent Orange are described. The article encourages all veterans exposed to Agent Orange to get a physical examination at the nearest Veterans Administration health facility.

1387 "Agent Orange: Update." <u>Congressional Record</u>, v. 126, pt. 16, August 6, 1980, p. 21469-21483. Senator A. Cranston (D-CA), chair of the Senate's Committee on Veterans' Affairs, updates the senators on the Agent Orange issue by having printed in the <u>Record</u> the Interagency Work Group to Study the Possible Long-Term Health Effects of Phenoxy Herbicides and Contaminants' progress report, their assessment of the Ranch Hand protocol, the agenda of the Veterans Administration Advisory Committee on Health-Related Effects of Herbicides' August 6th meeting and the Senator's July 31st letter to the Administrator of Veterans' Affairs on the Agent Orange issue.

1388 "Agent Orange Update." <u>Health/Pac Bulletin</u>, v. 12, no. 1, October 1980, p. 3. The reader is updated on the status of the Veterans Administration's epidemiological study and the Air Force's Ranch Hand study.

1389 "Agent Orange Update." <u>American Legion Magazine</u>, v. 112, no. 6, June 1982, p. 31. Recent developments in studies on the effects of Agent Orange on Vietnam veterans are briefly mentioned. The White House Agent Orange Working Group has approved the proposed design for a study on the health effects of exposure to Agent Orange. The Air Force Surgeon General feels that the results of the Ranch Hand study could carry implications for military personnel exposed to biological and chemical agents currently being developed by the Department of Defense. Governor J. Brown (D-CA) has signed legislation that will commit state resources to help Vietnam veterans exposed to Agent Orange. The New England Medical Center at Tufts University has begun testing children for problems related to Agent Orange exposure by their fathers serving in Vietnam.

1390 "Agent Orange Update." <u>American Legion Magazine</u>, v. 114, no. 4, April 1983, p. 28-31+. The recent transfer of the epidemiological study to the Centers for Disease Control, the progress of the Centers for Disease Control's birth defect study and the Air Force's Ranch Hand study, the activities of the Army Agent Orange Task Force and the White House's Cabinet level Agent Orange Working Group, and the research activities at the Veterans Administration are all discussed.

1391 "Agent Orange Update." <u>Citizen Soldier</u>, no. 7, June 1984, p. 4-5. This update consists of a series of short articles which discuss the Agent Orange Registry, the New Jersey Agent Orange Commission and questions veterans may have about the settlement.

1392 "Agent Orange Update." <u>Congressional Record</u>, v. 133, no. 17, February 4, 1987, p. S1755-S1780. Senator A. Cranston (D-CA) updated his fellow senators on the status of the Centers for Disease Control's Exposure Study and had correspondence from the Centers for Disease Control, the Department of Health and Human Services, the Office of Technology Assessment and the Senate Committee on Veterans' Affairs printed in the <u>Record</u> as this correspondence provides a historical examination of the Agent Orange study as well as its current status. Senator Cranston asked the Office of Technology Assessment and the Agent Orange Working Group to evaluate the methodologies and analysis used in a study conducted on farmers in Kansas who were exposed to herbicides for its relevance to studies being conducted on veterans who were exposed to Agent Orange. The report of this study, Senator Cranston's requests to the Office of Technology Assessment and the Agent Orange Working Group and their evaluations are included. Also included is a mortality update of the Project Ranch Hand II study being conducted by the Air Force and a status report from the Department of Health and Human Services on the major studies being conducted by the Centers for Disease Control, the Department of Defense and the Veterans Administration.

1393 "Agent Orange Veterans' Bill." <u>Congressional Record</u>, v. 130, no. 8, February 1, 1984, p. H316. Representative F. Harrison (D-PA) spoke on why he is glad that H.R. 1961, the Agent Orange and Atomic Veterans Relief Act, passed the House.

1394 "Agent Orange Victims." <u>Editorials on File</u>, v. 10, no. 23, December 1-15, 1979, p. 1438-1439. This article consists of editorials from newspapers from around the country reacting to the General Accounting Office's report which stated that ground troops were in areas sprayed with Agent Orange and to reports by veterans that they are experiencing health problems as a result of being exposed to Agent Orange.

1395 "Agent Orange: Women Were Victims, Too." Family Circle, v.
      98, no. 14, October 15, 1982, p. 82. The efforts women are
      making to get the fact across that they were also exposed to
      Agent Orange in Vietnam and are entitled to compensation,
      both as a result of the litigation and from the federal
      government, and to be included in the Centers for Disease
      Control's study are noted.

1396 "Agent Orange Work Group Formed." Congressional Record, v.
      127, pt. 14, July 31, 1981, p. 19204-19205. Senator A.
      Cranston (D-CA) announced that an Agent Orange Working
      Group of the Cabinet Council on Human Resources has been
      formed as a successor to the Interagency Work Group on
      Phenoxy Herbicides and Contaminants. Correspondence
      between M. Anderson, Assistant to the President for Policy
      Development, and Senator Cranston on this issue is included.

1397 "Air Force Under Fire for Agent Orange Study." Chemical
      Week, v. 126, no. 21, May 21, 1980, p. 18. The credibility
      and research design of a Department of Defense study on the
      health effects of Agent Orange have been questioned by a
      National Academy of Sciences' panel.

1398 "Air Force Will Study Men Who Sprayed Agent Orange."
      JAMA, v. 243, no. 2, January 11, 1980, p. 102-103. The study
      of the Operation Ranch Hand personnel will get underway very
      soon and is expected to last well into the 1980's. A group
      of Vietnam veterans met in Chicago recently to discuss how to
      get the federal government to take more action. The General
      Accounting Office released a report recently which stated
      that ground troops were in areas sprayed with Agent Orange
      and urges the federal government to determine if a study of
      the health effects of exposure to Agent Orange on ground
      troops is needed. Since 1977 the Veterans Administration has
      received more than 750 herbicide-associated compensation
      claims. However no compensation claims have been allowed
      based solely on herbicide exposure in Vietnam.

1399 "Amendments Submitted: Veterans' Dioxin and Radiation
      Exposure Compensation Standards Act." Congressional Record,
      v. 130, no. 68, May 22, 1984, p. S6277-S6279. The text of
      amendments to the Veterans' Dioxin and Radiation Exposure
      Compensation Standards Act submitted by Senator A.K. Simpson
      (R-WY) (amendment no. 3088) for himself and 10 others,
      Senator L. Pressler (R-S.D.) (amendment no. 3089) for himself
      and five others, Senator A. Specter (R-Pa) (amendment no.
      3090) for himself and three others and Senator H. Heflin (D-
      AL) (amendment no. 3091) is given.

1400 "And Now, Agents Blue, Brown and..." National Journal, v. 13, no. 29, July 18, 1981, p. 1293. The efforts Congress has made to respond to Vietnam veterans' concerns about having been exposed to Agent Orange and their efforts to force the Veterans Administration to deal with these concerns are briefly noted.

1401 Anderson, J.K. "VFW Leads in Agent Orange Fight." VFW Magazine, v. 79, no. 9, June 1983, p. 26-28+. Representatives from the VFW and four other veterans' organizations testified recently before a House subcommittee to support legislation introduced by Representative T. Daschle (D-S.D.) which would compensate veterans exposed to Agent Orange. The DAV and the Paralyzed Veterans of America oppose the legislation.

1402 "Another Agent Orange Study." Chemical Week, v. 134, no. 13, March 28, 1984, p. 14+. The Centers for Disease Control has announced the details of how they will conduct their Agent Orange/Vietnam Experience Study.

1403 "...Approves Agent Orange Compensation Bill." Chemical and Engineering News, v. 62, no. 42, October 15, 1984, p. 14. The Congress has approved a bill authorizing the payment of benefits to veterans suffering from chloracne and porphyria cutanea tarda, two Agent Orange-related diseases. The Veterans Administration is to issue regulations on these diseases as well as soft tissue sarcoma. A scientific advisory committee is to be established to review all of the pertinent technical, scientific and medical literature on a continuing basis.

1404 "Armed Services." (See 1996)

1405 "At Long Last Some Good News about Progress on the VA's Agent Orange Study." Congressional Record, v. 127, pt. 5, April 2, 1981, p. 6376. The Office of Technology Assessment has reported to Senator Cranston (D-CA) that progress has finally begun to be made on the Veterans Administration's epidemiological study. The text of the Office of Technology Assessment's letter to Senator Cranston is included.

1406 "At Year's End Agent Orange Scorecard Lopsided." Veterans Rights Newsletter, v. 6, no. 7-8, November-December 1986, p. 49+. This article reports on the lack of progress in distributing the funds from the out of court settlement, the lack of movement in the Centers for Disease Control's epidemiological study and the continuing denial of disability benefits by the Veterans Administration to veterans exposed to Agent Orange.

1407   Austin, B. "Et Al." (See 2002)

1408   **Austin, B. "U.S. Ignores Health Concerns of Women Who
       Served in Vietnam."** Los Angeles Daily Journal, v. 97, no.
       79, April 17, 1984, p. 4. Women who volunteered to work as
       civilians in Vietnam were also exposed to Agent Orange. The
       Veterans Administration has refused to treat them and the
       Centers for Disease Control is not planning to include them
       in their epidemiological study. There is a bill before the
       Senate Veterans Affairs Committee which includes a statement
       asking the government agencies to study the problem. The
       women are also lobbying for bills on the state level.

1409   **"Australia Funds Check on Agent Orange."** Chemical Week, v.
       126, no. 15, April 9, 1980, p. 18. The Commonwealth
       Institute of Health will be conducting a $2.2 million, two-
       year inquiry into the effects of Agent Orange exposure on
       Australian veterans at the University of Sydney. The
       Institute will attempt to interview about 60,000 veterans and
       their families which include about 100,000 children.

1410   **Bangert, J., S. Morfield and A. Verker. "GIs Fight Agent
       Orange Contamination."** Guardian, v. 31, no. 17, January 31,
       1979, p. 9. The efforts of Citizen Soldier, Agent Orange
       Victims International and Vietnam Vets for Self-Reliance to
       get the government to accept responsibility for the Agent
       Orange problem are noted.

1411   **Barnard, R.C. "Herbicide Threat to Humans Cited."** Air Force
       Times, v. 39, no. 40, April 30, 1979, p. 20. The General
       Accounting Office has issued a report stating that those
       involved in the spraying missions are more likely to have
       been exposed to Agent Orange. The report also states that a
       survey should be conducted to determine the long-term health
       effects of exposure. Also quite a few class action suits
       have been filed on behalf of veterans who feel they were
       exposed to Agent Orange against the manufacturers of the
       defoliant. Also discussed is the difficulty veterans are
       having getting assistance from the Veterans Administration.

1412   **Barnard, R.C. "Vets Get Action on Agent Orange."** Air Force
       Times, v. 39, no. 47, June 18, 1979, p. 4. The Air Force
       study of Ranch Hand personnel is seen by some veterans as a
       sign that the Carter Administration is changing its attitude
       on the Agent Orange issue.

1413   **"A Bill for the Special Needs of Vietnam-era Veterans."**
       Congressional Record, v. 129, no. 7, February 1, 1983, p.
       E227. Representative T.J. Downey (D-N.Y.) is reintroducing
       legislation which would waive the one-year limitation for

Vietnam veterans' claims for compensation for disabilities
and disease resulting from exposure to Agent Orange. The
text of H.R. 1135 is included.

1414 "Bill to Help Viet Vets Signed by Ohio Governor." Jet, v.
62, no. 16, June 28, 1982, p. 46. Governor J.A. Rhodes (R-
Ohio) has signed a bill providing $500,000 for screening
programs for possible victims of Agent Orange exposure in
Vietnam.

1415 "Bills on Agent Orange and Vet Centers Pass House and
Senate." Veterans Rights Newsletter, v. 1, no. 2, June 1981,
p. 9+. Both the House (H.R. 3499) and the Senate (S. 921)
have passed legislation on the Agent Orange issue. The
differences in the bills will need to be ironed out before a
final bill is sent to the President. These pieces of
legislation would require the Veterans Administration to
provide hospital care if the patients were found to be
suffering from disabilities due to exposure to Agent Orange
and would expand the scope of the Agent Orange study.

1416 "The Body Count Continues." [editorial] Short-Timers
Journal, no. 3, 1983, p. 1-3. This editorial questions why
the government moved so quickly in the case of Times Beach
but has not in the case of Vietnam veterans exposed to Agent
Orange with so many veterans having acutely manifested
problems.

1417 Bonior, D.E., S.M. Champlin and T.S. Kolly. The Vietnam
Veteran: a History of Neglect. New York: Praeger, 1984.
xix, 200p. The book details the problems facing the Vietnam
veteran. On pages 22, 116-117, 147-151 the efforts veterans
have made to get the federal government to respond to their
concerns about having been exposed to Agent Orange are
discussed.

1418 "Broadening Agent Orange Study Will Benefit All Vietnam Vets,
Says Chief." VFW Magazine, v. 70, no. 8, March 1983, p. 14.
The Centers for Disease Control has recently announced it
will broaden the Agent Orange study to include health
problems caused by other toxic agents and medications.
Commander-in-Chief Currieo believes this will benefit all
Vietnam veterans.

1419 Brownstein, R. "Who Compensates the Victims?" Nation, v.
230, no. 25, June 28, 1980, p. 777-780. The problems of
Vietnam veterans have in getting compensation from the
federal government for health problems resulting from Agent
Orange exposure are discussed in this article on the efforts
the victims of exposure to radiation and toxic chemicals are

making to obtain compensation from the government and
through the courts. The Agent Orange litigation is also
mentioned.

1420   Calesnick, B. "Dioxin and Agent Orange." (See 1015)

1421   California. Department of Veterans Affairs. Agent Orange: a
Vietnam Legacy, 1965-1971. Sacramento: The Department,
[n.d.] pamphlet. This pamphlet was developed to inform
California veterans on the issues surrounding the Agent
Orange controversy. Also included is a questionnaire which
the department is asking California veterans to complete in
order to assist the department in identifying the concerns
and needs of the state's veterans.

1422   California. Department of Veterans Affairs. Report to the
California State Legislature, AB 14 (Nolan), Agent Orange
Program. Sacramento: The Department, January 1, 1985. 1
volume (various paginations). The efforts the state of
California has made to carry out its Agent Orange program are
listed. Also described are the characteristics of the
California veteran identified as having been exposed to Agent
Orange.

1423   California. Legislature. Assembly. Veterans Affairs Select
Committee. The Effects of Agent Orange and Related
Herbicides and Psychological Problems (Delayed Stress
Syndrome) on Returning Vietnam Veterans. Hearing, August 5,
1981. Sacramento: Assembly Publications Office, 1981.
125p. Veterans, counselors and wives of veterans testified
about their experiences with Agent Orange. Mostly they
testified about their problems dealing with physicians, the
Veterans Administration, and their health and their
children's health.

1424   California. Legislature. Assembly. Veterans Affairs Select
Committee. The Effects of Agent Orange and Related
Herbicides and Psychological Problems (Delayed Stress
Syndrome) on Returning Vietnam Veterans. Hearing, August 6,
1981. Sacramento: Assembly Publications Office, 1981.
178p. Most of the people testifying at this hearing
discussed delayed stress syndrome among Vietnam veterans.
However, several veterans and counselors testified about
their experiences with Agent Orange.

1425   California. Legislature. Assembly. Veterans Affairs Select
Committee. The Effects of Agent Orange and Related
Herbicides on Returning Vietnam Veterans. Hearing, July 30,
1981. Sacramento: Assembly Publications Office, 1981.
139p. Among those testifying as this hearing were U.S.
Veterans Administration officials, a California Veterans

Affairs official, a California legislative assistant, counselors, Vietnam veterans and veterans' wives. The testimony from the veterans, wives and counselors dealt with their health problems and the problems they are having in dealing with the Veterans Administration. The testimony from the Veterans Administration officials for the most part defended the work they are doing in dealing with the Agent Orange problem.

1426   California. Legislature. Assembly. Veterans Affairs Select Committee. The Effects of Agent Orange and Related Herbicides on Returning Vietnam Veterans. Hearing, July 31, 1981. Sacramento: Assembly Publications Office, 1981. 193p. Testifying at this hearing about their concerns on Agent Orange were veterans and representatives of veterans' groups. Also testifying were Texas Representative L. Shaw about legislation that has been passed in Texas and Dr. G. Spivey, the Principal Investigator of the contract from the Veterans Administration to design the epidemiological study of Vietnam veterans who may have been exposed to Agent Orange. Dr. Spivey believes that Agent Orange is not the cause of many of the problems veterans attribute to it.

1427   Carney, L. "VA Drafts 'Orange' Care Plan." Air Force Times, v. 42, no. 20, December 7, 1981, p. 37. A draft regulation has been prepared by the Veterans Administration authorizing free medical care to Vietnam veterans exposed to Agent Orange. Care will be limited to hospital and nursing home care in Veterans Administration facilities and outpatient care in Veterans Administration facilities. A determination of eligibility to this program will not constitute a basis for later claiming service-connected disability.

1428   Carney, L. "VA Red Tape Said Adding to Agent Orange Anxiety." Air Force Times, v. 39, no. 43, May 21, 1979, p. 45. Senator A. Cranston (D-CA), Senate Veterans Affairs Committee Chairman, stated recently that "bureaucratic delay" by the Veterans Administration was "needlessly adding to the fear and uncertainty" of veterans. However, the Veterans Administration has started a registry of those who come to Veterans Administration clinics complaining of what veterans believe to be health problems related to Agent Orange exposure. Studies to determine if dioxin can be stored in the body have not been started.

1429   Carter, M.L. "House OKs Aid for Radiation, Defoliant Exposure." Air Force Times, v. 44, no. 30, February 13, 1984, p. 6. H.R. 1961 will provide temporary disability compensation for veterans who were either exposed to atomic radiation or chemical defoliants. It has passed the House and is now in the Senate Veterans Affairs Committee. Those exposed to the defoliants must suffer from soft tissue sarcoma, porphyria cutanea tarda or chloracne. If passed by the Senate and signed by the President, benefits would be payable as of October 1, 1983. The program is expected to cost $4.7 million in FY1984, $4.9 million in FY1985, and $5.2 million in FY1986.

1430   "Carter Vetoes Bill Requiring HEW Study of Dioxins." Congressional Quarterly Weekly Report, v. 38, no. 1, January 5, 1980, p. 42. President Carter in his first veto of a bill passed by the 96th Congress has rejected a bill which would have required the Department of Health, Education and Welfare to study the health effects of exposure to dioxins. However, the President has signed another bill which mandates that the Veterans Administration conduct a study of the health effects of Vietnam veterans' exposure to dioxins. The text of the veto message is included.

1431   "Changes." Win, v. 17, no. 13, July 15, 1981, p. 20. Twelve Vietnam veterans have begun a hunger strike in order to bring awareness to the problems veterans have in dealing with the Veterans Administration in regards to Agent Orange as well as demanding an investigation into the death of James Hopkins.

1432   "The Chemicals Question/Agent Orange." Congressional Record, v. 126, pt. 14, July 2, 1980, p. 18391-18392. Representative R. Roberts (D-Tex.) spoke on the Love Canal and the Agent Orange dilemmas.

1433   Chester, M.A. "Status of the Ranch Hand Study Concerning Herbicide Orange." Medical Service Digest, v. 33, no. 5, September-October 1982, p. 14-15. This article consists of the text of a statement the author made to the House Committee on Veterans' Affairs Subcommittee on Oversight and Investigations discussing the status of the Ranch Hand study.

1434   "Chicago City Council Addresses Agent Orange Issues." National Vietnam Veterans Review, v. 4, no. 2, February 1984, p. 34. The concerns of the Chicago area's 250,000 Vietnam veterans potentially exposed to Agent Orange were addressed recently in hearings held by the City of Chicago's Committee on Intergovernmental Affairs.

1435   "Chorus of Complaints on Veterans' Medical Care." U.S. News & World Report, v. 91, no. 3, July 20, 1981, p. 24+. In part, a discussion of the problems Vietnam veterans who believe they were exposed to Agent Orange are having in getting treatment at Veterans Administration medical facilities or compensation from the Veterans Administration.

Most of the veterans' concerns are about the quality of care
they are receiving at Veterans Administration medical
facilities.

1436 "Compensate for Agent Orange Exposure--VFW." VFW
      Magazine, v. 70, no. 4, January 1983, p. 42-43+. The VFW is
      the only major veterans' organization urging support of
      Representative T. Daschle's (D-S.D.) bill which would make
      Agent Orange exposure a presumptive disability. Also
      mentioned is the General Accounting Office's report which
      found mismanagement in the Veterans Administration's method
      of study of Agent Orange and urges the transfer of the
      Veterans Administration's epidemiological study to the
      Centers for Disease Control.

1437 "Compensation for Agent Orange Victims." Congressional
      Record, v. 129, no. 96, July 12, 1983, p. H4955.
      Representative W.R. Ratchford (D-Conn.) spoke in support of
      disability compensation to Vietnam veterans exposed to Agent
      Orange. In a study ordered by the Connecticut state
      legislature 540 serious health problems were found in 406
      veterans' families.

1438 "Compensation Proposed for Dioxin Exposure." Chemical and
      Engineering News, v. 63, no. 17, April 29, 1985, p. 13. The
      Veterans Administration has proposed the regulations they
      were required to develop as a result of the passage of the
      1984 Veterans' Dioxin & Radiation Exposure Compensation
      Standards Act under which veterans may receive compensation.
      The Veterans Administration at this time will only honor the
      claims of those suffering from chloracne and not of those
      suffering from porphyria cutanea tarda or soft tissue sarcoma
      as they do not feel there is enough medical evidence to
      support these claims.

1439 Comstock, E.G. "The Vietnam Veterans Agent Orange Relief
      Act." JAMA, v. 250, no. 3, July 15, 1983, p. 359. The
      author believes that the Vietnam Veterans Agent Orange Relief
      Act, S-374, should be defeated.

1440 "Congress May Provide Agent Orange Compensation." Chicago
      Daily Law Bulletin, v. 130, no. 92, May 9, 1984, p. 3+. Dow
      Chemical and Diamond Shamrock have stated that they plan to
      file a suit against the federal government in which they will
      contend the government had the ultimate responsibility for
      the use of Agent Orange in Vietnam. Representative T.
      Daschle (D-S.D.) feels that Congress will provide some relief
      for Vietnam veterans who feel that their ailments are the
      result of Agent Orange exposure.

1441 "Congress Says Agent Orange Study Taking Too Long."
<u>Veterans Rights Newsletter</u>, v. 2, no. 5-6, September-October
1982, p. 33. Testimony was heard before the House Veterans
Affairs Subcommittee on Oversight and Investigations which
criticized the length of time it is taking the Veterans
Administration to get its Agent Orange study underway.

1442 "Congressional Panel Hears Vietnam Vets on Agent Orange
Effects." <u>Chemical Week</u>, v. 125, no. 1, July 4, 1979, p. 18.
The House Commerce Committee's Subcommittee on Oversight
and Investigations heard testimony recently sharply
criticizing the manufacturers of Agent Orange from Vietnam
veterans and their families.

1443 Connecticut. Department of Health Services. Vietnam
Herbicides Information Center. <u>A Report from the Vietnam
Herbicides Information Center</u>. Hartford, Conn.: The
Department, April 1984, 41 p. This report details the
activities of the state of Connecticut's Vietnam Herbicides
Information Commission and the Vietnam Veterans Agent
Orange Victims, Inc. The status of scientific studies being
conducted by various branches of the federal government is
summarized.

1444 "Contract Hospital Care and Medical Services in Puerto Rico
and the Virgin Islands." <u>Congressional Record</u>, v. 127, pt.
8, May 21, 1981, p. 10774-10778. Senator A. Cranston (D-CA)
spoke on several amendments to S. 921. Amendment no. 59 (p.
10776-10778) would provide access to the Veterans
Administration's health-care system for veterans either
exposed to radiation during atomic testing or to Agent Orange
in Vietnam. The text of the amendment is included.

1445 Corson, W.R. "The Vietnam Veterans Adviser." <u>Penthouse</u>, v.
13, no. 3, November 1981, p. 114. The author believes that
the Veterans Administration must do something about the Agent
Orange problem.

1446 Corson, W.R. "The Vietnam Veterans Adviser." <u>Penthouse</u>, v.
13, no. 5, January 1982, p. 118. It has been revealed that
substantial numbers of servicemen in Vietnam were exposed to
Agent Orange when planes on defoliation missions had to dump
their cargo on or near military bases.

1447 Corson, W.R. "The Vietnam Veterans Adviser." <u>Penthouse</u>, v.
14, no. 4, December 1982, p. 124. The author calls on the
Veterans Administration to take action on the Agent Orange
problem.

1448 Craighead, J.E. "Dioxins." [letter] <u>Environment</u>, v. 21, no.

9, November 1979, p. 43. This letter is in response to A.S.
Miller's article (See 1611) which appeared in the June 1979
issue of this journal. This letter states that there is no
scientific verification for any dioxin-associated diseases in
Vietnam veterans or in the Vietnamese. He challenges the
author to provide appropriately documented data to support
his position.

1449 "DAV Seeks Continuation of Army Joint Services Environmental
      Support Group." DAV Magazine, v. 29, no. 1, January 1987, p.
      4. The Joint Services Environmental Support Group needs to
      be re-established now that its parent command has been shut
      down. This group helped pinpoint the location of U.S. units
      in South Vietnam during the war. This is an essential
      service as this helps determine who was exposed to Agent
      Orange.

1450 "DOD, GAO Differ on 'Orange.'" Air Force Times, v. 40, no.
      20, December 10, 1979, p. 4. A report prepared by the
      General Accounting Office stated they found that thousands of
      U.S. ground troops may have been exposed to Agent Orange
      despite claims to the contrary by the Department of Defense.

1451 "The Dangers of Agent Orange." Congressional Record, v. 126,
      pt. 5, March 19, 1980, p. 5908-5909. Representative D.
      Bonior (D-Mich.) stated that before Congress worries about
      the problems the Soviets are having with biological weapons,
      Congress should worry about getting some legislation passed
      to help veterans who were exposed to Agent Orange.

1452 Daschle, T. "Agent Orange Issue Is Colored by Need for More
      Data." [letter] Wall Street Journal, September 1, 1983, p.
      25(E), p. 23(W). The author wrote this letter in response to
      the Journal's Agent Orange March (See 1360) editorial.

1453 Daschle, T. "Making the Veterans Administration Work for
      Veterans." Journal of Legislation, v. 11, no. 1, Winter
      1984, p. 1-14. The lack of independent review of Veterans
      Administration policies and procedures has led to unfair
      decisions regarding the payment of benefits, a disregard of
      scientific and medical opinions unsupportive of Veterans
      Administration positions, and subjected sick and dying
      veterans to unnecessary suffering. These policies and
      procedures as they affect post World War II and Korean-era
      veterans suffering from radiation exposure and Vietnam-era
      veterans suffering from post-traumatic stress disorder and
      from exposure to Agent Orange are discussed.

1454 "Daschle Calls Agent-O Settlement 'Major Victory.'" (See
      2049)

1455 David, P. "Agent Orange: Veterans' Case Comes to Court."
(See 2050)

1456 **Davis, N.M.** "States Took Initiative in Agent Orange Battle."
State Legislatures, v. 10, no. 6, July 1984, p. 5-6. The
author describes programs that have been initiated to assist
Vietnam veterans who believe they were exposed to Agent
Orange in Vietnam.

1457 **Davis, R.** "Cheering Vets." Progressive, v. 45, no. 9,
September 1981, p. 18. A law which was passed recently by
the Texas legislature is commented upon. This law would
require the state to monitor Agent Orange patients and to
provide them with state-paid diagnostic testing upon request.
Also the Texas attorney general can sue the U.S. government
for the military records of veterans who want to determine if
they were exposed to Agent Orange.

1458 **Davis, S.** "Maude DeVictor - She Blew Whistle on Agent
Orange." Ms, v. 8, no. 12, June 1980, p. 26. The story of
how M. deVictor, a counselor with the Veterans Administration
in Chicago, researched the link between Agent Orange and the
health problems veterans in the Chicago area were having is
told. When the Veterans Administration pressured her into
stopping her investigation, she went public and a Chicago
television station produced a documentary on the topic.

1459 **DeBenedictis, D.J.** "Veterans Battle Stiff Legal Limits to
Get Into Court: Attorneys Criticize $10 Cap on Fees, Federal
Immunity: Others Defend System." Los Angeles Daily Journal,
v. 97, no. 228, November 12, 1984, p. 1+. The difficulty
veterans have in pressing claims including Agent Orange
against the Veterans Administration are noted.

1460 **"Defense."** Facts on File, v. 38, no. 1989, December 22,
1978, p. 984. Paul Reutershan, founder of Agent Orange
Victims International, passed away on December 14 of cancer.
The Veterans Administration stated on October 11 in testimony
before a House Veterans Affairs' subcommittee that about 500
Vietnam veterans had filed disability claims for ill effects
the veterans felt had been caused by exposure to Agent
Orange. Of these claims, 72 had been turned down, eight had
been approved and the rest were pending. Major General G.
Dettinger, Deputy Surgeon General of the Air Force, stated
that so far there is no evidence of lasting damage due to
Agent Orange exposure.

1461 **"Defoliant, Cancer: Studies Show Link,"** Science News, v.
117, no. 15, April 12, 1980, p. 230. Two members of Congress
who are Vietnam veterans recently released the results of

five studies which show that two components and a contaminant of Agent Orange probably cause cancer in humans. Veterans Administrator, M. Cleland, did not include the results of these studies in the Agent Orange packet recently released by the Veterans Administration.

1462 "Defoliant Companies Can Be Sued." (See 2058)

1463 DeHart, R. "Herbicide Orange Health Effects." Aviation Space and Environmental Medicine, v. 53, no. 5, May 1982, p. 512. The Air Force has begun a study of the veterans of the Ranch Hand Operation.

1464 "Delay in Agent Orange Study Hit." American Medical News, v. 25, no. 38, October 1, 1982, p. 16. The Veterans Administration has been threatened by the chairman of an informal caucus of Vietnam veterans in Congress that they will be relieved of the responsibility for its Agent Orange study if a pilot is not underway before mid-October.

1465 "Department Launches Agent Orange Program." California. Department of Veterans Affairs. Cal-Vet News, v. 4, no. 1, September 1982, p. 3. In October the Department of Veterans Affairs will launch a program of informing Vietnam veterans of the possible effects of exposure to Agent Orange.

1466 "Design for Agent Orange Research Project Faces Thorough Review." DAV Magazine, v. 23, no. 12, December 1981, p. 11. The design of the epidemiological study by scientists at the University of California at Los Angeles is now undergoing review by the National Research Council. The design has become controversial as Dr. Spivey, the researcher in charge of the study, recently told a committee of the California state legislature that there is little evidence that Agent Orange threatens human health.

1467 Diefenback, R.C. "Agent Orange Studies Are Incomplete." [letter] Occupational Health & Safety, v. 56, no. 2, February 1987, p. 67. The author responds to K. Mahler's article (See 1589) which appeared in the September 1986 issue of this journal. R.C. Diefenback wishes to correct some of the statements made regarding the method in which the Centers for Disease Control is conducting its studies of Vietnam veterans' health. He also explains why the start of the Agent Orange study has been delayed. It has to due with the problem of estimating the extent to which an individual veteran was exposed to Agent Orange.

1468 "A Different Approach with Newly Introduced Agent Orange Legislation." Congressional Record, v. 129, no. 27, March 8,

1983, p. H892-H893. Representative B. Edgar (D-Pa) is joining Representatives T. Daschle (D-S.D.) and D. Bonior (D-Mich.) in support of legislation which would authorize a presumption of disability compensation for Vietnam veterans exposed to dioxin suffering from chloracne, soft tissue sarcomas and porphyria cutanea tarda. Veterans have waited long enough for Congress to move on this issue.

1469   **"Dioxin Poisoning: Human Victims?"** Sciquest, **v. 52, no. 6, July-August 1979, p. 29.** In part mentions the difficulty those who believe they were exposed to Agent Orange in Vietnam are having in getting the Veterans Administration to assist them. The Air Force, however, has agreed to study participants in the spraying program.

1470   "Dioxin Poisons Vietnam Veterans." (See 1041)

1471   **"Dioxin's First Victims."** Congressional Record, **v. 129, no. 58, May 3, 1983, p. E2015-E2016.** Representative L.E. Panetta (D-CA) questions why the Times Beach victims have been given assistance and the veterans exposed to Agent Orange have not. He submitted to the Record an article by Representative T. Daschle (D-S.D.) which appeared in the April 24, 1983 issue of the Los Angeles Times.

1472   **"Disabled Veterans Rehabilitation Act of 1980."** Congressional Record, **v. 126, pt. 18, September 4, 1980, p. 24051-24093.** The floor debate on S. 1188, the Disabled Veterans Rehabilitation Act of 1980, is given. On page 24074 Senator A. Cranston (D-CA) offers unprinted amendment 1549 which would authorize expansion of the epidemiological study of Agent Orange. This amendment was passed. Unprinted amendment 1550 was offered by Senator H.J. Heinz (R-PA) which would eliminate some of the obstacles facing veterans who were exposed to Agent Orange in getting compensation from the Veterans Administration. The debate on this amendment is on pages 24076-24081. This amendment passed. S. 1188 was passed.

1473   **"Disabled Veterans Rehabilitation Act of 1980 - S. 1188."** Congressional Record, **v. 126, pt. 17, August 22, 1980, p. 22618.** Senator H.J. Heinz (R-PA) submitted amendment no. 2274 to S. 1188, the text of which is included. This amendment would presume a connection between certain diseases and Agent Orange exposure.

1474   **"Disabled Vets Battle Agent Orange."** Black Panther, **v. 20, no. 1, February 11, 1980, p. 6.** Testimony given by veterans at a U.S. Senate Veterans' Affairs Committee hearing in Los Angeles is detailed. Also noted are some of the lawsuits that have been filed.

1475 "Dispatch from the War that Isn't Over." Rolling Stone, no.
      348, July 23, 1981, p. 8+. The story of the veterans who
      started a hunger strike on the lawn of the Wadsworth Medical
      Center this spring is told. They were demanding an
      independent investigation into the suicide of James Hopkins
      and adequate treatment for those veterans who had been
      exposed to Agent Orange in Vietnam.

1476 Donnelly, H. "Senate Approves Hike in GI Benefits."
      Congressional Quarterly Weekly Report, v. 38, no. 5, February
      2, 1980, p. 262-263. The Senate has turned down a proposal
      that would have made it easier for Vietnam veterans exposed
      to Agent Orange to obtain service-connected disability
      benefits. Senate Cranston's (D-CA) amendment, however, was
      passed. It requires the Department of Health, Education and
      Welfare to study the effects of various types of dioxin
      exposure as a supplement to the Veterans Administration's
      study.

1477 "Dow Accused in House Subcommittee." Multinational Monitor,
      v. 2, no. 7, July 1981, p. 8. The House's Veterans Affairs'
      Subcommittee on Oversight and Investigations has prepared a
      report which charges that the Dow Chemical Company failed to
      warn the Department of Defense about the possible hazards of
      exposure to Agent Orange and that the Department of Defense
      may have ignored the hazards of which they were aware. Also
      the Congress has passed legislation providing federally
      funded medical treatment for Vietnam veterans who believe
      they were exposed to Agent Orange.

1478 "Dow Stubs Its Toe on a Dioxin Brochure." Chemical Week, v.
      131, no. 16, October 20, 1982, p. 17. The New York State
      Temporary Commission on Dioxin Exposure distributed 150,000
      brochures on Agent Orange which were written to inform
      Vietnam veterans who may have been exposed to Agent Orange.
      The Dow Chemical Company tried to halt the distribution of
      the brochures by obtaining a court order. They failed. Dow
      believes that the brochure is inaccurate and implies that
      exposure to dioxin may cause health problems in humans.

1479 "Downey 'Agent Orange' Bill." Congressional Record, v. 126,
      pt. 7, April 24, 1980, p. 9088-9099. Representative T.
      Downey (D-N.Y.) introduced H.R. 7157. This bill would amend
      title 38 so that the one-year limitation on claims for
      compensation from the Veterans Administration for medical
      problems incurred by military service would be waived for
      Vietnam veterans wanting compensation for exposure to Agent
      Orange.

1480 "Effects of Agent Orange." Congressional Record, v. 128, no.

116, August 20, 1982, p. E4031-4032. Representative M.M.
Heckler (R-Mass.) had an article from the August 20, 1982
issue of the <u>Boston Globe</u> inserted in the <u>Record</u>. This
article outlines some of the still unresolved issues
concerning Agent Orange exposure. Representative Heckler
states that she will continue to press for Veterans
Administration recognition of the effects of exposure to
Agent Orange.

1481 Elam, F. "Agent Orange Exposure Charges Backed." <u>Guardian</u>,
      v. 32, no. 9 December 5, 1979, p. 8. In a recently released
      report by the General Accounting Office, it was definitely
      proven that thousands of American soldiers were exposed to
      Agent Orange while serving in South Vietnam. Also a federal
      judge in New York has ruled that the veterans who have filed
      a lawsuit against the manufacturers of Agent Orange can
      legally sue the companies in federal court.

1482 Elliott, B. "Agent Orange/Compensation." <u>Congress Watcher</u>,
      July 1983, p. 10. The bills that have been recently
      introduced to compensate Vietnam veterans for diseases
      supposedly caused by exposure to Agent Orange are discussed.

1483 Ensign, T. "Action--at Last--on Agent Orange." <u>Guardian</u>, v.
      36, no. 20, February 22, 1984, p. 7. The resolution passed
      by the House of Representatives which would provide automatic
      compensation for veterans with cancer and other diseases
      caused by Agent Orange exposure is discussed. Also mentioned
      is the lawsuit which will soon go to trial after five years
      of pre-trial proceedings. Eleven representative cases have
      been selected. The manufacturers continue to state that they
      were acting as agents of the government.

1484 Ensign, T. "Agent Orange Compensation Law in Sight."
      <u>Guardian</u>, v. 36, no. 36, June 13, 1984, p. 4. Both the
      Senate and the House of Representatives have passed
      legislation which would require the Veterans Administration
      to draft guidelines for compensating veterans exposed to
      Agent Orange.

1485 Ensign, T. "Agent Orange Coverup." <u>Guardian</u>, v. 34, no. 38,
      June 23, 1982, p. 8. The Veterans Administration has issued
      a new brochure on Agent Orange which denies that any health
      symptoms from exposure to Agent Orange have been established
      and any health concerns about exposure are based on unproven
      scientific "theory."

1486 Ensign, T. "Agent Orange: Vietnam's Deadly Legacy." <u>Win</u>,
      v. 16, no. 8, May 15, 1980, p. 4-7. The reluctance of the
      Pentagon and the Veterans Administration to deal with the

issue is noted. A report issued by the General Accounting Office which has concluded basically that the Pentagon was lying about the number of troops directly exposed to Agent Orange and the lawsuits that have been filed are also mentioned.

1487 Ensign, T. "The Deadly Fog: Agent Orange Update." Health/Pac Bulletin, v. 11, no. 6, July-August 1980, p. 25-26. Despite public outcry the Pentagon and the Veterans Administration have been reluctant to acknowledge that exposure to Agent Orange has caused health problems among Vietnam veterans. Citizen Soldier, a GI/veterans' rights organization, has been active in gathering information about Agent Orange exposure.

1488 Ensign, T. "VA Loses Control of Agent Orange." Guardian, v. 35, no. 5, November 3, 1982, p. 5. Responsibility for the epidemiological study on Agent Orange has been transferred to the Centers for Disease Control.

1489 Ensign, T. and M. Uhl. "Dioxin: Uncovered by Accident, the Number of Cases Rising Dramatically." (See 1054)

1490 "Ex-Ranch Hand Volunteers Needed for 'Orange' Study." Air Force Times, v. 41, no. 15, November 3, 1980, p. 40. The Air Force Surgeon General, Lt. General P.W. Myers, is asking former Ranch Hand personnel to volunteer to participate in a long-term study of the effects of exposure to herbicides in Vietnam.

1491 "The Facts about Agent Orange: a Time for Reason." Congressional Record, v. 126, pt. 6, March 31, 1980, p. 7196-7199. Representative R. Roberts (D-Tex.) is not convinced of the validity of the claims of veterans that their health problems are a result of exposure to Agent Orange. He also was upset about the recent press conference held by two of his colleagues and the "evidence" they presented. He wishes that his colleagues would use judgement, reason and restraint when making comments to the media on this issue. Also included is the text of correspondence between M. Cleland and A. Young.

1492 Famiglietti, L. "AF Bows to Criticism, Won't Do Orange Study." Air Force Times, v. 40, no. 44, May 26, 1980, p. 26. As a result of criticism by the National Research Council, the Air Force has decided to let the Interagency Work Group of the Department of Health and Human Services determine how the study of the Ranch Hand personnel is to be conducted and by whom.

1493 Famiglietti, L. "Agent Orange: Physical Exams to Begin This
      Fall." Air Force Times, v. 41, no. 41, May 4, 1981, p. 2.
      The physical exams for the Air Force's study of the Ranch
      Hand personnel are scheduled to begin in September. The
      epidemiological procedures have been developed, an
      information packet for participants has been prepared and a
      preliminary questionnaire is being tested.

1494 Famiglietti, L. "Contract Granted for More Agent Orange
      Study." Air Force Times, v. 45, no. 34, March 11, 1985, p.
      14. The Air Force has awarded a $22.5 million contract so
      that the third and fifth year physical exams of the people
      that are participating in the study of the Ranch Hand crew
      members can be conducted.

1495 "Feds Admit Agent Orange Was Dropped on Americans." Jet, v.
      61, no. 5, October 15, 1981, p. 31. Newly discovered
      military records show that Agent Orange was dropped on or
      near U.S. military installations in 41 instances when
      airplanes had to dump their cargo of Agent Orange in
      emergencies.

1496 "A Final Battle with Agent Orange." Congressional Record, v.
      129, no. 13, February 14, 1983, p. E447-E448. Representative
      T.A. Daschle (D.-S.D.) mentions the fact that a veteran who
      was active in the Agent Orange movement passed away recently.
      Charlie Hartz died of brain cancer at the age of 35.
      Representative Daschle will reintroduce legislation which
      would grant compensation to veterans suffering from ailments
      which could be caused by Agent Orange exposure.
      Representative Daschle had two articles from the Philadelphia
      Inquirer inserted into the Record. One by M. Bowden was from
      the December 21, 1979 issue and the other by L. Herskowitz
      was from the August 26, 1980 issue.

1497 "Finally, Agent Orange Studies Begin." VFW Magazine, v. 73,
      no. 1, September 1985, p. 12. The Centers for Disease
      Control is ready to begin its study of 43,000 Army personnel
      from E-5 or below who served during the Vietnam Era. Thirty
      thousand will be chosen for telephone interviews, 10,000 will
      be chosen for three-day physicals and psychological testing
      at government expense.

1498 Fisher, M.J. "Insurers Prefer Senate Toxic Substances
      Proposal." National Underwriter: Property & Casualty
      Insurance Edition, v. 88, no. 22, June 1, 1984, p. 1.
      Insurers prefer the Senate version over the House version of
      a bill which would grant service-connected compensation for
      exposure to Agent Orange. The Senate version would require
      the Veterans Administration to develop guidelines for

determining who would be compensated. The House version assumes that there is a connection between exposure to Agent Orange and three diseases.

1499 "Five Hundred Vets File Dioxin Disability Claims." Medical World News, v. 19, no. 23, November 13, 1978, p. 78. Of the 500 claims alleging harm from exposure to Agent Orange, eight have been granted, 72 have been denied and the others are pending. A registry of veterans diagnosed and treated by the Veterans Administration's Medical Services Department has been started. Also discussed is whether or not levels of dioxin can be measured in a human being.

1500 Flowers, F.P., N.A. Fenske and P.A. Whisman. "Agent Orange: What's It All About." Florida Medical Association. Journal, v. 68, no. 12, December 1981, p. 991-992. The investigative efforts underway to determine the health effects of exposure to Agent Orange are noted. Specifically mentioned are the Operation Ranch Hand study, the Veterans Administration's Agent Orange Registry, the Veterans Administration's epidemiological study which will be designed by a research team at the University of California at Los Angeles and the establishment of the Intragency Work Group to Study Possible Long-term Health Effects of Phenoxy Herbicides and Contaminants.

1501 "From Academy Reports: to Study Effects of Agent Orange on Health..." National Academy of Sciences. News Report, v. 30, no. 7, July 1980, p. 5. This article consists of the text of a letter of transmittal by P. Handler concerning the report issued by the Academy entitled Review of U.S. Air Force Protocol: Epidemiological Investigation of Health Effects in Air Force Personnel Following Exposure to Herbicide Orange in May. This report concludes that the proposed study would not verify adverse health effects due to exposure to the herbicide.

1502 "GAO Clears Way for VA Agent Orange Study." Congressional Record, v. 127, pt. 2, February 19, 1981, p. 2525. Representative G.V. Montgomery (D-Miss.) spoke about the delays the Veterans Administration has faced in getting started on the epidemiological study. These delays are the result of litigation being brought against the Veterans Administration and a protest which was brought to the General Accounting Office. The litigation has been dismissed and the General Accounting Office has now cleared the way for the Veterans Administration to begin working on the epidemiological study.

1503 "GAO Reports: Agent Orange Exams Need Improvement." Citizen Soldier, no. 5, May 1983, p. 6. The General

Accounting Office released the report of their investigation of the Veterans Administration's Agent Orange examination program in late 1982. The report concludes that veterans were generally dissatisfied with the Veterans Administration's efforts, that only one of the 14 facilities the General Accounting Office visited was adequately following up on the health problems reported by veterans, most physical examinations were incomplete and few examination records documented a complete medical history. The report also details deficiencies found in the Agent Orange Registry.

1504 "GAO Says Agent Orange Exams Need Improvement." Veterans Rights Newsletter, v. 2, no. 5-6, September-October 1982, p. 33+. The General Accounting Office has issued a report on its investigation of the Veterans Administration's Agent Orange examination program. The General Accounting Office found that veterans are generally dissatisfied with the program and made several suggestions for improvement.

1505 "GAO Scores VA Agent Orange Exams." Facts on File, v. 42, no. 2191, November 21, 1982, p. 846. In a survey prepared by the General Accounting Office, it was found that medical exams of Vietnam veterans exposed to Agent Orange had been inadequately administered by the Veterans Administration. The Veterans Administration has replied that they feel that the General Accounting Office used out-of-date information and has exaggerated the problem.

1506 "GI Bill Amendments Act." Congressional Record, v. 126, pt. 21, September 26, 1980, p. 27575-27595. The House amendments to the Senate amendments to H.R. 5288 are discussed. The text of the letters between Senator A. Cranston (D-CA) and Representative R. Roberts (D-Tex.) on the issue of compensation to veterans who were exposed to Agent Orange is given on pages 27579-27580.

1507 "GI Bill Amendments Act of 1979." Congressional Record, v. 126, pt. 1, January 24, 1980, p. 646-670. Senator J. Heinz (R-PA) offered on page 653 amendment 922 of S.870, a bill which would make some changes in GI educational programs. This amendment would provide for a presumption of service connection for certain disease arising in Vietnam-era veterans exposed to Agent Orange. A letter from R. Muller, Executive Director of Vietnam Veterans of America and articles from the Boston Globe, Philadelphia Inquirer and the New York Times were read into the Record. Senator A. Cranston (D-CA) offered on page 658 amendment 923 which would require the Secretary of the Department of Health, Education and Welfare to study the long-term effects of Agent

Orange exposure as a substitute to Senator Heinz's amendment.
Senator Heinz moved to table Senator Cranston's amendment.
This was rejected. The Cranston and Heinz amendments were
both approved.

1508   Garment, S. "Painful Problem: How to Aid Victims of Agent
       Orange." Wall Street Journal, April 27, 1984, p. 28(E), p.
       26(W). Legislation currently before Congress is discussed.
       The author feels that legislators can not continually shift
       the costs of contamination to industry and that they should
       take care when and where they acknowledge national
       obligation.

1509   Garmon, L. "Agent Orange Issue: Far from Settled." Science
       News, v. 122, no. 10, September 4, 1982, p. 149. A recent
       meeting of the Veterans Administration's Advisory Committee
       on the Health-Related Effects of Herbicides drew a standing
       room only crowd. The proposed study protocol for the
       epidemiological study is due in the next few weeks. It will
       be 1989 before any meaningful results can be expected.

1510   Garmon, L. "Dioxin Digest." Science News, v. 124, no. 10,
       September 3, 1983, p. 156-157. A bill that would make
       Vietnam veterans disabled by one of three relatively rare
       diseases presumably due to exposure to Agent Orange eligible
       for compensation was approved by a panel of the U.S. House of
       Representative's Veterans' Affairs Committee. A study of
       85,000 Vietnam veterans concerned about exposure to Agent
       Orange showed a wide variety of health problems but nothing
       specifically related to Agent Orange exposure says A.L. Young
       of the Veterans Administration.

1511   Garmon, L. "VA Yields Control of Agent Orange Study."
       Science News, v. 122, no. 17, October 23, 1982, p. 263. The
       Veterans Administration has agreed to give up control of the
       investigation into whether or not exposure to Agent Orange
       has caused health problems in Vietnam veterans. The Centers
       for Disease Control will probably take over the study.

1512   Gates, E. "VA's Agent Orange Dilemma." Air Force Magazine,
       v. 63, no. 8, August 1980, p. 91. The Veterans
       Administration's position on Agent Orange is explained. The
       Veterans Administration intends to publicize all new
       developments on Agent Orange. They do care.

1513   Gazella, K. "Seeing Orange." Environmental Action, v. 14,
       no. 4, October-November 1982, p. 7-8. At a recent hearing
       held by a subcommittee of the House Veterans Affairs
       Committee, Representative T. Daschle (D-S.D.) stated that he
       would introduce legislation to take the Veterans

Administration's epidemiological study away from them and give it to another group if the Veterans Administration did not get the study underway in one month. Only five million dollars of the Veterans Administration's $140 million research budget goes to Agent Orange studies.

1514   Geisel, J. "Agent Orange Study." Business Insurance, v. 16, no. 18, May 3, 1982, p. 55. The White House Agent Orange Working Group has approved a pilot study which is the last preliminary step before launching a massive survey of the 18,000 Vietnam veterans who may have been exposed to Agent Orange. Also detailed is the progress that has been made in the Ranch Hand veterans study and the Centers for Disease Control's study of 7500 children with birth defects.

1515   Geisel, J. "Agent Orange Study." Business Insurance, v. 18, no. 23, June 4, 1984, p. 33. As a result of legislation passed by the Senate, the Veterans Administration and an independent 15-member commission will decide how to compensate servicemen exposed to radiation from atomic weapons and to Agent Orange. Compensation rules will be developed for several diseases associated with exposure to Agent Orange including chloracne, soft tissue sarcoma and porphyria cutanea tarda. A congressional conference will be set up to resolve the differences between this legislation and similar legislation passed by the House.

1516   Gemperlein, J. "Forgotten: Women Vets of Vietnam." National Vietnam Veterans Review, v. 5, no. 4, April-June 1986, p. 11. The problems women Vietnam veterans have had, including getting health care and recognition that they too suffer from having been exposed to Agent Orange, are discussed. The Centers for Disease Control has refused to include these women in their Agent Orange study.

1517   Gottlieb, M. "The Vietnam War that's Still Being Fought." New York, v. 15, no. 42, October 25, 1982, p. 16+. The efforts of the Vietnam Veterans Agent Orange Victims, Inc. and other veterans' groups are making to get the Veterans Administration to accept responsibility for the Agent Orange issue are described as well as their position in the class action suit against the manufacturers of the defoliant. Dow's position in the issue is also mentioned.

1518   "Government Admits More Vets Were Exposed to Agent Orange: Secretary Schweiker Wants to Hear from Vets." Veterans Rights Newsletter, v. 1, no. 5-6, September-October 1981, p. 39. At a press conference held on September 23, Secretary of Health and Human Services, R. Schweiker, admitted that there were more soldiers exposed to Agent Orange than previously thought.

1519 "Gov't Report on Agent Orange." CBS News Daily News Broadcasts, v. 10, no. 229, August 16, 1984, p. 9-10 (evening news). Further debate on the Centers for Disease Control's study on birth defects and service in Vietnam is given.

1520 Griswold, D. "The Pentagon's Genetic Time Bomb." Workers World, v. 21, no. 25, June 22, 1979, p. 4+. The Pentagon has continued to deny the claims for compensation for veterans exposed to Agent Orange because they do not want to admit they were involved in chemical warfare.

1521 Gunby, P. "Agent Orange: What's to Be Done by Whom?" JAMA, v. 243, no. 23, June 20, 1980, p. 2375+. The design of the Air Force's Operation Ranch Hand study has been criticized by the National Research Council. Several veterans' groups have also filed a lawsuit challenging the Veterans Administration's recent request for scientists to submit study proposals for their Congressionally-mandated epidemiological study.

1522 Gunby, P. "Military Looks Toward 1985 in Ongoing Defoliant Study." JAMA, v. 251, no. 16, April 27, 1984, p. 2067-2068. The controversy surrounding the recently released result of the baseline report from the study of the Operation Ranch Hand personnel is discussed.

1523 Gunby, P. "Plenty of Fuel for Agent Orange Dispute." JAMA, v. 242, no. 7, August 17, 1979, p. 593+. A study will be conducted by the U.S. Air Force on the Ranch Hand veterans. Organizations such as Citizen Soldier are calling for more extensive studies and have set up hotlines to help veterans with health problems. The National Veterans' Task Force on Agent Orange has announced they will be undertaking an epidemiological study with the cooperation of the American Health Foundation.

1524 "H.R. 1961." Congressional Record, v. 130, no. 7, January 31, 1984, p. E189-E190. Representative K. Kramer (R-Colo.) spoke on why he supports the passage of H.R. 1961, the Agent Orange and Atomic Veterans Relief Act.

1525 "H.R. 1961." Congressional Record, v. 130, no. 7, January 31, 1984, p. E192. Representative R.D. Coleman (D-Tex.) spoke on why he supports the passage of H.R. 1961, the Agent Orange and Atomic Veterans Relief Act.

1526 "H.R. 1961." Congressional Record, v. 130, no. 7, January 31, 1984, p. E209. Representative D. Edwards (D-CA) spoke on why he supported H.R. 1961, the Agent Orange and Atomic Veterans Relief Act, but expressed his disappointment that

this bill did not go as far as the bill originally introduced
by Representative T. Daschle (D-S.D.). Representative
Edwards recently visited Vietnam to investigate the effects
of Agent Orange on the Vietnamese and Vietnam's ecology.

1527 "H.R. 1961." Congressional Record, v. 130, no. 7, January
      31, 1984, p. E221. Representative E. Hillis (R-Ind.) spoke
      on why he supports the passage of H.R. 1961, the Agent Orange
      and Atomic Veterans Relief Act.

1528 "H.R. 1961." Congressional Record, v. 130, no. 7, January
      31, 1984, p. E221-E222. Representative L.E. Panetta (D-CA)
      spoke on why he supports the passage of H.R. 1961, the Agent
      Orange and Atomic Veterans Relief Act.

1529 "H.R. 1961." Congressional Record, v. 130, no. 9, February
      2, 1984, p. E300-E301. Representative W. Dowdy (D-Miss.)
      spoke on why he supports the passage of H.R. 1961, the Agent
      Orange and Atomic Veterans Relief Act.

1530 "H.R. 1961." Congressional Record, v. 130, no. 11, February
      6, 1984, p. E331. Representative B. McEwen (R-Ohio)
      explained why he supports the passage of H.R. 1961, the Agent
      Orange and Atomic Veterans Relief Act.

1531 "H.R. 1961." Congressional Record, v. 130, no. 11, February
      6, 1984, p. E339-E340. Representative C. Schneider (R-R.I.)
      explained why she supports the passage of H.R. 1961, the
      Agent Orange and Atomic Veterans Relief Act.

1532 "H.R. 1961 - Agent Orange and Atomic Veterans Relief Act."
      Congressional Record, v. 130, no. 7, January 31, 1984, p.
      E189. Representative S. Conte (R-Mass.) spoke on why he
      supports the passage of H.R. 1961, the Agent Orange and
      Atomic Veterans Relief Act.

1533 "H.R. 1961, the Agent Orange and Atomic Veterans Relief Act."
      Congressional Record, v. 130, no. 7, January 31, 1984, p.
      E222. Representative O.J. Snowe (R-Maine) spoke on why she
      supported the passage of H.R. 1961, the Agent Orange and
      Atomic Veterans Relief Act.

1534 "H.R. 6377 Introduced, Extending Service-Connected Disability
      Benefits to Veterans Who Have Suffered Dioxin Poisoning."
      Congressional Record, v. 126, pt. 8, May 6, 1980, p. 9917.
      Representative C.J. Dodd (D-Conn.) is convinced there is a
      cause and effect relationship between exposure to Agent
      Orange in Vietnam and the development of documented
      symptoms. Therefore he has decided to co-sponsor H.R. 6377.
      Representative Dodd feels that not enough has been done for
      the veteran who was exposed to Agent Orange.

1535 Hartnett, N.B. "Agent Orange." DAV Magazine, May 1979
      (See 1088)

1536 **Hartnett, N.B. "Agent Orange." DAV Magazine, v. 25, no. 2,
      February 1983, p. 2-3.** The Centers for Disease Control have
      agreed to take over responsibility for the Veterans
      Administration's epidemiological study. The project
      completion date is September 1987. The DAV's position on
      Agent Orange research and compensation is detailed.

1537 Hay, A. "Dioxin: the 10-year Battle that Began with Agent
      Orange." (See 2123)

1538 **"Health Effects of Agent Orange." Congressional Record, v.
      126, pt. 9, May 13, 1980, p. 11113-11114.** Representative D.
      Bonior (D-Mich.) stated that due to the fact that neither the
      Veterans Administration or the Air Force has the capability
      or desire to get to the bottom of the Agent Orange dilemma,
      an independent and non-biased government agency should be
      charged with the responsibility for solving this problem.

1539 **"Health Effects of Agent Orange Must Be Resolved."
      Congressional Record, v. 125, pt. 28, December 18, 1979, p.
      36680-36685.** Senator C.H. Percy (R-Ill.) feels disappointed
      that the epidemiological study will be conducted by the
      Veterans Administration instead of the Department of Health,
      Education and Welfare as the Veterans Administration has not
      satisfactorily addressed the Agent Orange issue. Senator
      Percy also discusses the General Accounting Report which
      found that U.S. ground troops were in areas sprayed with
      Agent Orange. He has included in the Record a copy of this
      General Accounting Office report and copies of letters he has
      written to Defense Secretary H. Brown and Veterans
      Administration Administrator M. Cleland.

1540 **"Help for Agent Orange Victims." Congressional Record, v.
      130, no. 13, February 8, 1984, p. E403.** Representative R.A.
      Borski (D-PA) spoke on the passage of H.R. 1961, the Vietnam
      Veterans' Agent Orange Relief Act of 1983. He believes it is
      an important first step towards compensating Vietnam veterans
      who were exposed to Agent Orange.

1541 **Hennessey, B. "Vets Fight Agent Orange." Guardian, v. 31,
      no. 28, April 18, 1979, p. 3.** The General Accounting Office
      has recently released a report recommending that the Pentagon
      undertake a survey of the health effects of Agent Orange.
      Citizen Soldier has been demanding government action but has
      not met with much success and has been conducting their own
      survey.

1542 "Herbicide Exposure." <u>Congressional Record</u>, v. 126, pt. 8, May 7, 1980, p. 10388. Representative L. Aspin (D-Wisc.) expressed his concern about the irresponsible and insensitive way the Veterans Administration and the Department of Defense have dealt with the Agent Orange issue.

1543 Hirst, D. "GAO: Agent Orange Exams Often Inadequate." <u>Air Force Times</u>, v.43, no. 17, November 15, 1982, p. 39. The General Accounting Office has issued a report stating that the physical examinations given by the Veterans Administration to veterans who are worried about the effects Agent Orange might have on their health were inadequate. Also addressed in this report is the difficulty veterans are having in obtaining compensation.

1544 Holden, C. "Reviewers Pan Agent Orange Study Plan." <u>Science</u>, v. 214, no. 4525, December 4, 1981, p. 1107. The research team at the University of California at Los Angeles who designed a protocol for the study of veterans exposed to Agent Orange have been asked to go back to the drawing board as the task forces who reviewed it found it very unsatisfactory. The team has 35 days to come up with a new protocol.

1545 Holden, C. "UCLA Designing Big Agent Orange Study." <u>Science</u>, v. 212, no. 4497, May 22, 1981, p. 905. A research team at the University of California at Los Angeles has been awarded $114,288 by the Veterans Administration to design a protocol for a study on the effects of exposure of Vietnam veterans to Agent Orange. The Air Force is planning to study the effects of exposure among the Operation Ranch Hand veterans. Veterans' groups are pressuring Congress to pass several bills on this issue.

1546 Holden, C. "VA Study of Twins May Be Cancelled." <u>Science</u>, v. 226, no. 4674, November 2, 1984, p. 521. The Veterans Administration may cancel its study using twins to determine the long term health effects of service in Vietnam. The study population has been determined to be too small. A registry of 12,000 twin pairs will be continued. They will be sent detailed health questionnaires. There is some concern if the study is cancelled that the Veterans Administration's credibility with veterans will be diminished even further.

1547 Holden, C. "VA to Study Twins." <u>Science</u>, v. 223, no. 4641, March 16, 1984, p. 1157. In an attempt to learn more about the psychological, psychosocial and health effects of service in the Vietnam War, the Veterans Administration is planning a study of twin veterans. It is hoped that one of the outcomes

of this study will be meaningful information on the effects
of exposure to Agent Orange.

1548 "House Orders VA Medical Care for Vietnam Veterans
      Exposed to Agent Orange." Congressional Quarterly Weekly
      Report, v. 39, no. 23, June 6, 1981, p. 1003-1005. The House
      has passed a bill which would require that the Veterans
      Administration provide medical care to Vietnam veterans
      exposed to Agent Orange over the opposition of the Reagan
      Administration. The reasons why the House felt it necessary
      to pass this bill are mentioned.

1549 "House Orders VA to Care for Agent Orange Patients."
      American Medical News, v. 24, no. 23, June 12, 1981, p. 2.
      The House has passed legislation directing the Veterans
      Administration to provide hospital care and medical attention
      to those veterans who believe they were exposed to Agent
      Orange in Vietnam. This is the first formal legislation
      approved by Congress which acknowledges there may be a link
      between the health problems veterans have and Agent Orange.

1550 "House Passes Agent Orange Bill." Congressional Record, v.
      130, no. 7, January 31, 1984, p. E225-E226. Representative
      J.J. Florio (D-N.J.) spoke on why he supported the passage of
      H.R. 1961, the Agent Orange and Atomic Veterans Relief Act.
      He mentions that the passage of this bill in the House is
      only one of the major hurdles this bill faces in the upcoming
      months.

1551 Humphrey, G.F. "Scientists and Royal Commissions." Search,
      v. 17, no. 3-4, March 1986, p. 63-64. The author comments on
      the way in which scientists were treated as witnesses before
      the Royal Commission on the Use and Effects of Chemical
      Agents on Australian Personnel in Vietnam (also known as the
      Evatt Royal Commission), the Royal Commission into British
      Nuclear Test in Australia and the Royal Commissions into
      Exploratory and Production Drilling for Petroleum in the Area
      of the Great Barrier Reef. In the Evatt Royal Commission
      report there are comments regarding both the personal and
      professional competence of these scientists.

1552 Illinois. Agent Orange Study Commission. Interim Report.
      Springfield, Ill.: The Commission, December 1982. 8p. This
      report details the legislative mandate to the Commission and
      how the Commission perceives its role. Also provided is a
      statistical summary of the 28 witnesses before the Commission
      who provided written testimony detailing their complaints.

1553 Illinois. Agent Orange Study Commission. Testimonies from
      Professional Hearings (See 1099)

1554   "In Recognition of the American Veterans." <u>Congressional</u>
       <u>Record</u>, v. 130, no. 7, January 31, 1984, p. E228.
       Representative S. Gejdenson (D-Conn.) spoke on why he
       supported the passage of H.R. 1961, the Agent Orange and
       Atomic Veterans Relief Act, even though it is a compromise
       bill and does not go far enough in addressing the needs of
       affected veterans.

1555   "In Support of H.R. 1961, the Agent Orange Relief Act."
       <u>Congressional Record</u>, v. 130, no. 7, January 31, 1984, p.
       E194. Representative B. Richardson (D-N.M.) spoke on why he
       supports the passage of H.R. 1961, the Agent Orange and
       Atomic Veterans Relief Act.

1556   "In Support of the Conference Report on H.R. 1961."
       <u>Congressional Record</u>, v. 130, no. 130 part II, October 4,
       1984, p. E4259. Representative D. Edwards (D-CA) spoke on
       why he supports the passage of the conference report on H.R.
       1961, the Agent Orange and Atomic Veterans Relief Act.

1557   "Incidents Involve Orange: Chemicals Dumped Near Bases."
       <u>Air Force Times</u>, v. 42, no. 11, October 5, 1981, p. 3.
       Health and Human Services Department Secretary Schweiker
       announced in a recent press conference that Agent Orange was
       dumped on U.S. military personnel in Vietnam because the
       pilots were sometimes forced to dump their cargo on or near
       military bases because of enemy fire or engine failures.

1558   "The Independent Agent Orange Study Act." <u>Congressional</u>
       <u>Record</u>, v. 127, pt. 2, February 19, 1981, p. 2520-2521.
       Representative B.A. Gilman (R-N.Y.) reintroduced his
       independent Agent Orange Study Act which calls for the
       Veterans Administration to transfer control of the
       epidemiological study to the National Academy of Sciences.
       The text of H.R. 1962 is included.

1559   "The Independent Agent Orange Study Act of 1980."
       <u>Congressional Record</u>, v. 126, pt. 21, September 30, 1980, p.
       28558-28559. Representative B.A. Gilman (R-N.Y.) submitted
       H.R. 8238 which would require the Veterans Administration and
       the National Academy of Sciences to enter into an agreement
       whereby the Academy would conduct an epidemiological study
       on the effects of exposure to Agent Orange on veterans. The
       text of the resolution is included.

1560   "Introduction of Agent Orange Compensation Legislation."
       <u>Congressional Record</u>, v. 129, no. 27, March 8, 1983, p. H891-
       H892. Representative T.A. Daschle (D-S.D.) is introducing
       legislation which would grant compensation to Vietnam
       veterans suffering from soft tissue cancer or porphyria

cutanea tarda based on the assumption that these diseases were caused by exposure to Agent Orange.

1561 "Introduction of Bills and Joint Resolutions." Congressional Record, v. 127, pt. 3, March 5, 1981, p. 3668. Senator A. Cranston (D-CA) introduced for himself and two other senators S. 636 which would among other things expand the scope of the epidemiological study the Veterans Administration is conducting on the effects of Agent Orange exposure. The bill was referred to the Committee on Veterans Affairs.

1562 "Introduction of Bills and Joint Resolutions." Congressional Record, v. 127, pt. 4, March 12, 1981, p. 4260-4261. Senator J. Heinz (R-PA) introduced S. 869 for himself and three other senators (page 4260) which would require that the regulations containing guidelines for resolving claims for veterans' benefits based on exposure to Agent Orange be promulgated.

1563 "Introduction of Bills and Joint Resolutions." Congressional Record, v. 129, no. 30, March 11, 1983, p. S2676. Senator L. Pressler (R-S.D.) introduced S. 786 which would establish a service-connection presumption for certain diseases caused by exposure to herbicides or other environmental hazards or conditions in veterans who served in Southeast Asia during the Vietnam era. This legislation was referred to the Committee on Veterans Affairs.

1564 "Introduction of Bills and Joint Resolutions." Congressional Record, v. 129, no. 4, April 6, 1983, p. S4182-S4183. Senator A. Cranston (D-CA) introduced S. 991. This bill would require regulations providing for the resolution of Veterans Administration benefits claims based on certain exposures to herbicides containing dioxin, radiation and other hazardous substances and for other purposes. The bill was referred to the Committee on Veterans' Affairs.

1565 "Introduction of Bills and Joint Resolutions." Congressional Record, v. 129, no. 103, July 20, 1983, p. S10466-S10467. On page S. 10466 it is stated that Senator A. Cranston (D-CA) introduced S. 1651 for himself and three other Senators. This bill would provide for presumption of service-connection for certain diseases in certain veterans assumed to be caused as a result of exposure to Agent Orange or radiation. The bill was referred to the Committee on Veterans' Affairs.

1566 Jacobs, J.B. and D. McNamara. "Vietnam Veterans and the Agent Orange Controversy." Armed Forces & Society: an Interdisciplinary Journal, v. 13, no. 1, Fall 1986, p. 57-79. The authors summarize the efforts veterans have made to get the Veterans Administration and Congress to respond to their concerns about having been exposed to Agent Orange, the events that led to the litigation, the issues involved in the lawsuit (including the connection between the lawsuit, the Feres Doctrine, the Government Contract Defense and the settlement) and the sociopolitical implications of the Agent Orange issue.

1567   Joeckel, C.E., Jr. "Radiation, Agent Orange Veterans Are Winners." DAV Magazine, v. 26, no. 11, November 1984, p. 2+. A compromise Agent Orange and radiation exposure bill has been sent to the White House. It establishes a two year program of temporary allowances for disability or death in cases involving chloracne and porphyria cutanea tarda suffered by Vietnam veterans exposed to Agent Orange. It also directs the Veterans Administration to develop regulations governing the adjudication of claims based on exposure to Agent Orange or radiation from nuclear detonations. The scope and content of these regulations have been tightly defined.

1568   Juarbe, F., Jr. "Budge Cuts Hampering Herbicide Study." VFW Magazine, v. 69, no. 6, March 1982, p. 49. The Veterans Administration's efforts to study veterans' exposure to Agent Orange is limited by Congress' slashing of the Veterans Administration's research and development funds. It is the apparent intention now to study the Operation Ranch Hand veterans and then extrapolate the findings to the entire 2.7 million veterans who served in Vietnam during the spraying. The VFW is opposed to this as the Air Force personnel were not subjected to the same extremes of exposure as the ground troops.

1569   Kansas. Department of Health and Environment. Veterans' Exposure to Chemical Agents, Including Agent Orange (Update): Report to the Governor and Legislature. Topeka, Kan.: The Department, February 1986. 23p. As a result of the Kansas Legislature in 1982 passing K.S.A. 73-1703, a voluntary registry for veterans who felt they suffered adverse effects from exposure to Agent Orange while in Vietnam was established for veterans living in Kansas. This bill requires the Secretary of the Kansas Department of Health and Environment to report to the governor and the legislature regarding this registry and to provide a summary of Agent Orange studies once a year. The 1986 report contains a recommendation that the registry and report be discontinued, which was done.

1570   Kearney, P.C. "Dioxin Update." Northeastern Weed Science Society. Proceedings, v. 36, supplement, 1982, p. 69-74. The composition and purpose of the Veterans Administration

Advisory Committee on Health-Related Effects of Herbicides and the Agent Orange Working Group are noted. The status of the Fat Biopsy Study in Texas, the Centers for Disease Control's Birth Defects and Military Service in Vietnam Study, the Air Force's Ranch Hand Study and the Veterans Administration's epidemiological study is also mentioned.

1571 Kehoe, D.M. "In DC 200 Veterans Relive War." In These Times, v. 6, no. 26, May 26, 1982, p. 4. In mid-May 200 Vietnam veterans camped out on the Mall in Washington, D.C. for four days of workshops, lobbying and marches to bring about more awareness of the problems faced by Vietnam veterans who were exposed to Agent Orange. The Vietnam Veterans Against the War and a dozen other veterans' groups sponsored the event and dubbed it Operation Dewey Canyon IV.

1572 Klein, R. "The Poison Orange" in Wounded Men and Broken Promises (See 1115)

1573 Kreul, K. "No Time to Rest." American Legion Magazine, v. 115, no. 6, December 1983, p. 4. The stand the American Legion has taken on the Agent Orange issue is discussed. The American Legion supports legislation that would create a presumptive service-connection as a basis form compensation for chloracne, porphyria cutanea tarda and soft tissue sarcoma. The Legion has entered into an agreement with two epidemiologists to conduct a study of Vietnam-era Legionnaires. The study is due to be completed by the end of 1984 and will be known as the Columbia University and American Legion Study of Vietnam Era Veterans.

1574 Kulewicz, J.J. "Agent Orange: the States Fight Back." Ohio State Law Journal, v. 44, no. 3, Fall 1983, p. 691-712. This article describes the programs 15 states have enacted to identify disorders caused by Agent Orange and to provide assistance in processing claims.

1575 Lauter, D. "Hill Faces Pressure to Pay Tort Costs." National Law Journal, v. 6, no. 38, May 28, 1984, p. 3+. Now that a settlement has been reached in the Agent Orange litigation, there will be increased pressure on Congress to provide legislation compensating victims of exposure to toxic substances used in the name of national security.

1576 Lazarus, G. "A Legacy of Vietnam Draws States' Attention." State Legislatures, v. 7, no. 7, July-August 1981, p. 3-4. Legislation passed by Congress and the states of New York and Texas on the Agent Orange issue is detailed. Also noted are the study by the Air Force on the Ranch Hand personnel and the class action suit brought against the manufacturers of Agent Orange.

1577   Leepson, M. "Agent Orange: the Continuing Debate."
       Editorial Research Reports, v. 2, no. 1, July 6, 1984, p.
       491-508. The following aspects of the Agent Orange issue are
       discussed: the studies sponsored by the federal government,
       the role of the Veterans Administration, whether the federal
       government should be held liable and the recent out of court
       settlement.

1578   Leepson, M. "Vietnam War Legacy." Editorial Research
       Reports, v. 2, no. 1, July 6, 1979, p. 481-500. As part of a
       general article on the problems facing Vietnam veterans, the
       Agent Orange issue is mentioned. Specifically mentioned are
       how the Veterans Administration has handled the issue, the
       Air Force's study of the Operation Ranch Hand veterans and a
       congressional hearing that has been held.

1579   "Let's Think About Our Vietnam Vets Who Suffer with Agent
       Orange Effects." Congressional Record, v. 129, no. 120,
       September 19, 1983, p. H7011. Representative B. Richardson
       (D-N.M.) spoke in favor of H.R. 1961, the Vietnam Veterans
       Agent Orange Relief Act.

1580   Letwin, M. "Vietnam Vets: Their War Goes On." Win, v. 18,
       no. 17, September 15, 1982, p. 10-13. Operation Dewey Canyon
       4 brought veterans to Washington, D.C. for four days of
       workshops, marches, etc. to bring about more awareness of the
       Agent Orange problem as well as other problems experienced by
       Vietnam veterans.

1581   Lewis, W.W. "Unmasking Agent Orange: Federal Government
       Wanted to Forget the Toxic Effects of Vietnam Defoliants."
       New Jersey Monthly, v. 8, no. 6, April 1983, p. 43-46. The
       work of New Jersey's Agent Orange Commission, established in
       1980, is described.

1582   Linedecker, C. Kerry: Agent Orange and an American Family
       (See 1134)

1583   "Link Between Agent Orange and Cancer Found in Europe
       Study, U.S. Panel Says." Wall Street Journal, August 4,
       1980, p. 18(E), p. 5(W). A task force set up by the White
       House to study Agent Orange has evaluated five European
       studies which have found a link between Agent Orange and
       cancer. The task force has recommended that the Air Force
       proceed with its study of veterans who were heavily exposed
       to Agent Orange despite criticism from scientists on its
       structure.

1584   Lipsig, H.H. "Help for Vietnam Vets." [letter] New York
       Law Journal, v. 185, no. 122, June 25, 1981, p. 2. The New
       York legislature and the governor have signed Bill No. 7321-A

which permits individuals the right to file a lawsuit within two years of the date of discovery of personal injuries due to exposure to hazardous materials. This should help remedy some of the problems faced by veterans who were exposed to Agent Orange.

1585 Lipsig, H.H. "New York's New Statute of Limitations for 'Toxic Torts.'" New York Law Journal, v. 186, no. 16, July 23, 1981, p. 1+. The statute of limitations has been extended in New York for veterans exposed to Agent Orange to two years from the date of discovery of the injury resulting from the exposure.

1586 "Living Up to Our Commitments: Vietnam Veterans and the Question of Agent Orange." Congressional Record, v. 129, no. 27, March 8, 1983, p. H936-H937. Representative L.E. Panetta (D-CA) spoke on the need to grant compensation to veterans who believe that their illnesses are due to exposure to Agent Orange. This is the reason he is joining Representative T. Daschle (D-S.D.) in introducing H.R. 1961, the Agent Orange and Atomic Veterans Relief Act.

1587 McCulloch, J. "The Politics of Writing about Agent Orange." Social Alternatives, v. 5, no. 2, 1986, p. 33-35. The author was called to be a witness before the Evatt Royal Commission and he describes the harassment he received from the Commission as a result. The author believes the Evatt Royal Commission report compounds the injustice that has already been done to Vietnam veterans and their families.

1588 Magee, D. "Long War of Wayne Felde." (See 1142)

1589 Mahler, K. "Agent Orange Studies Continue at CDC." Occupational Health & Safety, v. 55, no. 9, September 1986, p. 7-8. The author details how the Centers for Disease Control is conducting its study of the health of 4,500 Vietnam-era veterans at the Lovelace Medical Center in Albuquerque, New Mexico as part of a federal study to determine if there is a link between exposure to Agent Orange and ill-health. The author also details the lack of reliable medical records regarding how much Agent Orange individual veterans were exposed to and the methods Centers for Disease Control researchers have developed to detect minute levels of dioxin in human blood serum.

1590 Maiman, J.M. "Agent Orange." National Vietnam Veterans Review, v. 3, no. 1 & 2, January/February 1983, p. 26-27. A series of articles, one of which details a recent meeting of the Agent Orange State Commissions in Washington, D.C.; the others detail what is being done at the state level, particularly in Florida and Maine.

1591 Maiman, J.M. "Agent Orange Issue Is Colored by Need for More
      Data." [letter] Wall Street Journal, September 1, 1983, p.
      25(E), p. 23(W). The letter was written in response to the
      Agent Orange March editorial (See 1360) which appeared in the
      August 12, 1983 issue of the Wall Street Journal.

1592 Maiman, J.M. "Agent Orange Was Vietnam's Times Beach."
      Wall Street Journal, April 13, 1983, p. 26(E), p. 26(W).
      The author criticizes the Veterans Administration for not
      addressing the Agent Orange issue satisfactorily. The
      citizens of Times Beach received compensation, so why can't
      the Vietnam veterans who on the average were exposed to
      higher levels of contamination?

1593 Maiman, J.M. "Florida AO Commission." National Vietnam
      Veterans Review, v. 4, no. 2, February 1984, p. 34. An Agent
      Orange Commission has been established in Florida.

1594 Maiman, J.M. "IL Resolution on Civilian Veterans Assigned to
      House Vets Committee." National Vietnam Veterans Review, v.
      4, no. 2, February 1984, p. 34. A resolution to include
      civilian non-combatants in Agent Orange testing and treatment
      has been assigned to the Illinois House Committee on
      Veterans' Affairs and should come before the Illinois General
      Assembly this spring. The resolution is the first of its
      kind in the nation.

1595 Maiman, J. "States Act on Agent Orange." VFW Magazine, v.
      71, no. 7, March 1984, p. 8+. The actions various states
      have taken on the Agent Orange issue are noted. To date,
      some 21 have established Agent Orange commissions or
      programs.

1596 Maine. Agent Orange Information Committee. The Vietnam
      Veterans' Self-help Guide on Agent Orange. Augusta, Maine:
      Maine Department of Human Services. Bureau of Health, [n.d.]
      8p. This brochure was developed in order to explain to
      veterans how to determine if they were exposed to Agent
      Orange, how to schedule an Agent Orange exam and what the
      Agent Orange exam covers.

1597 "Managing a Flood of Claims." (See 2185)

1598 "Mandatory Reporting: Agent Orange." State Health
      Legislation Report, v. 10, no. 2, May 1982, p. 28. The
      Oklahoma legislature has recently passed a law which requires
      the physician who has primary responsibility for treating a
      Vietnam veteran who may have been exposed to Agent Orange
      to submit, at the request of the veteran, a report to the
      State Department of Health.

1599 "Mandatory Reporting: Agent Orange." State Health
Legislation Report, v. 10, no. 3, August 1982, p. 46-47.
West Virginia has enacted a law requiring a physician who has
treated a veteran who believes he was exposed to Agent Orange
to, at the request of the veteran, submit a report to the
State Department of Health.

1600 Martin, B. "Agent Orange: the New Controversy." Australian
Society, v. 5, no. 11, November 1986, p. 25-26. The author
discusses the controversy surrounding the report issued by
the Evatt Royal Commission and the fact that vast portions of
this report were copied almost verbatim from the submission
made by the Monsanto Australia Chemical Company.

1601 Maze, R. "Agent Orange Effect on Women May Be Studied."
Air Force Times, v. 46, no. 10, September 23, 1985, p. 16.
Legislation which would require the Veterans Administration
to study whether or not exposure to Agent Orange has caused
health problems in women is being considered by Congress as
the two large-scale studies presently underway do not include
women veterans.

1602 Maze, R. "Agent Orange Study Stirs Doubts in Congress." Air
Force Times, v. 46, no. 29, February 3, 1986, p. 16. The
Office of Technology Assessment has raised several questions
about the manner in which the Centers for Disease Control is
conducting its study on Agent Orange. The Centers for
Disease Control has 30 days to resolve these questions. The
questions have to do with how the Centers for Disease Control
is going to examine the issue of exposure to Agent Orange
both in terms of time and in terms of distance.

1603 "Medical Proof Warrants AO Compensation." American Legion
Magazine, v. 114, no. 5, May 1983, p. 33. The American
Legion has endorsed a bill introduced by Representative T.
Daschle (D-S.D.) which would provide compensation to Vietnam
veterans exposed to Agent Orange and suffering from
chloracne, soft tissue sarcoma or porphyria cutanea tarda as
they have concluded that there is sufficient medical evidence
to support this position.

1604 "Memorials." Congressional Record, v. 129, no. 39 pt. II,
March 24, 1983, p. H1810. Memorial 50 was presented by
Representative E.D. Rudd (R-Ariz.) from the House of
Representatives of Arizona. It concerns the information,
counseling and health care needs of Vietnam veterans exposed
to Agent Orange. It was referred to the Committee on
Veterans' Affairs.

1605 "Memorials." Congressional Record, v. 129, no. 40, April 5,

1983, p. H1821. Memorial 61 from the House of
Representatives of Arizona concerns the needs of Vietnam
veterans exposed to Agent Orange for health care. It was
referred to the Committee on Veterans' Affairs.

1606   **"Memorials."** Congressional Record, **v. 129, no. 102, July 19,
1983, p. H5273-H5274.** On page H5273 it is stated that the
state of Louisiana's Legislature presented a memorial
relative to the Vietnam Veterans Agent Orange Relief Act. It
was referred to the Committee on Veterans' Affairs.

1607   **"Memorials."** Congressional Record, **v. 129, no. 92, June 28,
1983, p. H4577.** Memorial 200 was presented from the state of
Minnesota's Legislature. It concerns the need for
compensating Vietnam veterans for adverse health effects. It
was referred to the Committee on Veterans' Affairs.

1608   **"Memorials."** Congressional Record, **v. 129, no. 119,
September 15, 1983, p. H7004.** Memorial 260 was presented by
the California Legislature and concerns the needs of veterans
exposed to Agent Orange. It was referred to the Committee on
Veterans' Affairs.

1609   Milford, L. and R. Simon. **"Discussion Paper on Agent
Orange."** Veterans Rights Newsletter, **v. 1, no. 1, May 1981,
p. 4-6.** This article consists of an excerpt of a paper the
authors presented at the first national conference on Agent
Orange which was held this month and was sponsored by the
National Veterans Task Force on Agent Orange. The authors
discuss the Veterans Administration's policy on Agent Orange,
the Interagency Work Group on Phenoxy Herbicides, the
litigation against the manufacturers of Agent Orange, the
epidemiological studies underway, the state commissions that
have been formed and legislation introduced in Congress.

1610   Miller, A.S. **"The Author Replies."** Environment, **v. 21, no.
9, November 1979, p. 43.** The author responds to a letter by
J.E. Craighead (See 1448) which is a response to A.S.
Miller's June 1979 article in Environment (See 1611) and
provides citations to the sources he used to support his
position that exposure to Agent Orange can cause health
problems. He notes that the Department of Defense and the
Veterans Administration are even beginning to acknowledge
this.

1611   Miller, A.S. **"2,4,5-T: Chemical Time Bomb."** Environment,
v. 21, no. 5, June 1979, p. 2-4. The difficulties veterans
who believe they were exposed to Agent Orange are having in
getting assistance from the Veterans Administration are
discussed.

1612 "Modified Agent Orange Bill Adopted by House." <u>DAV</u>
      <u>Magazine</u>, v. 26, no. 3, March 1984, p. 8. The House has
      passed a bill which would grant special disability or death
      allowances to Vietnam veterans who suffer from soft tissue
      sarcoma, porphyria cutanea tarda or chloracne which they
      presumably contacted as the result of exposure to Agent
      Orange pending the results of the Centers for Disease
      Control's study on Agent Orange.

1613 Mokhiber, R. "Liability for Agent Orange." [letter] <u>Wall</u>
      <u>Street Journal</u>, May 14, 1984, p. 27(E), p. 25(W). This
      letter is a reply to an article by S. Garment (See 1508)
      which appeared in the April 27th issue of the <u>Journal</u>. The
      author of this letter agrees that the federal government
      should not compensate the victims of exposure to Agent Orange
      but disagrees with S. Garment's statement that the chemical
      manufacturers should also not compensate the victims.

1614 "More on Agent Orange." <u>Congressional Record</u>, v. 126, pt.
      21, September 30, 1980, p. 28315-28317. Senator A. Cranston
      (D-CA) details the discussion on Agent Orange which has taken
      place in various committees this month and has three articles
      from the September 15 and 16 issues of the <u>Baltimore Sun</u>
      reprinted for the <u>Record</u>.

1615 Murphy, S. "A Critique of the Veterans Administration Claims
      Process." <u>Brooklyn Law Review</u>, v. 52, no. 2, 1986, p. 533-
      569. The author presented this note at a symposium on Mass
      Torts after Agent Orange. The note examines the issue of
      whether or not the Veterans' Compensation Act effectively
      addresses the needs of Agent Orange claimants, discusses how
      the Veterans Administration claims process functions for
      Agent Orange claimants and the difficulties veterans face in
      establishing Agent Orange as a service-connected disability.
      The author believes that the Act's omission of a judicial
      review provision limits its effectiveness and undermines the
      social policy that caused the Act to be written. The Act is
      only a temporary solution.

1616 Musselmann, K.G. "Patient Men Have Waited Too Long."
      <u>DAV Magazine</u>, v. 29, no. 1, January 1987, p. 1+. The author
      calls on Congress, the Veterans Administration and the
      scientific community to create an environment for action on
      the radiation and Agent Orange issues. Patient men have been
      waiting too long for answers. The author also details some
      of the things that have been learned about exposure to Agent
      Orange.

1617 "NRC Asks for Delay in Agent Orange Study." <u>Chemical and</u>
      <u>Engineering News</u>, v. 60, no. 46, November 15, 1982, p. 7.

The National Research Council has recommended that the
Veterans Administration delay the start of the pilot study
for the epidemiological study they were mandated by Congress
to do until the Air Force study on the Ranch Hand veterans is
finished this spring.

1618   National Research Council. Effects of Exposure to Agent
       Orange on Ground Troops in Vietnam. October 1982. 29p.
       Available from NTIS: PB 83-156521. The protocol prepared by
       the University of California at Los Angeles School of Public
       Health for the Veterans Administration is reviewed. The
       report discusses the scope of the proposed study and
       questions the methods the conductors of the study would use
       to identify the participants, to define exposure to Agent
       Orange, to determine the composition of a sample study and
       recommends that the the questionnaires and clinical testing
       protocols be revised.

1619   National Research Council. Committee on Toxicology. Review
       of U.S. Air Force Protocol: Epidemiological Investigation of
       Health Effects in Air Force Personnel Following Exposure to
       Herbicide Orange. May 6, 1980. 25p. Available from NTIS:
       AD-A 085 105/5. A review of the proposed study of those Air
       Force personnel exposed to Agent Orange was undertaken by
       this committee. Based upon this review the committee
       concluded that the study would probably not identify adverse
       health effects due to the herbicide and recommends that due
       to questions concerning impartiality and credibility the Air
       Force not conduct its own study, that the study be redesigned
       to include a longer follow-up period and that if the study is
       redesigned a limited number of morbidity end points should be
       evaluated, each in greater detail.

1620   National Veterans Law Center. The Veteran's Self-Help Guide
       on Agent Orange. Washington: Veterans Education Project.
       February 1983. 8p. This brochure was developed to help
       Vietnam veterans who wish to file claims at the Veterans
       Administration for health problems they believe to be caused
       by exposure to Agent Orange.

1621   "New Agent Orange Bill Promises: Automatic Compensation."
       Citizen Soldier, no. 5, May 1983, p. 3. A bill introduced by
       Representatives D. Bonior (D-Mich.), T. Daschle (D-S.D.) and
       B. Edgar (D-PA) would automatically compensate veterans
       suffering from one of three disease believed to be related to
       exposure to Agent Orange. The three disease are: soft tissue
       sarcoma, porphyria cutanea tarda and chloracne.

1622   "New Agent Orange Warning Urged by Veterans." American
       Medical News, v. 24, no. 38, October 9, 1981, p. 26. The

National Veterans Task Force on Agent Orange is asking the federal government to identify and warn veterans who might have been exposed to Agent Orange dumped by United States planes on our own ground troops. The article also lists the studies that are underway on the health effects of Agent Orange exposure.

1623 "New Jersey Agent Orange Commission Hearings." Veterans Rights Newsletter, v. 1, no. 5-6, September-October 1981, p. 41. The New Jersey Agent Orange Commission recently held hearings to learn more about how they can help New Jersey Vietnam veterans who were exposed to Agent Orange.

1624 "New Jersey Agent Orange Commission Slates Medical Testing." National Vietnam Veterans Review, v. 4, no. 4, April 1984, p. 3. The New Jersey Agent Orange Commission is in the process of getting ready to begin its testing of Vietnam veterans living in New Jersey.

1625 New Jersey. State Commission on Agent Orange. Reference Guide: the New Jersey Commission of Agent Orange. Trenton, N.J.: The Commission, [n.d.] 4p. This pamphlet was developed to provide a first step in obtaining information or additional information for New Jersey Vietnam veterans who were exposed to Agent Orange.

1626 "New VA Medical Guidelines." National Law Journal, v. 4, no. 17, January 4, 1982, p. 8. Veterans exposed to Agent Orange in Vietnam feel that they are not receiving quality medical care at Veterans Administration hospitals. New guidelines passed by Congress require Veterans Administration hospitals to treat veterans with health problems from exposure to Agent Orange but limit care to Veterans Administration centers.

1627 "New Vets' Law Reaches Agent Orange, Radiation, Vet Centers, Vocational Rehabilitation." Veterans Rights Newsletter, v. 1, no. 7-8, November-December 1981, p. 53. The final bill that was reached as a result of the compromise of H.R. 3499 and S. 921 is described. Veterans are eligible for basic health care services by the Veterans Administration for disabilities suffered if they were found to have been exposed to herbicides. The bill also authorizes, but does not require, the Veterans Administration to expand the scope of the Agent Orange study.

1628 New York (State). Temporary Commission on Dioxin Exposure. Findings, Conclusion and Recommendations of New York State Temporary Commission on Dioxin Exposure. Albany: The Commission, September 1983. 27p. This document brings together the foreword, findings, conclusions and

recommendations from the commission's preliminary, interim
and final reports.

1629 New York (State). Temporary Commission on Dioxin Exposure.
      Interim Report. Albany: The Commission, 1982. 64p. The
      Temporary State Commission on Dioxin Exposure was created
      by a bill enacted by the New York State Legislature and
      signed by Governor H. Carey in 1980. This interim report
      details the results of the Commission's research in the
      following areas: health effects attributed to dioxin
      exposure; birth defects attributed to dioxin exposure;
      veterans' views of the Veterans Administration, the
      Department of Defense, and the chemical manufacturers; the
      government's response to veterans' concerns; and herbicide
      exposure in the United States. The recommendations of the
      Commission are also detailed and include actions to alleviate
      veterans' concerns and to increase existing knowledge of
      dioxin.

1630 "No AO Study Results Before 1988: VA." Citizen Soldier, no.
      4, 1982, p. 1. It will be at least 1988 before any results
      or conclusions will be known as to what the actual health
      effects of exposure to Agent Orange are, admitted the
      Veterans Administration's medical director to a House
      Veterans' Affairs panel recently.

1631 "No Deadline for Agent Orange Claims." California.
      Department of Veterans Affairs. Cal-Vet News, v. 3, no. 1,
      January-February 1981, p. 5. There is no statute of
      limitations for filing a claim for a service-connected
      disability. The class action suit is also discussed.

1632 "No Quick Answer on Agent Orange Effects." Chemical Week,
      v. 127, no. 7, August 13, 1980, p. 19. A federal government
      panel feels that it will take two or three years of research
      to fully assess the long-term health effects of Agent Orange
      exposure. The panel also stated that the Air Force should go
      ahead with its proposed study of Operation Ranch Hand
      veterans.

1633 "No Quick Answers Expected on Agent Orange Questions."
      DAV Magazine, v. 22, no. 5, May 1980, p. 3. According to a
      recent statement by Veterans Administration Administrator M.
      Cleland no quick, simple answers are possible to the concerns
      expressed by veterans exposed to Agent Orange. At this time
      in only 23 cases has the Veterans Administration granted
      service-connected disability claims based on disabilities the
      veterans believed to be caused by exposure to Agent Orange.
      However, in none of the claims granted by the Veterans
      Administration did the agency cite exposure to defoliants as
      the cause of disability.

1634 "No Volunteers Needed for Agent Orange Study, CDC Officials
      State." DAV Magazine, v. 25, no. 7, July 1983, p. 11.
      Volunteers will not be accepted for the study that will be
      conducted by the Centers for Disease Control. The Centers
      for Disease Control has stated that the use of volunteers
      could jeopardize the scientific validity of the study.

1635 Nobles, B., ed. Agent Orange: the Oregon Department of
      Veterans' Affairs Guide for the Oregon Vietnam Veteran.
      Salem, Oregon: Oregon Department of Veterans' Affairs, May
      1984. 24p. This booklet was written for the Oregon Vietnam
      veterans in order to help them become more aware of what
      Agent Orange is and to help them determine if they were
      exposed to Agent Orange while serving in Vietnam.

1636 O'Donnell, J. "The Vietnam Veterans Adviser." Penthouse, v.
      13, no. 11, July 1982, p. 100+. It has been revealed that
      Agent Orange was only one of several hazardous chemicals
      servicemen were exposed to in Vietnam.

1637 "Ohio State Legislators Introduce Bill on Agent Orange."
      Veterans Rights Newsletter, v. 1, no. 5-6, September-October
      1981, p. 41. A bill has been introduced in the Ohio House of
      Representatives to help Ohio Vietnam veterans exposed to
      Agent Orange. This bill is similar to a bill that was passed
      in Texas. In addition the offspring of veterans who have
      medical problems will be offered genetic counseling and
      testing.

1638 "'Orange' Appeal." Crawdaddy, no. 89, October 1978, p. 64.
      Despite the efforts of veterans' groups, the only result of
      exposure to Agent Orange that the Veterans Administration
      will recognize is chloracne. As many as 300,000 veterans may
      have been exposed to Agent Orange in Vietnam.

1639 "Orange Journalism." Progressive, v. 45, no. 8, August 1981,
      p. 35. The controversy surrounding an article written by New
      York Times science reporter, R. Severo, is noted. Severo had
      written an article about a Congressional subcommittee's draft
      report which was critical of the government's stand on Agent
      Orange.

1640 "'Orange' Memo Upsetting." Air Force Times, v. 40, no. 38,
      April 14, 1980, p. 13. A document released by
      Representatives D. Bonier (D-Mich.) and T. Daschle (D-S.D.)
      have Air Force and Veterans Administration officials upset
      because it has the words, United States Government, printed
      across the top and is unsigned.

1641 Osser, R., comp. "Agent Orange -- the War that Lingers."

CSG Backgrounder, December 1982, 8p. The responses state and federal government have made to the Agent Orange issue are detailed. Whether or not state governments should be involved in this issue is also discussed.

1642 "'Outside' Scientists Monitor Agent Orange Study." Air Force Times, v. 41, no. 11, October 6, 1980, p. 9. Outside scientists will help the Intragency Work Group on Agent Orange monitor the Air Force's study of the Ranch Hand personnel according to Assistant to the President for Domestic Affairs and Policy Eizenstat. This independent review should keep the study honest and help to alleviate the doubts of Vietnam veterans as to the objectivity of the study, Eizenstat said.

1643 Palca, J. "Dioxin Exposure: CDC Study Still at Square One." Nature, v. 320, no. 6062, April 10, 1986, p. 476. The Centers for Disease Control's epidemiological study has been suspended as the Agent Orange Working Group and the Office of Technology Assessment can not agree on what an acceptable exposure measure should be. The study may be cancelled.

1644 Palm, R. "Agent Orange Comes Home." Connecticut Magazine, v. 43, no. 11, November 1980, p. 82-87. The frustration Connecticut members of Agent Orange Victims International are having in trying to get some action from the Veterans Administration on the Agent Orange issue is expressed. The class action suit against the manufacturers of the defoliant is also mentioned.

1645 "Partial Clearance for Agent Orange." Newsweek, v. 96, no. 6, August 11, 1980, p. 53. In a study of 200 mice conducted by a group of federal agencies, it was concluded that exposure to Agent Orange resulted in "...no significant increase in birth defects or decreased fertility." However, a scientific panel of the White House Work Group on Agent Orange recommended that any service in Vietnam should be regarded as a "a causal factor" in processing claims for medical compensation.

1646 Payne, K.J. "Beyond Vietnam, Beyond Politics, Beyond Causes..." (See 2241)

1647 Pear, R. "U.S. Liability Unresolved in Agent Orange Cases." (See 2242)

1648 "Percy Calls for Full Investigation of Agent Orange." Congressional Record, v. 125, pt. 11, June 5, 1979, p. 13465-13474. Senator C. Percy (R-Ill.) appreciates the efforts the Air Force has made to undertake an epidemiological study.

But the federal government needs to do more and the Senate
needs to make sure that the Veterans Administration lives up
to its mandate to pursue the causes of veteran's health
complaints. The transcript of the WBBM-TV program is
included, as well as a three-part article by R. Severo for
the New York Times, and Senator Percy's correspondence with
the Veterans Administration and Comptroller General Staats on
the Agent Orange issue.

1649 "Petitions and Memorials." Congressional Record, v. 126, pt.
      7, April 18, 1980, p. 8354-8362. POM-681 (p. 8361) is a
      joint resolution passed by the Wisconsin Legislature which
      asks Congress to require the Veterans Administration to test
      all veterans who were exposed to Agent Orange and urges the
      President and Congress to require the Veterans Administration
      to treat these veterans. This petition was referred to the
      Senate's Committee on Veterans' Affairs.

1650 "Petitions and Memorials." Congressional Record, v. 126, pt.
      23, November 19, 1980, p. 30197-30201. POM-894 (p. 30200) is
      a concurrent resolution of the Legislature of the State of
      Pennsylvania to the Senate's Committee on Veterans' Affairs
      asking that a study of the effects of Agent Orange on Vietnam
      veterans be conducted independent of the Veterans
      Administration.

1651 "Petitions and Memorials." Congressional Record, v. 129, no.
      47, April 14, 1983, p. S4680-S4684. POM-85 (p. S4684) was
      submitted by the House of Representative of the state of
      Georgia and was referred to the Committee on Veterans'
      Affairs. This memorial requests Congress to consider
      providing information services, health care and psychological
      services to Vietnam veterans exposed to Agent Orange,
      mandating an epidemiological study and instructing the
      Veterans Administration to cooperate fully in these efforts.

1652 "Petitions and Memorials." Congressional Record, v. 129, no.
      84, June 14, 1983, p. S8335-S8341. POM-246 (p. S8341) was
      submitted by the General Court of the Commonwealth of
      Massachusetts and was referred to the Committee on Veterans'
      Affairs. It asks the federal government to provide adequate
      treatment and compensation to veterans exposed to Agent
      Orange and to conduct a study on the long-term effects of
      exposure to Agent Orange.

1653 "Petitions and Memorials." Congressional Record, v. 129, no.
      91, June 27, 1983, p. S9171-S9176. POM-273 (p. S9173-9174)
      was submitted by the General Assembly of the Commonwealth of
      Pennsylvania and was referred to the Committee on Veterans'
      Affairs. It states, in part, that as the Defense Department

was responsible for spraying Agent Orange the Veterans
Administration should be responsible for funding and
administering individual screening programs so that veterans
suffering from the effects of exposure to Agent Orange may
receive full medical benefits, therapy, disability benefits
and rehabilitation training.

1654   "Petitions and Memorials." Congressional Record, v. 129, no.
96, July 12, 1983, p. S9703-S9707. POM-297 (p. S9705) was
submitted by the Minnesota State Legislature and was referred
to the Committee on Veterans' Affairs. It asks that veterans
exposed to Agent Orange be compensated and that the
appropriate federal agencies investigate the complaints of
Vietnam veterans exposed to Agent Orange. POM-305 (p.
S9707) was also submitted by the Minnesota State Legislature
and makes similar requests. It was also referred to the
Committee on Veterans' Affairs.

1655   "Petitions and Memorials." Congressional Record, v. 129, no.
105, July 22, 1983, p. S10682-S10684. POM-342 (p. S10684)
was submitted by the Louisiana Legislature and was referred
to the Committee on Veterans' Affairs. It states that the
Louisiana Legislature would appreciate it if Congress would
pass H.R. 1961, the Vietnam Veterans Agent Orange Relief Act.

1656   "Petitions and Memorials." Congressional Record, v. 129, no.
105, September 21, 1983, p. S12361-S12365. POM-397 (p.
S12364) was submitted by the California Legislature and was
referred to the Committee on Veterans' Affairs. It asks the
Congress and the President to enact legislation for
compensating veterans suffering from liver disorders, skin
conditions and soft tissue cancers which have been linked to
exposure to Agent Orange.

1657   Plattner, A. "Congress Orders VA Care for Vietnam War
Veterans Exposed to Agent Orange." Congressional Quarterly
Weekly Report, v. 39, no. 43, October 24, 1981, p. 2079-2080.
Due to budgetary considerations the legislation which would
provide medical care in Veterans Administration health
clinics for Vietnam veterans suffering ailments attributed to
Agent Orange may be vetoed.

1658   Pogson, G. "Agent Orange Inquiry." Legal Service Bulletin,
v. 9, no. 1, February-March 1984, p. 53. The charge to the
Royal Commission headed by Justice Evatt is detailed.

1659   "The Poisoned Trail of Agent Orange." Congressional Record,
v. 126, pt. 18, September 3, 1980, p. 24009-24010.
Representative W.R. Ratchford (D-CT) spoke of his
disappointment in the slow progress of H.R. 6377, the Vietnam

Era Veterans Agent Orange Act. He also includes an article from the <u>News-Times</u> of Danbury, CT on the possible health effects of exposure to Agent Orange and the lack of response at the Veterans Administration and the Pentagon to veterans' concerns on this issue.

1660 "Public Bills and Resolutions." <u>Congressional Record</u>, v. 126, pt. 1, January 30, 1980, p. 1332-1334. H.R. 6377 was introduced by Representative T. Daschle (D-S.D.) (page 1333) to amend title 38 and provide a presumption of service-connection for the occurrence of certain diseases in veterans exposed to phenoxy herbicides contaminated by dioxins. This resolution was referred to the Committee on Veterans' Affairs.

1661 "Public Bills and Resolutions." <u>Congressional Record</u>, v. 127, pt. 1, January 6, 1981, p. 212-229. Representative R.A. Roe (D-N.J.) introduced H.R. 523 (page 219) which would waive the one-year limitation on claims for compensation from the Veterans Administration for disabilities and disease caused by exposure to Agent Orange in Vietnam. This bill was referred to the Committee on Veterans' Affairs.

1662 "Public Bills and Resolutions." <u>Congressional Record</u>, v. 127, pt. 1, January 22, 1981, p. 721-729. Representative G.V. Montgomery (D-Miss.) introduced H.R. 1173 (page 726) which would amend section 307 of Public Law 96-151 by assigning the epidemiological study of exposure to Agent Orange to an independent scientific agency. This bill was referred to the Committee on Veterans' Affairs.

1663 "Public Bills and Resolutions." <u>Congressional Record</u>, v. 127, pt. 3, February 25, 1981, p. 3084-3087. Representative R.M. Mottl (D-Ohio) introduced H.R. 2157 (page 3086) for himself and four other representatives. This bill would expand the scope of the study the Veterans Administration is required to conduct on exposure to Agent Orange. The bill was referred to the Committee on Veterans' Affairs.

1664 "Public Bills and Resolutions." <u>Congressional Record</u>, v. 127, pt. 3, March 4, 1981, p. 3553-3557. Representative T.J. Downey (D-N.Y.) introduced H.R. 2297 (p. 3554) for himself and 74 other representatives which would waive the one-year limitation on claims for compensation from the Veterans Administration for disabilities and diseases believed to be caused by exposure to Agent Orange or other phenoxy herbicides. This bill was referred to the Committee on Veterans Affairs.

1665 "Public Bills and Resolutions." <u>Congressional Record</u>, v.

127, pt. 4, March 12, 1981, p. 4201-4203. Representative
T.A. Daschle (D-S.D.) introduced H.R. 2493 (p. 4202) for
himself and 74 other representatives which would grant
presumption of service-connection for the occurrence of
certain diseases in veterans who were exposed to herbicides
in Vietnam. The bill was referred to the Committee on
Veterans' Affairs.

1666 "Public Bills and Resolutions." Congressional Record, v.
127, pt. 4, May 7, 1981, p. 9031-9032. Representative R.M.
Mottl (D-Ohio) has introduced H.R. 3499 (p. 9032) for himself
and 24 other representatives which would provide, in part,
medical care to veterans exposed to herbicides. The bill was
referred to the Committee on Veterans' Affairs.

1667 "Public Bills and Resolutions." Congressional Record, v.
128, pt. 18, September 21, 1982, p. 24421-24422.
Representative T.A. Daschle (D-S.D.) introduced H.R. 7146
which would establish a presumption of service-connection for
chloracne in Vietnam-era veterans who served in Vietnam.
This bill was referred to the Committee on Veterans' Affairs.

1668 "Public Bills and Resolutions." Congressional Record, v.
128, pt. 18, September 23, 1982, p. 24994. Representative
T.A. Daschle (D-S.D.) introduced H.R. 7170 which would
transfer the epidemiological study from the Administrator of
Veterans' Affairs to the Secretary of Health & Human
Services. This bill was referred to the Committee on
Veterans' Affairs.

1669 "Public Bills and Resolutions." Congressional Record, v.
128, pt. 20, October 1, 1982, p. 27431-27433. On page 27432
is the notice that Representative P. Simon (D-Ill.) has
introduced H.R. 7285 which would grant service connected
compensation to veterans who were exposed to nuclear
radiation or toxic chemicals and who are suffering from
radiological or chemical disabilities. This bill was
referred to the Committee on Veterans' Affairs.

1670 "Public Bills and Resolutions." Congressional Record, v.
129, no. 1, January 3, 1983, p. H40-H48. Representative C.D.
Long (D-MD) introduced on page H45, H.R. 209 which would
require the Secretary of Health and Human Services to arrange
an independent epidemiological study on the effects of
exposure to Agent Orange. This bill was referred to the
Committee on Energy and Commerce.

1671 "Public Bills and Resolutions." Congressional Record, v.
129, no. 2, January 6, 1983, p. H85-H99. Representative R.A.
Roe (D-N.J.) introduced H.R. 331 on page H88 which would

waive the one-year limitation on claims for compensation from the Veterans Administration for veterans suffering from disabilities or diseases resulting from exposure to herbicides in Vietnam. This bill was referred to the Committee on Veterans' Affairs. On page H91 Representative D. Applegate (D-Ohio) introduced H.R. 462 which would do the same thing as H.R. 331. This bill was also referred to the Committee on Veterans' Affairs.

1672 "Public Bills and Resolutions." Congressional Record, v. 129, no. 7, February 1, 1983, p. H238-H239. Representative T.J. Downey (D-N.Y.) on page H238 introduced H.R. 1135 which would waive the one-year limitation for Vietnam veterans' claims for compensation for disabilities and diseases resulting from exposure to Agent Orange. The bill was referred to the Committee on Veterans' Affairs.

1673 "Public Bills and Resolutions." Congressional Record, v. 129, no. 12, February 10, 1983, p. H510-H513. On page H511 representative T.J. Downey (D-N.Y.) introduced H.R. 1382 which states that any compensation granted by the Veterans Administration for a claim for a disease or disability resulting from exposure to Agent Orange in Vietnam shall be retroactive to the date the veteran first applied to the Veterans Administration for compensation. This bill was referred to the Committee on Veterans' Affairs.

1674 "Public Bills and Resolutions." Congressional Record, v. 129, no. 25, March 3, 1983, p. H877-H880. On page H878 Representative P. Simon (D-Ill.) introduced H.R. 1914 which would grant compensation to veterans exposed to radiation or to toxic chemicals and are suffering from ailments resulting from this exposure. This bill was referred to the Committee on Veterans' Affairs.

1675 "Public Bills and Resolutions." Congressional Record, v. 129, no. 28, March 9, 1983, p. H1109-H1112. Representative T.A. Daschle (D-S.D.) introduced H.R. 2017 which would provide a presumption of service-connection for the occurrence of certain diseases related to exposure to herbicides or other environmental hazards or conditions in veterans who served in Southeast Asia during the Vietnam era. This bill was referred to the Committee on Veterans' Affairs.

1676 "Public Bills and Resolutions." Congressional Record, v. 113, no. 2, January 7, 1987, p. H145-H159. On pages H148-H149 Representative J.E. Porter (R-Ill.) introduced a bill which would require the Veterans Administration to study the effects of exposure to phenoxy herbicides (including Agent Orange) on women who served with the Red Cross or the USO in Vietnam during the Vietnam War and to provide counseling and medical exams to these women. This bill was referred to the Committee on Veterans' Affairs.

1677 "Recovery of Certain Health Costs, Program of Assistance to State Medical Schools, and Study of Veterans Exposed to Agent Orange." Congressional Record, v. 127, pt. 9, June 9, 1981, p. 11830-11832. Senator A. Cranston (D-CA) submitted amendment no. 62 to S. 636 which would, in part, expand the scope of the epidemiological study on the effects of exposure to Agent Orange. The text of the amendment is included.

1678 "Regulations: Agent Orange-Radiation." Veterans Rights Newsletter, v. 4, no. 11-12, March-April 1985, p. 94-95. The Veterans Administration has announced the way in which it plans to implement the Veterans Dioxin and Radiation Exposure Compensation Standards Act.

1679 "Relieve VA of Agent Orange Epidemiology Study." Congressional Record, v. 18, no. 128, September 23, 1982, p. 25013. Representative T.A. Daschle (D-S.D.) explains why he introduced H.R. 7170 which would transfer the epidemiological study from the Administrator of Veterans' Affairs to the Secretary of Health and Human Services. The text of the bill is included.

1680 "Remedying the Effects of Agent Orange." Congressional Record, v. 126, pt. 5, March 19, 1980, p. 5981-5983. Supplemental information to the bill introduced by Representative T. Daschle (D-S.D.) to provide assistance to veterans exposed to Agent Orange in Vietnam was supplied to the Record by Representative D. Bonior (D-Mich.). Included in this information is the text of letters from Representatives Daschle and Bonior to H. Mark, Secretary of the Air Force, and to M. Cleland, Administrator of the Veterans Administration, and an article from the New York Times on the possible link between Agent Orange and genetic problems.

1681 "Report of Committees on Public Bills and Resolutions." Congressional Record, v. 130, no. 3, January 25, 1984, p. H159. Representative G.V. Montgomery (D-Miss.) delivered to the Clerk H.R. 1961, the Agent Orange and Atomic Veterans Relief Act, with amendments for printing. It was referred to the Committee of the Whole House on the State of the Union.

1682 "Representative Kemp Cosponsors Bill to Assist Vietnam Veterans." Congressional Record, v. 126, pt. 10, May 22, 1980, p. 12422. Representative J. Kemp (R-N.Y.) has cosponsored H.R. 7157 which would waive the one-year limitation for compensation from the Veterans Administration for disabilities resulting from exposure to Agent Orange while serving in Southeast Asia. Representative Kemp told the story of Ron Ewing who did not start having problems until four years after his discharge and has a three-year-old son who was born with a collapsed lung and has only grown one and a half inches this past year and has gained less than one pound.

1683 "Reprieve for Agent Orange." Science News, v. 118, no. 6, August 6, 1980, p. 86. A study released recently by the Department of Health and Human Services found no significant effects on mating, fertility or health of offspring of male mice fed the components of Agent Orange. A federal task force has been set up to study the Agent Orange and Vietnam veteran issue. They have proposed that research should be done to determine if service in Vietnam rather than solely exposure to Agent Orange places veterans in high risk of health problems.

1684 "Reviews of Center for Disease Control's Vietnam Veteran/Agent Orange Birth Defects Study." Congressional Record, v. 131, no. 5, January 24, 1985, p. S566. Senator A. Cranston (D-CA) had inserted in the Record a copy of a letter from Dr. J. Ditzer, the Veterans Administration's Chief Medical Director, to Senator Cranston on the status of the Veterans Administration's Advisory Committee on Health-Related Effects of Herbicide's review of the Centers for Disease Control's birth defects study.

1685 Rocamora, J. "Dioxin: the Persistent Poison." Southeast Asia Chronicle, no. 90, June 1983, p. 24-27. The efforts Vietnam veterans are making to obtain compensation from the Veterans Administration and the manufacturers of Agent Orange for the health problems they believe are the result of exposure to the defoliant are updated.

1686 Rosenblatt, J. "Compensating Victims of Toxic Substances." (See 2268)

1687 Roth, M. "Veterans Demand Care for Agent Orange Effects: L.A. Hunger Strikers Evicted." Guardian, v. 33, no. 38, June 24, 1981, p. 8. Four veterans are participating in a hunger strike to force the President or a high-ranking representative to assure them that programs to treat veterans exposed to Agent Orange will be improved and benefits for Vietnam veterans will not be cut. R. Coy, acting counsel for the Veterans Administration, has stated that a symposium will be held soon and that a $114,000 study on the effects of exposure to Agent Orange will be undertaken.

1688   Rothman, R. "Agent Orange Compensation: Senate Fight Set
        Over Paying Veterans Exposed to Herbicide." <u>Congressional</u>
        <u>Quarterly Weekly Report</u>, v. 42, no. 19, May 12, 1984, p.
        1109. A compensation bill which will be debated on the
        Senate floor later this month is discussed. The bill would
        authorize federal compensation to Vietnam veterans who have
        contracted chloracne, porphyria cutanea tarda or sarcoma,
        which are three diseases some have blamed on exposure to
        Agent Orange.

1689   Rothman, R. "Bill Tells VA to Set Agent Orange Guidelines."
        <u>Congressional Quarterly Weekly Report</u>, v. 42, no. 40, October
        6, 1984, p. 2457-2458. In a bill passed by the House, the
        Veterans Administration would be required to set policies for
        compensating Vietnam veterans who have diseases believed to
        be associated with exposure to Agent Orange. Also mentioned
        is the formal approval that has been granted to the out of
        court settlement and the studies that are underway at the
        Centers for Disease Control.

1690   Rothman, R. "House Approves Agent Orange Disability Pay."
        <u>Congressional Quarterly Weekly Report</u>, v. 42, no. 5, February
        4, 1984, p. 229. H.R. 1961, the Agent Orange and Atomic
        Veterans Relief Act, passed by voice vote on January 30. It
        authorizes compensation benefits for those Vietnam veterans
        exposed to Agent Orange who are suffering from chloracne,
        porphyria cutanea tarda and soft tissue sarcoma.

1691   Rothman, R. "Senate Passes Compromise Agent Orange Bill."
        <u>Congressional Quarterly Weekly Report</u>, v. 42, no. 21, May 26,
        1984, p. 1279. Compromise legislation requiring the Veterans
        Administration to set policies for compensating veterans
        exposed to Agent Orange was unanimously passed by the Senate
        recently. Two amendments, one by Senator L. Pressler (R-
        S.D.) defining the make-up of the advisory committee
        established by the bill and one by Senator A. Spencer (R-PA)
        limiting the amount of evidence veterans would be required to
        submit, were also passed. The measure will now go to
        conference with the House.

1692   "A Rush to Judgement on Agent Orange Issue." <u>Human Events</u>,
        v. 43, no. 42, October 15, 1983, p. 4-5. This article was
        written in opposition to legislation sponsored by
        Representative T. Daschle (D-S.D.) and Senator L. Pressler
        (R-S.D.) which would grant presumptive disability
        compensation to veterans exposed to Agent Orange in Vietnam.
        The results of the mortality study of the Operation Ranch
        Hand personnel and the research done on the data which has
        been entered into the Agent Orange Registry are mentioned.
        Neither of these studies show a link between veterans' health

problems and Agent Orange. The media has blown the issue all out of proportion.

1693 Russo, T. "The Scientific Method and VA Policy Making." Citizen Soldier, no. 4, 1982, p. 3+. The author believes that the Veterans Administration practices biased science when researching whether or not exposure to Agent Orange has caused a wide range of maladies.

1694 "S. 6 - Veterans' Administration Health-care Amendments of 1985." Congressional Record, v. 131, no. 5, January 24, 1985, p. S611-S621. Senator A. Cranston (D-CA) explains the content of S. 6 - Veterans' Administration Health-care Amendments of 1985. One of the provisions of this bill is to extend for 2-1/2 years the eligibility of veterans exposed to Agent Orange to receive priority Veterans Administration health-care services for disabilities not determined to be unrelated to such exposure. An Office of Technology Assessment report on the status of the Centers for Disease Control's study is also included.

1695 "S. 1953 - the Vietnam Veterans Agent Orange Relief Act." Congressional Record, v. 127, pt. 24, December 15, 1981, p. 31254-32156. Senator A. Pecter (R-PA) introduced the Vietnam Veterans' Agent Orange Relief Act. The text of S. 1953 is included. His bill would provide a 20 percent disability for a disease caused by exposure to Agent Orange according to credible medical opinion.

1696 Sandison, M. "Agent Orange." Hawaii Health Messenger, v. 45, no. 4, Winter 1982, p. 3-4. This article tells of the programs being set up in Hawaii for that state's Vietnam veterans who were exposed to Agent Orange.

1697 "Scientists Picked to Design Agent Orange Study." DAV Magazine, v. 23, no. 6, June 1981, p. 9. An epidemiological study will be designed by Doctors G. Spivey and R. Detels at the University of California at Los Angeles.

1698 "Secret House Report Sharply Critical of VA, DOD, Dow Handling of Agent Orange." Veterans Rights Newsletter, v. 1, no. 1, May 1981, p. 3. A staff report prepared by the House Subcommittee on Oversight and Investigations is critical of the way the Veterans Administration handles Agent Orange claims and is critical of the fact that the Department of Defense took no precautions to prevent exposure.

1699 "Secretary Schweiker's Press Conference on Agent Orange." Congressional Record, v. 127, pt. 17, September 24, 1981, p. 21870-21871. Representative G.V. Montgomery (D-Miss.)

commented on the information released by Secretary Schweiker at his recent press conference. Representative Montgomery contends that little of this information is new. The text of the Secretary's press release is included as well as a portion of the Committee on Veterans' Affairs hearing of September 16, 1980.

1700 Seligman, D. "Good News Is Not What They Came to Hear." Fortune, v. 104, no. 7, October 5, 1981, p. 102+. Dr. G. Spivey, who was awarded a contract with the Veterans Administration to design a study of the health effects of exposure to Agent Orange, testified before a California legislative committee that veterans should not worry about there being any serious side effects of being exposed to Agent Orange. "The... likelihood of substantial exposure to ground troops in Vietnam is not great," he stated.

1701 "Senate Acts to Extend Some Viet-Vet Programs." Air Force Times, v. 41, no. 50, July 6, 1981, p. 14. The Senate has voted to expand the scope of the Agent Orange study as well as some other Vietnam veterans' programs. Also passed was an amendment introduced by Senator A. Cranston (D-CA) providing veterans exposed to herbicides or radiation tests priority medical care in Veterans Administration hospitals.

1702 "Senate Backs Medical Care for Agent Orange Victims." Congressional Quarterly Weekly Report, v. 39, no. 25, June 29, 1981, p. 1091-1092. The Senate has unanimously agreed with the House and voted to require the Veterans Administration to provide medical care to Vietnam veterans who were exposed to Agent Orange.

1703 "Senate Resolution 372 - Relating to Exposure to Dioxin by Members of the Armed Forces." Congressional Record, v. 130, no. 50, April 25, 1984, p. S4823-S4849. Senator A. Simpson (R-Wyo.) introduced Resolution 372, the proposed Veterans' Dioxin and Radiation Exposure Initiative of 1984, for himself and five other senators. Among other things this resolution would provide a service-connection between porphyria cutanea tarda and chloracne. It would direct the Veterans Administration to develop guidelines for approving or rejecting the findings of epidemiological studies of Agent Orange. The text of the resolution and correspondence with Veterans Administration Administrator H. Walters, the Paralyzed Veterans of America, AMVETS and the Director of the Defense Nuclear Agency are included. Also included are recent editorials from the Washington Post and the Chicago Tribune.

1704 Shaughnessy, S. "Liability for Agent Orange." [letter]

<u>Wall Street Journal</u>, May 14, 1984, p. 27(E), p. 25(W). The author wrote this letter in response to an article by S. Garment (See 1508) which appeared in the April 27, 1984 issue of the <u>Wall Street Journal</u>. Shaughnessy believes that the federal government should compensate those harmed in military service.

1705 Silberner, J. "Common Herbicide Linked to Cancer." (See 1201)

1706 Skjei, E. and M.D. Whorton. "Agent Orange." In <u>Of Mice and Molecules: Technology and Human Survival</u>. New York: Dial Pr., 1983, p. 206-209. This book is a survey of toxic waste and environmental pollution. In this section the authors discuss the controversy over the use of Agent Orange in Vietnam. The problems veterans are having in dealing with the Veterans Administration and the National Academy of Sciences' advice on how a epidemiological study of the Operation Ranch Hand crew members should be conducted are mentioned.

1707 Smith, E. "Agent Orange Veterans: Who Is Responsible." <u>Not Man Apart</u>, v. 10, no. 9, September 1980, p. 13-14. The efforts veterans exposed to Agent Orange are making to get the government to accept responsibility for their problems resulting from that exposure, what the Veterans Administration has done so far and the class action suit brought against the chemical companies who manufactured Agent Orange are all discussed.

1708 Smith, P. "VFW Backs Agent Orange Benefits Bill." <u>Air Force Times</u>, v. 43, no. 20, December 6, 1982, p. 12. The Veterans of Foreign Wars is supporting a bill introduced by Representative T. Daschle (D-S.D.) which would force the Veterans Administration to compensate Vietnam veterans for health problems resulting from Agent Orange exposure.

1709 Smith, R.J. "Proposals to Study Veterans Criticized." <u>Science</u>, v. 208, no. 4447, May 30, 1980, p. 1015. The National Research Council and the National Veterans Task Force on Agent Orange are asking that the proposed study by the Air Force of the Operation Ranch Hand veterans be reworked.

1710 "Soft Tissue Cancers and Vietnam Veterans." <u>Congressional Record</u>, v. 128, no. 122, September 15, 1982, p. E4195-E4197. Representative T.A. Daschle (D-S.D.) submitted three articles on soft tissue sarcoma and exposure to dioxin to the <u>Record</u>. These are articles are from the February 13, 1980 issue of <u>Pesticide and Toxic Chemical News</u>, the January 31, 1981 issue of Lancet and the May 6, 1982 issue of New England Journal of Medicine (See 1193). Given the difficulties veterans are having with getting the Veterans Administration to deal with their claims, Representative Daschle is compelled to introduce legislation to establish a presumption that soft tissue cancers in Vietnam veterans are linked to service in Vietnam and are therefore compensable.

1711 "Some Peace of Mind." (See 2296)

1712 "Statements on Introduced Bills and Joint Resolutions." Congressional Record, v. 127, pt. 3, March 5, 1981, p. 3668-3696. Senator A. Cranston (D-CA) explains why he and two other Senators are introducing S. 636 on pages 3684-3688. This bill would in part expand the epidemiological study to include other factors such as exposure to other chemicals or environmental hazards, give the Veterans Administration the authority to contract with non-Veterans Administration entities for the design and conduct of the study and would provide the Veterans Administration with a framework to translate their findings into guidelines for veterans filing claims.

1713 "Statements on Introduced Bills and Joint Resolutions." Congressional Record, v. 127, pt. 4, March 12, 1981, p. 4261-4318. Senator J. Heinz (R-PA) explains why he and three other senators are introducing S. 689 on pages 4263-4264. The senators want to remove any obstacles veterans exposed to Agent Orange might be facing and to make sure that the Veterans Administration considers in a timely manner any evidence causally linking Agent Orange to diseases in humans. The text of S. 689 is included.

1714 "Statements on Introduced Bills and Joint Resolutions." Congressional Record, v. 127, pt. 9, June 8, 1981, p. 11700-11709. Senator J. Heinz (R-PA) explains why he introduced S. 1345 on pages 11708-11709. This bill would provide authority for hospital care for Vietnam veterans if a Veterans Administration physician determines such care is necessary for a condition associated with Agent Orange exposure. Of the 5,025 claims received by the Veterans Administration as of November 30, 1980 only 23 claims had been allowed.

1715 "Statements on Introduced Bills and Joint Resolutions." Congressional Record, v. 129, no. 30, March 11, 1983, p. S2679-S2722. Senator L. Pressler (R-S.D.) explains on page S. 2714 why he introduced S. 786 which would treat certain disease assumed to be caused by exposure to Agent Orange in Vietnam as service-connected illnesses.

1716   "Statements on Introduced Bills and Joint Resolutions."
        <u>Congressional Record</u>, v. 129, no. 41, April 6, 1983, p.
        S4183-S4211. Senator A. Cranston (D-CA) explains (p. S4198-
        S4200) why he is introducing S. 991 which would require the
        Administrator of the Veterans Administration to issue
        regulations which would provide guidelines for the resolution
        of Veterans Administration benefit claims including claims
        for compensation based on exposure to Agent Orange or
        radiation from a nuclear detonation. The text of the bill is
        included. The bill was referred to the Committee on
        Veterans' Affairs.

1717   "Statements on Introduced Bills and Joint Resolutions."
        <u>Congressional Record</u>, v. 129, no. 103, July 20, 1983, p.
        S10467-S10481. Senator A. Cranston (D-CA) explains (p.
        S10477-S10480) why he and three other senators introduced S.
        1651. This bill would provide for the presumption that
        veterans suffering from certain diseases have these diseases
        because they were exposed to Agent Orange or radiation. The
        provisions of the bill are explained and the text of the bill
        is included. The bill was referred to the Committee on
        Veterans' Affairs.

1718   "Statements on Introduced Bills and Joint Resolutions."
        <u>Congressional Record</u>, v. 131, no. 111, September 10, 1985, p.
        S11201-S11212. Senator A. Cranston (D-CA) introduced for
        himself and three other senators S. 1616 (p. S11201-S11204)
        which would require the Administrator of the Veterans
        Administration to provide for an epidemiological study of the
        gender-specific health effects on women veterans of their
        exposure to dioxin in Vietnam. The text of the bill,
        correspondence with Dr. J. Mason, director of the Centers for
        Disease Control, and with C. Baker, Chair of the Cabinet
        Council Agent Orange Orange Working Group, are included.

1719   Steif, W. "Agent Orange Disaster." <u>Progressive</u>, v. 44, no.
        2, February 1980, p. 8. The General Accounting Office has
        recently released a report on Agent Orange. As a result of
        this report, President Carter has established an interagency
        working group. In a federal court in New York, Judge Pratt
        has ruled that the class action suit against the
        manufacturers of Agent Orange can be tried in federal court
        instead of in state courts.

1720   Steif, W. "The Agent Orange Scandal." <u>Progressive</u>, v. 43,
        no. 12, December 1979, p. 11-12. Senator J. Heinz (R-PA)
        and Representative D. Bonior (D-Mich.) have introduced a
        comprehensive Vietnam veterans bill which would make all of
        the 2.4 million U.S. veterans who served in Vietnam eligible
        for Veterans Administration compensation for disabilities

resulting from exposure to Agent Orange. Children of
veterans who show Agent Orange-related symptoms would also
be eligible for compensation.

1721 Stein, J. "The Forgotten Vets." Progressive, v. 44, no. 6,
      June 1980, p. 14-15. The difficulties in getting the
      Veterans Administration to accept some responsibility for the
      veterans who are having health difficulties due to exposure
      to Agent Orange are mentioned. Two congressmen have
      uncovered an apparent 1977 Veterans Administration internal
      memo equating the effects of exposure to Agent Orange to
      thalidomide.

1722 Stichman, B.F. et al. "Developments in Veterans' Law During
      1985." (See 2300)

1723 Stoffel, J. "Aid on the Way for Vietnam Veteran Victims of
      Agent Orange." State Government News, v. 24, no. 7, June
      1981, p. 15. Legislation passed by Congress and various
      states on the Agent Orange issue is noted.

1724 Stroman, R.M. "The Vietnam Herbicide Information
      Commission." Health Reporter: Pennsylvania Department of
      Health Newsletter, v. 4, no. 2, February 1983, p. 1+. The
      author describes the mandate, structure and activities of the
      Vietnam Herbicide Information Commission which was formed
      as a result of the Pennsylvania Legislature passing House
      Bill 1575 in April 1982.

1725 "Study by Secretary of HEW on Effects of Dioxins."
      Congressional Record, v. 125, pt. 26, December 6, 1979, p.
      34999-35000. Senator A. Cranston (D-CA) submitted S. 2096
      which would mandate the Department of Health, Education and
      Welfare to study the effects of exposure to dioxin and
      discusses how this bill compares to H.R. 3892. The text of
      the bill is included.

1726 "Study of Effects in Humans of Dioxins." Congressional
      Record, v. 125, pt. 28, December 19, 1979, p. 36916-36918.
      Representative H.O. Staggers (D-W.V.) asked to have the
      Committee on Interstate and Foreign Commerce discharged
      from further consideration of S. 2096 and asked for its
      immediate consideration by the House. Representative
      Staggers urges adoption of this measure. The text of S. 2096
      is included.

1727 "Study Supports Agent Orange Claims." Guardian, v. 33, no.
      38, June 24, 1981, p. 8. A subcommittee of the House
      Interstate and Foreign Commerce Committee has written a
      report confirming the health complaints of veterans exposed
      to Agent Orange.

1728 "Subcommittee on Oversight and Investigations, House
      Veterans' Affairs Committee." Congressional Record, v. 128,
      no. 122, September 15, 1982, p. E4183-E4184. Representative
      R.M. Mottl (D-Ohio) had Representative T.A. Daschle's (D-
      S.D.) opening statement before the Veterans' Affairs
      Subcommittee on Oversight and Investigation's hearing of
      September 15, 1982 inserted in the Record. Representative
      Daschle details his frustration with the inability of the
      Veterans Administration to get an epidemiological study
      underway.

1729 "Submission of Concurrent and Senate Resolutions."
      Congressional Record, v. 130, no. 50, April 25, 1984, p.
      S4832. S. Res. 372 was submitted by Senator A. Simpson (R-
      Wyo.) for himself and five other senators in order to express
      the sense of the Senate regarding the atomic radiation and
      Agent Orange issues. The resolution was referred to the
      Committee on Veterans' Affairs.

1730 "Suit Aims at Blocking Agent Orange Study." Chemical and
      Engineering News, v. 58, no. 19, May 12, 1980, p. 5. The
      National Veterans Task Force on Agent Orange has brought a
      suit asking that the Veterans Administration's study of the
      health effects of Agent Orange be blocked. A committee of
      the National Research Council has asked that the Air Force
      review its proposed study of the Ranch Hand veterans.

1731 "Support Agent Orange Bill, Currieo Urges." VFW Magazine, v.
      70, no. 8, May 1983, p. 18. At the VFW's annual mid-winter
      conference in Washington, Commander-in-Chief Currieo urged
      veterans to support legislation which would make Agent Orange
      exposure a presumptive disability.

1732 "Support for Our Veterans." Congressional Record, v. 130,
      no. 7, January 31, 1984, p. E227. Representative S.H. Hoyer
      (D-MD) spoke on why he supports the passage of H.R. 1961, the
      Agent Orange and Atomic Veterans Relief Act.

1733 "Support Vietnam Veterans Agent Orange Act." Congressional
      Record, v. 129, no. 27, March 8, 1983, p. H894-H895.
      Representative C.H. Smith (R-N.J.) spoke in support of
      legislation introduced by Representative T.A. Daschle (D-
      S.D.) which would grant compensation for certain disabilities
      attributable to Vietnam veterans' exposure to herbicides
      while serving in Vietnam. The time for footdragging has
      ended.

1734 Swann, R. "Dioxin Poisoning and Vietnam Veterans."
      Northwest Passage, v. 18, no. 4, July 10, 1978, p. 4-5. The
      story of Michael Vogt who was exposed to Agent Orange in

Vietnam and his fight to get the government to take
responsibility for the problems resulting from that exposure
is told. The efforts made by Citizen Soldier are also noted.

1735   Tarbell, M. "The Agent Orange Time Bomb." Penthouse, v. 10,
       no. 12, August 1979, p. 74+. The efforts of several Vietnam
       veterans who believe that they were exposed to Agent Orange
       to get the government to accept responsibility for their
       health problems are detailed. Also noted is the story of
       Maude deVictor, a Veterans Administration claims counselor in
       Chicago, who first made the connection between Agent Orange
       and service in Vietnam.

1736   Taylor, S., Jr. "Government Has the Edge..." Los Angeles
       Daily Journal, v. 97, no. 99, May 15, 1984, p. 4. The
       difficulties that still face veterans and their families in
       obtaining compensation from the federal government is told.

1737   Tedeschi, L.G. "Dioxin: a Case in Point." (See 1225)

1738   "Texas Agent Orange Law Became Effective September First."
       Veterans Rights Newsletter, v. 1, no. 5-6, September-October
       1981, p. 41. The new Texas Agent Orange law is explained.
       If a veteran desires, he can ask his doctor to submit a
       report to the Texas Department of Health. This agency is
       required to conduct epidemiological studies on the health
       effects of exposure to Agent Orange. The state attorney
       general is authorized to bring class action lawsuits if need
       be to obtain information about exposure to Agent Orange and
       to obtain veterans' medical records.

1739   Texas. Department of Health. Texas Veterans Agent Orange
       Assistance Program. Austin, Texas: The Department, 1981.
       pamphlet. The assistance H.B. 2129 provides veterans exposed
       to Agent Orange and now living in Texas is described.

1740   Texas. Department of Health. Texas Veterans Agent Orange
       Assistance Program. Annual Report. Austin, Texas: Texas
       Department of Health, March 31, 1983. various paginations.
       The work of the Texas Veterans Agent Orange Assistance
       Program is described. Data on the 346 veterans in the
       program and brief descriptions of the six pilot studies of
       the program are included.

1741   Texas. Department of Health. Texas Veterans Agent Orange
       Assistance Program. Annual Report. Austin, Texas: Texas
       Department of Health, August 1985. 1 volume (various
       paginations). This report details the activities of the
       Texas Agent Orange Program from its inception through July
       31, 1985. It describes a study underway at the University of

Texas and summarizes the findings of other studies on the
health effects of Vietnam veterans' possible exposure to
Agent Orange.

1742   "Texas to Help Gather Agent Orange Data." Business
Insurance, v. 15, no. 24, June 15, 1981, p. 8. The Texas
attorney general has been granted authority by the Texas
legislature to bring a class action suit against the branches
of the U.S. military for medical records and information
concerning those who were exposed to Agent Orange for
veterans needing assistance in determining if they were
exposed to Agent Orange or not. Texas doctors will also be
required to notify the Texas Department of Public Health if
they treat veterans with possible Agent Orange symptoms. The
University of Texas medical clinics are also required to
provide genetic screening. Funds have also been provided for
free testing of veterans' fat tissue in order to search for
chromosome damage.

1743   Theiler, P. "A Vietnam Aftermath: the Untold Story of Women
and Agent Orange." (See 1228)

1744   Thomas, J. "Civilians Seek Agent Orange Redress." Off Our
Backs, v. 16, no. 1, January 1986, p. 18. The approximately
18,000 women who served as civilians in Vietnam are asking to
be included in government studies of the effects of Agent
Orange and to have the eligibility as veterans for financial
compensation. Civilians were not included in the 1984 out of
court settlement and are not included in the Centers for
Disease Control's study.

1745   "To CDC: VA Gives Up Agent Orange Study." American
Medical News, v. 25, no. 44, November 19, 1982, p. 6. The
Veterans Administration has agreed to relinquish control of
its study of the effects of Agent Orange to the Centers for
Disease Control.

1746   Tredway, L. "When a Veteran 'Wants' Uncle Sam: Theories of
Recovery for Servicemembers Exposed to Hazardous
Substances." (See 2326)

1747   "Two Faces of War." Congressional Record, v. 127, pt. 9 June
4, 1981, p. 11655-11657. Representative T. Harkin (D-Iowa)
inserted an article by M. MacPherson which appeared in the
May 26, 1981 issue of the Washington Post in the Record.
This article, in part, discusses the difficulties facing
Vietnam veterans who have medical problems they believe are
the result of having been exposed to Agent Orange.
Representative Harkin believes that H.R. 3499 which passed
the House recently may not have gone far enough, but at least
it is a start.

1748   Uhl, M. and T. Ensign. "Blowing the Whistle on Agent
       Orange." Progressive, v. 42, no. 6, June 1978, p. 28-30.
       Reprinted in "VA Action Needed on Agent Orange."
       Congressional Record, v. 124, pt. 10, May 11, 1978, p. 13454-
       13455. The story of how M. deVictor, a Chicago Veterans
       Administration claims officer, investigated the possible
       health effects of exposure to Agent Orange is told. When she
       was ordered to stop her investigation, she turned her
       research over to a Chicago television station which did a
       documentary on the subject. The health problems of two
       Illinois veterans who believe that exposure to Agent Orange
       is causing their problems are mentioned.

1749   "Unexpected Response Delays Analysis of Ranch Hand Agent
       Orange Findings." Air Force Times, v. 44, no. 14, October
       24, 1983, p. 22. An unexpectedly high rate of participation
       in the Operation Ranch Hand morbidity study has delayed the
       completion of this study until late February 1984.

1750   U.S. Congress. House. Committee on Interstate and Foreign
       Commerce, Subcommittee on Oversight and Investigations.
       Agent Orange: Exposure of Vietnam Veterans. Hearing, 96th
       Cong., 2nd sess., September 25, 1980. Washington: GPO,
       1981. iii, 249p. This hearing was held to continue hearings
       which were held in 1979. The purpose of this hearing was to
       attempt to determine if the government has shown an
       appreciation for the extent of the health problems resulting
       from the use of Agent Orange by the military in Vietnam.

1751   U.S. Congress. House. Committee on Interstate and Foreign
       Commerce, Subcommittee on Oversight and Investigations.
       Involuntary Exposure to Agent Orange and Other Toxic
       Spraying. Hearing, 96th Cong., 1st sess., June 26 and 27,
       1979. Washington: GPO, 1980. iv, 256p. As part of their
       responsibility for public health, this subcommittee held a
       hearing on the hazards of Agent Orange exposure to Vietnam
       veterans. The subcommittee also discussed the similarities,
       difference, and the interrelations between the Toxic
       Substance Control Act; the Food, Drug, and Cosmetic Act; and
       the Federal Insecticide, Fungicide, and Rodenticide Act.
       Testifying at this hearing were veterans and their families;
       V. Yannaconne, an attorney involved in the lawsuits against
       the manufacturers of Agent Orange; scientists;
       representatives of various groups; and Representative D.
       Bonior (D-Mich.)

1752   U.S. Congress. House. Committee on Veterans' Affairs. Agent
       Orange and Atomic Veterans Relief Act: Report Together with
       Additional Views (to Accompany H.R. 1961). Report, 98th
       Cong., 2nd sess., January 25, 1984. Washington: GPO, 1984.

26p. H.R. 1961, which would grant disability allowances to Vietnam veterans who suffer from chloracne, porphyria cutanea tarda or soft tissue sarcoma, is analyzed. Also included is background information on Agent Orange.

1753   U.S. Congress. House. Committee on Veterans' Affairs. Veterans' Compensation and Health Care Amendments of 1985: Report Together with Supplemental Views (to Accompany H.R. 1538). Report, 99th Cong., 1st sess., October 29, 1985. Washington: GPO, 1985. 109p. This document gives the House Committee on Veterans' Affairs an explanation of H.R. 1538, Veterans' Compensation and Health Care Amendments of 1985. A portion of title III (See pages 40-41, 49-51) would provide for a study of female veterans who were exposed to certain herbicides in Vietnam.

1754   U.S. Congress. House. Committee on Veterans' Affairs. Veterans' Health Care Act of 1981: Report (to Accompany H.R. 3499). Report, 97th Cong., 1st sess., May 19, 1981. Washington: GPO, 1981. 46p. In addition to several other proposals, this report recommends that hospital care be provided free of charge at Veterans Administration clinics if Veterans Administration physicians deem it necessary for those Vietnam veterans who may have been exposed to Agent Orange.

1755   U.S. Congress. House. Committee on Veterans' Affairs, Select Subcommittee. Issues Concerning Vietnam Veterans. Hearing, 97th Cong., 1st sess., July 16, 1981. Washington: GPO, 1981. iv, 95p. This hearing was held to discuss the benefits and services available to Vietnam veterans. One of the issues discussed was exposure to Agent Orange. (See pages 55-58, 91-95) Testimony at this hearing was heard from representatives of veterans' organizations and from individual veterans including participants in the hunger strike.

1756   U.S. Congress. House. Committee on Veterans' Affairs, Subcommittee on Compensation, Pension and Insurance. H.R. 1961 - Vietnam Veterans Agent Orange Relief Act. Hearing, 98th Cong., 1st sess., April 26 and 27, 1983. Washington: GPO, 1983. v, 477p. This hearing was held to discuss the issues involved with H.R. 1961, which would grant compensation to Vietnam veterans who may have been exposed to Agent Orange and are suffering from soft tissue sarcoma, porphyria cutanea tarda or chloracne.

1757   U.S. Congress. House. Committee on Veterans' Affairs, Subcommittee on Compensation, Pension and Insurance. H.R. 1961 - Vietnam Veterans Agent Orange Relief Act. Hearing,

98th Cong., 1st sess., July 12, 1983. Washington: GPO,
1983. iv, 211p. Additional testimony was received from the
Veterans Administration and other professional and scientific
witnesses concerning H.R. 1961.

1758   U.S. Congress. House. Committee on Veterans' Affairs,
Subcommittee on Hospitals and Health Care. Agent Orange
Studies. Hearing, 99th Cong., 2nd sess., July 31, 1986.
Washington: GPO, 1986. iii, 159p. This hearing focused on
three issues. One, the current status of the Centers for
Disease Control's study. Two, the objections that have
arisen as a result of the Centers for Disease Control's study
being based only on Army personnel records. Three, the
amount of money that has been spent thus far on Agent Orange
studies.

1759   U.S. Congress. House. Committee on Veterans' Affairs,
Subcommittee on Hospitals and Health Care. Legislation to
Improve Medical Programs Administered by the Veterans'
Administration (H.R. 2157, H.R. 2953, and H.R. 2999).
Hearing, 97th Cong., 1st sess., April 28, 1981. Washington:
GPO, 1981. iii, 54p. H.R. 2157 is a bill that would expand
the scope of the Veterans Administration's study on Agent
Orange to consider Vietnam service as an exposure factor
rather than focusing solely on Agent Orange.

1760   U.S. Congress. House. Committee on Veterans' Affairs,
Subcommittee on Oversight and Investigations. Current Status
of Agent Orange Studies. Hearing, 97th Cong., 1st sess., May
6, 1981. Washington: GPO, 1981. iii, 385p. Testifying at
this hearing were officials from the Veterans Administration
and the Air Force commenting on the progress made on the
development on their studies, a representative from the
Office of Technology Assessment whose responsibility it is to
monitor the Veterans Administration's epidemiological study,
and a representative from the National Veterans Law Center.

1761   U.S. Congress. House. Committee on Veterans' Affairs,
Subcommittee on Oversight and Investigations. Federal Agent
Orange Activities and the Vet Center Program. Hearing, 97th
Cong., 2nd sess., September 15, 1982. Washington: GPO,
1982. iv, 164p. This hearing was held to receive testimony
on the status and activities of the federal government in
regards to the Agent Orange issue. Testimony focused on the
Veterans Administration's study, the Veterans
Administration's implementation of medical treatment
mandated by Public Law 97-72 and the progress made by the
Intragency Work Group on Agent Orange. Testimony was heard
from Veterans Administration officials, the Army on their
program, a state senator from Illinois, several

representatives from veterans' service organizations and a representative from the National Veterans Law Center.

1762 **U.S. Congress. House. Committee on Veterans' Affairs, Subcommittee on Oversight and Investigations.** Status of Federally Conducted Agent Orange Studies. Hearing, 98th Cong., 1st sess., May 3, 1983. Washington: GPO, 1983. iii, 146p. Testimony was heard from members of Congress, the Veterans Administration, the Department of Health and Human Services, and the Department of the Air Force on the current status of federally conducted Agent Orange studies, and from the state of Tennessee's Select Committee on Veterans' Affairs on studies they have recently completed.

1763 **U.S. Congress. Senate. Committee on Veterans' Affairs.** Agent Orange Update and Appendix: Agent Orange Activities (Part 2). Hearing, 96th Cong., 2nd sess., September 10, 1980. Washington: GPO, 1980 [i.e. 1981]. iv, 1368p. This hearing was held to update the committee members on the Agent Orange issue. Testifying were members of the interagency work group and other government officials and representatives of veterans' groups.

1764 **U.S. Congress. Senate. Committee on Veterans' Affairs.** Oversight on Issues Related to Agent Orange and Other Herbicides. Hearing, 97th Cong., 1st sess., November 18, 1981. Washington: GPO, 1982. iv, 500p. Testimony at this hearing focused on updating the members of this committee on the status of various studies that are in the development stage or have begun on the issue of veterans' exposure to Agent Orange.

1765 **U.S. Congress. Senate. Committee on Veterans' Affairs.** VA Health Resources and Program Extensions and Appendix, Agent Orange Activities. Hearing, 96th Cong., 1st sess., April 10, 1979. Washington: GPO, 1980. iv, 462p. Appendix B includes documents which update the committee on the Veterans Administration's and Department of Defense's studies on the health effects of exposure to Agent Orange by Vietnam veterans.

1766 **U.S. Congress. Senate. Committee on Veterans' Affairs.** Veterans' Compensation and Benefits Improvements Act of 1985. Report, 99th Cong., 1st sess., November 26, 1985. Washington: GPO, 1985. iv, 188p. This report explains the Senate Committee on Veterans' Affairs' examination of the Veterans' Compensation and Benefits Improvements Act of 1985. Part of Title 5 (pages 62-64) would require that a Vietnam-Experience Epidemiological Study of the Health of Women Veterans be undertaken.

1767 U.S. Congress. Senate. Committee on Veterans' Affairs.
      <u>Veterans Exposure to Agent Orange: Hearings on S. 374, S.</u>
      <u>786, and S. 991</u>. Hearing, 98th Cong., 1st sess., June 15 and
      22, 1983. Washington: GPO, 1983 [i.e. 1984]. vi, 654p.
      This hearing was held to learn what additional information
      may be expected from continuing research on Agent Orange
      exposure. Testimony was heard on the oversight of technical
      and management aspects of Agent Orange, the Ranch Hand
      study, the planned soft tissue study, and medical research on
      the possible health effects of exposure with emphasis on the
      veterans' epidemiological study. Testimony was heard from
      officials from the Veterans Administration, the White House
      Agent Orange Work Group, the Office of Technology
      Assessment and representatives from various veterans'
      groups.

1768 U.S. Congress. Senate. Committee on Veterans' Affairs.
      <u>Veterans' Exposure to Ionizing Radiation as a Result of</u>
      <u>Detonations of Nuclear Devices</u>. Hearing, 98th Cong., 1st
      sess., April 4, 1983. Washington: GPO, 1984. iv, 577p.
      See "Guidelines Pertaining to Treatment of Veterans Exposed
      to Agent Orange and Ionizing Radiation" on pages 127-138.
      These guidelines have been issued by the Veterans
      Administration for use by Veterans Administration physicians
      to help them in making decisions as to whether an
      individual's disability may have been caused by exposure to
      Agent Orange.

1769 U.S. Congress. Senate. Committee on Veterans' Affairs.
      <u>Veterans Programs Extension and Improvement Act of 1981:</u>
      <u>Hearing on S. 26 (Titles II and III, Only), S. 380, S. 458,</u>
      <u>S. 636, S. 689, S. 872, S 914, S. 921, and Related Bills</u>.
      Hearing, 97th Cong., 1st sess., April 30, 1981. Washington:
      GPO, 1981. iv, 685p. A bill was introduced by Senator A.
      Cranston (D-CA) which would amend the Agent Orange Study
      Provision. (See pages 57-87) This bill would expand the
      scope of the Agent Orange study to include evaluation of
      other factors involved in service in Vietnam and it would
      require the Veterans Administration to study the health of
      Vietnam veterans as their health may have been affected by
      exposure to Agent Orange.

1770 U.S. General Accounting Office. <u>Health Effects of Exposure</u>
      <u>to Herbicide Orange in South Vietnam Should Be Resolved</u>
      (See 1242)

1771 U.S. General Accounting Office. <u>Report on the Use of</u>
      <u>Herbicides and Other Chemicals in Vietnam</u>. Washington:
      General Accounting Office, 1978. 14p. Also included as part
      of the hearing before the Subcommittee on Medical Facilities
      and Benefits of the House of Representatives' Committee on

Veterans Affairs held on October 11, 1978. This report mentions the Department of Defense funded studies on the health effects of herbicides, the fact that the Department of Defense has little information on the number of personnel exposed to herbicides in Vietnam and summarizes the use of herbicides and other chemicals in Vietnam.

1772 **U.S. General Accounting Office. U.S. Ground Troops in South Vietnam Were in Areas Sprayed with Herbicide Orange: Report.** Washington: GPO, 1979. 21p. This report states that U.S. ground troops were in and close to areas during and shortly after the spraying of Agent Orange. The Department of Defense evidently took few precautions to prevent exposure to Agent Orange. Also included in this report is a statement on the status of the efforts by the Department of Defense and the Veterans Administration on previous recommendations.

1773 **U.S. General Accounting Office. VA's Agent Orange Examination Program: Actions Needed to More Effectively Address Veterans' Health Concerns: Report to Congress.** Washington: GPO, 1982. v, 78p. This report concludes that while the Veterans Administration's Agent Orange examinations were more thorough than veterans perceived, the General Accounting Office was able to confirm three of the veterans' complaints. One, examinations were not thorough enough. Two, the Veterans Administration has provided little or no information to veterans on the effects of Agent Orange to their health. Three, Veterans Administration personnel are not well informed.

1774 **U.S. General Accounting Office. Human Resources Division. Agent Orange: VA Needs to Further Improve Its Examination and Registry Program.** January 1986. 66p. Available from NTIS: PB 86-169687. This report reviews and evaluates whether or not veterans were given their Agent Orange examinations promptly by the Veterans Administration, whether or not veterans were receiving the results of their examinations promptly and whether or not the Agent Orange Registry is reliable and complete. The General Accounting Office found that most examinations were made promptly. However, not all veterans were notified of the results of the examination and the Agent Orange Registry is not reliable. Based upon the General Accounting Office's findings several recommendations were forwarded to the Veterans Administration to which the Veterans Administration mostly agreed.

1775 **"U.S. House Tells VA to Aid Agent Orange Victims."** Jet, v. 60, no. 15, June 25, 1981, p. 39. The House of Representatives, by unanimous vote, has directed the Veterans

Administration to provide medical care to veterans exposed to
Agent Orange in Vietnam.

1776   **U.S. Veterans Administration. Annual Report - 1981.**
       Washington: GPO, May 1982. viii, 237p. Information on the
       Veterans Administration's activities in FY1981 on the Agent
       Orange matter is given on pages 21-22 and 117. By the end of
       FY1981 over 67,000 Vietnam veterans had received Agent
       Orange-related examinations. The Veterans Administration has
       contracted for the design of an epidemiological study. JRB
       Associates have been contracted to review and analyze the
       scientific literature on Agent Orange and other phenoxy
       herbicides. The award-winning film, "Agent Orange: a Search
       for Answers," is being shown nationwide.

1777   **U.S. Veterans Administration. Annual Report - 1982.**
       Washington: GPO, July 1983. ix, 241p. Information on the
       Veterans Administration's activities in FY1982 on the Agent
       Orange matter is given on pages 26-28 and 118. A two-volume
       report analyzing the scientific literature on Agent Orange
       and other phenoxy herbicides was prepared under contract from
       the Veterans Administration by JRB Associates. As of
       September 30, 1982, 97,486 Vietnam veterans have agreed to
       participate in the Veterans Administration's Agent Orange
       Registry. Two information pamphlets have been prepared.

1778   **U.S. Veterans Administration. Annual Report - 1983.**
       Washington: GPO, June 1984. xviii, 244p. Information on
       the Veterans Administration's activities in FY1983 on the
       Agent Orange matter is given on pages xvii, 24-27, 114-115,
       124 and 127. These activities include ongoing research
       studies, providing information to veterans, maintaining the
       Agent Orange Registry and responding to veterans who apply
       for compensation.

1779   **U.S. Veterans Administration. Annual Report - 1984.**
       Washington: GPO, August 1985. xvii, 260p. Information on
       the Veterans Administration's activities in FY1984 on the
       Agent Orange matter is given on pages 10, 24-27 and 140. A
       two-volume update to the literature review has been issued.
       An update on the Agent Orange Registry is given.

1780   **U.S. Veterans Administration. Annual Report - 1985.**
       Washington: GPO, 1986. xviii, 261p. Information on the
       Veterans Administration's activities in FY1985 on the Agent
       Orange matter is given on pages 25-27.

1781   **U.S. Veterans Administration. A Commitment to Serving**
       Vietnam Veterans Concerned about Agent Orange. Washington:
       GPO, November 1985. 13p. The purpose of the studies the
       Veterans Administration has been involved in and the ones

they are monitoring concerning the health effects of Vietnam
veterans' exposure to Agent Orange is noted. The services
the Veterans Administration provides Vietnam veterans exposed
to Agent Orange are also noted.

1782 **U.S. Veterans Administration. Worried About Agent Orange?**
Washington: Veterans Administration, 1980. pamphlet. What
the Veterans Administration and other federal agencies are
doing and what veterans who were exposed to Agent Orange in
Vietnam should do are noted. There is no scientific evidence
linking Agent Orange to sperm damage or birth defects at this
time.

1783 **U.S. Veterans Administration. Advisory Committee on Health-**
Related Effects of Herbicides. Annual Report of Activities
for Calendar Year 1982. Washington: The Committee, [n.d.].
7p. A summary of the meetings the Committee held in 1982 is
given. Also included is a list of the Committee members for
1982.

1784 **U.S. Veterans Administration. Advisory Committee on Health-**
Related Effects of Herbicides. Annual Report of Activities
for Calendar Year 1983. Washington: The Committee, [n.d.].
7p. This report summarizes the Committee's activities in
1983 by reviewing the four meetings the Committee held and
noting the Committee's efforts to keep abreast of the
research being conducted around the country. A list of the
1983 Committee membership is also included.

1785 **U.S. Veterans Administration. Advisory Committee on Health-**
Related Effects of Herbicides. Annual Report of Activities
for 1984. Washington: The Committee, [n.d.]. 6p. This
report summarizes the Committee's activities in 1984 by
reviewing the four meetings the Committee held and noting the
Committee's efforts to keep abreast of the research being
conducted around the country. A list of the 1984 Committee
membership is also included.

1786 **U.S. Veterans Administration. Advisory Committee on Health-**
Related Effects of Herbicides. Annual Report of Activities
for 1985. Washington: The Committee, [n.d.]. 4p. This
report summarizes the events of the two meetings the
Committee held and discusses the Committee's new charter. A
list of the 1985 Committee membership is also included.

1787 **U.S. Veterans Administration. Advisory Committee on Health-**
Related Effects of Herbicides. Transcript of Proceedings,
June 11, 1979. June 1979. 146p. Available from NTIS: **PB**
82-146366. At the first meeting of the Advisory Committee
each of the members stated what their agencies were doing
with respect to Agent Orange. Also included is a statement

on herbicide research in the Department of Medicine and
Surgery.

1788 U.S. Veterans Administration. Advisory Committee on Health-
Related Effects of Herbicides. Transcript of Proceedings
(Second Meeting, September 24, 1979). September 1979. 173p.
Available from NTIS: PB 82-146374. At this meeting, the
Committee stated its conviction to treat veterans at Veterans
Administration hospitals who are suffering from the long-term
effects of exposure to Agent Orange without establishing
causation or linkage to Agent Orange exposure. Also
discussed at this meeting were position papers on Agent
Orange, the information gathering process for the
epidemiological study, and the establishment of a formal
process liaison with all other federal agencies concerned
with the study of Agent Orange.

1789 U.S. Veterans Administration. Advisory Committee on Health-
Related Effects of Herbicides. Transcript of Proceedings
(Third Meeting, April 12, 1979). March 1980. 126p.
Available from NTIS: PB 82-146382. The position papers on
Agent Orange were discussed at this meeting as well as
concern on whether or not available data on the exposure of
Vietnam veterans to herbicides would be sufficient for a
scientifically valid epidemiological study on the long-term
health effects of exposure to Agent Orange.

1790 U.S. Veterans Administration. Advisory Committee on Health-
Related Effects of Herbicides. Transcript of Proceedings
(Fourth Meeting, April 23, 1980). July 1980. 130p.
Available from NTIS: PB 82-136797. The scientific studies
on the effects of Agent Orange exposure on Vietnam veterans
are discussed. Also mentioned is the growing interest of the
news media and the general public in this issue.

1791 U.S. Veterans Administration. Advisory Committee on Health-
Related Effects of Herbicides. Transcript of Proceedings
(Fifth Meeting, August 6, 1980). November 1980. 144p.
Available from NTIS: PB 82-146390. Among the reports
presented at this meeting were the following: Chloracne Task
Force, Literature Analysis, Agent Orange Registry,
Epidemiological Study, Professor Ton That Tung's latest
study, Centers for Disease Control Proposed Birth Defects
Study, the AFIP Registry, and Ranch Hand study.

1792 U.S. Veterans Administration. Advisory Committee on Health-
Related Effects of Herbicides. Transcript of Proceedings
(Sixth Meeting, November 6, 1980). December 1980. 149p.
Available from NTIS: PB 82-146408. The narrative of the
video tape, Agent Orange: A Time for Reason, produced by the
St. Louis Regional Medical Education Center of the Veterans

Administration is included in the proceedings. The videotape was produced in order to disseminate scientific and military information on Agent Orange to veterans, to attempt to allay unnecessary fears among veterans and to encourage them to participate in Veterans Administration programs. The scientific studies being conducted to determine the effects of exposure of Vietnam veterans to Agent Orange were discussed at this meeting.

1793 **U.S. Veterans Administration. Advisory Committee on Health-Related Effects of Herbicides. Transcript of Proceedings (Seventh Meeting, February 4, 1981).** April 1981. 191p. Available from NTIS: PB 82-146416. At this meeting status reports on the Agent Orange and the AFIP Registries were given and the Air Force's Ranch Hand Study was discussed.

1794 **U.S. Veterans Administration. Advisory Committee on Health-Related Effects of Herbicides. Transcript of Proceedings (Eighth Meeting, May 5, 1981).** Washington: GPO, May 1981. ix, 139p. Also available from NTIS: PB 82-136805. Reports were given at this meeting on the Epidemiological Study, Literature Analysis Report, the Dioxin Conference, and the studies of the Environmental Epidemiology Branch of the National Cancer Institute. Reports were also heard from veterans' service organizations and state governments.

1795 **U.S. Veterans Administration. Advisory Committee on Health-Related Effects of Herbicides. Transcript of Proceedings, Ninth Meeting, August 19, 1981.** September 1982. 146p. Available from NTIS: PB 83-228783. The draft design of the epidemiological study was presented. Reports were given on the Birth Defects Study being conducted by the Centers for Disease Control, the Ranch Hand Study, plans for the upcoming International Dioxin Symposium, and veterans' service organizations activities. Representatives from the states of Texas, New York, California and New Jersey gave reports on the viewpoints and activities of veterans' groups in these states as related to herbicide effects.

1796 **U.S. Veterans Administration. Advisory Committee on Health-Related Effects of Herbicides. Transcript of Proceedings, Tenth Meeting, November 19, 1981.** April 1982. 120p. Available from NTIS: PB 82-263112. Included among the reports given at this meeting were: the Veterans Administration's Epidemiological Study, the Ranch Hand Study, the 1981 and 1982 International Dioxin Symposium, the AFIP Agent Orange Registry, the Vietnam veterans leadership program and the Veterans Administration Mortality Study. The issues raised by these reports were then discussed and commented upon.

1797 U.S. Veterans Administration. Advisory Committee on Health-
      Related Effects of Herbicides. Transcript of Proceedings,
      Eleventh Meeting, February 25, 1982. May 1982. 110p.
      Available from NTIS: PB 82-263120. Reports presented at
      this meeting included: the Veterans Administration Agent
      Orange Registry, the Veterans Administration Mortality Study,
      the activities of the Armed Forces Epidemiological Board, and
      the initiatives in the State of Wisconsin. Reports were also
      submitted by veterans' service organizations. Discussion and
      comments on the issues raised are included in the transcript.

1798 U.S. Veterans Administration. Advisory Committee on Health-
      Related Effects of Herbicides. Transcript of Proceedings,
      12th Meeting, Held at Washington, D.C., May 13, 1982.
      September 1982. 128p. Available from NTIS: PB 83-190314.
      Reports were given from the Agent Orange Research and
      Education Office and on the public information and
      educational plan for Agent Orange at this meeting. Also
      presented at this meeting were updates on the epidemiological
      study, the Veterans Administration mortality study, the
      proposed twin study, the Centers for Disease Control birth
      defects study, the Ranch Hand Study, and Veterans
      Administration solicited in-house research. Also discussed
      were proposed protocols for the epidemiological study and the
      future and composition of the Agent Orange Advisory
      Committee. Comments and discussion from the audience
      conclude the transcript.

1799 U.S. Veterans Administration. Advisory Committee on Health-
      Related Effects of Herbicides. Transcript of Proceedings,
      Thirteenth Meeting, August 31, 1982. January 1983. 140p.
      Available from NTIS: PB 83-204685. Reports were given at
      this meeting from the Agent Orange Research and Education
      Office, on the public information and education plan for
      Agent Orange, and from various veterans' service
      organizations. Updated at this meeting were the
      epidemiological study, the Veterans Administration mortality
      study, activities in Australia. The Agent Orange Registry
      was reviewed by the Armed Forces Institute of Pathology.
      Representatives from Illinois and Minnesota presented reports
      on activities in their states. The transcript concludes with
      comments and audience discussion.

1800 U.S. Veterans Administration. Advisory Committee on Health-
      Related Effects of Herbicides. Transcript of Proceedings,
      Fourteenth Meeting, November 30, 1982. March 1983. 118p.
      Available from NTIS: PB 83-204677. Reports and updates
      presented at this meeting addressed: the Veterans
      Administration Agent Orange examination, the Chloracne Task
      Force, AMVETS, the recent dioxin symposium, the Centers for
      Disease Control Birth Defects Study, the Air Force's health

study and the activities of commissions from various states
were presented in a report from the State Agent Orange
organization. Comments and audience discussion conclude the
report.

1801 **U.S. Veterans Administration. Advisory Committee on Health-
Related Effects of Herbicides. <u>Transcript of Proceedings,
15th Meeting, February 24, 1983</u>.** 1983. 119p. Available
from NTIS: PB 83-228791. The transfer of the Agent Orange
epidemiological study to the Centers for Disease Control and
the Veterans Administration's retrospective study of dioxins
and furans were discussed at this meeting. The activities of
the Chloracne Task Force, the Veterans Administration's
differential herbicide exposure study of identical twins, and
the literature review study of soft tissue sarcomas in
relation to phenoxy herbicides, the Ranch Hand Study, and the
Centers for Disease Control's birth defects study were among
those discussed. The relationship between Times Beach,
Missouri and Vietnam in terms of dioxin levels and the
degradation and behavior in soil of pesticides containing
TCDDs was discussed and commented upon.

1802 **U.S. Veterans Administration. Advisory Committee on Health-
Related Effects of Herbicides. <u>Transcript of Proceedings,
Sixteenth Meeting, May 20, 1983</u>.** Washington: The Committee,
July 1983. v, 62p. At this meeting the members were brought
up to date on recent activities and heard reports from the
Subcommittees on Education/Information and Epidemiology/
Biostatistics. The subcommittee process was evaluated by the
Committee. The Committee was also updated on the activities
of state Agent Orange commissions. Questions were accepted
from the audience.

1803 **U.S. Veterans Administration. Advisory Committee on Health-
Related Effects of Herbicides. <u>Transcript of Proceedings,
Seventeenth Meeting, September 1, 1983</u>.** December 1983. iii,
71p. Available from NTIS: PB 84-205780. At this meeting
committee members heard a report from the American Medical
Association's Council on Scientific Affairs on how they help
physicians treating veterans who have been exposed to Agent
Orange, were given an update on health in Seveso, Italy,
heard a report on the activities at the state government
level, were updated on recent Environmental Protection Agency
actions regarding dioxin, heard reports from the
subcommittees and learned about a Veterans Administration-
Environmental Protection Agency coordinated program for the
analysis of dioxin in human adipose tissue. The meeting
ended with comments and discussion by the audience and
participants.

1804   **U.S. Veterans Administration. Advisory Committee on Health-
Related Effects of Herbicides. <u>Transcript of Proceedings,
Eighteenth Meeting, December 6, 1983.</u> February 1984. iii,
82p. Available from NTIS: PB 84-205798.** The Committee
heard remarks from J. Gronvall, newly appointed Veterans
Administration Deputy Chief Medical Director, an update on
the literature review, a report on a study being conducted by
the American Legion and Columbia University, a report on the
status of the Centers for Disease Control's epidemiological
study, a report on the status of the Centers for Disease
Control's Birth Defects Study, a report on the issue of women
Vietnam veterans who were exposed to Agent Orange, heard
reports from the subcommittees, and heard remarks from Dr. J.
Levinson, an obstetrician and gynecologist from Delaware, on
the effects of Agent Orange exposure. The meeting ended with
comments and discussion by the audience and participants.

1805   **U.S. Veterans Administration. Advisory Committee on Health-
Related Effects of Herbicides. <u>Transcript of Proceedings,
19th Meeting, March 6, 1984.</u> Washington: GPO, June 1984.
v, 143p.** At this meeting reports were given by two
Australian physicians describing their research on Australian
veterans who were exposed to Agent Orange, by G. Lathrop on
the Air Force's study of the Ranch Hand crew members, by Dr.
D. Erickson on the Centers for Disease Control's
Epidemiological Study, by Dr. J. Mulinare on the Centers for
Disease Control's Birth Defects Study and by the two
subcommittees. Questions were also accepted from the
audience.

1806   **U.S. Veterans Administration. Advisory Committee on Health-
Related Effects of Herbicides. <u>Transcript of Proceedings,
Twentieth Meeting, June 5, 1984.</u> Washington: The Committee,
September 1984. v, 160p.** The committee members were
updated on recent activities, state government activities,
the Centers for Disease Control's Birth Defects Study, the
Veterans Administration Chloracne Task Force, the
retrospective study of dioxins and furans in adipose tissue,
the VA/AFIP pathological evaluation of malignant neoplasms in
PTF. The Committee also heard about plans for a revision of
the American Medical Association's report on the Agent Orange
issue. The subcommittees gave reports. Dr. J. Levinson
reported on his visit to Australia and Agent Orange research
going on in Australia and New Zealand.

1807   **U.S. Veterans Administration. Advisory Committee on Health-
Related Effects of Herbicides. <u>Transcript of Proceedings,
Twenty-first Meeting, September 12, 1984.</u> December 1984. v,
125p. Available from NTIS: PB 85-171809.** The Committee
heard about the status of international dioxin research, the

Centers for Disease Control's epidemiology study and Australian veterans studies, the results of the Centers for Disease Control's Birth Defects Study, the activities of the Agent Orange Projects Office and state commissions. The Committee also heard reports from the subcommittees. The Committee also received questions from the floor.

1808   U.S. Veterans Administration. Advisory Committee on Health-Related Effects of Herbicides. Transcript of Proceedings, Twenty-second Meeting, December 11, 1984. Washington: GPO, May 1985. v, 205p. Also available from NTIS: PB 85-233997. The Committee heard reports on the federal government's activities, the litigation, the New York state proportional mortality study, the Veterans Administration's Agent Orange budget, the Veterans Administration's Office of Public & Consumer Affairs' Agent Orange videotape program, National Cancer Institute supported research on cancer and phenoxy herbicide exposure, the Veterans Administration's In-House specially solicited Agent Orange research, the results of the soft tissue sarcoma study and from the Chief Medical Director. Questions were accepted from the floor.

1809   U.S. Veterans Administration. Advisory Committee on Health-Related Effects of Herbicides. Transcript of Proceedings, Twenty-third Meeting, March 26, 1985. Washington: The Committee, June 1985. vii, 178p. The Committee heard reports on state government activities, the Mortality Among Vietnam Veterans in Massachusetts Study, the West Virginia Mortality Study, the Veterans Administration/Environmental Protection Agency Adipose Tissue Study, the twin study, the Australian Mortality Study, the possibility that military dogs exposed to Agent Orange in Vietnam are also suffering adverse health effects due to this exposure and from the general counsel's office. Questions were also accepted from the floor.

1810   U.S. Veterans Administration. Advisory Committee on Health-Related Effects of Herbicides. Transcript of Proceedings, Twenty-fourth Meeting, October 22, 1985. March 1986. vii, 170p. Available from NTIS: PB 86-217486. The Committee heard reports on the Massachusetts Mortality Study, on the activities in other states, from veterans' service organizations, from other Veterans Administration Advisory Committees, on the status of on-going research of the Agent Orange Projects Office and on the highlights of a international symposium held in Bayreuth. The meeting ended with comments and discussion by the audience and participants.

1811   U.S. Veterans Administration. Advisory Committee on Health-

Related Effects of Herbicides. <u>Transcript of Proceedings, Twenty-fifth Meeting, June 12, 1986.</u> Washington: The Committee, October 1986. vii, 244p. This meeting consisted of remarks by Veterans Administration Administrator Turnage and reports on the status of the Veterans Administration's research efforts, the Vietnam Experience Twin Study, the Air Force Ranch Hand II Health Study, the Centers for Disease Control's Epidemiology Study, the Massachusetts Vietnam Veterans Health Survey and on the Advisory Committee on Women Veterans. The meeting ended with comments and discussion by the audience and participants.

1812   U.S. Veterans Administration. Office of Public and Consumer Affairs. <u>Agent Orange: Information for Veterans Who Served in Vietnam: Questions and Answers.</u> Washington: GPO, 1982. 8p. The Veterans Administration's position on many of the questions veterans who were exposed to Agent Orange may have is stated.

1813   U.S. Veterans Administration. Office of Public and Consumer Affairs. <u>Agent Orange Review.</u> Washington: GPO, v. 1 -, 1982-. This periodical is issued occasionally to keep Vietnam veterans informed on the Agent Orange issue.

1814   U.S. Veterans Administration. Veterans' Advisory Committee on Environmental Hazards. [<u>Minutes of June 25, 1985 Meeting</u>]. Washington: The Committee, [n.d.]. 4p. The Committee heard an overview of chloracne and then turned to discussing the regulations relating to claims filed for compensation for disabilities resulting from dioxin exposure. The Committee found no serious objections to the Veterans Administration's proposed regulations.

1815   U.S. Veterans Administration. Veterans' Advisory Committee on Environmental Hazards. [<u>Minutes of March 3, 1986 and March 4, 1986 Meetings</u>]. Washington: The Committee, [n.d.]. 10p. On March 3rd, the Committee heard a summary of the comments that had been received during the public comment period, the status of the Centers for Disease Control's Vietnam veterans studies, a summary of the third annual Ranch Hand mortality update and an overview of the Australian Royal Commission's report. On March 4th, the Committee heard reports on the studies conducted in Wisconsin, West Virginia and Iowa, a review of the American Legion Vietnam Veterans study and a summary of the February 1986 <u>Scientific American</u> article by F.H. Tschirley. The Committee also discussed the difficulty in accurately diagnosing soft tissue sarcomas.

1816   U.S. Veterans Administration. Veterans' Advisory Committee on Environmental Hazards. [<u>Minutes of November 17, 1986 and</u>

November 18, 1986 Meetings]. Washington: The Committee,
[n.d.]. 19p. On November 17th, the Committee heard a report
of a lawsuit filed against the Veterans Administration by the
Vietnam Veterans of America (VVA). The Scientific Council
discussed the findings of the Massachusetts study, the
Wisconsin study and of several Agent Orange related studies.
The Council also discussed the problem of soft tissue sarcoma
analysis. On November 18th, the Science Council heard an
overview of the epidemiological study mandated by Pub. L. No.
96-155 and addressed questions posed by the Department of
Veterans Benefits. The Committee discussed the lawsuit by
the VVA and the possibility of a joint meeting of the
Herbicide Committee.

1817 U.S. Veterans Administration. Veterans' Advisory Committee on
Environmental Hazards. [Transcript of April 22, 1985 Full
Committee Meeting]. Washington: The Committee, [n.d.].
192p. This Committee was established as the result of the
passage of the Veterans Dioxin and Radiation Standards Act.
At this first meeting the Committee discussed how to meet its
charges. One, to advise the Veterans Administration on the
status of scientific knowledge of the human health effects of
ionizing radiation and dioxin exposure. Two, to develop
regulations that will detail how the Veterans Administration
is to evaluate scientific studies on the health effects of
exposure to these substances. Three, to develop regulations
for the handling of claims for benefits for disabilities
resulting from exposure. The Committee heard an overview on
the Agent Orange by A.L. Young, a report from the Cabinet
Council Agent Orange Working Group and from the Veterans
Administration's Agent Orange program.

1818 U.S. Veterans Administration. Veterans' Advisory Committee on
Environmental Hazards. Scientific Council. [Minutes of April
22, 1985 Meeting]. Washington: The Committee, [n.d.]. 1p.
The Council discussed time lines in order to complete the
work they were charged to do.

1819 U.S. Veterans Administration. Veterans' Advisory Committee on
Environmental Hazards. Scientific Council. [Minutes of April
23, 1985 Meeting]. Washington: The Committee, [n.d.]. 3p.
The Council discussed the Veterans Administration's approach
to chloracne, porphyria cutanea tarda and soft tissue
sarcomas.

1820 U.S. Veterans Administration. Veterans' Advisory Committee on
Environmental Hazards. Scientific Council. [Minutes of June
24, 1985 Meeting]. Washington: The Committee, [n.d.] 3p.
The Council heard reports on the status of the Ranch Hand
study, studies being conducted on the link between soft

tissue sarcoma and dioxin, and mortality studies involving
Vietnam veterans. The Council agreed that the Veterans
Administration's proposed regulations were in line with
current scientific knowledge about the health effects of
dioxin exposure and that there is no evidence that soft
tissue sarcoma occurs with any greater frequency among people
exposed to dioxin than those who were not.

1821   "Update on Agent Orange Issue." Congressional Record, v.
       127, pt. 24, December 16, 1981, p. 32129-32132. Senator A.
       Cranston (D-CA) discusses two documents on the Agent Orange
       issue. The first was the report prepared by the American
       Medical Association's Council on Scientific Affairs' Advisory
       Panel on Toxic Substances. The other is a letter from C.
       Hagel, Deputy Administrator of Veterans Affairs, to Senator
       A. Spector (R-PA) relating to questions raised about Agent
       Orange at Mr. Hagel's recent confirmation hearing. The text
       of this letter is included in the Record. Senator Cranston
       announced that the first two volumes of the literature review
       have been released and that early response has been very
       favorable.

1822   "VA Action Needed on Agent Orange." Congressional Record,
       v. 124, pt. 10, May 11, 1978, p. 13454-13455. Representative
       D. Edwards (D-CA) along with 13 of his colleagues on the
       Veterans' Affairs Committee have initiated a request for an
       official response from the Veterans Administration on the
       issue of what the Veterans Administration has in mind to do
       about Agent Orange and to provide the committee with a
       thorough report on Agent Orange.

1823   "VA Agent Orange Bill Becomes Law." Facts on File, v. 44,
       no. 2294, November 2, 1984, p. 810. President Reagan has
       signed a bill which will require the Veterans Administration
       to set policy and pay disability benefits to Vietnam veterans
       suffering from chloracne and porphyria cutanea tarda which
       the veterans feel they have as a result of exposure to Agent
       Orange in Vietnam. This is the first time that it has been
       acknowledged by the government that exposure to Agent
       Orange might have caused ill health in Vietnam veterans.

1824   "VA Announces New Agent Orange Research." American
       Legion Magazine, v. 113, no. 5, November 1982, p. 34. Ten
       new research projects which will investigate the health
       related effects of Agent Orange exposure have been approved
       for funding by the Veterans Administration.

1825   "VA Appoints Agent Orange Panel." Air Force Times, v. 40,
       no. 3, August 13, 1979, p. 7. A special advisory committee
       of doctors and other medical experts has been appointed by

the Veterans Administration to help determine the effects of
exposure to Agent Orange and other herbicides on Vietnam
veterans. The Veterans Administration said that so far 2,000
veterans have requested Agent Orange related examinations and
nearly 500 have filed disability claims.

1826 "VA Contracts for Design of Agent Orange Study." Chemical
and Engineering News, v. 59, no. 19, May 11, 1981, p. 6. The
Veterans Administration has awarded a team of epidemiologists
from the University of California at Los Angeles headed by G.
Spivey the contract to design an epidemiological study to
determine if the Vietnam veterans exposed to Agent Orange
suffered any medical effects as a result of this exposure.

1827 "VA: Curious Orange." Science News, v. 119, no. 21, May 23,
1981, p. 325. The Veterans Administration has contracted
with a University of California at Los Angeles research team
to design a study to determine whether exposure to Agent
Orange has caused health problems in Vietnam veterans.

1828 "VA Defends Treatment in Agent Orange Dispute." American
Medical News, v. 24, no. 33, September 4, 1981, p. 32. The
Veterans Administration stated that there was no evidence to
link Vietnam veteran James Hopkins' death to inadequate
treatment for exposure to Agent Orange.

1829 "VA Finalizes Rules for Agent Orange and Radiation Cases."
Veterans Rights Newsletter, v. 5, no. 3-4, July-August 1985,
p. 17+. The Veterans Administration has decided that for now
chloracne is the only disease that they will grant
compensation for in regards to Agent Orange exposure.
However, they have decided that any Vietnam veteran is
presumed to have been exposed so the veteran no longer has to
prove he was exposed. How the Veterans Administration
decides what scientific evidence is needed in order to grant
a disease presumptive service-connected status is noted.

1830 "VA Has Not Done Its Job with Respect to Vietnam-era
Veterans." Congressional Record, v. 126, pt. 12, June 20,
1980, p. 15857. Representative T.J. Downey (D-N.Y.) feels
that the Veterans Administration and the General Accounting
Office should do an exhaustive survey of all the chemicals
that were sprayed in Vietnam, that the Veterans
Administration should conduct extensive tests on the veterans
who were exposed to these chemicals and that the Veterans
Administration should conduct an outreach program to alert
Vietnam-era veterans to the possible consequences of exposure
to these chemicals.

1831 "VA Makes Changes to Agent Orange Registry Program."

Veterans Rights Newsletter, v. 6, no. 5-6, September-October 1986, p. 37. The Veterans Administration has recently announced some changes and clarifications regarding the Agent Orange Registry Program.

1832 "VA Neglects Agent Orange Issue." Congressional Record, v. 126, pt. 6, April 15, 1980, p. 7731-2. Representative M. Frost (D-Tex.) tells of the efforts one of his constituents had to make in order to get the Veterans Administration to test him for exposure to Agent Orange.

1833 "VA Now Publishing Agent Orange Review." American Legion Magazine, v. 114, no. 6, June 1983, p. 24. The Veterans Administration's Office of Public and Consumer Affairs has begun publishing Agent Orange Review as part of the Veterans Administration's effort to provide information on Agent Orange to concerned veterans and their families.

1834 "VA Offers Agent Orange Examinations." Military Review, v. 63, no. 4, April 1983, p. 17. Army Reservists who were exposed to Agent Orange while serving in Vietnam are eligible for free physical examinations and advice at Veterans Administration medical centers.

1835 "VA Opposed A.O. Compensation Law." Citizen Soldier, no. 6, December 1983, p. 1+. Veterans Administration Benefits Chief Starbuck testified before Congress recently that the Veterans Administration considers the approach taken by H.R. 1961 to be inadvisable and defended the current compensation system. The reasons why the Veterans Administration is opposed to granting compensation for porphyria cutanea tarda and soft tissue sarcoma are noted.

1836 "VA Orders Definitive Study of Herbicide Agent Orange." Journal of Commerce, v. 348, no. 24,960, May 7, 1981, p. 10. A research team at the University of California at Los Angeles has been awarded a contract from the Veterans Administration to design an epidemiological study to determine if exposure to Agent Orange in Vietnam is the source of some veterans' health problems.

1837 "VA Pledges an Intense Study of Agent Orange." Jet, v. 63, no. 1, September 13, 1982, p. 5. Veterans Administration Chief Nimmo has recently pledged that seven million dollars will be spent over the next two years to research the effects of Agent Orange on veterans.

1838 "VA Scored on Agent Orange Study Delay." Facts on File, v. 42, no. 2187, October 15, 1982, p. 765. The Veterans Administration has stated that it will probably be 1988 or

1989 before their study on the effects of Agent Orange on Vietnam veterans will be completed.

1839 "VA's Agent Orange Exams Criticized." Science News, v. 122, no. 19, November 6, 1982, p. 301. A recently released report from the General Accounting Office states that the Veterans Administration's physical examinations of and follow-up programs for Vietnam veterans who believe their health problems result from exposure to Agent Orange are inadequate.

1840 "The VA's Intolerable Delay." [editorial] Los Angeles Daily Journal, v. 95, no. 184, September 15, 1982, p. 4. The Veterans Administration has announced that it will probably take until 1988 or 1989 to complete their study of the health effects of exposure to Agent Orange. K. Berning, an Illinois State Senator, complained that this shows "...a lack of concern, a lack of interest on the part of the national government." This editorial states that this estimate of the situation seems to be correct.

1841 "VA's Reluctance to Accept Evidence Prompts Call for Scrutiny." American Legion Magazine, v. 115, no. 2, August 1983, p. 27. The American Legion testified before the Senate Veterans' Affairs Committee recently. They feel that because of the Veterans Administration's "inflexible attitude" toward accepting scientific research which has been done linking certain diseases to Agent Orange exposure that they cannot support conferring "an inordinate amount of decision-making authority on the agency" without assurance of congressional oversight by the Veterans' Affairs Committee.

1842 "VA's Views on Proposed Agent Orange Legislation." DAV Magazine, v. 25, no. 6, June 1983, p. 6. The text of a news release the Veterans Administration issued detailing their reasons for opposing H.R. 1961, a bill introduced by Representative T. Daschle (D-S.D.), is given. This bill would compensate veterans who had been exposed to Agent Orange and had developed certain illnesses.

1843 "VFW Supports Compensation for Agent Orange Disabilities." Congressional Record, v. 128, pt. 18, September 24, 1982, p. 25221. Representative T.A. Daschle (D-S.D.) had the text of a press release from the Veterans of Foreign Wars (VFW) inserted in the Record. The VFW supports legislation which has been introduced to compensate veterans for disabilities related to Agent Orange exposure. Representative Daschle states that the burden of proof for determining the relationship between a disease and its service relationship should be on the U.S. government not the veteran - not the other way around as it presently is. In Australia the burden of proof is on the Australian government.

1844 "Veterans Administration Accused of Ignoring Europe Defoliant
      Cancer Reports." Oncology Times, v. 2, no. 5, May 1980, p.
      1+. Congressmen D. Bonior (D-Mich.) and T. Daschle (D-S.D.)
      have released the results of studies conducted in Europe on
      the toxicity of phenoxy herbicides or their contaminants.
      The lawsuit against the manufacturers of Agent Orange is also
      mentioned. The manufacturers have charged that the
      government failed to exercise due caution in the use of the
      defoliant.

1845 "Veterans' Administration Agent Orange Study." Congressional
      Record, v. 127, pt. 2, February 6, 1981, p. 2050-2053.
      Senator A. Cranston (D-CA) spoke about the General
      Accounting Office's review of the Veterans Administration's
      proposed protocol for an epidemiological study on exposure to
      Agent Orange. Senator Cranston urged the Veterans
      Administration to proceed with all expeditiousness now that
      this report has been completed. Senator Cranston submitted a
      copy of the General Accounting Office report for the Record.

1846 "Veterans' Administration Health Resources and Programs
      Extension Act of 1979." Congressional Record, v. 125, pt.
      12, June 18, 1979, p. 15148-15181. The Senate debate on
      S.1039 is given. The debate focuses on Amendment 263 which
      would direct the Department of Health, Education and Welfare
      to conduct an epidemiologic study on effects of exposure to
      dioxins. This amendment is sponsored by Senators A. Cranston
      (D-CA), J. Javits (R-N.Y.) and D. Moynihan (D-N.Y.). The
      amendment passed. Also included is the text of a letter to
      President Carter from Senator Cranston, the text of the reply
      by S. Eizenstat to this letter and the text of Senator
      Cranston's April 30, 1979 press release.

1847 "Veterans' Administration Unmoved by Agent Orange
      Legislation." Congressional Record, v. 129, no. 27, March 8,
      1983, p. H892. Representative D.E. Bonior (D-Mich.) is upset
      with the Veterans Administration because of their failure to
      grant compensation for soft tissue cancers suffered by
      Vietnam veterans exposed to Agent Orange despite all the
      evidence linking soft tissue cancers and 2,4,5-T.
      Representative Bonior is introducing legislation with
      Representative Daschle (D-S.D.) to grant compensation in this
      instance.

1848 "Veterans' Bill Signed." Congressional Quarterly Weekly
      Report, v. 39, no. 45, November 7, 1981, p. 2195. President
      Reagan has signed the Veterans' Health Care, Training and
      Small Business Loan Act of 1981 (HR 3499-PL 97-92). As part
      of this legislation Vietnam veterans are now eligible for
      health care at Veterans Administration clinics for ailments
      that have been linked to Agent Orange exposure.

1849 "Veterans' Compensation and Benefits Improvements of 1985." Congressional Record, v. 131, no. 164, December 2, 1985, p. S16624-S16630. The debate on S. 1887, the veterans' compensation COLA bill, is given. Section 507 (p. S16630-S16631) would provide for an epidemiological study on the health of women veterans exposed to Agent Orange in Vietnam. The text of a letter from D. Arnett, Acting Chair of the Cabinet Council Agent Orange Working Group, is included. This letter states that the Centers for Disease Control and members of the Science Panel of the Executive Branch Agent Orange Working Group agree that such a study is feasible.

1850 "Veterans' Disability Compensation and Survivors' Benefits Amendments of 1979." Congressional Record, v. 125, pt. 25, November 15, 1979, p. 32589-32599. Senator A. Cranston (D-CA), chair of the Senate Veterans' Affairs Committee, reported on the committee's findings on H.R. 2282 and their recommended amendments to this resolution. Senator Cranston introduced an amendment (p. 32593-32594) concerning an Agent Orange study. Also included are the text of a letter from Veterans Administrator Cleland on the Veterans Administration's Agent Orange study activities, the text of a letter from Senator Cranston to President Carter, the text of a letter from Senator Cranston to Dr. J. Crutcher of the Veterans Administration, the text of a letter to Secretary of Health, Education and Welfare Califano and the text of a memo from Veterans Administration Administrator Cleland on the various Agent Orange epidemiological studies that have been proposed.

1851 "Veterans' Dioxin and Radiation Exposure Compensation Standards Act." Congressional Record, v. 130, no. 68, May 22, 1984, p. S6144-S6177. The floor debate on S. 1651, the Veterans' Dioxin and Radiation Exposure Compensation Standards Act, is given. Among other things this bill would grant a presumption of service connection between soft tissue sarcoma, porphyria cutanea tarda and chloracne and exposure to Agent Orange. The amendments to the bill were adopted. A conference with the House was requested and a vote on S. 1651 was subsequently indefinitely postponed.

1852 "Veterans' Dioxin and Radiation Exposure Compensation Standards Act." Congressional Record, v. 130, no. 130 part III, October 4, 1984, p. S13587-S13611. The debate on the House amendments to the Senate amendments to H.R. 1961 is given. The Senate concurred with these amendments. The text of the amendments is included.

1853 "Veterans' Dioxin and Radiation Exposure Compensation Standards Act." Congressional Record, v. 130, no. 131 part

II, October 5, 1984, p. S13672-S13673. Senator S. Thurmond (R-S.C.) feels that H.R. 1961, the Veterans' Dioxin and Radiation Exposure Compensation Standards Act, is meritorious legislation and he commends it to his colleagues.

1854 "Veterans Form Agent Orange Task Force." Keep Strong, v. 4, no. 5, September 1979, p. 70-71. A coalition of church, veteran, scientific and public interest organizations have formed the National Veterans' Task Force on Agent Orange. This task force was formed because the Veterans Administration has refused to do its job of representing veterans. The purpose of this task force is to gather the information necessary to prove that exposure to Agent Orange does cause widespread health problems.

1855 "Veterans' Health Care." Congressional Quarterly Weekly Report, v. 39, no. 51, December 19, 1981, p. 2518-2519. H.R. 3499 has cleared Congress. This bill mandates the Veterans Administration to provide medical care to Vietnam veterans suffering from ailments attributed to Agent Orange.

1856 "Veterans' Health Care Act of 1981." Congressional Record, v. 127, pt. 9, June 2, 1981, p. 11160-11170, 11174-11175. The debate on H.R. 3499 is given. This bill in part would provide medical care to Vietnam veterans exposed to herbicide defoliants and would expand the scope of the Agent Orange study to include the effects of all environmental hazards. This bill passed.

1857 "Veterans' Legislation." Congressional Record, v. 127, pt. 3, February 25, 1981, p. 3049-3050. Representative R.M. Mottl (D-Ohio) spoke on the four Veterans' Administration medical bills he is introducing. One of the bills would expand the scope of the study the Veterans Administration is required to conduct on exposure to Agent Orange to include other herbicides, environmental hazards, etc. and would require the Veterans Administration to study the literature on exposure to herbicides.

1858 Veterans of Foreign Wars of the United States. Proceedings of the 85th National Convention. Washington: GPO, 1985. xvii, 226p. The Senate's passing of S. 1651, the Veterans' Dioxin and Radiation Exposure Compensation Standards Act, was discussed on pages 211-212. One of the organization's priority legislative goals for 1983-1984 (p. 207-208) is to support legislation which would liberalize the disposition of herbicide related claims so that the burden of proof for award of disability compensation is on the government rather than the veteran.

1859   "Veterans' Programs Extension and Improvement Act of 1981."
       Congressional Record, v. 127, pt. 9, June 15, 1981, p. 12348-
       12384. Two hours of debate on S. 921 is given. This bill in
       part would modify the epidemiological study on the exposure
       to Agent Orange. Senator A. Cranston (D-CA) introduced
       several amendments to this bill - one of which would provide
       access to the Veterans Administration health care system for
       veterans exposed to radiation or Agent Orange. Letters from
       the American Legion, Vietnam Veterans of America and the
       National Association of Atomic Veterans are included.
       Several other amendments to this bill were offered.

1860   "Veterans' Programs Extension and Improvement Act of 1981."
       Congressional Record, v. 127, pt. 10, June 16, 1981, p.
       12450-12456. The debate on S. 921 is continued. Amendment
       59 as modified passed. A vote on H.R. 3499 was taken in the
       Senate and the bill passed. The vote on S. 921 was
       indefinitely postponed.

1861   "Veterans' Programs Extension and Improvement Act of 1981."
       Congressional Record, v. 127, pt. 17, October 2, 1981, p.
       22860-22876. The text of the debate on the Senate amendments
       to H.R. 3499 and on the House amendments to the Senate
       amendments is given. Some of this debate centers on the
       issue of health care to Vietnam veterans who were exposed to
       Agent Orange and whether or not the epidemiological study
       should be expanded. The text of the amendments is also
       included.

1862   "The Veteran's Self-help Guide on Agent Orange." Discharge
       Upgrading Newsletter, v. 5, no. 2, February 1980, p. 3-6.
       The text of a four-page guide prepared by the National
       Veterans Law Center is given. The guide was prepared in
       order to provide assistance to veterans wishing to file
       claims with the Veterans Administration for problems that
       could have been caused by Agent Orange exposure.

1863   "Vets Being Examined for Effects." Air Force Times, v. 42,
       no. 24, January 4, 1982, p. 15. As part of the Air Force's
       Ranch Hand study some 2,400 (half Vietnam veterans) will
       receive physical examinations at Houston's Kelsey-Seybold
       Clinic. Follow-up examinations are planned at 3, 5, 10, 15
       and 20 year intervals. Louis Harris and Associates have been
       awarded a contract to administer a questionnaire to identify
       the health, medical, demographic, social and psychological
       conditions to the people involved in the study.

1864   "Vets Call for Resignation of Scientist Studying Agent
       Orange." Veterans Rights Newsletter, v. 1, no. 4, August
       1981, p. 25. Veterans are upset about the testimony Dr. G.

Spivey gave before a California Assembly committee. Dr.
Spivey was hired by the Veterans Administration to design a
health study of Agent Orange. Dr. Spivey testified that fear
is very likely to be the most serious consequence of the use
of Agent Orange, that there is no evidence presently of any
health effects from exposure and the likelihood that ground
troops were substantially exposed is not great. Veterans now
are calling for Dr. Spivey's resignation from the study.

1865   "Vietnam Chemical Still Taking Toll." Prevention, v. 30, no.
       7, July 1978, p. 204. Twenty-seven Chicago-area Vietnam
       veterans who handled Agent Orange have complained to the
       Veterans Administration about suffering from various
       illnesses and having offspring born with birth defects.

1866   "The Vietnam-era Veterans Health Care and Benefits Act of
       1981." Congressional Record, v. 127, pt. 5, April 1, 1981,
       p. 5966-5967. Representative T.A. Daschle (D-S.D.) spoke on
       the reasons why he is introducing H.R. 2953. This
       legislation would provide hospitalization or outpatient
       treatment for all Vietnam veterans exposed to Agent Orange
       who, after being examined by a Veterans Administration
       physician, are determined to be in need of medical
       assistance. The bill would also address some of the
       recommendations made by the Interagency Work Group in
       regards to the Veterans Administration's proposed
       epidemiological study. The text of H.R. 2953 is included.

1867   "Vietnam Veterans." Facts on File, v. 41, no. 2118, June 19,
       1981, p. 420. The Intragency Work Group on Agent Orange has
       urged that a broader study of Agent Orange be undertaken than
       the one begun by the Veterans Administration. The Senate has
       voted to grant federally financed medical care to Vietnam
       veterans exposed to Agent Orange.

1868   "The Vietnam Veterans Adviser." [editorial] Penthouse, v.
       10, no. 5, January 1979, p. 118. This editorial states that
       Penthouse is convinced that the Veterans Administration is
       not attempting to cover-up or ignore the Agent Orange
       problem.

1869   "Vietnam Veterans Agent Orange Act." Congressional Record,
       v. 127, pt. 4, March 25, 1981, p. 5252-5254. Representative
       T.A. Daschle (D-S.D.) spoke on legislation he has
       reintroduced which would grant a presumption of service-
       connection for the occurrence of certain diseases in veterans
       who were exposed to Agent Orange. Representative Daschle
       spoke on the accomplishments of the interagency work group,
       the findings of some of the epidemiological studies that have
       already been done and the fact that while 6,164 claims have

been filed with the Veterans Administration only 24 have been allowed. The text of H.R. 2493 is included.

1870   "Vietnam Veterans Agent Orange Relief Act." Congressional Record, v. 130, no. 129 part II, October 3, 1984, p. H11155-H11166. The proposed amendments by the Senate to H.R. 1961 are discussed on the House floor as well as amendments to the Senate amendments. The text of the amendments is included. The House amendments to the Senate amendments were passed.

1871   "Vietnam Veterans: Agent Orange Study." Congressional Record, v. 128, pt. 20, October 20, 1982, p. 27623-27626. Senator A. Cranston (D-CA) discusses the frustration that many have felt at the failure of the Veterans Administration to get the epidemiological study underway. The Administrator of Veterans Affairs has written to the Secretary of Health and Human Services proposing that the Centers for Disease Control take over the study. The text of letters from the Office of Technology Assessment, the Administrator of Veterans Affairs, Representative G.V. Montgomery (D-Miss.) and Senator Cranston on this issue and the text of a Veterans Administration memo from the Administrator regarding the reorganization of Agent Orange responsibilities were inserted in the Record.

1872   "Vietnam Veterans and Agent Orange." Congressional Record, v. 126, pt. 5, March 25, 1980, p. 6436. Representative T. Daschle (D-S.D.) stated that he feels it is time for the House to address the issue of the possible health effects of Agent Orange exposure. He mentioned that the wife of a Vietnam veteran who was exposed to Agent Orange while in Vietnam and now lives in South Dakota gave birth to a baby with a great number of birth defects and chromosome damage although both parents have normal chromosomes.

1873   "Vietnam Veterans and Agent Orange." Congressional Record, v. 127, pt. 8, May 27, 1981, p. 10859. Representative R.W. Kastenmeier (D-WI) has recently received a petition from the organization, Vietnam Veterans Against the War, concerning Agent Orange which was signed by 554 people. The petition requests that the Veterans Administration do the following things: develop a test to determine if veterans have residual effects of exposure to Agent Orange and then conduct this test on all Vietnam veterans, provide treatment for all affected veterans and pay compensation to affected veterans. The petition also asks the federal government to contact the Vietnamese for assistance. Representative Kastenmeier urges the Veterans Administration to act with compassion on this issue.

1874   "Vietnam Veterans: Conduct of Agent Orange Study Shifted to
       CDC." Congressional Record, v. 129, no. 23, March 1, 1983,
       p. S1840-S1843. Senator A. Cranston (D-CA) feels that the
       transfer of the epidemiological study to the Centers for
       Disease Control is a positive step. The Centers for Disease
       Control will submit the study protocol to the Office of
       Technology Assessment for review and comments. The Senator
       feels that the health effects of the entire Vietnam
       experience should be studied, not just the effects of
       exposure to Agent Orange. He is pleased that the Centers for
       Disease Control plans to conduct two studies - one is on the
       effects of exposure to Agent Orange and one will be a broader
       examination of the Vietnam experience. The Senator had
       letters from the Office of Technology Assessment, the Centers
       for Disease Control and the Veterans Administration on these
       issues inserted in the Record.

1875   "Vietnam Veterans Seek Compensation on Agent Orange."
       American Medical News, v. 26, no. 3, January 21, 1983, p. 52.
       Approximately 16,000 Vietnam veterans have asked for
       compensation from the Veterans Administration for medical
       problems they believe to be caused as a result of exposure to
       Agent Orange. Thus far no veteran has been awarded
       compensation based solely on the fact that he was exposed to
       Agent Orange.

1876   "Vietnam Veterans Studied for Herbicide Exposure." Nature,
       v. 279, no. 5715, June 21, 1979, p. 667. The Air Force and
       the Department of Health, Education and Welfare will study
       1,200 Vietnam veterans exposed to Agent Orange to determine
       the long-term effects of exposure to 2,4,5-T. The study is
       scheduled to last six years.

1877   "Vietnam Veterans to Be Studied." Prevention, v. 31, no. 9,
       September 1979, p. 200-201. The federal government is
       planning to conduct a survey on the health of over 1,000
       American airmen who sprayed Agent Orange over the jungle
       areas of Vietnam.

1878   "Vietnam: Vets Exposed to Toxic Agents Sought for Checkups."
       American Legion Magazine, v. 106, no. 2, February 1979, p.
       32. The American Legion is encouraging all veterans who were
       exposed to Agent Orange to go to their nearest Veterans
       Administration health care facility for evaluation.

1879   "Vietnam Vets Form Lobbying Coalition." Facts on File, v.
       43, no. 2238, October 7, 1983, p. 762. Twelve veterans'
       groups have formed a coalition to lobby Congress on behalf of
       the concerns of Vietnam veterans including the Agent Orange
       issue.

1880 "Vietnam Vets Health Endangered by Exposure to Agent
      Orange." (See 1257)

1881 **Volpe, L. "Vets Hold Agent Orange Conference." Workers
      World, v. 23, no. 22, May 29, 1981, p. 7.** Approximately 200
      Vietnam veterans have come to Washington, D.C. to protest the
      lack of action by the federal government, the Veterans
      Administration and the manufacturers of Agent Orange.

1882 **Volpe, L. "Vets Protest Reagan Policies." Workers World, v.
      23, no. 26, June 26, 1981, p. 5.** Vietnam veterans are
      holding protest rallies and hunger strikes in an effort to
      get the federal government to provide assistance for some of
      the problems they are having -- one of which is the effects
      of exposure to Agent Orange.

1883 **Watriss, W. "Agent Orange." Texas Observer, v. 73, no. 19,
      September 25, 1981, p. 1+.** H.B. 2129 has been passed by the
      Texas Legislature. This legislation directs the State Health
      Department to coordinate clinical testing and genetic
      screening for Vietnam veterans with the University of Texas
      Medical System. The Health Department has also been
      authorized to collect the information and conduct an
      epidemiological study concerning the health problems reported
      by Vietnam veterans in Texas. The efforts veterans are
      making to get the Veterans Administration to acknowledge
      their claims is also noted. Congress has begun to pass
      legislation in this area.

1884 **Wehr, E. "Carter Efforts to Cut VA Hospital Staffs Opposed."
      Congressional Quarterly Weekly Report, v. 37, no. 25, June
      23, 1979, p. 1251-1252.** The Senate adopted S. 1039 by voice
      vote and approved an amendment authorizing a study of Agent
      Orange.

1885 **Wehr, E. "Veterans' Health Bill Cleared: VA to Conduct
      'Agent Orange' Study." Congressional Quarterly Weekly
      Report, v. 37, no. 51, December 22, 1979, p. 2906-2907.** The
      Senate has compromised with the House and agreed that the
      study of the effects of exposure of Vietnam veterans to Agent
      Orange will be conducted by the Veterans Administration
      instead of the Department of Health, Education and Welfare.

1886 Weissberg, A. "Agent Orange: Continuing Horror of Vietnam."
      (See 1264)

1887 **Willenz, J.A. "Agent Orange." In Women Veterans: America's
      Forgotten Heroines.** New York: Continuum Publ. Co., 1983, p.
      230-231. These pages describe the efforts the Veterans
      Administration has made to respond to veterans' feelings that

their medical problems are a result of being exposed to Agent Orange. None of the 66 studies that have been conducted on the effects of Agent Orange and other dioxins on Vietnam veterans has included women.

1888   Williams, R. "Agent Orange Revisited: Alternatives to Litigation." (See 2370)

1889   "Women Vietnam Veterans Should Be Included in Agent Orange Studies." Congressional Record, v. 131, no. 112, September 11, 1985, p. E3964-E3966. Representative M. Kaptur (D-Ohio) and several of her colleagues are introducing legislation requiring the Veterans Administration to proceed with the implementation of a study on the health effects of Agent Orange exposure on women Vietnam veterans. The text of a letter 78 members of Congress sent to the Cabinet Council Agent Orange Working Group on this issue and the text of a reply from Secretary of Health and Human Services Heckler are included.

1890   Young, A.L. and H.K. Kang. "Status and Results of Federal Epidemiologic Studies of Populations Exposed to TCDD." Chemosphere, v. 14, no. 6-7, 1985, p. 779-790. The 15 studies being sponsored by 10 federal agencies on the effects of exposure to TCDD, most of which are focused on the exposure of Vietnam veterans to Agent Orange, are described.

1891   Zamichow, N. "Vietnam Workers Stonewalled on Agent Orange Dangers." Ms., v. 15, no. 2, August 1986, p. 26. The plight of women who served as civilians in Vietnam during the war and were exposed to Agent Orange is described. The 1984 out of court settlement does not include civilians and the Centers for Disease Control's study will not include women. The government says civilians cannot be scientifically studied.

THE AGENT ORANGE LITIGATION

1892   "A.O. Judge Replacement Named." Citizen Soldier, no. 6, December 1983, p. 3. Judge Jack B. Weinstein is the presiding judge in the Agent Orange litigation now that Judge Pratt has stepped aside.

1894   Addlestone, D.F. "Developments in Veterans Programs in 1981." (See 1289)

1894   **Adell, J. and S. Fass. "Agent Orange Settlement Averts Giant Product Liability Trial."** Journal of Commerce, **v. 360, no. 25,719, May 8, 1984, p. 1+.** The Agent Orange litigation has been settled out of court and the reaction of the manufacturers and their insurers is mentioned. The manufacturers did not admit to any liability in the case.

1895   "Agent Orange." Discharge Upgrading Newsletter, October 1979. (See 1291)

1896   **"Agent Orange."** Discharge Upgrading Newsletter, **v. 5, no. 9-10, September-October 1980, p. 6-7.** The Air Force has been sued by a graduate student asking that documents concerning Operation Ranch Hand be released under the Freedom of Information Act.

1897   "Agent Orange." CBS News Daily News Broadcasts, May 7, 1980 (See 1296)

1898   "Agent Orange." Veterans Rights Newsletter, November-December 1981 (See 1300)

1899   **"Agent Orange."** CBS News Daily News Broadcasts, **new ser., v.9, no. 77, March 18, 1983, p. 13 (evening news).** The Agent Orange litigation is discussed.

1900   "Agent Orange." Veterans Rights Newsletter, September-October 1983. (See 1314)

1901   "Agent Orange." Veterans Rights Newsletter, November-December 1983. (See 1315)

1902   **"Agent Orange."** Wall Street Journal, **February 28, 1984, p. 10(E), p. 10(W).** The Supreme Court has refused to hear an appeal by the manufacturers of Agent Orange who are being sued for damages caused by exposure to this chemical during the Vietnamese War.

1903   **"Agent Orange."** CBS News Daily News Broadcasts, **new ser., v. 10, no. 129, May 8, 1984, p. 18 (morning news).** Some veterans do not feel the out of court settlement is fair.

1904   **"Agent Orange."** CBS News Daily News Broadcasts, **new ser., v. 10, no. 130, May 9, 1984, p. 16 (morning news).** Dow Chemical Company is planning to sue the federal government in order to force them to participate in the paying of the $180 million settlement.

1905   **"Agent Orange." [editorial]** Nation, **v. 238, no. 19, May 19, 1984, p. 596-7.** The impact of the settlement on veterans is noted. Because the federal government is not a party to the settlement, it can still be sued by both sides. The problems left by the Vietnam War cannot be solved until the government acknowledges responsibility for the tragedy of Vietnam.

1906 "Agent Orange." CBS News Daily News Broadcasts, new ser., v. 10, no. 156, June 4, 1984, p. 12 (evening news). The suit brought by Vietnam veterans exposed to Agent Orange seeking damages from the federal government has been thrown out of court. The court still needs to decide whether or not the children and wives of exposed veterans can sue the federal government.

1907 "Agent Orange." CBS News Daily News Broadcasts, new ser., v. 10, no. 221, August 8, 1984, p. 10 (evening news). The first fairness hearing on the out of court settlement is discussed.

1908 "Agent Orange." Reporter. Office of the Judge Advocate General of the Air Force, no. 4, Summer 1984, p. 23-24. The extent to which the federal government is still involved as a defendant in the Agent Orange litigation is noted.

1909 "Agent Orange." CBS News Daily News Broadcasts, new ser., v. 10, no. 269, September 25, 1984, p. 8 (evening news). The out of court settlement has been approved. The chemical companies and some veterans still plan to sue the federal government.

1910 "Agent Orange." CBS News Daily News Broadcasts, new ser., v. 10, no. 269, September 25, 1984, p. 48 (morning news). The out of court settlement has been tentatively approved.

1911 "Agent Orange." Facts on File, v. 45, no. 2304, January 18, 1985, p. 27. Judge Weinstein has given formal approval to the May 1984 settlement. The attorneys for the veterans have been awarded $9.3 million in fees and expenses. Next a plan for distributing the compensation among the veterans and their families needs to be decided upon. There are now about 170,000 claimants.

1912 "Agent Orange." Veterans Rights Newsletter, v. 4, no. 11-12, March-April 1985, p. 86-87. Judge Weinstein has ruled that claims of veterans against the federal government are barred by the Feres doctrine, that there was not evidence to support the claims of veterans' wives and that the claims of the veterans' children are to be dismissed without prejudice. Judge Weinstein has also dismissed the claims of the veterans who opted out of the settlement and the attempts of the chemical companies to get the federal government to pay part of the settlement.

1913 "Agent Orange." <u>Facts on File</u>, v. 45, no. 2322, May 24,
      1985, p. 382-383. Judge Weinstein has ruled that the federal
      government is "within its legal rights" in refusing to
      contribute to the $180 million settlement. However he stated
      that this position will cost the United States a great deal.

1914 "Agent Orange." <u>Reporter. Office of the Judge Advocate
      General of the Air Force</u>, no. 3, Spring 1985, p. 23. An
      update of the federal government's involvement in the
      litigation brought by veterans.

1915 "Agent Orange." <u>Veterans Rights Newsletter</u>, v. 5, no. 9-10,
      January-February 1986, p. 77-79. An update on the litigation
      and the Centers for Disease Control's epidemiologic studies
      is given.

1916 "Agent Orange: a New Twist." <u>Lancet</u>, v. 2, no. 8408,
      October 20, 1984, p. 919. The Justice Department is trying
      to take the government contract defense away from the
      manufacturers of Agent Orange by stating that the
      manufacturers sought to profit from government contracts and
      boasted about their ability to meet the demands for a
      herbicide that they had been previously producing for the
      commercial market.

1917 "Agent Orange Accord Nears Approval...as Vets' Compensation
      Bill Passes." <u>Science News</u>, v. 126, no. 19, November 10,
      1984, p. 296. Judge Weinstein has given conditional approval
      to the trust fund established by the out of court settlement.
      All parties will maintain a right to sue the U.S. government.
      President Reagan has signed a bill into law granting
      compensation to veterans who within one year of leaving
      Vietnam contracted chloracne or porphyria cutanea tarda. The
      bill also requires the Veterans Administration to issue
      regulations within two years detailing whether any other
      compensable health effects can be linked to Agent Orange
      exposure.

1918 "Agent Orange and the Pentagon." <u>Chemical Week</u>, v. 133, no.
      3, July 20, 1983, p. 30-31. The documents unsealed recently
      in the Agent Orange suit indicate that the military did not
      test for the health effects of using "overkill"
      concentrations of Agent Orange in Vietnam. The documents
      also revealed that a 1967 government sponsored study found
      that exposure to chemical defoliants was approaching the
      lethal level for Vietnamese citizens and that military
      planners ignored publicly available research on the dioxin-
      related health problems among workers producing 2,4,5-T.

1919 "Agent Orange Battle Flares Again." <u>Chemical Marketing</u>

Reporter, v. 226, no. 27, December 31, 1984, p. 3+. A suit
has been filed in U.S. claims court seeking $1.8 billion in
damages from the Federal government for injuries allegedly
caused by exposure to Agent Orange. The suit centers on the
theory that since the federal government placed the contracts
for the herbicide under the Defense Production Act, the
defendants were able to use the government contract defense
and the out of court settlement was substantially less than
the true value of the veterans' claims. The suit is also
based on the Tucker Act which provides for suits against the
government based on breach of contract or on constitutional
grounds.

1920 "Agent Orange Blame Is US Government's, Five Companies
Say." Chemical Marketing Reporter, v. 217, no. 2, January
14, 1980, p. 3+. Five chemical companies -- Dow Chemical
Co., Hercules Inc., Diamond Shamrock Corp., Thompson-
Hayward Chemical Corp., and Monsanto Co.-- have charged
that the government should be held liable for all reparations
and damages sought by Agent Orange Victims International.
However, they continue to deny that Agent Orange is a
dangerous substance.

1921 "Agent Orange Case: Chemical Firms Lose." Chemical
Marketing Reporter, v. 216, no. 22, November 26, 1979, p. 18.
A federal judge in New York has ruled that the manufacturers
of Agent Orange can be sued by Vietnam veterans.

1922 "Agent Orange Case Documents Unsealed." News Media and
the Law, v. 9, no. 2, Summer 1985, p. 20-21. All of the
documents that would have been used in the Agent Orange class
action suit trial except for those related to information in
government files have been ordered unsealed. The chemical
companies involved in the suit have appealed.

1923 "Agent Orange Case Proceeds." Chemical Marketing Reporter,
v. 223, no. 20, May 16, 1983, p. 5+. The motion brought by
Dow to have the suit against the manufacturers of Agent
Orange dismissed has been rejected. The trial was scheduled
to begin last month but the beginning of the trial is at
least a year away. Four companies have been dropped from the
case: Hercules Inc., Thompson Co., Riverdale Co. and Hoffman-
Taff Co.

1924 "Agent Orange Case Settled." Duns Business Month, v. 123,
no. 6, June 1984, p. 30. The out of court settlement is
mentioned. It is possible but not likely that veterans will
reject the settlement and file their own suits. Still
undecided is the federal government's liability in the issue.

1925 "Agent Orange Case Settled: $250 Million Awarded Victims."

Citizen Soldier, no. 7, June 1984, p. 1+. The reactions of several veterans to the settlement are noted.

1926 "Agent Orange Case Should Be Reopened Some Veterans Say." Chemical Marketing Reporter, v. 227, no. 3, January 21, 1985, p. 5. A group of Vietnam veterans say they plan to organize veterans to work towards setting aside the $180 million settlement.

1927 "Agent Orange Data Are Opened to Industry." Chemical Marketing Reporter, v. 223, no. 5, January 31, 1983, p. 5. The chemical manufacturers who are the defendants in the Agent Orange class action suit have been granted access to the Environmental Protection Agency's files on 2,4,5-T. The plaintiffs will also be granted access to the files.

1928 "Agent Orange Deadline Extended: Jan. 15." Veterans Rights Newsletter, special settlement issue, December 21, 1984, p. 1. Judge Weinstein has extended the deadline to file a claim against the trust fund established by the May 1984 settlement.

1929 "Agent Orange: Decision Day." Economist, v. 291, no. 7341, May 12, 1984, p. 34. The Agent Orange litigation has been settled out of court. The legislation that is being considered by the House of Representatives is also mentioned.

1930 "Agent Orange Documents Prompt Dow Denial." Chemical Marketing Reporter, v. 224, no. 2, July 11, 1983, p. 3+. Dow Chemical Company has denied the charges that they along with other manufacturers of Agent Orange withheld scientific information on the health effects of exposure to TCDD from the government and stated that these charges were "inconsistent with the facts" by citing court documents that were released last week as part of the Agent Orange litigation.

1931 "Agent Orange - Dow." CBS News Daily News Broadcasts, new ser., v. 9, no. 186, July 5, 1983, p. 10 (evening news). As part of the Agent Orange litigation the contents of a 1965 Dow Chemical Company memo have been disclosed. The memo expresses concern about possible health problems as the result of exposure to dioxin.

1932 "Agent Orange Fee Request Rejected." Chicago Daily Law Journal, v. 131, no. 27, February 7, 1985, p. 1. Lawyers who represented the veterans in the Agent Orange litigation have asked Judge Weinstein to award them higher fees. He refused.

1933 "Agent Orange Finally Gets Its Day in Court." Chemical Week,

v. 132, no. 20, May 18, 1983, p. 44-45. When the first phase
of the Agent Orange trial gets underway next month the
manufacturers of Agent Orange will argue that data on the
potential human health effects of exposure to dioxin were
equally accessible to both government and industry and at
best the available data was very scanty.

1934 "Agent Orange Fund Payment Plan Filed." Chemical and
Engineering News, v. 63, no. 9, March 4, 1985, p. 8. The
plan for who will get what from the out of court settlement
has been filed. The only people that will get anything are
those who are totally disabled ($25,000) and the families of
deceased veterans ($5,000.) Only five percent of the current
claimants would get anything under this plan. However, no
proof that Agent Orange caused the injury will need to be
submitted. The only information that will need to be
submitted will be information about the injury and proof that
the Department of Defense records indicate that the veteran
was exposed.

1935 "Agent Orange in the Courts: Update and Overview." Veterans
Rights Newsletter, v. 2, no. 1-2, May-June 1982, p. 1+. This
article provides background information about the law
limiting a serviceman's ability to sue the government for
damages arising from military service and then details the
various suits that have been brought against the federal
government and the chemical companies.

1936 "Agent Orange in the Dock." Newsweek, v. 103, no. 20, May
14, 1984, p. 79-80. The upcoming Agent Orange litigation
trial and the changes Judge Weinstein has made since he
inherited the case last October are discussed.

1937 "Agent Orange Issue Not Nearly Settled." Chemical and
Engineering News, v. 62, no. 8, September 17, 1984, p. 8.
Judge Weinstein has not yet decided on what to do about the
veterans who have opted out of the settlement.

1938 "Agent Orange Judge Denies Gov't Motion: US Defendant
Again." Chemical Marketing Reporter, v. 224, no. 26,
December 26, 1983, p. 7+. Judge Weinstein has reinstated the
federal government in the Agent Orange class action suit. He
rejected the Justice Department's argument that the federal
government is exempt because of the Feres doctrine.

1939 "Agent Orange Judge Dismisses Fund's Critics." Chemical
Marketing Reporter, v. 226, no. 5, July 30, 1984, p. 3+. A
motion brought by 1,500 Vietnam War veterans who feel that
the proposed out of court settlement is too small has been
dismissed by Judge Weinstein.

1940 "Agent Orange Lawsuit." National Vietnam Veterans Review, v.
      4, no. 7, p. 30+. The meaning of the May 1984 settlement is
      analyzed.

1941 "Agent Orange Lawsuit Dismissed by Federal Judge." Chemical
      Marketing Reporter, v. 225, no. 4, June 11, 1984, p. 3+.
      Judge Weinstein has dismissed a suit which would have forced
      the federal government to provide complete medical care to
      Vietnam war veterans and their families claiming Agent
      Orange-related injuries.

1942 "Agent Orange Lawsuits Consolidated by Federal Judge."
      American Medical News, v. 24, no. 2, January 16, 1981, p.
      192. In a federal district court in New York, Judge Pratt
      approved a motion to consolidate all of the lawsuits filed
      against the manufacturers of Agent Orange into one class
      action lawsuit. A motion brought by the manufacturers to
      have the suit dismissed on grounds that the defoliant's
      manufacture was controlled and regulated by the United States
      government was denied. Also denied was a motion brought by
      the plaintiffs that the federal government be named as a
      defendant.

1943 "Agent Orange Legal Fees: $9.26 Million." Chicago Daily
      Bulletin, v. 131, no. 4, January 7, 1985, p. 1+. The more
      than 100 lawyers representing the veterans in the litigation
      were awarded $9.26 million from the $180 million trust fund
      established by the out of court settlement. Judge Weinstein
      used a rate of between $100 and $150 per hour to determine
      how much each lawyer would receive.

1944 "Agent Orange: Legally Right, Morally Wrong." Time, v. 125,
      no. 20, May 20, 1985, p. 29. Judge Weinstein has dismissed a
      suit brought by the manufacturers of Agent Orange against the
      federal government. The manufacturers wanted the courts to
      force the government to contribute to the $180 million trust
      fund. The judge said that the government was within its
      legal right to refuse to pay but criticized the government
      for abandoning its moral responsibility.

1945 "Agent Orange Makers Form $180 Mil. Pact for Vets Said
      Harmed by Herbicides." Jet, v. 66, no. 11, May 21, 1984, p.
      5. The out of court settlement is mentioned.

1946 "Agent Orange Makers Offered Defense by Judge." Business
      Insurance, v. 16, no. 10, March 8, 1982, p. 1-2. It has been
      ruled by a New York District Court that if the Agent Orange
      manufacturers can successfully plead the government
      contractor defense they can assume the government's immunity
      from liability.

1947   "Agent Orange: More Data Help Define Dioxin Danger."
        Chemical and Engineering News, v. 61, no. 28, July 11, 1983,
        p. 4. Thousands of pages of evidence in the suit against the
        manufacturers of Agent Orange have been released. The
        results of the Air Force Ranch Hand mortality study are
        discussed.

1948   "Agent Orange: New Evidence; Vet Reaction." CBS News
        Daily News Broadcasts, new ser., v.9, no. 187, July 6, 1983,
        p. 5 (morning news). Reaction by veterans to the contents of
        a 1965 Dow Chemical Company memo that has been disclosed as
        part of the Agent Orange litigation is given. This memo
        expresses concern that exposure to dioxin might cause health
        problems.

1949   "Agent Orange Pact Gets First OK." Business Insurance, v.
        18, no. 40, October 1, 1984, p. 2. The out of court
        settlement has been tentatively approved by Judge Weinstein.

1950   "Agent Orange Pact Hits Monsanto Hardest." Chemical and
        Engineering News, v. 62, no. 21, May 21, 1984, p. 5-6. The
        payments for the settlement will be apportioned among the
        manufacturers based partly on the amount of dioxin
        contamination in the Agent Orange each manufacturer made
        and the amount of Agent Orange sold by each manufacturer.
        Monsanto will pay approximately 45 percent of the settlement,
        Dow about 20 percent, Diamond Shamrock 12 percent, Hercules
        10 percent, TH Agriculture & Nutrition six percent, Uniroyal
        five percent and Thompson two percent.

1951   "Agent Orange Papers: What Companies Knew." Chemical
        Week, v. 133, no. 2, July 13, 1983, p. 24+. In the Agent
        Orange suit, scores of internal company memos and other
        documents were unsealed last week by order of Judge Pratt.
        The documents show that the company positions regarding
        disclosure of dioxin information were set in 1965, which was
        before Agent Orange began to be widely used, and that crucial
        dioxin information was not given to the Agriculture
        Department, the U.S. Public Health Service or the Defense
        Department by industry officials until 1970.

1952   "Agent Orange Payment Plan Approved." Chemical and
        Engineering News, v. 63, no. 22, June 3, 1985, p. 16. Judge
        Weinstein has approved a modified payment plan for the fund
        set up by last year's out of court settlement. Payments will
        average $1800 for death and $5700 for total disability.
        Approximately $9.3 million has been allocated for attorney's
        fees. $45 million will be used for counseling services and
        $4 million will go to Australian and New Zealand Vietnam
        veterans.

1953 "Agent Orange Payments Are Blocked by Court." Chemical and
      Engineering News, v. 64, no. 35, September 1, 1986, p. 6.
      The out of court settlement funds will not be distributed
      this year as a group of veterans who are unhappy with the
      distribution plan have appealed the plan and a federal
      appeals court in Manhattan has ordered a stay on the
      distribution plan.

1954 "Agent Orange Payments Cut, Vets Will Get Less." Jet, v. 68,
      no. 14, June 17, 1985, p. 5. Veterans who are eligible for
      compensation under the out of court settlement will have to
      wait at least a year to receive their money and will get less
      than they expected. The largest individual payment will be
      approximately $12,000 for total disability and about $3,400
      for death benefits.

1955 "Agent Orange: Payout Plan Stayed by Court." Chemical
      Marketing Reporter, v. 230, no. 9, September 1, 1986, p. 5.
      As a result of the some veterans' opposition to the plan
      developed to distribute the funds established by the May 1984
      settlement, the funds have been blocked by a federal appeals
      court. The plan as originally developed was to make payments
      based on disability rather than on exposure because Judge
      Weinstein had ruled that the link between veterans' illnesses
      and Agent Orange was tenuous. The veterans contend that
      there is a direct link between Agent Orange and their
      illnesses.

1956 "Agent Orange Payout Planned." Facts on File, v. 45, no.
      2327, June 28, 1985, p. 482. Judge Weinstein has approved a
      plan for distributing the $180 million settlement fund to
      veterans and their families. $150 million will be allocated
      to those deceased or totally disabled veterans who were
      exposed to Agent Orange. $45 million will be set aside to
      establish a foundation to provide services to eligible
      veterans, especially to families of children with birth
      defects. $4 million will be set aside for claims made by
      Australian and New Zealand Vietnam veterans.

1957 "Agent Orange Plan Stayed." Business Insurance, v. 20, no.
      36, September 8, 1986, p. 2. Due to opposition to the
      distribution plan by some veterans a federal appeals court
      has stayed a plan to administer the funds from the 1984
      settlement. Aetna Life & Casualty Company and Aetna
      Technical Services will be paid $6.8 million through 1994 to
      administer the claims.

1958 "Agent Orange Pleas Fail in Appeals Court." Chemical
      Marketing Reporter, v. 231, no. 17, April 27, 1987, p. 7+. A
      federal appeals court has ruled that neither the

manufacturers of Agent Orange or the government can be found
liable for injuries resulting from exposure to Agent Orange.
The results of the Centers for Disease Control's study of
birth defects in the offspring of veterans and the Air
Force's Ranch Hand Study are mentioned.

1959 **"Agent Orange Products Liability Litigation."** Clearinghouse
Review, v. 14, no. 13, April 1981, p. 1256-1259. This
article addresses many of the issues involved in the Agent
Orange litigation and answers many questions veterans may
have concerning Form A-95 which is the form that must be
filed in order to sue the federal government under the
Federal Torts Claims Act.

1960 "Agent Orange Science Study and Lawsuit Stalled." (See 1370)

1961 **"Agent Orange 'Settled': Everyone Wins! Except the Victims"**
The Veteran, v. 14, no. 2, Spring 1984, p. 4. The details of
the settlement are listed and its omissions are discussed.

1962 **"Agent Orange Settlement."** CBS News Daily News Broadcasts,
new ser., v. 10, no. 128, May 7, 1984, p. 1-4 (evening news).
Reaction to the out of court settlement is given.

1963 **"Agent Orange Settlement."** Congressional Record, v. 130, no.
60, May 10, 1984, p. E2066. Representative T.A. Daschle (D-
S.D.) commended all sides on reaching a settlement in the
Agent Orange litigation. Representative Daschle reminds his
colleagues that the Agent Orange issue is still not
completely resolved and there is still legislation that needs
to be passed.

1964 **"Agent Orange Settlement."** Chemical Marketing Reporter, v.
225, no. 20, May 14, 1984, p. 3+. Although the manufacturers
of Agent Orange settled out of court, the companies continue
to maintain that there is no causal relationship between
exposure to Agent Orange and the health problems of Vietnam
veterans. Dow Chemical Company stated that despite the
"strength of Dow's scientific case, it would have been very
difficult for a jury to sort out the complex scientific
issues in this highly emotional case."

1965 **"Agent Orange Settlement."** Chemical Marketing Reporter, v.
227, no. 2, January 14, 1985, p. 4. Final approval has been
given to the out of court settlement by a federal judge in
New York.

1966 **"Agent Orange Settlement."** Congressional Record, v. 133, no.
9, January 21, 1987, p. E198. Representative D.E. Bonior (D-
Mich.) submitted an editorial by J. Zengerle and C. Hagel

from the December 29, 1986 issue of the <u>Los Angeles Times</u> which discusses the issue of the allocation of funds from the out of court settlement.

1967 **"The Agent Orange Settlement: a Bad Deal."** [editorial] <u>Citizen Soldier</u>, no. 8, April 1985, p. 1+. This editorial states the reasons why Citizen Soldier is opposed to the distribution plan.

1968 "Agent Orange Settlement - a Hollow Victory." (See 1372)

1969 **"Agent Orange Settlement Affirmed."** <u>Facts on File</u>, v. 47, no. 2423, p. 313-314. The basic distribution plan established by the May 1984 out of court settlement has been confirmed. However, the fee-sharing agreement between some of the veterans' lawyers has been invalidated, the special foundation that was to be established to distribute some of the funds has been ruled out and the appeals brought by the manufacturers against the federal government for allegedly withholding information about the dangers of Agent Orange have been rejected. Judge Winter wrote the majority opinion and called the settlement in general "an extraordinary piece of litigation" and that it was reasonable since science has not yet proved that exposure to Agent Orange caused the veterans' injuries.

1970 **"Agent Orange Settlement Is Tentatively Approved; Dow Says It Is Pleased."** <u>Chemical Marketing Reporter</u>, v. 226, no. 14, October 1, 1984. p. 3+. Judge Weinstein has tentatively approved the out of court settlement. Dow Chemical Company has stated that they are pleased with this action. Final approval is not expected until early next year. The amount the lawyers are to be paid and how the fund is to be distributed are two issues that still need to be resolved.

1971 **"Agent Orange Settlement Order."** <u>Veterans Rights Newsletter</u>, v. 4, no. 4-5, August-September 1984, p. 30-33. This article consists of excerpts from the summary, introduction and the section on the distribution plan of the Preliminary Memorandum and Order Settlement issued by Judge Weinstein on September 25, 1984.

1972 **"Agent Orange Suit Against Government Dismissed."** <u>Veterans Rights Newsletter</u>, v. 1, no. 12, April 1982, p. 90. A suit brought by some veterans against the federal government has been dismissed. The plaintiffs argued they were victims of medical malpractice by the Veterans Administration. Judge Pratt said that the courts had no jurisdiction in this case and that the Federal Tort Claims Act is the best route for veterans to go with complaints concerning the Veterans Administration.

1973 "Agent Orange Suit Ends in Settlement for $180 Million:
      20,000 Vets to Share in Fund Set Up by Chemical Companies:
      Court Approval Due." Los Angeles Daily Journal, v. 97, no.
      94, May 8, 1984, p. 1+. The details of the out of court
      settlement are discussed. Before Judge Weinstein grants
      final approval of the settlement, public hearings will be
      held. Also mentioned are the reactions of the chemical
      companies, veterans and lawyers involved in the settlement.

1974 "Agent Orange Suit Fails." Chemical Week, v. 127, no. 23,
      December 3, 1980, p. 22. A panel of the U.S. Court of
      Appeals for the Second Circuit in New York recently dismissed
      the suit brought by Vietnam veterans and their families
      against the manufacturers of Agent Orange for lack of
      jurisdiction.

1975 "Agent Orange Suit Filed." Facts on File, v. 44, no. 2302,
      December 31, 1984, p. 979. A class action suit against the
      federal government has been filed by lawyers representing a
      group of Vietnam veterans. The suit seeks $1.8 billion in
      damages for health impairments allegedly resulting from
      exposure to Agent Orange.

1976 "Agent Orange Suit: Firms Agree to Pay, Deny Liability."
      Chemical and Engineering News, v. 62, no. 20, May 14, 1984,
      p. 6-7. The manufacturers of Agent Orange settled out of
      court as they believed that the agreement was a
      "compassionate, expedient, and productive means of meeting
      the needs of the people involved." But in agreeing to the
      settlement the companies did not admit to any liability.
      Still unanswered are the issues of whether or not dioxin
      exposure caused ill effects, whether or not the manufacturers
      concealed knowledge of the risks posed by exposure to dioxin,
      and whether or not the federal government knew enough to be
      held accountable. The reaction of the various veterans
      groups ranged from approval to disappointment.

1977 "Agent Orange Suit Settled." Editorials on File, v. 15, no.
      9, May 1-15, 1984, p. 512-521. Editorials from various
      newspapers discussing the out of court settlement are given.

1978 "Agent Orange Suit: Settlement Is Approved." Chemical and
      Engineering News, v. 62, no. 40, October 1, 1984, p. 4. The
      $180 million Agent Orange settlement reached last May has
      been approved by Judge Weinstein.

1979 "Agent Orange Suit Stirs Liability Issues." Industry Week,
      v. 205, no. 2, April 28, 1980, p. 24+. The chemical
      companies that have had a lawsuit filed against them by the
      Vietnam veterans exposed to Agent Orange have filed a

counter-suit against the federal government claiming that the
government should be held responsible for any damages
awarded by the court.

1980 "Agent Orange Suits." Wall Street Journal, December 15,
      1981, p. 12(E). The Supreme Court has let a ruling stand
      made by a federal appeals court in New York that the Agent
      Orange suits should be decided under state laws.

1981 "'Agent Orange' Suits Settled for $250m." Financial Times
      (London), no. 29,315, May 8, 1984, p. 2. An out of court
      settlement has been reached in the Agent Orange litigation.

1982 "The Agent Orange Surprise." Chemical Week, v. 134, no. 20,
      May 16, 1984, p. 24. Both sides in the Agent Orange
      litigation appear to be relieved to have been to reach an out
      of court settlement. The chemical companies still have not
      admitted to any liability but many veterans' advocates
      believe that $180 million would not have been paid if there
      had not been any liability. The defendant's financial status
      will not suffer as they all have product liability insurance
      in excess of the settlement. The settlement is not yet final
      and won't be until public comment hearings are held two to
      three months from now.

1983 "Agent Orange: the Best Feasible Solution..." [editorial]
      Los Angeles Daily Journal, v. 97, no. 96, May 10, 1984, p. 4.
      The Agent Orange settlement is not a triumph of justice but
      it is the best feasible solution. Who deserves compensation
      is the central issue that still needs to be resolved.

1984 "Agent Orange: the Final Hurdle." Newsweek, v. 105, no. 3,
      January 21, 1985, p. 68. Judge Weinstein has ratified the
      out of court settlement. He has awarded $9.3 million in fees
      and expenses to the veterans' lawyers. All that is left is
      to determine how to distribute the money fairly among the
      veterans.

1985 "Agent Orange Trust Fund of $180 Million Gets Adviser." Wall
      Street Journal, July 9, 1984, p. 34(E). Judge Weinstein has
      appointed R.J. Davis to serve as an investment adviser for
      the $180 million trust fund established by the out of court
      settlement.

1986 "Agent Orange Update." Citizen Soldier. (See 1391)

1987 "Agent Orange Victims Win a 'Vindication.'" In These Times,
      v. 8, no. 24, May 16, 1984, p. 4. The out of court
      settlement allows the chemical companies to deny liability
      but establishes an $180 million trust fund to compensate

veterans and their families. But it could be two and a half
years before veterans see some money. V. Yannacone, the
lawyer who filed the first lawsuit in 1979, stated, "...the
American judicial system has seen its finest hour."

1988   "Agent Orange: Women Were Victims, Too." (See 1395)

1989   Allen, R.J. "Rationality, Mythology and the Acceptability of
       Verdicts Thesis." Boston University Law Review, v. 66, no.
       3-4, May/July 1986, p. 541-562. The author responds to C.
       Nesson's paper (See 2218) which also appeared in this issue
       of this journal. R.J. Allen critiques the way in which C.
       Nesson applied the acceptability of verdicts thesis he
       developed in a 1985 Harvard Law Review article to the Agent
       Orange litigation.

1990   Alsop, R. "New Judge in Agent Orange Suits Changes the Focus
       of the Case and Speeds Up Trial." Wall Street Journal,
       December 1, 1983, p. 31(E), p. 31(W). A new judge has been
       appointed in the Agent Orange litigation. He is Judge
       Weinstein and how he has changed the course of the suit is
       described.

1991   "American Government Knew About Dioxin in Herbicides."
       New Scientist, v. 99, no. 1371, August 13, 1983, p. 459.
       According to the Dow Chemical Company, the federal
       government was aware of the hazards of using Agent Orange.
       In 1967, the Rand Corporation reported to the Department of
       Defense that the fears about the toxicity of dioxin were
       justifiable. In 1969, the Bionetics Research Laboratories
       reported to the National Cancer Institute that exposure to
       2,4,5-T caused birth defects in animals.

1992   Anderson, D.E. "Agent Orange Vets Sue U.S. For $1.8
       Billion." Los Angeles Daily Journal, v. 97, no. 262,
       December 28, 1984, p. 3. A $1.8 billion lawsuit has been
       filed against the federal government by some of the Vietnam
       veterans who were exposed to Agent Orange. The suit is based
       on the "Tucker Act."

1993   "Appeals Court Dismisses Agent Orange Complaint." Journal of
       Commerce, v. 346, no. 24,848, November 26, 1980, p. 8. The
       Second Circuit Court of Appeals ruled recently that the
       Federal court lacks the jurisdiction to hear the suits
       brought against the manufacturers of Agent Orange by Vietnam
       veterans who believe that exposure to Agent Orange in Vietnam
       is the source of their health problems. There still exists
       the possibility of individual cases being tried in local
       federal courts.

1994 Appleson, G. "Two 'Agent Orange' Classes Unique." National Law Journal, v. 6, no. 17, January 2, 1984, p. 3+. It appears that the Vietnam veterans who are suing the manufacturers of Agent Orange are the only certified federal class in any current products liability litigation. Also two separate classes have been created in order to determine compensatory and punitive damages.

1995 "Armed Forces - Right to Sue - In Re 'Agent Orange' Product Liability Litigation." American Journal of Law & Medicine, v. 10, no. 2, Summer 1984, p. 230-232. The U.S. District Court for the Eastern District of New York has reversed a 1980 decision and has ruled that the Feres doctrine does not protect the federal government from third party liability to the wives and offspring of Vietnam veterans exposed to Agent Orange. This ruling will permit manufacturers of Agent Orange to seek indemnification from the government for damages they owe veterans' families.

1996 "Armed Services." Facts on File, v. 39, no. 2038, November 30, 1979, p. 903-904. A report released by the General Accounting Office states that U.S. ground troops were in areas sprayed with Agent Orange during or just after defoliation missions were flown. A class action suit has been filed on behalf of Massachusetts veterans by S. J. Zardis, Director of the Massachusetts Chapter of the Agent Orange Victims International. The defendants are five manufacturers of Agent Orange and the suit asks that the manufacturers be required to set up a trust fund to compensate alleged victims of herbicide exposure.

1997 Aschkenasy, J. "Agent Orange Case Settlement Not Likely to Rock Insurers." National Underwriter: Property & Casualty Insurance Edition, v. 88, no. 19, May 11, 1984, p. 1+. The insurers of the chemical companies involved in the Agent Orange litigation are well fixed to handle the indicated costs in the recent out of court settlement.

1998 Aschkenasy, J. "Agent Orange Defendants, Insurers Work on Claims Distribution Plan." National Underwriter: Property & Casualty Insurance Edition, v. 88, no. 21, May 25, 1984, p. 1. The insurers and the chemical companies contributing to the $180 million settlement awarded to those veterans suffering from exposure to Agent Orange are working together to determine which company is responsible for which portion. The problem is not a coverage problem as much as it is an accounting one.

1999 Ashman, A. "Federal Jurisdiction... Veterans' Claims." American Bar Association Journal, v. 67, February 1981, p.

215-216. The U.S. Court of Appeals for the Second Circuit
has ruled that the federal common law right on action does
not apply in the Agent Orange litigation.

2000 "At Year's End Agent Orange Scorecard Lopsided." (See 1406)

2001 **"Attorneys Move to Delay Settlement Distribution."** Veterans
Rights Newsletter, **v. 4, no. 9-10, January-February 1985, p.
72.** Citizen Soldier and B. Musslewhite have filed a motion
asking the court to delay its plans for distributing the
funds from the settlement.

2002 Austin, B. **"Et Al."** Student Lawyer, **v. 13, no. 5, January
1985, p. 50-52.** Ten thousand women served as civilians as
part of the Red Cross and the USO in Vietnam. They were also
exposed to Agent Orange while in Vietnam. However, they will
not receive any compensation from the 1984 settlement and the
Centers for Disease Control's study will also be excluding
these women.

2003 **"Balance of Veterans' Claims on Agent Orange Dismissed."**
Wall Street Journal, **May 9, 1985, p. 18(E), p. 40(W).** Two
hundred eighty-one veterans who declined to participate in
the out of court settlement have had their suits against the
manufacturers of Agent Orange dismissed by Judge Weinstein.

2004 **"The Bargaining Behind the Agent Orange Deal."** Business
Week, **no, 2843, May 21, 1984, p. 39-40.** This article
details the negotiating that went on by both sides to reach
agreement on the $180 million settlement.

2005 Barnard, R.C. "Herbicide Threat to Humans Cited." (See
1411)

2006 **"The Battle of Agent Orange."** Time, **v. 124, no. 10,
September 3, 1984, p. 47.** Hearings are being held across the
country to determine the fairness of the out of court
settlement. The Centers for Disease Control has concluded as
a result of a study they conducted that Vietnam veterans
exposed to Agent Orange are not at a greater risk of
fathering a child with birth defects than the general
population. Many veterans feel that they have been had.

2007 **"Bendectin Case Revived; Agent Orange Pact Hit."** Chemical
and Engineering News, **v. 63, no. 6, February 11, 1985, p. 6.**
Judge Weinstein has been asked to set aside the out of court
settlement by several lawyers representing Vietnam veterans
who feel the pool is inadequate for the approximately 170,000
claims made against it.

2008 Bennett, B. "The Feres Doctrine, Discipline, and the Weapons of War." Saint Louis University Law Journal, v. 29, no. 2, March 1985, p. 383-421. The author examines the history of the Feres doctrine and the rationales that have justified it and argues "...that the changing technology of warfare has given rise to unique claims" and "...that in this uniqueness is reflected the injustice of the Feres doctrine." As part of this examination the author discusses the relationship between the Agent Orange litigation and the Feres Doctrine.

2009 "Benton Musslewhite Argues in Support of Motion to Set Aside Settlement." Citizen Soldier, no. 8, April 1985, p. 4-5. B. Musslewhite's arguments before the Court of Appeals asking that final approval of the settlement be set aside are summarized.

2010 Berenstein, G.L. "An Interpretation of the Feres Doctrine After West v. United States and In Re 'Agent Orange' Product Liability Litigation" Iowa Law Review, v. 70, no. 3, March 1985, p. 737-750. Judge Weinstein has ruled that the Feres doctrine does not apply to claims made by the wives and children of Vietnam veterans exposed to Agent Orange for genetic damage, birth defects and miscarriages. The author feels that this is an appropriate and fair change in judicial interpretation of the Feres doctrine and that this interpretation will allow individuals to receive compensation for injuries that clearly deserve compensation.

2011 Bernstein, P.M. "The Agent Orange Case." New York Law Journal, v. 185, no. 37, February 25, 1981, p.1-2. Judge Pratt has granted the Agent Orange litigation class status and has ruled that federal common law applies.

2012 Birnbaum, S.L. and B. Wrubel. "Agent Orange Class Certification -- and Industrywide Liability for DES." National Law Journal, v. 6, no. 25, February 27, 1984, p. 38-41. In part, a discussion of why the Agent Orange litigation was granted class action certification when this is against the prevailing trend. The issue of applicability of the government contract defense is also discussed.

2013 Blechman, W.J. "Agent Orange and the Government Contract Defense: Are Military Manufacturers Immune from Product Liability?" University of Miami Law Review, v. 36, no. 3, May 1982, p. 489-532. Whether or not the concept of government contract defense should be applied in the Agent Orange litigation is discussed. The author believes that the government contract defense is necessary to preserve the government's discretionary authority over military procurement and should be applied in the Agent Orange issue

if the chemical companies prevail on the issue of what the
federal government knew and several other key issues.

2014 "Blood, Sweat & Tears." CBS News Daily News Broadcasts, new
      ser., v. 10, no. 129, May 8. 1984, p. 37-39 (morning news).
      S. Schlegel and V. Yannacone, two of the attorneys for the
      veterans, and several Vietnam veterans discuss their feelings
      about the settlement.

2015 Blumenthal, R. "Aetna Life Picked to Handle Claims on Agent
      Orange." Wall Street Journal, August 29, 1986, p. 38(E), p.
      34(W). A federal court has chosen Aetna Life & Casualty to
      process veterans' claims against the settlement fund once the
      freeze on the plan has been lifted. Aetna will receive six
      million dollars for processing the claims.

2016 Blumenthal, R. "Difficult Questions Remain in Agent Orange
      Controversy." Chicago Daily Law Bulletin, v. 130, no. 106,
      May 30, 1984, p. 3+. What the veterans will get for their
      $180 million, if it is enough money and what the lawyers
      might be awarded are mentioned. It is difficult for lawyers
      to recommend the settlement to their clients when they do not
      know what the veterans will be getting.

2017 Blumenthal, R. "Distribution of Agent Orange Fund Blocked."
      Chicago Daily Law Bulletin, v. 132, no. 169, August 28, 1986,
      p. 1+. The decision to go ahead and distribute the money
      from the fund set up by the May 1984 settlement according to
      the plan agreed to by Judge Weinstein has been blocked by an
      appeals court. Lawyers for some of the veterans asked for
      the stay because they feel the settlement did not establish a
      link between veterans' diseases and exposure to Agent Orange.

2018 Blumenthal, R. "Federal Judge Has Reshaped 'Agent Orange'
      Lawsuits." Los Angeles Daily Journal, v. 96, no. 234,
      November 23, 1983, p. 14. In the short time since Judge
      Weinstein has been presiding over the Agent Orange lawsuit he
      has already reshaped and accelerated the case. He has
      suggested that the trial focus comprehensively on the claims
      of six or ten representative veterans. He has reinstated two
      of the chemical manufacturers who were dropped earlier from
      the suit. He has set May 7, 1984 as a tentative date to
      start the trial and has voiced strong interest in a
      settlement. The position the manufacturers of Agent Orange
      are taking is also discussed.

2019 Blumenthal, R. "How Agent Orange Fund May Be Set Up."
      Chicago Daily Law Bulletin, v. 130, no. 92, May 9, 1984, p.
      6. Answers are given to some of the questions that have been
      raised about the out of court settlement.

2020 Blumenthal, R. "Judge Helped Shape Agent Orange Case." <u>Chicago Daily Law Bulletin</u>, v. 130, no. 95, May 14, 1984, p. 3+. How Judge Weinstein got both sides to settle is detailed.

2021 Blumenthal, R. "Of Agent Orange and Radiation: Tough Talk by Agent Orange Judge Drew Sharply Divided Parties Together." <u>Los Angeles Daily Journal</u>, v. 97, no. 99, May 15, 1984, p. 4. The role played by Judge Weinstein in getting both sides to come to an agreement is noted.

2022 Blumenthal, R. "Unanswered Questions on Agent Orange Settlement." <u>Los Angeles Daily Journal</u>, v. 97, no. 114, June 5, 1984, p. 4. Some of the questions remaining to be answered as a result of the out of court settlement are: whether or not the fund is large enough, what will the $180 million buy the veterans and what amount of the settlement will be awarded to the lawyers.

2023 Blustein, P. "Poisoned Image: Dow Chemical Fights Effects of Public Outcry Over Dioxin Pollution: but Evidence Shows It Told Industry of the Dangers Before Agent Orange Sale: Penalty for Making Napalm?" <u>Wall Street Journal</u>, June 28, 1983, p. 1+(E), p. 1+(W). Court records have revealed that in 1965, Dow Chemical Company invited other chemical manufacturers to their headquarters in Midland, Michigan to show them the methods they had discovered in reducing the dioxin contamination levels in Agent Orange. Neither Shamrock or Monsanto paid any heed to these recommendations. A study done in 1969 by the National Cancer Institute found that 2,4,5-T caused birth defects in rats and mice.

2024 Brownstein, R. "Who Compensates the Victims?" (See 1419)

2025 Bull, B. "Agent Orange: Money, but No Answers." <u>Amicus Journal</u>, v. 6, no. 2, Summer 1984, p. 10-12. The Agent Orange litigation, the out of court settlement and the fact that this settlement still does not resolve the veterans' questions of whether or not Agent Orange is the cause of their problems are mentioned. The author states that the settlement "...avoided justice and permitted a blatant wrongdoer to maintain an ugly pretence of innocence. The trite lesson of Agent Orange, of course, is lost in the scramble of claims and denials; what is bad for nature is bad for people."

2026 "...But It's Still Not Enough" [editorial] <u>Los Angeles Daily Journal</u>, v. 97, no. 96, May 10, 1984, p. 4. The Agent Orange settlement is not enough as there is still no verdict on the issue.

2027 **"Cancer Link Denied."** Chemical Week, v. 123, no. 12,
September 20, 1978, p. 22. Paul Reutershan, a Vietnam
veteran, has filed a suit against Dow Chemical Company
charging that Dow was aware of the potential dangers of
exposure to Agent Orange. Paul, who has cancer claims, that
he developed the cancer due to his exposure to Agent Orange
in Vietnam. Dow has stated they will vigorously contest the
suit.

2028 **"Champerty."** [editorial] Wall Street Journal, October 16,
1984, p. 28(E), p. 32(W). The Agent Orange litigation is an
excellent example of champerty. Champerty means lawyers
getting people to bring litigation in exchange for a share in
the take of a suit. In this instance the lawyers will
probably end up with more than any one veteran. Each veteran
will probably get about $50 a year. The editorial states
that all champerty does is to "...disturb the peace of
society, lead to corrupt legal practices and prevent remedial
process of law."

2029 **Charo, R.A.** "Class Action and Mass Toxic Torts." Columbia
Journal of Environmental Law, v. 8, no. 2, Summer 1982, p.
269-307. Whether or not class action should be used in cases
involving victims of toxic torts such as Vietnam veterans
exposed to Agent Orange is debated.

2030 **"Chemical Firms Settle Agent Orange Claims."** National
Catholic Reporter, v. 20, no. 30, May 18, 1984, p. 3. The
Agent Orange litigation has been settled out of court.
V. Yannacone, the lawyer who first filed suit in 1979,
believes "...the veterans have won the final battle of the
Vietnam War."

2031 **"Chemical Firms Sued in 13 Deaths Allegedly Tied to Agent
Orange."** Wall Street Journal, July 10, 1980, p. 29(E). The
families of 13 Vietnam veterans are suing the manufacturers
of Agent Orange, charging that exposure to the defoliant has
caused the deaths of four veterans and nine children.
Another suit has been filed on behalf 84 veterans who believe
that exposure to Agent Orange is the cause of their ill
health.

2032 **"Chemical Firms Win Agent Orange Battle."** Chemical
Marketing Reporter, v. 218, no. 22, December 1, 1980, p. 3.
A New York Federal Appeals Court has ruled that those wishing
to sue the manufacturers of Agent Orange will have to pursue
the matter in separate state courts instead of in a
consolidated federal suit.

2033 **Chiang, H.** "Litigation Notebook." Los Angeles Daily

Journal, v. 98, no. 147, July 26, 1985, p. 3. Judge
Weinstein has upheld the internal fee-splitting agreement
some of the lawyers for the plaintiffs had worked out. This
agreement allows lawyers who helped finance the litigation a
300 percent return on their investment before lawyers who
were involved in the actual litigation collect their fees.

2034 "Citizen Soldier Sues to Stop Agent Orange Settlement."
Citizen Soldier, no. 8, April 1985, p. 1+. Citizen Soldier
has asked the Court of Appeals not to give final approval to
the May 1984 settlement and to extend the deadline for filing
claims. Their motion was denied.

2035 "Class Action in Suit, Court Says Vets Can Join Agent
Orange." Los Angeles Daily Journal, v. 93, no. 264, December
31, 1980, p. 10. Veterans can join in a class action suit
for damages suffered due to exposure to Agent Orange ruled
Judge Pratt in a New York federal district court. He also
ruled that the federal government is immune from liability.

2036 "Class-action Litigation Involving Agent Orange May Be
Biggest Ever." Insurance Adjuster, v. 28, no. 328, June
1980, p. 4. An account of the progress made so far in the
class action suit is given. Four Washington state veterans
are involved in the suit which may be biggest of its kind in
this century.

2037 "Class Action Suit Filed Over Herbicides Exposure." Chemical
Week, v. 124, no. 3, January 17, 1979, p. 21. A class action
suit has been filed by lawyers for the deceased Paul
Reutershan against the manufacturers of Agent Orange and the
U.S. government. It seeks to set up a fund out of corporate
earnings to reimburse the Veterans Administration and the
Social Security Administration for medical costs due to
problems faced by those exposed to Agent Orange in Vietnam.

2038 "Class Certification Granted." Class Action Reports, v. 7,
no. 3, May-June 1981, p. 141-143. Class action certification
has been granted in the Agent Orange litigation.

2039 Cohen, N.B. "The Costs of Acceptability: Blue Buses, Agent
Orange, and Aversion to Statistical Evidence." Boston
University Law Review, v. 66, no. 3-4, May/July 1986, p. 563-
570. The author responds to C. Nesson's paper (See 2218)
which also appeared in this issue of this journal. N.B.
Cohen discusses whether or not event-verdicts should be
encouraged over evidence-verdicts and who should bear the
cost if this is encouraged.

2040 Conason, R.L. "Toxic Court Cases - Dilemma for Lawyers and

Litigants." New York Law Journal, v. 192, no. 29, August 10,
1984. p. 1+. The issues the May 1984 settlement raised such
as whether or not veterans should opt out of the settlement
are discussed. Fairness hearings on the settlement will be
held in various parts of the country.

2041 "Congress May Provide Agent Orange Compensation." (See
1440)

2042 Conrad, K. "Agent Orange Victims Await Court." Guardian, v.
34, no. 30, April 28, 1982, p. 9. More than 2500 individual
suits by Vietnam veterans against the manufacturers of Agent
Orange have been consolidated into a single suit before Judge
Pratt in a New York federal court.

2043 "Contempt of Justice" [editorial] Wall Street Journal, May
14, 1985, p. 28(E), p. 28(W). Reprinted in Los Angeles Daily
Journal, v. 98, no. 98, May 16, 1985, p. 4. The Agent Orange
litigation only benefited the lawyers who brought the suit.
Class action suits do not benefit the plaintiffs in the end.

2044 Cook, A.I. "Agent Orange Plan Approved." National Law
Journal, v. 9, no. 34, May 4, 1987, p. 38. The May 1984
settlement has been approved by a three judge panel of the
Second U.S. Circuit Court of Appeals. Some of the lawyers
for the plaintiffs have stated that they will petition for an
en blanc review of the decision and if that fails they will
petition the U.S. Supreme Court for certiorari.

2045 Corson, W.R. "The Vietnam Veterans Adviser." Penthouse, v.
15, no. 8, April 1984, p. 92. The issues that are involved
regarding how the Agent Orange litigation will be tried are
discussed. The first trial is scheduled to begin on May 7,
1984.

2046 "Court Denies Review of Agent Orange Ruling." Journal of
Commerce, v. 359, no. 25,669, February 28, 1984, p. 22B. The
manufacturers of Agent Orange have asked the Supreme Court to
block the class action suit brought against them by Vietnam
veterans and their families on the grounds that there were no
common issues to allow for a class action product liability
suit. The court has refused. This gives the green light for
the liability trial to begin in May in the Second Circuit
Court of Appeals.

2047 "Court Refuses to Bar Lawyers in Agent Orange." New York Law
Journal, v. 196, no. 41, August 27, 1986, p. 1+. The Court
of Appeals has refused to hear a motion that would disqualify
certain lawyers involved in the litigation.

2048 Critchfield, T. "Vietnam Vets Reject Agent Orange

Settlement." On Guard, v. 1, no. 1, 1986, p. 4. The author states the reasons why some veterans are opposed to the settlement. Some veterans are opposed to the distribution plan and far more veterans than anyone expected have filed claims so that amounts anyone will receive will be smaller than originally planned.

2049 "Daschle Calls Agent-O Settlement 'Major Victory.'" Air Force Times, v. 44, no. 45, May 28, 1984, p. 11. Representative T. Daschle (D-S.D.) believes that Congress should still act on pending compensation legislation as there are still many unresolved issues. He does, however, feel the recent out of court settlement is "a major victory for Vietnam veterans."

2050 David, P. "Agent Orange: Veterans' Case Comes to Court." Nature, v. 309, no. 5963, May 3, 1984. p. 5. The issues that will be dealt with when the class action suit finally comes to trial this month are discussed. The Centers for Disease Control's epidemiological study and the results of the Ranch Hand study are also noted.

2051 Davis, P.M. "The Agent Orange Litigation: a Learning Experience - Part I." Design News, v. 40, no. 23, December 3, 1984, p. 285. This article is the first part of a two part article assessing the background, causes and cures of the Agent Orange litigation. In Part I the author gives background information on the history of the use of defoliants in Vietnam and the events which led veterans to seek a class action suit against the manufacturers.

2052 Davis, P.M. "The Agent Orange Litigation: a Learning Experience - Part II." Design News, v. 40, no. 24, December 17, 1984, p. 147. This article is the second part of a two part article assessing the background, causes and cures of the Agent Orange litigation. In Part II the author focuses on the issues involved in the litigation and why the out of court settlement appears to be a reasonable alternative for all parties.

2053 DeBenedictis, D.J. "Agent Orange Trial to Begin Monday." Los Angeles Daily Journal, v. 97, no. 92, May 4, 1984, p. 2. Jury selection will begin in the Agent Orange litigation on Monday. Opening statements will begin the following week. Nine cases will go to trial. The author also discusses the effects the replacement of Judge Pratt by Judge Weinstein and V. Yannacone by D. Dean as lead counsel for the plaintiffs have had on the litigation.

2054 DeBenedictis, D.J. "Court Limits Suits Against Military

Suppliers." <u>Los Angeles Daily Journal</u>, v. 96, no. 216,
October 28, 1983, p. 3. Judge Pratt has excused himself from
the Agent Orange suit. He will be replaced by Judge
Weinstein. The chairmen of the plaintiffs committee have
also recently stepped aside.

2055 DeBenedictis, D.J. "Divided Opinions Mark Testimony at Agent
Orange Hearing: Vietnam Veterans Don't Know How to Assess
Proposed Settlement." <u>Los Angeles Daily Journal</u>, v. 97, no.
172, August 24, 1984, p. 16. The testimony of the first
fairness hearing mandated by the out of court settlement is
summarized.

2056 DeBenedictis, D.J. "Panel Undecided Over Money from Agent
Orange Suit: Will Advise Spending of $180-Million Fund for
Vietnamese Veterans: Attorney Fees at Issue." <u>Los Angeles
Daily Journal</u>, v. 97, no. 234, November 20, 1984, p. 1+. The
controversy on how best to spend the $180 million received
from the out of court settlement is noted.

2057 DeBenedictis, D.J. "Surprise Support Given Agent Orange
Pact." <u>Los Angeles Daily Journal</u>, v. 97, no. 174, August 28,
1984, p. 20. V. Yannacone, Jr., the lawyer who was in charge
of the veterans' suit against the manufacturers of Agent
Orange until last year, has given his tacit approval to the
out of court settlement. The deadline to file claims has
been extended to January 1, 1985.

2058 "Defoliant Companies Can Be Sued." <u>Nature</u>, v. 282, no. 5738,
November 29, 1979, p. 434. Judge Pratt has ruled that the
manufacturers of Agent Orange can be sued by Vietnam
veterans. The General Accounting Office has released a
report stating that the Department of Defense has severely
underestimated the number of soldiers exposed to Agent
Orange.

2059 "Defoliant Makers, Veterans Lose in Court." <u>American Medical
News</u>, v. 28, no. 21, May 24, 1985, p. 12. The 281 Vietnam
veterans who elected not to participate in the out of court
settlement have had their suits dismissed. The chemical
manufacturers will have to foot the bill for all of the $180
million as Judge Weinstein has ruled that the federal
government is not obligated to pay any of this money.

2060 "Dioxin Agreement." <u>New Scientist</u>, v. 102, no. 1409, May 10,
1984, p. 5. The Agent Orange litigation has been settled out
of court for $180 million.

2061 "Dioxin Discovery." <u>CBS News Daily News Broadcasts</u>, new
ser., v. 9, no. 187, July 6, 1983, p. 7-9 (morning news). A.
Fiorella, an attorney for the plaintiffs, is interviewed. He

discusses the contents of documents that a federal court has released as part of the Agent Orange litigation.

2062 **"Dioxin-exposed Vets Charge VA with Malpractice."** <u>Medical World News</u>, v. 22, no. 4, February 16, 1981, p. 45. A suit against the Veterans Administration and its top officials charging them with institutional malpractice has been filed by V. Yannacone, Jr. on behalf of Vietnam veterans exposed to Agent Orange.

2063 **"Dioxin Health Studies Disappear."** <u>Chemical Week</u>, v. 132, no. 26, June 29, 1983, p. 13-14. The latest development in the Agent Orange class action suit is the discovery that some of the documents concerning the results of the health effects of exposure to dioxin are apparently missing and may have been destroyed.

2064 **"Dioxin Papers Raise Questions."** <u>Chemical Week</u>, v. 132, no. 22, June 1, 1983, p. 14-15. Attorneys for the Vietnam veterans in the Agent Orange class action suit have charged that one of the defendants, Diamond Shamrock, may be destroying potential evidence.

2065 "A Dioxin Report for Everyone." (See 1042)

2066 **"Dioxin: to Tell or Not to Tell."** [editorial] <u>Chemical Week</u>, v. 133, no. 2, July 13, 1983, p. 3. Because the Dow, Monsanto and Diamond companies kept quiet in the 1960's about the potential dangers of dioxin it will be tough for chemical companies to persuade those involved in the Agent Orange and Vietnam veterans lawsuit and the general public that they can be trusted in the future. It will probably be a year or more before the class action suit will be ruled upon.

2067 **"Dioxin Trial Papers May Soon Be Made Public."** <u>Chemical Week</u>, v. 132, no. 23, June 8, 1983, p. 23-24. Documents under official seal since 1979 may be made public soon since the Agent Orange class action suit due to start this month will not begin now for another year or so. These documents could reveal that many individuals knew about the potential dangers of exposure to dioxin. Also the documents could disclose relative degrees of potential liability among the manufacturers of Agent Orange.

2068 "Disabled Vets Battle Agent Orange." (See 1474)

2069 **"Distribution Plan Released for Agent Orange Settlement Fund."** <u>Veterans Rights Newsletter</u>, v. 5, no. 1-2, May-June 1985, p. 1+. Judge Weinstein has released a report detailing how he plans to distribute the $180 million settlement fund.

2070   Dobin, E. "In Re 'Agent Orange' Product Liability
       Litigation: Limiting the Use of Federal Common Law as the
       Basis." Brooklyn Law Review, v. 48, no. 4, Summer 1982, p.
       1027-1051. The history of the Agent Orange litigation is
       given. The Second Circuit has refused to apply federal
       common law and has dismissed the suit for lack of subject
       matter jurisdiction. The positions of Judge Kearse,
       representing the majority opinion, and Judge Feinberg who
       dissented are detailed. The implications of the decision are
       described.

2071   Dodsworth, T. "Agent Orange Action." Financial Times
       (London), no. 29,317, May 10, 1984, p. 4. The chemical
       companies participating in the out of court settlement along
       with Vietnam veterans plan to press ahead with a suit against
       the federal government on whether or not the government
       should be included as a defendant.

2072   "Dow and Toxicology Meet Again." Chemical Week, v. 133, no.
       24, December 14, 1983, p. 13-14. The Dow Chemical Company
       has filed a motion requesting that any eventual division of
       liability in the case should not be based on the quantity of
       Agent Orange sold but rather on the amount of dioxin
       contained in each manufacturer's product. Dow Chemical will,
       however, have to deal with medical data collected in 1948 but
       still not public which shows that extremely low
       concentrations of the defoliant were capable of producing
       skin rashes and acne-like effects in secret human health
       tests sponsored by the company.

2073   "Dow Chemical Files Suit Against US Government." Journal of
       Commerce, v. 360, no. 25,721, May 10, 1984, p. 7A. Dow
       Chemical plans to sue the U.S. government in order to get
       them to help share in the costs of the $250 million out of
       court settlement.

2074   "Dow Defense." CBS News Daily News Broadcasts, new ser., v.
       9, no. 188, July 7, 1983, p. 11-13 (morning news). C. Carey,
       senior attorney for Dow Chemical Company, is interviewed
       concerning the contents of documents that have been recently
       disclosed as part of the Agent Orange litigation. Mr. Carey
       does not feel that the fact that the contents have not been
       made public before constitutes a cover-up nor does he feel
       that there is a connection between Agent Orange and some
       veterans' health problems.

2075   "Dow Seeks Dismissal in Agent Orange Case: What Did Gov't
       Know?" Chemical Marketing Reporter, v. 223, no. 9, May 9,
       1983, p. 3+. The U.S. government knew that 2,4,5-T contained
       dioxin several years before Dow and other chemical companies

manufactured Agent Orange for the Department of Defense, Dow Chemical Company told a federal judge. Dow also contends that the federal government knew of possible health hazards and has moved to have the suit brought against the companies by more than 20,000 Vietnam veterans and their families dismissed.

2076   "Dow's Innovation Reaches 'Highest Level for Several Decades'." ECN: European Chemical News, v. 42, no. 1132, May 21, 1984, p. 17. P.F. Dreffice, Dow President and CEO, in his report to company stockholders explained why the chemical companies sued by Vietnam veterans exposed to Agent Orange agreed to an out of court settlement.

2077   "Draft Distribution Plan for Agent Orange Fund." Veterans Rights Newsletter, v. 4, no. 9-10, January-February 1985, p. 69+. The preliminary plans for distributing the settlement funds are discussed and assistance is given to veterans who wish to file claims.

2078   Duell, R. "Cancer Spread by Army Use of Chemical Warfare in Vietnam." Workers World, v. 20, no. 31, August 4, 1978, p. 4. The truth about the Pentagon's chemical warfare program in Vietnam has been raised again as an issue because of a suit brought by Paul Reutershan, a Vietnam veteran exposed to Agent Orange who is dying of abdominal cancer.

2079   Dwyer, P. "The Agent Orange Settlement Is Still Unsettled." Business Week, no. 2964, September 15, 1986, p. 47. Veterans have still not received any compensation from the May 1984 settlement which is still tied up in appeals. Two issues which should be decided shortly are whether the settlement is fair to all plaintiffs and whether veterans who opted out of the settlement will get a hearing. There is a growing possibility that the settlement will fall apart and that there will be trials.

2080   "EPA Should Pass Rules on Hazards, Says Court." Chemical Marketing Reporter, v. 216, no. 8, August 20, 1979, p. 31. Judge Pratt has asked the chemical companies involved in the class action suit not to make any "...further dilatory procedural motions" to delay the suit. The judge also stated that the Environmental Protection Agency, not the courts, should decide on the environmental hazards of such chemicals as 2,4,5-T.

2081   Effron, E. "Vets May Receive Bulk of Settlement of Agent Orange: Special Master's Plan." Los Angeles Daily Journal, v. 97, no. 260, December 26, 1984, p. 1. The author reviews the options Special Master Feinberg is examining in order to develop a plan for distributing the settlement funds.

2082 Eisler, K.I. "Agent Orange Suit Nets $9.2 Million for Vets'
      Lawyers: Fee Award May Stifle Class Action Suits, Some
      Lawyers Warn: Rekindles Arguments." Los Angeles Daily
      Journal, v. 98, no. 6, January 8, 1985, p. 1+. The lawyers
      for the plaintiffs in the Agent Orange case have been awarded
      $9.2 million which will come out of the $180 million awarded
      in the out of court settlement. Some lawyers feel the fee is
      too low and some veterans feel the fee is too high.

2083 Elam, F. "Agent Orange Exposure Charges Backed." (See 1481)

2084 "Ending the Agent Orange Case." [editorial] Los Angeles
      Daily Journal, v. 100, no. 87, May 1, 1987, p. 4. The May
      1984 out of court settlement has now been approved by the
      appellate court. This editorial states that this is a good
      thing and that no other outcome would have been better for
      all of the veterans.

2085 Ensign, T. "Action--At Last--On Agent Orange." (See 1483)

2086 Ensign, T. "Agent Orange Victims Finally Get Settlement."
      Guardian, v. 37, no. 36, June 12, 1985, p. 4. Judge
      Weinstein has given his final approval to the out of court
      settlement. Only three percent of those who filed claims
      will be eligible for compensation. Several veterans' groups
      have appealed the settlement plan. The lawsuits of those
      veterans who decided not to participate in the out of the
      court settlement and to sue individually have been dismissed.

2087 Ensign, T. "Agent Orange Victims Protest Settlement."
      Guardian, v. 36, no. 34, May 30, 1984, p. 4. The United
      Vietnam Veterans Organization, Agent Orange Victims of New
      Jersey and the Vietnam Veterans Against War are organizing a
      campaign to overturn the out of court settlement and to
      reinstate V. Yannacone as the main lawyer for the plaintiffs.

2088 Ensign, T. "Agent Orange: Vietnam's Deadly Legacy." (See
      1486)

2089 Ensign, T. "The Deadly Truth About Dioxin." Guardian, v.
      35, no. 40, July 27, 1983, p. 1+. Dow recently announced
      that it would spend three million dollars to prove that
      dioxins are not harmful to humans. However, files have been
      made public that show that Dow knew about the effects of
      dioxin as far back as the 1930's. Judge Pratt has ruled in
      the class action suit that the defendants must show the
      government knew more than the manufacturers did about the
      toxic properties of Agent Orange. The Air Force study of
      Ranch Hand veterans in its preliminary findings reports no
      significant difference in death rates when compared with non-
      Vietnam flight crews.

2090 Ensign, T. "Fair Deal for Agent Orange Vets?" Guardian, v.
      36, no. 32, May 16, 1984, p. 1+. The out of court settlement
      is acceptable to some veterans even though the manufacturers
      of the defoliant did not acknowledge any liability. They
      feel that with this settlement they can now turn their
      attention to getting the federal government to accept
      responsibility for providing quality care to those who were
      exposed to Agent Orange.

2091 Ensign, T. "Many Are Unsettled by Agent Orange Settlement."
      Guardian, v. 36, no. 46, September 26, 1984, p. 9. Veterans
      and their families expressed their feelings concerning the
      out of court settlement at public hearings held across the
      country.

2092 Ensign, T. "Vietnam Veterans Contest Agent Orange
      Settlement." Guardian, v. 38, no. 29, April 23, 1986, p. 7.
      Some Vietnam veterans would like to see the May 1984
      settlement scraped. They argue that the settlement is
      inadequate and that veterans were not adequately notified of
      their right to opt out of the settlement. Attorneys for the
      veterans recently presented their arguments before a three
      judge federal panel. It is possible that the ban on the
      release of documents submitted by the chemical companies to
      the courts during the litigation will be lifted.

2093 "Environment." Facts on File, v. 43, no. 2228, July 29,
      1983, p. 567. As part of the Agent Orange class action
      hearings in Uniondale, New York material was recently made
      available which showed that the sprayings of Agent Orange
      continued despite health warnings. It was also revealed that
      the Dow Chemical Company knew about the possibilities of
      health problems due to exposure to dioxin before the
      government received its first supply of Agent Orange.

2094 Erspamer, G.P. and R. Gnaizda. "Dichotomy Persists: Agent
      Orange Case Isn't Over Yet." Los Angeles Daily Journal, v.
      97, no. 118, June 11, 1984, p. 4. The problems arising from
      the fact that lawyers representing veterans who wish to sue
      the Veterans Administration for damages resulting from Agent
      Orange exposure may only be paid $10 are noted.

2095 Ester, H. "Courts to Rule on Agent Orange." Far Eastern
      Economic Review, v. 108, no. 16, April 11, 1980, p. 16. The
      efforts Australian veterans are making to win compensation
      for the health problems they are having due to exposure to
      Agent Orange are noted.

2096 "Evidence on Dioxin's Effects Destroyed by Herbicide
      Manufacturers." Citizen Soldier, no. 6, December 1983, p.

3+. Judge Pratt has released documents that show that Dow
and other herbicide manufacturers considered Agent Orange to
be exceptionally toxic. A month earlier Dow had announced
that it would spend three million dollars on studies to prove
that dioxin is not hazardous to humans.

2097 "Fallout from Agent Orange Dogs a Herbicide." Business Week,
no. 2629, March 24, 1980, p. 114+. Dow's fight to keep the
Environmental Protection Agency from taking the defoliant off
the market is mentioned. The class action suit against Dow
and the other manufacturers of Agent Orange by the Vietnam
veterans is also noted.

2098 Feinberg, K.R. In Re "Agent Orange" Product Liability
Litigation: Report of the Special Master Pertaining to the
Disposition of the Settlement Fund. Washington: GPO,
February 27, 1985. 623p. In this volume, the author
provides a comprehensive explanation of how he proposes the
trust fund developed from the out of court settlement be
spent. He has proposed that only the most seriously ill or
the families of veterans who have died receive cash payments.
This will take about $130 million of the fund. Thus far,
approximately 7,000 claims have been filed for total
disabilities and approximately 3,000 claims have been filed
for death benefits. The Agent Orange Class Assistance
Foundation will be established to help those who did not
receive direct cash payments. Approximately $60 million will
be set aside for this purpose. Approximately $10 million
will be used for administrative costs.

2099 Feinberg, K.R. and J.S. Gomperts. "Attorneys' Fees in the
Agent Orange Litigation: Modifying the Lodestar Analysis for
Mass Tort Cases." New York University Review of Law & Social
Change, v. 14, no. 3, 1986, p. 613-631. The authors describe
how Judge Weinstein determined the amounts that the attorneys
who represented the veterans and their families received.

2100 "Firm Knew Dioxin's Dangers in '67." American Medical News,
v. 26, no. 34, September 16, 1983, p. 22. Recently released
documents in the Agent Orange litigation revealed that the
Dow Chemical Company knew as early as 1967 that exposure to
dioxin could injure or even kill people.

2101 Flaherty, F.J. "Agent Orange Shifts." National Law Journal,
v. 6, no. 8, October 31, 1983, p. 2+. The federal judge
presiding over the litigation and the leading plaintiff's
lawyers have stepped down. Of most concern to observers in
regards to the personnel changes and the litigation is the
prospect of disruption or going over ground already covered.

2102 Flaherty, F.J. and D. Lauter. "Fees, Other Issues Cloud Agreement." National Law Journal, v. 6, no. 37, May 21, 1984, p. 39. Just because a settlement has been reached in the Agent Orange litigation does not mean that all issues have been resolved. These issues include: the intention of both sides to pursue the federal government both in Congress and the courts; what will happen if too many veterans opt out of the settlement; the concern that the chemical companies could cancel the agreement; and how will the attorneys who represented the plaintiffs be paid.

2103 Flaherty, F.J. and D. Lauter. "Inside Agent Orange: the 11th-Hour Talks that Almost Failed." National Law Journal, v. 6, no. 37, May 21, 1984, p. 1+. The negotiations that have been underway since late last year which led to the May 7 settlement are recounted.

2104 Flaherty, F.J. and D. Lauter. "Judge's Novel Rulings Spurred Settlement." National Law Journal, v. 6, no. 37, May 21, 1984, p. 41. Some of the rulings that Judge Weinstein made led both sides to believe that it was in their best interest to reach an out of court settlement.

2105 "4 Vietnam Veterans to Help Administer Agent Orange Fund." New York Law Journal, v. 194, no. 36, August 20, 1985, p. 2. Four Vietnam veterans have been appointed by Judge Weinstein to an unpaid advisory board that will help make sure that the program for individual payments works efficiently and is responsive to the needs of veterans and their families.

2106 Fox, J.L. "Huge Settlement Avoids Dioxin Trial." Chemistry & Industry, no. 11, June 4, 1984, p. 394. Reaction to the out of court settlement is given.

2107 "The Front Line in the Legal Battle Over Dioxin." Business Week, no. 2794, June 13, 1983, p. 128E. What has happened in the four and a half years since the first class action suit was filed against the manufacturers of Agent Orange is summarized.

2108 "GAO Clears Way for VA Agent Orange Study." (See 1502)

2109 Geisel, J. "Agent Orange Maker Asks Court for Keene Ruling, Too." Business Insurance, v. 16, no. 14, April 5, 1982, p. 2+. Hercules Inc., one of the defendants in the Agent Orange class action suit, is asking a U.S. District Court to decide how Aetna Casualty & Surety Co., its primary liability insurer, should pay for the cost of its defense in the suit. Aetna so far has only paid about one-third of Hercules' defense costs.

2110   Geisel, J. "Lawsuits Linger After Agent Orange." Business
       Insurance, December 15, 1980, v. 14, no. 50, p. 1+. The
       ramifications of the Agent Orange class action suit for the
       insurance community are discussed.

2111   Gest, T. "Litigation: It's Not Over Yet." U.S. News &
       World Report, v. 96, no. 20, May 21, 1984, p. 65. The
       settlement in the Agent Orange litigation is just one step in
       an overall effort to compensate victims of exposure to toxic
       substances.

2112   Girdner, B. "Judge Bucks Products Liability Trend." Los
       Angeles Daily Journal, v. 96, no. 261, December 30, 1983, p.
       3. The suit brought by Vietnam veterans against the
       manufacturers of Agent Orange was certified this month as
       class action by U.S. District Court Judge Weinstein.

2113   Glasser, J. "The Government Contract Defense: Is Sovereign
       Immunity a Necessary Prerequisite?" Brooklyn Law Review, v.
       52, no. 2, 1986, p. 495-531. This note was presented as part
       of a symposium on Mass Torts after Agent Orange. The author
       discusses the issue of whether or not the government contract
       defense and the Feres doctrine were applicable to the Agent
       Orange litigation. The author concludes that the government
       contract defense should only be utilized when the government
       is immune for its military policy decisions.

2114   Gottlieb, M. "The Vietnam War that's Still Being Fought."
       (See 1517)

2115   "The Government Knew Plenty." [editorial] Chemical Week, v.
       133, no. 3, July 20, 1983, p. 3. This editorial expresses
       concern as to whether additional data on the dangers of
       2,4,5-T would have led to an earlier suspension of the
       spraying. The government also did not make any effort to
       assess the effects of spraying Agent Orange in concentrations
       far exceeding those normally used. A heavy weight of
       responsibility rests on the U.S. government.

2116   "Government Note: Weapons' Human Cost Must Be Figured
       In." [editorial] National Catholic Reporter, v. 20, no. 31,
       May 25, 1984, p. 12. The Agent Orange settlement may be one
       indication that the federal government can no longer develop
       and use chemical weapons with seemingly total disregard for
       the human costs involved.

2117   "Government Relieved of Agent Orange Payments." Chemical
       and Engineering News, v. 63, no. 20, May 20, 1985, p. 6.
       Judge Weinstein has ruled that the federal government does
       not have to share with the manufacturers of Agent Orange the

costs of the fund established by last year's out of court settlement.

2118 Greene, R. "Stop the Presses." Forbes, v. 133, no. 13, June 4, 1984, p. 150. The Agent Orange case is an example of how class action suits can drag on for years and actually in the final analysis be good for corporate defendants.

2119 Griffin, M.K. "Poisoned Patriotism." Student Lawyer, v. 10, no. 7, March 1982, p. 22-25+. V. Yannacone is the lawyer who is coordinating the effort to sue the manufacturers of Agent Orange for damages Vietnam veterans have suffered as a result of being exposed to the defoliant. He is known as the father of environmental law.

2120 Gunby, P. "Agent Orange: What's to Be Done by Whom?" (See 1521)

2121 Gunby, P. "More Questions Not Answers Emerge from Agent Orange Studies." (See 1082)

2122 Hanes, J.H. "Agent Orange: Liability of Federal Contractors." University of Toledo Law Journal, v. 13, no. 4, Summer 1982, p. 1271-1280. The Associate General Counsel for the Dow Chemical Company outlines some of the legal issues which have arisen during the course of the Agent Orange litigation.

2123 Hay, A. "Dioxin: the 10-year Battle that Began with Agent Orange." Nature, v. 278, no. 5700, March 8, 1979, p. 108-109. In part, a discussion of the lawsuit filed by Paul Reutershan who is dying of cancer due to exposure to Agent Orange in Vietnam and the requests for disability compensation as a result of exposure to Agent Orange that have been filed by 500 Vietnam veterans.

2124 "Hearings Begin on Agent Orange Pact." Chemical and Engineering News, v. 62, no. 33, August 13, 1984, p. 6. Hearings on the fairness of the proposed out of court settlement will be held in Brooklyn, Chicago, Houston, Atlanta and San Francisco. The first hearing was held in Brooklyn last week. Veterans were divided in their opinion on the adequacy of the settlement.

2125 "Hearings Open on Settlement Proposed in Agent Orange Suit: Vietnam Veterans Pack Brooklyn Courtroom." New York Law Journal, v. 192, no. 28, August 9, 1984, p. 1. The first of five hearings to be held on the fairness of the out of court settlement is being held in Brooklyn. Veterans are divided in their opinion as to whether the amount of the settlement is fair.

2126 "Hercules Is Reinstated in Agent Orange Case." Chemical
      Marketing Reporter, v. 224, no. 23, December 5, 1983, p. 3.
      Judge Weinstein, the new presiding judge for the Agent Orange
      class action suit, has denied a motion for dismissal by
      Hercules, Inc. Hercules, Inc. and three other chemical
      companies had earlier been dismissed by Judge Pratt.
      Thompson Co., Riverdale Co. and Hoffman-Taff Co. are all also
      back in the case.

2127 "High Court Declines 'Orange' Suit." Air Force Times, v. 42,
      no. 24, January 4, 1982, p. 15. The Supreme Court has
      declined to hear a suit which would have allowed Vietnam
      veterans exposed to Agent Orange to sue the manufacturers of
      the defoliant under federal precedents and policies.
      Veterans must now sue under rules laid down by state
      legislators.

2128 Hirst, D. "Agent Orange Settlement Tentatively Approved."
      Air Force Times, v. 45, no. 12, October 8, 1984, p. 14.
      Judge Weinstein has tentatively approved the out of court
      settlement. Hearings are now being held to determine what
      portion of the settlement should go to the lawyers. A
      hearing on a proposed plan for distribution of the settlement
      will be held in February 1985.

2129 Hirst, D. "Initial Settlement Reached in Agent-Orange Law
      Suit." Air Force Times, v. 44, no. 44, May 21, 1984, p. 4.
      The 14-point, $180 million, out of court settlement reached
      on May 7 is discussed.

2130 Hislop-Brumfield, L. "Judicial Recovery for the Post-service
      Tort: a Veteran's Last Battle." Pacific Law Journal, v. 14,
      no. 2, January 1983, p. 333-355. The problems veterans have
      had in dealing with the doctrine of military immunity when
      trying to seek redress for damages resulting in exposure to
      Agent Orange, radiation, etc. are discussed. Courts must
      come to accept the post-service tort.

2131 How-Downing, L. "Agent Orange Litigation: Should Federal
      Common Law Have Been Applied?" Ecology Law Quarterly, v.
      10, no. 4, 1983, p. 611-639. The implications of the Second
      Circuit's refusal to apply federal common law in the Agent
      Orange litigation are discussed.

2132 "Implications on Agent Orange Claim Form." Veterans Rights
      Newsletter, v. 4, no. 2-3, June-July 1984, p. 19-23.
      Explanation is given on how to fill out the claim forms to
      request funds from the fund established by the out of court
      settlement.

2133 "In Camera." Class Action Reports, v. 6, no. 5, September-

October 1980, p. 273+. The options Judge Pratt had in
determining what the most just, speedy and inexpensive
resolution of the litigation would be are noted. Judge Pratt
decided to grant class certification.

2134 "In Secret 1965 Meeting: Dioxin Makers Admitted 'Problem.'"
Citizen Soldier, no. 5, May 1983, p. 3. Documents released
as part of the lawsuit against the manufacturers of Agent
Orange have revealed that a secret meeting was held in 1965
between Dow Chemical and four other manufacturers of Agent
Orange at which concern was expressed about the toxic
impurities in samples of 2,4,5-T.

2135 "Instructions on Agent Orange Claim Form." Veterans Rights
Newsletter, v. 4, no. 2-3, June-July 1984, p. 19-23.
Explanations are provided on how to fill out the claim forms
to request funds from the fund established by the out of
court settlement.

2136 Irvine, R. "The Zumwalts and Agent Orange." (See 1105)

2137 Jacobs, J.B. and D. McNamara. "Vietnam Veterans and the
Agent Orange Controversy." (See 1566)

2138 Jaffe, S. "Business Decision." New Statesman, v. 107, no.
2275, May 25, 1984, p. 20. Some of the decisions still to be
made as a result of the out of court settlement are
mentioned. The settlement was not all some of the veterans
were expecting. The companies did not have to admit to any
liability. But as V. Yannacone, the lawyer who first filed
suit in 1979, stated, "...the veterans have won the final
battle of the Vietnam War."

2139 Johnston, S.J. and G. Evans. "Veterans Rap Agent Orange
Settlement." Militant, v. 48, no. 34, September 21, 1984, p.
16. Veterans testified in Atlanta recently on the "fairness"
of the out of court settlement. The results of the Centers
for Disease Control's study on the risk of Vietnam veterans
fathering children with birth defects are also noted.

2140 Joyce, C. "Lawyers Reveal Conspiracy of Silence on Dioxin."
New Scientist, v. 99, no. 1369, August 4, 1983, p. 327-328.
Documents recently released as part of the Agent Orange
lawsuit reveal that the manufacturers of the defoliant knew
in the early 1960's that dioxin was extremely toxic.

2141 "Judge Dismisses Agent Orange Claims of Vietnam Veterans
Against the US." Chemical Marketing Reporter, v. 227, no. 7,
February 18, 1985, p. 24. Judge Weinstein has dismissed all
of the suits against the federal government brought by

Vietnam veterans claiming injury from exposure to Agent Orange and claims by veterans' wives but left open the possibility that the children of veterans could sue the federal government. The judge also denied requests for higher attorney fees brought by over 100 of the plaintiff attorneys. The Air Force has also released the second report on its ongoing mortality study of the Operation Ranch Hand crew members. This report stated that, when compared with the American white population, crew members were found to be living significantly longer than expected.

2142   "Judge Dismisses Agent Orange Suits." Chemical and Engineering News, v. 63, no. 19, May 13, 1985, p. 7. The suits brought by 281 Vietnam veterans which were separate from the class action suit have been dismissed by Judge Weinstein.

2143   "Judge Finalizes Agent Orange Settlement at $180 Million: Limits Attorneys Fees." Veterans Rights Newsletter, v. 4, no. 9-10, January-February 1985, p. 70-71. Judge Weinstein has given his final approval to the May 1984 settlement. The fees the plaintiffs' lawyers were awarded by Judge Weinstein is noted.

2144   "A Judge Objects to Some Classy Action." Wall Street Journal, October 16, 1984, p. 28(E), p. 32(W). Excerpts from the September 26 and October 1 hearings before Judge Weinstein on the subject of the plaintiff's attorneys' fees are included. The judge was not impressed by the attorneys' requests. He feels the work done by the lawyers was not all that outstanding and if the case had gone forward they would have received nothing as they would have lost the case.

2145   "Judge Okays Agent Orange Settlement for $180 Million." Veterans Rights Newsletter, v. 4, no. 4-5, August-September 1984, p. 25+. Judge Weinstein has given his final approval to the out of court settlement. Some of the dissatisfaction veterans feel with the settlement is expressed.

2146   "Judge Orders Agent Orange Documents Released to Public." Veterans Rights Newsletter, v. 4, no. 6-8, October-December 1984, p. 42. In December 1984 an U.S. magistrate ruled that some of the documents submitted by the various parties in the litigation should have their protective orders lifted.

2147   "Judge Promises No Huge Fees for Agent Orange Lawyers." New York Law Journal, v. 192, no. 62, September 27, 1984, p. 1+. Judge Weinstein stated in the first of two hearings on the fee requests that he will not drain the out of court settlement in order to award large fees to the lawyers who

represented the veterans and their families. He also stated
that he had severe doubts as to whether the case should have
been brought at all.

2148 "Judge Refuses to Ban Sale, Use of 2,4,5-T." Journal of
      Commerce, v. 341, no. 24,527, August 17, 1979, p. 5. As part
      of their suit against the manufacturers of Agent Orange,
      Vietnam veterans had asked that the sale and use of 2,4,5-T
      be banned. A federal court judge ruled that he would not ban
      the sale of the chemical and said the veterans should take
      their case to the Environmental Protection Agency. The judge
      also dismissed all claims in this litigation alleging
      violations of the veterans' constitutional rights. He did,
      however, rule that the veterans could still pursue their suit
      by invoking federal common law. V. Yannacone cannot be
      barred from talking to the press as the chemical
      manufacturers would have liked.

2149 "Judge Rejects Challenge on Agent Orange Fund, Citing
      Litigation Costs." Wall Street Journal, July 26, 1984, p.
      19(E), p. 41(W). A motion that challenged the adequacy of
      the fund established by the May 7 out of court settlement and
      sought more information on how the settlement was reached has
      been dismissed by a federal judge.

2150 "Judge Upholds Agent Orange Pact." Facts on File, v. 44, no.
      2298, November 30, 1984, p. 888-889. The May 1984 settlement
      has been tentatively approved by Judge Weinstein. He
      believes that veterans should not receive "significant"
      compensation awards out of the settlement funds. Rather he
      would prefer to have the funds go towards purchasing
      insurance and creating a national center for Vietnam veterans
      which would represent their legal and political interests.

2151 "Judge Weinstein and the Agent Orange Case." Delaware
      Lawyer, v. 4, no. 2, Fall 1985, p. 56-58. The remarks made
      by G.B. Hering at a Delaware State Bar Association luncheon
      in Wilmington on November 26, 1984 are transcribed. Mr.
      Hering gives a history of the litigation and then details how
      Judge Weinstein was able to bring about an out of court
      settlement.

2152 "Judicial Review: Absolutely (but Maybe Not)."
      Congressional Record, v.132, no. 125, September 22, 1986, p.
      E3217-E3218. Representative G.V. Montgomery (D-Miss.)
      discusses a recent New York Times editorial on the Agent
      Orange litigation. Representative Montgomery believes that
      the courts are not any better equipped to resolve veterans'
      claims than the Veterans Administration.

2153 Julien, A.S. "New Products Developments in Agent Orange,
      DES." New York Law Journal, v. 184, no. 85, October 30,
      1980, p. 1+. Whether or not the class action suit brought by
      the veterans exposed to Agent Orange against the
      manufacturers of the defoliant can be heard in federal courts
      will be decided on the basis of federal common law.

2154 "Jungle Suits." [editorial] Wall Street Journal, January 5,
      1981, p. 10(E). The 167 suits against the manufacturers of
      Agent Orange have been consolidated into one class. This
      editorial states that the veterans are pressing litigiousness
      to an absurd and unsettling extreme and the courtroom is no
      place to decide if Agent Orange is the cause for veterans'
      distress and what compensation they are entitled to should be
      decided by the Veterans Administration or the Congress.

2155 "Justice's Brief on Agent Orange." Chemical Week, v. 135,
      no. 12, September 19, 1984, p. 26+. The Federal District
      Court in Brooklyn will soon hear the cases of the veterans
      who chose not to participate in the out of court settlement.
      The Justice Department has filed a brief attacking the
      chemical manufacturers' argument that they are not liable
      because they were making Agent Orange under government
      defense contracts. The Justice Department argues that the
      companies were motivated by profit not patriotism, that there
      was no government specification for dioxin contamination in
      Agent Orange and that the chemical companies did not share
      their knowledge of possible toxicological problems with the
      government.

2156 "Justices Deny Agent Orange Trial Delay." New York Law
      Journal, v. 191, no. 39, February 28, 1984, p. 1+. Diamond
      Shamrock asked the Supreme Court to review the decision that
      one trial for all veterans exposed to Agent Orange could be
      certified by a federal court and the decision to conduct a
      national campaign to find those veterans who were exposed to
      Agent Orange. The Court has let both decisions stand.

2157 Kaberon, S. "Agent Orange Settlement Called 'Fair' Start."
      Chicago Daily Law Bulletin, v. 130, no. 158, August 13, 1984,
      p. 1+. The testimony given at the fairness hearing in
      Chicago on the out of court settlement is summarized.
      Chicago lawyer S. Schlegel called the settlement "...the best
      result achievable under all of the circumstances."

2158 Kaberon, S. "Splitting Agent Orange Proceeds 'Most
      Difficult.'" Chicago Daily Law Bulletin, v. 130, no. 227,
      November 19, 1984, p. 1+. It is going to be very difficult
      to decide how to distribute the $180 million settlement among
      the more than 35,000 veterans who have made claims. K.

Feinberg, special master in the case, discussed some of the
possible ways the money might be distributed at a program at
the Northwestern University School of Law recently.

2159 Kalish, J. "Agent Orange Lawsuit Scheduled for Trial."
      National Catholic Reporter, v. 20, no. 10, December 23, 1983,
      p. 18. May 7, 1984 has been set as the date the class action
      suit will begin after five years of pre-trial motions. To be
      tried first will be the 11 so-called representative
      plaintiffs.

2160 Kalish, J. "I Want Live Vets, Says the U.S. District Judge
      Who Will Preside Over the Agent Orange Trial." In These
      Times, v. 8, no. 19, April 11, 1984, p. 8-9. The five years
      of motions, oral arguments, and appeals will come to an end
      next month when the Agent Orange trial finally begins. The
      issues that will be settled are discussed. A handful of live
      veterans will be selected to be representative plaintiffs.
      They will be used to decide the issue of causality.

2161 Kalish, J. "Vets Denounce Settlement." In These Times, v.
      8, no. 33, September 5, 1984, p. 5. The sentiments of
      veterans and their families testifying at the fairness
      hearings on the out of court settlement are summarized.

2162 Kohn, A. "Agent Orange Suit Defendants Lose Appeal for
      Writ." New York Law Journal, v. 191, no. 8, January 12,
      1984, p. 1. The defendants in the Agent Orange litigation
      were denied a writ of mandamus by the Second Circuit Court of
      Appeals. The defendants had questioned the certification of
      two of the classes and the types of notice sent out to the
      members of the class.

2163 Kohn, A. "Appeal of Class Certification Planned in Agent
      Orange Case: Judge Orders Notice Requirement for
      Plaintiffs." New York Law Journal, v. 190, no. 116, December
      19, 1983, p. 1. Judge Weinstein has specified who will be
      part of the class in the Agent Orange litigation and what
      types of notice will be required for notification of the
      members of the class. Defense lawyers have been granted a
      stay of the ruling for seven days to prepare a mandamus
      proceeding against the judge. Judge Weinstein has also
      indicated he may reformulate the government contract defense.

2164 Kohn, A. "Court Upholds Stay in Setting Agent Orange Plan in
      Motion." New York Law Journal, v. 196, no. 83, October 28,
      1986, p. 1+. The stay on the implementation of the plan to
      distribute the money from the fund established by the May
      1984 settlement will not be lifted. Appeals to the plan
      distribution have been filed on numerous issues.

2165 Lalle, F.A. "Agent Orange As a Problem of Law and Policy."
      Northwestern University Law Review, v. 77, no. 1, March 1982,
      p. 48-83. The history of the Agent Orange controversy is
      detailed. Also discussed is how the Feres doctrine prevents
      veterans from suing the federal government and the decision
      by the Second Circuit that federal common law should be
      applied in the class action suit against the manufacturers of
      Agent Orange. The author also includes an alternative
      legislative proposal.

2166 Lamar, J.V., Jr., T. Loughran, and P. Stoler. "Winning Peace
      With Honor." Time, v. 123, no. 21, May 14, 1984, p. 39 40.
      The long history of the Agent Orange litigation, the
      reactions of both sides to the settlement and the fight that
      will continue to get the federal government to accept some
      responsibility for the problems attributed to Agent Orange
      are detailed.

2167 Lauter, D. "A 'Last Hurrah' for Agent Orange?" National Law
      Journal, v. 7, no. 18, January 14, 1985, p. 3+. The class
      action suit filed in U.S. Claims Court by B. Musslewhite is
      discussed. Also mentioned is the progress that is being made
      towards resolving the out of court settlement reached in a
      New York federal court last May.

2168 Lauter, D. "Soldiers' Families Backed on Claims." National
      Law Journal, v. 4, no. 8, November 2, 1981, p. 5. Judge
      Shapiro ruled in Philadelphia recently that in some cases the
      Feres doctrine should not apply which might help those
      suffering from problems due to Agent Orange exposure have an
      easier time suing the federal government.

2169 "Lawyer Blasts Agent Orange Settlement." Chicago Daily Law
      Journal, v. 131 no. 21, January 30, 1985, p. 1. B.
      Musslewhite, a Houston attorney who helped veterans negotiate
      the out of court settlement, has resigned from a nine member
      panel of attorneys who represented the veterans in the
      litigation. He now feels that the out of court settlement is
      a "...mockery of justice." He has asked Judge Weinstein to
      rescind the settlement.

2170 Lazarus, G. "A Legacy of Vietnam Draws States' Attention."
      (See 1576)

2171 "Lead Council and Judge in Agent Orange Suit Change."
      Veterans Rights Newsletter, v. 3, no. 5-6, September-October
      1983, p. 34. Judge Pratt has withdrawn as judge in the Agent
      Orange litigation due to increased pressure of his work on
      the Second Circuit Court of Appeals. Judge Weinstein will
      take over. Before he resigned Judge Pratt relieved Yannacone

& Associates of their responsibilities as lead council for
the veterans because they were unable to absorb the enormous
expenses involved.

2172 Leepson, M. "Agent Orange: the Continuing Debate." (See
1577)

2173 "Legal Notice to Class Members of Pendency of Class Action."
Veterans Rights Newsletter, v. 3, no. 9-10, January-February
1984, p. 72-75. The text of the legal notice of the pendency
of class action involving veterans who may have been exposed
to Agent Orange explains to the veteran how to request
exclusion from the class if he so desires is given. Forms
are included.

2174 Levin, B.L. "Agent Orange: a Tale of Greed Overcoming
Need." Los Angeles Daily Journal, v. 98, no. 75, April 15,
1985, p. 4. The author feels that the veterans' lawyers have
been too greedy and that the plan for distributing the
settlement funds is not fair.

2175 Levy, S.J. "Agent Orange and Nuremberg Defense." New York
Law Journal, v. 187, no. 56, March 24, 1982, p. 1. Judge
Pratt has ruled that the Agent Orange litigation will be
tried in phases and the first trial will deal with the
government contract defense. Based on the Feres doctrine
Judge Pratt dismissed the chemical manufacturers' third-party
claims against the U.S. government. These decisions seem to
reflect a desire to resolve a troublesome litigation in one
quick, all embracing decision.

2176 "Liability on Agent Orange." Business Week, no. 2733, April
5, 1982, p. 60. In an interim decision in a federal court in
New York it was ruled that the manufacturers of Agent Orange
could escape liability to U.S. servicemen under the
government contract defense if it could be proven that it was
the government that established the specifications and that
the government knew as much about the dangers of Agent
Orange as the manufacturers of the defoliant.

2177 "Limit on Agent Orange Settlements Urged." Chicago Daily
Law Bulletin, v. 131, no. 40, February 27, 1985, p. 1+. K.
Feinberg, the special master appointed to determine how the
out of court settlement should be distributed, has submitted
his proposal. He feels that the number of people eligible to
receive funds should be severely limited. He feels that only
veterans with long-term disabilities and the families of
veterans who died should receive benefits. The veterans will
have to prove that they were in areas that had been sprayed
and how much spraying had been done but not that their
illnesses are a result of exposure to Agent Orange so long as

they were not caused by a "traumatic event" such as a car accident.

2178   Lindgren, J.S. "Judges and Statutes: Essays on Agent Orange." Law & Policy Quarterly, v. 6, no. 2, April 1984, p. 189-202. The author discusses why judges have ignored the Federal Insecticide, Fungicide & Rodenticide Act in ruling on suits brought by Vietnam veterans exposed to Agent Orange.

2179   Lowther, W. "A Bittersweet Victory." Macleans, v. 97, no. 21, May 21, 1984, p. 52. The five year legal battle between the Vietnam veterans exposed to Agent Orange and the manufacturers of the defoliant has ended with a bittersweet victory for the veterans. The manufacturers have agreed to establish an $180 million fund but did not admit any liability. The settlement also allows the companies to sue the federal government on the grounds that they followed Pentagon specifications in manufacturing Agent Orange.

2180   Lyons, L.J. "Aetna L & C Chosen to Handle Claims on Agent Orange." National Underwriter: Property & Casualty Insurance Edition, v. 90, no. 36, September 5, 1986, p. 4+. Aetna Life and Casualty has been chosen to administer the distribution of the monies from the trust fund once dispensation begins. However, the U.S. Court of Appeals has blocked distribution because some veterans are upset over the way the funds are to be distributed. These veterans feel the largest claims should go to those who are now suffering from cancer or other illnesses which they feel are the result of exposure to Agent Orange. Aetna is also now in litigation with Diamond Shamrock over payment of its share of the settlement costs. Aetna has estimated that it will cost them seven million over a ten year period to service 250,000 claims.

2181   McAbee, M.W. "Civil Procedure - Federal Courts - Claims of Military Veterans Against Manufacturers of Agent Orange Not Governed by Common Law. In Re Agent Orange Product Liability Litigation, 635 F. 2d 987 (2d Cir. 1980)." Cumberland Law Review, v. 12, no. 1, Winter 1982, p. 183-195. The implications of the Second Circuit's refusal to apply federal common law in the Agent Orange litigation are discussed.

2182   McGinley, L. "Explosive Growth of Lawsuits Against the U.S. Creates Concern Over Potential Budget Impact." Wall Street Journal, January 14, 1985, p. 38(E). The number of cases against the federal government is growing by leaps and bounds. But it is much harder to win against the federal government than it is a company as seen in the Agent Orange litigation.

2183 **McIntyre, K.J. "Agent Orange: Opposing Attorneys Define
Different Battle Lines for Trial." Business Insurance, v.
15, no. 2, January 12, 1981, p. 3+.** The chemical companies
against which the Vietnam veterans exposed to Agent Orange
have brought a class action suit will base their defense on
the fact that they believe their product met government
specifications.

2184 **Mahoney, R.J. "The Agent Orange Case." [editorial]
Chemtech, v. 14, no. 8, August 1984, p. 455.** This editorial
describes Monsanto's position on the Agent Orange issue and
why they agreed to settle out of court. They settled because
they didn't feel that it was possible for the veterans and
the public to get beyond the emotional aspects of this case
to the facts and because it was the right thing to do.

2185 **"Managing a Flood of Claims." [editorial] New Jersey Law
Journal, v. 113, no. 24, June 14, 1984, p. 4.** Congress ought
to devise a plan to help courts cope with cases such as Agent
Orange and asbestos which have generated a flood of claims.

2186 **Massachusetts. General Court. Science Resource Office. Who
Is Involved in the Court Cases Concerning Agent Orange, and
What Issues Are at Stake? Boston: The Office, April 1981.
3p.** The class action suit filed against the manufacturers of
Agent Orange on behalf of over 100 Vietnam veterans and their
families is commented upon.

2187 **Matlock, M.A. "Chemical Firms Charge U.S. Liable for
Veterans' Suit." Business Insurance, v. 14, no. 3, January
21, 1980, p. 10.** The five chemical companies involved in the
Agent Orange class action suit charge that the federal
government should be held liable for injuries or disabilities
resulting from exposure to the defoliant. These charges were
filed as third party complaints to the class action suit
filed in Federal District Court in New York.

2188 **Meier, B. "Agent Orange Settlement Is Approved: Cash Awards
Are Likely to Be Limited." Wall Street Journal, January 8,
1985, p. 6(E), p. 6(W).** The out of court settlement has been
formally approved. The lawyers will get $9.3 million.
Veterans will probably be compensated for continuing medical
expenses. The court expects about 17,000 claims against the
fund. Direct cash payments will be made to the estates of
about 4,000 veterans who died from dioxin-related diseases.

2189 Meier, B. "Agent Orange Study Fails to Quiet Debate on
Birth-defect Issue." (See 1146)

2190 **Meier, B. "Agent Orange Trial Set to Start Monday: Dioxin's**

Role in Human Illness at Issue." <u>Wall Street Journal</u>, May 4, 1984, p. 7(E), p. 6(W). The Agent Orange trial is due to start next week and will center on nine test cases which represent the types of medical problems caused by the defoliant. During the trial the jurors will also need to decide whether the manufacturers of the defoliant failed to notify the government concerning the data they had gathered on the dioxin-related effects.

2191   Meier, B. "Clerk Is Inundated by Attorney Filings in Agent Orange Suit." <u>Wall Street Journal</u>, September 5, 1984, p. 24(E), p. 20(W). The deadline has passed for the plaintiff's attorneys to file for fees from the out of court settlement. Judge Weinstein's office has been overwhelmed with claims. It is estimated that the legal fees sought could be $20 million or more.

2192   Meier, B. "Fewer Veterans May Be Eligible in Dioxin Award: Agent Orange Case Lawyers See Smaller Number Able to Support Health Claims." <u>Wall Street Journal</u>, May 25, 1984, p. 4(E), p. 4(W). Lawyers estimate that between 5,000 and 15,000 veterans will make claims against the fund but that they may only be able to establish a link between dioxin exposure in about 1,000 veterans and a link between dioxin exposure and birth defects in veterans' children in fewer than 1,500 cases. It is expected that between $27 million and $45 million of the settlement will go for attorneys' fees.

2193   Meier, B. "Hearing Set for Today on Agent Orange Settlement As Veterans' Claims Pour In." <u>Wall Street Journal</u>, August 8, 1984, p. 58(W). The fairness hearings are to begin this month. How scientists will determine who will be compensated is discussed. It is estimated that the Court in New York will received 35,000 to 50,000 letters regarding the out of court settlement.

2194   Meier, B. "Judge Clears Agent Orange Payout Plan; Individual Awards to Be Held to $12,800." <u>Wall Street Journal</u>, May 29, 1985, p. 64(E), p. 58(W). A $12,800 cash limit will be placed on individual cash payments from the fund established by the out of court settlement. Families of deceased veterans will receive individual payments of $3,400. $45 million has been set aside to provide services to veterans. $4 million was set aside to settle the claims of Vietnam veterans from Australia and New Zealand.

2195   Meier, B. "Judge Stops Plan to Pay Victims of Agent Orange." <u>Wall Street Journal</u>, August 28, 1986, p. 4(E), p. 40(W). The distribution plan for the settlement has been frozen as some of veterans' lawyers are trying to overturn the plan.

2196 Meier, B. "Major Questions on Dioxin and Illness Remain in Wake of Agent Orange Pact." Wall Street Journal, May 10, 1984, p. 20(E), p. 6(W). The out of court settlement did not resolve any of the questions about the health effects of exposure to dioxin.

2197 Meier, B. "Nine Attorneys Seek $23.5 Million Fees in Case Over Dioxin." Wall Street Journal, September 27, 1984, p. 10(E), p. 10(W). The nine lawyers who negotiated the out of court settlement for the veterans are asking for $23.5 million in attorney's fees. More than 100 lawyers have asked for reimbursement for their work on the Agent Orange litigation.

2198 Meier, B. "Plan Would Limit Agent Orange Payouts and Require No Proof Dioxin Caused Ills." Wall Street Journal, February 28, 1985, p. 14(E), p. 14(W). Under the plan proposed by a court appointed lawyer veterans would not have to prove a link between exposure to dioxin and their illness in order to receive compensation from the trust fund established by the out of court settlement. Two funds would be set up to provide services to parents with children with birth defects and to make grants to the veterans' community. Approximately 200,000 claims have been filed.

2199 Meier, B. "U.S. Likely Knew of Dangers of Dioxin During Its Use in Vietnam, Judge Says." Wall Street Journal, September 26, 1984, p. 10(E), p. 10(W). Judge Weinstein has given final approval to the out of court settlement. However, he believes that the federal government was probably aware of the dangers of exposure to dioxin and criticized the federal government for not doing more to help veterans. He also stated that the chemical companies would have probably won due to this fact and also due to the fact that the medical problems cannot be definitely linked to Agent Orange.

2200. Meier, B. "Veterans at Agent Orange Hearing Split Over Size and Distribution of Settlement." Wall Street Journal, August 9, 1984, p. 8(E), p. 10(W). The first of the hearings on the fairness of the out of court settlement was held in Brooklyn. Veterans testifying expressed their opinions mainly on the size of the settlement and how the money is to be dispensed. October 26 is the deadline for filing claims. Approximately 12,000 claims have been submitted so far. Judge Weinstein will rule on the settlement later this year.

2201 Meier, B. and R. Winslow. "Agent Orange Pact Sparks Differences in Veterans Groups." Wall Street Journal, May 9, 1984, p. 2(E), p. 2(W). The Vietnam Veterans of America has stated that it will recommend to its members that they remain

part of the settlement. The United Vietnam Veterans
organization has stated that it will challenge the adequacy
of the settlement during the court hearings planned by Judge
Weinstein to determine whether the agreement is fair. Dow
Chemical Company and the other manufacturers involved in the
settlement plan to continue the suit they have filed against
the federal government which claims that the federal
government bears the liability for any health problems caused
by Agent Orange.

2202   Meier, B. and R. Winslow. "Seven Firms in Agent Orange Case
       Agree to $180 Million Settlement." Wall Street Journal, May
       8, 1984, p. 3+(E), p. 3+(W). The details of the out of court
       settlement and how it was reached are revealed.

2203   Milford, L.M. "Justice Is Not a GI Benefit." Progressive,
       v. 45, no. 8, August 1981, p. 32-35. How the federal
       government is using the Feres doctrine to avoid being sued
       over the Agent Orange issue is discussed.

2204   Milford, L. and R. Simon. "Discussion Paper on Agent
       Orange." (See 1609)

2205   Miller, J.F. "Liability and Relief of Government Contractors
       for Injuries to Service Members." Military Law Review, v.
       104, no. 1, Summer 1984, p. 1-108. This article discusses
       the degree to which the government contractors should be held
       liable for their research and products. The Agent Orange
       litigation is mentioned throughout this article.

2206   Milstein, S. "The Crusader Who Lost His Way After Founding
       the Agent Orange Suit: Victor Yannacone Managed to Estrange
       Almost Everyone Around Him--Except His Veterans." American
       Lawyer, v. 6, no. 4, April 1984, p. 96-105. The story of how
       V. Yannacone and other lawyers put together the Agent Orange
       litigation and how V. Yannacone was gradually forced out of
       the litigation is told.

2207   Mirelowitz, G. "Agent Orange Settlement: No Justice for
       Veterans." Militant, v. 48, no. 18, May 18, 1984, p. 1+.
       Not all Vietnam veterans are pleased with the out of court
       settlement. There were no veterans involved in the
       negotiations.

2208   "Mixed Reaction to Agent Orange Pact." Chicago Daily Law
       Bulletin, v. 130, no. 91, May 8, 1984, p. 3. Veterans have
       mixed feelings in regards to the out of court settlement.
       Spokesmen for the lawyers and chemical companies tell why
       they settled out of court.

2209 "Monsanto Is Said to Provide Almost Half of $180 Million Agent Orange Settlement." Wall Street Journal, May 14, 1984, p. 6(E), p. 4(W). The details of how the manufacturers will divide up the costs of the settlement are noted.

2210 Moore, W.J. "Decision on Agent Orange Fees Presages Changes in Tort Cases." Legal Times, v. 7, no. 32, January 14, 1985, p. 1+. Judge Weinstein has announced the fees the plaintiff lawyers in the Agent Orange litigation are to receive. V. Yannacone's law firm was the biggest loser. The largest fee award went to the law firm of Dean, Falanga & Rose of Carle Place, New York.

2211 Moore, W.J. "Fee-splitting Agreement Draws Attention of Agent Orange Judge." Legal Times, v. 7, no. 23, November 5, 1984, p. 1. The author discusses the rather unique fee splitting agreements some of the plaintiff lawyers in the Agent Orange litigation entered into. Also discussed is what fee awards Judge Weinstein might make.

2212 Moore, W.J. "Long Road Ends in Agent Orange Pact." Legal Times, v. 6, no. 49, May 14, 1984, p. 1+. The role played by the two special masters in obtaining the settlement is noted.

2213 Moore, W.J. "Master Says Mass Torts Don't Belong in Courts." Legal Times, v. 7, no. 20, October 15, 1984, p. 5+. K. Feinberg, a special master in the Agent Orange litigation, believes that it is not realistic to expect the judicial system to resolve complex social issues such as the Agent Orange issue.

2214 Moore, W.J. "Toxic Tort Cases Challenge Litigators to Keep Up." Legal Times, v. 6, no. 44, April 9, 1984, p. 2+. Judge Pratt discussed his reactions to the Agent Orange litigation at a recent hazardous waste and toxic tort symposium sponsored by the Cleveland Chapter of the Federal Bar Association.

2215 "More Agent Orange Suits Filed in Chicago: Still Others Will Follow." Chemical Week, v. 124, no. 9, February 28, 1979, p. 18. More suits have been filed against the manufacturers of Agent Orange.

2216 "More Legal Action on Agent Orange Accord." Chemical and Engineering News, v. 63, no. 4, January 28, 1985, p. 28. Citizen Soldier has started a campaign to have the out of court settlement set aside.

2217 "Nationwide Hearings Ordered on Fairness of Agent Orange Pact." Wall Street Journal, June 5, 1984, p. 8(E), p. 58(W).

Hearings will be held in several cities on the fairness of
the Agent Orange settlement in August. The suit brought on
behalf of the veterans and their families against the
Veterans Administration has been dismissed by Judge
Weinstein. The suit claimed the agency had failed to provide
adequate care to veterans who believe their health problems
are due to exposure to Agent Orange.

2218   Nesson, C. "Agent Orange Meets Blue Bus: Factfinding at the
Frontier of Knowledge." Boston University Law Review, v. 66,
no. 3-4, May/July 1986, p. 521-539. The author presented
this paper at a conference on Probability and Inference in
the Law of Evidence. The author uses the Agent Orange case
to examine the issue of what type of evidence is needed to
satisfy the plaintiff's burden of causation and the conflict
between law as science and law as justice. The author
concludes by stating that it seems wrong him to require the
proof of causation to be made solely according to the
standards and methodology of statistical science in both the
individual and class context.

2219   "A New Blister in the Agent Orange Case." Chemical Week, v.
132, no. 17, April 27, 1983, p. 13-15. Several recently
released documents suggest that some of the manufacturers
failed to act 18 years ago on data indicating that Agent
Orange contained a highly toxic contaminant. Phase One of
the class action suit will start on June 27 and will revolve
around the question as to whether or not the government knew
everything about Agent Orange that the manufacturers knew.

2220   "New $1.8 Billion Agent Orange Suit Filed." Chicago Daily
Law Bulletin, v. 130, no. 253, December 27, 1984, p. 1. A
class action suit has been filed against the federal
government by B. Musslewhite, a Houston attorney, on behalf
of a group of veterans who feel that actions by the federal
government forced the veterans to settle their suit against
the chemical companies for much less than they deserved.

2221   "New $1.8 Billion Lawsuit Filed Against Uncle Sam." Citizen
Soldier, no. 8, April 1985, p. 6. A new suit has been filed
against the federal government by Vietnam veterans exposed to
Agent Orange and their wives and children. The suit has been
filed because it is felt that the federal government breached
its contract with the chemical manufacturers.

2222   "New Suit Filed Over Agent Orange Exposure." Chemical and
Engineering News, v. 63, no. 1, January 7, 1985, p. 26. A
new class action suit against the federal government has been
filed by veterans exposed to Agent Orange. The suit
maintains the government has deprived veterans of their

rights by asserting neither the government or the manufacturers can be sued for damages.

2223   "News Updates." Science News, v. 127, no. 4, January 26, 1985, p. 57. Judge Weinstein has given final approval to the out of court settlement. The lawyers for the veterans will receive $9.2 million for fees and expenses.

2224   Nicholson, C.A. "Agent Orange Products Liability Litigation." Air Force Law Review, v. 24, no. 2, 1984, p. 97-124. The author examines the issues the lawyers for the veterans will have to prove in order to win the litigation.

2225   "No Agent Orange Fee 'Reward': Judge." Chicago Daily Law Bulletin, v. 130, no. 190, September 27, 1984, p. 1+. Judge Weinstein has stated that the veterans for the Vietnam veterans will not be rewarded with large legal fees. These fees will come out of the $180 million settlement.

2226   "No Bonanza for Lawyers." [editorial] Los Angeles Daily Journal, v. 98, no. 12, January 16, 1985, p. 4. This editorial states that the $10 million the lawyers will get for their work in the Agent Orange litigation is fair.

2227   "No Deadline for Agent Orange Claims." (See 1631)

2228   "No Longer So Secret an Agent." Time, v. 122, no. 3, July 18, 1983, p. 17. Documents opened last week in court in New York revealed that Dow officials knew even before the mid-1960s that exposure to dioxin might cause people to become seriously ill. Some 20,000 Vietnam veterans and their families have brought a suit against the manufacturers of Agent Orange.

2229   "No Sweat." CBS News Daily News Broadcasts, new ser., v. 10, no. 129, May 8, 1984, p. 34-36 (morning news). C. Carey, chief attorney for the Dow Chemical Company in the Agent Orange proceedings, explains why Dow Chemical agreed to the settlement and reiterates that the settlement cannot be construed as an admission of guilt.

2230   "A Nod in Court for the Agent Orange Settlement." Chemical Week, v. 135, no. 14, October 3, 1984, p. 40. Judge Weinstein has given his tentative approval to the out of court settlement. He did state, however, that he did not feel any individual plaintiff would have been able to prove that Agent Orange was the cause of his health problems. He also stated that the government was well aware of the possible health problems and thus the companies would not have been found liable for the injuries caused by the herbicide if the case had gone to court.

2231   Norris, J.A., M. Fudala, and B.L. Watson. "Product Quality
       and Safety--Occupation Safety and Health--Agent Orange--In
       Re 'Agent Orange' Product Liability Litigation." American
       Journal of Law and Medicine, v. 7, no. 1, Spring 1981, p. 46-
       49. The Court of Appeals for the Second Circuit has ruled in
       the Agent Orange suit that there is no federal common law
       right of action and has dismissed the consolidated cases.

2232   "Notice of Proposed Settlement of Class Action." Veterans
       Rights Newsletter, v. 4, no. 2-3, June-July 1984, p. 13-16.
       The text of the proposed settlement is given. This was sent
       to about 400,000 veterans to inform them about the terms of
       the proposed settlement, the fairness hearings and that they
       will need to submit a claim form.

2233   "$180 Million Agent Orange Pact Ok'd." Chicago Daily Law
       Bulletin, v. 130, no. 188, September 25, 1984, p. 1+. Judge
       Weinstein has formally approved the out of court settlement.

2234   "'Orange' Firms Say Government Failed to Warn." Air Force
       Times, v. 40, no. 30, February 18, 1980, p. 45. The chemical
       companies involved in the Agent Orange class action suit have
       accused the federal government of "recklessly" using Agent
       Orange which is the reason veterans may be having health
       problems due to exposure. Air Force personnel also were not
       properly taught how to use the defoliant.

2235   "Orange Settled: Some Veterans Protest Out-court Settlement
       in Agent Orange Damage Suit." CBS News Daily News
       Broadcasts, new ser., v. 10, no. 129, May 8, 1984, p. 3
       (morning news). Some veterans feel that the settlement is
       not fair.

2236   "Orangemail: Why It Got Paid." [editorial] Los Angeles
       Daily Journal, v.98, no. 50, March 11, 1985, p. 4. This
       editorial describes why the settlement was the best solution
       for a dismal situation.

2237   "Orangemail's Cause and Defect." [editorial] Los Angeles
       Daily Journal, v. 98, no. 61, March 26, 1985, p. 4. This
       editorial praises the creativity Judge Weinstein has shown in
       obtaining the out of court settlement. Such creativity may
       save the legal system from the mess tort lawyers have made.

2238   Orloff, N. "Theories of Cancer and Rules of Causation."
       Jurimetrics Journal, v. 27, no. 3, Spring 1987, p. 255-262.
       The author examines how Judge Weinstein's and Judge Jenkin's
       different views of the causes of cancer led to them to apply
       different rules of law in the Agent Orange and Nuclear Test
       Blast litigations.

2239 Palm, R. "Agent Orange Comes Home." (See 1644)

2240 Pauly, D., R. Manning and H. Lambert. "Dow's Bad Chemistry."
Newsweek, v. 102, no. 3, July 18, 1983, p. 60. In hearings
held as part of the Agent Orange litigation, it was revealed
that Dow knew in 1965 that dioxin might be harmful to humans.

2241 Payne, K.J. "Beyond Vietnam, Beyond Politics, Beyond
Causes..." Barrister, v. 6, no. 2, Spring 1979, p. 10-13+.
The lawsuits brought against the manufacturers of Agent
Orange are detailed. Also discussed are the efforts veterans
are making in order to get the government to accept
responsibility for their health problems due to exposure to
the defoliant.

2242 Pear, R. "U.S. Liability Unresolved in Agent Orange Cases."
Chicago Daily Bulletin, v. 130, no. 91, May 8, 1984, p. 1+.
The out of court settlement states that both the veterans and
the chemical companies still have the right to file claims
against the federal government. A bill that has passed the
House of Representatives granting disability compensation to
Vietnam veterans suffering from three diseases thought to be
caused by exposure to Agent Orange is mentioned.

2243 Peterson, K. "Agent Orange: Vets Move to Justice."
Guardian, v. 34, no. 25, March 24, 1982, p. 2. Judge Pratt
has ruled that the government contract issue will be tried
first.

2244 Podesta, J.S. "Some Vietnam Vets Get Compensation for Agent
Orange Exposure, but Others Claim It's Still Not Justice."
People, v. 23, no. 8, February 25, 1985, p. 36-38+. K.
Feinberg discusses the plan he has developed for distributing
the trust fund established by the out of court settlement.
The Ryan family discuss why they are opposed to the
settlement. Elmo Zumwalt III, who suffers from cancer he
believes to have been caused by having been exposed to Agent
Orange, is not opposed to the settlement.

2245 Power, R. "U.S. Court Affirms Most of Settlement Over Agent
Orange." Wall Street Journal, April 22, 1987, p. 50(E), p.
41(W). The out of court settlement has been affirmed by a
federal appeals court. However, the fee-sharing agreement
between some of the veterans' lawyers has been invalidated
and the decision to establish a foundation to distribute some
of settlement's funds has been overturned.

2246 Press, A., A. McDaniel and B. Burgower. "A Fast Deal on
Agent Orange." Newsweek, v. 103, no. 21, May 21, 1984, p.
56. The efforts made by Judge Weinstein to get both sides to

agree to a settlement are noted. The reactions of veterans
to the settlement are mixed.

2247   **Press, A. et al. "Toxic Torts: a Quagmire." Newsweek, v.
       99, no. 9, March 1, 1982. p. 53-54.** The litigation involving
       Agent Orange, DES and asbestos are noted.

2248   **"Procedural History of the Agent Orange Product Liability
       Litigation." Brooklyn Law Review, v. 52, no. 2, 1986, p.
       335-340.** The editors of the Review prepared this outline of
       the procedural history of the Agent Orange litigation from
       its beginning through August 19, 1986 as an introduction to
       the papers presented at a symposium on Mass Torts after Agent
       Orange which are compiled in this issue of the Review.

2249   **"Producers May Be Liable for Agent Orange Damages." Journal
       of Commerce, v. 346, no. 24,871, December 31, 1980, p. 5.**
       Judge Pratt has ruled in U.S. District Court that Vietnam
       veterans can join in a class action suit against the
       manufacturers of Agent Orange. He also ruled that the
       federal government is immune from any liability. If it is
       found in a trial that the manufacturers of Agent Orange are
       liable then a second hearing will be held to address the
       issues of negligence and product liability.

2250   **"Producers Sue U.S. in Agent Orange Case." Chemical Week, v.
       126, no. 3, January 16, 1980, p. 24.** Third-party suits
       against the government have been filed by the manufacturers
       of Agent Orange. The companies feel that the federal
       government set the contract terms and that they rigidly
       complied with these terms.

2251   **Pryor, J. "Court of Appeals Dismisses Complaints on Agent
       Orange." Los Angeles Daily Journal, v. 93, no. 239, November
       26, 1980, p. 3+.** A federal appeals court in New York has
       dismissed a complaint against the chemical companies who
       manufactured Agent Orange brought by some Vietnam veterans,
       stating the federal court lacked jurisdiction. This ruling
       leaves open the possibility of veterans renewing their claims
       on an individual basis in their own federal district. The
       issue could end up in the Supreme Court.

2252   **Raloff, J. "Agent Orange: What Isn't Settled." Science
       News, v. 125, no. 20, May 19, 1984, p. 314-317.** The reasons
       why both sides agreed to the out of court settlement, the
       issues that are still to be resolved, the health studies that
       are underway or have been completed and the possibility for
       creating new law a trial would have had are all discussed.

2253   **Ranii, D. "Dow Must Pay $85,000 for 'Bad Faith' Efforts."**

National Law Journal, v. 6, no. 17, January 2, 1984, p. 6.
Dow must pay approximately $85,000 in attorney fees for the
"bad faith" effort the company made in trying to enforce an
administrative subpoena for confidential scientific data
which could have an impact on the Agent Orange litigation.
The scientific data involves unfinished experiments at the
University of Wisconsin Medical School on the effects of TCDD
on primates.

2254 Reaves, L. "Agent Orange Megatrial." American Bar
      Association. Journal, v. 70, May 1984, p. 27-30. This
      article details the history of the litigation, its unique
      aspects, the granting of class certification, the
      manageability of the class, the accountability of the federal
      government and the decision to have the cases of 10
      representative plaintiffs serve as models for future
      litigation.

2255 "Recent Developments in the Agent Orange Suit."
      Clearinghouse Review, v. 18, no. 4, August-September 1984, p.
      382-383. The issues that will need to be resolved now that a
      settlement has been reached are discussed.

2256 Riley, J. "Agent Orange: a $25,000 Cap." National Law
      Journal, v. 7, no. 26, March 11, 1985, p. 3+. Due to the
      fact that 200,000 claims have been filed against the $180
      million received in the out of court settlement, a cap of
      $25,000 per claim has been proposed in a special master's
      plan developed by K. Feinberg. Mr. Feinberg's proposed
      distribution plan is announced.

2257 Riley, J. "Agent Orange Fees Sharply Curtailed." National
      Law Journal, v. 7, no. 19, January 21, 1985, p. 3+. From the
      $180 million out of court settlement fund, $9.2 million has
      been allocated for attorney's fees. Most of the attorneys
      involved felt the allocation was too small and 88 of the 121
      lawyers who filed a claim will not get any money at all.

2258 Riley, J. "Agent Orange Pact Is Ok'd by Judge." National
      Law Journal, v. 7, no. 5, October 8, 1984, p. 3+. Judge
      Weinstein has approved the "fairness" of the $180 million out
      of court settlement and has urged the government to
      substantially upgrade its aid. The judge also feels that the
      veterans had only a slight chance of winning a trial. He
      feels the settlement is fair for the defendants because it
      saved them millions of dollars in defense costs and adverse
      publicity.

2259 Riley, J. "Agent Orange Plan Halted." National Law Journal,
      v. 8, no. 52, September 8, 1986, p. 4. The decision to

implement the plan to distribute the money from the fund established by the May 1984 settlement has been stayed by an appeals court because lawyers for some of the veterans want the money to be distributed according to the likelihood a particular disease was caused by exposure to Agent Orange. This has happened now because the plan did not become final and appealable until late July.

2260 Riley, J. "Defoliant Makers Lashed; Justice Lawyers Slam Conduct in Sealed Brief." National Law Journal, v. 7, no. 2, September 17, 1984, p. 1. The Justice Department has prepared a brief which attacks the assertions made by the manufacturers of Agent Orange that the defoliant was produced in patriotic compliance with government orders and took issue with the manufacturers' contentions that they had met government specifications. The government also disputes that they had had equal knowledge with the manufacturers about the potential hazards from the toxic contaminants in Agent Orange.

2261 Riley, J. "Fee Tussle Starts on Agent Orange; Requests Swamp Court." National Law Journal, v. 7, no. 3, September 24, 1984, p. 3+. The controversy surrounding the attempt to decide how much of the out of court settlement will go towards attorneys' fees is noted.

2262 Riley, J. "Is It Fair? Lawyers, Vets Offer Divergent Views at Hearing on Agent Orange Accord." National Law Journal, v. 6, no. 51, August 27, 1984, p. 1+. The testimony given at the fairness hearings held on the out of court settlement is summarized.

2263 Riley, J. "Judge Issues More Rulings in Agent Orange Litigation." National Law Journal, v. 7, no. 24, February 25, 1985, p. 18. The independent claims of veterans' wives and children against the out of court settlement charging that Agent Orange has caused their birth defects and miscarriages have been dismissed by Judge Weinstein. However, if a scientific link between Agent Orange and birth defects is established, the claims may be refiled.

2264 Riley, J. "New Agent Orange Rulings." National Law Journal, v. 7, no. 37, May 27, 1985, p. 10. Judge Weinstein has dismissed the claims of 281 veterans who did not participate in the out of court settlement. He has also ruled that the chemical companies cannot recover from the federal government that portion of the settlement that has been set aside to cover claims from veterans' wives and children for miscarriages and birth defects.

2265 Riley, J. "A Silver Bullet - Or Merely a Dud?" National Law Journal, v. 6, no. 46, July 23, 1984, p. 1+. The litigation surrounding dioxin - including the Agent Orange litigation - is summarized.

2266 Rivkin, L.L. "The Government Contract Defense: a Proposal for the Expeditious Resolution of Asbestos Litigation." Forum, v. 17, no. 5, Summer 1982, p. 1225-1249. How the government contract defense has been used in the Agent Orange litigation and how this may be implemented in asbestos litigation involving World War II shipyard workers is commented upon.

2267 Rocomora, J. "Dioxin: the Persistent Poison." (See 1685)

2268 Rosenblatt, J. "Compensating Victims of Toxic Substances." Editorial Research Reports, v. 2, no. 14, October 15, 1982, p. 757-772. In a general article on compensating those suffering ill health from exposure to toxic substances, the Agent Orange litigation and legislation that has been passed to assist those exposed to the defoliant are mentioned.

2269 Rosenfeld, M. "All Quiet on the Legal Front." New York Law Journal, v. 184, no. 121, December 24, 1980, p. 2. The Second Court of Appeals has ruled that the federal courts do not have jurisdiction in the Agent Orange issue because the court could not decide which group should be favored.

2270 Ross, J. "Chemicals in Court: Disaffected Vets May Topple Whopping Agent Orange Accord." Los Angeles Daily Journal, v. 97, no. 122, June 15, 1984, p. 4. The reasons why many veterans and the organizations which represent them are upset with the settlement are given. If too many veterans opt out of the settlement, the chemical companies may also withdraw. Both the veterans and the chemical companies would like to sue the federal government.

2271 Rossi, R. "Megafirm v. Wall Street: Battle Over Agent Orange." New Jersey Law Journal, v. 106, no. 17, October 23, 1980, p. 21. One hundred and fifty law firms have joined the suit against the manufacturers of Agent Orange. These firms have agreed to accept only the fees a judge might award them if they win the case. This is the first time the large law firms which represent Wall Street corporations have ever faced a megafirm.

2272 Rossi, R. "Megafirm v. Wall Street: Battle over Agent Orange: 'Chemical Holocaust." Los Angeles Daily Journal, v. 93, no. 198, September 30, 1980, p. 3. Lawyers from more than 150 firms are involved in the lawsuit against the

manufacturers of Agent Orange. More than 100 of them met
recently in Chicago to plot strategy.

2273 Roth, R.A. "The Essence of the Agent Orange Litigation: the
Government Contract Defense." Hofstra Law Review, v. 12, no.
4, Summer 1984, p. 983-1019. The author of this note
examines the issue of whether or not the government contract
defense should be eliminated in strict products liability
suits such as Agent Orange. The author believes it should be
eliminated. The veterans exposed to Agent Orange and their
families deserve to be able to have a trial and have their
case heard before a jury.

2274 Rothman, R. "Bill Tells VA to Set Agent Orange Guidelines."
(See 1689)

2275 Rust, M. "Expansion of the Feres Doctrine." Emory Law
Journal, v. 32, no. 1, Winter 1983, p. 237-271. How the
Feres doctrine has developed and how it has been extended to
cases in which the policy interest underlying the doctrine is
not applicable are discussed in general. The Agent Orange
litigation is briefly mentioned.

2276 Sand, R.H. "How Much Is Enough? Observations in Light of
the Agent Orange Settlement." Harvard Environmental Law
Review, v. 9, no. 2, Summer 1985, p. 283-306. The author
discusses the implications of the size of the Agent Orange
settlement. He feels that the amount of money the defendants
settled for is too high.

2277 Schaal, D. "Agent Orange: Dow Chemical's Dirty Tricks."
Guardian, v. 31, no. 45, August 29, 1979, p. 2. Citizen
Soldier recently revealed that a Dow Chemical Company
"consultant" probably posed as a member of the press and
obtained copies of the group's documents thus giving Dow an
inside scoop on the group's legal strategy in fighting Dow in
their suit against them concerning Agent Orange. The
possibility exists that the Veterans Administration and Dow
are in collusion on this issue.

2278 Scheindlin, S.A. "Discovering the Discoverable: a Bird's
Eye View of Discovery in a Complex Multi-district Class
Action Litigation." Brooklyn Law Review, v. 52, no. 2, 1986,
p. 397-454. The author presented this paper at a symposium
on Mass Torts after Agent Orange. The author summarizes the
rulings that have been made regarding some of the discovery
issues that arose during the Agent Orange litigation.

2279 Schuck, P.H. Agent Orange on Trial: Mass Toxic Disasters in
the Courts. Cambridge, Mass.: Belknap Press of Harvard

University Press, 1986. ix, 347p. The author reviews the
roots of the Agent Orange litigation, the events leading up
to the settlement and the events since the settlement. The
legal issues involved are analyzed and the clash between
fundamental legal principles and social issues is discussed.

2280 Schuck, P.H. The Role of Judges in Settling Cases: the
Agent Orange Example. (Working Paper/Civil Liability
Program, no. 36) New Haven, Conn.: Yale Law School, Center
for Studies in Law Economics and Public Policy, 1985. 38p.
The role Judge Weinstein and his special masters played in
obtaining a settlement is reviewed. The author discusses the
implications of judges playing an ever increasing role in the
settlement of civil cases.

2281 Schuck, P.H. "The Role of Judges in Settling Cases: the
Agent Orange Example." University of Chicago Law Review, v.
53, no. 2, Spring 1986, p. 337-365. An earlier version of
this paper was published in 1985 (See 2280) as Working Paper
no. 36 from the Civil Liability Program Center at the Yale
Law School's Center for Studies in Law Economics and Public
Policy. The role Judge Weinstein and his special masters
played in obtaining a settlement is reviewed. The author
discusses the implications of judges playing an ever
increasing role in the settlement of civil cases.

2282 "The Settlement." [editorial] New York Law Journal, v. 6,
no. 37, May 21, 1984, p. 12. Judge Weinstein is to be
congratulated for getting both sides to come to an agreement
and for saving the legal system from a trial that would have
sorely tried it.

2283 "Settlement Agreement." Veterans Rights Newsletter, v. 4,
no. 2-3, June-July 1984, p. 16-19. The text of the agreement
signed by the Plaintiffs' Management Committee and the
defendants' lawyers is given.

2284 "Settlement Proposal in Agent Orange Challenged by Veterans."
Wall Street Journal, July 6, 1984, p. 23(E), p. 25(W).
Lawyers representing approximately 500 veterans and their
families have filed a motion in federal court in New York
challenging the proposed settlement and seeking more
information on how the settlement was reached.

2285 "Settlement Proposed in Agent Orange Suit: Government
Refuses to Be Party to It." Veterans Rights Newsletter, v.
4, no. 1, May 1984, p. 1-2. An out of court settlement has
been reached in the Agent Orange litigation. The agreement
reserves for both sides the right to sue the federal
government as the government refused to be part of the

settlement. A special master has been appointed to develop a plan on how the fund established by the settlement is to be administered.

2286 "Settlement: Questions and Answers." Veterans Rights Newsletter, v. 4, no. 1, May 1984, p. 4-7. Answers to questions veterans are frequently asking about the settlement are given.

2287 "Settlement Talks." [editorial] National Law Journal, v. 6, no. 51, August 27, 1984, p. 12. This editorial was written in support of Judge Weinstein's handling of the Agent Orange litigation and states he has been basically fair and proper.

2288 "Shaking Up the Agent Orange Case." Chemical Week, v. 133, no. 18, November 2, 1983, p. 22-23. Judge Weinstein has replaced Judge Pratt as the presiding judge in the Agent Orange litigation. He is changing the direction of the suit by bringing the Hercules Company and the Thompson Chemical Company back into the spotlight, letting the government know that they will be expected to play a major role in the trial and switching the focus of the trial from policy issues to science by letting the veterans know that they must present proof that exposure to Agent Orange has caused their illness.

2289 Sherman, P. "Agent Orange and the Problem of the Indeterminate Plaintiff." Brooklyn Law Review, v. 52, no. 2, 1986, p. 369-395. The author presented this paper at a symposium on Mass Torts after Agent Orange. The author addresses the problem of identifying the plaintiffs and the defendants in the litigation. The issue of the fairness of distributing economic loss without regard to causation is also addressed.

2290 Silver, K. "Tentative Settlement Reached in Agent Orange Case." Exposure, no. 40, July/August 1984, p. 2+. The reactions of Wall Street, the chemical manufacturers and the veterans to the out of court settlement are noted.

2291 Simon, E. "Veterans Class Suit Prohibited." Business Insurance, v. 14, no. 48, December 1, 1980, p. 2+. In a two to one decision, a U.S. Court of Appeals in New York has ruled that Vietnam veterans exposed to Agent Orange will need to sue the manufacturers of the defoliant under state laws. The court ruled that the plaintiffs did not have grounds for action under federal common law. Not all veterans will be able to file suits under state laws because interpretations as to when the statute of limitations begins varies from state to state.

2292 Smith, E. "Agent Orange Veterans: Who Is Responsible."
      (See 1707)

2293 Snyder, K.D. "Deadline for Filing Agent Orange Claims."
      Clearinghouse Review, v. 18, no. 7, November 1984, p. 754-
      758. Those belonging to the class that settled with the
      manufacturers of Agent Orange in May who believed they have
      suffered or are currently suffering from adverse health
      effects due to exposure to Agent Orange have until January 2,
      1985 to file their claim. Copies of the forms are included.

2294 Snyder, K.D. "Final Distribution Plan Announced in Agent
      Orange Case." Clearinghouse Review, v. 19, no. 3, July 1985,
      p. 349. The final distribution plan for the fund set up by
      the out of court settlement is described. Up to $12,800 will
      be paid to veterans who are disabled and $3400 will go to
      each family of veterans who were exposed and have died. The
      first payments are expected to be paid in May 1986. About
      245,000 persons have filed preliminary claim forms.

2295 "Soldiers Charge Chemical Weapon in Killing Them." Business
      Insurance, v. 13, no. 2, January 22, 1979, p. 35. A federal
      class action suit has been filed against the manufacturers of
      Agent Orange on behalf of Paul Reutershan who died of
      abdominal cancer recently. The suit charges that the
      manufacturers knew the defoliant was cancer-causing.

2296 "Some Peace of Mind." [editorial] Los Angeles Daily Journal,
      v. 97, no. 198, October 1, 1984, p. 4. This editorial is a
      reprint of an editorial that appeared in the Los Angeles
      Times. It notes the federal research that has begun and the
      tentative approval of the out of court settlement by Judge
      Weinstein. These events should start to give Vietnam
      veterans some peace of mind.

2297 "Special Master's Statement." Veterans Rights Newsletter, v.
      4, no. 1, May 1984, p. 2. The text of the statement made by
      Special Master Feinberg on May 7 is given.

2298 Steif, W. "Agent Orange Disaster." (See 1719)

2299 Steinhardt, J.D. "Agent Orange and National Consensus Law:
      Trespass on Erie or Free Ride for Federal Common Law?" U.C.
      Davis Law Review, v. 19, no. 1, Fall 1985, p. 201-241. The
      author discusses Judge Weinstein's solution to the Agent
      Orange litigation which was to create "national consensus"
      law instead of using federal common law.

2300 Stichman, B.F. et al. "Developments in Veterans' Law During
      1985." Clearinghouse Review, v. 19, no. 9, January 1986, p.

988-997. The events and developments of 1985 in the area of veterans' rights are summarized. Developments that occurred in the Agent Orange litigation are given on pages 989-991. The court found the settlement fair and reasonable. A distribution plan has been approved. Appeals by some of the class members has held up implementation of the distribution plan. The court dismissed the claims of 281 veterans who chose to opt out of the class action. The Veterans Administration is continuing to grant service-connected disability benefits only to those veterans who are suffering from chloracne.

2301   **"Stipulation of Settlement."** Veterans Rights Newsletter, v. 4, no. 1, May 1984, p. 3. The text of the settlement reached on May 7, 1984 is given.

2302   Storck, W. **"Companies Blame US for Agent Orange Ills."** Chemical and Engineering News, v. 58, no. 3, January 21, 1980, p. 14+. The chemical companies involved in the lawsuit brought by the Vietnam veterans exposed to Agent Orange and their families have filed a third party action against the federal government stating that the government should be held liable for any damage allegedly caused by exposure to Agent Orange.

2303   **"Suits Filed on Behalf of Agent Orange Vets Whose A-95 Forms Were Rejected."** Veterans Rights Newsletter, v. 1, no. 7-8, November-December 1981, p. 50. Lawyers for some of the veterans who have had their A-95 forms rejected have filed two suits in federal court. The A-95 form is the first form a veteran who wishes to file a claim under the Federal Tort Claims Act must complete.

2304   **"Summary of Proposed Distribution Plan."** Citizen Soldier, no. 8, April 1985, p. 4-5. The distribution plan as proposed by Special Master Feinberg is summarized.

2305   **"Supreme Court."** Facts on File, v. 41, no. 2145, December 25, 1981, p. 955-956. The Supreme Court has refused to review a ruling by the U.S. Second Circuit Court of Appeals that the Vietnam veterans exposed to Agent Orange need to seek damages through state rather than federal courts.

2306   **"Supreme Court."** Facts on File, v. 44, no. 2260, March 9, 1984, p. 170. The Supreme Court has declined a request by the manufacturers of Agent Orange to block the trial set to begin in May.

2307   **"Supreme Court Denies Petition in Agent Orange Suit."** Veterans Rights Newsletter, v. 1, no. 7-8, November-December

1981, p. 50. The Supreme Court has refused to hear a petition by the veterans who are suing the manufacturers of Agent Orange. A Court of Appeals decision that federal common law does not apply and state law applies in this case will stand.

2308 Tannenbaum, E. "The Pratt-Weinstein Approach to Mass Tort Litigation." Brooklyn Law Review, v. 52, no. 2, 1986, p. 455-493. This note was presented at a symposium on Mass Torts after Agent Orange. The author traces the history of "In Re: 'Agent Orange' Product Liability Litigation" and discusses the roles Judges Pratt and Weinstein played in the litigation.

2309 Tapp, M. "Fairness Hearing Next in Agent Orange Litigation." Chicago Daily Law Bulletin, v. 130, no. 92, May 9, 1984, p. 1+. Chicago lawyers D. Trafelet and S. Schlegel discuss how they feel about the fairness hearings which are to be held to determine the fairness of the $180 million settlement.

2310 Tarnoff, S. "Agent Orange Class Actions to Include Punitive Claims." Business Insurance, v. 18, no. 2, January 9, 1984, p. 2+. Judge Weinstein has ruled in the Agent Orange litigation that the plaintiffs can sue the manufacturers of Agent Orange for both compensatory and punitive damages and has rejected arguments by the defendants that claims should be brought individually. The Agent Orange litigation is the only remaining products liability class action.

2311 Tarnoff, S. "Agent Orange Firm, Insurer Clash Over Cover." Business Insurance, v. 18, no. 44, October 29, 1984, p. 3+. Diamond Shamrock Chemicals Company has filed a suit against its primary insurer, Aetna Casualty & Surrety Company, as Diamond feels that Aetna is not paying for the portion of the costs of the Agent Orange litigation it said it would. Diamond filed this suit three weeks after Aetna filed a suit against Diamond.

2312 Tarnoff, S. "Asbestos Insurer Wants Agent Orange Ruling." Business Insurance, v. 16, no. 18, May 3, 1982, p. 62. The government contract defense states that a manufacturer is not liable for a plaintiff's injuries if a product conforms to the specifications of a third party -- in the case of Agent Orange, the United States government. If this decision holds up in the Agent Orange case then Commercial Union would like to apply this decision to suits filed on behalf of shipyard workers exposed to asbestos during World War II.

2313 Tarnoff, S. "Judge Delays Agent Orange Trial." Business Insurance, v. 17, no. 21, May 23, 1983, p. 2+. Judge Pratt

has recently ruled on several issues involving the Agent
Orange litigation. Hercules, Inc., Riverdale Chemical Co.,
Hoffman-Taff Inc. and Thompson Chemical Company have been
dismissed as defendants. The trial has been postponed
indefinitely and there will now be one trial on all issues.

2314 Tarnoff, S. "Toxic Substances Will Haunt U.S. Companies in
the Future." Business Insurance, v. 17, no. 18, May 2, 1983,
p. 1+. The toxic substances which have resulted in
litigation are discussed. Asbestos and Agent Orange have
created the largest number of lawsuits.

2315 Tarnoff, S. and S. Shapiro. "Monsanto and Dow Paying 65% of
Agent Orange Pact." Business Insurance, v. 18, no. 20, May
14, 1984, p. 1+. Monsanto contributed $81.9 million to the
trust fund established as a result of the out of court
settlement. Dow Chemical contributed $35.1 million. The
impact the settlement will have on the companies' insurers is
noted.

2316 Taylor, N.F. "Children of Agent Orange." Glendale Law
Review, v. 6, no. 1, 1984, p. 30-42. The author examines the
applicability of the Feres doctrine to the claims brought by
the children of Vietnam veterans who were exposed to Agent
Orange for genetic injury and birth defects. The author
believes that the Second District Court's ruling that these
claims are covered by the Feres doctrine and thus cannot be
recompensated extends the Feres limitations too far.

2317 Taylor, S., Jr. "Despite Recent Rulings, Suing the Army Is
Uphill Fight." Chicago Daily Law Bulletin, v. 130, no. 97,
May 16, 1984, p. 3. Although veterans have made some
progress in suing the federal government, the Feres doctrine
will be a major obstacle for veterans exposed to Agent Orange
to overcome in their attempts to win compensation from the
federal government.

2318 Tell, L.J. "On the Docket: Legal Cases of Special Interest
to Investors." Barrons, v. 64, no. 39, September 24, 1984,
p. 24+. As part of a summary of legal actions of interest to
investors, the Agent Orange litigation is noted. The refusal
of the federal government to accept any responsibility for
the out of court settlement is mentioned. The federal
government argues that profit not patriotism was the motive
behind the companies' actions.

2319 "Tentative Agent Orange Settlement Reached." Science, v.
224, no. 4651, May 25, 1984, p. 849-850. The out of court
settlement leaves many questions unanswered and unaired but
both sides had reasons for reaching an agreement. Several

long term studies will attempt to answer some of the
remaining questions.

2320 "Texas Attorney Files $1.8 Billion AO Suit Against
Government." Veterans Rights Newsletter, v. 4, no. 6-8,
October-December 1984, p. 42. B. Musslewhite has filed a
suit on behalf of several veterans and their families against
the federal government. He believes that the government is
liable to the veterans for the difference between what
veterans should have gotten in the settlement and the $180
million they got.

2321 Thomas, J. "Civilians Seek Agent Orange Redress." (See
1744)

2322 Thomson, D.A. "Agent Orange Litigation." [editorial] Trial,
v. 16, no. 12, December 1980, p. 16-17. The reader is
brought up to date on recent developments in the Agent Orange
litigation.

2323 "Time Extended for Agent Orange Claims in State." New York
Law Journal, v. 189, no. 126, June 30, 1983, p. 1. Governor
Cuomo (D-N.Y.) has agreed to a two-year extension of the
statue of limitations in tort actions brought by Vietnam
veterans exposed to Agent Orange.

2324 "Toxic Torts Can Be Settled." [editorial] Business
Insurance, v. 18, no. 21, May 21, 1984, p. 6. All of the
parties involved in the settling of the Agent Orange
litigation are to be commended. There are still several
issues that need to be resolved, among them being how the
money is to be allocated and the chemical companies'
litigation against the federal government.

2325 Trauberman, J. "Compensating Victims of Toxic Substances
Pollution: an Analysis of Existing Federal Mechanisms."
Harvard Environmental Law Review, v. 5, no. 1, 1981, p. 1-29.
The harms produced by toxic substances are noted. The author
explains why traditional tort law does not provide adequate
compensation. Existing federal compensation statutes are
surveyed and the author states that they also do not provide
adequate relief. Along with several other cases of exposure
to toxic substances, the Agent Orange issue is mentioned.

2326 Tredway, L. "When a Veteran 'Wants' Uncle Sam: Theories of
Recovery for Servicemembers Exposed to Hazardous
Substances." American University Law Review, v. 31, no. 4,
Summer 1982, p. 1095-1139. This article discusses the
options veterans, including those exposed to Agent Orange,
have in attempting to sue the federal government for service
in hazardous military programs. The obstacles facing Vietnam

veterans exposed to Agent Orange are also noted. These
include: obtaining compensation from the Veterans
Administration, getting Congress to provide assistance by
revising the process for obtaining remedies and getting the
government's consent to be sued under the Federal Tort Claims
Act.

2327 Twerski, A.D. "With Liberty and Justice for All: an Essay on
      Agent Orange and Choice of Law." Brooklyn Law Review, v. 52,
      no. 2, 1986, p. 341-367. The author presented this paper at
      a symposium on Mass Torts after Agent Orange. The author
      explains why be believes Judge Weinstein tried to fashion a
      "national consensus" standard as the governing law of the
      case and discusses whether or not this decision was correct.
      He concludes that Judge Weinstein has not been able to form a
      national consensus standard.

2328 "$250 Million Agent Orange Accord Ok'd." Chicago Daily Law
      Bulletin, v. 130, no. 90, May 7, 1984, p. 1+. How an out of
      court settlement was able to be reached is explained.

2329 Tybor, J.R. "Agent Orange: a Red Alert." National Law
      Journal, v. 3, no. 5, October 13, 1980, p. 1+. Lawyers
      involved in the Agent Orange litigation met in Chicago
      recently to discuss tactics and plan strategy. They feel
      that federal common law must be applied so that all veterans
      who suffered damages due to Agent Orange can recover. It is
      also hoped that class action status will be obtained. A
      detailed discussion of what has happened thus far and in what
      direction the litigation is headed is also included.

2330 Tybor, J.R. "Agent Orange: No Federal Umbrella." National
      Law Journal, v. 3, no. 13, December 8, 1980, p. 6. The
      federal district court in New York has ruled that the concept
      of federal common law does not apply in the Agent Orange suit
      and veterans will now need to file claims in federal courts
      in their own states. This will force federal courts to apply
      state statues of limitations. Lawyers feel this decision
      will ruin their chance to obtain national class certification
      status and plan to appeal to the Supreme Court.

2331 Tybor, J.R. "Both Sides Claim Victory in Agent Orange
      Order." National Law Journal, v. 3, no. 19, January 19,
      1981, p. 7+. Judge Pratt has certified the litigation
      against the manufacturers of Agent Orange as a class action
      suit. The manufacturers will claim that they are immune from
      liability since they followed government specifications in
      producing the herbicides.

2332 Tybor, J.R. "Some Statutes of Limitation Apply in Agent

Orange Case." National Law Journal, v. 4, no. 16, December
28, 1981, p. 34. The Supreme Court has refused to review the
Second Circuit Court of Appeals decision that respective
state statutes of limitation will apply in the Agent Orange
litigation. The claims of veterans in approximately 19
states may possibly be barred as a result.

2333 "U.S. Court Orders Opening of Agent Orange Case Files." Wall
Street Journal, June 11, 1987, p. 15(E), p. 10(W). Tens of
thousands of documents produced by the manufacturers of
Agent Orange during the litigation will be unsealed ruled a
federal appeals court in New York. These documents have been
sealed under two protective orders since 1981.

2334 U.S. District Court. Eastern District of New York. In Re
"Agent Orange" Product Liability Litigation: Preliminary
Memorandum and Order on Settlement. Washington: GPO,
September 25, 1984. 456p. This opinion summarizes the terms
of the settlement; why the court feels that the settlement
appears to be reasonable for the plaintiffs, defendants and
the public; the legal obstacles that would be confronted if
the litigation were to go to trial by the plaintiffs and
defendants; the evidence the plaintiffs have produced in
support of their case; the legal relevance of this
information; obstacles facing the plaintiffs; and the issue
of how to determine who caused harm. Included in the
appendices are a copy of the settlement agreement and a copy
of a letter stating the federal government's position as to
why they refuse to participate in the negotiations.

2335 "U.S. Exempted in Agent Orange Settlement Fund." Wall Street
Journal, May 10, 1985, p. 50(E), p. 46(W). Judge Weinstein
has ruled that the federal government is within its rights in
refusing to contribute to the out of court settlement against
the manufacturers of Agent Orange. The judge, however,
criticized the government for refusing.

2336 "U.S. Fails to Escape Trial as Agent Orange Defendant." New
York Law Journal, v. 191, no. 74, April 17, 1984, p. 1+. The
Second Circuit Court of Appeals has ruled that the federal
government will have to stand trial in the Agent Orange
litigation. The Court ruled that the federal government is
not shielded by the doctrine of sovereign immunity.

2337 "U.S. Sued by Veterans for $1.8 Billion in Agent Orange
Case." Wall Street Journal, December 28, 1984, p. 34(E), p.
13(W). Lawyers have filed a new suit against the federal
government on behalf of veterans exposed to Agent Orange.
The lawyers contend that the federal government infringed the
constitutional rights of veterans by asserting, and enabling

the chemical companies to assert, immunity from the veterans' claims under the Defense Production Act.

2338   U.S. Veterans Administration. Advisory Committee on Health-Related Effects of Herbicides. Transcript of Proceedings, Twenty-second Meeting, December 11, 1984. (See 1808)

2339   U.S. Veterans Administration. Veterans' Advisory Committee on Environmental Hazards. [Minutes of November 17, 1986 and November 18, 1986 Meetings] (See 1816)

2340   "Update: No Federal Liability in Agent Orange Suit." Business Insurance, v. 15, no. 1, January 5, 1981, p. 1-2. Judge Pratt has ruled that Vietnam veterans exposed to Agent Orange and their families can sue the chemical companies who manufactured Agent Orange. He also ruled that the chemical companies cannot bring a suit against the federal government to make them liable for any damages Agent Orange may have caused.

2341   "Update on Agent Orange Suit." Veterans Rights Newsletter, v. 4, no. 2-3, June-July 1984, p. 9+. The legal developments in the Agent Orange litigation that have taken place since the out of court settlement are noted.

2342   "VA Rules for Deciding Agent Orange Claims Challenged." Veterans Rights Newsletter, v. 6, no. 5-6, September-October 1986, p. 33-34. A lawsuit has been filed as the veterans who filed this suit feel the Veterans Administration has failed to properly follow the Veterans' Dioxin and Radiation Exposure Compensation Standards Act.

2343   "VA Sued on Agent Orange." Discharge Upgrading Newsletter, v. 4, no. 5, May 1979, p. 4. The National Veterans Law Center has filed a lawsuit in an effort to get the Veterans Administration to change its ruling that Vietnam veterans are not to receive disability benefits for damages these veterans feel are the result from having been exposed to Agent Orange.

2344   "VA Sued Over Agent Orange Study." Discharge Upgrading Newsletter, v. 5, no. 5-6, May-June 1980, p. 8. The National Veterans Law Center has filed a suit against the Veterans Administration stating that the Veterans Administration's proposed study on the health effects of exposure to Agent Orange is inadequate.

2345   "Veterans Administration Accused of Ignoring Europe Defoliant Cancer Reports." (See 1844)

2346   "Veterans Lose Agent Orange Case." New Scientist, v. 88, no.

1231, December 11, 1980, p. 693. The Second Court of Appeals
has ruled that a federal court is not the appropriate place
for the Agent Orange lawsuit. However, the plaintiffs are
still able to file suits in their local federal court.

2347 "Veterans Plan to Appeal Agent Orange Dismissal." Chicago
Daily Law Bulletin, v. 130, no. 110, June 5, 1984, p. 1+.
Judge Weinstein has rejected a class action suit brought by
veterans' groups demanding greater nationwide medical care
for Vietnam veterans suffering from the effects of exposure
to Agent Orange. The suit named the Veterans Administration,
the Public Health Service and the Food and Drug
Administration as defendants. The lawyers for the veterans
have said they will appeal the rejection.

2348 "Veterans Tell Bitter View of Agent Orange Accord." Chicago
Daily Law Bulletin, v. 130, no. 155, August 8, 1984, p. 1+.
The testimony given at the first fairness hearing in Brooklyn
on the out of court settlement is summarized.

2349 "Veterans to Air Views on Agent Orange Fund." Journal of
Commerce, v. 361, no. 25,784, August 9, 1984, p. 22B. The
hearings on the fairness of the out of court settlement have
begun. Hundreds of letters have also been sent to Judge
Weinstein. The opinions expressed in the letters are evenly
split for and against the settlement.

2350 "Veterans Update." American Legion, v. 117, no. 1, July
1984, p. 25. The American Legion feels that the out of court
settlement is not a definitive resolution of the issue.

2351 "Vets Clash on Pay-out for Agent Orange." Journal of
Commerce, v. 363, no. 25,927, March 7, 1985, p. 7A. Veterans
are in disagreement as to whether or not the out of court
settlement is just.

2352 "Vets Sue Producers of Agent Orange." Journal of Commerce,
v. 345, no. 24,752, July 10, 1980, p. 3. A suit has been
filed in U.S. District Court by 13 Maryland families who are
charging seven companies who manufactured Agent Orange with
negligence in marketing Agent Orange. They are seeking $130
million in damages on the grounds that exposure to Agent
Orange in Vietnam caused the deaths of four veterans and nine
children.

2353 "Vets Want VA Benefits for Herbicide Damage." National Law
Journal, v. 3, no. 19, January 19, 1981, p. 7. Vietnam
veterans have filed suits in three cities that, if won, would
force the Veterans Administration to treat exposure to Agent
Orange as a service-related disability.

2354   "Viet Herbicide Suit to Involve Thousands." Rochester
       Patriot, v. 7, no. 3, February 15, 1979, p. 10. The class
       action suit brought by attorneys for the deceased Paul
       Reutershan on behalf of all veterans exposed to Agent Orange
       in Vietnam is described.

2355   "Viet Vets Sue Over Exposure to Cancer-causing Agent." Black
       Panther, v. 19, no. 7, May 28, 1979, p. 3+. Efforts being
       made by groups to determine the damages caused veterans by
       exposure to Agent Orange are described. Federal court
       hearings were scheduled to begin in May.

2356   "The Vietnam 'Buy-off.'" [editorial] Wall Street Journal,
       May 26, 1984, p. 28(E), p. 26(W). Reprinted as "The Case of
       the Vietnam 'Buy-off.'" [editorial] Los Angeles Daily
       Journal, v. 97, no. 96, May 10, 1984, p. 4. The issue of
       whether or not the chemical companies bought off the veterans
       with the settlement is discussed. At least the veterans will
       get some money and the class action process will have made
       everyone happy.

2357   "Vietnam Defoliant Suit Filed." Facts on File, v. 39, no.
       1996, February 9, 1979, p. 90. A class action lawsuit has
       been filed in federal district court in New York against the
       manufacturers of Agent Orange on behalf of the 4.2 million
       Americans allegedly exposed to Agent Orange in Vietnam.

2358   "Vietnam Veterans Attack Terms of Settlement on Agent
       Orange." Los Angeles Daily Journal, v. 97, no. 161, August
       9, 1984, p. 5. At the first of the five hearings which are
       being held to help Judge Weinstein decide if the out of court
       settlement is acceptable or not, many veterans told why they
       do not approve of the settlement.

2359   Vietnam Veterans of America. Legal Services. VVA's Guide on
       Agent Orange. Washington: Vietnam Veterans of America
       Legal Services, November 1984. 16p. This brochure was
       developed to help veterans fill out the forms that need to be
       completed in order to file a claim now that a settlement has
       been reached in the litigation.

2360   "Vietnam Vets: You Need to Read This About the Agent
       Orange Lawsuit." Veterans Rights Newsletter, v. 3, no. 9-10,
       January-February 1984, p. 65+. The history of the litigation
       is given. What opting-out of the litigation means and what a
       class action is are explained. The article also tells a
       veteran if he will need his own lawyer or not.

2361   "Vietnam Vets, Chemical Cos. Settle Agent Orange Suit."
       Facts on File, v. 44, no. 2269, May 11, 1984, p. 336. The

out of court settlement is discussed. The chemical companies did not admit liability and the role of the federal government in this issue has not been resolved.

2362 Vouri, M. "Class Action Suit Against Agent Orange." Northwest Passage, v. 24, no. 9, April 1984, p. 4. Some of the people who are involved in the class action suit against the manufacturers of Agent Orange are described. Telephone numbers for those who have questions are given.

2363 "Weinstein Role in Agent Orange Pact Challenged." Legal Times, v. 7, no. 45, April 15, 1985, p. 5. The lawyers for the veterans who opted out of the May 1984 settlement have submitted an affidavit asking the Second Circuit Court to issue a writ of mandamus requiring the recusal of Judge Weinstein. The lawyers feel that Judge Weinstein's impartiality might well be questioned.

2364 "Weinstein Upholds Agent Orange Fee Agreement." Legal Times, v. 8, no. 6, July 15, 1985, p. 4. Judge Weinstein has ruled that the fee splitting arrangement that some of the lawyers who represented the veterans in the Agent Orange litigation worked out between themselves is legal.

2365 Weisbaum, D.B. Report to General Assembly: Illinois Agent Orange Study Commission. Springfield, Ill.: Illinois Agent Orange Study Commission, 1984. 146p. This report summarizes the results of hearings which were held throughout the three year period of 1982 to 1984.

2366 Weiss, G. "Squeezing Agent Orange: Judge Frowns on Lawyer's Plea for Fees." Barrons, v. 64, no. 42, October 15, 1984, p. 38+. The debate that is being waged over how much of the out of court settlement the lawyers should get is noted.

2367 Whelan, E.M. "Deadly Dioxin?" (See 1267)

2368 Whelan, E. "'Orange' Case Best Feasible Solution." [commentary] Farm Chemicals, v. 147, no. 10, October 1984, p. 17+. The author does not believe that it can be scientifically proven that exposure to Agent Orange caused the birth defects seen in some veterans' children. Chloracne is the only disease that has been linked to exposure. The author believes the out of court settlement was a business decision made by the manufacturers who recognized that the Agent Orange disease hypothesis was a red herring. They recognized, however, that in a jury trial the scientific facts would not have had a chance.

2369 "Who Pays for the Damage?" Time, v. 115, no. 3, January 21,

1980, p. 61. The litigation involving Agent Orange, the Ford
Pinto and asbestos is described.

2370   Williams, R. "Agent Orange Revisited: Alternatives to
       Litigation." American Journal of Trial Advocacy, v. 6, no.
       2, Fall 1982. p. 323-330. Why the Feres doctrine has
       remained an obstacle to recovery through the courts for
       Vietnam veterans exposed to Agent Orange is explained.
       However, the Veterans Administration has increased the
       availability of health care in their clinics and several
       states are considering legislation which would authorize
       medical treatment for symptoms of exposure.

2371   Winslow, R. "U.S. Sprayed Agent Orange in Vietnam for 2 1/2
       Years After '67 Study Cited Peril." Wall Street Journal,
       July 6, 1983, p. 2(E), p. 2(W). Documents released as part
       of the Agent Orange litigation reveal that a Rand Corporation
       report prepared for the Department of Defense in 1967
       expressed concern about the spraying of Agent Orange. Other
       documents revealed that a National Cancer Institute study in
       1969 showed that dioxin caused birth defects in rats and
       mice, that the government considered building its own
       herbicide plant and that a chemical industry committee sought
       minimal restrictions on the domestic use of the herbicide.
       On this last issue, veterans say that the committee gave the
       government outdated information and withheld studies that
       showed dioxin's possible hazards to humans.

2372   Wise, D. "Agent Orange Insurance Fund Set by Judge." New
       York Law Journal, v. 193, no. 102, May 29, 1985, p. 1+. The
       final version of the distribution of the funds set up by the
       out of court settlement has been approved. Approximately
       30,800 veterans will received disability payments of up to
       $12,500 and the survivors of approximately 18,100 veterans
       will receive death benefits of up to $3,400. Forty-five
       million dollars will be used to establish a foundation to
       assist veterans and their families -- especially those
       families who have children with birth defects. Two percent
       of the fund will go to Australian and New Zealand veterans
       who were exposed to Agent Orange in Vietnam.

2373   Wise, D. "Agent Orange Judge Acts to Speed Benefits to
       Veterans." New York Law Journal, v. 197, April 24, 1987, p.
       1+. The author details Judge Weinstein's plans to get the
       process of dispersing the money in the settlement fund back
       on track now that the Court of Appeals has approved the
       settlement. The issue of the fees for the plaintiffs'
       attorneys is discussed. The issue of what the court
       perceives to be a lack of proof of the causal relationship
       between Agent Orange and veterans' injuries is discussed.

2374 Wise, D. "Hearing Set on Disclosure of Agent Orange
      Documents." New York Law Journal, v. 193, no. 4, January 7,
      1985, p. 1+. Hearings will begin soon to determine which of
      the hundreds of thousands of pages of documents produced
      during the discovery phase of the case should be made public.

2375 Wise, D. "Judge Dismisses Claims Left in Agent Orange." New
      York Law Journal, v. 193, no. 30, February 14, 1985, p. 1+.
      Judge Weinstein has dismissed all claims against the $180
      million granted in the out of court settlement brought by
      some of the veterans' wives and their children. Judge
      Weinstein has left the door open for claims to be resubmitted
      if direct cause for the miscarriages and birth defects can be
      definitively linked to Agent Orange. The judge dismissed the
      claims as he believes that this has not yet happened.

2376 Wise, D. "Lawyers in Agent Orange Case Flood Court with Fee
      Claims." New York Law Journal, v. 192, no. 49, September 10,
      1984, p. 1. The Clerk's Office in the U.S. district Court in
      Brooklyn has been overwhelmed with applications for
      attorney's fees in the Agent Orange case.

2377 Wise, D. "Major Issue to Be Argued in Agent Orange Claims."
      New York Law Journal, v. 191, no. 47, March 9, 1984, p. 1.
      Since Judge Weinstein has taken on the Agent Orange
      litigation he has overhauled the posture of the case. He has
      agreed to reconsider reopening aspects of the government-
      contractor defense. Thompson Chemical Company and
      Hercules Inc. have been reinstated.

2378 Wise, D. "9.2 Million Fees, Expenses Awarded in Agent Orange
      Case." New York Law Journal, v. 193, no. 5, January 8, 1985,
      p. 1+. The lawyers who represented the veterans will receive
      more than nine million dollars in fees and expenses from the
      out of court settlement. The largest amount, $1.46 million,
      went to the law firm of Dean, Falange & Rose of Carle Place,
      L.I. For the work mostly performed by partners, a $150 an
      hour across-the-board fee was granted and for work mostly
      performed by associates an across-the-board fee of $100 was
      granted.

2379 Wise, D. "Oddity in Agent Orange Case: Presiding Judge Now
      a Litigant." New York Law Journal, v. 196, no. 47, September
      5, 1986, p. 1+. Judge Weinstein has become a litigant
      himself in the Agent Orange case and has asked K. Feinberg to
      defend the plan he developed for distributing the money from
      the fund established by the May 1984 settlement. The
      veterans' lawyers' management committee has also attacked the
      merits of the distribution plan.

2380   Wise, D. "Recovery from U.S. Barred to Makers of Agent
       Orange." New York Law Journal, v. 193, no. 90, May 10, 1985,
       p. 1+. Judge Weinstein has ruled that the chemical
       manufacturers involved in the out of court settlement of the
       Agent Orange litigation may not recover any of the $180
       million trust fund that was established as a result of the
       settlement from the federal government. However, the judge
       commented that the government could pay a price in the future
       for failing to come to the aid of the manufacturers who
       voluntarily produced critical war supplies.

2381   Wise, D. "Settlement Approved to End Veterans' Agent Orange
       Suit." New York Law Journal, v. 192, no. 61, September 26,
       1984, p. 1+. Judge Weinstein has tentatively approved the
       out of court settlement. Final approval will be made when it
       has been decided how much the attorneys who represented the
       veterans and their families will be paid. Judge Weinstein
       stated that he feels that the data submitted thus far
       suggests that the plaintiffs' case is without merit. But the
       settlement is justified as it saves the chemical companies
       adverse publicity and tens of millions of dollars in legal
       fees and will reduce the hardships faced by veterans and
       their families.

2382   Wise, D. "$25,000 Cap Put on Benefits to Agent Orange
       Claimants." New York Law Journal, v. 193, no. 38, February
       27, 1985, p. 1+. The special master appointed by Judge
       Weinstein to determine how the out of court settlement should
       be distributed has proposed that the maximum payment be
       $25,000, that only 50 percent of those exposed to Agent
       Orange be eligible for compensation and that greater
       compensation go to those veterans with the disabilities of
       greatest duration.

2383   Wise, D. "2 Days of Arguments Slated in Agent Orange
       Appeals." New York Law Journal, v. 195, no. 67, April 9,
       1986, p. 1+. Sixty-seven appeals and cross appeals from the
       1984 settlement are scheduled to be heard on April 9 and 10.
       Issues to be heard include appeals over the dismissal of the
       suits brought by 282 veterans who filed claims outside of the
       settlement, the fairness of the settlement, whether certain
       documents should be made public and fees for the attorneys
       who represented the veterans.

2384   Wise, D. "281 Claims Outside Class Voided in Agent Orange
       Case." New York Law Journal, v. 193, no. 89, May 9, 1985, p.
       1+. The claims of 281 veterans who decided not to
       participate in the class action suit but rather chose to
       pursue their cases individually have been dismissed by Judge
       Weinstein. He ruled that there was no epidemiological

evidence to support their claims and rejected the affidavits of two physicians the defendants had produced to support their claims.

2385 Wise, D. "2 Old Rivals Square Off As Agent Orange Trial Opens." New York Law Journal, v. 191, no. 88, May 7, 1984, p. 1+. Two lawyers, one representing Dow Chemical and one representing the veterans, tell how they feel the trial will unfold and how they will present their cases. The two lawyers know each other from the years they each spent practicing law in Nassau County.

2386 Wise, D. "U.S. Judge Upholds Lawyers' Fee Plan in 'Agent Orange.'" New York Law Journal, v. 193, no. 124, June 28, 1985, p. 1+. Judge Weinstein has upheld the internal fee arrangement that the nine members of the plaintiffs' management committee had worked out. As a result, before funds are distributed to all of the other plaintiffs' lawyers, the six members of this committee who advanced the funds to finance the litigation are entitled to recover three times their investment. This does not violate the Code of Professional Responsibility.

2387 Wise, D. "Veterans Settle Class Action with Makers of Agent Orange." New York Law Journal, v. 191, no. 89, May 8, 1984, p. 1+. An out of court settlement has been reached with the manufacturers of Agent Orange. Veterans would still like to pursue their claims against the federal government. The manufacturers as part of the settlement were able to deny any liability for the plaintiffs' injuries.

2388 Wisser, W. "Letter from New York." Far Eastern Economic Review, v. 124, no. 15, April 12, 1984, p. 80. The Agent Orange trial will begin on May 7. Some background information on the use of Agent Orange in Vietnam and the litigation is given.

2389 Yannacone, V.J., Jr., W.K. Kavenagh and M.T. Search. "Agent Orange Litigation: Cooperation for Victory." Trial, v. 18, no. 2, February 1982, p. 44-49. An account of how the class action suit against the manufacturers of Agent Orange developed is given.

2390 Yates, R. "All's Set: Everybody's in for Vets' Dioxin Trial." Chicago Daily Law Bulletin, v. 130, no. 4, January 6, 1984, p. 1+. Chicago attorneys S. Schlegel and D. Trafelet are very involved in the Agent Orange litigation. They now lead a team of lawyers working on Dow's liability. The points that they will have to prove in order to win the litigation are also discussed.

2391 Yates, R. "Atomic Fallout and Agent Orange: a Glimpse at the Future." Brief, v. 13, no. 4, August 1984, p. 4-8+. The implications of the out of court settlement on the future of mass tort cases in the courts are discussed.

2392 Zamichow, N. "Vietnam Workers Stonewalled on Agent Orange Danger." (See 1891)

2393 Zollers, F.E. and S.N. Hurd. "A Model for Analyzing Government Contract Defense in Product Liability." Journal of Products Liability, v. 9, no. 4, 1986, p. 317-327. As part of a debate on what the appropriate use of the government contract defense should be in design defect cases involving military products, the Agent Orange litigation is mentioned.

2394 Zumwalt, E., III as told to J. Grossman. "A War with Hope." (See 1286)